The Ancient Wisdom
of Origen

The Ancient Wisdom
of Origen

John Clark Smith

Lewisburg
Bucknell University Press
London and Toronto: Associated University Presses

Associated University Presses
440 Forsgate Drive
Cranbury, NJ 08512

Associated University Presses
25 Sicilian Avenue
London WC1A 2QH, England

Associated University Presses
P.O. Box 39, Clarkson Pstl. Stn.
Mississauga, Ontario,
L5J 3X9 Canada

The paper used in this publication meets the requirements of the American National Standard for Permanence of Paper for Printed Library Materials Z39.48-1984.

Library of Congress Cataloging-in-Publication Data

Smith, John Clark, 1944–
    The ancient wisdom of Origen / John Clark Smith.
        p.   cm.
    Includes bibliographical references and indexes.
    ISBN 0-8387-5204-7 (alk. paper)
    1. Origen.   I. Title.
BR65.068S65   1992
270.1'092-dc20   90-53315
                                                              CIP

PRINTED IN THE UNITED STATES OF AMERICA

Dorothy Johnson Smith

Contents

Abbreviations

ANF   Ante-Nicene Fathers
BLE   Bulletin de littérature ecclésiastique
            (Report on ecclesiastical literature)
GCS   Die griechischen christlichen Schriftsteller der ersten drei
            Jahrhunderte
            (The Greek Christian writers of the first three centuries)
JTS   Journal of Theological Studies
LXX   The Septuagint translation of the Bible
PG   Patrologia Graeca (Writings of the Greek fathers)
RSR   Recherches de science religieuse
            (Studies in religious knowledge)
SC   Sources chrétiennes
            (Christian sources)
TDNT   Theological Dictionary of the New Testament
*   An asterisk indicates that the translation has been modified.

Preface

This book is the result of over fifteen years of study and research. In it I have tried to clarify, in light of Origen's writings on spiritual change and growth, the thought of Origen to English-speaking readers. As far as the author is aware, this book is the first detailed book-length study of the full spectrum of Origen's unique Christian vision written in English. Every idea of Origen is supported by texts, many of them translated into English for the first time. It also is informed by the major German, French, Spanish, and Italian studies on Origen.

This said, I am well aware of the pitfalls of Origen studies once one enters the world of Origen scholarship. It is now an enormous area of research and no one can claim complete dominance over all of it. My intent has been to give the heart of what Origen believed and yet not neglect the major works of Origen scholars which were available to me.

Readers interested in methodology should turn first to Appendix B. There I give an overview of the major progress and trends in Origen scholarship, discuss the difficulties and dating of the surviving texts, and reveal the way I have handled them.

Despite my years of attention to the manuscript, however, and the helpful comments of several scholars, I am certain there are shortcomings, reflections, of course, of my own shortcomings and of the difficulties of Origen's thought. But there comes a time to let the child go off into the world and see what happens. I can only hope that I have not done a disservice to Origen, and perhaps to some extent repaid my debt to him who has been my teacher for so many years.

The Ancient Wisdom
of Origen

I

Introduction: How Was Spiritual Change Viewed in Origen's Day?

Background

Just as modern society has been increasingly filled with numerous religious and pseudoreligious groups which vie for the allegiance of people, so it was in the first centuries after Christ. After the New Testament as we know it today was set down, there was a time of restless movement and change, a time of spiritual transformation. Numerous options besides the way of the little Christian sect were available. Christianity had not yet overwhelmed the world with its truths and behavior. Many other sects were competing with it and thinkers were responding to a real need and dilemma.[1] The assortment was varied: the mysteries, the Gnostic groups, the influx of oriental religions, the State religion, the transforming old philosophies, as well as the new Christian sect and its own heresies. All of these drove the ancient man to a psychological crisis of decision, to the necessity of comparison and reaffirmation of his beliefs.[2]

Among many others, the Christians were trying to convince others through their own writers of the importance of Christian life and why a person should become a Christian. But no non-scriptural writings have survived up to the third century that truly display the full power of Christian thought on this idea. No one up to the third century was able to defend the way of Christ as well as change the heart.

No one until Origen. His dates are uncertain, but we know he was alive from about 185 to 251 A.D.[3] He was not only a rigorous follower of the gospel in his everyday behavior and a dedicated Christian; he was a thinker, a man who dared to speculate, yet one greater than any Christian thinker of the ancient world because he alone first explored the territory of Scripture with great depth. He stands higher than any thinker as the greatest defender and philosopher of Scripture, a man who knew Scripture as well as any Christian thinker who ever lived, who knew the Greek and Hebrew, and who lived the way of Scripture. As a boy he tried to run off and become a martyr, but his mother hid his clothes. As an old man it is almost certain that he died from wounds given him in the persecution of Christians under the emperor Decius. While others would recant, Origen maintained his faith in the face of every conceivable onslaught. His own faith was secure in this extraordinary age of upheaval.[4]

The works of Origen focus on change in a time of great change, a time not

15

unlike our own. It was not a pastime for him; to convert others was an essential skill in that era. He wrote about every known aspect of spiritual growth and the many dilemmas that accompany it, and we can say without exaggeration that his account has never been surpassed. He was the inspiration for the many thinkers who followed.

The purpose of this book then is to explore how Origen handled the problem of change and spiritual growth in the midst of such a bewildering number of options for the people of his time. How and why did people become Christian? What was expected of them? What were the important dimensions of change in spiritual growth? What did it mean to experience Christian change? Our subject is spiritual transformation and growth in the time of Origen, what we can call, in a general sense, conversion, though Origen's understanding of this concept is much more profound than what is commonly understood.

We will explore this subject in six parts. The first part will discuss the milieu in which Origen wrote. The second part explores Origen's controversial views on the beginning and the end in order to show a need for change and the final end or goal toward which Origen believes the journey of the spirit is leading. Then, in parts three, four, and five, the heart of the study, we clarify how Origen understood the way a person becomes a true Christian through restraint of the body, virtue, and quest for spiritual knowledge. Finally, we offer some reflections in part six.

But first, to appreciate Origen and what he faced, we begin with a brief overview of the options offered to the people of the third century and how the competitors of the little Christian sect considered change. In this way, we will clarify the soil of attitudes in which Origen seeded his own viewpoint.

Six major viewpoints will be considered: Greco-Roman religions, contemporary philosophies, Valentinian Gnostics, the Hebrew Scriptures (the Old Testament), the New Testament, and other Christian thinkers who preceded Origen.

Greco-Roman Religions[5]

Let us start with a working definition of the process of spiritual change that we will explore in depth in this study: To change, one must have a transforming experience of mind and conduct involving a total reformation of life, and one must seek to know what transcends human knowledge and action.

If we accept the above definition of spiritual change, then it is almost unknown in the Greco-Roman religion of the Empire.[6] The Greek word *Metanoia* (usually translated repentance), for example, which involved a powerful transformation for the Jew and Christian, often signified merely a change of mind in the sense of a value judgment or reconsideration. The Latin word *Religio* for the pagan was primarily something describing rituals that communicated with the gods as well as the obligations to perform the rituals.[7] Though these ritual sacrifices demanded purity, often with some moral overtones, they were not part of a process of transformation. One sacrificed not for personal transformation, but out of a duty to a local deity or to one with which a person has some attachment.[8]

Moreover, the pagan religions of the Empire (as well as Hermeticism and Gnosticism), i.e., sun worship and astrology, began more and more to concentrate on the transformation of the universe rather than only of man (cosmology rather than anthropology). The effect, in comparison to Judaism or Christianity, was that the Greco-Roman religions were more formal and objective. Man stood under the hand of a fate by which the gods ruled the cosmos and directed at their whim the wills of men. Sin too was more objective. As one writer explains, in pagan ritual moral evil was put aside by the devotee; he was not delivered from it.[9]

In sum, turning to the new or a return to the old involving a complete change of heart and conduct, as well as new allegiances, was rare. In terms of their relations with the supernatural, people relied primarily on *Religio*, namely, the sum total of the rituals that tied them to the gods or spirits; in terms of personal transformation, these generally involved not religion but philosophy, as a section below will try to clarify. In the former case, any significant spiritual change was irrelevant. In the latter case, a change obviously does not compromise one's allegiance to any religious sect or god. The fundamental purpose was not to be turned to the gods, but to profit from service to them.[10] Hence with respect to religion, a pagan did not leave behind an old way and then give his whole life to something new. The new forms were supplements rather than alternatives to the ancestral piety.[11]

Indeed there is a strong tendency, especially in the Roman character, toward conservatism and maintenance of the old ways.[12] Since pagan piety centered around the family and the locale, the very nature of the religion encouraged this conservatism. If one thinks of change as a turning away from the old, how could the pagan turn away from his family and locale? Would this not be equal to forsaking his roots?[13] Conversion evidently could not mean a rejection of one's family and home. One might include an alien deity in one's sacrifices, but one did not convert to it without losing the favor of one's family, home city, and god. In Origen's time, the cult of the Emperor was also imposed upon the old religion of the family and city, so that allegiance to Rome was made a religious as well as political necessity.[14] To reject one's family, city, nation and god would hardly seem prudent to most of the ancients, but, in effect, this is what the Christians seemed to be asking converts to do.

With respect to the mystery religions, there is a stress on initiation rather than inner transformation; that is, the process by which one becomes a member, introduced to the secrets, occurs through external rites of initiation.[15] It was primarily the ceremonies, then, that made one a member, rather than a turning, returning or inner transforming experience. Moreover, it was other ceremonies that maintained one's membership and interest.[16]

The Philosophers[17]

1.

For conversion in the sense of a complete break with the old for something new, let us turn to the philosophical schools of the Greco-Roman world.[18] The fundamental reason why ancient philosophy had a concept of conversion was that it "held a clear concept of two types of life, a higher and a lower, and exhorted men to turn from one to the other."[19] Philosophic conversion could mean both a turn from the sensible reality to the intelligible reality, and a turn toward one's true nature, toward that which is in harmony with Nature, and away from that which distracts one, i.e., what is outside one's self. Since in most ancient philosophers these two dimensions are interrelated, they will be discussed together. But the latter, the turn toward oneself, found in philosophers such as Plato, Philo, Plutarch and Epictetus, is, in fact, the most pronounced way of expressing conversion.[20]

This stress on the self-conversion seems especially true for the Stoics. For example, Epictetus sees conversion as a process concerned with oneself only, which means avoiding what is external and outside the self, avoiding what originates from outside, and returning to one's true self and the way of providence. He is less concerned with the questions arising from a Platonic sensible-intelligible mode of conversion, though this aspect is implied. The Stoic conversion is more a call to a providence that bears on men than a contemplative admiration of the intelligible or the Good. As one writer summarizes the matter, the Platonist finds Truth in conversion; Epictetus finds freedom, freedom from the constraints of external forces.[21] Epictetus advocates a turn from attention to external forces to the interior forces that enable man to be free and in harmony with *Logos*. Whereas the Platonist strives toward an intelligible realm other than the sensible world, the Stoic Epictetus strives for harmony with the providence of the world.[22] Providence in turn results from the universal law, *Logos*, which rules both men and gods. In sum, in order to be free, men must be in accord with the universal law, which is also being in accord with god. To be in accord with the universal law man turn inwardly toward his own power of *Logos* and away from all that is external.[23]

Even though conversion is inward, it is displayed in external actions. In fact, Stoic, Epicurean and Cynic systems center not on philosophic speculations and metaphysics, but on human life, and especially on ethics.[24] The Stoics, for example, have a conception of moral progress in which one can ascend from depravity to moral wisdom by his own power. Progress, however, is made only in terms of evil—less and less evil. The wise man lives by virtue (*Arete*) and does no action mixed with evil.[25] For the Epicureans, the goal is pleasure, that is, the absence of bodily pain and mental affliction through moderation in one's life and acquiring the capacity to distinguish what is natural.[26] In both the Stoic and the Epicurean systems, it is then how one manages and directs his own judgment, and controls the effects from the external world, that determines true transformation.

2.

Several kinds of transformation are evident in Platonic thought, but each is focused either around the journey away from sense-reality or the self-conversion. And both may be described as epistemological changes. Both also include an ethical dimension that will be reflected in the convert's behavior in society. Plato himself was convinced that our moral conduct in this world determines the form in which we are reborn. But the ethics of Plato and other Platonists up to the time of Origen is fundamentally based in what we know, since how we act depends on how deeply we have knowledge of moral values. Platonic conversion may also be described as a turning of the intellect (*Nous*) away from the sensible and toward its true object: the intelligible. This turning is a turning back, a re-turn, to a condition in which the intellect can contemplate the Forms in the realm of the divine. As for how the soul returns to the divine reality, the Platonists usually attribute the power to the soul itself, that is, the power of self-motion. The problem of free will, necessity and providence to which we allude here remained a difficulty for the Platonists up to Plotinus, and it remains inconclusive even in Plotinus. But the intent in most Platonists was to preserve free will. Moreover, for all Platonists up to Plotinus, including Plato himself, the soul is being influenced by intermediaries, the race of demons.[27]

3.

The foregoing paragraph is a general summary of the main themes in Platonic conversion. However, since Origen was writing in the time of Middle Platonism, it might be useful to state briefly some of the traits of this form of Platonism as far as conversion is concerned. Middle Platonism is said to span the time from 80 B.C. to A.D. 220. We are particularly interested in the thought of Philo of Alexandria on conversion, since, in general, Origen's philosophical point of view "is based on Philo rather than any more recent influence."[20]

There are two main implications of Middle Platonism for conversion. First, in the emphasis upon the likeness to God aspect of Platonic ethics, the Middle Platonists tended to reveal the spiritual and mystical side of Platonic thought, making the journey of the soul not only a journey to the divine, but a journey that will liken one to the divine. The Platonic Forms become, in fact, thoughts of the Divine Mind, though, it should be added, the Middle Platonist expected only rare momentary visions of this Mind. Conversion takes on, in any case, a religious quality in certain Platonic thinkers, notably Plutarch and, of course, Philo, a Jew. Second, the increased prominence given to divine powers and intermediary beings, particularly the Logos, in Middle Platonic philosophers seems to make the conversion journey more an interplay or partnership between the soul, essentially a divine creature itself, and the various powers of the One.[29]

How do we change? Middle Platonic doctrine on this concern may be summarized by the following statement of Albinus (fl. A.D. 149–157):[30]

> We may attain to the goal of becoming like unto God (a) by being in control of suitable natural faculties, (b) by correct habituation and training and discipline, and (c) most especially by the use of reason and teaching and the transmission of doctrines, so as to transcend for the most part human concerns, and to be always in contact with intelligible realities.

This view corresponds almost exactly with the view of Philo (ca. 13 B.C.–50 A.D.).[31] Hence before we leave Middle Platonism, let us review the way in which Origen's Alexandrian forebear Philo understood conversion.

4.

Philo's view of man's turning to God seems to have at least three main dimensions. The first dimension is the effort of each person, essentially life-long, to transcend the effects of sense-reality and reach a state in which passion is under control. This dimension is primarily ascetic and purgative, enabling the soul to concentrate its energies on its rational element.

The second dimension involves the use of this rational element to fathom the way of virtue and God's imprints throughout the universe. It is the effort to apprehend God (in truth the Logos) through his creations and his rational patterns innate in all things.

The third dimension concerns faith, the faith of Abraham, which, for Philo, is a kind of intuitive reasoning. In this dimension, when man has felt himself as nothing, when he has purged and purified himself of thoughts of passion and the body, when the soul is not trying to reason out discursively God's way in creation, then God's continuous revelation floods into the soul. For now, freed of obstacles, the soul's natural longing and love for God can dip into its much greater portion; it can feel its place in the divine unity. At this point, the sojourner may experience a mystic vision of God.

All three dimensions are interconnected. Self-discipline goes hand in hand with the path to virtue, and virtue is necessary for faith.[32]

5.

Let us review the idea of conversion in the philosophy of the Empire. Conversion to the ideas of the philosophers required a true change in the life of the convert. This change may be the result of several kinds of journeys. The two most important of these journeys seem to be the change from a life tied to sensible realities to a life concerned with intelligible realities, and the turn inward, self-conversion, an inner effort to conform oneself to the universal law or reason.

The journey of all philosophers involved a strong concern with ethics and the quest for virtue. The end of Platonic conversion was theoretical and extraterrestrial, a return to the presence of the One and divine warmth. The end for the Epicureans and Stoics was more natural, as they understood the term. For the Epicureans, it involved a state of intellectual pleasure and absence of pain and affliction. For the Stoics, it meant freedom, the release from constraint from all sides and submission to the will of providence. Conversion in philosophy may or may not involve a Supreme God, but demons and lesser divine beings were in various ways often influential. For none, with the exception of Philo, was any liturgy, institution, sacrament or scripture particularly significant, but most converts were aided by a sage or school, and most philosophers had some doctrine of revelation, grace, or providence. Conversion to philosophy did not demand total allegiance. Converts were free to worship as they pleased as well as borrow ideas and ways from other philosophers.

The Gnostics[33]

Besides the Greco-Roman religions and philosophies, there was a third alternative, a very different and, for some, powerful alternative: Gnosticism. This view of reality, which, in its most sophisticated form, borrowed from many other sources, especially Platonism, became such a strong force that philosophers and Christians, including Origen, felt compelled to write works opposing it. It was to them a point of view very attractive to religious buyers and that required some subtle argumentation to refute. Not only is this view of existence important for understanding Origen's thought, but it is a view that has many similarities to religious ideas common today.

Though there were many varieties of Gnosticism, its general view of conversion seems to be similar throughout the era of our concern. As the name "Gnostic" itself implies, a word which comes from the Greek word for knowledge (*gnosis*), this kind of conversion was primarily epistemological. From another perspective, however, gnostic conversion occurred only on the cosmic level without human involvement.[34] The effects of this cosmic image of generation can be narrowed to three major themes with respect to conversion: dualism, election, and knowledge.

Gnosticism in general presents a radical dualism between the spiritual and the material, between spirit and flesh, between the Unbegotten One and the world and, of course, between good and evil. Gnosticism is obsessed with the evil inherent in created things. The result of this fundamental attitude of dualism is a very strong emphasis on what transcends matter and the created world, and a very powerful indictment of and at the same time indifference to things and institutions of the created world. Since the true home of one's spiritual self is in the *pleroma*, the place of divine "fullness," the follower of Gnosticism wishes to do everything possible to return there, and to leave behind all contact with and thoughts concerning material things, especially the body. Hence in most of the sects, a rigid asceticism is demanded.

Such asceticism was intended to help the elect transcend the influences of the inferior order in which they were entombed and allow that divine spark given to them to be aroused, so that ultimately they could fix their minds on the higher order where true good and truth resides. The Gnostic concentrates in his ethics, in fact, more on transcendence than on purgation or purification. For him, the flesh, the world and the institutions of the world cannot be purified. They are not of the generation of the *pleroma*, but are the result of an inferior entity distant from the One. The Gnostic's effort then must be directed toward escaping the evil of the world and its inferior position.

The guide for the Gnostic in this effort to overcome imperfection and inferiority can obviously not be found in infected external institutions. Nor can help be expected from the One. One Gnostic responds, "The mind is the guide, and reason is the teacher."[35]

But even the mind can be inadequate alone, without revelation. Adherents of Gnosticism believed that the savior came down from the *pleroma* to reveal knowledge necessary to return the spiritual elements in those elected back to their home. The savior could be one of a number of different personages, depending on the sect, but in many forms of Gnosticism revelation is necessary in partnership with the efforts of men. Again, however, this revelation is not given to all, but only to the elect.

The knowledge revealed to the elect had two sides, theoretical (or mystical) and practical.

The mystical side concerned basically the secret story of how the soul came to its unfortunate condition, how it was imprisoned in matter by an inferior power, becoming ignorant of its true home. It presented the cosmology noted above, and particularly the solution to the origin of evil.

The practical side of the knowledge provided the actual steps by which the spirit could escape the world and especially how it could pass from the various spheres beyond this world on its way home. This practical knowledge involved various secret names, magical preparations and formulae. Adherents of Gnosticism realized that the journey back to God was not only a lifelong struggle, but even continued after the mortal body was shed. Those who made the journey were eternally predestined. In Gnosticism there is actually nothing a person could do to earn redemption by the savior. For without the revelation, the natural reason is completely impotent in these matters. Hence conversion and "freedom" is predestined. One writer doubts whether it is even proper to speak of freedom in Gnosticism, since even the freedom which the elect possess is not truly theirs; it is wholly given in the revealed knowledge.[36]

It would appear actually that the clearest image of conversion in Gnosticism is not anthropomorphic, but cosmic. The Gnostics were concerned about the disorder and disarray in which the cosmos found itself, and they generally viewed the ensuing process of redemption as an effort to bring everything back to unity, to unite every divine spark with the supreme good, and to rid the cosmos of evil.[37]

The Gnostics group humanity in a kind of spiritual hierarchy. The highest group, the *pneumatiki*, have a guaranteed return to the *pleroma*. Conversion is not really applicable to them. Conversion is also without significance to the most inferior group, the *hyliki*, since they are predestined to destruction.

In the middle are the *psychiki*, who are given the opportunity to earn redemption through good works,[38] but they do not receive *gnosis* and the most they may attain is an "intermediate habitation." The *psychiki* require instruction and must be content with mere faith.[39] The image is less forbidding in other works. For example, in *The Tripartite Tractate*, the *psychiki* who will be saved are predetermined, but the salvation is full for them; they need not be content, as Irenaeus has stated, with an intermediate habitation. *The Tractate* has also a slightly different cosmology. It replaces the conversion of *Sophia* (Wisdom) with the conversion of the Logos. Here the conversion is more a turning toward the good and away from evil. In sum, the *psychiki* are predestined to earn their redemption through good works and faith. Though in Irenaeus this redemption is not a full salvation, being without *gnosis*, in the *Tractate* salvation is complete.

One needs to consider whether such a conversion is indeed conversion, and not rather the completion of a mechanized cycle. In both systems, all is fixed.[40]

In conclusion, it would appear from this brief overview that there is much more of a real conversion occurring in Gnosticism on the cosmic level, both in terms of specific entities, such as Sophia or Logos, and in terms of the entire process of returning the spiritual elements home. Man results from the passions and conversions that happen on a transcendent realm. Those predestined to be saved are trapped in an alien environment. They are brought back not fundamentally by the conquest of sin, but by the conquest of ignorance. Even those who are saved through good works and asceticism are saved according to plan. Being far distant from the Father and armed with knowledge about the nature and destiny of the world as well as the secret magical names and formulae, the spiritual elements wend their way home to the All, completing the great plan of cosmic conversion.

The Hebrew Scriptures (the Old Testament)[41]

It is apparent to anyone who reads Origen that the most enduring influence upon his mind was the Scriptures. It is important to clarify not only how Origen viewed scriptural conversion, but also how conversion is seen in the Scriptures by scholars today. In the next two sections we will be discussing the latter dimension in order to set down a reasonably objective view of spiritual change in the Scriptures so that we can see how much the view of Origen was influenced by it.

The approach to conversion in the Hebrew Scriptures will be as follows: First, there will be presented a general outline of how conversion may be understood, viewed historically. Second, three details concerning these dimensions of conversion will be discussed. (a) the role of God, (b) the terminology of conversion and its implications, and (c) conversion in the prophets.

There are four dimensions of Judaic conversion which roughly correspond to four stages in the history of the Jews. (1) The first dimension involves a "turning away" from God. In this condition, the people are apathetic toward their God and the covenant, and turn away in apostasy toward other gods and sinful practices. (2) The second dimension concerns the response by the prophets to the conversion away from God.[42] The prophets demand an inner repentance, a "turning back" or return to the ways of the fathers, and a recall to the covenant and promises. The first dimension of apostasy sometimes involved a mere externality in one's religious practices. The prophets hence demand a total return to God not only in practice, but, more importantly, in heart. The master of this call is the prophet Jeremiah.[43] Unfortunately the exile interrupts or prevents the fulfillment of this prophetic call. (3) After the exile and return of the Jews, Jewish religion, reflected in the writings of this period, becomes more legalistic and ritualistic.[44] Conversion often concerns only the liturgy of sacrifices, rigorous practices and complete service of one's life to the Law. The Book of Ezekiel reflects many of these aspects, though it also has passages which tend toward a kind of personal conversion. (4) Finally, as is often expressed in the Apocrypha and Pseudepigrapha, the old prophetic call for the conversion of inner change returns, but it is also intermixed with the prevailing legalism and ritualism of the temple.[45] In sum, these four dimensions may be narrowed to two: an inner conversion of the heart, a spiritual turning back to God and the covenant, and an outer change of practice, stressing ritual and legalism in one's religious life. The second aspect had the tendency to degenerate into mere habit without an inner moral intention.

To this general summary, let us now discuss in more detail three themes.

The first concerns the role of God in Hebrew conversion. It is God above all who takes the initiative in conversion in the Hebrew Scriptures. Conversion is a grace of light that reveals to the sinner his sin and the goodness of him whom the sin offended.[46] Hence Judaic conversion is not merely man turning to God and away from sin; it is man and God turning toward each other. In fact, this mutual conversion of God and man is a unique contribution of the Hebrew scriptures to the meaning of conversion.[47] Man's contribution to the conversion process is self-abasement and penitence, while the role of God is to pardon, bestow grace and soften the heart.[48]

Since Origen's basic text for his Old Testtment was not the Hebrew, but the Septuagint, it seems neccessary to discuss the conversion terminology of the original Hebrew text and its Greek translation.[49] In this way, we may come to some understanding of how the Greek interpreted the Hebrew original.[50] *Shub*, the word for conversion in Hebrew, meant a "fundamental change of direction towards an object in light of a recalling to one's initial point of departure."[51]

In religious contexts, this definition means more than merely a change of conduct; it implies also a change in attitude.[52] Jeremiah, called the "doctor of conversion,"[53] uses *shub* 111 times to stress the importance of a change in both attitude and conduct. One "turns away from idols or a profane way of life, and "turns toward" God. These two aspects were considered one act in the Hebrew *shub*, but they later become increasingly distinguished in the Greek by the terms *metanoiein* (to repent) and *epistrephein* (to turn back). It is noteworthy also that the Hebrew uses a verb to describe conversion rather than nouns or adjectives.[54] Conversion is a concrete action, not a reflection on its values.[55]

Finally, since conversion is a key focus in many of the prophets, let us try to summarize what appears to be an important factor in their understanding of conversion: The prophets tend to link conversion with trust and faith.[56] Sin for them is to disregard God. Idolatry is failing to regard and be faithful to God. Hence conversion is a show of confidence in the Lord both externally in practice and inwardly in one's attitude and heart.[57] To be converted means to have reformed one's attitude and relation to God, so that one places his entire trust in the will of the Lord.[58] Ultimately then, all of man's efforts culminate in a renewal of faith in the Lord.

The New Testament

Turning to the New Testament writings, we find some of the same themes of the Hebrew Scriptures. But there appear to be two obvious general differences: First, in the New Testament, though God's grace is present in every step of conversion, the role of man in conversion is developed more intensely. Second, conversion in the New Testament tends to be not a single event or a series of single events, but a continuous condition which progresses toward the kingdom.[59] Other than these general differences, there are also several unique tendencies of and additions to the concept of conversion in the New Testament which bear discussion. It is not possible to develop all of them in detail, but the most important aspects seem to be: (1) the more distinct difference of *metanoiein* and *epistrephein*; (2) conversion as it applies to the Gentiles; (3) the reconciling role of Jesus Christ in conversion; (4) the role of baptism; (5) the importance of the concept of the kingdom; and (6) the role of the Holy Spirit.[60]

The basic source for the Hebrew understanding of conversion would appear to be Jeremiah. In the New Testament, several writers believe that this position is assumed by the Luke-Acts writings.[61] Except where noted, the following summary follows conversion as presented in Luke-Acts, although we will be outlining the themes of conversion in Paul, John, and the other gospels.

According to what is extant in the New Testament, the early Christian preachers are faced with two groups: the Jews and the pagans. Yet to both of them the preachers present a similar conversion process: Turn from the past and come to an awareness of one's past errors, sin and shame, for Christ has given all people the opportunity to be reconciled to God. The pagan's errors are ignorance and idolatry, and the Jew's problems focus on sin. Each potential convert must feel shame, guilt, or be apologetic for his past before the process of becoming a Christian can continue.[62] This initial step in the process of conversion in the New Testament is generally called repentance (*metanoia*).[63] It is the response to God's offering of forgiveness and reconciliation.

After the admission of error or sins and the turn from idolatry, the next dimension of New Testament conversion involves belief or faith in Jesus Christ. Though we will discuss the role of Christ below, we need to state here that conversion is only possible because of Christ's redeeming act and the offer of pardon given to man through him. Indeed to believe in Christ and to be converted are closely related.[64] With faith the sins and past errors can be remitted, and pardon can occur.[65] This second dimension may be described as a turn toward the Lord or a need for a bond to Jesus Christ. It is not, we might note, an acceptance of a philosophical system of truths, but a complete relinquishing to a person, to the living God and to Jesus as Lord of one's life.[66] It was this precise dimension and movement that was often a stumbling-block for pagans. They were baffled by the demand to turn to a person (God or Jesus) rather than to a system of truths or a ritual.[67] The bond to Jesus is sealed by two factors. In terms of one's attitude, it involves the recognition that he has risen, he is resurrected, he is alive, and for all a reconciliation has occurred. It is primarily for this reason that one finds a stress on the resurrection in the apostolic preaching.[68] The second factor involves the third dimension of the conversion in the New Testament: the complete acceptance and practice of the Christian way of life, and entrance into the Christian community. The seal here is baptism.

Baptism is the sign that the converted has a completely new orientation in his manner of life and conduct. But it is more than merely a sign to New Testament writers. It also inspires not only a change of attitude, i.e., a change in one's system of values, but a total change of lifestyle and conduct. In this sense, it is a catalyst of a new direction, a spiritual change in direction comparable to a physical change in direction. And this process is generally labeled *epistrephein* or *epistrophe*.[69] Here finally the converted pagan or Jew abandons all his old ways and customs, and adopts enthusiastically the Christian way.[70] The third dimension of baptism confirms and seals the first two dimensions, repentance and faith. Man turns away from evil through heartfelt repentance, turns toward the Lord in complete trust and confidence in his love and power, experiences a transformation of his inner self and his conduct through the effort to follow the way of Christ, and then receives the grace of baptism that seals his intention and provides divine aid in his struggles. Though in this outline grace seems to be unrevealed until baptism, the grace of the Spirit is at work throughout the process. In fact, all dimensions— repentance, faith, and baptism—may be considered in part gifts of God. God is somehow involved in, though not necessarily controlling, every dimension of the path toward becoming a Christian.[71]

These foregoing paragraphs, then, describe briefly and in outline the main features of New Testament view as presented primarily in Luke-Acts. Let us, nevertheless, add a few details or clarifications, as the case may be, to this view by surveying conversion in other New Testament writings.

In Mark, to be converted is to believe in the Good News, which is the presence of the kingdom of God that Jesus accomplishes. The first aspect of conversion for Mark is faith in the total transformation of existence by the coming of the kingdom. Hence we view here (and in the Gospel of John) a wider, more cosmic perspective of conversion that Jesus inaugurates and supervises.[72] Matthew's contribution to the Christian idea of conversion lies in his tendency to stress the insight that the whole Christian life is a kind of conversion. He sees the purpose of the Christian life as the creation of the kingdom on earth by witness and example. Matthew thus writes to those who are inside the kingdom.[73] In contrast to Matthew, it might be noted, Luke directs his attention to the Gentiles. He stresses the universality of salvation. "If salvation is universal, conversion is the necessary condition."[74]

Paul, who makes clear how God is the initiator of conversion,[75] often outlines the process as turning from the service of idols to the service of God. And this service sometimes, as in Colossians, becomes a predominantly moral transformation, i.e., turning from a dissolute life to a life of holiness.[76] There is also in Paul—Galatians, for example—a conversion of understanding, a kind of epistemological point of view with respect to how one changes one's attitudes. When one becomes a Christian, Paul believes, he is no longer ignorant of God, but now knows the true God and knows how to conform to His will.[77]

Even more epistemologically oriented, with respect to the spiritual journey, is the Gospel of John. One journeys from darkness, evil and sin of the "world" to the light, good, truth and love of Jesus Christ. John's catalyst for conversion is the revelation of knowledge, the truth, which Jesus brings. Moreover, a particularly important insight of this Gospel, it seems to me, is the stress on the need for a condition of receptivity and attentiveness for the efficacy of conversion. It is also evident that, with the emphasis on revelation, John stresses the importance of grace to conversion.[78]

Other Christian Writers before Origen[79]

1.

The main elements of conversion as presented in the scriptural writings are not always evident in the second century Apostolic Fathers. Often one aspect or another takes prominence, creating an apparent imbalance in perspective when contrasted with the approach of Scripture. Also, since the Bible of the Fathers was the Hebrew Scriptures (particularly the LXX), we find generally a dialogue with the ideas on conversion expressed in the LXX. Having said this, we do note,

in fact, several general types of conversion in the Apostolic Fathers, types which
are analogous in some sense to the areas in which the authors write or were born,
the areas being Rome, Asia Minor and Alexandria.[80]

Let us turn first to the Roman Apostolic Fathers: I and II Clement (ca. 100?
and 120 A.D.?) and Hermas (ca. 140 A.D.?).[81]

In general, a strong moralism is present in the Roman Apostolic Fathers.[82]
Naturally this moral emphasis affected their view of conversion. For example,
in II Clement, repentance tends to be connected less with one's change of mind
than with one's change of habits and with certain moral deeds.[83] Similarly in
I Clement, who addresses not the pagans but those already professing Christianity,
and who understands conversion and repentance as integral to the process of
returning to the merciful God, repentance involves more often an outer turning
requiring good deeds and obedience to the order and hierarchy of the Church
rather than an inner turning.[84] In sum, their legalism tends to bring to the
foreground a conversion by deed and holiness. We also find the idea of conversion
as a permanent condition of the Christian, a kind of continuous spiritual struggle
against temptation, as well as a sort of epistemological conversion in which Christ,
the Master of Truth, brings knowledge through his laws.[85] But both of these
aspects are intimately bound up with the conversion by holiness and obedience
to the laws of Christ. There is a similarity of this conversion to the post-exilic
view of conversion in the LXX.

Hermas's *Shepherd* requires a separate discussion, since it is a little book
completely devoted to the subject of conversion. Three main uses of "conversion"
have been noted.[86] First, there is the typically Christian intimate link of
conversion and repentance. Second, Hermas's view of conversion is often similar
to the LXX conception. As in the LXX, Hermas writes that one will receive a
kind of material prosperity if one returns to the Lord.[87] Hence there is an
emphasis on a kind of external religiosity. Furthermore, Hermas's view of
conversion does not involve Christ, but the "Lord." In fact, conversion is the
product of the partnership of the Lord, man, and the commandments given by
the Lord to man. Finally, Hermas develops in detail the conversion of the heart,
again more under the influence of the LXX than New Testament thought. He
sees the "Lord" working in the heart of the one converted. Despite Hermas's
interest in the LXX and Judaic use of conversion, still we find no evidence of
the LXX idea of God turning away or to the people. In this way, Hermas
resembles the New Testament and other early Christian writers.

To this outline, we might also add Hermas's view of faith. Hermas understands
faith as the parent of all other virtues and the fundamental motivating force of
conversion.[88]

The approach in Asia Minor may be illustrated by a consideration of the letters
of Ignatius (died ca. 108 A.D.?) Ignatius's view of conversion, as represented from
the extant works, may be fairly labeled a Christological conversion; that is, nearly
the entire focus of Ignatius's view of how man is transformed centers, on the
one hand, on his union with and imitation of Christ, and, on the other hand,

on the work of Christ himself.[89] Of course, this view must be understood in light of the apparent practical motives of Ignatius's letters, which were primarily to respond to heretical Christologies. One writer, for example, has pointed out that Ignatius, in his wish to concentrate all his energies in the letters on problems of Christology and the need for unity, has simply assumed the general religious teachings and the ordinary moral instruction.[90] It is possible that other dimensions, uses or concepts of conversion might have been more developed by Ignatius in other circumstances.

In terms of the Christological conversion, Ignatius writes that we receive Christ through union with the Church and the sacraments. Hence the mystical aspect of Ignatius, in which one is encouraged to unite spiritually with Christ and bring Christ into one's life and heart, is linked with ecclesiology.[91] In contrast to the Roman writers, Ignatius stresses the need for divine help, the importance of faith as the way to God and as the key element in deeds, and the belief that works in general do not determine one's relationship with God.[92] Yet beside his intense interest in the role of Christ, Ignatius also believes that man must first voluntarily choose the life that is God.[93]

In the Apostolic Fathers, the idea of Christian transformation, as we would expect in such early times, is generally undeveloped. The ideas of repentance, faith, and works are usually stated without comment, as if one was using a word universally understood or a well-known formula. It was noted above that probably Ignatius intentionally left aside such discussions in order to concentrate on immediate problems of heresy and fragmentation. In fact, practical motives take precedence over speculation in almost all of the Apostolic Fathers. The Fathers, for example, do not speculate in extant writings on the nature of evil, the origins of man's predicament, the nature of the soul, or the final heavenly condition of the faithful or the sinful. When they mention these areas of concern, they generally seem to be repeating creedal patterns. There is much attention to a life of holiness in the conversion process, some Fathers viewing the matter as obedience to the commandments, others stressing the need as well for an inner transformation. Hermas seems to provide the most complete picture of what is required to become a Christian, while Ignatius anticipates later views on how Christ will be involved in the conversion process.

2.

For the Apologists of the second century, the entire Christian message is aimed at conversion from heathenism.[94] These folk were clearly involved in the battle to survive as a sect. The primary new development, with respect to conversion as well as other areas, is the use of the *logos* concept in cosmology, anthropology and Christology.[95] In Justin (died ca. 165 A.D.), for example, *logos* is used as a way to bring Christianity and classical culture together, and also to unite the "Old" and "New" covenants. In both aspects the theme is continuity of conversion through the Father's Logos.[96] The Logos was at work both in the great philosophers of classical culture and in the prophets of the Old Testament who called for a turning from past beliefs and ideas to the one and true God.[97] The reasons why *logos* is central in conversion are, first, because it represents as immanent in man (his "reason") the link between God and man.[98] This link is a seed of the divine Logos and allows men to see truth, be enlightened and receive revelations from the Logos, who, according to Justin, was fully incarnate in Christ.[99] Second, the Logos as incarnate in Christ defeats one of the main obstacles to conversion, namely, the devil and demons.[100]

Although both roles of *logos* involve divine aid in conversion, the Apologists also believe intensely in man's free will.[101] Justin, for example, stated that an important part of the conversion process occurs when man, through his own free will, seeks the help of the Logos.[102] Yet divine involvement is never absent. This fact is clear in Justin's description of Christian initiation, a process practically equivalent to conversion in this context. The initiation process is as follows: belief in the Christian teaching, repentance, baptism, illumination.[103] Each element in this process exhibits for Justin a divine participation in the most fundamental sense, since each involves God's gift at creation, the human *logos*.[104] Yet God's role does not impede free will.[105]

In sum, Justin and other Apologists had a sense of conversion as a cooperative effort between God and man, but the connection remains undeveloped. Their kind of conversion might be described as transformation by *logos*, since *logos* is, in their view, the power which enables man to be transformed. Of course, we need to recall that the content of the extant works of the Apologists is determined by the motives and circumstances of the writing. As we saw already with Ignatius, the image of conversion can be somewhat narrowed by the genre and the practical reasons for the works.

3.

This same point must be made also with respect to the work of Irenaeus (ca. 130–200 A.D.), whose main surviving writing is totally directed toward opposing the Valentinian Gnostics.[106] Whereas the Apologists were concerned with pagan attacks, his view of conversion is colored by the problem of heresy and the need to distinguish orthodox conversion from Gnostic conversion. In light of this fact, it is not surprising that his primary contribution to the meaning of conversion seems to rest in his consideration of the "conversion to the Church,"[107] in contrast with other Christian writers (and New Testament writers) who usually wrote of conversion to God, Christ, the Lord, the Logos and the Truth. For Irenaeus, however, the beginning of the Christian sojourn seems to lie in realizing and becoming a part of the true vessel of truth on earth, the apostolic Church. Since his writings are addressed to Christians rather than pagans, his concept of conversion is often a conversion of return, such as we discovered in the LXX; but here it is a return of the heretic (or those seduced by heretics) to the true community, the true Church, the only Church "of God." The phrase "of God" is critical for Irenaeus. Only in the Church "of God" can one be found in Christ.[108] Only there can one come to know God, receive immortality and the teaching of the true tradition. Only in one vessel can one receive the Truth, which is found in the one Tradition. Irenaeus's conversion to the Church of God brings to light both the uniqueness of the apostolic truth for him, and the uniqueness of the conversion to it.[109]

The other area of development with respect to conversion, an area which also probably results from Irenaeus's anti-Gnostic motives, is Irenaeus's detailed discussions of theological anthropology, especially with respect to the pattern of man's spiritual life and his ideas on man as a maturing creature.[110] The Apostolic Fathers and the Apologists were generally vague and sometimes silent concerning the factors leading up to the need for conversion and the subsequent consequences, particularly the soteriological role of Christ in terms of fallen man. In contrast to these writers, Irenaeus views the nature and destiny of man as an important part of the great plan of God, and he presents this part and God's plan thoroughly in order to contrast it with the detail of Gnostic speculations.[111] It is not possible here to present or examine thoroughly Irenaeus's ideas, but one can briefly narrate them as follows: Man was created as a childlike creature who was progressing and maturing. The Fall, caused by man's inexperience, spiritual weakness, and negligence of his gifts, interrupts this process of advancement and delivers an almost fatal blow to man's growth. But the process is made possible again with Christ's incarnation and perfect human life.[112] Due to Christ's work of perfect obedience and strength in the face of temptation, man again can resume his journey toward immortality and life with God. Central to the process is Irenaeus's belief, against the determinism of the Gnostics, in man's freedom to choose salvation and the process of conversion.[113]

In accordance with this summary and the prior statements on the conversion to the Church, we may conclude that conversion in Irenaeus is, even more clearly than in prior Christian writers, the essential, continuous, even natural course of Christian life, if that Christian, of course, is a member of the Church of God, the Church which extends back to and begins with Christ. The elements of this conversion are traditional for Irenaeus: Now that man has the opportunity for salvation, he need only follow Christ's commands within the Church, obeying these commands and resisting sin. The second Adam has reopened the door toward life with God and released man from the clutches of the devil. Though one tends to stress only the role of redemption in Irenaeus's system, it is the return to a state of conversion, of slow advancement toward resemblance to Christ and life with God, which lies behind God's economy. By advancing in goodness and knowledge, one approaches closer and closer to God. Advancement (or progress) here seems to imply a continuous effort to improve oneself and a continuous turning away from what is unworthy to the ways of Christ and his Church. Christ is both the catalyst and the end of this conversion.[114]

4.

In contrast to Irenaeus, whose ideas on conversion tend to center on his view of Christ as second Adam, the Church, and his idea of progress, the point of view of Tertullian (ca. 160–225 A.D.?) tends to show, on the one hand, a legalistic quality, and, on the other hand, a marked influence from Stoicism, with respect to the concept of conversion.[115] It is important to mention again that the purpose of each of these sections is to search for the writer's individual contributions to the concept of conversion rather than outline his theology. Hence, with respect to Tertullian, these tendencies are only tendencies. Tertullian's view of Christ as savior, for example, is evident throughout his work; indeed it is his material-Stoic view of the soul as that which is inherited from Adam that seems to require Christ's saving work and death in his theology.[116] Unlike Irenaeus, however, who tends to see the Fall as an interruption in man's evolution due to his inexperience and ignorance, Tertullian, to some extent like his fellow Africans Cyprian and Augustine, understands the act of Adam as a racial wound that weakens the powers of the soul, so that man must have divine help in order to heal the wound and be saved.[117] Hence, due to Adam's act, man has a bias toward sin. Like Irenaeus, however, Tertullian insists that man is still free to choose.[118]

These two elements, that man has a bias to sin and that man remains free to choose, are critical for Tertullian's view of man's turning toward God. To take the first step in conversion, in order to wash away the inherited bias to sin, man must choose the divine power of baptism. Prior to baptism, Tertullian outlines a process of repentance.[119] Hence baptism is the culmination of a process of preparation. The entire process, including baptism, constitutes, for Tertullian, the necessary first stage toward any further development.[120] The following stages involve the other contribution of Tertullian to the concept of conversion: his judicative view of how Christian life functions.

Tertullian tends to pattern the relationship between man and God as if a defendant were standing before a judge. This view of the divine-human relationship is also determined by a rigid but optimistic moralism that Tertullian probably learned partly from reading the Stoics.[121] Man the defendant must satisfy the one he has injured by a system of satisfaction. In this system, man receives merits for good works, while bad conduct requires satisfaction.[122] Hence God the judge either awards damages or inflicts punishments. This combination of judicature and moralism often gives to his view of conversion the appearance of turning without a deep spiritual movement, as if external obedience to rules and commands given in Scripture suffices to earn a place for the converted in heaven.[123] But Tertullian is careful to require, as noted above, and even insist on, a sincere repentance before baptism.[124] In fact, Tertullian clarifies that there are two aspects of repentance, the inner and the outer. The former is the inner satisfaction of conscience, while the latter is the outer satisfaction of confession.[125] We noticed a similar stress on works together with a sincere repentance in Hermas. In light of the predominance of the idea of satisfaction in the Christian struggle, it may be accurate to describe his view of conversion as satisfaction, as long as one is aware of of the inner dimensions of the process. In sum, Christ's death makes possible the restoration of relations, so that man now can choose to repent, receive divine help in baptism and enter the process of lifelong merit and satisfaction by which he returns to God.

5.

Though the aspect of enlightenment and revelation of knowledge is present in many prior Christian thinkers, it was developed in much greater detail by Origen's direct predecessor, Clement of Alexandria (?-before 215 A.D.), who even calls the perfect Christian a gnostic.[126] Hence Clement's primary contribution to the Christian concept of conversion is the development of an epistemological conversion in contrast with the Gnostic system described above. A secondary contribution, connected to the first, is Clement's discussions on the relation of knowledge and faith (*gnosis* and *pistis*).[127]

In effect, Clement's general view of spiritual change is outlined in the three major works which are extant: the *Protrepticus*, an exhortation and invitation to the unconverted heathen to break through opinion, tradition, prejudice and customs, and permit faith to prosper;[128] the *Paedagogus*, a practical instruction booklet for those being converted who are preparing for baptism or who are baptized on how to eliminate passion and acquire self-control;[129] and the *Stromateis*, a series of miscellaneous notes woven together around the theme of contemplation of the higher mysteries for those who have made progress in the control of the lower earthly attractions.[130] The *Stromateis* is unconnected to the other two books, which are two parts of a planned series, but it does fit into the right place for Clement's view of the conversion process. In these three works, we witness again, though in a much clearer framework than past Christian writers, that becoming a Christian is a continuing life process involving faith, virtue, and contemplation. From the moment of receiving the word in "exhortation" through the struggles to combat passion and then on to the higher mysteries, the spiritual journey is a perfecting process.

And that which is being perfected, Clement writes, is faith.[131] A person begins and ends in faith, and knowledge is the demonstration of faith. Clement explores the entire question of Christian change in terms of faith and knowledge in a chapter of *Stromateis*. He writes:

And, in my view, the first saving change is that from heathenism to faith, as I said before; and the second, that from faith to knowledge. And the latter terminating in love thereafter gives the loving to the loved, that which knows to that which is known.[132]

Faith, it should be noted, does not end when knowledge begins; knowledge, as stated above, is a demonstration of what faith already "knows." And love is a kind of agent of unification that merges the man of faith ever closer to God, so that distinctions become blurred. In other words, the goal of spiritual maturity is a mystical ascent through faith to a kind of union through love with God. Knowledge is one way of bringing faith up to its true potential in contemplating God.

Clement also explains this process in terms of the higher and lower life of the Christian. The lower involves exhortation and instruction regarding the passions.[133] At this level Christ is a lawgiver, a shepherd and a tutor, titles which encompass Christ's human capacities. But in the higher life, Christ is "known" as God, i.e., in the mystery of the Eucharist. In the higher life of the gnostic, Christ now is Light, Truth, and Life.[134] The difference of the lower and the higher life, and the threefold path by which faith is comprehended—faith, knowledge, love—become even clearer when we compare Clement's knowledge (gnosis) and faith (pistis) with Gnostic views.

The basic differences are, first, Clement stresses that gnosis and perfection are open to everyone.[135] All people are called to the higher life, in contrast to the elite system of Gnosticism in which one kind of person is predestined by nature. For Clement the difference between one man and another in terms of his or her progress is that "one man applies less, one more, to learning and training."[136] Another difference is Clement's stress on free will in contrast to the role of fate and the image of necessity which seem often to darken man's prospects in the Gnostic systems.[137] This necessitarianism affected every aspect of Gnosticism, including anthropology, as we have noted in discussing the Gnostic idea of election. Clement, however, believed in the balance of free will and grace in the process of turning toward God, as well as a cooperation between the quest for holiness and God's providence.[138] A third difference is the significant place Clement provided for the concept of unity in his theology: the unity of God (in contrast to the two-god, two-Jesus Gnostic speculations), and the unity of God's plan in creation, revelation and salvation (in contrast to the Gnostic's radical dualism in each of these areas).[139] For Clement, the transformation of man is not the unfortunate result of something that occurred on a transcendent level, but from the beginning holds a critical place in the plan of God.

This third difference between Clement and contemporary Gnostics is especially evident in Clement's discussions on God's care, providence, and instruction. These may be loosely grouped under the principle of education. Unlike the Gnostics, who considered it essential to divorce the One from any contact or involvement with material creation, the God of Clement is busily at work throughout the ages trying to lure man away from ignorance of him and polytheism. The training activity of God is, for Clement, the heart of what the Christian conversion implies, namely, educating man to the knowledge contained in faith. Whereas for the Gnostics faith was the inferior mode of the *psychiki* toward salvation, for Clement it is the foundation of knowledge. Throughout the ages God is educating everyone, even the pagans, the philosophers, and the Jews, to the true knowledge. Hence conversion does not begin with Christianity. Christianity is the final stage in God's great plan of conversion.[140]

Summary

These then are the variety of concepts of transformation and spiritual change that were present in Origen's environment of the third century, and is it not a diverse group? Imagine how the person who sought spiritual food must have felt. He or she would have viewed a full spectrum of possibilities, from the lack of a conversion concept (as we understand it) in the Greco-Roman religions to systems in which the entire point of view is overwhelmed with conversion. He or she would have witnessed a conversion to the Church, a conversion of satisfaction, forms of epistemological conversion, a self-conversion, a cosmic conversion, moralistic and judicative conversions, conversion of God and Christocentric conversion. Several writers combine a number of elements. Each differs from the other on the steps involved in the conversion, and the end toward which conversion leads.

Standing in the midst of these myriad of possibilities is the thought of Origen of Alexandria. He will synthesize many of them into a coherent and profound vision of Christian thought on change and spiritual growth that even today, after many centuries, stands as a powerful statement of how a person becomes a Christian.

II

The Beginning and the End: What Happens before and after Earthly Life?

Background

Why do some people seek the good and others do not? Why do some have a tendency to degenerate while others do not? Why are some people tempted so easily by what will harm them and others are not? Why can some people emerge out of the darkness of evil, fighting all the while for the light, while others keep slipping back, making little or no progress? And why do some seem to lack moral sense at an early age and others do not?

These questions gnaw at our patiences and their answers could explain a great deal. Origen asked these same questions and sought for the answers in Scripture when they were not spelled out in the rule of faith as it was written in his day. He rephrased them with scriptural referents: Why did God seem to prefer Jacob over Esau? Why did God accept the gift of Abel and not that of Cain? Why did the Pharaoh's heart harden? There are numerous seemingly mysterious questions such as these in Scripture, and no one was more interested in their answers than Origen.

It was not a mere intellectual interest; it was more a practical matter of survival for the little Christian sect. Daily, Origen was faced with serious opposition from non-Christians and even heretical Christians who came to him and debated. He was renowned for his teaching and his power of thought, as well as his openness and kindness toward those who truly sought the truth. They came with their own answers, but their answers were not always, according to Origen, in line with the goodness of God or with the image of God as presented in Scripture.

He could not simply state that these were all mysteries. Origen conceded that there is more in Scripture than any person could grasp. He conceded that there were, as Paul states, things which could not be told now. But to say nothing in the climate of his day, with heresies growing or sprouting up everywhere, was imprudent. Silence would leave open the errant speculations of others, the possibility of any answer, or that the Scripture was unclear or inconsistent. And, as I noted in the first part, there was no predecessor, no Christian or non-Christian thinker, who was Origen's peer in such matters. No one had wrestled so deeply with the scriptual mysteries. To Origen the answers of the heretics made a mockery of Scripture and God's grace. Origen realized from the beginning that he needed to set down some basic principles so that thinkers from all groups could see the beauty of Scripture and the depth of its thought, so that how a person grows or declines spiritually could be reasonably clear. He had to probe profoundly into the patterns of scriptural thought so that he could offer, at least to some extent, explanations of some of these mysteries, particularly the mysteries about the beginning and the end. If he could not grasp the beginning and the end, how could he explain the middle of man's transformation, the middle of the Christian life?

So here is the key concern. If he was to proceed with his discussions of the spiritual journey and how one becomes a Christian, he had to establish a need.

Three general stages of spiritual growth appear in Origen. These are (1) before the need for change, (2) while one is transforming, and (3) when conversion is completed or perfected. Origen more often refers to the present condition of man's soul, its present needs and problems, than to some pure state before or after the experience of conversion.[1] But in several works he does pose questions concerning the origin of the soul, the nature of the body and the rational creature's final state both because he wishes to know how man's present condition arose and what his final state will be, and also because he is interested in the transformation of man's present condition. In addition, these inquiries were often speculations with no other purpose at times than to respond to and perhaps to convert non-Christians and heretics on issues where the rule of faith and Scripture were, in Origen's opinion, either silent or obscure.[2] However, even in discussing these issues, he often presents the questions side by side with remedies that can transform man's condition and help him return to a better state.[3]

Even though Origen's primary concern seems to have been with the transformation of man's present condition, let us investigate briefly, first, how Origen described the rational creature's state of original innocence and what reasons he gives for a change in that state, and, second, how Origen understood the ultimate goal toward which he believed the conversion of rational life was directed. We discuss the first area in this section, and the second in the sections that follow.

Why Did Man Fall?

He began with the beginning, or the proto-beginning, before there was a beginning as we know it. What journey had man already taken, according to the hypothesis which Origen accepts, when he fell to his present state? Origen was convinced that there had to be some cause for man's present condition. How else can one explain the diverse motivations of the human mind?

This procedure may also help us to understand both the nature of and the reasons for man's present condition. As Origen wrote in his explanation of Jer. 10:12, "The Lord...who set right the inhabited world...," "...no one who has not fallen needs to be set right."[4]

Before we begin, we need a clarification of the basic terminology Origen uses in his understanding of man. For context purposes only then, let us briefly summarize the main terms involved in his discussions.[5] For Origen, man has three dimensions: the spirit (*pneuma*), the soul (*psyche*), and the body (*soma*). The soul itself has two dimensions: an upper part, which depending on the context and Origen's purpose, can be described with the Platonic "intellect" (*nous*), the Stoic "heart" (*hegemonikon*) or the scriptural "heart" (*kardia*),[6] and the lower part, which is invariably called "flesh" (*sarx*)." While the upper part tends toward the spirit, the lower part is influenced by the body. And it is this struggle in each person's soul that makes Origen's views on man's progress and degeneration so dynamic and active concerning man's conversion. The spirit is the upper part of the intellect, the divine influence, the conscience, and the place where the Holy Spirit resides when he is in man. The soul is the dimension involving will and choice, while the body with flesh is the seat of—not the cause of—the earthly part of man's existence. If the soul is in sin, the spirit becomes, so-to-speak, dormant, but it does not die or leave the man. Indeed the spirit's continuing presence, despite the condition of man, gives hope for change.

In his dialogue with philosophers and Gnostics, Origen suggests hypothetically that the problems of man[7] originated in a pre-existent state. As in many other issues, Origen at times will discuss the matter of origins first as it is literally written in Scripture (in this case, Genesis), namely, that God places man in paradise, and man loses paradise because of disobedience, or that man, like Adam, falls due to sin, and has need of a restoration.[8] However, since the mystery of the origin of souls was not explicitly discussed in the rule of faith and was, in Origen's opinion, hidden in Scripture, Origen felt free to speculate, through allegorical exegesis, and offer, based on his interpretation of several other scriptural texts, some additional clarity to what seemed to him a mystery.[9] He noted that the causes of man's fall often centered, as they do in Scripture, around the devil. For example, in his homily on Jer. 2:22, Origen states that the devil is the catalyst for the appearance of evil and death, and, in the same section, Origen confirms the image of a group that "turned opposite to the plan of the creator."[10] Other passages confirm that one creature, the devil, exercised his free will, rebelled against God, and others through imitation followed.[11]

The mention of free will is critical. God gave to each intellect the power of free will so that it could decide its own destiny and respond individually to the good. Origen will extend this view to say also that not only did the Fall result from the use of free will, but the diversity of creation resulted from the diversity of ways in which intellects exercised their free wills.[12]

Let us note clearly what it is that the intellects neglect: the good. All intellects receive both existence and the good only from God. Since the good and existence are essentially only of God, intellects are good accidentally.[13] By preserving or neglecting this good that God had given them, intellects decide their own direction. All, including the creature who became the devil, begin as equals, with the same rational nature.[14] However, when the intellects were influenced by the devil's act of withdrawal, noted above, they followed the devil's example and, in accordance with the degree of rebellion in their choices, God assigned them a rank: "...he placed everyone in a position proportionate to his merit."[15] The result was that diversity of choices in response to the good resulted in a world of diverse creatures.[16]

It is clear that man, in his original state, freely chose his direction, and, as a result, turned away from God. Evidently some change in him had occurred as a result of these choices. This change occurring in the original state is described in some detail by Origen as a kind of cooling due to the human creature's "loss of its first natural and divine warmth." He comes to this conclusion because the word *psyche* (soul) in Greek comes, he believes, from a word that involves something growing colder. No longer was it a *nous* (intellect); it had become a *psyche* (soul) because of the loss of the divine warmth. When it is restored, however, it becomes again a *nous* (intellect).[17]

We see that the soul is the result of a transformation of the intellect (*nous*, or *mens* in the Latin adaptation) by a rebellious, self-willed act. Nevertheless, Origen also states that the intellect is not destroyed by this act, since the soul can return to the condition of being an intellect.

It is important to stop for a moment to dwell on what has occurred and the implications of the above texts with reference to conversion and the meaning of the good, and how Origen has responded to several mysteries. Origen has considered two aspects of originate existence, both gifts of God: the good, and self-motion (or free will); he then views them as being dependent on each other when resident in man. The object of the will of man, for example, is the good. All good comes from God, and the good of man, while possessed by him through the power of the intellect (*nous*) and his reason (*logos*)—as we shall see in Part III—was received from God as a kind of permanent gift, in the same way we are each given an individual body. Hence though man has no "essential goodness"[18] in the sense that he is the source of good or that he made the good (as God does in Genesis), the good which is in him is his to use or not to use freely. Later on, we shall also learn that the soul is never *essentially* changed; that is, the intellect endures, even if it is dormant while sin is present.

This point of view clarifies one stumbling block for us in understanding change. Origen assures us that the fall of man is a question of the will alone, that the Fall is a moral degeneration arising from the choices the will makes. So in the beginning, the good is given through the intellect and reason (*logos*), for in them rests the power of good. This power may be neglected by the will, but it is unchanged. If the Fall was ontological, corrupting every dimension of man, the possibility of transformation would rest solely in the hands of God. For only God could transform the creature to its former state of being. Hence from the beginning, Origen leaves open the possibility of a conversion effort shared between God and man.

The second stumbling block is why man would ever turn away from God if man has good. Though Origen often explains that man copied the devil, that man neglected the good, and even that man became satiated with the divine warmth, these are answers not detailed enough to explain how Origen viewed the immense step from intellect to soul, or, more significantly, the move from being with God to being cold and distant from him. How did man, a creation of the perfect omnipotent being who created all things and who is reality itself, have even the potential to fall?

In answering this question within the parameters of Origen's thought, we learn how fundamental two dimensions are for Origen. The first dimension involves Origen's understanding of freedom, which we will discuss in more detail in a later section of this part. The true issue is what is the origin and nature of freedom? Freedom is fundamental to God's way and is spread throughout existence. Freedom for Origen is so encompassing and powerful that it can even oppose God and one's own nature. God does not create a divine creature to serve him mindlessly; he creates a creature who is truly free, who can become in his own way and through his own realization divine and a friend to God or, if he wills, a slave to the devil. For Origen, the creation of a truly free will is an act only God could fulfill. And regardless how bad man becomes, how low he sinks in his sin, he is never beyond the freedom of God and man to act and change. Evil by definition is impermanent.

The second dimension is Origen's view of God, a subject that is somewhat outside our present discussions. Origen's God is indeed the Father of the New Testament, the Supreme Perfect Parent whose every decision involves raising his sons and daughters to be complete and to love out of love and respect, and the Model through his Logos rather than only a judge, a tyrant or source of misery. Such a God creates an existence that balances more on his hope in and love for his children, and on his infinite ability to create contexts in which his children will change, than on any form of coercion. We shall see this attribute of Origen's view of God again and again as we proceed.

But now that we have given Origen's response to two stumbling blocks, let us continue with the effects of the Fall.

After the transformation, Origen discusses the nature of the product, the *psyche* (soul). In general, the soul has two dimensions, a rational and an irrational dimension. The rational part remains intellect (*nous*), while the irrational part is the source of the passions and desires, which Origen calls the "body" (*soma*). Origen clarifies these two fundamental dimensions in his discussion of Luke 8:16, where Jesus says that no one hides a light, but reveals it so that all may see the light, and Luke 11:34, which concerns a similar matter where the "eye is the lamp" of the "body." For Origen, the light in the first passage is the light of the Logos and Wisdom, which, in man, is in the intellect (*nous*). The cause of the passions is the "body" (*soma*), which is described by Origen with the Platonic terms "irascible" and "concupiscent." The rational, Origen writes, results from intellect, and the irrational results from the act of withdrawal from the intellect's "first natural and divine warmth."[19]

This summary then clarifies the kind of perversion (in contrast to conversion) which caused to emerge the earthly "soul" and all its struggles. It shows intellects initially fervently serving their Creator, and drawing their goodness from him, but who begin, after the devil's example,[20] to neglect the divine warmth. As this happens, the neglect of that goodness and the loss of the divine warmth through the unworthy direction of the free will and the power of freedom gives rise to a cooling in which evil can grow, intellect becomes soul (without perverting the *nous*), and man is no longer worthy to be in the presence of the Creator. How each intellect directs its free will determines its eventual status. It was not the work of God, but intellect's own choices which gave rise to its turning away from the good. Moreover, despite the error of intellect's choice, restoration and return to that initial state is possible.[21]

Let us repeat the events that occurred in man's original environment, according to Origen's speculations: Before the world as it now appears was created, God created intellects,[22] equal and alike, placed them in his presence to serve and obey him, implanted seeds of goodness in them, and gave to all free will so that their positions would be the result of their own choices and motions. Then these intellects, being influenced in varying degrees by the rebellious act of the devil,[23] grew cool in their service, of their own free will turned away from God, and became souls. Thus, intellect became soul from a neglect of that power of good which enabled it to be in God's presence and serve him. Yet the power of good and freedom remains unaffected by the evil of man's choices. Hence man retains the potential, if he will, to return to God.

The purpose of this section is to show how Origen unraveled some of the mysteries of the earliest stages of the spiritual journey. Why does man need to change? How did he get into this situation? This first section gives Origen's answer. However, we must be careful about how we understand Origen's answer. No scriptural writer was more humble before the Scripture than Origen, and as one well-versed in every sentence of it, he knew that it was bigger and more profound than his mind could grasp. Origen needed an answer for the heretics and blasphemers of his day. He needed a profound and honorable answer to some of the difficult stumbling-blocks of the text. But as we shall see as we proceed, Origen was not arrogant about his answer; he did not think his answer had to be the final or complete one. The answer was only what he considered a reasonable choice, one that, he believed, did not do an injustice to the Scripture or the goodness of God.

What Does Scripture (Acts 3:21) Mean by the Final "Restoration" (*Apokatastasis*)?

It is not enough, of course, to talk about the beginning. Perhaps a greater mystery is the end. Where is man going? What is his divine destiny? What plan does God have? In brief, what is the end of man's spiritual journey?

The previous section was devoted to Origen's description of rational creatures' original condition and their fall. This section summarizes the connection of conversion with Origen's ideas on the end.

In the course of the description of the Fall, Origen mentions the possibility of a return to the condition of intellect.[24] He indicates elsewhere that seeded in us is a power which can bring us back to perfection.[25] This notion of return is an element common to eschatology and, as we have noted, conversion, and is called "restoration" or "restitution" (*apokatastasis* in Greek, *restitutio* in Latin). Let us then consider briefly in this section and the sections that follow the implications of restoration for spiritual change. In this section, we will set down as far as possible a definition of the concept "restoration" in terms of conversion.[26]

Let us begin with a clarification of terms. The word "restoration" (*apokatastasis*) is found once in the Bible, in Acts 3:21. The context begins, however, at Acts 3:17, and is translated as:

> And now, brethren, I know that you acted in ignorance, as did also your rulers. But what God foretold by the mouth of all the prophets, that his Christ should suffer, he thus fulfilled. Repent, therefore, and turn again, that your sins may be blotted out, that times of refreshing may come from the presence of the Lord, and that he may send the Christ appointed for you, Jesus, whom heaven must receive until the time of restoration of all that God spoke by the mouth of his holy prophets from of old.

We note that this text is primarily concerned with changing and becoming new, refreshed. We must repent and "turn again" in order for the "time of restoration" to arise.[27] Note that the conversion occurs before the restoration. It is uncertain whether the concept itself here concerns "the conversion of persons", or "the restitution of things," the concept of a new Messianic creation.[28]

Until Origen none of the extant works of the Fathers used the term in the sense of a restoration of all created beings, nor was it a particularly significant concept for any of their theologies, especially those of Marcion, Irenaeus, or Clement of Alexandria. Clement saw it as the follow-up to the Gnostic life.[29] The Gnostic Heracleon used the term beside "salvation" (*soteria*) with respect to the "eternal rest" (*anapausis*).[30] Its force as a spiritual idea with full depth and clarity appears first in Origen, who relies on 1 Cor. 15:25–28,[31] John 17:21[32] and the key text of Acts 3:21,[33] from where, according to one writer, he borrowed the term, though he is influenced mainly by the current medical and political sense.[34]

Although some aspects of the restoration concept came to be considered unorthodox later, no direction had been clarified in Origen's time.[35] In Origen's thought, as we shall see below, when it was used theologically, it was a word often used for a more specific clarification of the end, the end of ends.[36] For example, in his long commentary on John 1:1 on the meaning of the word *arche* (beginning), he refers to Prov. 16:5, "The beginning of a good way is to do justice." This "way" has a beginning, which is concerned with action, but it has an end also, and the end concerns contemplation (*theoria*). Origen then continues, using the two words ("end" and "restoration") in the same sentence: "In the latter the end of it, I suppose, comes to rest at last in the so-called restoration. . . ."[37]

Similarly, in his book *On First Principles*, in his discussion of the end of the ages, he writes that there may be something greater that exists at the restoration when "the universe reaches its perfect end," something, as Ps. 115:18 says, "more than an age."[38]

If one speculates about the beginning, it is logical, now as then, to speculate about the end, and Origen, along with other thinkers of his time and before, did not hesitate to discuss the end, with and without the use of the word *apokatastasis*.[39] The word for restoration, *apokatastasis* or *restitutio* in the Latin adaptation, is used in the context of end only three times in *On First Principles*, the book which most often discusses this issue. In each of these texts, *restitutio* implies not merely an end, but the final perfect completion of creation, the end of ends, the end of worlds and the end of ages.[40] A similar definition is found in Origen's other works, especially when we include the verb form of this word. Nevertheless, since restoration was a concept not defined in the rule of faith, and the word is itself used only once in Scripture, Origen was very cautious. He recognized that many different kinds of arguments would be necessary.[41]

Now that we have discussed the terminology involved, let us clarify in more detail what Origen thought about the final perfection of the ages, the restoration.

First of all, for Origen the final end will transcend all other ages.[42] It will occur after the period of the Judgment, after men have turned back to God. And the return will be to a place in which all have once resided. It will essentially be a "restoration to one's own home," as Origen writes in his homily on Jer. 15:19, "If you will return, I will also restore you."[43]

Of course, this return involves not only a similar place, but, more importantly, a similar state, a state similar to the condition of "intellects" discussed in the first section.[44] In his specific chapter on the end, Origen clarifies precisely what this state will be like by commenting on 1 Cor. 15:25. Origen tries to explain what it meant for God to be spiritually "all in all" for man:

> And he will be all things in each person in such a way that everything which the rational mind, when purified from all...can feel and understand or think will be all God and that the mind will no longer be conscious of anything besides or other than God, but will think God and see God and hold God and God will be the mode and measure of its every movement; and in this way God will be all to it.... If then the end having been repaired to the origin and the issue of things having been made to resemble their beginning, he restores that condition which rational nature once enjoyed...so that all consciousness of evil has departed..., when there is nowhere any death..., nowhere any evil at all, then truly God will be all in all.[45]

Note here the use of the word "restores" to confirm the image which is present in Origen's thoughts.

The role of Christian conversion is clear. Conversion is the process that makes restoration possible, that motivates the spiritual journey toward its end, as Origen states in a later section of this same chapter. He writes, in a context actually concerned with the effect of being "restored" on the body, that natures are formerly sinful, but "through being converted" are "reconciled to God" and blessedness.[46] Indeed, this section briefly states that conversion of the rational being toward reconciliation with God is a lengthy process, involving "infinite and immeasurable ages, seeing that the improvement and correction will be realized slowly and separately in each individual person."[47] Clearly then, to be restored, one must turn or, in Origen's thought in this context, return.

However, this conversion involves not only the restoration of the individual person. As we noted with respect to the community of minds in the first section, so also, in the end, restoration involves other critical aspects. These are partly explored in Origen's interpretation of John 13:3, where it is written, ". . . Jesus, knowing that the Father had given all things into his hands, and that he had come from God and was going to God . . .," and 1 Cor. 15:25–28. As we recall, this chapter of the Gospel of John concerns the betrayal, and the context of this verse concerns the fact that the devil had influenced Judas. Jesus, seeing the larger perspective of the ages, reacts, according to Origen, in light of the final restoration. It is not practical to quote the entire chapter from the *Commentary on John*, but we can summarize the implications of Origen's views presented there.[48]

First, there is the destruction of all negative effects derived from an evil will, such as sin, death and the evil powers. Second, there is a final union and subjection to Christ of all beings endowed with *logos*, including all who have opposed God.[49] Third, there is the restoration of the initial order of things.

Another aspect not mentioned in the above context is the restoration of the Church to Christ. This element is mentioned briefly in a text from the *Commentary on Matthew*.[50] Origen is interpreting Matt. 22:1–14, which is a parable told by Jesus about the kingdom of heaven. The parable concerns those who are invited to a marriage celebration given for the son of a king, and particularly how some were and some were not worthy to attend. Origen, who understands his interpretation as traditional, sees the king as the Father, the son as Christ, the marriage as the ". . . restoration of the spouse the Church of Christ with Christ her bridegroom."[51]

There is, of course, a logical precision about these statements. Just as evil and death entered into the world through the devil, so evil and death are in the end subjected and destroyed in order for restoration to happen. Just as in the beginning there were intellects whose thoughts were all God, so in the end all is again focused on God and subjected voluntarily to Christ. The key concern for us is the importance of how men change in Origen's viewpoint. The process of change brings the individual souls, the Church, even the evil powers, back to a condition in which restoration is possible. Conversion is mentioned or implied in all of the above texts. In one of the texts, Origen even indicates that a slow process of reconciliation is necessary before restoration is possible. This slow process of reconciliation that precedes and prepares for restoration is conversion. Hence conversion is the process that winds its way through all the worlds and ages and times that are required to bring creation finally back to the time of restoration. Indeed it is the catalyst for God's plan, as Origen understands it.

The notion of return is, then, an element common to both the restoration and conversion. This common element suggests strongly that the restoration and conversion are not only related concepts, but that the restoration is clearly dependent on the process of conversion. Let us continue to view the restoration as a return with the purpose of showing how it is an important factor in a consideration of the spiritual journey.

Two questions concerning the restoration, viewed as a return, may be posed as follows: (1) How is this return to be achieved? and (2) to what precise condition does one return? The answers to both questions involve conversion. By knowing how the return is achieved in terms of the contributions of God and man, we shed light on conversion, since conversion contributes to this process. Also, by understanding the final condition, we come to realize what is needed to reach that condition.

An answer to the second question requires a consideration of (a) the universality of the return, and (b) the presence and nature of the body in man's final state as Origen seems to have understood it. An answer to the first question calls for reflection on (a) the kind of balance Origen understood between divine foreknowledge and human freedom, and (b) the nature and duration of purification/ punishment. Of course, the full depth of these answers can only be found by considering the other parts of this study, for our purpose in this part is to explore these questions in terms of the Fall and the restoration, insofar as it will affect the spiritual journey.

Is the End Predetermined or Is Man Free in Some Sense?

An answer to the first question above—how is the return to be achieved—involves, as noted above, a study of the relationship between God's foreknowledge and man's freedom. As we will encounter the importance of freedom to Origen's ideas on conversion and in his thought in general, we need to consider the issue in some detail. Fortunately this question is quite thoroughly handled in Chapter 21 of the *Philocalia*, which preserves the original Greek of *On First Principles* 3.1.1–23.[52] The chapter is divided as follows: 3.1.1–5 presents a philosophical proof of free will and the scriptural basis for the existence of free will. 3.1.6–13 discusses the problems presented by the hardening of Pharaoh's heart. 3.1.14–23 treats problems with other scriptural texts that seem to do away with free will.[53]

Here again, let us note, Origen is tackling one of the puzzling passages in Scripture. Why does God intentionally harden Pharaoh's heart? The action would seem to conflict with the freedom of the individual and, more important, be unjust. How can this action harmonize with the goodness of God?

In the section 3.1.13–14, Origen is trying to show that if Pharaoh died without being completely healed of sin, God still has unlimited time in which to save him. For example, Origen writes regarding Pharaoh, "for when he was drowned, he was not destroyed,"[54] because God is not concerned with souls for just fifty years but "in view of the endless world."[55] This passage indicates, in a general sense, the patience that God shows. He is concerned with the "immortality of the soul" and the "eternal world," not with some hurried remedy. The following passage shows more specifically that God brings sinners to salvation, not quickly, but through the experience of suffering.[56]

The references to "eternal world" and "the immortality of the soul" are indications of God's foreknowledge in dealing with the souls of certain sinners, such as Pharaoh. God knows that he has unlimited time in which to help sinners. He acts as a physician with his own timetable to cure the "ills" of sinners.[57]

Sometimes, as the above text indicates, God permits ills or misfortunes, but whatever remedy God decides upon, it is one that he, in his foreknowledge, knows will aid the soul.[58] God as the great superintendent carefully watches over and aids each soul and knows precisely the time and the way to heal it.[59]

Henceforth God appears to Origen as a patient teacher who will seemingly wait as long as necessary for souls to unite themselves freely with him.[60] But there is no explicit mention of man's freedom. Actually Scripture seems at times to make statements that deny freedom. For example, consider Ezek. 11.19–20, where God says that he will remove the "stony heart" and give them a "heart of flesh." Origen, however, interprets it and other passages in a way that is at least consistent with his own doctrine of freedom.[61] The passage from Ezekiel, Origen indicates, could easily be misinterpreted by one who would destroy free will to state that to accept and live a virtuous life is not our work but the work of God, that we need do nothing. God will do it for us. He will change our heart.[62]

In answer to this argument, Origen observes that God will remove the "stony heart" and give a "heart of flesh," but only when someone first willingly comes to the Logos and asks to be healed.[63] So the answer is that there is a balance, a mixture of participation, between the work of God and the work of man. Somehow God's foreknowledge and man's freedom collaborate to achieve salvation:[64]

It is, then, neither in our power to make progress apart from the knowledge of God, nor does the knowledge of God compel us to do so unless we ourselves contribute something towards the good result....[65]

The first point here is that divine knowledge permits sinners to make progress toward salvation and that God knows what our progress will be. The second point is that this divine knowledge does not force salvation upon the sinner. Rather, the sinner must "contribute" and willingly approach God for help.[66]

Another view of this relationship is presented in Origen's homily on Jer. 5:3, where it is written, "You have completed them, and they did not want to receive instruction." Origen believes that this statement is an indication of the relationship between "...one who offers knowledge and the one who does not wish to receive the knowledge from the offerer."[67] Origen then says that all the benefits of providence are laid down for us, but we must take them up if we wish to be fulfilled. In this sense then, providence itself is not a necessity, but an alternative.[69]

In terms of the spiritual journey, it is evident that freedom of will, rather than nature, is a key factor determining whether man will progress or regress. Indeed, on an important text on the "close of the age," Matt. 13:47–50, when the good and bad "fishes" will be sorted, Origen writes:

> For the reasons why fishes are good or bad lies not in the souls of the fishes.... For it is not the nature in us which is the cause of evil, but it is the voluntary choice which causes evil; and so our nature is not the cause of righteousness... but it is the principle which we have admitted which makes men righteous.[69]

It needs to be stressed that Origen saw his view of this issue affirmed everywhere in Scripture. The entire third chapter of *On First Principles* from which we have quoted his view is based in text after text from Scripture. We may tend to eschew the allegorical method today as an opportunity for fanatics to proof-text their ideas, but we are far from the truth in grouping Origen with them. The texts in which Origen sees mysteries were in his time, and still are today, even with all of our modern exegetical methods, complex if not troublesome, and there is never a text where some difficulty is present that the literal meaning could easily explain. It was a different, less scientific, age, of course, but we need not apologize for Origen. Nor are we given any reason to doubt his primary objective: to uncover the mysteries inherent in the text. Unlike fanatics seeking refuge, Origen is not ashamed to point out the paradoxes and difficulties of even his own interpretations, as well as reveal his insecurity before the Word of God.

One such difficulty was the differing accounts of whether John the Baptist was not "sufficient," which Mark writes (Mark 1:6, 7), whether he was not "worthy," as John writes (John 1:26), or both; or if he grew to be one or the other. Origen concludes without an answer, writing:

> However much we take into our minds there are still left things not yet understood; for, as we read in the wisdom of Jesus, son of Sirach, "When a man has finished, then he begins, and when he leaves off, then he shall be doubtful." (Sir. 18:7)[70]

Even Origen's uncertainty is documented. It is fair to say that Origen was well aware of the paradox often found in Scripture, and that a certain tension remains, a tension that, at least according to some modern biblical scholars in our brief consideration above, is present in Scripture itself on this issue of foreknowledge and freedom. Nevertheless, nothing seems to shake Origen's tenacious belief in human spiritual freedom, and that belief appears to relieve some of the tension in his view of New Testament eschatology.[71]

Someone may ask whether Origen continued with this view throughout his life. A clear summary of Origen's thought from a later work than *On First Principles* is given in his interpretation of the (for him) problematic text, "You deceived me, Lord, and I was deceived" of Jer. 20:7. Why should God deceive someone? The interpretation of this text for Origen indicates that God has many kinds of deceits used for his own purposes in his plan of conversion and education in man's spiritual journey. Origen here stresses, supported by 2 Cor. 9.7, that God does not force man to do what He wants. In fact, he creates situations so that we act voluntarily. Origen says it more precisely:

> God does not behave as a tyrant, but as a ruler, and when he rules, he does not coerce but encourages, and he wishes that those under him yield themselves willingly to his direction so that the good of someone may not be by compulsion, but according to his own choice.... In a sense then God seeks a way whereby a person should want to do voluntarily what God wishes.[72]

What Happens to Sin and the Sinful in the End?

In the prior section Origen discussed one element of the process by which men return to God, namely, the role of free choice and how this factor relates to God's role.

Another element of this process is purification and punishment. Why, we ask, do some men have such difficult lives? Why are men who are apparently successful so unhappy? And why do some people have to suffer so much in order to change and seek what is good?

Origen found here another mystery and responded with an answer that some of us may find startling. Just as men use the power of free will to turn themselves back to God, so also God has varied ways of purification and other remedies that help men turn around to him. In other words, suffering is not necessarily an unhappy event; it may be planned by God to teach.

But how long will God punish? How long will he be patient? This was a mystery whose answer could never be certain for Origen, and it is difficult in some texts to lay before us a clear decision in his thought. The choice is between a view, implied in several texts, that sees the possibility of eternal punishment and the "death" of the soul, and a view that stresses the purification of the soul of all evil elements through an ultimate fire and then subsequent salvation. One writer particularly has noted that Origen, in his interpretation of 1 Cor. 3:11–15, will mention serious sins in a context that is not concerned with salvation by fire. Hence he believes that Origen's primary interest, in the doctrine of temporary punishment, and in the texts analyzed, does not exclude a doctrine of eternal punishment.[73]

At the same time, it is clear that Origen did use this scriptural text to refer to a final purification in the end-times, as we shall discover below. It is possible that Origen understands the text of 1 Cor. 3.11–15 at both levels: on the one hand, it refers to serious sins in this life and their consequences, and, on the other hand, in its spiritual interpretation, it refers to the effect of all our acts, both good and bad, in the restoration. This double interpretation (and even triple interpretation) is not uncommon for Origen with any text. With this in mind, let us now offer a few texts where Origen discusses the matter.

One interpretation of the fire in store for sinners, based on Isa. 50:11, is that it is the "fire" that man kindles in himself through harmful desires that lead to sin. Every time someone sins, "certain torments are produced from the harmful desires themselves."[74] When these inner flames of sins build up to a certain point, a divine power enables man to be aware of them and to be stung by the awareness of them, when the "conscience becomes an accuser against itself."[75] According to these texts, then, man with help from a divine power punishes himself through the extent he sins. But no indication of purification is involved.

The idea of purification is often connected to Origen's view of God as a physician who will use many remedies to cure the soul's ills, even the ". . . infliction of a punishment of fire on those who have lost their soul's health."[76] But the word "fire" itself involves for Origen being purified and corrected, and is often mentioned in his *Homilies on Jeremiah*.[77] For example, conversion, the fire, and punishment are involved in Origen's understanding of Jer. 13:1–11 and Ezek. 1:27.[78] In his interpretation of God's waistcloth mentioned in the text from Jeremiah, Origen indicates, in light of Ezek. 1.27, that what is below the hips is "fire", and what is above the hips is "electrum" (an alloy of gold and silver). The Scripture here is using the "body" of God as an image to teach what is and is not important. Origen understands what is below the hips as that which is a part of the inferior world of generation; this involves the fire and needs purification. What is above the hips has transcended generation. How do we arrive there? Origen believes that we can change; we can ascend and progress and become pure like electrum. To accomplish this, we must first pass through fire.[79]

These texts could refer either to the purification and punishment of this life or to the restoration. It is not always clear in Origen's expositions. Possibly they were intended to involve both times. But a text in which Origen considers 1 Cor. 3:11–15 in terms of the afterlife occurs in his homily on Jer. 16:18, "And first I will recompense their wrongs doubly." This text, according to Origen, indicates, on the one hand, that God has diverse ways of dealing with sins, and, on the other, that God has an order by which he recompenses.

The word "first" in the text particularly interests Origen. Origen asks initially: what happens if we die with both sins and good deeds?[80] The reference to death indicates that from here on in the discussion Origen is discussing what happens after we leave this life. Origen offers various alternative answers to this question before he settles on what is applicable to the just God "who wants to purify and destroy evil."[81] Origen asks again, in light of 1 Cor. 3:12: What happens to us? Does God ignore our good and refuse us because of our sins?[82] Origen replies by stating first that we do receive the "fire" for our sins—the wood, hay, and stubble of 1 Cor. 3.12. He bases this opinion in part on the text "God is a consuming fire" (Deut. 4:24 / Heb. 12:29). However, second, though God does consume the hay, wood, and stubble, he does not consume "his own creation," the image and likeness (Gen. 1:26).[83]

This text and others like it are very important for a precise understanding of how Origen views the end and the spiritual journey. God does not destroy what he creates; rather he purifies man of the corrupting elements. Man may receive countless punishments, he may not be forgiven for many ages, he may be denied access to the Church in the world,[84] but in the very end, after many worlds, God's purpose, as Origen noted, is to purify and destroy the evil, not the creature.[85] Indeed, as Origen continues in his homily, he indicates that "first" God renders what is due for wrongdoing and then what is due for the deeds of righteousness.[86] So in some texts purification and punishment by the fire are part of God's process to destroy evil after death. Though he does not state how long this process requires, he does imply strongly that it will end, and the deeds of righteousness will be rewarded. We then continue to be transformed in the afterlife or the after-ages until we are pure.

Thus the process herein described is the abolition of evil by God in order to restore his creature to its true pure state. In a text from *Against Celsus*, his great work defending the way of the Christians against an educated pagan, Celsus, Origen corrects Celsus's misconception of how the final image and unity of rational being will appear. The final time will be one of divine supreme healing and the purification of evil elements. No evil can survive beside the power of the Logos:

> We believe that at some time the Logos will have overcome the entire rational nature, and will have remodeled every soul to his own perfection, when each individual simply by the exercise of his freedom will choose what [the Logos] wills and will be in that state which he has chosen. And we hold that just as it is unlikely that some of the consequences of physical diseases and wounds would be too hard for any medical art, so also it is unlikely in the case of souls that any of the consequences of evil would be incapable of being cured by the supreme Logos and God. For since the Logos and the healing power within him are more powerful than any evils in the soul, he applies this power to each individual according to God's will, and the end of the treatment is the abolition of evil.[87]

We see then how strongly Origen viewed the purifying power of God in the end, and that evil elements of the soul, and even evil itself, will at some point cease. Such a view implies that conversion has an objective. We note also that no one is excluded in these treatments.[88]

Other texts are equally supportive of a punishment and purification that is not only universal but temporary. For example, it has been suggested by one writer that Origen did not take literally the reference in Matt. 3:12 to "unquenchable fire." In his discussions of this text, as well as Isa. 66:24 and Jer. 20:7, Origen indicates that God's real intentions are concealed from the ordinary man, who requires threats in order to convert and remain steadfast. Indeed when a man realizes this deceit in the literal meaning of Scripture, he often regresses.[89] The truth about punishment consists in the spiritual interpretation of these texts. And the spiritual interpretation yields two results: First, that the punishment is temporary,[90] and second, that the punishment is of a spiritual order.[91]

Both of these aspects are completely confirmed in Origen's response to Celsus's distortion of what the end-time fire involves. Origen states that the fire is a purification, not a punishment, that it affects only what results from sin, and that the threatening words in Scripture about fire are used only to prevent

simpleminded believers from straying. Origen, in fact, expresses this view in terms
of conversion. He writes of these simpleminded believers that fear and the
suggestion of punishment are the only "means of conversion and repentance."[92]
A similar concern with conversion is evident in another passage from *Against
Celsus*. In reply to Celsus's comparison of Christianity with the mystery religions
in terms of eternal punishments, and Celsus's inquiry about which of the two
religions is closer to the truth, Origen replies that the one that so convinces people
that they believe the punishments are real and are changed as a result, this is
the religion that is right.[93]

All of the above discussions indicate how important the processes of purification
and punishments were for Origen's thought, regardless of when in the plan of
God they occurred. In most cases, these processes are connected to the movement
of conversion and are decisive factors toward salvation. We have seen that Origen
avoids ideas that, in his opinion, contradict God's role as Father and Creator,
particularly those ideas which would imply that God would destroy his own
creation or create something that would require eternal punishment. Several writers
have indicated that the notion of hell, for example, conflicts with Origen's deeply
felt notion of the goodness of God. As we noted in the first section of this chapter,
God alone is good.[94]

It is important to distinguish in Origen's thought between what occurs in terms
of the ages, and what will happen at the very end. Punishments and remedies
may arise for man, some seemingly eternal, but after the ages come to a close,
no evil can escape God's purifying power of good.

Will Everyone Finally Return to God?

If evil is completely eradicated in the end, does this mean that all people will
return to their place with God? Origen treads lightly here. He sees still yet another
mystery that will need special discussion of the various alternatives. He realizes
that, for the simpleminded people in his parish, the guarantee of a universal
restoration could encourage libertinism. What is the point of being good if you
know at some stage you will be saved? Or, from the point of view of an aware
and literate member of the parish, what determines when or how one is returned?

The reader may rightfully wonder why we will devote an entire section to this
matter. The reason involves the very nature of our subject. If universality is
unjustified in Origen's thought, then the extent of the concept of spiritual growth
and change would become severely limited. It would mean that at some point
there will be no hope for some for conversion; it would mean that God's work,
Christ's work, is finally incomplete—as we shall see in following parts of our
work, where Origen discusses Christ's harvest. That situation would imply that
the gift of free will that man was given at creation can finally, in some cases,
ultimately be stymied by evil, that the power of the goodness of God to end evil
through his creation is limited, and that God created something that eventually
would not choose good. Thus, conversion would be, in this case, a determined

process, not depending on the cooperation of God and man, but rather on certain people's awareness of and certain people's blindness to the truth or to the gift that God has given them. Indeed it would mean, as Origen noted in the prior section in our discussion of free will, that God could create some souls that would not attain their end (an impossibility, in Origen's opinion). Conversion would depend only on man's own inherent weaknesses and strengths, his willingness to use them, and God's frightening judgement at the end of time. In fact, this would be for some a kind of freedom doomed to damnation.

Our consideration of this issue will have three parts: First, we will discuss texts which seem to show universality; second, we will note that the word *apokatastasis* in Origen's thought does not necessarily involve universality; and third, we will reply to the implications of that use of *apokatastasis* and what non-universality would imply for Origen's thought.

Origen's views on this issue show three aspects, according to one writer: First, Origen often develops his teaching on the restoration in connection with the statement that in the end "...God may be all in all." (1 Cor. 15:28) Second, he concentrated his efforts at interpretation on the word "all" (*pas*) in that formulation. We find, for example, that most of the scriptural texts that Origen cites use the word "all." Third, in his interpretation, he may have been influenced by Plato's description of God as the "measure of all things."[95]

Origen's concern to see the restoration as a restoration of all things is viewed also as a result of God's perfection and providence. We have already cited the text from *Against Celsus* where Origen states that the goal of the Logos according to God's will is the "abolition of all evil."[96] In another passage of this work, Origen sums up his teaching on the way God cares for the whole world at the end of creation.[97] Both Celsus and Origen agree that a kind of providence exists in the universe. But Origen, unlike Celsus, argues for God's special concern for the rational being.[98] Thus, God arranges, through his concern for all rational beings, to bring them back to himself, after having seen their purification.

> And providence will never abandon the universe. For even if some part of it becomes very bad because the rational being sins, [God] arranges to purify it, and after a time to turn the universe back to himself.[99]

The idea of God perfecting all of his creation and bringing it back to its original purity is found in a number of texts of Origen's thought. In these contexts, we invariably discover Origen excludes no one from such perfecting; rather, all are implied and sometimes explicitly noted. For example, two texts from Origen's *Commentary on John* will clarify this point. Origen mentions the matter when he is considering the names of Christ in the beginning of his commentary. One of these names is "great high-Priest" (Heb. 4:14):

> Hence he is a "great High-Priest," having offered himself as the sacrifice which is offered...for every rational creature.... He "restores all things to" his Father's "kingdom" (cf. Matt. 17:11; Acts 1:6), and arranges that whatever is empty in each part of creation shall be filled up with what the Father's glory holds. (Cf. Eph. 1:17-23; 3:19; 4:10)[100]

We note how Origen stresses every rational creature, each part of creation, and how he says that Christ restores all things to the kingdom by correcting imperfections. Origen here connects the redemption with the restoration. Christ's sacrifice was offered for all rational creatures; in other words, the sacrifice of Christ not only promises to redeem all, but ultimately does redeem all.

A similar theme is found in Origen's commentary on John 4.34, where Jesus says, "My work is to do the will of him who sent me, and to accomplish his work." Origen views Jesus' second task, "to accomplish his work," as a task of perfecting the work of God. Man was not absolutely imperfect when he was in paradise, but his disobedience gave rise to imperfection. Christ was sent to return beings with *logos* to the original state of perfection.[101] Thus, Jesus' second task is a task that returns every being, "...and I mean every being with *logos* and not only man...",[102] sometimes after punishment, to a state of perfection. This conclusion seems to indicate that Origen saw every being with *logos* returning to a state of perfection as they were originally made by the Creator.[103]

In Origen's *Homilies on Jeremiah*, we find several references to this same theme. For example, in his discussion of Jer 10:12, Origen seeks the support of 1 Cor. 15:22 and Ps. 144 (145):14. Twice he emphasizes these scriptural texts, unequivocal in terms of universality, which say that the Lord raises up "all" who fell in sin and with Adam.[104]

Some passages without the word *apokatastasis* seem to imply universality.[105] Let us view, for example, Origen's interpretation of Matt. 13:37–40. Here is the scriptural text:

He who sows the good seed is the Son of man; the field is the world, and the good seed means the sons of the kingdom; the weeds are the sons of the evil one, and the enemy who sowed them is the devil; the harvest is the close of the age, and the reapers are angels. Just as the weeds are gathered and burned with fire, so will it be at the close of the age.

Origen interprets this passage as follows:

And according to this the whole world might be called a field, and not the Church of God only, for in the whole world, the Son of Man sowed the good seed, but the wicked one tares, that is, evil words, which, springing from wickedness, are children of the evil one. And at the end of things, which is called "the consummation of the age," there will of necessity be a harvest, in order that the angels of God who have been appointed for this work may gather up the bad opinions that have grown upon the soul, and overturning them may give them over to fire which is said to burn, that they may be consumed.[106]

In this text, Origen's interpretation of the whole world, and not only the Church of God, as a field, has been regarded as an indication of a universal restoration.[107] The word *apokatastasis*, as we have noted, is not used, and it is possible to view the references to the "end of things" as applicable only to those who belong to the Church.[108] Yet the scriptural context and the context of Origen here involves how the Son of Man sowed the seeds in the "whole world."

And according to both Scripture and Origen's interpretation, it is the angels who deal with both good and evil souls "at the end of things," when souls are not destroyed, but the evil in them.[109]

Several other passages from the same work might also be interpreted as a basis for the conviction of a non-universal restoration. One such passage forms part of Origen's interpretation of Matt. 22:1–14, the parable of the wedding feast, which we discussed and quoted above. One might conjecture that the few who are chosen, the worthy guests, are for Origen the members of the Church. Only they are worthy to share in the restoration.[110] In sum, this text can be cited to indicate that, in some passages, the word *apokatastasis* can be used by Origen in a way that may have a non-universal implication. While Origen in his interpretation of certain passages, such as 1 Cor. 15:28, may have considered a universal return to God, his use of the word *apokatastasis* does not necessarily imply universality.

Nevertheless, this evidence does not militate against a universal return. Origen, as we have seen in the several texts mentioned above, seems to view a universal return in texts with and without the word *apokatastasis*. The interpretation of a single word, such as *apokatastasis*, does not fully explain how Origen understood the total concept of restoration. It is highly likely that Origen believed that in the end, after many ages of correction and punishment, all would become members of the Church in glory, just as, in the beginning, all "intellects" were members of the pre-existent Church. Origen, in fact, did believe that only a few would be saved at the outset.[111] However, according to Origen, as we shall see when we discuss how conversion continues even after death, such an event does not stop the work of perfection.

Let us examine the issue now from the standpoint of the implications of non-universality, in order to see if Origen's thought supports these implications. More indirect but nevertheless important confirmations of Origen's interest in universality are certain concepts embedded in his thought. For example, if in the end, when he would be eternally punished for his sins, a person could no longer know God, then God's gift of knowledge, which is innate in every person, according to Origen, would at some point be limited and weaker than evil for some. It would also mean that evil has triumphed over God's creation of free will; that is, the effect of evil is more permanent than the effect of God's grace for some people. This event would mean that God created something that could not do what it was ultimately created to do, or that God turned permanently away from a portion of his creation.

Since we have seen several texts where Origen indicates that all evil will be destroyed, then—if the previous statements reflect Origen's thought—God would triumph over evil only in the cosmic realm, despite man, not through a kind of cooperation with his creations. Moreover, if all are not restored, then (however we would understand this perspective) it would appear that God created, as the Gnostics believed, different creatures by nature, some capable, others incapable of attaining blessedness. And what of those creatures (e.g., the devil) who might be capable but *unwilling* to choose good? While this may not imply inequality in creation, it does imply an innate inequality in the capacity to choose good.

But Origen, fully cognizant of Gnostic implications, would not allow for any kind of inequality in God's creative acts, as we have seen. Nor is there ever a time when humans are not innately equal. Hence all people have the same capacity to choose good; all are equally capable of attaining the good. And since we also know that Origen believed Scripture when it says that God created humans in his own image and likeness, intending them to know him and be near him, even blessing each with *logos*, the idea of evil ultimately triumphing even on the personal plane would probably be unacceptable to Origen. This is why, in light of these facts, he often stresses that God does not abandon the universe, that all evil will be destroyed, and that no one sins so badly that in some future age he will not have another chance. We find this latter point in Origen's commentary on the text Matt. 12:32,

And whoever says a word against the Son of man will be forgiven; but whoever speaks against the Holy Spirit will not be forgiven, either in this age or in the age to come.

Origen indicates, however, that this statement does not cover the ages beyond the age to come. Hence he leaves us with the impression that forgiveness at some point will be possible.[112] Similarly, in his work *On Prayer*, and in a section concerned with the end of the ages, Origen succinctly states that even the worst sinner in the ages to come will receive God's grace and be turned around:

And in those ages to come God will show the riches "of his grace in kindness" (Eph. 2:7), since the worst sinner, who has blasphemed the Holy Spirit (Matt. 12:31) and been ruled by sin from beginning to end in the whole of this present age, will afterwards in the age to come be brought into order, I know not how.[113]

Beside Matt. 12:31–32, another text that could be used to deny a universal restoration is Luke 16:19–31. Origen discusses this text in his *Homilies on Jeremiah*, indicating that the rich man was not yet worthy to be delivered over to the Logos who examines hearts and minds, and hence would need to receive punishment. Yet, unlike the tale in Luke, Origen gives even the rich man reason to hope, concluding also with this statement:

But whether in the future that man does suffer this [punishment], let one who can, determine.[114]

This statement essentially takes the sting of damnation out of the passage. And the way this sentence is expressed—"let one who can..."—is a method Origen uses when addressing the common folk unschooled in the mysteries of Scripture when there is a deeper, spiritual interpretation to the text. The spiritual interpretation is that the punishment as expressed in Luke was different from what the literal words expressed.

That God remains ever a refuge, even if a man is a sinner, even if he has depended for help in the past from demons, and even if God has turned away, is stated in a fragment of the homilies. Origen writes:

> But one needs to depend on God, for though he has turned away because of sins done, he does not disdain the deep and abiding refuge in himself.[115]

Indeed a strong reason for universality is that its opposite implies that God has turned away permanently from some part of his creation. Origen perhaps realized this when he wrote the above text.

But Origen was not interested only in the spiritual journey of the creature called man. What of the ultimate end of the devil and the demons? Origen was not afraid to address the question, since many people, heretics and non-Christians, as well as those from his congregation, raised the matter. It is a difficult problem for us today to know what Origen thought precisely, since Origen does not address it in any texts still extant in Greek, his own language; it is implied, however, in many texts, some of which we have given above.[116]

In his discussion of Jer. 13:16, for example, he makes a guarded reference to the salvation of the "dark mountains," whom he has identified as the devil and his angels. The Scripture says that "you will wait for the light." Origen opens up the possibility that this text is a reference to the light of "mercy" given even to the dark mountains and those who wait with the dark mountains.[117] The darkness discussed in the text brings to mind another discussion of this question in Origen's commentary on John 1:4, "In him was life, and the life was the light of men." Here Origen points out that all men, even saints and apostles, were once in darkness. Hence it follows for Origen that "all darkness can become light."[118] Of course, we realize that this statement does not claim that darkness *will* necessarily become light, but it does state that anyone in "darkness" *can* be saved. This statement is similar to Origen's belief in his homily on Jer. 15:19, which says "if you will return, I will also restore you."[119]

Similarly Origen implies that all are restored in his discussion of John 13:3, "...Jesus, knowing that the Father had given all things into his hands...." Origen relates this text closely with 1 Cor. 15:27, "For God has given all things in subjection under his feet." Though it is not clear how "all" are subjected, it is probable that the devil and demons have been transformed and are like all other creatures under the rule of heaven.[120] Origen points out in another volume of the *Commentary on John*, as we noted earlier, that the devil as a creature is the work of God, and is given existence and being due to God's grace. Evil, on the other hand, is non-being, and is not the work of God; all who share in evil deprive themselves of being. Again this view strongly suggests that the original creation, including the original creature who was the devil, returns and shares again in the presence of God.[121]

Finally, we need to mention Origen's view of Wisdom 3:9–10 and Ps. 67:32–33. In many passages throughout his homilies Origen states that the home of the devil is symbolized in Scripture by Ethiopia.[122] In this context, Origen is discussing the way of salvation for Israel and the Gentiles. He then quotes the two scriptural passages above as an indication that minimally the home of the devil (and the souls under him) will be saved.[123]

What then are the implications of non-universality? What if everyone is not returned? How would such a view of man's relationship with God harmonize with Origen's entire theological perspective? How would one measure the extent of grace?[124] And would a limited restoration invite the notion of an eternal hell, which, as one writer noted,[125] seems inconsistent with Origen's oft-stated belief in the goodness of God?

Taking into account the complete thought of Origen, it seems more likely that Origen considered the notion of universality a necessary result of his own concepts of providence, goodness, divine purifying power, and gifts of free will and *logos*. In light of this and the fact that no text in Latin or Greek flatly denies a universal restoration, and that many texts strongly imply it, we will assume Origen wrote about conversion in the hope and belief that all, admittedly after many ages, would be purified and returned to the Father through the work of Jesus Christ.

What Happens to the Body after Death and in the End?

Another enigma that few writers would face but that is a true concern in Scripture is the future of one's body. After all, the body is part of the person, part of his or her identity. Is only one part of the person transformed? The Apostle Paul had a profound interest in the resurrected body, and Origen was of the same mind. Origen realized that the whole person had to be transformed. But how?

For Origen how we are transformed involves both that which transforms, the purpose of the transformation and the end-product of the transformation. We have discussed earlier in this chapter some elements of what transforms insofar as it concerns the restoration, namely, the power of God to return his creation to its pure state, and man's gift of free will. Implicit also in these discussions and the sections on universality and punishment is the purpose of the transformation, namely, to purify and return man to a more natural relationship with God. Though we did note that no evil would exist in the natures of those so transformed, we did not clarify any other qualities of this ultimate nature of man in the restoration.

Hence, in order to continue to understand how that final condition would appear, our purpose in this section is to discuss the kind of body, if any, man would have. The significance of this discussion also arises from our concern in Chapter 3, below, with how the senses are managed (*aisthesis*). In order to be transformed, as Origen stresses in many passages and ways, there must be discipline with respect to the effect of the senses.

In a text from the work *On First Principles*, Origen indicates that when man fell, he acquired a "covering" according to the extent of his fall. The quality of the material substance would be a reflection of the quality of the spiritual state of the person, the level of his maturity. The farther one fell, the more "gross" and "solid" would be his bodily condition.[126] In this text Origen cites Scripture three times. It is probable that here, as in many other issues, Scripture encouraged Origen to consider the possibility of some kind of bodily restoration. For example, 1 Cor. 15:44 says:

> It is sown a physical body, it is raised a spiritual body. If there is a physical body, there is also a spiritual body.

Origen's interpretation of Scripture took several avenues, depending often on the context. Let us consider, for example, texts from *On First Principles*, the *Commentary on John*, and *Against Celsus* in order to give an overview of how he approached the question of the body in the restoration.

Two different extant texts of the same passage in *On First Principles* will be presented. One is supposedly the original Greek of Origen quoted by Justinian:

> But if what has been subjected to Christ shall in the end be subjected also to God, then all will lay aside their bodies; and I think that there will then be a dissolution of bodily nature into non-existence, to come into existence a second time if rational beings should again fall.[127]

And parallel to this text is the Latin translation of the same passage by Rufinus:

> ... all who have been subjected to Christ will in the end be subjected also to God the Father, to whom it is said the Christ will deliver up the kingdom. Thus, it appears that then even the use of bodies will cease; and if this happens, bodily nature returns to non-existence, just as formerly it did not exist. But let us see what those who make these assertions have to face.[128]

In comparing the two versions, we note two differences: First, in the Rufinus edition, there is no reference to the use of bodies a second time; and second, Rufinus's adaptation has an extra sentence that some writers believe turns the text into an alternative rather than Origen's view. A third Latin translation survives by Jerome.[129] Jerome's edition coincides almost exactly with the Greek version of Justinian, and does not include the sentence found in the Rufinus adaptation. In summary, either we may consider the versions of Justinian and Jerome the true teaching of Origen,[130] or, on the other hand, we can see the extra sentence of Rufinus as an indication this opinion is only one possibility among others, not necessarily a reflection of his own views.[131]

However, if we quoted the full section of Rufinus' adaptation, it is clear that even in his adaptation, the following sentences are not intended to indicate an alternative, but a clarification of the consequences of the foregoing view of the body.[132]

Then, in a later section of this part, Origen does indicate that this view is one of three opinions.[133] This text clearly demonstrates that, according to the

Rufinus adaptation, for Origen there were several possibilities. The implication of this passage and of the chapter in general is more that each of these alternatives is acceptable than that any one of them is preferable. Each of the alternatives is also supported by texts given from Scripture, implying again that Origen recognized that each of the possibilities could be seen in Scripture. Hence these texts cannot be used to support or deny a bodiless existence, but merely to note that Origen did consider bodiless existence a viable alternative in some sense.

It is that sense which we need to consider. One writer has named ten specific passages where Origen supports a bodiless existence in the restoration. In examining these texts one by one, we see that Origen is not considering the spiritual body as discussed in the above texts from *Against Celsus*, but the corporeal body, the vain body, the gross body, the body that was made to accommodate man's fall, as we noted above in a prior section. In a couple of the texts, the context is not even the restoration, but the state of spiritual ecstasy. For example, in one text from *On Prayer*, Origen is exploring what happens when one prays, and he states that the soul leaves the body and its bodily existence, and in this way becomes spiritual.[134]

The second of these alternatives needs to be clarified in more detail. Essentially it involved a "redefinition of corporeality," a redefinition that Origen himself understood from Scripture, i.e., 2 Cor. 5:4.[135]

We find this view in his homily on Jer. 18:5–6, which concerns how the Lord will make the house of Israel as a potter. Origen sees here two interpretations: The one refers to the individual, the other to the two nations of Israel and the Gentiles. In the first interpretation, Origen states, quoting 1 Cor. 15:38, that God is like the potter in the resurrection, that he can pick up the pieces of the broken body, a body which he after all created, renew it, and make it into a better receptacle. In effect, God makes a different receptacle from the same material, indicating that the body is transformed rather than annihilated.[136]

Perhaps behind this idea of a receptacle changing without changing the person is the idea of a seminal principle. According to Origen, each man has within him a "seminal principle," which maintains the personality of the individual through all the stages of bodily decay and change. Origen can thus state that the doctrine of the resurrection teaches that the soul has a seminal principle.[137]

So too the idea is found in Origen's discussion of the resurrection in another section of *Against Celsus*. Here Origen stresses that the body has some "principle" that is not corrupted, so that the raised body is not, in line with what Paul writes in 1 Cor. 15:42–50, "flesh and blood," but a spiritual body.[138] This seminal principle is that principle which maintains the essence of the personality in the restored state. With the personality remaining stable, the body changes, acquiring qualities, Origen maintains, suitable to its environment.[139]

These texts, therefore, seem to show that Origen viewed the kind of body as an effect of environment upon the soul. The more pure the environment, the more pure the body. Origen supported this view with 2 Cor. 5:1–4, and 1 Cor. 15:35–44.[140] Furthermore, Origen indicates that the body, in its transformed state, is an important element in his views on the return of the soul in the restoration. To return, we have to overcome the burden of the gross body.

It is not our purpose in this study to attempt to solve the puzzle of the body in Origen's thought. In the passage from death to eternal life, the condition of the body is for Origen critical. Whether ultimately that condition is a bodiless one or a spiritual one may remain a controversy, but clearly there is a process of change, of conversion, that begins in the Fall, continues on earth and even in the afterlife, and that Origen recognizes as one of the key dimensions transforming humankind. The transformation of the body involves the control and management of the senses, a dimension that we have called *aisthesis*, and that we discuss in Chapter 3.

Summary

We began with a series of mysteries about the end and the beginning, for we recognized that we cannot discuss the progress of the spiritual life without knowing if there is some need. If there is no need, why change? Why progress? Origen too knew this concern, and it was one of the reasons he wrote about these mysteries. He felt that he needed to respond to the heretical views of other groups and to the ideas of the pagan philosophers, even though the solutions to these mysteries were not clear even in the rule of faith or in Scripture. The purpose of this chapter has been to give his answers.

Origen viewed the original state as one where "intellects" were in fervent devotion surrounding God, their wills freely choosing to worship and know him. Then, due to the example of the devil, and in accordance with their own choices, they slowly began to neglect the good in them and fell to the condition of souls. The condition of a soul is one in which the so-called rational is in a dynamic struggle with the irrational. The spiritual journey of transformation is the process by which this unnatural condition is resolved and the creature transformed.

The other area of our concern was the end, the restoration. There are two evident conclusions concerning the restoration: First, Origen felt a logical attraction, based in several texts of Scripture in which universality seems to be present, to the idea of all creatures returning to the purity of the beginning; but he does not develop the idea in any great detail in the extant texts, and there are a couple of texts that are paradoxical. He is convinced about the importance of purification and free will in returning man to God. And he does show concern about the meaning and future of the body. Such stress on these concepts, recognized by all writers on Origen, gives added importance to how Origen understood the way one becomes a Christian and the spiritual journey in general.

Second, if we are to understand in detail how Origen saw the end, we need to take into account the context of the passages in which he discusses the matter, and particularly the context of Origen's whole thought.

III

Managing the Senses: How Does Man Acquire Self-Control and Restrain His Desires?

Background

The preceding part clarified how Origen understood both the original state from which man turned and the nature and implications of the restoration. Origen's discussion of these conditions clearly pointed to the need for a process of change on both a personal and a cosmic dimension. Now that this need has been established in Origen's thought, let us examine in this and the next two chapters the way in which this need could be fulfilled.

These three chapters consider three major mysteries of the spiritual process of growth and the questions that arise because of them. This chapter discusses how man can change by managing the effects generated from his gross body and the physical senses, and the agents that can aid him in this struggle.

It may seem unimportant to talk about the body in a book about the spiritual journey. After all, is it not just a limp thing, a piece of flesh with nerves? What is so difficult about handling the body? Is it not the first to decay and be cast aside in the grave? Unfortunately, it is much more complex than that. Not only in our day, but even in Origen's day it was believed that the body had not just a little but an immense influence on how we think and act. Every philosopher in the ancient world devoted his time to the problems each person has in controlling or managing the effects of the body, what we shall label with a Greek word *aisthesis*, which we might loosely translate "sense-perception."[1]

Nor do we turn to the body first without reason. It is no secret that all of us, even ascetics, learn first in our meditation and contemplation to understand and manage our bodies. Sometimes we use its rhythms to help us meditate; sometimes we are exhilarated by its strength, beauty and physical pleasures. But the control of the body for better or for worse comes first in the effort of anyone to acquire a spiritual life, and Origen, who was said to have led the life of an ascetic himself, understood that no Christian can ignore its needs and presence.

Now that we have discussed the beginning and the end, both times without a body as we know it, let us now observe the middle of the spiritual journey,

61

a middle filled with our and other bodies, a middle too often plagued by physical problems too long to list. Then as now, man seemed to have no choice but to spend his life housing, clothing, feeding, feeling the pain and pleasures of his body and the way it affects his mind. We begin then with an outline of how the gross body arose.

How Did the Fleshly Body Arise?[2]

Origen's description of the emergence of the body is stated as follows: After the event of withdrawal described in Chapter 2, represented by a change from mind to soul, from fervent love to cool neglect, the soul began to acquire a different sort of body, a gross body.[3] The implication is that the farther the intellect was from God, the more it "cooled," thus giving rise to more dense environments. Though the intellect had a body, it was in a spiritual, ethereal form. The withdrawal changed it into something gross.

The effect of corporealization then was that the visible world, including bodies, became diverse, more gross and solid.[4] Once the body became gross, it could give rise, when undisciplined, to the passions. And the passions were those feelings which could turn the soul from the spiritual and could dull the spiritual sensitivity of the soul, so that the soul could become a victim of the "flesh."[5]

However, this appearance of a gross body is not a necessity. It too, like all the changes which affected man in his fall, resulted from the soul's own choices. God gave to each soul a body corresponding to its merits, that is, according to its moral choices.[6]

Thus, Origen considered life in this world as a struggle for the soul in an "unnatural" state.[7] To the change from intellect to soul, and to the already existing spiritual tensions, has been added the presence of a gross body, one that complicates the soul's struggles. Once the intellect was in a state of blessedness; now it is encased in an unnatural body with all its accompanying difficulties, especially the passions. Once the intellect was close to the Creator and enjoyed the warmth of his love; now the soul appears to be distant from him, and subservient to passion. In fact, the passion that contact with such a gross body can cause is an irrational element, foreign to the rational soul.[8]

In sum, due to its choices and the acquisition of a gross body, the rational soul in its present state is faced with constant choices that test its strength and desire to return to union with God. It is faced with a very difficult problem and mystery: what to do with the body and the visible world.

What Is the Meaning of the Body for the Follower of Jesus?[9]

To respond to this question, let us consider the body now in a fuller context; that is, let us view "man," whom Origen calls a "soul using a body," the soul being called the inner man.[10] We will outline in more detail Origen's anthropology in the next section. Here we wish to view where the body stands in the process of spiritual growth.

In light of a gross body, man is trapped by his own choices in a physical environment whose images he cannot prevent but only use according to his reason, his *logos*. Origen writes:

> To be subject then to a particular external impression which gives rise to such and such an image is admittedly not one of the things lying within our power; but to decide to use what has happened either in this way or in that is the work of nothing else but the reason within us, which, as the alternatives appear, either influences us towards the impulses that incite to what is good and seemly or else turn us aside to the reverse.[11]

Origen in this passage presents how man receives impressions by means of the body; these impressions give rise to images, which, in turn, man must use or control through the power of reason within him. Since the images are irrational, if he does not control them, they can encourage passion. And if the soul is subject to passion, it is subject to flesh, and the divine Logos is not in it.[12] So the images that result from sense-impressions cannot be avoided, but they can be turned toward good or evil impluses, depending on the way reason judges them. They are presented before the rational faculty without good or evil tendencies.[13]

In Origen's discussion of Jer. 4:3, for example, he compares the inner self to soil that awaits seeds. He says that our soul must seek out the "rational" plough and plant seeds from the Scriptures in order to rid the earthly life of "thorns."[14] Thus, if man is to turn to good impulses, his important tasks are to learn to direct properly the rational faculty (*logos*) within him in order to direct the senses, and to remove the "veil" of passion already present from his mind. This second concern, which Origen notes in his discussion of Jer. 3:25, arises in those of us who are already in passion. It prevents us from seeing the "shining glory of God" when it is "set over our heart. . . ."[15]

Controlling the impressions of the physical world, however, implies being capable of viewing reality in a different way. It implies the effort to transcend what is mere sense-impression and the images that result from it; it implies transcending the superficial appearance of things or what Origen calls the sphere of "becoming." This movement away from the mere experience of the senses, the sphere of becoming, is one task with which, Origen tells Celsus, the "disciples" (namely, the followers) of Jesus are especially concerned. They realize that this effort is "not merely a matter of theory," but one way to "purify and restore their soul entirely."

> [True Christians] look, as they have learnt, not at the things which are becoming, which are seen and on that account temporal, but at the higher things, whether one wishes to call them "being," or things "invisible" because their nature lies outside the realm of sense-perception [*aisthesis*]. It is in this way that the disciples of Jesus look at the things that are becoming, so that they use them as steps to the contemplation of the nature of intelligible things.[16]

By all possible means, Origen writes, the Christian tries to avoid the "error that is bound up with becoming." Origen's foundation for these remarks is Scripture, namely, 2 Cor. 4:18 and Rom. 1:20:

> We look not at the things that are seen but the things that are unseen; for the things that are unseen are eternal.

> Ever since the creation of the world his invisible nature, namely, his eternal power and deity, has been clearly perceived in the things that have been made.

The disciple of Jesus does not theorize about the seen and unseen; he considers the task of transcending the sphere of "becoming," of seeking the "unseen" and "eternal," of step by step realization of intelligible things, as a central and scripturally based task of his everyday life. For him the task is not "theory," but the way to truth. This distinguishes him from those who realize these facts concerning the illusion of the visible world, but who "have not lived worthily of [the truths] manifested to them by God...."[17]

Moreover, Origen would also claim, in light of the first text cited in this section,[18] that these latter persons have not properly understood these truths so as to be able to judge the images that the visible world has impressed upon them. Not only does the believer strive to understand these truths, but such truths are realized in thought and deed. The follower of Jesus who is turning to God receives the same external impressions and images as others, but the images are used and understood in a different way, inciting the believer to eternal things and the Creator.

We find a more detailed clarification of this matter in other sections of *Against Celsus*. Why did Paul, after all, find inferior the wisdom of the world? Origen responds that Paul believed that the worldly wise men are not wise concerning

> ... intelligible, invisible and eternal things, but only interest themselves in things of sense, and that because they put everything into this last category, they become wise men of the world.... [But when Paul speaks of the wisdom of God,] he means those doctrines which change the soul from the things of this earth to be concerned with the blessedness with God and with what is called his kingdom, and which teach men to despise as transitory all sensible and visible things, to seek earnestly the invisible and to look on things that are unseen. (Cf. 2 Cor. 4:18)[19]

Hence the doctrines of God convert one from the things of sense to the eternal things. This point is made extremely clear when Origen distinguishes the material and sensuous aspects of other religions from Christianity. He writes:

> We admire Jesus who changed our thoughts from considering objects of sense, not only everything corruptible but also what will be corrupted, and who led us to honour the supreme God with upright conduct and prayers.[20]

Yet though the things of sense are "transitory," there is nothing inherently or morally wrong with the visible world or the body, as Origen often affirms by quoting again and again Rom. 1:20.[21]

In sum, what the Christian perceives by his senses becomes finally only a step in order to ascend to what really supports things of sense. Still, the visible world, the realm of the senses and the images that are their product, are central to that effort; they cannot be ignored or avoided. Thus to rise up to a comprehension of the invisible, the sphere of being, requires the domination, control, and proper discipline through reason (*logos*) of the effects of the realm of the visible, the sphere of "becoming," which, in the most personal sense for each person, is the body.

Most simply, the mystery of change for the Christian in this dimension is the control of the senses, including all external influences that move us physically and psychologically, such as food and money, to prevent the growth of passion.[22]

But how does man accomplish this? Now that we have explored how the body arose and its theological and scriptural implications for Origen, we can answer the question in the remaining sections.

Are There Any Inner Gifts Given by God to Help Man Manage the Senses?

When Origen mentions in the text given above that the attitude of the believer is not theory, he is purposefully, it appears, making a contrast with some philosophers whose ideas are only empty doctrine that does not transform the individual, and who create images of idols in physical form and in notion. The Christian who is moving away from a life bound by the senses experiences in his attitude and deeds the inadequacies and ultimate hopelessness of the temporal, corruptible environment of a solely physical existence. In this effort, he is greatly aided by the rational faculty (*logos*). For unlike others, such as certain philosophers, the Christian's rational process of thought is transforming. It directly relates to the special yearning in the soul.

An eager longing for the reality of things is natural to us.... This longing, this love, has, we believe, undoubtedly been implanted in us by God....[23]

These words appear in a chapter concerned with the rewards the saints will receive. In the previous section, Origen had consoled the reader with the thought that all the saints will receive instruction in divine things by the proper instructors either here or in the future Jerusalem. Since some may not find this inciting a "worthy desire," Origen then points out how God has given all rational creatures the inner longing for the reality of things. We need not, Origen assures us, rely solely on outside help, but may turn to our own inner selves. For within us is a longing for the design of things made by God that is more powerful even than our attraction for some beautiful item made by man. For "... our mind cherishes a natural and appropriate longing to know God's truth and to learn the causes of things."[24]

This inner sense of the rational soul is the means by which one can advance from things of sense to those things beyond sense-perception. In certain people who have studied in the philosophy schools, the rational inner sense which enables them to espy certain truths beyond sense-perception seems to be active but is not reflected in their behavior. We shall return to this issue in the consideration of conduct in Chapter 4. At this point, in the concern with control of the senses, let us note how Origen lauds those whose "inner longing for the reality of things" lifts them in part from the struggles with sense-perception and the gross body. In fact, Origen, basing himself on Scripture, carefully distinguishes between sense-perception and the other divine sense:

> But in case it should appear mistaken to say as we have done that intellectual things are beyond sense-perception, we will quote as an illustration the saying of Solomon: "You will find also a divine sense" (Prov. 2:5). By this he shows that intellectual things are to be investigated not by bodily sense but by some other which he calls divine.[25]

In light of these two passages, three conclusions can be offered: First, man has the rational faculty (*logos*) to use and control properly the images and passions that can result from sense-impressions. He cannot prevent these impressions from striking the soul, but he can direct them so they can be turned to good uses and impulses. Second, man also has the means to transcend what the senses produce through what is called here a "divine sense," which Origen also calls a longing for intelligible, eternal things. This sense enables man to transcend this world of sense-impressions and to reach some comprehension of the reality of things, the sphere of being. This inner sense, implanted by God, is not created by the products of sense-perception, but is a faculty that has the capacity to investigate intellectual things directly.[26] Third, neither the physical senses nor the images that arise from sense-perception are inherently evil. Matter itself is not evil. In discussing the origin of evil, Origen writes:

> But in our view it is not true that the matter which dwells among mortals is responsible for evils. Each person's mind is responsible for the evil which exists in him, and this is what evil is. Evils are the actions which results from it.[27]

Good and evil thoughts are not caused by the sensuous external world or by the senses themselves, but by the way in which the sense and the images that arise from them are directed.

In sum, man has been given important means in controlling and transcending the sphere of becoming, of moving beyond what could be only an earthly, sensuous condition. In order to examine in more detail these means, let us turn to Origen's view of the powers of man as given him by God.

Origen has described man as a soul using a body and as any rational creature.[28] While this description sufficed for our prior consideration of the body, we need to know more about Origen's anthropology and psychology before proceeding.[29] For understanding change involves investigating *how*, by what means, man changes. There are two fundamental ways: through powers given to him, and which he shares, and through outside help. This section is concerned with the former. Later sections will consider how help is given from outside.

The following presentation, then, of Origen's psychology is a summary—and no more than a summary—that will clarify the kind of inner context in which the mystery of the soul's conversion is understood. We suspect that this overview will become increasingly useful as the study progresses. Then we will proceed to a discussion of Christ's role as Redeemer.

In his interpretation of Jer. 2:31, Origen indicates that God has constructed the soul so that it will be rational, grasp knowledge, and exercise its intelligence. Hence the *psyche* (soul) begins with these fundamental powers and potential.[30] These fundamental powers allow man to "build" a structure or building worthy of God. Man initially builds, as we shall see in more detail in later sections, with teachings, Scripture and moral practice.[31] In the context of Heb. 8:2 and Matt. 15:13, however, Origen will write that God is the architect of the "building."[32] There need be no contradiction here. God is both the builder and the creator of the powers that man can use to build in cooperation with God.

The above then provides a fundamental framework without listing and defining the various terms Origen uses to clarify the dimensions of the soul.[33] Let us now indicate how the inner powers, particularly in this section the image (*eikon*) and *logos*, function in Origen's view of conversion, then explore the role of Christ as Redeemer in conversion.

Origen in a fragment says that each human being is analogous to the world. If he is good, he has the image of the heavenly. If he is bad, he is following the image of the earthly.[34] This fundamentally cosmic pattern influences many of Origen's images and examples of the hope and plight of man. Origen did not conceive of man in isolation or unto himself, but rather as a creature interacting with and related to what are for Origen truly cosmic forces, such as the Logos (or Image), the devil, and the various spiritual powers. All good in man is, for Origen, accidental, which means that man does not originate or create good; he receives it from outside himself. Hence the good powers we discuss in this section are dependent on, shared with, and derived from God; they are not solely owned by human nature. Similarly, evil is also accidental in the sense that all men begin with a nature without tendencies toward good or evil.[35]

The process of interacting with the cosmic forces and realization of his shared powers through an inner yearning is often explained by Origen through his thoughts on the creation according to the image, and the *logos* in man.[36] For Origen, the use of the image terminology, borrowed from Scripture[37] and the Alexandrian school, was a precise way to present the problems of man's present condition in a gross body and their solution.[38] In the previous section, we saw how Origen uses the similar frameworks of being and becoming, of reality and appearance, of invisible and visible, and of man's rational faculty and its control of external sense impressions to clarify both the problem of and the remedy to man's condition. One of the basic biblical frameworks which Origen uses to indicate the power of man in relation to God is the image:

On the one hand, our original substance is formed according to the image of the Creator, but, on the other hand, that which we have received with fault is formed from the dust of the earth (cg. Gen. 1:26–27). If we, having forgotten in some way the better nature in us, subordinate ourselves to the dust of the earth, the best part of ourselves receives the image of the earthly. But if we, realizing that [there are two elements in us], one created according to the image, the other received from the dust of the earth, incline completely toward that in which we reproduce the image, we will truly be according to the likeness of God, and we will have left behind all affection for the material and the body, as well as all particular affection for those things which share that likeness.[39]

This text gives man the same two choices that Origen has expressed, in different ways, previously. Man can be mindful of the creation according to the image, his principal substance, or he can turn toward and permit the images of the earthly to rule his nature. The earthly in this text is represented by the "material" and the "body." It is often also an image for Origen of the devil and spiritual death.[40] It is worthwhile to note that Origen does not offer any opposition between the earthly and the principal substance. It is our "affection" for one or the other that determines our natures' direction. Thus, man himself "paints" the images of the earthly through the "colours" of various evils, such as greed and lust.[41] Yet his choice does not affect the image of God:

For it remains always the image of God, although you may cover it over with the image of the earthly.... Through particular kinds of malice, like diverse colours brought together, you yourself paint in yourself the image of the earthly, which God did not create in you.[42]

Origen clearly indicates that it is man's responsibility to be mindful of the better part of his nature. But how is this done? On the one hand, we must consider everything we want to do to be certain it is not in accord with the devil.[43]

On the other hand, in a positive direction, in a chapter concerned with the consummation Origen writes that we can make some strides by imitation of God.[44] The imitation of God principally means that one must imitate the goodness of God, especially towards one's enemies.[45] All of the Lord's virtues, such as holiness, patience, justice, mercy, and compassion are necessary in order to progress to the perfection of God's likeness.[46] To be mindful of the image of the heavenly means to try to imitate God through acts of virtue that are indicative of his goodness.[47] By so doing, man will be making progress toward the likeness of God, which is the design for humanity in the consummation.

It is clear, however, that the image of the heavenly in man is buried under an accumulation of images of the earthly. Yet this power still offers a hope for man. It creates a nostalgia that Origen mentioned above.[48] Such a power is even akin to God, Origen writes, since it was created according to God's Image, the Logos.

For example, Celsus found amusing the Christian belief in man's uniqueness. To a God looking down from heaven, Celsus mocked, there would be no difference between men and ants. Origen replied:

> He who looks down from heaven upon the irrational animals, even though their bodies may be large, will not see any origin for their impulses other than irrationality, so to speak. But when he looks at the rational beings, he will see reason which is common to men and to divine and heavenly beings, and probably also the supreme God himself. This explains why he is said to have been made in the image of God; for the image of the supreme God is his Reason (Logos).[49]

The relation of the divine Logos with *logos*—or the participation of the *logikoi* (creatures with *logos*) with the divine Logos—is a common theme in Origen.[50] In fact, *logos* is a kind of communication link or contact point for all divine gifts and movements; it is the link through which man is spiritually nourished. For *logos* (reason) is the divine food.[51] The use of this rational power and contact point will in turn bring an increasing power of Christ (the divine Logos/Image) in us, so that the more we merit by our acts, the more we attain on the road to the likeness.

> It is clear that Christ becomes present in each individual in such a degree as is warranted by the extent of his merits.[52]

Origen has many different ways of exploring the role of Christ or how the divine Logos participates in man's pilgrimage. In some texts, he sees the inner Christ as the good shepherd who rules over the senses and irrational movements through *logos*.[53] Sometimes he states that we actually progress according to the strength of *logos* in us, and that the strength fails in a soul subject to passion. Certainly there seems to be for Origen an increasing or decreasing degree or dimension of spiritual experience, depending almost directly on the force of *logos* in us. If one indeed is to see God, he must share in *logos*.[54]

The participation of God, however, does not alter the need for the contribution of man in this participation. In other words, it is not a one-sided participation, initiated and generated by the divine Logos alone. As Origen writes in a fragment, the *logos* in us is not an active power without our aid.[55] Or, as Origen describes the matter in another context, the power of *logos* is a seed that needs our nourishment and conservation.[56]

Hence we need to be a little cautious in our understanding of what Origen means by participation. Often it seems to be a participation dependent more on man than on God. Each step warrants some divine contribution, but the steps are taken by man, and the growth of participation is initiated by man. God offers the power, the potential and, of course, the reward of himself, but man's own choice and will is the catalyst.

The creation according to the image is not like the images mentioned above,[57] which sense-impressions cause in us. Those images have as their basis the physical senses, but the creation according to the image has as its basis reason. Those images can grow into physical desires, longings for power, lust for false idols and gods—all images of the earthly resulting from an irrational judgment on information received from the senses. The image in man created according to the Image of God emerges from the love of nonmaterial, eternal things. Furthermore, the senses know and are known by what is similar to them, namely, the external world of physical things. Similarly, Origen explains, the creation according to the image participates in what is akin to it, namely, the things of reason and the intellect.[58] The senses naturally relate to sensible things, and the divine sense, noted above, to things of God. The creation according to the image therefore is not corporeal. Its power emanates from within, in the inner man.[59]

The image is one of two key elements in this mode of conversion. By its presence, the possibility of conversion is assured, for both its source and its object is God. Origen verifies this fact in his discussion of Jer. 22:24–26. He points out that the turning of the process of repentance, one of the key factors in spiritual growth and movement, is a movement in which "every person who takes upon himself what is according to the image becomes a seal or ring on God's hand."[60]

How Does Christ as Redeemer Help Us?

Now that we have had an introduction to the role of the inner powers of man and their potential to convert, let us also briefly consider another kind of catalyst, the importance of Christ as Redeemer in this process. Our concern here is merely to note the cosmic redemptive act which initiates spiritual change.[61] Obviously we will be discussing many other dimensions of Christ's role in other sections.

This chapter has concerned *aisthesis* because of the importance of the concept of sense-perception in Origen's views on the mystery of how one loves or returns to God. But *aisthesis* is not only concerned with the senses; it also concerns the process of perception. It describes a kind of link that overlaps what, in Origen's day, were the areas of the body and the mind, the flesh and the spirit. Our primary interest in this section is to give an overview of how the Redeemer initializes this process of conversion, how his assumption of flesh allows for changes in man.

Christ is the sum total in Origen's thought of what "Christianity" means as a spiritual way of life, vision, and mode of conversion. Each aspect of Christ is a critical means for all rational creatures to be near God and return to him. To substantiate this view, we need go no further than the first books of his *Commentary on John* (upon which many passages in the later books are also based), and the beginning sections and fourth book of *Against Celsus*, to see how completely he viewed the significance of Christ's almost endless aspects/roles, depending on the place in God's plan.[62] Our main concern in this section is the unique role of Christ as the man-God and his assumption of flesh.

Let us begin by clarifying how Origen described Jesus. He wrote:

> Thus it is true to call him man and to call him not man; man, because he was capable of death; not man, on account of his being diviner than man.... [The Docetics[63]] do what they can to deprive us of the man who is more just than all men, and are left with a figure which cannot save them, for as by one man came death, so also by one man is the justification of life. We could not have received such benefit as we have from the Logos had he not assumed the man, had he remained such as he was from the beginning with God the Father, and had he not taken up man.... But after that man we also shall be able to receive him, to receive him so great and of such nature as he was, if we prepare a place in proportion to him in our soul.[64]

Death is the pivotal issue in understanding Christ's nature. On the one hand, his death indicates he was man. On the other hand, he conquered death, so this indicates he is God. It is Christ's victory over death that saves us and that allows him to come into our soul. In other texts, Origen will note that in those passages where Christ is sorrowful (Matt. 26:38) or troubled (John 12:37), these states indicate Christ not as God but as man. For to Origen these states are again indicative of death, as he writes:

> The Logos was not liable to death, but the human is liable to death....[65]

He became man to bring the "benefit" of God to man, and he could not have accomplished this task, according to Origen, if he had not assumed manhood.

The signficance of Origen's understanding of Christ for how we change and progress spiritually in terms of redemption always seems to lie with what man needs, with man's weakness, with the solution to rather than the origin of sin, which often revolves around death. The God-man has a purpose in coming: to deliver man from what enslaves him by taking on what enslaves him.[66] For example, Origen, in his interpretation of Isa. 53:1–5, writes that "...he took on the weakness of our sins...."[67] In another homily, in his interpretation of Rom. 6:6 and Rom. 8:3, he refers to Christ's sojourn when he took on the "body of sin" "in the name of the flesh of sin" so that man can worship God here and in the afterlife.[68] In his homily on Jer. 1:10, Origen talks of the accomplishment of Christ:

> But Jesus Christ has uprooted the kingdoms of sin and has pulled down the buildings of evil and has made righteousness and truth in our souls to rule against these kingdoms.[69]

Hence Christ comes not only to bring the divine benefit, but to change creation from its bondage to death and sin through these benefits. The Logos made flesh, he writes, comes to perfect what is imperfect.[70] Man's imperfect nature arose, as we have discussed in Chapter 2, from his disobedience and desire to imitate the wrong model and way of acting, the devil. In this context, Origen also quotes Heb. 5:14, a favorite text of his, to clarify Christ's role: "But solid food is for the mature, for those who have their faculties trained by practice to distinguish good from evil." Christ comes to perfect God's work and to unite men with wisdom in order to bring men to a "mature" condition.[71]

Origen is discussing in all of these texts the grand plan. Man and creation due to Adam and the devil are corrupted. Things need to be set right. So God introduces a divine power, a power that is at one in will with the Creator.[72] This answer to the mystery of how men are sinful and corrupt, and the meaning of death, is a traditional, even biblical, answer, though Origen does not in these texts explore it in great detail.

Elsewhere he clarifies that for change to happen, things must turn around at the foundation through the appearance of what is outside. At the foundation is death. Thus much of Origen's analysis of Christ's redemptive acts rests in how death and its by-products can be removed.[73] Origen often states that men were the subjects of the evil king Satan who wields the power of death. In light of 1 Cor. 15:22, Origen indicates that Adam brought them to this state of death and Christ brings them to the state of life again.[74]

The theme of life and death is important for viewing Christ's redemptive aspect. Man, being in sin, could not on his own grasp Christ's divine life. Man, because of Adam, was alive only to a dead, sinful life. Christ came into our form to reverse the condition and restore (as noted in the text above), to help man die to sin through his life and death, and live eternally in him. This relationship with Christ is not only vicarious. Christ enters man's very being so that the act of dying to death now becomes possible for humanity since he has opened the door.[75] In this sense, if we are redeemed, we carry about the "death of Jesus" in the body, and the spirit lives.[76] And with the spirit alive, as we shall see in more detail in Chapter 5, man can reach his true destiny as a son of God. Origen clarifies these matters nicely in one section of his long discussion of the various aspects of Christ, one of which is the "Lamb of God" (John 1:29):

> For the Lamb of God became like an innocent sheep being led to the slaughter, that He may take away the sin of the world. He who supplies the rational (logos) to all is made like a lamb which is dumb before her shearer, that we might be purified by his death, which is given as a sort of medicine against the opposing power, and also against the sin of those who open their minds to the truth. For the death of Christ reduced to impotence those powers which war against the human race, and it set free from sin by a power beyond our words the life of each believer.... For his taking away sin is still going on with each one of those in the world, till sin be taken away from the whole world, and the Saviour deliver the kingdom prepared and completed to the Father, a kingdom in which no sin is left at all, and which, therefore, is ready to accept the Father as its king, and which on the other hand is waiting to receive all God has to bestow, fully, and in every part, at that time when the saying is fulfilled, "That God may be all in all." (1 Cor. 15:28)[77]

Origen is explicit about this objective role of Christ's redemption in his reply to Celsus's question about the purpose of Christ's descent:

[Celsus] fails to see that in our view the purpose of the descent was in the first place to convert those whom the Gospel calls "the lost sheep of the house of Israel" (Matt. 10:6; Matt. 15:24), and, in the second place, because of their unbelief, to take away from the former Jewish husbandmen what is called "the kingdom of God" and to give it to "other husbandmen," the Christians, who will render to God the fruits of the kingdom of God in due season (Matt. 21:43, 41), each of their actions being a fruit of the kingdom.[78]

Origen in this section goes on to point out that this possibility of redemption and conversion was a choice that men by free will could seek; it was not forced upon them by divine mandate. Obviously, God could have accomplished his purpose by coercion, but he chose otherwise.

Yet a mystery remains for us if the Redemption is seen only objectively. Why did Jesus need to come at all as a man? The incarnation and redemptive process that emerged from it was, in Origen's view, a mode in which it was easiest for humanity to grasp the Logos and be transformed. Essentially it was a matter of what was best for spiritual growth and change. By the means of his manhood, Christ was more accessible and managed to open up a mode in which a more direct communication was possible. However, though Christ had the form of a man, for Origen he had none of the moral weaknesses or sins of humanity. He experienced temptation, but he did not yield to it. In Origen's words, "he underwent no change from good to bad."[79]

The Redemption, however, is not only objective in Origen's thought. We have stressed this aspect in this section. We have clarified how Christ comes to earth to achieve a restoration, a conversion of creation that was subjectively impossible. But this dimension of redemption is only the initial step of redemption for Origen; it is not the whole process. Later will come instruction, imitation and the development by Christ from within, but those are not our concerns in this part.

But is the Redemption the only external help man receives? Does man need more than this to battle the evil powers? Before we can answer these questions, we need to probe briefly into how Origen understood evil and the role of the devil.

What Is the Role of Evil and the Devil?[80]

To move spiritually away from a life based only in the senses requires the participation of powers resident in man and the cosmic role of Christ. It remains to examine how, in light of the soul's struggle with the effects of sense-perception, progress in this mode is achieved, that is, how the soul controls and transcends the images that sense-perception causes.

We have offered an overview of these forces in the previous section. Though we did not specify, it is clear that Origen views in this struggle two primary forces: the forces of God through his Logos who is the Christ, and the forces of the devil and those who follow him. Though proof of this viewpoint is everywhere in Origen's thought, let us offer a couple of examples of how he expresses it.

The dichotomy involved in this perspective is found in Origen's view of Jer. 1:9–10; Matt. 15:13, 19; and Eph. 4:27. He first indicates that all the "evil thoughts" (Matt. 15:19) are "plants" that the "father in heaven has not planted." (Matt. 15:13) The devil is the sower of those seeds. God, on the other hand, has his own plants.

> Thus both God who has the seeds and the devil await us. If we give "place to the devil" (Eph. 4:27), the "enemy" (Matt. 13:28), he sows a plant which the Father did not plant [and] in every way is uprooted. If we do not give "place to the devil," but we give place to God, God rejoicing sows his seeds in our hearts.[81]

Origen carries the dichotomy of God and the devil to the point of opposition in his interpretation of Jer. 20:8, "I call upon faithlessness," which includes faithlessness to the devil. He says, with reference also to Matt. 6:24, that if one is a friend to the devil, he is an enemy to God, and vice versa.[82]

Hence the conflict of these two forces is always real and in the forefront of Origen's thought. He considers the conflict a full-scale war,[83] and is confident that it must be won if man is to change. For God, in his view, will never enter the soul of a sinner.[84] Even if the devil and God appear to do the same thing, the effects and meaning are quite different. For example, Origen radically contrasts the deception of Jeremiah by God, in Jer. 20:7, and the serpent's deception in Genesis 3.[85]

In sum, the choice between these two forces in Origen's view of man is fundamental. It must be faced and considered in every act and thought. Every event of human life can be traced to a decision involving one of these two primary forces, the forces of God or the forces of the devil.

This said, let us now turn to an investigation of Origen's view of evil and the devil.

There are at least two different, though interrelated, ways of understanding evil and the devil in Origen's thought: either as a cosmic, objective force or as a subjective force. Before we investigate them, let us, first of all, define what evil is in Origen's thought. His most clear definition is found in *On First Principles*, and there is no indication that he wavered from this definition in his other works. He wrote:

> Now to withdraw from the good is nothing else than to be immersed in evil; for it is certain that evil means to be lacking in good.[86]

Elsewhere Origen said, ". . . all evil is nothing, since it is also non-being. . . ."[87] For Origen only good *exists*; evil is a privation of good.[88] Hence, Origen adds that evil has no essence or being; it has no reality, since the only true reality and being is God and what God creates, and evil is neither his creation nor does he share in it.[89]

With this view of evil, let us return to the two perspectives of the devil and evil. The objective view involves the devil as an instigator of evil, a cosmic figure, an adversary who has denied and opposed God. This view is often found in Origen's apologetic work *Against Celsus*, where Origen at one point traces the origin of the figure throughout Scripture as the bearer and model of wickedness. Evil came to be, he says,

...because of some who lost their wings and followed the example of the first being who lost his wings.[90]

Origen continues that the earth became a "school of virtue" for those who "became evil." He claims that man failed because "he neglected to partake of the living bread and the true drink."[91]

Origen summarizes the objective, cosmic view of evil when he counters with this question to Celsus:

Why, then, is it absurd that among men there should be two extremities, if I so say, the one of goodness, the other of the opposite, so that the extremity of goodness exists in the human nature of Jesus, since from him the mighty work of conversion, healing and improvement flowed to the human race, whereas the opposite extremity exists in him who is called Antichrist?.... It was right, also, that one of the extremes, the best, should be called the Son of God, because of his superiority, and the the the one diametrically opposed to him should be called son of the evil demon who is Satan and the devil.[92]

Here we view the concern of evil on a cosmic scale, almost beyond the concerns of humans. Here it is a battle between God and the devil.[93]

However, the other way to understand evil and the devil is in terms of the effects of evil and the devil's work, particularly how it involves earthly matters and the senses. Indeed in some texts, particularly with reference to Rom. 16:20, Origen will use the word "satan" figuratively for the power of evil in us.[94] As noted above in Chapter 2, the way man changes for Origen is primarily a cooperative effort between man's God-given gifts and God. Hence our main focus will be on what has been called the subjective dimension of evil and the work of the devil. Let us then take a closer look at this dimension.

In terms of his influence on man's soul, who is the devil and what is his work? For Origen the devil is the commander of the images of the earthly[95] and the prince over all evil, impious, and criminal powers and doctrines.[96] He is intimate with sin. Indeed, Origen points out, "If 'everyone who does sin has come from the devil' (1 John 3:8), just as many times we have come from the devil, we sin."[97] And to those who give him dominion over them, the sinners, the devil indeed has power. For example, in his interpretation of Num. 21:21–24, Origen views Sihon, king of the Amorites, as a figure for the devil.[98] According to the spiritual sense, Origen explains that the devil may be seen in the king because the devil is also a prince; but the devil is a prince not simply over a race of people, but even over the whole "world," because sinners refuse to abandon what is worldly and have made the world sinful.[99]

Hence to be in league with the devil, the prince of sinners, is to have an inordinate and irrational affection for worldly images, images that are the products of sensible reality.[100] The devil "destroys" all those insofar as they incline to earthly thoughts.[101] Included in the perverted earthly images are the figments produced in the worshippers of idols.[102] Such an attraction and affection for things of the external world and imagined notions creates sin. And in terms of many texts in Origen,[103] the effect of sin is a turning away from God, a perversion (in contrast to conversion), and enslavement to the devil. Or, said another way, in his homily on Jer. 17:13,

> Whenever each of us sins, through his sinning he "leaves" Christ, and if he leaves Christ, he leaves God.[104]

There is no in-between area for Origen, no compromise zone in which the earthly and the heavenly can meet and be mingled. For Origen the question of relationship between opposites is not possible.

The true issue involves what a person seeks. He says succinctly: "If you seek what is earthly, you do not seek what is heavenly."[105]

We have considered the root of the problem with respect to the powers of the devil, namely, the way the mind of man turns and to what it is attracted, because this chapter concerns the mystery of how man controls his senses. Since the devil is directly involved in the extent to which man falls prey to earthly things and thoughts, the devil and *aisthesis* certainly can be intimately involved, depending on the man. We need then to understand the methods of the devil and how man is trapped.

For Origen the devil and his powers are not passive forces. As Origen himself notes, the devil is often described in Scripture as a "lion."[106] And the lion lurks about seeking for prey to devour. He threatens and howls, awaiting our weakness. It is God who shields us from him.[107] How then does the devil get his followers?

On the one hand, according to Origen's discussion of the partridge (another figure for the devil) in Jer. 17:11, he leads people astray and deceives them by a false image of what is good. He lures those who are unprepared and innocent.[108] Each of the desires and passions attached to evil impulses has one of the devil's army, a demon,[109] to nurture it.[110] As Origen clearly states the matter, "The demons are the 'riders of horses' (Jer. 28:21–24) who sit upon the fleshly pleasures."[111] Also, in his understanding of Jer. 3:22, Origen contrasts those who are committed only to God, and say, "we will be yours," (Jer. 3:22) and those controlled by the "spirit of anger," the "spirit of grief," by the belly, greed and other forms of idolatry. Origen recognized that commitment can lie in both directions.[112]

On the other hand, as we have noted in other contexts, man turns himself to the devil through his own choices. In a general sense, our responsibility is stated in Origen's understanding of Jer. 2:22, where man himself is said to have "turned to malice."[113] Origen writes:

> If then there is something superior about us, God has made it, but we created the evil and the sin for ourselves.[114]

Furthermore, Origen goes on to say that God made the soul of man good initially, but man perverted it, turning it opposite to God's plan.[115]

We note in these texts that the process of turning can occur in both good and evil directions, and that turning or change of heart is a free act. More specifically, man's evil results from his failure to moderate natural instincts, such as desire, fear, pleasure and pain.[116] Hence, none of the things that move man to evil are actually in themselves evil. Even the devil is not the cause. Man alone lets these forces arise and overwhelm.[117]

Evidently then, since the devil is the prince of sinfulness and can take control of worldly, earthly things and thoughts, to avoid evil and the devil means to stop sinning and to control the instincts that can give rise to excesses of passion and desire, such as anger, pride, avarice, and other excesses.[118] Of these passions, the most acute is pride and arrogance. It is the seminal fault of the devil himself, and when we are prideful we are sons of the devil.[119] By turning in pride to ourselves and the external world and not to God, we condemn ourselves to the devil. By imitating his prideful acts, we cover over the powers given to us at creation, and will receive the same judgment as the devil.[120]

The process of handling evil by God is not unlike, for Origen, the relationship between a sick person and a physician. The physician offers his advice and cures, and it is up to the sick person to take them and be cured. If the sick person does not accept the help of the physician, then the patient must pay the penalties. Similarly, God sends his angels to help cure the sinner, but if sin continues to prosper, the sinner's sentence (cf. Jer. 28:8–10) grows, and then God himself gives his judgments.[121]

From another perspective, the biblical idea of "captivity", captivity to the devil, to the demons, and to sin, is a favorite image of Origen to illustrate how God can punish a sinful race. Indeed, as Origen mentions in his exegesis of Jer. 1:3, "if we sin, we are about to become captives" of the devil.[122] We can escape this captivity to the devil, he says, if we repent and convert.[123] Another image, related to the captivity, is the Jews' rejection of Jesus. Because of their refusal to accept Christ as Lord, God gives to them a "bill of divorce," as in Jer. 3:7–8.[124]

The effect of evil is always death. In his discussion of Jer. 13:16 concerning the "dark mountains," which Origen believes are symbolically the devil and demons, he writes:

> But when anyone comes to the "dark mountains," let us see what is there: "The shadow of death" (Jer. 13:6). Where the dark mountains are, there is "the shadow of death" arising from the dark mountains themselves; "and they will be brought down into darkness."[125]

And going one step beyond the effect of death, Origen points out in light of Jer. 15:5, "who will spare you," and Heb. 6:4–6, that he who sins after repenting cannot be restored to repentance.[126]

In summary, let us note two elements of the role of evil forces in Origen's thought. First, the devil and his forces do not originate evil impulses. They result from man's own judgment on the way he tempers his natural instincts and on the way he interprets and uses impressions from the physical world. Second, as soon as an evil tendency does manifest itself, it is nurtured by the evil forces.

Hence without self-control and divine help, man can become more and more a victim of these forces, and will find it difficult to change and turn back to God. With certainty, Origen writes, human nature alone cannot combat the powers of the devil.

> For human nature by itself alone cannot, I think, maintain the struggle against "angels" and "heights" and "depths" and any other creature.[127]

How then can man progress and overcome these powers? It is certain, according to Origen, that man alone cannot win in the war against the devil's forces.

Two areas of aid are given man. First, already discussed in a section above, there is the gift of salvation made possible by the Redemption, in which the door of salvation and divine help is opened for us by Christ as Redeemer. It is Christ who "nullified the ruler of this age and nullified sin" so that man can worship God. Christ accomplished this feat by bearing the "body which has saved" and the "body of sin." (Rom. 6:6)[128] Origen is even more specific in his homily on Jer. 11:1. There it is Christ's coming that rendered harmless the devil by his example and through the cross.[129]

Second, there is the working of the divine Logos in the rational world. There are two dimensions of the Logos. There is the inner rational yearning, *logos*, which God has given man at creation. But also there are the outer agents of the Logos: Scripture, the Church, good angels, and the Holy Spirit. If man will choose to direct properly his rational faculty, then he may hope to receive aid of these other forces of the Logos that oppose the devil.[130]

The change that occurs with the aid of these instruments creates a kind of pattern and principle for the discussion to be offered in the next parts. This aspect of the spiritual growth process, analogous in some ways to a purification process that clears away the images of the earthly and sensuous, should not, however, be considered apart from the other aspects. The movement away from a concern with the senses is only one dimension in the complete journey to understand the mysteries and become a follower of Jesus. Nevertheless, it lays a kind of foundation for the restoration of the soul upon which the others must always depend.[131]

We have discussed the inner work of *logos* in us. Let us now give an overview of each of the areas in which the Logos helps us. We begin with Scripture.

How Can Scripture Aid Us in Controlling the Difficulties with the Senses and the Body?[132]

There are those who think that Scripture, as the harmonious and unified result of the plan and truth of the Logos, was for Origen the most important force in spiritual growth.[133] It certainly was not a dead parchment describing the days of old when great saints walked the earth, but the Logos of God himself speaking to and luring all hearts who will listen. In the following text, Origen even connects the wisdom of God in creation with the wisdom in Scripture; he thus gives Scripture a kind of organic quality.

> ... the creation of the world itself, fashioned in this wise as it is, can be understood through the divine wisdom, which from actual things and copies teaches us things unseen by means of those that are seen (cf. Rom. 1:20), and carries us over from earthly things to heavenly. Yet these principles are found not only in all creatures; the divine scripture itself is written with wisdom of a rather similar sort.[134]

Just as in another section we read that the disciples of Jesus use earthly things—the sphere of becoming—as steps to the higher, intelligible sphere,[135] so also in this text just quoted Origen points out that Scripture is a channel to the higher things. The remarkable implication is that Scripture for Origen is a living entity, a divine creation like other creatures, which inspires because it is living. God reveals his wisdom in it. Through the confusion of the world Scripture is the path of peace that the Logos, as the shepherd, holds out to men. This view arises in Origen's consideration of Matt. 5:9 and Eccles. 12:11.

> For, also, according to the Preacher, all the scriptures, are "words of the wise like goads, and as nails firmly fixed which were given by agreement from one shepherd" (Eccles. 12:11); and there is nothing superfluous in them. But the Logos is the one shepherd of the rational [scriptures] which may have an appearance of discord to those who have not ears to hear (Matt. 11:15; Mark 4:9; Luke 8:8) but are actually in harmony.[136]

Origen goes on to say that the harmony of the Scripture is clear to those who seek the "music" of God—the Law, the prophets and the gospel sounding as chords together without discord.

> For as he knows that all the scripture is the one perfect and harmonized instrument
> of God, which from different sounds give forth one saving voice to those willing to
> learn, which stops and restrains every working of an evil spirit. . . .[137]

The rational power, therefore, of the Logos is present in Scripture. Armed with its power, one who hears and wishes to listen can dispel the influences tending toward evil and be drawn a step toward salvation.[138]

The Scripture not only has inspirational power because of the presence of the Logos within it; it literally tells us the way to convert and change our lives. Origen, as we have seen previously, especially in his dialogue with Celsus, bases the effectiveness of religions and philosophies and people on how effectively they can change mankind.[139] He daringly states, in the following passage, that fundamentally the process of becoming a follower of Jesus begins with knowing and following the wisdom found in Scripture, in reading the books and following its truths. The context of the following passage concerns how God rejected the Jews with a bill of divorce because of their deeds and refusal to change (Jer. 3:8–10):

> Thus the true conversion is to read the old [books], to see those who have become just,
> to imitate them, to read them to see those who have been reproached, to guard oneself
> from falling into those reproaches; to read the books of the New Testament, the words
> of the Apostles, after reading, to write all these things into the heart, to live in accordance
> with them lest a "bill of divorce" (Jer. 3:8) is also given to us, but we can belong to
> the holy inheritance. . . .[140]

The process of turning away from evil and toward God depends on man's free choice, on "those willing to learn." In terms of Scripture, the possibility of freedom depends on the condition of the soul, especially whether or not it is covered with a "veil" of shame or sin. As Origen writes, if the veil is present, and the Bible is read, it will not be understood; its meaning will be hidden.[141] Turning to God, he states, removes the veil.[142] Once the veil is removed, then man still must choose. The Logos is prepared to enlighten man, but man must be willing to hear the message. Indeed, man must turn to the Lord, and the veil will be lifted and man will see the glory of God.[143]

In other words, there is a kind of cooperation, even though it would appear that, in the ultimate sense, man stands in a paradoxical situation with respect to freedom and the necessity of God's design. He is free in the sense that he chooses *when* to choose God's will and complete God's plan,[144] but it is God's will that directs how the soul is to be healed and rid of evil impulses. And there is no evil beyond the power of God, no evil which cannot be cured, for the divine Logos is stronger than any evil.[145]

The exercise of turning to the Scripture and hearing its saving voice is also an individual process within which each person has to pave his own way. Scripture is difficult and profound. It often speaks in parables and mysteries. To understand it requires hard study, a desire to comprehend many things, and help from the

Logos.[146] In fact, according to Origen, there are different dimensions of Scripture dependent upon one's own spiritual progress.

Each person according to his capacity understands the scriptures.[147]

One must therefore portray the meaning of the sacred writings in a threefold way upon one's soul, so that the simple man may be edified by what we may call the flesh of the scripture, this name being given to the obvious interpretation; while the man who has made some progress may be edified by its soul, as it were; and the man who is mature. . . . [may be edified] by the spiritual law, which has a "shadow of the good things to come."[148]

In the latter text quoted here, Origen presents three ways in which the meaning of Scripture may be communicated and experienced. Each way has a function in man's salvation.

For just as man consists of body, soul and spirit, so, in the same way does the scripture, which has been prepared by God to be given for man's salvation.[149]

This progression from the body of Scripture to the spirit is the spiritual journey through the powers of Scripture. The soul's journey through the dimensions of Scripture is similar, as we have noted, to the journey from the sphere of becoming to the sphere of intelligible reality, and beyond. And just as the senses and the images they engender are not inherently evil or useless, so also the "body" of Scripture has an important function in scriptural conversion.[150]

For the intention was to make even the outer covering of the spiritual truths, I mean the bodily part of scriptures, in many respects not unprofitable but capable of improving the multitude in so far as they receive it.[151]

In Origen's view of Scripture, all dimensions are a part of God's intentions. For God

. . . made the soul and body and spirit of scripture: the body in those things which came before us, the soul for us now, and the spirit for those things which came after the inheritance of eternal life in the future.[152]

These three dimensions, then—though in practice usually narrowed to two—appear to be the main modes that direct the path of scriptural conversion.[153]

Scripture influences man through the relationship between the divine Logos in it and the *logos* present in men. For the seed, man's *logos*, implanted by the Creator, is attracted to that quality of the Logos to which it is akin.[154] Yet the efficacy of this relationship depends upon the condition of the soul.

But since the Logos has opened the eyes of our soul, we see the difference between light and darkness and in every way prefer to stand in the light, and do not want to enter the darkness at all. The true Light, because he is living, knows to whom it will be right to show the radiance, and to whom only light, not showing his brilliance because of the weakness still inherent in the man's eyes.[155]

As we have seen in prior sections of this chapter,[156] the better part of man's nature can be clouded over by earthly images. Man makes judgments without reason that turn him toward evil impulses and images. Such distractions and images, products of man's difficulties with the senses, are factors in the degree of light that the eyes of our soul receive. Those minds which are less distracted by the effects of the senses and their accompanying images are able to receive a greater portion of his light and thus make quicker progress beyond the reality that the senses grasp.

Yet this relationship between the Logos in Scripture and *logos* in man does not imply that Scripture itself has no part in opening man's eyes despite his prior condition. It is not, in other words, merely a dumb agent. Origen indicates this power of Scripture in his discussion of Leviticus 16. Leviticus 16 tells how Aaron is instructed to cast lots on two goats, one lot for the Lord, the other lot for Azazel. The one goat becomes a sin offering for the Lord; the other is sent away into the wilderness. Origen interprets these events in the following way:

> Thus the "lot of the Lord" ought to be understood as if [the Scripture] had said election of the Lord or portion of the Lord; and, on the other hand, that lot which was sent into the wilderness should be understood as that part which spurned and cast itself off from the Lord on account of its unworthiness. . . . When an evil thought arises in your heart. . . . realize that this is the lot of Azazel, and cast it out immediately and expel it from your heart. How do you cast it out?. . . . If the divine reading is in your hands and the precepts of God before your eyes, then you will be ready to cast off and repel those thoughts which do not belong.[157]

The Scripture acts as a catalyst to the mind, which, in a way that Origen does not specify in this exposition, prepares it to rid the mind of evil, unworthy thoughts. Let us suggest, on the basis of previous passages on the Logos's activity, that it is the Logos in Scripture that gets us ready to cast off the lot that is alien and unworthy. For it is the *logos* in us that helps to control and drive out the evil impulses and images that arise from sense-perception. Origen view of the Logos's purgative powers is clear in his discussion of Jer. 2:22. He writes:

> But it pays to note that the Logos has every power. And just as he has the power of every scripture, so the Logos has the power of every ointment, and he is the power of every thing which purifies and cleanses.[158]

With Scripture before his eyes and the purifying power of the *logos* within him, man drives away evil thoughts, and replaces them with the lot of the Lord. But what precisely is the "lot" of the Lord?

If truly there rises up in your heart thoughts of mercy, justice, piety and peace of God, these are the "lot of the Lord." These are offered on the altar and are accepted by the high priest. In these things, you are reconciled to God.[159]

Origen is more specific about one of the reasons for Scripture's efficacy in conversion in his exposition of a difficult passage in Joshua. Here he offers an extraordinary view of Scripture and his faith in it and explores the magical, mystical qualities of the sacred word. He encourages his hearers not to be disheartened by what appear to be bewildering scriptural texts. The reading of the Scripture enlightens us, he says, even if we do not completely understand the passage, because it contains certain powers—holy charms—that are akin to faculties within us. In effect, not only the Logos-*logos* relation explains the power of Scripture in conversion. Scripture, in fact, has a kind of magical force. Powers within us are enchanted by the words and names that our reading produces, and, because of their kinship to faculties within us, give to us a reforming capacity that can transform our lives.[160] In brief, the mere reading of Scripture, even without endless study and meditation, can be useful to our struggles to better ourselves. "Our inner nature is charmed; its better elements are nourished, the worse weakened and brought to nought."[161]

In sum, the main struggle involves Scripture's role of redirecting the mind's activity from objects that are grasped only by the senses and from images that result from sense-perception, to intelligible objects and conceptions, such as the "lot" of the Lord (justice, peace, mercy, goodness, and truth). The reading and meditating upon Scripture facilitates this process because the power of Scripture has a kinship with faculties in man, including *logos*. This relationship between the powers of Scripture and the faculties in man not only draws man to Scripture, but it drives away evil forces and nourishes the good in man. For Origen, Scripture, in a variety of ways and regardless of the prior condition of the soul, can transform anyone who is willing to move away from a life fettered by the power of the senses.

What Role Does the Church Have in This Struggle?[162]

Another instrument of the Logos, within which the reading and meditation of Scripture occur, and with which Scripture has an intimate relationship, is the Church.[163]

For Origen the Church is a community with power deriving from pre-existent roots. In his commentary on the Song of Songs, Origen, influenced by a bold statement in Ephesians, clarifies the origin of the Church:

For you must please not think that she is called the bride or the church only from the time when the Savior came in flesh: but she is so called from the beginning of the human race and the very foundation of the world...even before the foundation of the world. (Cf. Eph. 1:4, 5)[164]

The reference in this text to an existence before the foundation of the world does not necessarily imply that the Church has a kind of heavenly existence of which the earthly is an image. Such a perspective could not adequately account for the fall of intellects and the need to strive for virtue. Rather, as a community of "intellects," the Church existed and was known by God before the foundation of the earth. As a consequence of her fall, after the foundation of the world, the Church continues the bride-bridegroom relationship, even though it is no longer in its pure pre-existent state.[165]

Like the individual, the Church also undergoes a change. But the relationship between the Church and the individual's spiritual journey is a reciprocal one in which the action of the one invigorates and purifies the other.[166] This relationship will be clarified below.

Although potentially all, even unbelievers, are members of the Church,[167] the present community of the Church is the community of believers. When one enters the realm of faith and good conduct, one enters the Church. Thus, the Church is often considered by Origen distributively; that is, each believer actually is the Church.

> But the soul, which is said to be "in the church," is understood not as being situated within the buildings which the walls enclose, but rather as being placed within the bulwarks of faith and the edifice of wisdom, and covered over with the lofty gables of charity. What makes a soul to be in the house of the church is, therefore, good conduct and belief in right doctrines.[168]

The potency of the Church for each member arises, in part, from the close relation of the Church with the Logos. In an argument in which Origen is attempting to illustrate how the soul of Jesus could be united without separation with the first born of all creation, Origen presents an ecclesiastical image of the union of the Church and the Logos.

> We say that the holy scriptures declare the body of Christ, the soul of which is the Son of God, is the whole church of God, and that the limbs of this body, which is to be regarded as a whole, are those who believe, whoever they may be. For a soul gives life to a body and moves it, since it has not the power of self-movement like a living being; so also the Logos, which moves and acts upon the whole body for needful purposes, moves the church and each limb of the members of the church who do nothing apart from the Logos.[169]

Another intimate clarification of the relation between Christ and the Church is found in Origen's discussion of Matt. 19:5, ". . . and the two shall become one," and Eph. 5:31–32.

> And he at the beginning created him "who is in the form of God" after the image, made him male, and the church female, granting to both oneness after the image. And, for the sake of the church, the Lord—the husband—left the Father whom he saw when he was "in the form of God" (Phil. 2:6), left also his mother, as he was the very son

of the Jerusalem which is above, and was joined to his wife who had fallen down here, and these two here "became flesh." For because of her, he himself also became flesh, when "the Logos became flesh and dwelt among us" (John 1:14), and they are no more two, but now they are one flesh . . . for the body of Christ is not something apart different from the church, which is his body, and from the members each in his part. And God has joined together these who are not two, but have become one flesh, commanding that men should not separate the church from the Lord.[170]

Hence Origen compares the intimate partnership between the Logos and the Church with the intimacy of the soul and the body. This union, as these texts show, is without separation. The one, the Church, does not move or function without the other, the Logos. The Church is enlivened and directed by the Logos. And not only did the Logos assume flesh in man, but he assumed flesh in terms of the Church. Indeed it is clear for Origen how the Church is the temple of God.[171] With respect to the believer, the one who wishes to become a follower of Jesus enters the Church both through his own good conduct and belief in right doctrines, and, in light of what we have just discovered, through the innate power and incentive of the Logos who, according to Origen, is the source of virtuous activity.[172]

The passages also specify the Logos's relationship to members. Each member of the Church does "nothing apart from the Logos." Thus, in all good conduct and other virtuous activity, the members of the Church are united with the Logos. Yet the reverse may also occur and the face of the Church may turn ugly on account of the members' lack of virtue and good aspirations.[173] That face is "daily being renewed 'according to the Image of him who created it . . .'."[174]

According to this view, it appears that the members of the Church determine, to an extent, the progress of the Church in its journey toward perfection. Origen clearly indicates that this "face" vacillates from comely to ugly. As it vacillates, so does the progress of the spiritual journey. We have noted how Origen considers the Church in terms of each individual soul. From these passages it seems reasonable to conclude that each member has a share in renewing the face of the Church, and that each member assumes responsibility for the future of the Church. This view is summarized by Origen in his commentary on Matt. 16:18, which says, "And I tell you, you are Peter, and on this rock I will build my church." (RSV)

For a peter [or "rock"] is every imitator of Christ, from which drink those who "drink of that spiritual rock which followed" (1 Cor. 10:4); and on every such peter is built the whole principle of the church and the corresponding way of life. For in each of the mature, who possess the combination of words, deeds and thoughts which effect bliss, is the church built by God.[175]

The emphasis here, as in other passages above, is the connection between the member and the Logos, and between the acts of the member and the Church in determining the growth in conversion of the Church. The role of Christ, mentioned in the text just quoted, will be considered below.

Let us note in the passages considered up till now the parallel to the way Scripture is also working. In Scripture, the soul is enlightened and turned away from evil by the Logos; in the Church, the member is enlivened by the Church's soul, the Logos, when completing virtuous acts and following sound doctrine. In addition, in light of Scripture's capacity to turn the faithful away from evil, the Church also is a sanctuary from the enemies of God.[176] Thus, in the contribution of the Church to the conversion process in this dimension, the Logos has again the catalytic role. Through the support of the Logos, the Church enables the believer to transcend the bad effects of the senses.

The Logos, however, does not create a pattern for members to follow. Such a model would be too far above man's capacities. That pattern is probably given by the soul of Christ.

> And the fact that the church is the aggregate of many souls and has received the pattern of her life from Christ may lead us to suppose that she has received that pattern not from the actual deity of the Logos of God—and this obviously is far above those actions and dispositions in respect of which men ought to be given a pattern—but rather it was the soul that he assumed and in which was the utmost perfection, that was the pattern displayed to men.[177]

The Logos influences the members of the Church, but Christ's soul is the model that members should follow.[178] Christ mediates the life and power of the Logos for the members, and brings the vision of peace to all who would enter the Church.[179] Thus, Christ, as the model for the Church, enables the Church to enlighten her members.

> For as the moon is said to get its light from the sun, so that through it also the night can be illuminated, so also the church, when the light of Christ has been received, illuminates all who dwell in the night of ignorance.[180]

In this passage, Origen is commenting on Gen. 1:4. Just as God made the light to shine on the earth and divide the night and day, so also there are two lights that shine upon us: Christ and his Church.[181] These lights—one, the Church, illuminated by the other, Christ—also divide in us the day of knowing from the "night of ignorance." Since night and ignorance are the opposites of day and the knowledge acquired in the Church, it seems likely that the night of ignorance is primarily the time of unbelief outside the Church, as well as disobedience to God.[182] In effect, this interpretation implies that the Church's purposes lie not only with believers, but also with unbelievers. Yet it is not always clear in Origen how the Church itself is to convert unbelievers. One possible approach is to connect the many texts that refer to God's plans to the Church. For example, Origen writes:

> And providence will never abandon the universe. For even if some part of it becomes bad because the rational being sins, [God] arranges to purify it, and after a time to turn the universe back to himself.[183]

One of the agents by which God purifies and turns the world back to himself is necessarily the Church. For the Church, according to Origen, is the crucial vehicle for salvation. For example, in his homily on Josh. 2:17ff., Origen writes that "... no one is saved outside the church."[184] The Church in this context is all of those who have come to believe in Christ. Those who do not, Origen has pointed out in the sentences that precede this text just quoted, are punished.[185] Thus, entrance into the Church is part of a purification process toward salvation.

An apocalyptic version of how the Church will be involved in the greater plan of God is offered by Origen in his commentary on Matt. 13:47. In this commentary, the Church is like a net that gathers in everyone, including the Gentiles, to be judged. When the net is pulled to the angel's "shore," it is decided who is righteous, and who should be purified in the fire. The Church, according to these passages, is the way to punishment or salvation for all men. Moreover, it is a destined end for all men in the world, regardless whether they believe or call upon the name now or in the future.[186]

That all men have the opportunity to turn back to God and become spiritual beings is evident again in Origen's exposition of Matt. 5:14 and John 1:29, where the word "world" needs to be clarified. Origen concludes that "world" in these verses means those who call on the name, but in "prophetic" and "theological" senses it means also unbelievers. The Church, thus, is the light of the "world" of present believers, the light of the "world" of those who will become believers in the future, and the light of the "world" in contrast to heaven.

Should anyone consider that the church is called the light of the world, meaning thereby of the rest of the race of men, including unbelievers, this may be true if the assertion is taken prophetically about the doctrine concerning the endtimes; but if it is to be taken of the present, we remind him that the light of a thing illuminates that thing, and would ask him to show how the remainder of the race is illuminated by the church's presence in the world. If those who hold the view in question cannot show this, then let them consider if our interpretation is not a sound one, that the light is the church, and the world those who call on the name.[187]

The role of the Church in helping us overcome the mystery of the senses is related directly to its intimate relation to the power of the Logos, to the pattern of Christ's soul that enlightens and directs the members, and to its function as an agent in God's plan of purification. It seems clear from those texts offered that Origen intended the Church to be involved centrally in the process of returning souls to their primitive state, which is the *apokatastasis*.[188] From one perspective, this function results logically from the Church's relationship to the Logos. Through the kinship with the Logos, the *logoi* of men can overcome and transcend the difficulties in controlling the products of the senses.

But Origen specifies the task of the Church in more detail. The Church began, he writes, as a community of minds worshipping and serving God. It will return to that state. In the meantime, on its road to maturity, enlivened by its soul, the Logos, in moving away from the detrimental effects of the senses and passion, enlightened by Christ and the perfect example of his soul, the Church enlightens its members and eventually encompasses all—believers and those who are presently unbelievers. In sum, the Church, like Scripture, is empowered by the Logos. And the Logos is that power, as we have seen, which can help men to change. Thus, in Origen's thought on how men change and become more spiritual, both Scripture and the Church are pivotal in the process of overcoming the difficulties involved with the senses and purifying the soul of man.

Are There Spiritual Beings That Help Man?[189]

Not only Scripture and the Church, but also both good and evil angels influence the soul.[190] The role of the devil and his forces, the demons, was outlined in a section above. Origen indicates that the demons are disciples and imitators of the devil, and carry out his commands to oppose all desires toward good by enticing the soul (which has already taken a step toward evil) toward evil thoughts and acts. And, as we noted in that section, Origen believes that God uses the devil and demons as threats to jolt men from a life filled with gratification of the senses, and from the torpor of irrational desires fomented by the devil's army:

> And he has not driven the devil away from sovereignty over this world because there is still need of his service for the further training of those who are to be crowned, for the battles to be joined and the victories to be won by the blessed.[191]

In this passage, Origen indicates his belief that God makes profitable use of the "service" of the devil in order to condition and turn men to the blessed state. Thus, even the evil powers are not beyond God's providence in his means to purify and turn the soul to good.

The good angels, however, have as their high-priest the Logos. Indeed they are viewed by Origen as one order of beings with a "rational nature" assigned by God. They are still men, but of a different order with different tasks.[192] They have, first of all, a cosmic responsibility over the heavenly bodies and other life forms.[193] Yet, more important to our subject, they are assigned for the sowing of good seeds in people's souls, as guardians over us, nursing and lifting people up when necessary. They mourn or rejoice depending on whether we sin or not.[194] Just as the evil powers try to lure man to evil thoughts, so the good angels come into one's life and suggest good thoughts and drive away bad thoughts.

> According to the promise of the Logos of God who is "the Lord of Hosts," therefore, command is given to the "holy angels," who are "sent to minister for them who receive the inheritance of salvation," to catch in every soul such thoughts as those that have been put into her by the demons; so that when these have been driven away, the flowers of virtue may be brought forth. Their catching of the bad thoughts consists in their suggesting to the mind that those thoughts come not from God, but from the evil one, and in imparting to the soul the power to discern the spirits; so that she may understand which thought is according to God, and which thought is from the devil.[195]

Origen is clarifying at least two points in this passage. First, angels fight evil thoughts by informing the soul of the origin of its thoughts. For example, if a soul should have evil thoughts about images or desires arising from the senses, an angel may suggest to her that this judgment is influenced by demons. Second, the angels give to the soul the actual power to distinguish the origin of thoughts. When either of these acts or events occur will vary, depending on whether the angel prepares the soul beforehand, or comes after.[196]

The power to distinguish, however, does not mean that the soul is forced to think good or evil thoughts. The judgment on whether to think good or evil thoughts is dependent, as we have discussed in other contexts,[197] on the free will. The good or evil powers excite or agitate the heart, Origen tells us, but it is the free will that determines the extent of the influences.

> It is possible for us, when an evil power has begun to urge us on to a deed of evil, to cast away the wicked suggestions and to resist the low enticements and to do absolutely nothing worthy of blame; and it is possible on the other hand when a divine power has urged us on to better things not to follow its guidance, since our faculty of free will is preserved to us in either case.[198]

Thus, the effect of an angel's suggestion depends on the personal choice of the soul. At the heart of such decisions is the rational faculty, as discussed previously. Depending on the individual's choice through the use of reason, either the evil powers will rush in at the sign of a tendency toward evil and influence the soul accordingly, or the efforts of good angels to suggest good thoughts and acts, as well as drive away evil ones, will triumph.

If a soul should do something unworthy while under the guardianship of an angel, another angel, specializing in judgments and punishments, may chastise the soul. This order of angels, for example, is implied in Origen's exposition of Matt. 18:23–25, the parable of the unforgiving servant. Origen involves angels in several roles in this text, one of which is as ministers who punish the servant.[199] Though Origen may not have considered these ministers "good" angels,[200] the angels of chastisement certainly serve a function in the often rocky road of spiritual growth.

Less frequently, Origen discusses a "divorce" between an angel and the soul to which the angel is assigned on account of some unworthy act.[201] In his discussion of the "bill of divorcement" mentioned in Matt. 19:7–8, Origen considers whether the wife/husband covenant can be applied figuratively to the relationship of the soul and its guardian angel.

> . . . each [angel] lawfully dwells along with the soul which is worthy of the guardianship of a divine angel, but sometimes after long sojourning and intercourse, a cause may arise in the soul why she does not find favour in the eyes of the angel who is her lord and ruler, because that in it there is found an unseemly thing; and bonds may be written out, as such are written, and a bill of divorcement be written and put into the hands of her who is cast out, so that she may no longer be familiar with her former guardian, when she is cast out from his dwelling. (Cf. Deut. 24:1–2)[202]

Origen is even more explicit in a fragment on Jer. 28:8–10. There Origen considers those who are "incurable" by the angel-physicians.

> But it is angel-physicians who are under the great physician God who want to heal those who are persuaded. And if not, they will say, condemning her as incurable and as one who has been persuaded to the ways of despair, "Let us forsake her, let each of us depart from his own land" and his own place and his own concerns, "for her sentence has reached to heaven."[203]

In sum, because of their intimate relationship with the soul, good angels (and other angels also) are an important factor in how we overcome the difficulties presented by the senses. Angels not only fight evil powers along with the soul itself, but they help provide the power to discern evil through good suggestions.[204]

Summary

The mystery that we identified at the beginning of this chapter concerned the struggles of the soul to deal with the powerful distractions and needs of the senses. How, after all, could a person avoid, neglect or ignore what seems to be so much a part of his or her being, the tools and life of the body? It is a mystery of the first order, and we have tried to give Origen's answer in this chapter.

Origen's answer evolves from his understanding of the innate nature of man and the predicament in which man fell when he turned away from God in the beginning. In that beginning, man had a certain God-given power that Origen called *logos*. He called it *logos* because it was a reflection of the divine Logos discussed at the beginning of the Gospel of John. But man also acquired a gross, fleshly body from the Fall. That body was not the body he had in the beginning; it was a perversion of the original thing, which was ethereal. With such a gross body arose all of the problems for the *logos*. It had to manage what was now unnatural, and it was not an easy task. Fortunately, God gave man other aids. He gave the Scripture, the Church and good angels, and, preeminently, he gave the Redeemer, Jesus Christ. These external aids, along with the potential of *logos*, are the way for man to manage the problems associated with the senses and the gross body.

So the soul's struggle to live within and yet try to transcend the sensuous reality constitutes the starting-point of understanding this first mystery, and the first dimension that man must overcome to become a Christian, to progress spiritually. Origen characterizes this dimension as a gradual release from a condition that stresses the importance of appearances and a reliance on the pleasures and knowledge received from senses. This first step is a process of turning from an inordinate love for those things which belong to the world of becoming.

At the base of this dimension, Origen has drawn our attention to the plague of irrational desires and images resulting from improper judgment on the process of sense-perception. Thus, in Chapter 3 we have witnessed a process of replacement and destruction of harmful elements in the soul, arising from dealing with the body, and of cultivation of good thoughts to replace them. The result is achieved through the cooperation of man's *logos* (rational faculty), created in the image of God which is the Logos, with the instruments of the Logos: Scripture, the Church, good angels and the Holy Spirit (to be considered in Chapter 5).

Yet despite the importance of purification of the soul from a disordered judgment of the products of sense-perception, this dimension is only one dimension of the spiritual process. It is only one of the mysterious layers. The next mystery involves how we behave, how the external activity of our minds emerges and how it should be molded. That dimension has an equal importance in how one becomes a Christian.

IV
Developing Good Conduct: How Does One Come to Act as a Christian?

Background

Chapter 3 concerned the body and managing the senses. We saw that the thoughts of the person are constantly being affected by impulses and matters whose ultimate source is the senses and the body, and the way one chooses from the effects of the senses determines the quality of his mind. The effort to control the senses and properly exercise free will is strenuous in itself for one becoming a Christian, and he is fortunate to have the assistance of the Logos. But there is another side, equally important: behaving as a Christian, doing what one knows or thinks to be good and true. And this dimension is not, according to Origen, separate but integral to the other. People are faced continually with the externalization of their beliefs and thoughts and with the effect of their or others' acts on their mind. So just as they are faced with the onslaught of passion and the distractions of the senses, they are, of course, living and responding to various moral choices in behavior.

John 3:21 says, "He who does what is true comes to the light, that it may be clearly seen that his deeds have been wrought in God." Origen understood that doing what is true is an exhausting and life-consuming task, and everywhere he looked he found hypocrisy and pretense. For action, even so-called good action, is not always doing what is true. To become a Christian one must behave as a follower of Jesus. But what kind of action does this commitment imply? What is doing what is true? How does one translate his thoughts into actions? How does one acquire the strength to do good in an evil context? What of the problem of hypocrisy? Does doing good always mean a person is good? How does one learn to behave as a Christian? These are important questions and are still with us today. We are going to puruse all of them through Origen's texts in the following three sections. The first two sections are preparation for the third, which is the heart of this chapter.

First, in the following section, we are concerned with the problem of how thought and action work together for the true Christian. We consider this problem not only theologically, but also in terms of the non-Christian attitudes. We need to remember constantly that Origen was not living in a Christian world or society.

The societal, political, and religious context was non-Christian, and he had to explore how to become a Christian by contrasting it to non-Christian attitudes about behavior. Then, in the second section, we briefly state how Origen handled a few complex problems of moral practice and achieving virtue, including the relation of virtue and salvation. Then in the third section we explore in depth the critical idea of example/imitation in Origen. We conclude as always with a summary.

How Are Thinking and Doing Related for the Christian?

1.

To respond to this question, Origen uses an important group of terms that arise again and again as signals of the issue. These words are *praxis* (conduct or actions), *poiein* (to do), *ergon* (deed or work), *arete* (virtue), *theoria* (contemplation), *noema* (thought), and *logos* (reason). All of these terms, as we shall see, are involved in Origen's explanation of the true Christian action. All of them, when good, are signs of how someone becomes morally committed to God and lives a spiritual life. For example, note the commitment involved in Origen's use of "work" (*ergon*) in his commentary on Jer. 3:22, "Behold we will be yours because you are the Lord our God." He writes:

> But after we were called and have said, "Behold we will be yours," let us show by our works that when we have promised to become his, we have devoted them to none other than him.[1]

Let us clarify briefly what some of these terms meant to Origen: *arete* (virtue), that which shapes our nature to do good as opposed to the desire to do evil,[2] generates good *praxeis*, or the habits of doing good acts, while *erga* are the actual deeds resulting from good habits. Said another way, these deeds are the concrete gifts offered by a giver who has acquired the practice of doing good due to a soul filled with virtue. *Poiein* is a word which describes the whole process of works and practices.[3] Origen contrasts what we accomplish by *ergon* and by *diathesis* (disposition) in his commentary on the meaning of clouds in Ps. 134:7, indicating he understands that there are two different dimensions of the process, one from within the person, and one, at another pole, in external, concrete deeds. In general, then, we can assume that for Origen thoughts and works are two different but cooperative sides of our moral activities, one the product of our inner nature/mind, the other the product of our moral will.[4]

Usually "acts" and "works" are linked together, as, for example, in Origen's discussion of Jer. 3:24, where "thoughts" are the sons and "acts" and "works" are the daughters of the soul.[5] Origen also connects the two concepts when he says:

Hence when we considered the "veil" (2 Cor. 3:16; Jer. 3:25) which is set over [us] by works of shame, by acts of dishonour, let us remove the veil. It is in our power to remove the veil, there is no one else. For when Moses turned to the Lord, he removed the veil. (Cf. Ex. 34:34)[6]

Note here too how we must turn and remove the veil "over the heart" (2 Cor. 3:15) through works and acts.[7] This is one of many texts in which managing the senses—the matter of the veil—is connected to "works."

Also three of the terms (virtue, doing, work) are used together in Origen's discussion of earthly and heavenly works, as noted in 1 Cor. 15:49 and Matt. 6:19-20. He says:

So also what is done according to virtue leads, for one who "stores up treasure in heaven," who bears the "image of the heavenly," to places in heaven akin to his works.[8]

This text indicates that practices are worthwhile if they are generated from virtue. This same point is made in a different way when Origen writes in an extant fragment that one can only practice what one knows. Hence to do righteousness (a virtue), one must know righteousness.[9]

We need also to consider virtue (arete) in another way. For the Logos is all of virtue.[10] True virtue then is absolute for Origen. There are no grades of growth. However, there is a path toward that virtue, and this is popularly called virtue. In other words, there is no place for vice; there is only more and more virtue.[11]

2.

Now that we have introduced some of the main concepts, though we will consider *theoria* in more detail below, let us consider the close relationship of conduct and thought in the life of anyone who seeks to know and be near God. We mentioned that especially in texts concerned with the judgment we find Origen stressing the importance of conduct. Let us note a couple of these texts.

For example, he states in his discussion of Luke 3:16 that in the end, we must be pure and have prepared "works." Similarly, in his views on Ps. 74:9, he speaks about how good "actions" and "works" will be weighed and punishment allotted accordingly in the judgment. In another context, he says that God will not know us unless we do worthy acts. He states that he who does glory to God does it through acts (*praxeis*).[12] These texts and others indicate that for Origen not only what we think and how we form moral judgments are important. It is not only a question of how the senses are managed. On the one hand, reason's reorientation is foundational, but, on the other hand, another dimension, particularly noticeable in *Against Celsus*, is concerned with the struggle for moral excellence (*arete*) and good conduct or practice (*praxis*).[13] Both contribute to spiritual growth. Origen summarizes this point in his discussion of the spiritual food mentioned in John 4:32, "I have food to eat which you do not know." Origen writes:

That which is greater than the body is nourished by incorporeal thoughts, words and right actions.[14]

The two modes of spiritual growth—what concerns the senses and what concerns conduct—are continually discussed together and related by Origen. In the struggle to control the senses and passion, man's rational judgment, his thoughts, as we have seen in Chapter 3, are always being encouraged by evil powers. The same evil influence also affects man's potential for good actions. The degree of influence will determine the character not only of one's thoughts, but also of his actions. Like a vase, Origen writes in his homily on Jer. 18:1–2, we receive shape, and we receive shape either according to evil or according to virtue.[15] In his discussion of Jer. 17:11, in which the Scripture says that the partridge made his "riches without judgment," Origen comments that the devil— the partridge—made his "riches" "by acting without exercising judgment."[16] Hence here too he connects the two modes. Moreover, in the passage quoted below on the vacillating effect of evil on the reason and behavior of man,[17] Origen indicates that, depending on the influence of evil, man's rational faculty and his actions will be more or less good. In this discussion, Origen separates the roles of *logos* and *praxis*, but he considers them dimensions of man's progress. The emphasis here on the relation of evil and the capacity of reason is an indication of the mode concerning *aisthesis*, which is the restraint of the body and the control of the irrational. For whether the influence of sense-perception becomes evil is a matter of how one uses the rational faculty in the interpretation of effects from sense-perception.

Although the nature of some particular individual man is one and the same, things are not always the same where his mind, his reason, and actions are concerned. At one time he may not even have the capacity for reason, while at another time his reason is vitiated by evil, and this varies in its extent either more or less; and sometimes he may have been converted to live virtuously and is making more or less progress, and at times reaches perfection and comes to virtue itself by more or less contemplation.[18]

Though man's nature remains the same, the two dimensions concerned with (1) the rational faculty and (2) the quest for virtue and conduct waver more or less depending on the degree evil has influenced the soul. That these elements are dimensions of one's progress is clear from Origen's belief, noted in Chapter 3, that virtue, and the conduct which results from virtue, is intimately linked with reason. An affirmation of this is given in his homily on Jer. 3:24, where he blatantly states that there is an intimate harmony in each person between the "thoughts" and the "works" and the "practices," since all are "children of the soul."[19] Thus, Origen presents in the above text two dimensions of the spiritual journey of becoming a Christian. The reorientation of the rational faculty in its struggle with the potential evil arising from misjudgment of the effects of sense-perception is the mode concerning the senses; the struggle to live virtuously is the mode of conduct.[20]

3.

However, another, third, dimension is also visible in this text. The last sentence of the passage states that one comes to virtue by *theoria* (contemplation), which produces *arete* (virtue). Since *theoria* is also an agent in the relationship between the mode of conduct and the third mode, discussed in Chapter 5, it is necessary to examine briefly how Origen understood its activity. In the above passage, contemplation appears to be a bridge between *logos* and *praxis*. What comes first? Contemplation in this context seems to precede virtue. This priority is also the impression given in Origen's exposition of John 1:26, "Make straight the way of the Lord." Origen comments on this text:

> Now the way of the Lord is made straight in two fashions: First, in the way of contemplation, clarified with the truth without any mixture of falsehood; and then in the way of conduct, after the sound contemplation of what ought to be done, when action is produced which harmonizes with a sound theory of conduct.[21]

However, another perspective of the relation of contemplation and virtue seems to be present in Origen's discussion of the meaning of "beginning" in John 1:1. He writes:

> For if [we speak of] a beginning in the case of a transition, and of a way and its length, and [if we are told that] the beginning of a good way is to do justice, then it concerns us to know in what manner every good way has for its beginning to do justice, and how after such beginning [it arrives at] contemplation, and in what manner [it arrives at] contemplation.[22]

Here the practice of doing justice appears to come before contemplation. The apparent paradox might be explained in two ways: First, it is important, it would seem, to recognize how, in each case, Origen is viewing man's path to God. Viewed from the activitity of conduct, contemplation nurtures, as the one text clarifies, the inner quality of moral excellence. Moral excellence, in turn, as we shall see, results in conduct. However, viewed from the activity of contemplation, conduct, as seen in the text above, enlivened by virtue, drives the soul to higher knowledge. This latter perspective more concerns the third mode of change for the Christian to be discussed in Chapter 5. The former view is more applicable to this mode. Second, as several scholars have noted,[23] contemplation and conduct are inseparable in Origen's thought. This interdependence of *praxis* and *theoria* is noted, for example, in Origen's commentary on Luke 10:38–42, which concerns the roles of Mary and Martha. Origen interprets this passage in the following way:

> It is reasonable to infer that Martha is appointed for conduct and Mary for contemplation. For the mystery of love in conduct strips itself away unless one has been chosen, in addition to contemplation, for teaching and for persuasion by conduct. For there is neither conduct nor contemplation without the other.[24]

Contemplation is central to both tasks of Martha and Mary, but one is selected to contemplate Jesus' teaching, and another is selected to serve by conduct. Both are persuaded, however, by the conduct of the other. Contemplation emerges, then, in a way of acting as well as the act of contemplating the Lord and the Lord's teaching.

These passages clarify that contemplation is a converting catalyst for reason (*logos*) in its effort to develop virtue (*arete*), and in the growth to the spiritual activity of the third dimension of spiritual growth, to be discussed in the next chapter. Contemplation, as one of the texts in this section has indicated,[25] must be seen as a crucial factor in one's moral development. Clearly a rational faculty that has not achieved some degree of control over the difficulties that can arise from sense-perception will not make progress in conduct. For such a faculty cannot reach the contemplation by which one comes to virtue. Thus, movement away from *aisthesis* opens up the way for contemplation. And the relation between the first dimension—what concerns the senses—and the dimension of conduct arises because of the intimate connection between man's rational powers and the moral excellence attached to contemplation. Moral excellence, in turn, appears in conduct. Consequently, all four integrals—reason (*logos*), contemplation (*theoria*), virtue or moral excellence (*arete*), and action or conduct (*praxis*)— determine the degree of progress with respect to these modes.

We may further refine what these terms imply with the following structure. Virtue and conduct/deeds, in light of the texts quoted above, may be considered the contemplative and active functions of the virtuous life. Virtue is the inner moral perfecting quality produced by contemplation. Conduct/deeds is the concrete realization of this inner quality in action. Both appear, as well as the mode away from distractions and difficulties with the body, in Origen's exposition of Exod. 1:16, where the Pharaoh says:

> When you serve as midwife to the Hebrew women, and see them upon the birthstool, if it is a son, you shall kill him; but if it is a daughter, she shall live.

The wish of the Pharaoh, whom Origen sees as a figure for the devil, to kill the males and allow the females to live, is itself a figure, according to Origen, for the attacks on the rational faculty and the uncontrolled licence of the flesh.[26] Then Origen interprets the males as those who are converted to God:

> If indeed you see that rare one of a thousand who is converted to the Lord, directs his eyes above, seeks those things which endure and are eternal, contemplates not what is seen, but what is unseen (cf. 2 Cor. 4:18), hates voluptuousness, loves self-control, flees riotous living and is cultivating virtues, the Pharaoh wants to kill him as a male, as a man; he persecutes him and hunts after him and fights against him with a thousand devices.[27]

All of the elements—movement away from passion and distraction, contemplation, virtue, and conduct—are represented in this description of the continuing process of spiritual growth. Origen details not only the kind of perception a man in the process of becoming a Christian possesses and that his object is the invisible and the lasting, but also his behavior, both interior (e.g., contemplation, which produces virtue and self-control) and exterior (the practice of virtue in conduct). At the same time, Origen points out that the prince of this world is constantly seeking and trying to irritate the "male" by countless wiles.

In sum, there occurs in one who seeks Christ several kinds of developments, which we can describe as the mode away from an inordinate desire for things of the senses, and the mode concerned with conduct.

4.

There is another way to explain the complex problem of how inner discipline and conduct relate, namely, through an examination of pretense, hypocrisy and similar conditions. The interplay between how someone controls his senses and the mode of conduct is reflected also in Origen's comparison of the goals and practices of philosophies and non-Christian religions with Christianity in his apologetic work *Against Celsus*. Faced with the diverse assemblage of philosophies and religions that Celsus documented, writing ca. 176–180 A.D.,[28] in order to diminish the originality of Christianity and its effectiveness in converting men, Origen responded with his own account of the different goals and teachings of the Christian and non-Christian.

Origen perceives non-Christians to be part of two groups: either they are persons who appear to have moral excellence but who lack the support of moral practice, or they are persons whose acts may appear to have elements of moral practice, but whose inner growth is in its beginning stages, and thus inadequate to activate the contemplative power of *logos* that can acheive moral excellence. These two groups are, of course, related. For inner growth through *logos* and the mode of conduct as modes of spiritual growth cannot be separated. But in order to clarify how they relate, let us consider the two groups separately.

The second group is considered by Origen in countering Celsus's attack on the intelligence and education of Christians. Origen points out that "true" education leads to virtue, and "true" intelligence is not mere appearance of knowledge. Since Christian teaching and intelligence lead to virtue, they may be considered the best education and true intelligence.

> To have been truly educated is certainly not a bad thing. For education is the way to virtue. But not even the wise men of the Greeks would say that those who hold mistaken doctrines may be reckoned among the educated. . . . But what doctrines shall we call the best other than those which are true and exhort men to virtue? Furthermore, it is an excellent thing to be intelligent, but not merely to appear so, as Celsus says.[29]

The important emphasis here is that the minds of those who appear intelligent with false teachings are not trained or directed properly to achieve moral excellence. Their teaching is untrue and their efforts to be intelligent are misdirected. Without virtue, as we have just indicated, good conduct is not possible. But without the proper education, men are exhorted to virtue and only appear intelligent in their actions. Thus, Origen links the way men appear with the kind of teachings their minds have received and the way their minds have been directed, and he draws a distinction between being intelligent and appearing intelligent. Christians hold a doctrine, he implies, that exhorts men to virtue. Thus, it is a true doctrine, which clearly transforms the man. For they practice what they truly know. If they practice true righteousness, they have known righteousness.[30]

Origen goes on to say that Christians show concern for the inner progress of men when prospective converts approach them. Philosophers will talk with any one who will listen,

> But as far as they can, Christians previously examine the souls of those who want to hear them, and test them individually beforehand; when before entering the community the hearers seem to have devoted themselves sufficiently to the desire to live a good life, then they introduce them.[31]

The prospective converts, Origen continues, are separated into two groups: one that receives elementary instruction because they do not indicate that they are purified, and another that desires what all Christians desire.[32] It is the desire to lead a good life and the sign of purification that are crucial factors used by Christians. The Christian standard for conversion is not a mere appearance of intelligence or an eagerness to listen, but some sign of an inner moral decision. Thus, the care that the Christians take in examining prospective converts, the tests they administer to separate those who simply appear intelligent or good and those who have a true desire to live a good life, the concern with purification, an element central to movement away from distraction with the body, and the general emphasis on an inner redirection before virtue is possible, are examples of Origen's view of how exterior conduct is empty, regardless of its degree of intelligence, if it is not found in an inner desire for virtue.

With respect to the first group mentioned above, they appear to have acquired the wisdom of moral excellence, but their conduct is unworthy.[33] Plato is an example of this group for Origen. Plato differs from some other philosophers because his teaching was often true and good, especially about the soul, but his conduct was still akin to those who follow polytheism:

> And those who taught such profound philosophy about the soul and the future course of the soul that has lived a good life, abandon the great [truths] that God has revealed to them to attend to mean and trivial things, and give a cock to Asclepius.[34]

The Christian does not only need good and wise thoughts. Thinking needs to be supported in virtue and give rise to sound conduct. The Christian, for example, will endure great hardships to practice his religion. Origen quickly points to this fact when Celsus compares Christians to worms.

> Perhaps such earnest devotion, which is subdued neither by pain nor by imminent death nor by plausible arguments, does not prevent those who have become so devoted from being compared to worms. . . . But do we think those people are the brothers of worms . . . who master the most violent desire for sexual pleasure, which has made the minds of many soft and pliable as wax. . .?[35]

Thus, Christians have developed an inner strength and self-control that appears in their conduct. Their devotion demands that they act in a way that is congruent with their teachings and with virtue, unlike the others, who are like thieves and steal something they have not earned.[36]

Origen objects, of course, to the polytheism of pagan religion, but he is also disturbed by the insincerity and pretense by which such customs are continued. Even though men such as Plato are aware of the foolishness of such customs, they continue to observe them and are therefore insincere and impious.[37] Something is lacking in the lives of such men. In contrast to Plato, whose knowledge indicated a great wisdom but whose religious practices and polytheism were unworthy of that knowledge, the Christian's knowledge, based on true doctrine and thinking, is, in some way, harmonious with his conduct. An added element, a catalyst, enables him to be converted, and to convert others. That ingredient is divine aid.

5.

The inadequacy of non-Christian conduct, compared with Christian conduct, arises not only from doctrine or from the way advocates of it have directed their rational faculties. Their words are empty because they are not in harmony with the supreme Logos, whose power is essential for spiritual growth to occur. In a passage in which Origen is indicating how the mean style of the Scriptures facilitates Christian change, he emphasizes the need for grace. While the simplicity of the style of Scripture attracts hearers and readers, and thus facilitates conversion, this quality of simplicity alone is insufficient to convert. Similarly, the mere words of philosophers are ineffectual. The true catalyst of conversion, Origen indicates, is the power given to the words and the speaker by God, on the one hand, and, in terms of the hearers themselves, on the other hand, the degree of merit "as the Logos willed."[38] This divine role in conversion separates the efficacy of Christian conversion from conversion attempts of other teachings.

This view might seem to imply that no real change occurs without the cooperation of God. In another context, Origen is more explicit concerning the divine role. In a context where he is pointing out that the success of Christianity through the disciples and especially Jesus himself in turning men's hearts to good clearly indicates divine providence, he writes that "no benefit comes to mankind without God."[39]

The matter discussed here, we should note, refers not only to Jesus's power, but also to the power of what he taught. For the power with which Jesus spoke continues to convert through the power of God in his teaching.[40] This divine influence, Origen specifies, does not arise from any personal capacity, regardless how extraordinary, of man. The power of Jesus and his followers is in accord with a divine providence and influence. Origen clarifies these things in his reply to Celsus's claim that the philosopher Epictetus, who could endure the pain of a broken leg calmly, would have been a more suitable person to follow than Jesus.

> But it is certainly not true that what [Epictetus] said while his leg was being broken is comparable to Jesus's miraculous words and works which Celsus does not believe. For when spoken with divine power to this day they convert not only some of the simple people but also many of the more intelligent.[41]

It is the effects of Jesus' words and works that imply a divine power of changing someone. Hence his model for followers is better than that of pagan thinkers who did and do not have power to convert either themselves or others because their words did not possess the power that God alone grants. In the passage above concerned with divine Scripture,[42] Origen involves both the speaker and his works in the power to convert. Both the man and the teaching are instruments of God's aid. It is at this point—the point of interrelationship of managing the senses and the mode of conduct—that non-Christian conversion attempts are ineffectual. For the interlocking of all of the integrals (virtue, conduct, contemplation, reason) can now be seen to depend fundamentally on the catalyst of divine aid.

Section Summary

In sum, we have clarified three critical matters in this section for the mode of conduct in how Origen views the behavioral side of becoming a Christian. First, one cannot become a Christian if the inner life, namely, virtue, contemplation, and reason, is not intimately tied to the actions and works of the outer life and aided by divine power. Insincerity, lack of discipline, and false doctrine, regardless how good one's thoughts and actions may *appear*, are obstacles. Non-Christian philosophers strive toward divine power, but because of their conception of divinity, they and their words can affect neither themselves nor others. The Christian's actions, however, have moral force and the power to transform himself and take important steps on the spiritual journey, because his actions are in harmony with the Logos's teaching in Scripture, and have been the recipients of divine help.

Second, the rational faculty in some wise men is active in resisting thoughts and acts based solely in appearances and the sensible world. The habit of resistance gives to their souls a kind of strength. Nevertheless, they maintain a form of polytheism and pagan customs that are pleasing only to evil powers. Consequently, their struggles for moral excellence are not successful, and they bar themselves from achieving the contemplation that produces moral excellence. Hence, their conduct, which must be dependent on moral excellence, is somehow flawed.

Third, just discussed above, divine aid is a catalyst in all spiritual change. Without God, nothing or no one is changed; no action occurs. To Origen, God is the prime converter.

Therefore, there is in Origen's view of growth no separation of the functioning of the first and second modes. From the power of the *logos* discussed in the movement away from *aisthesis* to the fruits of moral excellence in conduct, the process of spiritual growth is a single series of interrelating dimensions transforming people in a number of ways.

What of Those Who Vacillate in Their Behavior?

1.

The quotation from *Against Celsus* above clearly states one of the most important insights of Origen's view on becoming a Christian: the progress of the spiritual life depends "more or less" on the degree of evil that has obstructed the rational faculty and the capacity for virtue.[43] In our discussion of the concerns about the body, it was shown that the proper use of the rational faculty in recognizing and turning aside from evil is an important aspect of that dimension. The variations in the capacity for virtue and the ensuing difficulties in attaining moral excellence, resulting in good conduct, is the process under consideration in this chapter. The concern for both dimensions lies in the vacillating nature of change and progress. To this concern this section is devoted.

To present the complexity, we will be discussing in detail two texts from the *Commentary on Matthew* and *Against Celsus*, both works written late in Origen's life. We will follow along with Origen in his probing into the meaning of a passage from Scripture, and then we will again listen to him defend the Christian way against Celsus's attacks. Many more examples could be given, but each would be essentially a development or repetition of the concepts offered in this and the previous section.

In both of the modes, the constant variations of more or less stated by Origen are signs of a struggle that he elaborates in detail in his commentary on Matt. 14:22–27, the text where the disciples are in a boat, and Christ walks on the water to calm the sea. Origen first asks what is the boat which Jesus asked the disciples to enter:

> ...[is it] perhaps the conflict of temptations and difficulties into which any person is constrained by the Logos, and goes unwillingly, as it were, when the Saviour wishes to train by exercise the disciples in this boat which is distressed by the waves and the contrary wind?[44]

The journey in the boat across unpredictable waters is seen by Origen as an opportunity to endure the conflicts in order to train man through action. One has to prove his strength of faith through action as a prelude to divine aid from the Logos. Origen continues:

> The Saviour then compels the disciples to enter into the boat of temptations and go before him to the other side and through victory over them to go beyond critical difficulties; but when they had come into the midst of the sea, and of the waves in the temptations, and of the contrary winds which prevented them from going away to the other side, they, struggling, were not able without Jesus to overcome the waves and the contrary wind and reach the other side. Wherefore the Logos, taking compassion upon them who had done all that was in their power to reach the other side, came to them walking upon the sea, which for him had no waves or wind that was able to oppose if he so willed. . . .[45]

In both passages, the Logos compels or constrains the disciples to enter the boat. By this action of the Logos, Origen wishes to emphasize again both how one is encouraged initially to endure and maintain one's faith in contrary winds and waves, and how, when he has done all in his power, one receives divine aid. The word translated "done" in this text is from the verb *prassein*, which is the source of the term *praxis* discussed in the previous section. Success in reaching "the other side" depends upon the disciples' conduct or the way they act in response to inclement conditions. In this context, conduct is not only an affirmative good action, but also a kind of defensive practice that must come to ward off the temptations that might encourage it to falter, or worse, become an evil act.

The degree to which one's strength of conduct is tested does not exceed one's power. God does not tempt one beyond his capacity.[46] The disciples are represented as being more advanced in their progress in resisting evil than others, but the message of the text may be applied, on the one hand, to anyone who has reached this point in the journey to become a Christian, and, on the other hand, as a symbol of everyone's journey toward greater purity and virtue. This latter intention is seen particularly in the following text, where faith and virtues are continually being attacked by the evil one.

> Then when we see many difficulties besetting us, and with moderate struggle we have swum through them to some extent, let us consider that our boat is in the midst of the sea, distressed at that time by the waves which wish us to make shipwreck concerning faith or some one of the virtues; but when we see the spirit of the evil one striving against us, let us conceive that then the wind is contrary to us. When then in such suffering . . . striving nobly with all our might and watching ourselves so as not to make shipwreck concerning the faith or some one of the virtues, . . . the Son of God will come to us, that he may prepare the sea for us, walking upon it.[47]

These passages demonstrate, through the image of the boat and the stormy sea, the way in which Origen viewed the conduct of one who is "on his way to maturity but has not yet become mature."[48] The disciple Peter,[49] as Origen goes on to say, is not without faith, but a man of "little faith." For example, in his exposition of the following passage, Matt. 14:28–31, Origen points out that there was in the nature of the same man both the tendency toward better things, through his faith, and a "tendency towards that which was opposed to faith."[50] This text then shares a common concern with the text offered above from *Against Celsus*.[51] In both, Origen presents the image of one who does or can waver and is more or less unsure, but nonetheless is "on his way to maturity." Conduct vacillates from acts with the power of some faith to acts that conceal an inclination toward evil. And he who is able to meet his present capacities, even though he is still one of little faith, will be helped by the Logos.

These passages are important because they indicate that man may be constrained to endure many struggles before help arrives, and that the road to Christian maturity is a constant and vacillating process whose setbacks and trials are a part of its development. With respect to conduct, such passages indicate that development and defense of virtue in conduct has an important role in the conversion process.

In the texts quoted, Origen does not detail the kind of temptations and difficulties one must endure, except to say that the "spirit of the evil one" is behind them. Elsewhere, in *Against Celsus*, Origen does point out the extent of these trials. The Christian's struggle in practicing his religion, in battling the evil one, may even, he writes, demand great sacrifice, even death itself. For virtue and holiness, he tells Celsus,[52] are very precious matters.

> It is with good reason that we regarded it as a matter dear to God if one is crucified for virtue, and is tortured for piety, and dies for holiness. "Precious before the Lord is the death of his holy ones." (Ps. 115:6)[53]

One who wishes to be "dear to God" does not object to such sacrifice if it is done for virtue, piety, and holiness.[54] In other words, his moral existence is meaningless outside piety and moral excellence. Virtue, piety, and holiness arise in conduct. To behave as one who seeks God is to exhibit in conduct the inner qualities of virtue and holiness. This concern for the display in conduct of those qualities which are dear to God overrides any desire for life. To uphold such a concern, the Christian would willingly die.

Martyrdom thus emerges in Origen's thought as one way in which evil forces are finally and triumphantly overcome and the difficulties of good conduct in this life ended. It is the supreme test and limit that Origen often offers and concerning which he wrote an entire book, *Exhortation to Martyrdom*. The projection of Christian principles in conduct was for him a life and death struggle in a hostile environment. As we have already discussed in Chapter 2 and will discuss in Chapter 5, for Origen, in the beginning and in the end life with God transcends earthly life; hence no one should protect earthly life in order to win the prize of an evil existence.

There are, however, other means through which good conduct may be effective against evil powers and in the process of spiritual growth. The realization of what is good arises, for example, through a process described above, namely, the kinship between *logos* and the Logos. To one who is willing, the Logos enlightens and enlivens each man on the highest good. Origen clarifies this view in *Against Celsus*. Celsus had quoted Plato as saying that the notion of the highest good comes "like a light in the soul kindled by a leaping spark."[55] Origen agrees with this statement, and notes also that the origin of his sudden inspiration, which is mentioned in Scripture (Hos. 10:12; John 1:3-4, 9; Matt. 5:14), is the Logos.[56] Thus, one way to acquire inner strength of goodness is through the power of the Logos. Such surety would be reflected in one's conduct. Other means, such as the imitation of Christ, will be described in another section.

Yet this explanation of the process of Christian change, where the recognition of and commitment to the source of good through the power of reason is the result of a meeting of like with like, *logos* with the Logos, is directed more to an educated audience who would readily comprehend the meaning and perhaps the source of such statements in *Against Celsus*.[57]

When preaching to the common folk of his congregation in the homilies, Origen makes more apparent the difficulties of good conduct. On the one hand, Origen can be very direct and threatening in his counsel to his audience. For example, the tone of many of his Jeremiah homilies is challenging: If you do not turn, you will become the slave of Satan. You cannot be a friend to God and to Satan.[58] However, on the other hand, often Origen replaces the discussion of sudden enlightenment by his more usual explanation of progress, relapses, and imperfect conversion, such as we have already discussed in his commentary on Matthew. He wishes to warn his people that even with some progress, temptations will continue. The battle with evil does not end by a single drink from the rock nor from a single bite of the manna of the Logos. It occurs whenever we step onto the spiritual path. We must be constantly ready for war whenever we "draw near to the depth of spiritual teaching."[59] The path of becoming a disciple of Jesus, even for the one who has made some progress, noted in this last passage and in those quoted above, is difficult. Even if one reaches a certain level of enlightenment from the bread and water of the Logos, and approaches the spiritual dimension of the Christian life and message, he is not finished. The fight to maintain good conduct before all distractions and temptations continues.

2.

It continues, in fact, beyond this earthly life. Origen's analysis of the Christian life and spiritual growth does not stop at death. He probes into Scripture for the answers to some disturbing questions, one of which we discussed in Chapter 2 in the sections concerned with the restoration. But there are many more questions about the afterlife. What happens to those who do vacillate in moral behavior more often or more deeply than others?

The depth of goodness in one's conduct is, according to Origen, determined not simply by how one appears before the priests and church members, but also in one's private life. In the passage mentioned above, Origen does not specify the nature of those who have begun to eat the manna and drink the water. His primary concern is to show that, at a certain point in one's progress, the war of temptations will meet one. But there are many levels of moral progress. Thus, let us examine how Origen treats the complexities of judging conduct, and how persons may be grouped according to their moral achievements and vacillations. We will present this matter again by focusing in detail on one of Origen's scriptural interpretations where the matter is given extensive discussion.

In his homily on Josh. 9:3–27, Origen presents his doctrine of the different kinds of salvation, the different ranks each will possess in the heavenly world. This subject is an ideal pivot for us in our discussion of conduct and for understanding how, in Origen's view, one becomes a Christian. Its implication is that the journey back to God continues for some even in the heavenly places, and that spiritual growth, as we have discussed it, is different from salvation.[60] Moreover, this doctrine is important for the proper perspective of this mode of conduct. For one of the determining factors Origen uses in distinguishing men is the depth of good conduct. Finally, this consideration will also point out how complex spiritual change becomes when one begins to consider specific kinds of people. As Origen himself wrote; "Many of them who come to salvation are assigned to different places."[61]

The kind of person under consideration in the homily is the deceiver, the Gibeonite. The Gibeonites, the Scripture says, in order to be "saved," deceive Joshua and the other Israelite leaders and make a convenant with them. When the Gibeonite deception is uncovered, Joshua honors the covenant, but tells the Gibeonites that they shall hereafter be "hewers of wood and drawers of water for the house of God" (Josh. 9:23). In sum, the Gibeonites are saved, on account of the covenant which had been sworn to them by God, but they remain slaves to the Israelites.

Origen views in this story two kinds of salvation: One with enslavement and dishonor, the other with freedom. First, in order to expound the figurative meaning of the Gibeonites, Origen preaches to his people:

There are indeed in the church those who believe and who have a kind of faith in God, who assent in all things to the divine commandments, who are religious toward the servants of God and wish to serve them, yet they also are zealous enough to decorate the church or give service. But in their acts and in their private life, they are quite impure and enveloped with vices, never completely "putting off the old man" with his practices (Eph. 4:22), but enveloped with his old vices and impurities, just like those [Gibeonites] covered with rags and old sandals. Besides this they believe in God and seem to show respect toward the servants of God and the cult of the church. Yet they show no sign of reformation or renewal in their conduct. Thus, Jesus our Lord certainly grants to them salvation, but that salvation of theirs, in some way, does not escape the mark of dishonour.[62]

The conduct of a Gibeonite is contradictory. He displays one kind of conduct at one time, but quite the opposite at another. Thus, his practices do not consistently exhibit purity. Consequently, he is not yet worthy of the salvation of the Israelites. His is the salvation of a hypocrite.

The problem with the Gibeonite is complex. For, according to Josh. 9:9, he knows of God's wonderful deeds for the Israelites, but this knowledge guides him neither toward a renewal of heart nor an improved conduct.

> And when [the Gibeonites] say these things and confess that they have themselves heard and know of the divine miracles, they do nothing themselves worthy of faith, nothing with admiration for such strength. Therefore, Joshua, though seeing the narrow and small character in their faith, kept a most just restraint with respect to them, so that they who brought too little faith merited salvation, but they did not receive the highest gift of the kingdom or of freedom, because their faith was not improved with any increase of works, since "faith without works is dead" (James 2:17), the Apostle James declared.[63]

The Gibeonites know the powerful and wonderful deeds God has done for his servants the Israelites. Nevertheless, they continue to deceive and to exhibit in their conduct a weakness of faith. Thus, they receive a salvation that is proportional to their faith and conduct. The Gibeonites are not wholly changed, but are still, in some sense, being changed. Salvation is given before conversion is completed. Salvation is possible even for the one of little faith, but conversion continues. The Gibeonites do not receive immediately the kingdom or freedom, but a lower place, serving those who have advanced beyond them in conduct and faith. Salvation is given, but conversion continues through the humbling and enslaving tasks of hewing wood and carrying water for the Israelites, those who have received the kingdom and freedom.

The salvation of the Israelites is described in this homily as one of freedom; the salvation of the Gibeonites is one of dishonor and slavery. In the latter case, the faith of the Gibeonites was not advanced in conduct, and it was this fact which determined their position. Like the harmony that must exist between reason and actions, as Origen notes in another context, so also, Origen reveals in the above texts, there must be a harmony between faith and conduct.[64] In this relation to faith and the level of salvation lies an important factor of conduct in the process of growth. Slavery, as it is understood in the passages just quoted, can coexist with a kind of salvation and imperfect conversion. But a more complete conversion is joined with freedom and a higher level of salvation. Origen concludes:

> Let us do what is good "while it is day" (John 9:4), and give ourselves to the work of our reformation so that, from our acts, our conduct, and our life, we may merit the title of honour. Let us become worthy to receive "the spirit of adoption" (Rom. 8:15), that we may have a place preferably among the sons of God. . . .[65]

The description of the Gibeonite in this section will serve as one example of the complexity of spiritual growth when considered in individual cases. Moreover, these passages also clarify that the distinction of the progress of one person from another in the conversion and salvation process is dependent, for Origen, on the increase of faith through good conduct.[66]

How Does One Learn the Conduct of a Christian?

1.

We have now clarified the important terms involved in conduct, its intimate relation to the mode of controlling the senses, and a sample of the various difficulties as well as complexities that the idea of conduct involves with respect to spiritual growth. But we have left aside until now the key matter of how good conduct is nurtured; that is, how, on a day-to-day basis, does a person develop himself so that his conduct is like that of a Christian? This section is devoted to precisely this matter.

How does a person change his or her conduct? For Origen, as we shall see below, growth in good conduct is taking to heart the best models. The purpose of this section is to present the several dimensions of Origen's understanding of these concepts as they refer to conduct so that we can have a deeper view of how conduct changes and how various models and examples of conduct help us to change.

The importance of this section in exploring Origen's thought on becoming a Christian cannot be exaggerated. Let us briefly note two reasons for this importance. As Origen notes again and again, all the elements of spiritual change are hard work, even with the help of God, but none is more demanding on a daily basis than how the person enacts the fruits of contemplation and virtue. Perhaps it is for this reason that Origen continually refers to the martyrs, the saints, the apostles, the prophets, the wise men, and, above all, Jesus Christ, to inspire his listeners and readers. For he understood well that man needs an example if he is going to be strong enough to change. So change involves outer doing as much as it involves inner spiritual activity, such as contemplation and virtue.

In brief, Origen's ethics centers itself in imitation and example. But equally important, Origen recognizes that the convert needs to practice; he needs to fulfill himself in deeds in order to fertilize, so-to-speak, the spiritual change that has occurred. Hence we find—and have already found—Origen connecting the dimensions of change in many texts, with always the practical emphasis on deeds of virtue.

The section may be outlined as follows: First, we will begin with a brief discussion of the models given by the prophets, apostles, martyrs, and other saints, and the position of God as Supreme Teacher, whose aid and power enables change to occur. Second, we will turn to a consideration of the imitation and model of Christ, whose model is central for any change of conduct. Third, because Christ's critical role is also reflected in the Church, which is his body, we shall define the role of the Church in conduct through a discussion of her role as a model. Finally, the discussion of the church leads us naturally to the role of the teacher and doctrine as examples in conduct and important catalysts of transformation.

2.

We begin with the models given by the prophets, apostles and saints, and the place of God.

The prophet Jeremiah was revered by Origen for many reasons, but one important characteristic of Jeremiah that impressed Origen was the prophet's courage to teach and speak the word of God regardless of hardships. Jeremiah's conduct was committed to his belief. His book tells the story of a man of God who taught the truth and endured great suffering for his faith. To a stubborn and sometimes cruel audience, Jeremiah continued to preach and teach the reprovals and prophecies that God gave to him. His one objective was to serve God by turning the people back to God. His goal was ultimately a goal committed to changing the conduct and minds of men.

This interpretation of Jeremiah's life and goals recurs continually throughout Origen's homilies on the prophet, and especially in a section concerned with Jer. 15:15. Origen even saw himself and his audience as those who should imitate the prophetic model. With respect to himself, he wrote:

> When I am abused, I can see that the cause of the abuse is none other than that I champion truth and I "am an ambassador" (Eph. 6:20) for the scripture, so that everything happens according to the Logos of God; for this I am blasphemed.[67]

Origen does not specify the cause of the abuse in this context. Still his intent, in light of Jer. 15:15, seems clear. Regardless of the abuse or suffering, he would "champion truth" and promote the Logos of God in Scripture. And it is Jeremiah's model that inspires him to reveal these personal goals. In an earlier verse (Jer. 15:10), Jeremiah sees himself at variance with everyone on earth, as one accused everywhere. Origen finds such difficulties a natural result of the task of the prophet, namely, to oppose and transform sinners and to expect disfavor. In other words, if Jeremiah was not in conflict with sinners, he would not be doing his job, which is "to teach, to reprove and to convert."[68]

But Origen encourages not only himself but everyone to imitate the prophetic and apostolic life.[69] As Christians, each of us is to say with Jeremiah, "I sat alone" (Jer. 15:17), and make his life "hard to imitate" for the majority.[70] On several occasions he advises his people in this way:

> And thus let all of us, as far as ability permits, strive for the prophetic life, for the apostolic life, not avoiding what is troublesome. For if the athlete avoids what is troublesome about the contest, the sweetness of the crown will never be his.[71]

This section concerning Jer. 15:15 considers the difficulties all must be prepared to face if they imitate the prophet. Wanting to be like the prophet, however, is by itself not sufficient. More important, Origen believes, "let us emulate the works of the prophets" and pray, "Give us to suffer what the prophets have suffered."[72]

In addition to the prophets, Origen considers all of the saints and the righteous as examples.[73] For example, in a passage of Jeremiah concerning the people of

Judah, Origen sees an expression that he believes refers figuratively to the contemporary Christians (Jer. 3:8–10). He believes that the examples of the martyrs in an earlier age of the Church taught the catechumens the love of truth, whereas in his own time, he feels that such faith is rare. Christians of his time, he states, turn away from God just as Judah did.[74]

> But when there occurred noble martyrdoms, then there were faithful, when we all came from the graves to the assembly after conducting the martyrs, and the whole church was present, without feeling distressed, and the catechumens, "neither frightened" nor troubled, [having turned] to the living God, were taught by the martyrs and by the deaths of those who confessed the truth "until death." (Of. Apoc. 2:10; Acts 14:15)[75]

While the martyrs' intense perseverance and adherence to God despite great pain and anguish is a teaching model of conduct,[76] the image of the fierce resister to temptation is also used to rouse up the hearers to good conduct. Such saints are like the hardest metal, adamant, (cf. Amos 7:7) according to Origen, unmoved by the vicious hammers of the devil.[77] "However much he is struck, he displays his virtue brighter."[78]

With this model of the prophets and saints uppermost in our minds, it would appear that conduct is simply an external imitation, that God does not inwardly contribute to the conduct process. But Origen is led to other conclusions by Scripture. Though Jeremiah is sent by God to turn the people, the ultimate power of change, as we have noted previously and Jeremiah himself explains, is with God alone.

We cannot pass over this fact lightly. For if the basis of imitation and example, the foundation of religious models, does not have a motivating power, then its significance in the religious life would be obscure. For example, Jeremiah says, "Make it known to me, Lord, and I will know" (Jer. 11:18). Concerning this passage, Origen writes that the only true teacher, the source of the converting power of all teaching, and the only true salvation does not originate in any example or man alone, but in God.

> "And do not call one 'teacher' on earth. For you have one teacher, the Father in heaven" (Matt. 23:8, 9). The "Father in heaven" teaches either personally or by means of Christ or in the Holy Spirit, or through Paul, that is, through Peter or other saints, yet [ultimately] only God's Spirit and God's Logos dwell and teach.[79]

Though the human teacher (Paul, Peter, and the saints) is allotted here a certain role as agent, Origen centers all in God and agrees with Jeremiah who speaks to the Lord, "Heal me and I will be healed. Save me and I will be saved. For you are my boast" (Jer. 17:14). "The only true salvation is if Christ saves."[80]

There is also another dimension in which God appears as the teacher. In his homily on Jer. 5:3, "You have completed them, and they did not want to receive instruction," Origen points out how God's economy is completed by means of an instruction and purification through knowledge. Hence he interprets this passage from Jeremiah as an expression of how God offers the benefits of his providence, but men do not receive them. God is then the source of all teaching and the power behind all true conversion, because conversion and instruction are elements of God's plan for man.[81]

Yet God's powers do not, let us recall, limit man's power of free will (cf. Chapter 2, above). Though God may be considered an instructor through the Logos, Origen notes, let us not believe that God compromises free will with respect to education and conduct. God is the fundamental origin of all teaching, but he does not enter the heart of one who is unwilling to receive him, or one who refuses to submit himself willingly to him.[82]

At the same time, as we noted above in Chapter 3, God does offer help to people through guardian angels. They are hard at work also in moral conduct, guiding the soul toward virtuous acts and away from old bad habits.[83] Their work is clarified, in fact, in Origen's commentary on the Song of Songs 1:6, "The sons of my mother have fought in me, they have made me the keeper in the vineyards; my vineyard I have not kept." Origen views the "mother" as the heavenly Jerusalem, the "sons" as angels, the "vineyards" that are to be kept as those "divine teachings" and the vineyard as "those habits and customs and way of life that she [the soul] practiced when she lived after the 'old man' " (Col. 3:19).[84] These angel champions act as "tutors and governors" who will help the soul fight the desire to return to the former life, the "conflicts of thoughts and the assaults of evil spirits."[85]

Since God is the true source of knowledge and teaching and the agent of all kinds of aid, it is better, Origen writes, to receive knowledge from him rather than through some agent.[86] For example, when Origen is discussing the meaning of Jesus' stay with the Samaritans in John 4, he detects in the Gospel author the wish to distinguish between belief arising from the woman's testimony and the belief arising from direct contact with the Logos. Origen writes:

> And it is better to become an eyewitness of the Logos and to listen without intermediaries when he teaches, not through teachers, and when he causes ideas to arise in the heart which discovers with great clarity images of the truth, than to listen to the word concerning him through servants who have seen him, so that one neither sees him nor is enlightened by his power.[87]

The section goes on to examine the distinction of living by faith and living by sight, a distinction that clarifies what is involved in seeing the Logos directly. We shall return to this distinction in the next chapter. For our purposes here it will suffice to say that Origen recognizes, based on Scripture and the apostolic and prophetic models, that the ultimate power of all teaching models and efforts is God.[88]

It is worthwhile to note the connection with Christ of each of the models Origen presents. The prophetic life as represented by Jeremiah is, in fact, directly applicable, interpreted spiritually, to Christ.[89] The model Jeremiah presents, then, is more profoundly the model of Christ. And concerning the same passage of Jeremiah (15:10), Origen clearly sees, with respect to the martyrs, an intimate connection with Christ. It is Christ who is accused, judged, imprisoned and martyred in the martyrs, and in all who suffer for truth.[90] With respect to the saints, it was noted in the passage concerning adamant that the saint is "in the hands" of the Lord, protected by him.[91] In addition to these models, we need to add also that the teacher is, according to Origen, merely a model on the way to a higher model. He writes in his commentary on Matt. 13:52 and 1 Cor. 11:1, concerning the scribe who is like the householder, that the disciple imitates the teacher, who imitates Christ.[92] Above all, then, the guide presents the example of Christ. Each person is encouraged to imitate the model of all good conduct if he is to become a Christian. Let us then turn to a discussion of what such an imitation means.

3.

The theme of the imitation of Christ has so many dimensions in Origen that it is not possible to cover all of them in one subsection.[93] Our primary goal in each of these subsections is to clarify how conduct can *change* through the principle of imitation and/or example.

Already in Chapter 3 we have briefly considered the role of imitation with respect to the creation according to the image. By conforming oneself to the Logos and his virtues, one progresses from being one dominated by the image of the earthly to one who is being transformed by the glorious image of Christ. For example, we find these sentiments in Origen's commentary on Rom. 5:12 and 1 Cor. 15:22, 47, 49:

> If we live according to the Logos of God, we are renewed and transformed according to the inner man to the image of God who created him. This [new] man then who is now transformed and restored to the image of God is neither earthly nor in this world, but his way of life is said to be in heaven. (cf. Phil. 3:20)[94]

This text leads us to believe that a change in conduct involves a conformation to the Logos of God. But Origen clarifies the matter in more detail in a passage concerned with Rom. 8:29. There he shows that the example is not exactly the Logos, but the human soul of Jesus, image of the Image, the Son of God.[95] Upon this model he is conformed in God's economy and toward this model he himself continually progresses, as the former text also helps to clarify.

With this brief recapitulation of prior discussions in mind, let us consider how the imitation of Christ, on the one hand, is related to the role of conduct in general and to instruction through example in helping one to progress in spirituality, and, on the other hand, how it is integrated with the role of the church in the conversion of conduct.[96]

The discussion will follow these lines: (a) First, several texts will be presented on the ethical relation of Christ to the change of inner life. (b) Second, we will consider the moral demands of becoming a follower of Christ. (c) Third, as a bridge to the next subsection, we will review the imitation of Christ by the church body as a catalyst for becoming a Christian. (d) Finally, we will offer a summary.[97]

(a) In various contexts and ways, Origen indicates with Paul (1 Cor. 3:11) that Jesus Christ is the inner "foundation" of the Christian soul and conduct. Often he uses particular scriptural images to convey his view of the matter. For example, the images of a building and a field in Jeremiah 22 and 1 Corinthians 3 are used in this way. Jeremiah is told, in Chapter 22, to preach to the King of Judah of justice, and to tell him to build a house of justice. Origen applies this lesson to the inner life:

> And if anyone builds well, he builds upon "gold," the teachings of truth, "silver," the Logos of salvation, "precious stones," a structure built out of virtues. (1 Cor. 3:11–12)[98]

Christ, then, is in the believer as a foundation upon which the believer changes; he builds himself up by means of what he is taught, by *logos* in him that saves and by the development of moral excellence. The Christian life should resemble a construction process; it should be based on Christ and be built up with fine materials of virtue.

In the above text Origen does not discuss the relation of Christ to the teachings and acts themselves, but in many other texts he creates the idea of a man developing a Christlike condition in his life when he completes good practices and imitates Christ, and of a man who, in a sense, becomes able, through Christ, to create Christ in himself. In other words, not only does one gain Christ by conduct, but one, according to Origen, more and more forms a christ in his inner life. Let us then turn to the texts that present this idea.

The connection of Christ with behavior is made at one point in Origen's discussion of Jer. 17:13, concerning the "endurance of Israel." He says:

> Just as the saviour is absolute righteousness, absolute truth, absolute sanctification, so is he absolute endurance. And it is neither [possible] to be righteous without Christ nor holy without him nor to endure without possessing Christ. For he is the "endurance of Israel."[99]

This text extends the activity of Christ as foundation to all the virtues of behavior, so that whatever we do that is righteous and holy, and that requires the force of truth and endurance, we share with Christ, for he is each of these virtues absolutely. In fact, in one text Origen writes that the Lord was "total virtue, animated and living."[100]

However, the reverse is also true, as Origen mentions with respect to another part of the same text, "Lord, let all who have left you be ashamed" (Jer. 17:13). When we are unjust, unwise and unholy, when we sin, we have left Christ; we have turned away.[101] Hence we participate in or separate from Christ depending on the moral quality of our conduct and thoughts. If we are just, he is present; if we sin, we leave him. It is important to note that the believer, not Christ or God, is the one who moves in or out of a condition of sin. We are only sharers in Christ, who remains, in a sense, firm and stable in condition, when we share in his qualities of righteousness, holiness, and truth. We come to him and share his virtue, or we turn away from him as do those who move away from virtue. Origen clarifies elsewhere that in the present life we possess only a "form and shadow" of virtue. In the future life, when we have completed our spiritual journey, we will have virtue itself.[102]

The same may be said for knowledge. If Christ is righteousness, and we do not know righteousness, how then can we know Christ? This is a concern of Origen in his discussion of Jer. 22:14–17. In these verses Jeremiah is commanded to warn the people of false prophets. Origen detects in these passages also a reference to false teachers in the Church who have not known Christ:

> . . .but since they have not known Christ, they "have not known" "righteousness" (Jer. 22:15–16). For to do what is righteous is a characteristic of those who have known God.[103]

The constant tendency to see an absolute role for Christ in every act and thought of good is evident in Origen's theology. He never tires of relating in a closer and closer connection the movement toward good and the Good itself, that is, Christ, until finally, as we shall witness in texts to follow, Origen will even speak of a spiritual union.

The powerful image of life and death, again based on an image from Scripture, is also creatively viewed in terms of this purpose by Origen, regarding Jer. 17:5, "Cursed is the man who sets his hope in man." After indicating that it is Christ as Logos, not according to the flesh, in whom he places his hope—as Paul seems to affirm, according to Origen, in 2 Cor. 5:16—Origen says:

> Through [Christ], I am no longer a man, if I follow his words; but he says, "I have said, You are gods and all sons of the Most High" (Ps. 81:6). Hence, as he is "first-fruit of the dead" (Col. 1:18), so he has become the first-fruit of all men who redirect themselves toward God. "Cursed" then "is the man who sets his hope in man, and affixes himself to the flesh of his arm," who would establish the fleshly. . . . But it is not this way with the holy, for he does not "affix himself to the flesh of his arm." For he has always "the death of Jesus in his body" (2 Cor. 4:10), and he "puts to death the earthly members, fornication, impurity." (Col. 3:5)[104]

As soon as people "redirect" themselves to God, they receive Christ, the "first-fruit of the dead," the dead being those who attach themselves to the earthly and sinful. The movement away from death is directly connected to the death of Jesus, an event that conquered all impure spirits and the powers of evil. For by redirecting life to God, the saint kills all aspects of the self that were opposed to God, such as all forms of impurity. In other words, in the turn toward God the saint recreates the triumph over the evil powers and death that Christ universally established by his death on the cross. Each spiritual change is a kind of reenactment of the crucifixion and resurrection.[105] These are the thoughts that lie behind Origen's statement that we should place our hopes in Christ alone. For only in Christ's model can we find the power of change to reach true life.

An additional dimension to the image of life/death is found in Origen's comments on Jer. 11:4: "You will be my people, and I will be your God." Origen wonders at what point can we really say that God is our God. He finds his answer in Scripture:

"God is not of the dead but of the living" (Matt. 22:32). Who is the dead? He is the sinner who does not possess him who said, "I am the life" (John 11:25), who possesses dead works, who has never repented from dead works, concerning whom the apostle said, "those who do not lay again a foundation of repentance from dead works" (Heb. 6:1). If then "God is not" a God "of the dead but of the living," and we know who "the living" is, for he is one who governs his life according to Christ and remains with him, if we wish that he will be our God, let us renounce the works of death, so that he can fulfill his promise. (Jer. 11:4–5)[106]

In accordance with this text, we can view even more clearly how deeply Origen related the moral quality of the inner life, as well as the works, of the believer with Christ. Life itself is received according to the degree that one governs his life according to Christ and renounces the works of death. Even the fulfillment of God's promise is connected to one's efforts to renounce, and repent from, what is dead. In sum, in light of these last two texts, the possession of life itself, that is, the only true life, Christ, is dependent upon one's practices, and, equally important to our subject, how one continues to change one's conduct.[107]

The imitation of Christ's crucifixion in order to conquer what is of death within us brings not only renewed life, but, as is evident from what will follow, divine life. By our acts, we too become, with Christ, sons of God. This idea occurs in Origen's thoughts on Jer. 11:10, "They have turned to the wicked ways of their forefathers." The Lord tells Jeremiah in this chapter that the men of Judah have turned to the sins of the forefathers. Origen wishes his listeners to take careful note of the word "forefathers" in the scriptural text rather than just "fathers." Scripture, he says, is referring to the father of nonbelievers, the devil. "Prior to believing we were, so-to-speak, sons of the devil."[108] His view on this matter is, he believes, firmly based in Scripture.[109] Every time we sin, he says, we are begotten by the devil.[110] So, on the one side, we become sons of the devil by our conduct and by our unbelief. But the reverse also applies for those who are righteous.

For I will not say that just once the righteous has been begotten by God, but always he is begotten in each good act in which God begets the righteous. If then I set before you, with respect to the saviour, that the Father has not begotten the Son and then severed him from his generation, but always begets him, I also will present something similar for the righteous .... and the saviour is always begotten by the Father, and also in this way, if you have the "spirit of sonship," God always begets you in him according to each work, according to each thought, and so a begotten one may always be a begotten son of God in Christ Jesus. (Cf. Prov. 8:25; Rom. 8:15)[111]

It should be kept in mind, when thinking upon this text, that we as begotten sons do not become equal to the Son of God. For while we become sons by choosing and doing the good, he is, as texts above have shown, the "absolute" source of every virtue. This fact is clarified especially to Celsus in a context concerning the difference of our sonship and the sonship of Christ. Jesus, Origen explains, is far superior to all others because he is the "source and origin" of the virtues that distinguish those called sons of God.[112] The above quoted text makes clear that our sonship depends upon the spirit of sonship. Origen indicates elsewhere that a son of God is one who chooses good for itself and follows Christ without fear. He distinguishes in this context, following Rom. 8:14–15, John 8:44 and 1 John 3:10, three categories: sons of God, slaves who believe and follow out of fear, and sons of the devil.[113]

Though it is clear from the texts already quoted who the sons of God and sons of the devil are, let us interject briefly a note on the slaves. Though the slaves fear to do evil, they are believers. In a fragment, for example, Origen seems to delegate to this level all those who lived before the appearance of Christ.[114] And in a section of his *Commentary on John*, Origen points out that slaves are those who believe only without hearing Christ's words and understanding their intent.[115] However, as has been evident from the beginning, no one is predetermined by God to any moral level. So the slaves, Origen insists against the Gnostics, are not slaves by nature. A slave becomes a son by a means that Christ himself taught, according to Origen, in Matt. 5:44–45, that is, by means of love for one's enemies and prayer for those who persecute.[116] It is ultimately, then, one's motives in conduct that determine whether or not one is worthy to be a son of God. Sinful motives taint all conduct, even if outwardly good, causing one to become a son of the devil. Conduct induced from motives of fear is fundamentally insecure and uncertain; it causes one to become a slave.

Let us return to the meaning of becoming a son of God. The nature of this correspondence between Sonship and human sonship may be found in another correspondence discussed above, namely, the correspondence between our virtues and Christ as absolute virtue. Since the Son's nature is absolute righteousness and virtue, the son is assimilated to God when he projects virtue and righteousness in work and thought. Our sonship then, as Origen explicitly states, is a model of his Sonship. Our sonship depends upon the extent within us of a christlike condition, and Christ is " ... present in each individual only in such a degree as is warranted by the extent of his merits."[117] Hence sonship develops in terms of Christ, "in Christ Jesus." This fact cannot be stressed enough if we are to appreciate Origen's thought. For him there is a continual mediatorship of Christ in these matters. We do good, we are healed, we follow Christ's model and, as he says at the end of one of his homilies, we are perfected *in Christ*.[118] We are sons because of his Sonship. The power in us that makes this correspondence and sonship possible is the creation according to the image, which we discussed in Chapter 3.

Origen's thought on the possession of Christ by those who do good may be summed up by a text concerning John 1:17: "grace and truth came through Jesus Christ." After Origen reiterates that Christ is truth and righteousness, and that all who have truth and righteousness have Christ, he states:

> For it is as if Christ is found in each saint, and there come to be through the one Christ many christs, imitators of him and formed after him who is the Image of God.[119]

The change of the Christian, then, occurs not by pursuing his own truth nor by becoming autonomous or individual in his spiritual life, but by imitating in every detail possible Jesus Christ. As Origen clearly states it in another context: "God wants to make us christs."[120]

We have reviewed how Origen has creatively considered the various biblical images of the building, life/death, and sonship, in addition to his thoughts on when God becomes our God, Christ the foundation and how we become christs, in order to present how deeply Origen understands the correspondence of God/Christ and conduct in changing the one who turning to God, and particularly what is involved in progressing from one level of conduct to another.[121] In effect, these considerations form a basis for texts concerning the demands made upon the imitator and the one becoming a Christian. Let us now turn to those texts, keeping in mind the foregoing correspondence.

(b) In the foregoing passages, we have been considering how Christ is more than a model in the imitator's spiritual journey; Christ is in a sense assimilated in each act of conduct. Yet the movement itself toward this condition is as important to the understanding of spiritual growth as the elements involved. In order to explain the actual movement involved in changing one's behavior, as it pertains to our concerns for how he understands the way one becomes a Christian, Origen sometimes uses the biblical images of going up and going ahead.[122]

The movement of going up, out of the countryside and valleys, is seen as following the path of Christ and coming to the place of Christ, the prophets, and the righteous. For example, in his exegesis of Jer. 16:16, where it is written:

> Behold I send many fishermen, says the Lord, and they will fish for them, and afterwards I am sending many hunters, and they will hunt for them on every mountain and on every hill, and out of the holes of the rocks.

Origen envisions a spiritual movement from the condition of being a "fish" to the condition of one in the "mountain" or a "rock," and a movement from one kind of life to another.[123] The fish is caught by the fishermen of Jesus:

> But he who was caught by the fishers of Jesus and who has come up from the sea,
> he also dies, but he dies to the world, he dies to sin, and after dying to the world and
> to sin, he is given life by the Logos of God and takes up another life.[124]

Then, after explaining that the soul itself has been transformed by this experience,
becoming something superior to its previous state, Origen continues:

> This fish, which was caught by the fishers of Jesus and really transformed, after it
> abandons the way of life in the sea, makes its way of life in the mountains. . . .[125]

On the one hand, the mountains and hills are indicative for Origen of the prophets
and other great prominent holy ones worthy of imitation and admiration,[126] but,
on the other hand, they are also the holy places where Jesus is and where his
divine work takes place. Only there can one be noticed by God's hunters in the
final days.[127]

To follow Christ and the holy ones, one then must live in the "mountains,"
in a holy condition. It is in these "places" that the soul, once transformed by
the Logos, caught by his fishers and dead to sin, resides. It is to such a place
that Jesus ascended. And the movement from one place to another is a movement
that involves one's entire way of life. It is a complete shift in one's orientation,
comparable, according to Origen, to the radical transference of a fish from water
to land, or a relocation from life in a valley to life in the mountains. And the
goal for such a transformation from death to new life is to be where Jesus is.
Jesus is the goal of change in conduct.

The images of going up and going ahead are combined in Origen's thoughts
on Jer. 15:6, "You have turned from me. You will go back!" Here as in other
chapters Jeremiah presents a brief history of the fall of God's people, and how
they will be punished. Jeremiah's commands are especially directed to Jerusalem.
Origen views the perversion of Jerusalem in two ways: first, as the Jews' rejection
of Christ, and, second, as the soul's apostasy and return to sin.[128] Origen
especially stresses the negative significance of "going back," and contrasts it with
Paul's advice, in Phil. 3:13, of "straining forward to what lies ahead." Those
who go or look back, such as Lot's wife (Gen. 19:26), are those who go back
to a sinful state. Those who strain forward, following Paul and Christ's own
teachings in Mark 13:16, Luke 17:32, and Luke 9:62, are the just who have left
behind their old sinful ways and converted to Jesus' teaching.[129]

Origen asks his listeners to learn from and imitate the teachings of Jesus
concerning the importance of moving forward rather than turning back. But
Origen, in harmony with Paul, realizes that the movement is not simply a facile
progress forward; it is a movement defined by the biblical word "to strain
forward" (epekteinein), which implies some struggle and hard work, extending
and stretching oneself beyond the normal limits of one's moral or spiritual
movement or state. In order to avoid and ignore what is "behind," what may
be a comfortable or less demanding situation, the righteous strain themselves
forward, to new levels of achievement, in order to attain the goal of perfection,
which is the context of both texts of Origen and Paul.[130]

Thought on Lot inspires Origen to elaborate on this story and its application to his point. In Gen. 19:17, Lot is advised not to look back to what is behind nor "stay in the surrounding countryside; escape to the mountain, lest you are taken with the others." The Scripture presents in combination two demands on the conduct of the one who seeks spiritual growth: to go ahead, away from what is behind, and to go up. The result of this combination permits Origen to impress effectively on his hearers the image of true progress in conduct; that is, to go forward and not remain in one's old or even present situation, and to go up to a higher level or model of life, especially the model of Jesus Christ. Constant movement forward and constant ascent are then the key dimensions.[131]

Thus the imagery of Lot and the mountain is very powerful in clarifying what Origen means to live the way Christ taught and lived. It also offers further examples of the kind of shift in attitude and conduct expected in the one becoming a Christian, the change from stress on what is behind to what is ahead.

The idea of leaving what is behind is developed by means of the images of the "day of man" and renouncing the "world." The former arises in Origen's discussion of Jer. 17:15–17, in which Jeremiah proclaims his trust in the Lord alone. Origen reiterates the message of Jeremiah 17 by quoting several texts from the New Testament (Matt. 16:24, 19:27, 8:22, 10:37–38) in which Jesus asks men to follow him and leave all behind. The follower of Jesus, Origen says, is not one who pleads to stay in this life, "the day of man" (Jer. 17:16), but one who seeks "the day of resurrection of the holy," and the "holy day of God."[132] It might be noted in passing that Origen, in this same section and on the same text of Jeremiah, points out that the true follower of Jesus will not grow weary and be in distress. Once a person begins to strain forward and move toward the mountain, Christ provides aid.[133]

The other image, renouncing the world, results from Origen's consideration of Jer. 18:1–2, "The word which came to Jeremiah from the Lord saying: Rise up and go down to the house of the potter." Origen stresses the importance of "up" and "down" in the text as referring to a form of imitation and discipleship. In the realms of below and above, as well as under, there is a distinct form of wisdom. And Origen provides examples of those who have traveled in these directions to gain the wisdom.[134] He quotes Eph. 3:18 in support of this view, and indicates that in order to arrive at any of these realms of wisdom, one must follow a certain model:

The intellect[135] which can follow the Son of God reaches everywhere, for it is led by the Logos who teaches about everything. And it follows if it has renounced the world and taken up its cross. For it can follow Jesus if it can say, "The world is crucified to me, and I to the world." (Matt. 16:24; Gal. 6:14)[136]

Origen here refers to Matt. 16:24. He discusses this passage, as well as Gal. 6:14, in an exposition elsewhere that stresses the sacrifice and arduous demands expected of the one who imitates Christ.[137] Origen also refers to the need for renouncing the world, but he does not specify in this context what "world" means. Let us suggest, in light of a later section in which he does discuss the sense of "world" (*kosmos*), that the world is the earthly place of sense-reality and, as we considered in Chapter 3, that which belongs to the things seen.[138] Being crucified to the world, then, is forfeiting the earthly and changeable reality, the reality in which sin arises, for the reality of Christ.[139]

> On this account let our every consideration and thought, our every word and act breathe[140] a "denial" of ourselves and a testimony [and confession][141] about Christ and in Christ. For I am persuaded that every act of the perfect is a testimony to Christ Jesus, and that abstinence from every sin is a "denial" of self, leading "after" Jesus.[142]

This text clearly presents the intensity and commitment by which Origen related the believer and Christ, and no text could better explain the demands upon each person becoming a Christian. No dimension of the true follower of Jesus can be ignored if one is devoted. Thoughts, judgments, words, and acts are all directed to Christ. This perspective of Origen is further inspired and enriched by Paul's concern to be "crucified with Christ," and "crucified unto the world." (Gal. 6:14) Moreover, the subsequent statements (Matt. 16:25–26) in Matthew 16 allow Origen to elaborate on the nature of sacrifice for Christ. The scriptural text is:

> For whoever would save his soul will lose it, and whoever loses his soul for my sake will find it. For what will it profit a man if he gains the whole world and forfeits his soul.

"World" in this context is interrelated with a sinful soul, so that losing such a soul is related to being crucified unto the world, and denying self. For Origen they all have one goal and object, Jesus Christ. After indicating that we must be "crucified with Christ," and lose our life "for the sake of Christ," he writes:

> According to what has been said, it seems to me, following the analogy of self-denial, that each ought to "lose his own soul." Let each one therefore "lose his own" sinful "soul," that having lost that which is sinful, he may receive that which is saved by doing what is right. But a man will in no way "be profited if he shall gain the whole world." Now he "gains the world," I think, to whom the world is not crucified. And to whom the world is not crucified, to that man shall be the loss of his own soul.[143]

When we contemplate these statements and the biblical images that Origen chooses in order to illustrate the moral demands of changing in order to follow Christ, it becomes clearer how critical the prior discussions on correspondence become. For it is Christ's connection with the doer of good acts that makes Origen's goals of spiritual growth for the believer possible. To lose one's soul, to be crucified to the world, and to deny one's self are made possible because Christ is the source from which we draw to fulfill such acts, and because he is the mediator who offers them to the Father.[144]

Christ himself sets high, seemingly impossible, standards when he asks men to love their enemies and pray for those who persecute them.[145] In fact, the final teaching and example of Christ that bears on the transformation of conduct is the overt examples that Christ himself set in his earthly life.[146] Christ's life was full of risks and dangers. He knew, for example, that his entrance into Jerusalem would cause many difficulties for him. The apostle Paul was also faced with risks (Matt. 20:17-20; Acts 21:11-13). Nonetheless, Origen points out, both met the danger and did not flee. And we too, he says, are to follow the examples of Christ and Paul his imitator when temptations try to steer us away.[147]

Of particular interest to Origen, with respect to Christ's earthly example, was the humility of Christ. The importance of humility for Origen arises in his thoughts on Jer. 13:15, "Hear and listen, and be not proud, for the Lord has spoken." In chapter 13, Jeremiah is especially focused on the sin of pride of Judah and Jerusalem, a sin he connects to going after strange gods. Origen first carefully discusses the kinds of pride in order to discover if any have worth, and then concludes that "in nothing can one be proud."[148] This is the example Christ himself gave.[149]

Moreover, humility is directly connected to the act of turning from the world in Origen's exposition of Matt. 18:14.[150] Humility is also the subject of Origen's thoughts on Isa. 6:8, "Whom shall I send and who will go to this people? And I said, Behold, I am [here], send me." Origen considers Isaiah's willingness to be sent a result of his ignorance concerning the task demanded of him. For when Moses was asked, in Exod. 4:13, he humbly declines by saying, "Appoint another whom you can send." Moses knew the magnitude of what God was asking, and he felt unworthy (cf. Exod. 4:10). Moses' humility, Origen continues, is a lesson for all of us in the Church, especially the leaders.[151]

These, then, are a few examples of how the humility of Christ is a model for us in our conduct, and of how Christ's earthly work can have a direct effect on our own spiritual growth.

Let us briefly conclude the exposition of the imitation of Christ by reference to some texts concerned with the Church.[152]

(c) In his understanding of Matt. 16:16-18, Origen centers the discussion around the twofold meaning of "peter" (*petra*). On the one hand, it refers to the name of one of Christ's disciples, but, on the other hand, it also means "rock" in Greek, and, according to Origen, refers to every imitator of Christ who, like Peter,[153] knows who Christ is, namely, the Son of God, and who drinks "the spiritual drink" from "the spiritual rock which followed."[154] Here only the imitator and Christ are mentioned, but Origen completes the triangle by a statement that includes the Church:

And upon every such rock is built every principle of the church and the way of life which accords with it. For in each of the mature, who has the combination of words and [all] deeds and [all] thoughts which effect bliss, is the church built by God.[155]

The image of building that is introduced here by Jesus is taken up again by Origen to clarify how men's thoughts and acts are the foundation of a structure built by God, namely, the Church. And each of these "rocks" that form the structure is an imitator of Christ. Hence the Church is built upon and built up by the imitation of Christ. These texts also exemplify how, in terms of the Church, Origen considers the concept of imitation both distributively and with respect to the Church as a single unit. The absolute pattern of Christ can be impressed in both ways.

The biblical images of the bride/bridegroom and the body/members are also believed by Origen to present the relation of the Church with Christ, and are applicable to our discussion of the concept of imitation.[156] For example, in his consideration of the Song of Songs 1:10, "How lovely have your cheeks become, as are the turtle dove's, your neck as necklaces!" (from a Latin translation), he discovers a profound allegory. After viewing the significance of "cheeks" as referring to those "who cultivate the integrity of chastity and virtue," Origen turns to the meaning of "neck" and "necklace." These, he believes, refer to the "souls which 'take up the yoke' of Christ" (Matt. 11:29), and the "obedience of faith" that causes the neck to be lovely. But the "obedience" is patterned after Christ. It is his "obedience" that is the "necklace."[157]

> Great in this matter, therefore, is the praise of the bride, great the glory of the church, when the imitation of his obedience equals the obedience of Christ, whom the church imitates.[158]

We may conclude from this logic of Origen the following: Origen has told us that his obedience is an obedience of faith. Man's faith draws Christ to himself by means of the virtue of faith, which Christ himself exhibited most profoundly in his obedience. Hence, Christ, being virtue itself, is drawn to us, in a sense, by his own pattern in us. This idea is another way of saying that we share in, rather than possess as our own, the virtues.

Another reason for the efficacy of imitation for Origen arises from Paul's imagery of the body and members of Christ being the body and members of his Church (cf. 1 Cor. 12:14-18, 27). As Chapter 3 discussed, we are by nature, insofar as we are of the Church, sharers of the Logos. The Church is the body of the Logos, and we as believers are its members. Hence there is a union of Church and Christ in his one body. Our imitation consists, first of all, of acts that perfect us, but these are also acts made possible by his presence as the body of Christ.[159]

Since we will be discussing conduct and the Church in more detail in the next subsection, let these texts suffice to show that Origen directly connects the idea of the imitation of Christ with the Church herself. These statements, however, concern only the present age. The Church in the age to come ". . . will be fair and beautiful not only by imitation, but also with her own unique perfection . . . ," as Origen notes in his commentary on Song of Songs 1:5.[160]

(d) In sum, the imitation of Christ, with respect to the transformation of conduct, has several dimensions that Origen expresses by powerful images. The basis of each of them is the participation of Christ in the one who is good and does well in conduct. It is not merely a matter of copying Jesus's external model, however, but concerns how we are conformed to and correspond with Christ.[161] Imitation creates sons of God and christs in the pattern of the Son and Christ, and such a process is possible, first, because Christ is absolute virtue, second, because Christ is a perfect model for the virtuous, and, third, because, as members of the Church, we are members of his body. When we are virtuous through good acts, we have Christ.[162]

Yet the imitation of Christ is also, in an objective sense, an arduous and even dangerous task, which Origen presents through the biblical images of losing one's soul, renouncing the world, putting aside works of death, the story of Lot, entering Jerusalem, as well as the concrete example of Jesus' own acts. All acts and thoughts are to be fixed not on oneself but on Jesus, the "mountain." Life of the "world," riches, fame, and position must be replaced with love, prayer, and humility, which are the true agents that create good conduct, based in Christ's own suggestions and acts.

Thus good conduct is established, with respect to Christ, by an ontological dimension (Christ as absolute virtue and the Image transforming the inner man) and a more objective dimension in which Christ presents an external model or offers suggestions through his teaching. In these two dimensions we see interlaced in Origen's thought the role of the divine and the role of the convert in transforming behavior.[163]

Finally, Origen relates imitation/example also to the Church by means of the biblical images of a building and the bride/bridegroom. He considers the Church a structure created by those who have good lives and who imitate the obedience of Christ. However, the holy are not in a corporeal building, nor, in fact, in any place, but wherever and whenever they live in according with the Logos of God. This view is clarified in his thoughts on Lev. 21:12—"he did not leave from the holy place"—and 1 Peter 2:21-22, where Scripture explicitly says that Christ left us an example by suffering and committing no sin, never departing from holiness. "For 'holy places' are not to be sought in a place, but in deeds and life and behaviour."[164]

4.

To this point we have considered imitation/example with respect to the prophets and saints, and imitation with respect to Christ. Let us now turn to a detailed discussion of the role of the Church in conduct. We will discuss two aspects of the Church's role, with special emphasis on the first: the Church as an example through its role in the plan of God. As the community and people of God it bears a definite responsibility to guide and inspire people at all spiritual stages to seek and gain perfection. Then, as a prelude to the final subsection on the teacher, we will briefly consider the standards that Origen set for leaders and priests of the Church, the human agents of the Church's transforming task in conduct.

(a) The Church, as we have noted previously, is for Origen in a critical position with respect to the plan of God for conversion and salvation. Her responsibility is very heavy. Those who are members of her have a covenant of truth, doctrine, and conduct with God, and if they do not live up to the covenant, Origen tells his listeners, they are "cursed." So the Lord himself says in Jer. 11:1–4. This passage, according to Origen, is directed to the Church, which is, analogically, the men of Judah.[165] When we do not do what is commanded, we lose the "promise" and no longer are his people. When we do not fulfil our part, conversion is stymied.[166] In the next section of the homily, Origen clarifies those people to whom God is God: He is not a God to the sinner or the unrepentant, but he is a God to those who have put aside the works of death.[167] Hence doing what God has commanded is in effect another way of growing spiritually: One renounces sin, repents, and does the works of a life governed by Christ. Yet, according to Jer. 11:6–9, some did not do what was commanded, and "a bond was found among the men of Judah" (Jer. 11:9). Origen views the "bond" as a reference to sinners in the Church.[168] The formation of the bond is a kind of act of defiance against God; it opposes what God has commanded in his plan for the Church. It threatens the covenant and is unworthy conduct.

In sum, God forms a covenant with a people, the Church. The contract involves responsibilities on both sides. From the side of the Church, the responsibility is to avoid sin and "works of death," while God's responsibility is to fulfill his promise, as evident in Jer. 11:4–5, where God promises to serve up a land "flowing with milk and honey."[169]

The Church's responsibilities, according to Origen, run parallel with God's expectations. Indeed God expects much more from the acts of the Church, and if she does not meet the standard, she receives double for her sins. This is the conclusion Origen reaches in Jer. 16:18, where God says, "And I will first recompense their wrongs doubly." The Church receives double compared with pagans because the Church knows God's will, whereas the pagans are ignorant. The entire exposition of Origen falls into a general context concerned with eschatology and judgment,[170] and especially with the question of how evil will be handled in the end.[171] According to Origen, Heb. 10:26–27 and Luke 12:47 confirm this rigorous punishment for those believers who sin.

On the one side, Christians will be punished more severely if they are not virtuous, but also, on the other side, they as the Church are to be prominent in their virtue. In fact, they are to stand out as examples to all those who surround the Church. This point of view is developed in his comments on Jer. 17:24–27. In these sentences, Jeremiah speaks about the blessings that will come upon Jerusalem if she will "hearken" to the Lord, that is, if she will turn to him. Origen sees the moral and spiritual position of Jerusalem as a reference to the Church.[172] All the locales and the gifts referred to in the scriptural text symbolize for him the different standards that the Church holds up beside those who come to praise her virtues. Instead of being weighed down with sin, Origen writes, let us emulate this image of Jerusalem that Jeremiah offers

... so that we may become "kings and rulers sitting" firmly "on the throne of David," the church of Christ. . . . But such persons also "ride on chariots and horses"—restraining the body and keeping back the irrational movements—so that the "city will be inhabited forever," and from every direction those who bear gifts "will come" to her because of the virtue of the leaders and the most excellent behaviour of the inhabitants. (Cf. James 3:2)[173]

Note here how Origen mentions the importance of restraining the body and the need to control the irrational, a clear reference to the other side of becoming a Christian, the side we discussed in Chapter 3. Note too how that side is combined in one text with the side of conduct under consideration in this chapter.

To clarify the "behavior" mentioned in the above text, Origen then details the meaning of each of the givers and the gifts: confession, peace of vision, humility, holy sacrifice, consecration of the soul, and purity. These are the qualities, based in Scripture, that for Origen dignify the Church as a community and make the leaders worthy of praise.[174] In light of these views, we can detect some pride in his rejoinder to Celsus when he rates the religious assembly (*ekklesia*) below the secular assembly. In fact, this passage is given in the context of conversion. In prior sentences, Origen clarifies that God intentionally, in the economy of conversion, differentiated his assembly from the secular assembly.

But the assemblies[175] of God which have become disciples to Christ, when contrasted with the assemblies of the districts in which they are situated, are as "beacons in the world" (Phil. 2:15). For who would not admit that even the inferior persons of the Church and those less worthy compared with the better [members] are more excellent than many of the assemblies in the districts?[176]

A more lengthy discussion of the exalted estimation of the Church is in Origen's commentary on John 2:21: "But he spoke of the temple of his body." Origen believes that deep mysteries are implied in this text, and proceeds to explore the meaning of "temple" and how the temple is built. As we have seen previously, the temple of Christ's body is the Church, and the temple is ". . . built from living stones, a spiritual house for a holy priesthood."[177] The construction of the earthly temple is described in 1 Kings 6. With this description before him, Origen then discusses the mystical meaning of each section of the temple with respect to the body of Christ, the Church. It is not necessary for our purposes to present the allegory, but we do need to note the way in which the stones that form the building are selected. Each section of the temple has a different function, and each of the stones is selected for each section according to its worth and conduct, and "the merit of his life here."[178] Hence one's place in the Church is determined by the merit of his life on earth, and the Church itself is something built up by those who have meritorious lives, each receiving a role or place in the structure.

This view presents the Church as a spiritual structure based upon a hierarchy of merit earned through how one has lived here, that is, how one has managed conduct and thought. Though we can assume that conduct would contribute to this merit, Origen does not specify in this context upon what the merit is based. In the following section, however, he points out that all of the "stones" are hewn and brought ready prepared to the proper place in the temple.[179] This view would lead us to believe that no sinner is permitted in the body of Christ, the Church.

Despite this rigorous image of the Church as one that exemplifies what is best and meritorious, Origen was not blind to the imperfections in the Church community. The Church is made up of a variety of people. What if one of these people sins? What will this sort of conduct do to her as presented above? How will it affect the spiritual journey? These are inevitable questions when we contrast the actual earthly Church with that community Origen calls "the land of God," "the house of the living God," and, as we just noted, "the body of Christ."[180] In fact, Origen is aware that the Church has both good and bad members, and that the good and bad are together in one community.[181] Yet this situation is not permanent, as Origen clarifies in his views on Jeremiah 27.

In Jeremiah 27, the Lord is revealing his intent to destroy the Babylonians and Chaldeans and to restore Israel, and Jeremiah says, at Jer. 27:25, "The Lord has opened his treasury and brought forth the vessels of his wrath." Origen is curious why the "vessels of wrath" exist at all in God's treasury. He finds a partial answer in Rom. 9:21–23, in which Paul indicates that God was patient with the vessels of wrath for the benefit of the vessels of mercy, but the significance of the "treasury" remains. What is the treasury that contains vessels of wrath?

> Perhaps it is the church in which such persons often escape notice. But there will be a time when he "opens" the church. For now it has been closed up, and the "vessels of wrath" share space with "vessels of mercy" (Rom. 9:23), and the "chaff" are with the "wheat" (Matt. 3:12, Luke 3:17), and in one "net" are the discarded and the chosen "fish" (Matt. 13:47–49). But the "Lord opens his treasury" in the time of judgment, when the "vessels of wrath" are "cast out" (cf. John 12:31), when he who is a "vessel of mercy" may reasonably say, "they have gone out from us, for they were not from us." (1 John 2:19)[182]

The Church then contains both vessels of wrath and vessels of mercy, and in the end-time, the vessels of wrath are cast out. Though the purpose of this casting out is not specified in the above fragment, the parallel Latin translation of Jerome indicates that the vessels of wrath, though in sin, can be near salvation and near the fire of purification, if they come near to Jesus. Also indicated in the Jerome translation (and in the Greek fragment) is a third kind of vessel, which sins outside the treasury and is inferior to the vessels of wrath. It receives a lesser salvation.[183]

The matter of sin in the Church is apparent also in Origen's interpretation of Jer. 15:10. Origen wants to show that Christ could say, "Woe's me, mother!" Hence he quotes Micah 7:1, "Woe's me, soul, for I have become as one gathering straw in the harvest." Since the prophet Micah would not "gather," according to Origen, this passage refers to Christ, who comes to gather the result of his plantings. He has planted a vine for fruit, but he gathers "straw," which is figuratively sin. He comes to the Church to harvest virtue, but instead he finds the sin of straw. At this point, then, Origen admits that Christ sees "the so-called churches filled with sinners. . . ."[184]

Origen even admits that lapses can occur in one who has attained a certain maturity. He comes to this conclusion when considering the story of Lucifer's fall, how Lucifer fell by free choice from a very exalted state to iniquity.

> So it can happen that in whatever condition the soul will be, and in whatever maturity of virtues, since virtue is changeable, a lapse can occur; so that just as one may incline from vices to virtue, so also one may incline from virtues to vices.[185]

So committed is Origen to this idea that he devotes an entire section of a homily to a list of texts from Scripture that verify the belief that the saint can sin. However, saints do differ from sinners in the fact that while sinners remain in their sin, saints do not. So penitence, in this context, becomes an act of holiness, and the name "saint" is a title given according to what one pursues, i.e., holiness, rather than a permanent condition that one has attained.[186]

This view of holiness and perfection, then, is another indication of Origen's understanding of spiritual movement as a vacillating process, now with respect to conduct; it is the movement toward the end that is the main concern of the saint, rather than a continuous perfect condition without sin.

It is evident from these texts not only that sinners are present in the Church, but that sin is a serious matter regardless of what stage one has reached in spiritual growth. The Church is not only a place for the saints to reach perfection, but a place for the "vessels of wrath," who will in the end be given to the purifying fire, and for other vessels who will receive a lesser salvation. All these vessels comprise the earthly Church. The kind of vessel one becomes in this process is determined in part by conduct. The Church, on the one hand, is to be an example of virtue and excellent behavior to all those around her, but, on the other hand, she has some members who "escape notice," according to Origen, who are cast out in the judgment for purification. But what of the sinner who does not escape notice?

It is important to clarify briefly what Origen means by being cast out from the Church before the end-time. This fate comes to those who do not escape notice, but are discovered and need to be disciplined. Origen presents the problem in his interpretation of Jer. 36:4–6:

> Thus said the Lord God of Israel concerning the settlement which I exiled from Jerusalem: Build houses and dwell in [them], and plant gardens and eat their fruits, and take wives and beget sons and daughters.

Jerusalem, as we have seen in other texts, is often interpreted by Origen as the Church, and he repeats this view in this passage. Then he writes concerning this place (Jerusalem/the Church): "And anyone who sins is cast out, even if he was not cast out by men."[187] Thus Origen speaks more universally here than in previous texts we have considered. Here he expels "anyone who sins" from the Church.

However, this expulsion need not be a permanent separation. According to what follows in this text, to reenter the Church one must fulfill the commands given symbolically in the Jeremiah text above. "Take wives" refers to taking up wisdom and the other virtues. Begetting "sons" refers to having holy thoughts and teachings, and begetting "daughters" to acts that arise from virtues.[188] Evidently these qualities are also what describe a good Church member, namely, one who attempts to think and act in accordance with wisdom and the other virtues. We need to note especially that Origen particularly refers to acts (*praxeis*) as an important dimension of one who is a good Church member.

Bad conduct is not only detrimental to the position of the Church member, but it also has, according to Origen, other adverse effects. One of these effects is clarified in his exposition of Jer. 13:14, "I will not spare and I will not feel pity from their destruction." Jeremiah 13, as stated previously, concerns God's punishment for Judah and Jerusalem. Heretics rashly conclude in their interpretation of this text, Origen says, that it refers not to the "good God" but to the demiurge. In fact, however, the text tries to explain how the one and only God punishes for the benefit of all. If God showed mercy indiscriminately or was too quick to pity, then the sinner, according to Origen, would not be completely cured and the community would continue to suffer from the corruption and lapse. Hence in such cases God uses a discipline more powerful than fear, namely, outright rejection, in order to safeguard the common welfare. In this context he states, ". . . in order to care for many, God does not "spare" one."[189] Because he is fully aware that a single member can soil the entire "body" of the Church, Origen prefers here rehabilitation outside rather than within the Church community.[190]

Return to the community after rehabilitation is always possible for Origen.[191] We have seen that a sinner who escapes notice in this earthly life will be finally rejected in the time of judgment for purification. Then we noted how even the known sinner is not rejected permanently; rather he must be severed from the body for the sake of the rest. The opportunity for reformation and forgiveness is left open in both cases. Origen's point, in light of the Jeremiah texts, is that God and the churches must often reject one because of sin, but the rejection is for purification and to safeguard the common welfare.[192] Indeed one dimension of Origen's thought, based on Rom. 11:11 and Prov. 19:25, is that punishment/rejection of a group or person is an educational process used by God to save others.[193]

For Origen even self-rejection can be a cure for the soul. The matter is discussed in his exposition of Jer. 45:17–20. In this chapter of Jeremiah, the prophet proposes to Zedekiah, king of Judah, who had sinned, that he could save himself and the city of Jerusalem if he would surrender himself to the king of Babylon.

Zedekiah refused and Jerusalem fell. In this story Origen sees an allegory concerning the sinner and the Church.

> If anyone who defiles the church should leave [her], he saves both her and his own soul. But if he is going to be like Zedekiah with respect to leaving, "a little leaven leavens the whole lump." (Gal. 5:9)[194]

We have seen, then, that the conduct of both the saint and the sinner has a marked effect on the nature and fate of the earthly Church. While the Church strives to be an example and the body of Christ, she is beset, through her members, by the complex problems that imperfection causes to arise, such as those of the unknown (the sinner of conscience) and the known sinner.

The double fall of the sinner and those who are corrupted by him is especially applicable to false teachers in the Church, who hurt not only the souls of others but their own souls.[195] In light of the above discussions on the expectations Origen has for the Church then, let us offer a concise account of what he expects of teachers and other leaders in the Church.[196]

(b) It will not be surprising to the reader of the prior part of this section that Origen is rigorous in his moral demands on the priests and leaders of the Church.[197] In his exposition of Jer. 12:13, for example, "their office[198] will not benefit them," Origen points out that moral and spiritual expectations are in proportion to one's position:

> Since then there are some in a [clerical] office who do not live in a way that "benefits" and adorns the office, for this reason it is written, "Their office will not benefit them," the expositors say. For to "benefit" is not the same as to assume a position with the elders, but to live in a way worthy of the position as the Logos requires. The Logos also requires you and us to live in a good manner. But if we were to say it another way, "the powerful will be tried in a powerful way" (Wisd. 6:6), more is required of me than the deacon, more of the deacon than the layman, yet even more is demanded of him who has been entrusted for all of us with the church's chief [office] itself.[199]

It appears clear from this text and others that a priest should not perform spiritual tasks, according to Origen, without personal moral worth. As he writes on the famous Matt. 16:18ff., if one claims the office of Peter, he must equal Peter to such an extent that it could be said to him, "You are Peter."[200] However, each office and each level of the Church has its responsibilities. The station of each person in the Church determines the demands made with respect to conduct. If the holder of the office or position does not fulfill the requirements of the office, he will be punished, and his punishment will be in proportion to his position also.

The exacting judgment awaiting each according to position is evident in Origen's views on Jer. 36:21, in which the Lord says he will deliver Achiab and Zedekiah into the hands of the king of Babylon. Origen believes that every elder who acts improperly is given over to the "king of Babylon," whom Origen understands symbolically as the devil.[201] Then he adds:

For if a person who partakes of the eucharist "unworthily" will receive "judgment" (cf. 1 Cor. 11:27–29), how much more will he who sits among the presbytery with a defiled conscience and who corrupts the council of Christ?[202]

These two texts will indicate, then, that Origen places priests and leaders of the Church on a more demanding level of conduct,[203] and that each will be judged, in terms of conduct, according to his position in the Church.

The above reference to a defiled conscience appears also in Origen's discussion of Matt. 15:17–20, where Jesus explains the meaning of the source of sin. This text gives Origen the opportunity to present those who are truly good in heart— and receive the corresponding reward from God—and those who appear good to men and hence receive their rewards from men. God judges the evil of men, according to Origen, not only by the works of men, but more importantly by the heart or mind that has generated the deeds. In sum, Origen states, if the motives are to impress humankind—the chief sins here are glory, flattery and gain—then one receives his due deserts from men, not from God.

And you will say the like in the case of him who seeks the office of a "bishop" for the sake of glory with men (cf. 1 Tim. 3:1), or, of flattery with men, or for the sake of gain received from those who, coming over to the Logos, give in the name of piety. . . . And the same also you will say about the elders and deacons. . . . Evil considerations are the spring of all sins, and can pollute even those actions which, if they were done apart from them [the evil considerations], might have justified the one who did [them].[204]

True service to the Church, as Origen states in his comments on the washing of the disciples' feet, depends on being in heart a servant, on doing acts of service to others, and on influencing others also to do them. In this way we are changed into a higher condition by God. The importance of example is particularly evident for the Church. Origen writes that the leaders of the Church should not imitate secular leaders, but Christ. He then continues to say that they should be accessible to all (women and children included), and they should learn from Christ, who washed his disciples' feet.

For through these acts, [Christ] taught his disciples to become imitators of his praiseworthy humility. And perhaps also since he who is Lord became a servant to our kind for the salvation of men, for this reason it is said that he took on the "form" of a servant" and humbled himself, becoming "obedient unto death." And if "God" through this [act] "highly exalted him" (Phil. 2:8–9), let him who wants to be "exalted" do likewise, so that by means of these [humble acts] he is "highly exalted."[205]

At least two important matters come to mind when considering this text. First, anyone who wishes to be highly exalted in the Church acts as another gateway to Christ by showing, through his own life and attitudes, the way through imitation. He imitates Christ, and the convert follows the Church leader. Humility is evidently one of the key dimensions of such a leadership and also a key catalyst in conversion. As we have seen previously, though Origen never demeans the divine gift of free will, he exalts those such as Moses and Paul who realize how unworthy they are before God and who recognize the true source of all good. This, then, is a humility that exalts, that is, that moves one up to another level of closeness to God.

Such an exaltation, in fact, points to another important matter that is evident from these texts. This matter concerns the interplay between being exalted and being highly exalted. There is here the same kind of correspondence between being great among men and being great with God. Some Church leaders were more interested in being great among men, their pride even exceeding that of secular leaders, their ambitions accomplished by intrigue, and their lives ruled by avarice, tyranny, lack of discipline, and impiety, resembling the vendors in the Temple (Matt. 21:12–13).[206] On the other hand, those who are humble, who prefer to serve rather than be served, who are accessible to all, and, above all, who are virtuous examples that others can imitate, such men exhibit the true qualities of a Church leader. And it is by means of such qualities that the people can profitably contribute to their own own conversion growth.

After all, a priest, according to Origen, is chosen by the people because he excels others in virtue and conduct. For example, in his homily on Leviticus 8, concerning the ordination of Aaron, Origen says that a priest should be "more excellent," "more learned," "more holy," and "more eminent in every virtue" among all the people.[207] Without exaggerating, then, we can state that for Origen the life of a priest or leader of the Church should be an inspiration to others, both Christian and non-Christian, to follow Christ. The Church leader is one who brings into clearer light the critical importance of the correspondence between Christ, the spiritual life, and the spiritual journey by exemplifying in conduct that which involves the service and work of Jesus Christ. Origen's view is summarized in his commentary on Matt. 23:5, "They do all their deeds to be seen by men."

> The disciples of Jesus, however, "do all their deeds to be seen by" God alone. For they "bind" the law of God "upon" their "hand," spiritually upon every good work, and through meditation upon the divine teachings, always promoting them, they make as "portable property"[208] the divine commands "before the eyes" of their souls and a full "fringe" of the virtue of Jesus, insofar as they imitate the master. (cf. Deut, 11:18)[209]

In contrast to the material bands and vestment fringes which, according to Jesus, the Jews wore to be seen by men, Origen focuses on the inner, spiritual items that are seen only by God. Christians' "phylacteries" and "fringes," noted by Matt. 23:25 as those worn by the scribes and Pharisees, are the spiritual laws upon which they meditate and the virtues.

Let us say, in concluding this subsection, that in Origen's thoughts on how the Church affects Christian behavior the Church has a pivotal role. We have discussed the beginnings of the Church in pre-existence, her intimacy with

Christ/Logos, her crucial covenant with God and her role as example to all, members and nonmembers alike. The Church is, in other words, an important catalyst in spiritual change and movement for everyone. The next subsection, in fact, is essentially also a consideration of the role of the Church, that is, in terms of her teaching function. And in Chapter 5 we shall discuss her again. In sum, all aspects of the spiritual journey are, for Origen, in some way related to her as Origen understands her. The Church is not only a home for the lost to find God, but also a community in which one can grow spiritually, despite lapses, and be inspired to greater heights until, in the end, one can be among the perfect who comprise the heavenly Church.

5.

Like an object that appears differently from different perspectives, the spiritual journey to become a Christian can be viewed in many ways in Origen, and each way can appear, without analysis, a complete image, as if there are no other sides. It is possible, for example, to view it in Origen as only a movement from one teaching or teacher to another, or perhaps, from one philosophical school to another, if we may be allowed to consider the community of Christians as a kind of school.[210] The concept of religious education in Origen touches on a number of key themes, i.e., the role of Scripture, the different needs of different kinds of people, correct preparation, free will, God the teacher, heresy, the position of non-Christian thought, and several others. The main concern in this subsection involves the importance of education to a change of conduct. The subsection is divided into four sections: (a) the person and task of the teacher, (b) pedagogical methodology, (c) the importance of the kind of teaching offered, and (d) a summary. So let us present the role of teacher and teaching with respect to the transformation of conduct in becoming a Christian.[211]

(a) With respect to the person and task of the teacher, here as in many other areas it appears that Origen was influenced by Scripture, particularly 1 Cor. 12:28, where it is written, "And God has appointed in the church first apostles, second prophets, third teachers. . . ."[212] This text, for example, is cited in Origen's long discussion of the feet-washing episode in John 13. Prior to the scriptural citation, Origen views Jesus' act of washing his disciples' feet as an act of teaching and preparing others to become like him, that is, to become sons and masters and teachers. The work of teaching, Origen writes, with Jesus as example, is to eliminate and purify from the pupils the earthly and inferior elements, the elements symbolized here by the feet, since they are far from the heart and in contact with the earth.[213] This commentary on John 13 is offered to indicate how highly Origen sets the teacher in the task of helping another become a Christian. In this commentary the teacher sets an example through the task of helping to cleanse the heart from earthly and inferior elements. In other words, as we shall discover in more detail as we continue, exemplary behavior, especially that which imitates Christ, causes a corresponding act in hearers or students that draws them closer and closer to the model of all virtuous conduct, Christ himself. This movement caused by example and attraction is a movement of spiritual growth.

The teacher's task is so important that it transcends that of other priests, as Origen clarifies in his discussion of Lev. 8:7, 13. Origen distinguishes in this text two kinds of priests: those who only perform liturgical tasks and those who can also instruct the people, just as Scripture distinguishes, according to Origen, between Aaron and the sons of Aaron in Leviticus 8. Origen says:

> Hence I think that it is one thing to perform in liturgical service with the priests, another to be instructed and distinguished in all [areas]. For anyone can perform in solemn functions before the people, but there are few who are distinguished in behavior, instructed in doctrine, trained in wisdom for clarifying the truth about things . . . . Thus, there is one name for a priest, but not one rank either for the worth of [his] life or for the virtues of [his] soul.[214]

It is clear from this text that the teacher is expected to surpass other priests in conduct and learning. Moreover, Origen directly connects the task of teaching the people with a distinguished behavior, involving a meritorious and virtuous life. A teacher influences his listeners not only by what he teaches, but also by his behavior. Both influence the listener to convert.

The demands on the teacher are a result of his calling. As a teacher from a very early age, Origen had seen the effect of good and bad teaching. He realized, as we shall discuss below, that the spiritual journey can, in some way, begin with what one reads and how one listens, if, that is, one is reading and listening to the right teaching and teacher. For Origen the greatest book of learning, wisdom, and mystery was by far the Holy Scriptures. It was the task of the teacher to unravel and explore these profound books. Hence let us turn next to a brief discussion of the task of the teacher with respect to doctrine and scripture.

We have already considered some aspects of the role of Scripture in Chapter 3. There its converting power was seen in the Logos. Here we shall be considering Scripture from the view of the teacher and preacher, namely, the one who interprets Scripture for the people, and how he can contribute to one's spiritual growth. From the view of the teacher, teaching is a quest for the truth, and that truth is found in the Church and the spiritual goods of the Church, the Holy Scriptures.

One of the basic tasks of the teacher/preacher is to call men into the bastion of truth, the Church. This fact arises in Origen's comments on Jer. 4:5, "Blow the trumpet over the land. Assemble and let us go into the fortified cities." The Logos, Origen says, is a "trumpet" that ". . . arouses the hearer, prepares him for the 'war' against the passions, for the war against the opposing powers, prepares him for heavenly 'feasts' . . . (cf. Num. 10:9–10).[215] Then Origen points out that the Logos commands him and others—whoever desires and seeks for the sense of Scripture—to make "beaten silver trumpets." (Num. 10:2). In this context of Numbers 10, the Lord tells Moses to sound beaten trumpets in times of assembly and war so that the people will be gathered together. If Moses will do this, then the people will be saved from their enemies. Moses is also instructed to continue to sound the trumpet at feasts in order to recall the times of their salvation.

Origen interprets this text symbolically. As already noted, he views the trumpet as the Logos, and the preacher as the one who sounds the trumpet by seeking the meaning of Scripture. Then Jeremiah adds that all should assemble and go into the "fortified cities." Origen understands the purpose of the trumpet to be to bring men into a fortified city, namely, the Church of God, for that is where the Logos of God wants us to be.[216] It is the interpreter of Scripture who sounds the trumpet, the Logos, for the war against the passions and brings the hearer into the Church, where truth resides. If the hearer does not enter the "fortified city," the Church, he must contend with the devil, whom Origen recognizes as the "lion" in the scriptural text (Jer. 4:7).[217] The entrance here of the devil is not merely a matter of our doing sin. The devil actively tempts us, according to Origen, to do sin. And one of the devil's many baits is through a process of verbal deception.[218] According to these texts, man is, on the one hand, invited into the church by the teacher, who lures through the truth, or, on the other hand, man is drawn, on account of his weakness for diversion, through the devil's bait, to false teachings. The teacher of true doctrine, then, constantly stands in a pivotal position in terms of the direction toward which each person conducts him/herself.

The same applies to those in the devil's company, namely, false teachers. Understandably, Origen lists a rather large variety of such imposters in his works, since he sees them as his opponents. In his commentary on Matt. 15:14, concerning blind guides, he urges his reader to be vigilant in detecting the blind ones who are more in need of guides themselves, especially with respect to Scripture.[219]

The heretics and false prophets would be included in this group. In his exposition of Jer. 3:6, concerning the apostasy of Israel, who "fornicated" under a "timber tree" rather than a "fruit-bearing" one, Origen views the planting of fruitless trees as analogous to the rhetoric of the heretics, which bears no fruit and does not transform listeners.[220] The teacher converts by what he says and by how he says it. Insincere behavior and style is incapable of reaching the heights necessary for conversion. Similarly, in Ezekiel 13, a chapter concerned with false prophets whom Ezekiel is commanded to oppose, Origen finds an example of the eloquent but false and ineffectual teacher. Origen especially views the kerchiefs that cover the head, mentioned in Ezek. 13:18, as symbols of the veils that eloquent speakers use to hide the truth through charm.[221]

Two kinds of false teachers who do not change others appear before us in these texts. First, in contrast to those teachers who try through their conduct and through Scripture to turn men to the truth of God in the Church, there are the heretics or those who hold unorthodox opinions who divert their listeners into the lap of the devil. They persuade their hearers away from rather than toward God. Second, there are those who appear to be men of God through their works and lectures, but who merely charm and dazzle without effect on the conduct or vices of their hearers.[222] For Origen it is evidently a sign of the true teacher that he will morally improve his listeners.

Origen is equally critical of teachers who, like the false prophets who "steal" God's words in Jer. 23:30 and in Rom. 2:21, teach with dishonest and defiled souls. They teach from Scripture, but they take what is not justly theirs.[223] Likewise, in his comments on Jer. 22:14–17, where Jeremiah describes the "house" and the fate of the one under judgment, Origen attacks the evil person in the Church who spreads false teachings. For such a teacher builds houses in the name of the Church, but in truth he knows neither Christ nor righteousness.[224] And also Origen attacks the teacher who treats his art as a trade, selling the truth for a fee. Since such a one is bartering the Holy Spirit, he, in company with others Jesus evicted, should be chased out of the Temple of God (cf. Luke 19:45).[225]

All of these examples of bad teachers have in common at least one quality: pretense.[226] Such teachers are either teaching what is false and trying to convince others of its truth by rhetoric or other means, or the teacher himself is somehow unworthy or misusing the word. These examples are quite clear. But pretense can be very elusive and hidden. Though Origen does warn his listeners and readers repeatedly about the guile of the heretics, false prophets, and false teachers, he also describes the common and more troublesome cases where a man's teaching is false, but his conduct is good, and where the teaching is good and the conduct bad.[227] Both of these situations are discussed in his exposition of Ezek. 16:18–19:

And you took your embroidered apparel, and covered them [idols], and set before them my oil and my bread which I gave you, [and] likewise also the honey and oil I fed you. (from the Old Latin translation)

The narrative in the Ezekiel text concerns the constructing and adorning of idols, and placing side by side with them God's oil, incense, and bread. The juxtaposition of idols alongside the holy things of God is viewed by Origen as an image of what heretical and other false teachers do. He mentions specifically the so-called Gnostics Marcion, Basilides, Valentinus, and their disciples. Such teachers clothe themselves with the "apparel" of good conduct, but their words and their teachings lead astray. They first construct their false teachings, their "idols," then they clothe them with the "embroidered apparel" of good conduct, and then they try to defend them with the "bread" of the prophets and the "honey" of the gospels.[228] Origen also describes in this homily the case of the Church teacher who teaches good doctrine, but acts improperly. And here Origen refers to Matt. 23:1–3 as his source. In such a situation, Origen recommends that we should follow the good teachings and ignore the conduct. He does not exempt even himself from the lessons taught in Matthew 23.

This should be your charge, people: If you have not had [someone] accuse [me] of bad teaching and doctrines alien to the church, you do not have to base your life on the way I live, but to do what I say. Let us imitate no one, and, if we want to imitate anyone, it was intended for us to imitate Christ Jesus.[229]

It would be useful for us to recall, before we continue, the subsection above on the imitation of Christ, and especially how the imitation of any of Christ's imitators is, in fact, an imitation of Christ. Moreover, in that subsection, we saw how imitation of Christ is a movement progressing toward a better and better conduct, toward an inner ideal (for Christ is virtue itself) and outer model. In the above text, Origen consistently stresses the inner ideal and model of Christ expressed in the teacher's words, not his acts, as long as those words conform to the true teachings of the Church. Since he includes himself in this group, Origen intends to distinguish the imperfect but sincere Church teacher from the teacher of pretense presented above. Whereas the latter is to be suspected, we are to "do" what the former teaches.

It is clear that in each of the above texts the focus is on teaching to the inner man. And this fact follows from previous discussions. For Origen stresses above all the change of the heart, and a conduct that such a heart would generate. The teacher, through the Logos, addresses this heart directly. The false teacher corrupts this heart regardless of behavior.

A teacher has certain basic tasks that appear often in Origen's writings. Yet most of these tasks center in some way around Scripture and its interpretation. It has already been noted that Origen calls himself an ambassador for Scripture, and one who blows the trumpet, the Logos, calling men into the fortified city, the Church. Origen also believed that not only teachers, but every person who wants to be a disciple of Christ should follow the advice given in Scripture itself, where it is written that we all should "give heed to reading, exhortation and teaching" (1 Tim. 4:13), we should "search the scriptures" (John 5:29), even though it will require "long hours of working," and we can progress by "meditating in the law of the Lord day and night" (Ps. 1:2).[230] Origen also states:

And we therefore, if we wish to know about the secret and hidden things of God, if we are men of desires and not contentious, must search with faith and with humility for those judgments of God hidden deeply in the divine writings. That is why the Lord used to say, "Search the scriptures!" (John 5:39). He knew that these [secrets] were not uncovered by those who, with their minds full of other affairs, hear and read in a casual way, but only by those who, with an upright and guileless heart, with the yoke of toil, with long hours of working, search deeply into the divine scriptures—among whom I know well that I am not one.[231]

The implication of the final statement, that even Origen himself, who perhaps contemplated and wrote on Scripture more than any figure in history, felt inadequate with respect to the devotion Scripture requires, testifies to the extraordinary position the Scripture holds in Origen's view of man's spiritual growth.

Whether we grow from hearing Scripture from a teacher or from our own meditations, Scripture has a key role in every dimension of religious education. And its secrets will not be unveiled easily. We will have to toil continuously with a pure heart before the mysteries inherent in Scripture will begin to teach us about divine things. In fact, the very act of searching the Scriptures is a dimension of conduct.

Still the teacher's function, with respect to Scripture, is even more intense than others'. By means of the Logos in Scripture, the teacher can save, reprove, continually enlighten (if the message is fresh), and guide conduct, all tasks which directly determine the spiritual progress. Before we can document these views, however, we need to offer a couple of texts that clarify in more detail the relation of Scripture and conduct.

The close connection of Scripture and conduct is made especially clear in Origen's exposition of Jer. 3:7-10, which concerns how Israel and Judah became faithless, failed to turn to God, and God gave them a "book of divorce." As a result, the captivity and exile occurred. Origen sees in this text a pertinent lesson for contemporary Christians: If God did not spare Israel and Judah, why should he spare us? Learn from Scripture! Origen pleads:

> . . . let us read the scripture, let us see who was justified, who was not; let us imitate the ones who were justified, let us prevent ourselves from falling in those things by which those made captive, those cast away by God, have fallen.[232]

However, Judah is worse in God's eyes than Israel, for Judah saw all that Israel did and what happened to her, and still did not turn. "And for all these things perverse Judah turned not to me with her whole heart, but in pretense" (Jer. 3:10). True Christian change must be with the whole heart. If one does not fully turn, Origen says, then he too is accused and receives a book of divorce.[233] But those who do turn have learned from those powerful spiritual catalysts, the old and new books, the Scriptures. These are books not of divorce, but of turning and belonging to God, and they are based, in the end, in an action, in conduct.

> The true conversion[234], therefore, is to read the old [books], to see those who were justified, to imitate them, to read those [books] to see those who were reproached, to guard oneself from falling into those reproaches, to read the books of the New Testament, the words of the apostles; after reading, to write all these things into the heart, to live in accordance with them, lest a "book of divorce" is also given to us.[235]

Scripture then provides examples that we are to follow in turning to God. The reader takes the lessons and examples from the figures in the books of Scripture into his heart, and then acts in accordance with them. These examples and how they lived form a kind of library of directives based, of course, in the Logos of God.[236]

There are then three dimensions of the change, with respect to Scripture, for one becoming a Christian, as it is expressed in this text. First, Origen bids his listeners to read the Scripture and then see (come to some understanding of) who are worthy imitating and why. From this reading, a set of qualities and a way of life emerge. Second, these qualities and principles of the worthy ones of Scripture are to be impressed on the heart so that the whole heart is changed. Third, these qualities are to be enacted in one's conduct. In other words, we are not only to read about and understand the ways of the saints, but we are to imitate them in our lives. Hence there are inner and outer dimensions of the same process. Scripture stands in the very center.

Now that we have considered the role of Scripture, let us return to a consideration of the task of the teacher in this process.

Not everyone is capable from the start of understanding, according to Origen, all the dimensions and mysteries of Scripture. We have already noted this perspective in the prior discussions of Scripture and its levels of interpretation. Hence the teacher becomes at the basic level a guide for those not yet advanced. In his exposition of Jer. 16:16, "behold I am sending many fishers, and they shall fish for them," the "fishers," Origen says, are those who throw the net, the words of Scripture, around the souls of the hearers, so that they are saved from the sea, the home of the demons, and its harsh waves. They are then brought out of the sea, die to the world, and revived to a new life, with a changed, more divine soul, by the Logos of God.[237] It is then the teachers, the disciples of Jesus whom we discussed above, who weave a net of scriptural texts to save the soul from the sea and help to transform it. A similar task is set out for the preacher in Origen's comments on Ezek. 13:18: "Woe to those who sew cushions under every elbow of the hand" (partially from the Old Latin). Origen interprets "those who sew" as teachers who use "cushions"—empty rhetoric and words their hearers want to hear—in order to win them to Christianity.[238] The proper work of the teacher is to point out the toil that must go into a virtuous life and to consider carefully what will turn one to salvation, self-control, and good conduct for the listener:

> For the Logos of God and the man of God should utter what makes for his hearer's salvation, what encourages him to self-control, to a life of sound conduct, to everything for which a man intent upon labor not lust should exert himself, that he may succeed in obtaining what God has promised.[239]

The teacher/preacher then carefully guides his hearers in order to keep the convert's mind intent upon what benefits him. As we have seen in other sections, conversion is a progressive yet vacillating process with times of self-control and good conduct along with times of lapses. The teacher tries to keep one on the virtuous road so that the hearer will in the end be prepared to receive the promises. The teacher's task is to consider carefully what turns one, by means of Scripture, toward salvation, self-control and good conduct. In all matters of conduct, he points to the examples given in Scripture itself, with Christ alone being the only true earthly and spiritual model worthy of imitation.

(b) Now that we have viewed the general task of the teacher, let us turn to a discussion of his method.

Since the teacher's primary teaching aid is Scripture, it is important, according to Origen, that the teacher strive to present his interpretation in fresh ways as often as possible. If he is going to teach, he must not use old fare, but ever seek and probe for the truths present in the text. These conclusions arise for Origen in his reflections on Lev. 7:5, where it is written, concerning sacrificial flesh, that it is to be "eaten that day; it is not be left until the morning."[240] The effect the teacher has upon his hearers then depends also upon the way he approaches his task, and especially, with respect to this text, the depth of insight and the extent of his quest for the spiritual. The literal interpretation and the fossilized perspectives of yesterday can become sterile and decayed without constant renewal and rediscovery.

Beside seeking fresh approaches and interpretation, the teacher must also use a method relative to the audience. For example, Origen believed that the process of growth was at certain points like recuperating from wounds or a sickness, and that each person is more or less in a process of healing from the sickness of sin, depending on their progress. This insight into the different spiritual conditions of man encouraged Origen to examine carefully the proper method that would apply to each person.[241] We encountered his ideas on the different needs in another context, and a similar line of thought would be applicable here. Let us, then, document this method in terms of the teacher.[242]

The basic image of spiritual progress as a process that wends toward making one whole and healthy is found in Origen's commentary on Jer. 3:25:

> Therefore we and our fathers were sinning in the presence of our God from our youth until this day, and we did not listen to the voice of the Lord our God.

Origen detects in this statement by the prophet concerning the apostasy and sin of Israel references to a period of time in which Israel wanted to listen and had partially turned, but did not respond immediately to God's voice and had not turned completely.

> For it is not the case that as soon as we want to listen, we all at once do actually "listen." For just as there is time required for wounds up to their healing, so it is also for conversion up to when we completely and purely turn to God.[243]

Naturally the time required for the healing from sin will vary with the person. These variations create a problem for the teacher. Many, for example, want to listen, but are unprepared to understand what they are hearing. Different levels, then, as we shall see in more detail below, demand different spiritual nourishment. The teacher must know how to handle these different conditions and what spiritual food with respect to interpretation and exhortation must be given. Hence the teacher uses different examples, different methods, and even different texts (and biblical books) for each pupil. In the extreme case, he will even deceive someone if, that is, the prospect is prejudiced against some doctrines of the Christians. In such a case, the teacher will simply claim that the idea is not Christian in order to lure the non-Christian hearer; just as Jeremiah would say, depending on his audience, "thus says the Lord" or "hear the words of Jeremiah."[244]

In order to clarify how the teacher must consider the preparation of his audience, Origen often illustrates the heart of the hearer by the biblical image of the field. For example, the teacher as a maker of fields in the Church is noted by Origen in his consideration of Num. 18:12, Rom. 16:5, 1 Cor. 16:15, and other texts that use the expressions "first-fruits," and those who are "first." It is these "first-born" and those chosen "first" whom the teacher tries to cultivate in his Church-fields.[245] The teacher as a tiller of fields arises also in Origen's exposition of Jer. 4:3:

> Thus says the Lord to the men of Judah and to the inhabitants of Jerusalem: Break up their fallow ground and sow not among thorns.

Origen states that this text is directed to teachers. It shows how the teacher must avoid teaching difficult doctrines to those with "thorns" and "fallow ground" in their hearts. He must not entrust certain mysteries too soon to students who have not ploughed their hearts and made the soil beautiful and good (cf. Luke 9:92, Matt. 13:8, and Luke 8:8).

> But if prior to the plow and prior to the working of fallow ground in the heart[247] of the hearers, a [teacher] should take the holy seeds—the teaching[248] concerning the Father, the teaching concerning the Son, the teaching concerning the Holy Spirit, the teaching concerning the resurrection, the teaching concerning the punishment, the teaching concerning the repose,[249] what concerns the law, what concerns the prophets, and in general of each of the scriptural books—and sow [them], he transgresses the command which said first, "Break up their fallow ground," and, second, "and do not sow among thorns."[250]

The discussion in these texts concerning the heart may seem incongruous with our general reflection on conduct, but, in fact, two matters need to be kept before our minds: First, as we have discussed previously, conduct is intimately involved with the state of the heart. If the heart is not prepared and nourished properly, its condition will be incapable of generating good acts. So the teacher presents examples of the right teaching at the proper point in one's growth in order to encourage a healthy recuperation, which, in turn, will bring the strength for good conduct. Second, since Origen himself is constantly mixing his discussions on the heart with discussions of conduct and moral behavior, it would be inaccurate to attempt, at all points, to separate so rigidly the dimensions. Conduct, pedagogy, and the state of the heart are all interdependent for Origen, and are all contributing factors in the process by which one becomes a Christian.

So the biblical image of the uncultivated field is used by Origen to explore one aspect of the teacher's method, namely, that the teaching of God as seeded in the Scriptures should be sown only when the heart is ready, and the mysteries should be revealed only when the soul is prepared by ploughing and is cultivated.

A dimension of Origen's concern for the preparation of the soul involves purity and an uncontaminated environment. Such concerns apply especially well to our considerations offered in Chapter 3. For the teacher is not simply imparting human ideas; he is sowing the divine seed, the Logos of God, the Logos who is in Scripture and who holds the mysteries of Scripture, the Logos *of God*. Thus, to sow such a one in the heart requires care. Origen states this concern for purity in his exposition of Lev. 21:13-14, concerning the kind of spouse the chief priest must select. Origen had previously shown that the priest here is figuratively Christ and the spouse is the soul.[251] Christ does not receive as a spouse a "harlot" or those who take "lovers" (cf. Ezek. 16:28, 33), whom Origen considers opposing powers and demons. These evil powers desire the beauty the soul was given by God, namely, the image and likeness of God (Gen. 1:26). Accepting a harlot is accepting the devil and his spirits, the spirits of anger, pride, unchasteness and envy.[252]

Through the use of various images such as the thorn, the fallow ground, the harlot, and contamination, Origen provides a vivid picture of the obstacles the teacher must lessen if the deeper lessons of the faith are to be given and the process of becoming a Christian is to continue properly. In brief, he must attend to the needs of his hearers in order to prepare the heart for future mysteries. Ever watchful of the progress of his pupils, the teacher brings them along—in essence, gradually reorients and purifies them—so that they all can receive the most profound levels of God's Logos. In this task and method, his opponents are evidently the evil powers, who also wish to direct the soul and turn it *away* from the Logos.

In light of these comments above, we can more easily appreciate why Origen reacts firmly, basing his defense on 1 Cor. 3:1-3 and Heb. 5:12-14, when Celsus accuses the Christians of doing just the opposite, that is, of exhibiting their secrets to anyone in the marketplace.[253] The mention of these two biblical texts is an indication of the Pauline two-level view of scriptural nourishment that Origen believes is useful for teachers, namely, "milk" for beginners and "solid food" for the advanced. These two levels of nourishment are often, however, expanded to three in order to include those neither beginners nor advanced. Let us present briefly a couple of examples of Origen's understanding of the three-level approach.

The two-level approach, noted by Origen whenever he cities 1 Cor. 3:2 and Heb. 5:12-14, is expanded to three through the additional reflections primarily on Rom. 14:2, where it is written that the "weak man eats only vegetables." For example, we find discussions of this approach in his homilies on Leviticus, Numbers and Joshua.

Lev. 1:6-9 describes the act in which the Aaronic priest divides the offering into pieces and lays it on the altar. The division of the victim, according to Origen, is figuratively understood as the separate portions the teacher gives to those who are beginners, those who have made some progress, and those who are mature. The priest in the text is the one ". . . who draws away the veil of the letter from God's word. . . ."[254] Then Origen states, in light of the scriptural texts noted above, that the "children" are nourished on milk, ". . . those who are weak in faith . . ." are restored with vegetables, and the "athletes of Christ" are fed on solid food.[255]

The text from the homily on Leviticus states in a general way the three major stages of one's progress in faith. However, in a preface to one of his homilies on Numbers, Origen gives one indication of how these levels are practically applied for the Christian. We have seen above how the teacher tends to leave certain matters unexplained until the soul is prepared. Most of the teacher's concern centers on understanding the various dimensions of Scripture. In order to clarify and organize the Scripture according to the various levels, Origen divides the scriptural books according to their relative difficulty. He attempts to substantiate his groupings by drawing an analogy between the physical and spiritual worlds. For just as each creature needs in a physical way certain basic nutritional needs, so also she or he has certain spiritual needs and nourishment. He then concludes:

> Every rational nature must be fed on food that is right and proper for it. Now the true food of a rational nature is the Logos of God. But as we just pointed out above many differences with respect to physical nutriment, so also not every rational nature—which, as we said, is fed with reason and the Logos of God—is nourished with one and the same word.[256]

Hence Scripture falls into three levels of "food." Leviticus and Numbers are among the most difficult, and are only for mature folk; the gospels, Psalms, and the letters of the apostles are for those infirm in faith; and Esther, Judith, Tobias, and Wisdom are for those still children in faith.[257] This organization responds to those who find certain sections of Scripture obscure and reject them. If some book of Scripture is too difficult, Origen believes, it probably means we are not ready spiritually to comprehend its mysteries. Each needs to recognize his level and ". . . turn the eyes of the mind toward him who commanded that these things be written . . ." so that he may nourish and heal each soul according to its needs.[258]

It should be noted that Origen views the progress from one level to another as an act of turning toward God. The teacher, as we have mentioned previously, is only an agent or catalyst of the turning. He presents the proper example according to the need of his audience, but the hearer himself turns to God and God is the one who nourishes and advances him toward greater mysteries.

Finally, the three levels are evident in Origen's exposition of Josh. 9:8, but here the three kinds of food are applied to four orders of men.[259] This passage describes how Joshua reads all the law of Moses to the "children of Israel, to women and children and the strangers who joined themselves to Israel." Each receives according to capacity. "Women" are "weak" and are fed vegetables, children are recent in the faith and are thus fed with "milk," proselytes, catechumens who want to join the faith, are also fed milk, and all, of course, strive to be the mature, who can grasp the spiritual mysteries.[260]

In whatever way Origen considers the matter, whether by means of two or three kinds of food, the teacher who presents and meditates on the Scripture needs to consider all these possibilities in his approach.[261] His purpose, especially with respect to spiritual growth, is to say what will reach each soul primarily through the examples given in Scripture. And through these examples, as we saw above in our consideration of Scripture and conduct, we can learn what is right with God and live according to it. But how Scripture is presented is a complex problem that Origen tried to alleviate through the two and three level forms of nourishment suggested by Paul.

Practically, his method meant either explaining a text in different ways or dividing the Scripture into various groupings according to profundity and difficulty of comprehension. It meant careful preparation of each hearer and an attempt to monitor his progress as closely as possible. This method would obviously require sensitivity and insight into the spiritual needs of students. Since everyone is at various stages, as we discussed above, the function of this scriptural education is to turn every soul as far as possible on earth toward Christ so that Christ is formed in the faithful. No one on earth is without need for such an education. Therefore, saints, beginners, and those weak but struggling in faith are all being converted, in thought and conduct, by their studies and meditation on Scripture through both a teacher and their own efforts. Each according to his own level becomes aware of the Scripture mysteries and imitates the examples offered by it. Let us stress again, in light of the subject of this chapter, that one of the critical rewards from the study of Scripture, particularly through the help of a teacher, is in imitating the examples that Scripture presents.

Another aspect of the teacher's method concerns his use of nonscriptural material to attract and train converts. Origen discusses the use of such materials in many contexts, but the most personal example would appear to be an extant letter traditionally thought to be addressed to Gregory Thaumaturgus, and preserved in Greek in Chapter 13 of the *Philocalia*. The main principle arising from this document is that, though Origen allows for the use of nonscriptural and non-Christian learning, he firmly places it in the service of Scripture and particularly in what is best for the service of God. And the touchstone of all study is prayer, which we will consider in more detail in Chapter 5. Fundamentally, it is to meditation and prayer that the Christian, whether teacher or student, must turn if he is to progress properly in Christian gnosis and the conduct that always arises from such learning. And, lest we forget, the "principle of learning," as Origen explains elsewhere, of knowledge human and divine, is centered in the nature—human and divine—of Christ.[262]

Hence even non-Christian or nonscriptural ways and learning have as their source, if they turn men to God, Christ, and Christ is the catalyst by which they can change and become Christians. As we have seen on several occasions, Christ is absolutely all virtues, indeed virtue itself, but he is also the wisdom of God. Since Christ is the Logos, and the Logos is discovered in Scripture and the Church, it is not unexpected that all nonscriptural material and doctrines outside the Church would have to be tested in service to Scripture and the Church before they could be useful for the one who wishes to know, and conduct himself in a way pleasing to, God. With this qualification, such material and the moral lessons they offer can be of great significance in one's spiritual journey.

Origen's willing but cautious and critical use of non-Christian material is also evident in *Against Celsus*, a work in which Origen, in order to answer effectively Celsus's charges against the Christians, must compare Christian and non-Christian sources.[263] But Origen also considers the matter in his homilies. For example, concerning Ex. 18:24, "And Moses listened to the voice of his father-in-law, and did whatever he said to him," Origen points out that we too, like Moses, should not reject something because of the speaker, even if he is a Gentile like Moses' father-in-law Jethro. Rather we ought to give ear to the words of all wise men, and do as the Apostle says, "test everything; hold fast to what is good" (1 Thess. 5:21). Origen cries out at those teachers and clergy who will not even listen to another Christian, let alone a pagan![264]

Not only do we sense Origen's openness to what is wise and good, regardless of its source, but we also see clarified, first, how important doctrine or teaching was to a person's Christianity. Origen criticizes the conduct of those who reject others for pretentious reasons. Then Origen underlines again the humility of Moses as a model for us, a model taught in Scripture. Hence the method to seek out wisdom from all sources—for to Origen wisdom is one, the Logos of God—is a method interlaced with how one behaves, especially in the texts above, with humility and prayer. In fact, failing to seek out and understand other manifestations of wisdom and failing to seek advice from all wise sources are both the result of the sin of pride and pretension.

Origen's method in preparing students and using non-Christian material was used by himself in his school at Caesarea, according to the *Oration* and *Panegyric* written by one of his students.[265] It is not practical for us to describe this glowing tribute to Origen the teacher in detail.[266] In fact, there is much in this work that we have already discussed elsewhere.[267] Origen was apparently an outstanding teacher because of his patience and care and his way of carefully preparing his student's soul before the next, more advanced level was attempted. We know that both the Alexandrian and Caesarean schools prospered well under his direction and methodology. He was a man who tried to know the personal character and needs of each of his students in order to introduce him properly and securely to divine studies and the Christian path. In these accounts, the writer continuously refers to Origen's love, kindness, and friendship, as well as his powers of mind and spirit. But above all these compliments on his method, he found that Origen was most impressive because of his behavior and way of life. It is his conduct rather than his ideas and methodology that wins the student to the Christian religion. Origen, we are told, set high standards as a model and example of a Christian, moving his student to yearn to imitate that model.

The *Oration* reveals a student who made progress by his studies with Origen at Caesarea, but Origen does not hesitate to discuss those whom the teacher cannot as yet turn for various reasons.

One reason, for example, is stubbornness. In his exposition of Jer. 15:10, Origen points out that prophets and teachers are often like physicians who have obstinate patients.[268] Such patients flee from physicians and avoid the instruments of healing because they fear the pain that comes with the passage of health.[269] Jeremiah bewails his suffering in Scripture because of the abuse he receives from such patients. Though God sent him, Origen says, to a sick people ". . . to turn back those who do evil . . . ," they refused to hear him.[270] So Jeremiah says,

Woe is me, my mother, for what did you bear me, a man judged and questioned throughout the land? I have not helped, nor has anyone helped me.

The final sentence intrigues Origen. He notes that the original Hebrew has "I have not owed, no one has owed me." So Origen proceeds to interpret both versions. The first, the Greek translation, refers primarily to the task of the one who is a kind of physician, while the Hebrew, according to Origen, centers around the failing of him who receives help. From both texts Origen develops, in light also of the obstinate pupil, a doctrine of pedagogical reciprocity. Let us summarize his conclusions with respect to both texts.

As a kind of physician Jeremiah offered help, but no one was helped by his words and, equally important, he himself received no "fruits" from those he was sent to help.

Perhaps on account of the courtesy of the one "helped" toward the one who has helped, there is a reciprocity, so that the speaker too comes to be helped, for "blessed is the one who speaks into the ears of those who hear" (Sir. 25:9). Thus a teacher could be benefited by this help from his audience, if they progress and become better; he could derive benefit by "having fruits" (Rom. 1:13) in them. [And when he does not have this (help) from the Jews, Jeremiah says,][271] "No one has helped me."[272]

Thus, the teacher fails to be benefited when a student or proselyte is obstinate and refuses to be helped. For teachers do benefit from intelligent and alert students, and lecturers become better when their hearers go beyond the words and inquire into the meaning of what is said. But above all the teacher derives benefit when he is the agent of someone's progress and ultimate happiness.[273] For just as in a courteous gesture, the student will return a kindness with a kindness. The entire process, through the ideas of helping, progressing and bettering someone, is a catalyst of change. This is then Origen's interpretation of the LXX Greek text.

With the respect to the Hebrew text, Origen points out that when Jeremiah writes that "no one owes me," he indicates that no one had bought from him any of his "spiritual goods." For when one receives something, he becomes, in a sense, a debtor. But the Jews took and received nothing from Jeremiah; hence they did not owe the prophet.[274]

With respect to spiritual growth, the reciprocity that is evident in both texts adds an important dimension to Origen's view of the teacher. For in some sense that Origen does not explore here in detail, the teacher derives benefits from his role. When he does not receive such benefits, or when he is not owed, then no progress is occurring. Thus, Christian education is a mutual process, involving, at the level of the teacher-student relationship, various kinds of reciprocity in which both the helper and the helped can benefit. Regardless how effectively one teaches, or how obstinate the pupil may be, the teacher does not complete his role until a reciprocity arises.

In another text concerning Ezek. 15:1–8, which compares Jerusalem to the useless wood of the vine, good only for burning, Origen considers the vine useless only if it does not bear fruit. He then compares the preacher to the vine, and the fruit to salvation, implying that the teacher/preacher is rendered useless and less honorable if salvation does not occur.[275]

Nevertheless, despite these statements describing a kind of reciprocity, Origen may place the blame for a lack of progress on the student alone, exempting in these contexts the teacher. This view agrees, of course, with Origen's belief in free choice and responsibility. His views on this matter arise in his commentary on Jer. 5:3–5:

> And they did not want to turn. And I said: These are perhaps the poor, because they do not want to know the way of the Lord and the judgment of God. I will go to the strong and I will speak to them.

(c) In his commentary on this text, we also have the opportunity to consider the final aspect of this subsection, namely, Origen's view of the role of doctrine itself as a force in becoming a Christian. It is interesting, for example, that Origen relates the unwillingness to change with being uninstructed and not receiving teaching.[276]

> Since [Jeremiah] understood these things concerning those neither willing to be instructed nor thinking about the scourges of God (cf. Jer. 5:3), he said, once he had thought about the cause of these things: "their soul is poor."[277]

Jeremiah seeks out the "strong" soul. Origen here defines the strong soul primarily in terms of conduct.

> For whenever anyone applies himself to great things and has worthwhile goals and considers always what is necessary—how he might live in accordance with right reason— wanting and heeding nothing abject and small, such a one has [something] strong and great in his soul.[278]

On the other hand, the poor soul, which Jeremiah describes as one that resists change and will not listen to the Logos, is one that will not receive what is said by the priest. "It is not so much a fault with those who speak as with those who hear. . . ."[279] The strong soul receives instruction, listens and "wants to turn," but the poor soul does not want instruction, does not want to listen, and does not want to turn.[280]

Hence we see that it is the responsibility of the Christian to listen and seek instruction for his own good. To turn implies, for Origen, to listen and learn and act from instruction and upon what one has learned. So the strong soul who does listen and does accept instruction is one whose practices and goals are in accord with reason and with "great things." The key principle here, it would appear, is that what one receives rather than the speaker is the important catalyst for change. It is the teaching rather than the teacher, the "way of the Lord and the judgment of God," that the "poor" resist. And one of the key factors in determining whether one will receive the teaching is the need to conduct oneself in accord with right reason. Conduct, the teaching, and the potential for becoming a Christian are interdependent.

The stress on the need for right teachings is also mentioned in Origen's exposition of Jer. 24:6, a text that concerns the Lord's promise "to restore" the Jews after the captivity, and to "build them up" and not "pull them down," to "plant" them and not "pluck them." This biblical image of God as a builder and gardener inspires the image, for Origen, of God at work in the soul. He wants especially to clarify that Christ creates in Christians through virtue and teachings a temple to God.[281] Teachings and virtues are critical groundwork in order that the soul is acceptable and prepared for God. The unclean elements must be destroyed. Elsewhere Origen agrees with Paul that false doctrines are an "obstacle" to God (cf. 2 Cor. 10:5–6).[282] We have already noted above that if the heart, according to Origen, is not being purified, then good acts cannot occur. For it is the transformation of the inner man and the inner motives to action that help to bring the fruit of good practice. Thus, in his teachings the teacher offers an example that reaches the heart, and that purifies it of "unclean spirits" and false doctrines. Let us also take note of the image of building used again by Origen, an image that is one of many modes for him to express the vacillating process of becoming a Christian. One turns to God by a building process comprised of virtues and good acts.

Origen's tendencies to stress either purgation or conduct may seem to us rather paradoxical at first, but the paradox wanes when we realize that Origen is usually led in one direction or another by scriptural images. In fact, as we have already shown in the section on the interface of modes, there is for him a kind of reciprocity and inseparable dependence of conduct and purgation, or, in this context, conduct and teaching.[283] Sometimes Origen in a single text will clarify the matter. For example, in his commentary on Matt. 24:4, 5, wherein Jesus warns his disciples about false teachers, Origen takes the opportunity to emphasize— as he believes Christ is doing—the importance of right doctrine, its relation to conduct, and the context in which salvation is found.

And indeed it is distressing to find man in error in respect of morality, but in my opinion it is far worse to go astray in matters of doctrine[284] and not to perceive according to the most true pattern of the scriptures. For if we are to be punished for moral offenses, those who offend through false doctrine are still more culpable. For if good behavior was sufficient for salvation, how is it that heathen philosophers and many among the heretics who live disciplined lives fail to attain salvation, the falsity of doctrine as it were darkening and defiling their conduct? Moreover, since he wants to point out a general unblemished [condition] which is evident not only in acts but even in knowledge, I think the Logos says in the 23rd Psalm, "Who shall ascend into the hill of the Lord or who shall stand in his holy place? He whose hands are innocent and his heart pure. . . ." But it must be understood, that [with respect to truth] it is impossible that someone is innocent in their hands and pure from sins unless he is pure in heart and unpolluted from false doctrines, as it indeed is impossible, conversely, that [someone] is pure in heart and unpolluted from false doctrines unless he is innocent in his hands and pure from sins. For each entails the other and pure thought[285] and irreproachable living are not by turns separated.[286]

Both the scriptural context and the text itself is concerned with the interrelationship of conduct and doctrine, the former being associated with the "hands," the latter with the "heart." Assuming a reasonable fidelity by the Latin translator, the text begins by clearly indicating which aspect has priority in importance (not necessarily in time) for salvation. But then Origen concludes by stating that the inner life cannot be separated by turns from the outer practice. The one by nature extends to the other, though Origen does seem to give the matters of doctrine a certain moral precedence.[287] What we are taught, therefore, is a critical factor in the state of the heart, which, in turn, is a critical factor in spiritual movement. Similarly, what we are taught cannot be separated from what we do. We are turned not by only one of these elements, but by the mutual effect of both.

Another example of the importance of teaching is found in the *Commentary on John*. Though it is unnecessary to explore this text at length, Origen does discuss the matter in his exposition of John 4:28 concerning the water jar the Samaritan woman left when she went to announce Christ to her neighbors. For Origen this water jar figuratively refers to the woman's prior teaching. She leaves behind the one doctrine and accepts the eternal teaching of Christ.[288] Here too then Origen indicates, as he has in the prior text, how a change in teaching is an important aspect in a change of heart and conduct. The implications, of course, of the concept of change are some form of spiritual growth.

(d) The length of this subsection of Chapter 4 indicates how important for Origen the concepts of the teacher and doctrine are. Let us note five main considerations in Origen's understanding of the role of teaching and doctrine.

1) First, the teacher, the source of all teaching, is God. No human teacher or doctrine is an end or example in and of itself. Each, like Jeremiah, is an agent of God in turning the hearts and lives of those who are in various stages of recuperation from the illness of sin.

2) Second, the teacher, nevertheless, even more than other priests, is an example

to his listeners and pupils. He teaches others to imitate him so that they may imitate Christ, sharing in the benefits that we discussed in the subsection on the imitation of Christ. That example and imitation can initiate a new direction or a return to a past way of life.

3) Third, not only does the teacher personally inspire his students, but he also provides examples through his teaching, especially by means of the lessons and stories in Scripture. As we saw, Scripture without peer provides the way for men at all points in spiritual growth.

4) Fourth, the teacher carefully evaluates his audience and pupils according to their progress, and provides the proper teachings for the needs of each. This teaching involves, as the *Oration* verifies, a patient preparation in order to make the student both receptive and capable of understanding and selecting his sources, including a critical regard for non-Christian wisdom.

5) Finally, the doctrine itself, regardless of the teacher, can be a catalyst of change, and, to some extent, Christian change consists in an exchange of one attitude for another, each formed by a different body of teachings. Hence the doctrine that we choose has a bearing on the way we are transformed.

Summary

This chapter has shown that Origen recognized the importance of action as well as thought, inner change manifesting itself in outer activity, in changing men and turning them back to God. For him it is not possible to be good without doing good, to think good thoughts without doing good deeds. Hence in changing or converting, the signs are outward as well as inward. The lack of the combination in some degree is one of the weaknesses, in Origen's view, of the non-Christian thinkers and devotees as well as the heretics and false teachers. Another fault is that they lack the great catalyst of all change, the Logos. For no one can be or do good without the aid of God, who is the source of all good. We also noted that Origen knew the complexities involved in changing one's conduct. As in many other areas of his thought, spiritual growth is not always a sudden shift or change; more often it is gradual, with lapses and difficulties along the way. The same view applies even to the period after death. Salvation, for example, does not imply one has completed his spiritual journey.

But the most complex and difficult issue involved in the conversion of conduct is how to answer the question: How do we change our conduct? According to Origen, the pivotal concept here is example/imitation and within it the idea of reciprocity. In order to change, we need models in every aspect of our life, through Christ, the prophets and apostles, the saints, the Church and the teachers in the Church. These models are our standards and inspirational roles through which we are transformed and which we can safely imitate.

V

Becoming a Christian: How Does a Christian Come to Know the Way of God?

Background

The essential theme of this final chapter concerns the special gifts of God in spiritual growth given in order to bring one to, or keep one at, a state of maturity and a level of knowledge that is the highest spiritual condition a Christian can attain in this life. We have discussed the importance of how a person thinks, the need to purge oneself of harmful distractions from the physical, how to build up a strong moral fiber in the soul, how to extend virtue to external acts, and in these discussions God's aid was never absent. Yet, unlike those areas, at this dimension man can contribute very little. All knowledge and action in the third mode can only be generated by God, in other words, what is truly transcendent and revealed, what concerns mysteries and acts that no man can achieve without God. Even the meaning of Scripture, as we shall see, has reached a point that only the saints can understand it. In fact, all movements in the third mode are more mysterious and profound. The emphasis is less and less on what man must do to progress, more and more on submission to God's will and what is revealed by him. Divine knowledge itself—a critical dimension that we have intentionally neglected until this chapter—is a gift of God to those who desire him only and who have reached a certain stage by purgation and conduct. It is a gift of wisdom and mystery.[1]

With respect to the outline of this chapter, we begin with a consideration of how the key elements of this mode, especially the role of grace (*charis*), integrate and interface with the other dimensions of becoming a Christian, namely, with the restraint of the senses and the development of virtue and good works. Then we examine Christ's critical role in this mode as we have in the other modes. Next we offer two sections, the first on faith, the second on repentance and prayer, which describe the basic preparatory requirements for progress in this mode. The fifth and six sections are then prepared to consider the gifts of God to the spiritually mature, namely, through the sacraments, scripture and knowledge (*gnosis*). All of these give one the opportunity to change and reach a kind of spiritual completion on earth, and prepare one for full maturity, salvation, and union with God in the age-to-come.

What Is the Higher Life for the Christian?

This section will serve to introduce the theme of the chapter and indicate its place in the entire process of change. It is divided into three subsections. In order to grasp the integration of this dimension in the process of spiritual growth, we need to have some idea what it is and what are its main motivating factors. So we begin the section with a discussion of several texts that mention a level of spiritual life which, prior to this, we have only intimated. Then, after noting that a key element of this dimension is God's aid and gifts, we discuss the meaning of grace (*charis*) in Origen's thought, and how it enables one to turn. Finally, having laid the foundation generally of what this dimension involves, we explore its interface with the other dimensions that we have discussed in previous chapters.

1.

In our prior discussions we have encountered scriptural images used by Origen to indicate a higher and more spiritual mode of life. For example, we referred to texts concerning the transition from the sea to the mountains, the need to go "up" in order to receive God's gift.[2] These can all be grouped as images of the higher life; they describe the condition or goal of one who is or is trying to be spiritually mature.

That there is a goal toward which each person should strive in terms of his/her spiritual life has therefore been evident throughout the study. This goal is really two sided: the goal possible in this life and the goal in the afterlife. This dual nature of maturity is clarified in Origen's discussion of John 4:21–23. Origen is intrigued by the expression "the hour comes and now is," and believes it refers to two kinds of maturity.

> Yet "the hour comes" is written twice, and "and now is" is not joined with it the first [time], but the evangelist says the second time, "But the hour comes and now is." I think the first refers clearly to the worship which stands, in terms of maturity, outside the bodily; and the second [refers to] the condition of being mature in this life as far as it is possible for human nature to advance. Thus it is also possible "to worship in spirit and in truth" (John 4:24) the Father not only when "the hour comes" but "and now is". . . .[3]

This text verifies, then, that a kind of spiritual maturity is possible in this life. We will leave aside for the present the significance of "in spirit and in truth." In what does this "maturity" consist? Since this entire chapter is essentially devoted to this explanation, it will be sufficient here to introduce the matter generally.

The word *teleios* (mature/complete) and its cognates are the Greek terms that Origen uses to clarify the general state of the spiritually advanced. This fact is substantiated in Origen's tendency to contrast the *teleios* with those who are immature, i.e., children in the faith and non-Christians, or with conditions which are unfulfilled or incomplete. For example, in his commentary on Matt. 18:10, he contrasts the growth of the stature of the body with the growth of the stature of the soul. He points out that souls, like bodies, do exhibit a variety of "sizes," but unlike the physical world, the growth in the spiritual world does not depend on innate determined forces. While man is not free to be whatever height he wishes, he is free to progress in the soul according to his free will. In a word he "matures" according to his own choices from childhood to manhood. Even Jesus, according to Origen, takes this journey of growth, for it is said in Luke 2:52 that Jesus "progressed" in "wisdom," "grace," and "stature." Then Origen continues:

> And the Apostle [says]: ". . . until we all attain to mature manhood to the measure of the stature of the fullness of Christ" (Eph. 4:13). For one must recognize that he "attains" "manhood" and this "mature" [stature] "in terms of the inner man" (Rom. 7:22) who has made the transition from the [stature] of the child and has reached the [stature] of the man, and who has put away the things of the child and has in general brought to maturity the condition of the man (1 Cor. 13:11). And so one must understand that there is also a certain "measure" of spiritual "stature" which the most mature soul can reach by magnifying the Lord and becoming great.[4]

Hence the journey presented here and elsewhere is a movement from immaturity and smallness of soul to maturity and greatness of soul. Due to this view of growth and change, the common English translation of *teleios* as "perfect" is usually misleading. More appropriate is the image of one who has reached a condition in which certain advanced and mature attitudes and actions are now possible and expected. Just as a full-grown person is naturally stronger and more resistant to disease, a person spiritually mature is full-grown, "complete" with potential strengths and abilities that in others are immature and still developing. So in this sense ". . . no one who has matured advances, but he who has need of progress advances."[5] For Origen the soul reaches a condition of maturity on earth that no longer requires advancement but nurture, attention, and use of the strengths and spiritual powers that are now possible. However, in these efforts to nurture itself, the soul changes and experiences a transformation. As we noted previously, even the mature lapse and require renewal and return.[6]

Let us briefly offer a few specific aspects of the *teleios* or the spiritually advanced. We may organize these aspects in categories of transcendence, such as transcendence of body, worship, human knowledge/vision, and worldly way of life. Since these categories are interrelated, our considerations will necessarily overlap.

The latter transcendence, transcending the worldly way of life, involves a type of movement, according to Origen's views on Jeremiah 3. One form of turning is partial; another is complete, or a turning which brings one to maturity. In Origen's scriptural text, God expected Judah to turn to him fully after seeing Israel's errors. But Judah turned in falseness, which is a partial and inadequate conversion. On Jer. 3:10, Origen paraphrases:

She did not fear me enough from what I had done to Israel to "turn" completely. Whereas she ought to have turned "in truth," she turned "in falseness."[7]

The word *teleios* here is the qualifier used by Origen to refine the kind of conversion involved. But what does it mean to turn in this sense? For Origen, as he explains elsewhere, it means a total, complete devotion to God alone, eschewing all other attractions and gods.[8] It means making no excuses and having no other commitments than to the Lord himself. In return God heals our sins through Jesus Christ. This view arises in Origen's understanding of Jer. 3:22: "Turn, sons, who have turned away and I will heal your reproaches. Behold, we will be yours, because you are the Lord our God." In order to comprehend Origen's views here, we need to keep in mind the entire Chapter 3 of Jeremiah, and particularly the understanding of Jer. 3:10.

In this section Origen first indicates that God encourages those who turn "to turn completely," so that he "will heal through Jesus Christ our 'stumbling blocks'."[9] Then he explores what this complete turning involves. He stresses that people who desire salvation will reply, "Behold, we will be yours," as Scripture says. They will not excuse themselves, as have others who were called,[10] but commit themselves only to God, not possessed by any evil spirits, such as the spirits of anger, grief and desire.[11] Hence the full turning, or the conversion by which one becomes *teleios*, involves a calling by God, a promise of forgiveness and salvation, and a full commitment without excuses by us to God alone. But then Origen adds:

But after we have been called and have said, "Behold we will be yours," let us show in works that, having promised to become his, we devote ourselves to none other than to him.[12]

Our commitment is not simply verbal; it is extended into action. Complete devotion also is truly complete; it transcends everything and demands the denial of the belly, material things, and other earthly attractions and idols.[13] Origen then continues:

... for us he is the God above all, the God "above all, through all and in all" (Eph. 4:6), and [since] we depend upon our love for God (for love joins us to God), we say, "Behold us, we will be yours because you are the Lord our God."[14]

This text makes precise the reason why the complete conversion or conversion of maturity is important. We must have love, we depend upon it, in order to "unite" or join with God. Love for God is devotion and commitment. It implies the denial of all other attractions and idols for the love of God. By this love we unite with God; that is, by love we become mature and turn in a complete sense. The result of this turning away from lack of devotion to mature devotion is a transcendence of the old way of worship of idols and earthly things by the new love for God.

Such a transformation in itself does not, according to Origen, occur all at once.

As we have cited him in another place, Origen states that just as wounds require healing time. ". . . so it is also with conversion up to when we maturely and purely turn to God."[15] At the end of his twelfth homily on Jeremiah, he asks us to take care in how we live, so that day by day we "improve," and are "healed," and are "made mature" in Christ Jesus.[16] Here too then we see implied a slow process of turning toward maturity, a process Origen again compares to healing. Also in his *Commentary on John*, during a discussion of John 4:24 and the biblical use of "spirit" (*pneuma*), Origen states the condition in which one comprehends how God is spirit:

> Still we need extensive exercise so that we, matured, and, as the Apostle said, our "faculties exercised," [having] become those who "distinguish good and evil" (Heb. 5:14), true and false, and who contemplate the intelligible, we are able to understand in a way more fitting and worthy of God, as far as it is possible for human nature, how God is light and fire and spirit.[17]

The implication in this text is that to grasp certain mysteries, i.e., how God is spirit, we have to "exercise" ourselves intensely. At that point, we become spiritually mature and capable of knowing the good, the true, and the intelligible. "Exercise" again indicates a process, a movement toward improvement or at least progress toward a better condition. This movement is a movement toward the advanced spiritual level of the mature.

The view of *teleios* as a goal toward which we turn or are turned, in contrast to passages in Origen in which the *teleios* condition itself is described, is clarified in Origen's commentary on John 4:34ff., concerning the work of Jesus, the sowers (the prophets), and the harvesters (the disciples of Jesus whom Jesus enlightens). Since we have discussed this movement in other chapters, we need only note how the goal for this progress is to be *teleios*, and to offer a few comments by Origen. Origen specifies in this discussion of John 4:34ff. that the object of the effort is to be mature. Jesus said that his purpose was "to complete" God's work. Origen first wonders how God's work could be "incomplete" and then what this "incomplete" entity could be. He answers the second question when he writes:

> But the completion of his work was the completion of that which is endowed with *logos*.[18]

Hence what is endowed with *logos* in man is the agent of advancement toward the mature state by means of the perfecting activity of Christ. The savior enlightens his disciples to reap the harvest for the *logos* in each for the age to come.[19]

The former question involves the fall from paradise for Origen. Man was in paradise mature in some sense, but he lost this condition due to disobedience. Man then became immature and was in need of a way to turn back and become mature again. So Christ is sent to complete or "bring to maturity" God's work.

So perhaps he who was mature somehow became immature due to disobedience and had need of one to bring him to maturity from his immaturity, and on account of this the saviour was sent....[20]

But Christ's work does not end with bringing men to maturity, for

...each, once brought to maturity, would be built up with "solid food" (cf. Heb. 5:14 and 1 Cor. 2:6) and made acquainted with wisdom....[21]

For, as Origen confirms by quoting Heb. 5:14 and 1 Cor. 2:6, these are the privileges of the mature, to be nurtured by mysteries that the mature can now grasp.

The image throughout this long discussion of John 4:34–38 is one of how spiritual change occurs. Man's beginning is *teleios* in paradise, but he falls. God then sends sowers to cultivate the power in man that can convert, namely, *logos*. These sowers are Moses and the prophets; the fields they sow in are the scriptural writings. Once the work is cultivated and sown, Christ comes in flesh to bring the work to maturity by enlightening all his disciples to harvest the fruit of the *logos* for the age to come, and "complete" the *logos* so that it can be brought to maturity. Christ's enlightenment as expressed here is a revelation of mystery. He actually turns around, or converts, the direction of the rational creation toward the mature condition. Whether or not it is precisely the same state as in paradise is not considered, but the important matter, in Origen's view, is that one must become mature again in order to prepare for the age to come, and this mature condition is here seen as one in which the mysteries can be grasped, one that is the culmination of a growth from spiritual infancy.

In the last quotation, Origen again cited Heb. 5:14, a seminal text for Origen in exploring the spiritual journey and his thought in general.[22] Here is the text:

But solid food is for the mature, for those who have the faculties trained by practice to distinguish good from evil.

In prior chapters, we have seen Origen's use of the three-level categorization of receptivity and preparation: milk, vegetables, and solid food (or meat). In the text quoted from Scripture, and with which Origen concurs in above passages, it states that solid food is for the mature. In fact, many of Origen's discussions of the mature state, the highest level of spiritual achievement in this life, concern what can be received and contemplated. For Origen the mature person transcends ordinary knowledge and thought, and contemplates the mysteries. This important aspect will be explored in depth in a section of this chapter. Here let us offer a few texts to introduce the matter for clarification of the interface of dimensions.

There are many ways Origen approaches and handles this same viewpoint. Sometimes he approaches it negatively, when he says, in his interpretation of Jer. 37:17–18, that the man whose "city" is at its "height" thinks nothing "lowly," and eschews earthly glory and riches.[23] Similarly he speaks about concentrating on and laboring for what arises from the "bread" of the Logos rather than the earthly bread, in his interpretation of "Give us day by day our daily bread."[24] The emphasis is on learning, first, to see where the real value and truth rests and, second, to turn one's thoughts and attention to the wisdom of Jesus. Origen agrees with John 6:27 that we must "labor" for the food of "eternal life." This quest for the food of eternal life is an effort then to move above, to transcend, the "food" of earth.

Origen often specifies this epistemological transcendence as a growing capacity to comprehend and expose to others the symbols, patterns, and mysteries in Holy Scripture.[25] For example, he points out this task of the mature with reference to the mystic meaning of the various animal sacrifices in Scripture. He writes:

> But in order to find and comprehend for each of these [sacrifices] the truth of the spiritual law which has happened through Jesus Christ, a task greater than human nature can grasp, is the work of none other than the mature person. . . .[26]

Origen then quotes Heb. 5:14. The task "greater than human nature" is the task that Jesus Christ accomplished, that is, of bringing the spiritual law to man. The "mature person" has the spiritual maturity to comprehend and point out in many ways and in otherwise obscure passages the references to this spiritual sacrifice and law. In the next section Origen specifies the nature of the spiritual sacrifice. It is the constant sacrifice of the Logos in man when he is enlightened:

> For what other perpetual sacrifice can be spiritual for one endowed with *logos* than the Logos in full bloom, the Logos, symbolically called the lamb, who is sent down at the same time the soul is enlightened—for this could be the morning of the perpetual sacrifice—and who is offered again at the end of the intellect's sojourn with divine matters? For [the intellect] is not always able to maintain itself in superior things as long as the soul is appointed to be yoked to the earthly and weighty body.[27]

It is evident from this text that the state of enlightenment is only temporary while one is "yoked" to the body. This temporary state would imply the need for a continuous return, while in the body, to this state, and a continuous spiritual sacrifice. The mature condition, then, is one demanding a continuous conversion and a perpetual sacrifice.

Another distinction applicable to the higher spiritual condition is the one made between "seeing" and "believing." For Origen there are analogies and patterns in many places in Scripture. Sometimes they are real distinctions, but often the one is a step toward, a dimension or stage of the other. This seems to be the case with the discussion of seeing/believing, with what the mature knows/multitude knows, and the divine sense/corporeal sense analogies. In all such cases the one transcends but is not necessarily unrelated to the other. We will be exploring them all in later sections. Let us briefly comment on them in concert here, since they all concern the question of wisdom and the interface of modes.

Origen's purpose in distinguishing between those who see and those who believe in the Father/Son is not to denigrate the importance of belief but to clarify a more advanced condition of the heart. The condition of belief, he says, concerns all those who apply themselves toward the piety for God, but

... to see the Logos and to comprehend in him the Father is no longer for all believers but only for the pure in heart.[28]

Similarly in Origen's interpretation of the parable of the pearl in Matt. 13:45ff., the soul that is trained and comes to maturity can grasp the mature knowledge, the "pearl," for the benefit of which all other knowledge is exercise, including the understanding of the law and prophet.[29] But we need to take note here of the significance of exercise and growth and the development of the heart as signs of the transformation from spiritual infancy to maturity. While the knowledge of Christ transcends all other knowledge, the other kinds of knowledge are important to the growth process. As Origen writes:

... the mature apprehension of the law and the prophets is an elementary discipline for the mature apprehension of the gospel and all of the meaning in the words and deeds of Christ.[30]

These discussions of the different dimensions of approach to religious knowledge and divinity may arise from Origen's faith in the basic principle that substances have an affinity for their own kind. The senses of the body, the senses upon which most knowledge is based, the senses that are drawn to the piety of ritual and its objects, all have an affinity for their own kind, namely, what is corporeal. Hence their purposes are finite and earthly. However, the mind or intellect is of a different nature from the corporeal and thus has a potential, once purified and trained, to have some view of the divine nature.[31] Those then who transcend the corporeal senses and the knowledge and things which base themselves upon the corporeal senses reach another dimension of knowledge that not only believes but sees, that knows not only what was said about Christ but the knowledge of Christ itself, whose nourishment, as Origen states in his understanding of the food set forth at the wedding feast in Matt. 22:4, is the mysteries of God.[32] And these are the mature.

There are two other aspects we need to mention concerning this dimension that concern the mature. These involve the role of the spirit and the completion of faith.

As we have already discussed in Chapter 2, Origen will often distinguish in his anthropology and theology in many ways between what is bodily and what is spiritual. The former concerns all that relates to sense-perception and the physical dimension, while the latter involves the power that lifts the soul into divine heights and mysteries. It involves the higher part of the soul, the *nous* and the *hegemonikon*. The mature person, as we saw above, lives by sight. The means, however, for this wisdom and knowledge center upon the Spirit, as Origen clarifies in his discussion of John 4:42, when he quotes 1 Cor. 12:8–9:

> To one is given through the Spirit the utterance of wisdom, and to another the utterance of knowledge according to the same Spirit, to another faith by the same Spirit. . . .

All, whether by faith or by sight, are inspired by the Spirit but, as Origen adds, those who walk by sight are "in rank" above the others.[33] With this general attitude, Origen continues to clarify how one who is in body is, as Paul said, "away from the Lord" (cf. 2 Cor. 5:6–8), and walks by faith while the "Spirit of God dwells in them" (cf. Rom. 8:8–9) and they are "at home with the Lord" (2 Cor. 5:8).[34] This separation from the body noted here is not a reference only to a future life, but also the present earthly life of the mature. For example, in his work on prayer, Origen considers this departure from the body to the Spirit an essential effect and catalyst of prayer.

> For the eyes of the mind are lifted up from their preoccupation with earthly things and from their being filled with the impression of material things. And they are so exalted that they peer beyond the created order and arrive at the sheer contemplation of God, and at conversing with him reverently and suitably as he listens. How would things so great fail to profit those eyes that gaze at the glory of the Lord "with unveiled face and that are being changed into his likeness from glory to glory" (cf. 2 Cor. 3:18)? For then they partake of some divine and intelligible radiance. This is demonstrated by the verse, "The light of your countenance, O Lord, has been signed upon us" (Ps. 4:6). And the soul is lifted up and following the Spirit is separated from the body. Not only does it follow the Spirit, it even comes to be in him. This is demonstrated by the verse, "To you I have lifted up my soul," since it is by putting away what it is as "soul" it becomes spiritual. (Cf. Rom. 8:9; 2 Cor. 2:14, 15)[35]

The spirit enables the soul to leave the body in a movement turned toward God. It is lifted up, follows the Spirit and, once confronted with the glory of the Lord, is changed and enlightened. It is no longer the soul with tendencies toward the flesh, but a spiritual entity that partakes of and even dwells in God. Hence we note two clear aspects of the spiritual journey: the movement up, when one is mature enough to follow the Spirit, and the transformation from what one was before the ascent and what one acquires from the contemplation of the Lord.

But Origen takes the idea of spiritual change one step further in a later section of *On Prayer*. Here too he compares the incomplete and the complete knowledge in accordance with 1 Cor. 13:9–12. He first indicates that the complete knowledge does away with that which is incomplete; it contemplates reality face-to-face apart from sense-perception. Then he writes:

> In just this way for each of us that which is mature in the "hallowing" of God's "name" and the mature establishment of his "kingdom" is not possible unless there is a completion of knowledge of wisdom, and, probably, of the other virtues. We are on the road to maturity if straining forward to what lies ahead we forget what lies behind

(cf. Phil. 3:13–15). As we make continual progress, the highest point of the kingdom of God will be established in us when the Apostle's word is fulfilled, when Christ, with all his enemies made subject to him, will deliver "the kingdom to God and the Father that God may be all in all." (1 Cor. 15:24, 28)[36]

We see in this text that in us the kingdom itself is advancing and maturing; it is changing and moving toward the "highest point," according to our own advancement. There is a sense in this text that all of us create the kingdom of God by our spiritual growth. For in the mature many dimensions of the religious life are coming to fulfillment. In other texts Origen reiterates what he mentioned in the above text concerning virtue. In his homilies on Joshua, the spiritual one surpasses all others in virtue.[37] In his commentary on the meaning of worship in John 4:20–23, Origen notes that the mature and the saint will transcend the worship offered by the multitude, will worship the Father, not simply God, and will worship, as the Scripture says, in "spirit" rather than in flesh.[38] Origen also mentions on several occasions the maturity of faith. For example, he refers to this mature state of faith in his discussion of the Samaritan woman's proclamation to the Samaritans in John 4:39ff.,[39] and in his interpretation of the official with an ill son in John 4:46–53.[40] The faith of both has attained, he writes, a mature level. In both cases, this faith arises from total belief in the word of the Lord without need of proof. Origen compares the official to Abraham,[41] in contrast to the official's servants who believe in a superficial and basic way.[42] Evidently their faith requires proof.[43] The process of change then is not simply from unbelief to faith, but from unbelief to belief to mature faith. The mature follower of Christ has again achieved a more transcendent level of religious life.

In sum, we can encapsulate what we have discussed by calling to mind a few critical images constantly used by Origen in his description of the mature state. First, there is the contrast between what is of the body or corporeal, and what is of the spirit. The one leads to the higher life and to a grasp of the mysteries. Second, there is the distinction of the child (the immature) and the man (the mature), which Origen sometimes combines with, third, the comparison of the great and the small soul. Then, fourth, there is the contrast of seeing and believing. To these we will eventually add many more, all of them based in or connected in some way with Scripture. In all there is movement, an advancement up and a nurture, from the low to the high, from one kind of spiritual food to another, and even in the mature state, there is growth from the constant nourishment of "solid food."

2.

Before we begin our consideration of grace, we need to set this matter in its full context by reviewing very briefly some aspects of Origen's anthropology covered in prior chapters.

In Origen's view, all good is the property of God. Man then has good by accident and is essentially dependent on God's plan for the cosmos, though this plan does not coerce people to participate in it. Hence man is a creature, a created entity, whose essential worth, progress, and fulfillment is found in a source other than himself. Thus, regardless of any other gifts, the fundamental qualities of life, existence, free will, reason, and the good result from God. These are the goods with which man began. These are the goods of the mature.

As we have discussed in several sections, man fell from a spiritually mature condition by disobeying God's commands, by misusing the gift of free will, and by neglecting the good given him. This act placed him in a very difficult position, because the mature state is at so lofty a level that no man through human power alone could attain it. The knowledge at the level of maturity is so profound and extraordinary that no amount of innate intelligence and preparation alone could grasp it. And for Origen there was no way for man to coerce God to return him to the mature state.

However, God in his foreknowledge had prepared for man's fall. He sent the prophets to begin a transformation process, and then he sent Christ to complete the work of the prophets. Through Christ man is given the chance to attain again a level of maturity, but only through the grace of God in Christ can this chance occur. Man can merit the grace, but he does not know if he merits. Merit is determined by God alone, not by human plan.

The grace with which we are concerned in this section is not the gifts of free will, *logos*, the image, and the good itself, but the grace that enables man to change and return to a mature condition.[44] This is a grace that originates in Christ and the Holy Spirit, and is not something, unlike other gifts, in which man participates in some sense. It is wholly undeserved, but God does allow man to merit it. Let us then present several different examples of the way Origen clarifies this gift.

(a) One of the common ideas of grace as a catalyst of growth is used for the power behind the saint's or the prophet's words. For example, in his interpretation of Jer. 1:10, Origen writes:

Everyone who receives words from God and who has the grace of heavenly words received them "to pluck up and break down nations and kingdoms." (Jer. 1:10)[45]

He points out that the "nations" and "kingdoms" in the scriptural texts refer to "human souls ruled by sin."[46] Thus, grace is given to transform the sinful soul. Christ himself, Origen later writes, is a prophet and is given such grace, then as well as now, to bring men to salvation.[47] Origen describes the effect of this grace of prophecy on Jeremiah. He writes that the deceit mentioned in Jer. 20:7 is not the same deceit that deceived Eve and Adam

. . . but the deceit which happened to the prophet . . . brought him to such a great grace of prophecy by increasing power in him, by making him mature and able to serve the will of the Logos of God without fearing man.[48]

That Origen believes this deceit and grace is applicable to not only prophets and Jeremiah is clear from the following sentences:

. . . let us also pray to be deceived by God, only let the serpent not deceive us.[49]

We want to take note of the use here of several critical words that involves the third mode of conversion: grace, power, maturity, and prayer. All of these are used to describe the turning of the soul to the highest state in this life, or at least give to the soul the means to attain it. The word "power" refers to the effect of Jeremiah's words; that is, the words have the power to change and move the essential nature of man. Origen clarifies the power of such a gift in his thoughts on Jer. 23:28, 29. He points out that Jeremiah's words are "nourishment for what is endowed with *logos*,"[50] because of his gift.

Grace then is linked with a surge of energy or power that renews the capacity to serve God's will, in contrast to a condition of impotence.[51] It is linked, however, not only with the capacity to serve or do, but also the capacity to know certain divine mysteries. Three matters concerning this epistemological role of grace will be considered: (b) the essential mediating role of Christ and the Holy Spirit, (c) the place of merit, and (d) the necessity of this grace for divine knowledge.

(b) According to Origen, grace and Christ are always linked, for he viewed Christ as an essential catalyst in the transmission of grace. This fact is implied in all of Origen's books in his discussions of Israel and Judah, or Israel and the Gentile nations. God sends away or turns away from Israel because she continually sinned and would not hear the word of salvation. He then turns to Judah or the Gentiles, depending on the scriptural context, and offers salvation through Jesus Christ. Judah is chosen because, according to Origen, the savior arose from the tree of Judah. Christ is the way God chooses to save us, and it is through the grace of God that we receive Christ.[52] Concerning Jer. 2:3, Origen writes:

But when he turned away from Israel and became to that Israel a desert and dry land, then grace is poured forth on the pagan nations, and Jesus Christ became now to us not a desert but a place filled with everything, and not a dry land, but one which bears fruit.[53]

We see in these motions of turning away, and turning to, a general spiritual growth.

What is implied in these discussions, however, is made explicit in Origen's commentary on John 1:17; "grace and truth came through Jesus Christ." In that discussion Origen clarifies that all grace—to the prophets, apostles, saints and us—as well as truth comes into existence by means of Christ. Christ did not create grace or truth—this act belongs solely to the Father—but Christ is the means by which the Father bestows grace, as Origen writes:

. . . but grace and truth not only were given but came into existence through Jesus Christ.[54]

Another biblical text commented on by Origen to explore the role of grace and Christ is Romans 5, particularly verses 2, 15–17, and 20–21. Let us briefly summarize Origen's views on each of these texts.

The first, Rom. 5:1–2, concerns how ". . . through him we have obtained access to this grace in which we stand. . . ." Origen interprets this text in light of John 10:9, "I am the door," and John 14:6, "No one comes to the Father unless through me." Origen then inquires what has access to this door; what can pass through it? The door, he says, is truth, justice, and nothing false or unjust can pass. Nor can any proudness or lack of humility, since Christ was gentle and humble, according to Matt. 11:29. He concludes by adding that one who glories in his weakness, labors with zeal, is always in danger on behalf of the Lord, and who stands always in faith—all of which arise from Paul's confessions (1 Cor. 15:10, 2 Cor. 11:26)—also "stands" in "grace." Thus to obtain grace one must pass through Christ, the door, and to pass through one must be and practice as noted.[55]

Rom. 5:15–17 develops more intensely the contrast of the effect of Adam's sin and Christ's grace, and from this contrast Origen specifies the real gifts from Christ's advent. The entire section then is devoted to clarifying the ways in which Christ and his influence is similar and dissimilar to Adam and Adam's influence. By the end of this long section Origen has revealed five results from the advent of Christ, all of them due to his grace: life, justification, regeneration, a new teaching, and the opportunity to grow to spiritual maturity. All of these gifts, according to Origen's interpretation, are of a different order from the effects of Adam's sin. The reason for this difference lies in the cause. The effects of Adam's act result from a transgression of duty, whereas Christ's act arose from obedience. And that obedience had an influence far beyond any transgression. For, as we noted above, grace opens up five essentially new (or previously closed) doors and events in one's existence. These gifts are offered freely to those who obey and are in imitation of Christ, and essentially raise one up from a condition where one is spiritually dead or in sin to a condition where one is spiritually alive.[56]

The greater effect of grace compared with sin is repeated again in Origen's discussion of Rom. 5:20–21.[57] A couple of points, however, are added here. First, Origen contrasts two types of ruling forces over man: the rule of sin and death and perdition under the tyrant the devil, and the rule of grace—righteousness, eternal life—that emerges through Christ. He particularly points out how Christ and the devil are each one in essence (*per substantiam*), but that from each many powers and operations (*virtus, operatio*) arise. From Christ, Origen catalogues grace, righteousness, peace, life, truth, and the Logos. From the devil arises sin, death, and perdition.[58] The reign of Christ, then, is a reign over the soul in which Christ's powers and operations can be exercised and can destroy the operations of the devil. Here it is called a reign of grace, and it is a grace that is superabundant, which means it absolves the man of sin not in the present, but in the future.

The necessity of Christ and grace is a commonplace in Origen's thought. It is inconceivable, according to Origen, for man to attain the reign of grace and its subsequent benefits without the source of grace, Christ. Included in this view is, of course, the grace of knowledge. Christ brings knowledge or mysteries that would be incomprehensible and unreachable without him. The basis for this view is that, according to Origen, God is unknowable except to himself.[59] Around God—in Origen's interpretation of the "darkness' in John 1:5—there is a shroud, a kind of dark obscurity that reflects the unknown. However, the hidden and invisible mysteries are given by God to Chirst, who bestows them on those who are enlightened or those in the light.[60] Origen then concludes that a transformation is involved in this understanding of darkness:

> I might add that a paradoxical aspect of this darkness which is praised (Matt. 10:27) is that it hastens to the light and overtakes it, and so at last, after having been unknown as darkness, undergoes such a change for him who does not know its power that he comes to know it and to declare that what was formerly known to him as darkness has now become light.[61]

Origen claims similar mediation for the Holy Spirit in the beginning of his work *On Prayer*, when he quotes 1 Cor. 2:11–13. In fact, the entire first section of this work clarifies that only through the grace of God ministered by Jesus Christ and the Holy Spirit can we come to know divine matters.

> There are realities that are so great that they find a rank superior to humanity and our mortal nature; they are impossible for our rational and mortal race to understand. Yet by the grace of God poured forth with measureless abundance from him to men through that minister of unsurpassed grace to us, Jesus Christ, and through that fellow worker with the will of God, the Holy Spirit, these realities have become possible for us.[62]

The actual distribution of function in the trinity with respect to grace is made very precise in Origen's discussion of John 1:3–4, "All things were made through him...." We have discussed previously this chapter of John because of its critical importance to Origen's thought. Here Origen writes:

> And I consider that the Holy Spirit supplies, so to speak, the material of the gifts of grace conceived by God to them who through him and through their participation in him are called saints. This material of the gifts of grace is produced by God [the Father], is dispersed by Christ, and becomes subsistent in the Holy Spirit.[63]

According to this text, the life of grace is really the function of the Holy Spirit. The Spirit materializes for the soul the supernatural life of grace, and sanctifies it. The grace of the Spirit then is received by the mature, the saint, who gains a participation in sanctity.[64] Creation, dispensation, and sanctification: these are the functions that Origen sets up for the Father, Son, and Holy Spirit in terms of grace.[65] In a later section on the Spirit, we will also discuss how the Spirit's role is one of completing Christ's work, so that three historical stages of becoming a christ on the cosmic level are presented by Origen: before Christ, the Incarnation, and after Christ, the age of the Holy Spirit. It is the grace of the Spirit that inspires the mature to know the mysteries.[66]

Let us summarize to this point. Grace is necessary to achieve the spiritual life and to fathom the divine mysteries. The bestower of grace is Christ, but the Spirit is the actual power or existent divine "material" that helps him to transcend and be sanctified. Grace itself is a kind of energy whose origin is outside human nature, and that enables man to destroy sin, death, and perdition. It is a renewal of life and a regeneration of spirit.

(c) Grace, however, according to Origen, is unearned and cannot be knowingly merited by preplanned acts. We receive according to our capacity, but God alone can judge our progress, and God alone would seem to provide the capacity itself. This latter point must be kept in mind when discussing in Origen the human role in spiritual progress. There are passages where free will and human power do seem to be stressed. In fact, however, in one text Origen indicates that God may also have role in the capacity (or sufficiency). This discussion arises in his views on John 1:27 and its parallel passages in the other three gospels. In the Johannine passage, John the Baptist states that he is not worthy to untie Christ's sandals, while in the other three gospels, John is said to be not competent to untie the sandals. Origen clarifies that there is a difference between being "competent" and being "worthy" and then writes:

> But it belongs to the goodness of God in conferring benefits to overwhelm the one who is being benefitted, preconceiving the future worthiness and adorning him before he becomes worthy with the competence so that after the competence he may come to be worthy, and not come to be competent by being worthy, anticipating the giver and preconceiving his graces.[67]

This passage and what follows in subsequent sections suggest that God with his grace is in total control, though there is a certain mystery in the process that man has yet to understand.[68] God anticipates both worth and competence for worth. Grace involves both the competence to attain worth and the worth that one eventually attains. We might also note that the gifts concerning competence and worth are not concerning those gifts noted above with respect to creation, but concern, as Origen clarifies in the prior chapter of his commentary, the most profound mysteries.[69] This grace, then, is the grace that brings one to and then accords one worth to understand divine matters.[70]

The word "worthy" (*axios*) is an important word in Origen's writings. And its religious use invariably involves a movement toward a condition of harmony with and attachment to God. Let us briefly indicate this use by perusing the *Homilies on Jeremiah*.

Not everyone is "worthy" of God's knowledge or of God's knowing, Origen states in his interpretation of Jer. 1:5–6, for the sinner is not recognized by God.[71] Origen views the word in the context of Jer. 10:12 as a reference to the different powers of Christ, one of which is justice. By that justice, he says, Christ has the power to confer according to "worth."[72] He indicates that one must be "worthy" of the treasures in God's storehouses mentioned in Jer. 10:13.[73] Jer. 13:11 mentions God's people as a waistcloth that clings to the hips of God, and Origen views this text as a message to his own hearers of a goal for all, namely, to be attached to God as a waistcloth is to a man's hips. But before this event occurs, Origen notes, we must go through the various stages of sanctification and belief, and thus become "worthy."[74] In Origen's view of Jer. 13:16, we become "worthy" of salvation by the lessons God teaches in his chastisements.[75] Isaiah was not "worthy" of the Holy Spirit until he ceased being a sinner.[76] There is an eschatological aspect of being "worthy" in Origen's interpretation of Jer. 16:18. We have considered this text previously as an indication of how those who have both sinful and virtuous deeds receive judgment. The "worth" of all is weighed by a just God.[77] Finally, concerning Jer. 20:12, also an eschatological text for Origen, Origen perceives us as going through fire and torture to become "worthy" to be delivered to the Logos.[78]

In all of these examples, "worth" involves a process, a transition from one point to another, which ends at last with the conferral and recognition of worth by God. The essence of worth, though not mentioned specifically in any of these texts, concerns a condition we discussed in Chapter 4, namely, purity of heart. As Origen writes on John 8:18 and Matt. 5:8:

> . . . no one can know [God] if he is preoccupied and not clear in mind, since those who are deemed worthy of this grace comprehend and see God with divine eyes by making the heart pure, as the saviour testifies when he says, "Blessed are the pure in heart, for they shall see God." (Matt. 5:8)[79]

Grace, then, is given to those who are worthy, and this worth is dependent, according to this text, on the condition of the heart. The gift here is the ability to see God through divine eyes. This entire section involves again the acquisition of knowledge of God, but by means of the gifts of God.

(d) Influenced by Paul, Origen develops his ideas on the unmerited nature of grace in his *Commentary on Romans*. He distinguishes along with Paul between what is owed as a debt and what is freely given benevolently.[80] The former, like a reward or wages, does not apply to the relationship of God and man. All things, even our very existence, are not his debt but our debts to him. Hence God gives abundantly without coercion or necessity. Even faith, which in this context, Rom. 4:16–17, seems to be man's contribution that earns the grace of the promise, is quickly shown by Origen, again in accordance with Paul (1 Cor. 12:9) to be a gift of God. He points out, based also on Luke 17:5, that faith without the grace of God is not mature:

You will find this also noted in the gospels where the apostles, realizing that the faith which is from man cannot be mature unless there is added also what is from God, say to the savior: "Augment our faith" (Luke 17:5). . . . even the faith itself by which we are seen to believe in God is based on a gift of grace in us.[81]

Again we see here grace as an empowering force that enables one to rise above his own competence to a level of worth recognized by God. Grace contributes both to the process toward enlightenment, namely, to faith, as well as to the enlightenment itself, as we saw above. Grace is an empowering force that converts a person to another level of faith, knowledge, or relationship with God. Man contributes, but God adds the ingredient that finally gives one the power to see God.

The balance of contribution from man and God with respect to grace is clarified more intensely in Origen's commentary on Rom. 12:3–8 and 1 Cor. 12:4–11. Both of these texts concern how each person is a member of the body of Christ, and is conferred grace in the Spirit as God wills and decides, according to how God has assigned the measure of faith. Here Origen states that man's contribution is important, but without the grace of the Spirit, it is, as Wisd. 9:6 affirms, as nothing. For without the grace of the Spirit, man cannot be a member of the body of Christ. Hence Origen sees a faith in us and a faith given by God through grace, a wisdom in us, a wisdom through grace, a teaching in us, a teaching through grace, etc., for all the gifts mentioned by Paul in the above texts. To what we offer as humans God promises to proportion grace, and it is God's gift that makes man's contribution come to life.[82] Origen explains this matter, for example, with respect to faith:

That faith certainly which hopes and believes and trusts without any doubt is in us; however the principle of faith itself both as knowledge and as a mature understanding of things which we believe is offered by God.[83]

Origen intends this reference to faith as an example of other gifts also, as we said above, such as service, teaching, preaching, and wisdom. There are two dimensions in each: the human dimension, which we are to work out with dedication, and the divine dimension, which is a free gift at the ground of the virtue and which brings it to maturity and a vision of divine things. One is so interlaced with the other, and yet, according to the text on faith above, in each dimension—one for believing, hoping, and total trust, the other for knowing and awareness of the object and truth of what is believed—there is no division in operation or chronology, only in importance. God's grace is essential, for without it, the other has no reality. In order to *turn* what we contribute as men into its true reality, grace is offered, and it is offered freely, unowed and unmerited.

Similarly, with respect to wisdom, whereas ". . . we say that human wisdom is exercise for the soul,"[84] wisdom concerning divine things requires God's help, and this gift itself works a change upon the soul that radically alters its vision. This point is made in reply to Celsus's criticism that Christians do not try to convert wise men. After distinguishing between the wisdom of the age and the wisdom of God, Origen writes, in harmony with Paul's view in Romans 1, that, while the wise men among the Greeks "knew God," they did not acquire this wisdom without God's help. And this wisdom, given with God's help, Origen continues, is one that moves the soul from the earthly and transitory to the blessedness of God and his kingdom, to the invisible and unseen.[85]

3.

Let us conclude this introductory section by a discussion of how Origen views the interface of this higher spiritual life with the other dimensions. To some extent we have laid the groundwork for this discussion in the prior subsections. But now we address the matter directly.

We shall consider the matter in two ways: First, let us offer a general view of the three modes, and specifically how each is one dimension of one unified process and disposition. Second, let us consider the relation of action and contemplation, works and wisdom, and purity of heart and contemplation.

(a) When Origen wishes to present the spiritual journey of man, including the intellectual and moral dimensions, he often refers to three dimensions.[86]

In his *Homilies on Joshua*, for example, Origen indicates three modes with respect to the flesh. This view occurs in his interpretation of the relationship between Israel and the Canaanites in Josh. 16:10 (LXX), 17:13–18. According to Origen's interpretation, this text indicates three kinds of dispositions. The first, in Josh. 16:10, the Canaanite, must offer tribute, but he is not obedient, nor is he required to be a slave to Israel. Origen interprets the Canaanite role as analogous to the flesh.

> First, it dwells with us, that is, it is attached to the soul, but it is not obedient [to her], except to the extent that it pays tribute, which is to say, it displays a kind of service in action or movement. Nevertheless, it "has desires" "against the Spirit" and is not obedient to the soul, but yields to its desires.[87]

Essentially this is the state when the senses are allowed to affect the soul without control. In this condition desires can overwhelm the soul and prevent it from achieving its end. This, in fact, is the condition of the beginner. But then Origen continues:

> If, however, we have made some progress, the flesh becomes a slave and is ready to be obedient to the will of the soul, and this is the second advance of the soul, when it has made the flesh obey and serve it.[88]

This aspect indicates the control of the senses and the will to direct the flesh in the proper action and thoughts. The flesh is now being obedient in its desires and actions to the will of the soul. This combination of inner virtue and outer moral behavior describes the transition that occurs in the interface of the first

and second dimension. It is the condition of one who is making some progress.
In the "second advance," the flesh survives along with its desires and still
requires to be mastered by the soul.

> The third is that of the mature state. For if we should now come to the mature state,
> he says to us that the Canaanite ought then to be exterminated and brought to death.
> For how this can be done in the flesh, hear the Apostle, who says, "Put to death your
> earthly members: fornication, impurity," and so on (Col. 3:5). He also says, "And
> those who belong to Christ Jesus have crucified the flesh with its passions and desires."
> (Gal. 5:24)[89]

From this text, we can see that each of the three aspects is not separate from
the others, but each is dependent on the others. The achievements of the one
overlap and buttress the other. In this context, which focuses on the flesh, the
slow mastery and extermination of the influences of the flesh is the aspect which
is common to all degrees. The powers of the flesh, through progressive control,
is finally destroyed in the mature condition, a condition, as we discussed above,
that involves the higher levels of grace and divine knowledge.

Elsewhere in this study we have considered the different forms of
"nourishment," especially with respect to the teachers' responsibilities. We might
recall here again those texts and the accompanying remarks that indicated that
there are for Origen basically three levels of "food": milk for the beginner,
vegetables for those making progress yet still weak, and solid food for the strong
and mature. These three levels are derived directly from Paul (1 Cor. 3:2, Rom.
14:2, and Heb. 5:4).[90]

Origen also explores this triple view of spiritual progress in other terms. For
example, in the *Homilies on Joshua*, he categorizes three levels of knowledge,
corresponding to the journey of the Israelites: profane knowledge when the
Israelites were in Egypt; knowledge of the law, which corresponds to manna;
and the knowledge of the saints from the fruit of the promised land. He implies
that the first is preparatory knowledge, the second, our preparation in the law
in this life toward a higher condition, and the third, the achievement of that
sublime condition of maturity.[91] Expressed in terms of spiritual movement, we
leave Egypt for the desert, and we leave the desert for the promised land. The
common element here is knowledge rather than the flesh.

In whatever context Origen offers the tripartite view, three key elements seem
to be involved: what one desires, what one does, and what one
knows/contemplates. These are the three aspects of the senses, the actions, and
the spiritual. For Origen there is always an interrelationship among the three,
each dependent in some way on the other. For example, acts are for Origen not
only the outward expression of the inner life, but also nourish the inner life, as
Origen writes in his *Commentary on John:*

> But that which is superior to the corporeal is nourished by incorporeal thoughts, words
> and right actions. . . .[92]

In this context of John 4:32, Origen devotes two chapters to the subject of corporeal and incorporeal nourishment, and how each is nourished according to what one needs and desires in both the corporeal and incorporeal realms. In this text, Origen indicates there is a difference of quality in the various kinds of nourishment in both realms. He writes:

> But the same quality of nourishing words and of thoughts, of acts which accord with them in contemplation, does not work together in all souls.[93]

Hence, not only are there different qualities of knowledge, but there are different conditions with which they agree. These critical variables in the spiritual journey are factors that indicate a variety of directions for each person to take, and a variety of movements leading finally to the highest "food":

> Thus, the more we progress, the more we eat the superior and abundant food, until we will arrive at eating the same food with the Son of God, [a food] which the disciples for the present did not know. (Cf. John 4:32)[94]

A constant progression is always occurring for those who are converting. But, on the other hand, conversion does not simply involve a straight journey up with no difficulties. It can be more accurately illustrated in Origen's thought as a jagged line with dips and peaks. As we have shown on a couple of occasions, even the mature can lapse and be faced with the dilemma of controlling the flesh again and again, or be nourished on "food" for the weak for a time. The dimensions are always present, and spiritual movement would always be occurring. It is in this sense that the dimensions/modes are simultaneous as well as stages.

Another example of the interface of the modes in a general sense can be found in the *Homilies on Jeremiah*. Here the concern is neither with the flesh nor with knowledge, but with one's way of life and attitude. The text arises from Origen's comments on Jer. 10:3, "And he has raised up the clouds from the last of the earth."

Origen first clarifies that by "clouds" here the Scripture means figuratively the holy ones.[95] Then Origen proceeds to examine the meaning of "the last." Who are "the last"? Origen considers the word throughout Scripture and concludes that the "last" are those who are last with respect to life. Both Christ (Mark 9:35) and Paul (1 Cor. 4:9) believe that the "last" are the blessed. For Origen they are the mature. He writes:

> Thus if we want to become "clouds" up to which "the truth" of God reaches (cf. Ps. 35:6), let us become "last of all" (Mark 9:35), and say in works and disposition: "For I think God has exhibited us apostles as last" (1 Cor. 4:9). And if I cannot be an "apostle," it is possible for me to become "last," so that God who raises up "clouds" from the "last of the earth" may raise up me.[96]

In this text we see the higher spiritual level of a "cloud," the "works" of virtue by which one progresses in soul, and the proper attitude or "disposition" of mind, has come to some control over the senses. Also we should note that the crucial act of raising one to the level of a "cloud"—where the truth of God is—is accomplished by God alone. This combination of grace, works and disposition is the sign of the dimensions of spiritual movement.

(b) The above text can also guide us into our second consideration with respect to the interface, namely, the relation of purity of heart/contemplation and action and contemplation. We have already discussed in Chapter 4 how action is dependent on and interrelates with one's attitude, depending on the condition of one's soul. That discussion concerned the interface of the movement away from concern with the senses, and the growth of a virtuous behavior and attitude. Now let us consider how this action interrelates with the higher spiritual dimension of the mature, and how the purity of soul interrelates with wisdom.

Here again it is important to mention that we will be briefly stating matters that will later be considered in more detail. The purpose of this section, as noted from the beginning, is to introduce the elements of this mode.

Let us begin by stating that there does not seem to be one formula that can be followed in deciphering Origen's view of this interface. As is evident from many texts we have already read, Origen viewed the progress of the religious life in terms of the complexities of the human soul. In different contexts, and especially under different scriptural contexts, one or the other mode, even two, may be stressed or seem to have precedence. But it is the achievement of the whole life—a pure heart, virtuous acts and contemplation under grace—that develops and contributes to maturity. The important fact for us is that one depends on the other in order for spiritual movement to occur.

A great number of texts see virtue and action as preparation, almost requirements, for maturity and the higher knowledge. It is unnecessary to offer all of them, since they are quite similar in thought. The text quoted above stated that the "last" who are raised up by God become such by "works and disposition." Similarly, in the *Commentary on Matthew*, concerning Matt. 18:10, Origen considers the souls of men in terms of their greatness and littleness. He indicates in this context that "actions" and "habits" determine why one becomes "great" and "mature."[97]

Furthermore, in Origen's understanding of Jer. 16:17, "My eyes are on all their paths, and their iniquities have not been hidden from my eyes," he says that "the holy person," in contrast to Adam in paradise,

> . . . has not hid, but he holds a heart with openness before God in accord with the holy way of life. (Cf. 1 John 3:21-22)[98]

The saint's way of life identifies him. His mature condition is open with respect to heart and act. The bad, Origen writes, hides from the face of God. His way of life prevents him from receiving God's favor.[99] In his discussion of Jer. 16:16, Origen points out that God seeks out those in the "mountains," a particular place that symbolizes for Origen a higher life charged with holiness and a new transformation.[100]

Holiness in life is not only a prerequisite for maturity; more specifically it is a prerequisite for wisdom, as Origen informs Celsus in a section concerned with God's eternal desire to change the rational being. Celsus has criticized Christians for limiting God's time of concern. Origen replies:

> And we will reply to this that God has at no time not desired to "judge the life of men," but he has always cared for the correction of the rational being and given opportunities for virtue. For in each generation the wisdom of God, entering into souls which it finds to be holy, makes them friends of God and prophets. (Cf. Wisd. of Sol. 7:27)[101]

Again in this text we see how the higher life with God is somehow dependent on the "life of men" and how much men use "opportunities for virtue."

We might note also in the texts quoted the interface of the heart[102] and the gifts of the higher life. God's favor and wisdom depend also upon a purity and devotion of heart. This aspect of purity reflects, we are aware, the first mode, which concerns the cleansing of the soul of "earthly" elements that impede it. To these texts could be added the contexts where Origen discusses Matt. 5:8, "Blessed are the pure in heart, for they shall see God."[103] This text is central to Origen's view of the heart and to the interface of the three dimensions. Let us offer three discussions of his view of the purity of the heart in order to clarify how the first dimension interrelates with the third dimension.

Origen's view on the role of a pure heart seems to have remained unchanged as far as extant works indicate. In his work *On First Principles*, he states that the "intellect"[104] must be purified and separated from bodily matter to perceive the divine nature.[105] He points out also that by bodily senses man sees with a mortal and corruptible sight, but by the "divine sense" of a ". . . pure heart, that is, the intellect, God can be seen by those who are worthy."[106]

Similar to be the idea expressed in this earlier work are the statements in his very late works, *Against Celsus*, the *Commentary on Matthew* and the last books of the *Commentary on John*. In the latter work, in his commentary on John 13:31–32, and particularly the meaning in Scripture of the word "glorify," he writes:

> Since the intellect—which has been purified and raised above all material things in order to grasp carefully the contemplation of God—is deified in what it contemplates, it is said that what is glorified is the countenance of him who contemplates God and converses with him and clings in such a vision, just as the glorified countenance of Moses is like this when the intellect was deified in him.[107]

The cleansing of the intellect (*nous*), which Origen uses interchangeably with heart (*hegemonikon*),[108] then becomes here a critical aspect of the deification and glorification process, a process that occurs at the very end of the spiritual journey. Man can focus his mind on God when nothing interferes or distracts him. The reference to "material things" concerns the world of the senses and matter in contrast to the world of the intellect.

The actual gift of sight is, however, from God. This fact is established in Origen's comments on Mt. 20:33–34, which concerns Jesus' touching of the eye of the blind.

> And when he "touches," darkness and ignorance will flee, and immediately not only do we "receive sight," but we also "follow" him who helps us to "receive sight" from him for no other reason than to use [it] or to "follow" him who enabled [us] to "receive sight," so that we, by always following him, may be guided to God, and may "see" our God with "eyes" which "receive sight" through him, like those who are "blessed" for being "pure" in "heart." (Cf. Matt. 5:8)[109]

Blindness in this context is analogous to and on the same level as being enmeshed in material things and sense distractions. Such things have a crippling effect upon the soul, which requires the touch of God for "sight" to be restored. The combination of the restoration of the soul from its crippled condition, and the gift of God to "see" are the two elements of the interface. Also one might note the sign of the second mode, by "following him," that is, by leading a life that follows the example set by Christ.

Finally, let us turn to *Against Celsus*. In a section in which Origen is supporting his belief that we do not need a physical body to see God, since we see God with the intellect, not with the eyes, he writes:

> The knowledge of God is not derived from the eye of the body but from the mind which sees that which is in the image of the Creator and by divine providence has received the power to know God. And what sees God is a pure heart from which evil thoughts no longer proceed, nor murders, nor adulteries . . . nor any other evil deed (cf. Matt. 15:19; Mark 7:12–22). That is why it is said, "Blessed are the pure in heart, for they shall see God." (Matt. 5:8) However, since our will is not sufficiently strong for us to be entirely "pure in heart," and because we need God to create it entirely pure, the man who prays with understanding says, "Create in me a clean heart, O God." (Ps. 50:12)[110]

This text clarifies precisely how closely the three modes interlock and depend upon one another. To know God, man must cleanse his mind of "evil thoughts," cease from "evil deeds," and receive the gift of God—renewing grace. The will turns us toward God, acts turn us toward God, but God alone turns us so that we see and know him. This final aspect of God's turning us toward himself is the third dimension of spiritual transformation in becoming a Christian. It contributes to each dimension, but it is particularly evident whenever man reaches that disposition which God believes merits a transcendence up to divine knowledge and holiness.

This constant interdependence of the dimensions may be the cause of the varying ways Origen discusses the order and chronology of action and contemplation, or action and grace, and their relationship. In some texts, Origen seems to state explicitly that actions arise from contemplation, that one cannot do what is righteous without knowing it, that we are the blessed when we do what we hear, see and understand, and even that true works arise after grace in order not to make grace void.[111] On the other hand, as we have already noted, he can also stress that right action leads to contemplation, and that contemplation is a consequence of our everyday practical life.[112] Then, finally, there are texts that place stress upon the fact that the two elements progress together and simultaneously influence each other toward one end: spiritual maturity.[113] Several of these texts were quoted in Chapter 4 when we considered the interface of thought and conduct. Though we may offer texts that seem to tend toward one factor or another, the crucial matter for us is that Origen never denies that each depends upon the other. As he wrote with respect to the sisters Martha and Mary, who are symbols of each dimension, ". . . there is neither conduct nor contemplation without the other."[114]

In his discussion of the "keys" of Matt. 16:19, Origen views the keys as gifts from Christ that open us to mysteries of wisdom. But these keys are keys of virtue, which, as we noted previously, are directly involved in moral behavior. Each virtue has a corresponding mystery:

> For I think that for every virtue of knowledge certain mysteries of wisdom corresponding to the species of the virtue are opened up to him who has lived according to virtue. . . .[115]

In this text can be seen the intimate inner correspondence of the second and third modes. There are three aspects offered in this text, all, it would appear, without chronology but feeding off each other.

First, there is the act of living according to virtue, that is, according to a certain level of moral excellence in one's behavior. Second, there is what Origen calls here the "virtue of knowledge." This state is one in which a person has come to "know" certain virtues, such as righteousness and self-control. Finally, there is the gift of wisdom, what Origen refers to as mysteries that correspond somehow to the virtues of knowledge.

Hence in this text we cannot fairly say that for Origen one mode comes before or after the other; rather in different contexts and lives, one dimension may only seem to precede the other. The aspect of the third dimension—the mysteries —is then never separate from the practical life, but ever depends on its virtuous roots for a knowledge that can merit it. Origen extends the matter even further:

> And perhaps also each virtue is a kingdom of heaven, and all together are a kingdom of heavens; so that, according to this, he is already in the kingdom of the heavens who lives according to the virtues, so that in light of this saying, "Repent, for the kingdom of heaven is at hand" (Matt. 3:2; 4:17), is to be referred not to time, but to deeds and disposition.[116]

This passage also gives insight into those texts above which speak of knowledge as a requirement for acting virtuously,[117] and those texts which appear to require contemplation prior to action[118] or vice versa.[119] Doing, knowing the virtue of what we are going, and receiving revelation of means of the knowledge are dimensions not dependent on time, but on disposition, that is, on the way the spiritual life is progressing and ordering itself, and on the relative importance of each to the ultimate goal. One who truly knows will act upon his knowledge. Yet, as we have seen in a number of texts, turning from one plateau to another is a complex matter, dependent upon each person's history, environment, nature and, most important, upon God's help. As a text from the *Commentary on Romans* tends to stress, divine help is with us from the beginning of our spiritual movements, and must be included in some way in each action, so that grace as such is already present in thought and in act from the beginning of the true conversion.[120]

If there is any precedence apparent in some texts, it must then be a precedence not of time, but of importance. For example, the highest goal of the spiritually mature is to turn completely to God in soul, in the inner self. Purity of heart and vision of God are thus primary; acts are secondary. In the spiritual movement toward maturity, deeds will not have priority in Origen's mind. They will either be extensions of knowledge or outward signs of inner progress. The outer sign is naturally seen first.

In sum, when we view the matter of interface in terms of spiritual trans-formation—of spiritual movement toward a condition of maturity—the various dimensions merge into one directed path, though perhaps in a hierarchy of importance. Of course, these conclusions must not obscure the contribution of each mode to the process. The three integrals in this unified process are interconnected not by chronology, but by nature: (1) purity of heart from control of the senses, (2) good deeds and inner moral purity leading to virtue, and virtue leading to a moral knowledge, and (3) this knowledge raised up and corresponding to a higher knowledge by grace and a spiritual maturity in which God is "seen" and felt.

But from the beginning, in the movement from desire to control, there is mystery in how this journey occurs. How does a blind and corrupt soul see and become pure? The leap to different levels of growth is mysteriously yet persistently aided by a divine force whose power becomes ever stronger as man progresses until he attains maturity. At that point, the whole power is in God's hands through his son Christ. Let us then turn to the crucial and for Origen wonderful role of Christ in this dimension. For it is from Christ that all modes arise, and it is in Christ that all modes converge.

How Is Christ the Foundation of the Spiritual Life?[121]

In the last section, we presented a few texts that indicate for Origen the existence and general content of the third dimension of becoming a Christian. Now our task is to clarify the critical catalysts and aspects of this content.

We begin with Christ for two reasons: First, Christ is the most important integral of this dimension. Without him, as we shall see, no spiritual step can be taken. Second, an understanding of Christ's role is a premise for the following sections in which Christ is, in essential ways, involved.

A reading of Book 1 and Book 2 of Origen's *Commentary on John* is a prerequisite to any understanding of how he viewed Christ. There the many spiritual dimensions of the Son of God, the many faces of Christ, are presented; they arise again in the later books of the commentary and in other books of Origen. The first book of this commentary is completely focused on John 1:1, "In the beginning was the Logos." Origen carefully details every biblical title and role of Christ reflected in Christ as Logos.[122] In his discussion of the varied aspects of Christ, even though one of his purposes is to examine and present Christ in himself, on each occasion he also indicates how Christ in his many roles relates to man. In fact, the key theme that is evident throughout Origen's *Commentary on John* seems to be that in each of the faces of Christ, Christ is an agent of change for the Father's creation. All things that men can share— holiness, power, life, truth, and wisdom—or that they need, such as redemption and the resurrection, are received and known through conversion to and by Christ.

It is not possible to explore Origen's long commentary on this text in depth, though we will mention several texts below. It would be necessary to quote especially the entire chapters 20 through 39, and all of Book 2 to convey the powerful impression of Christ's intimate work as converter, a work that is not outside him but is his very being, and the view of man as made for Christ, if only we accept him.

This intricate interrelatedness of Christ and man's progress is particularly evident in Origen's stress on the *logos* and image in man as partners of Christ, who is the Logos and Image of God.[123] Christ then is not merely a middle power between the Father and the rational creation. He is an active, working mediator, by nature united to the Father and, by mission and nature (as Logos and the Incarnate), to man. It is especially the spiritual union or comradeship of Christ and man that we wish to discuss in this section. We want to clarify not so much how Christ as man shares with man, but how Christ in his spiritual power shares with and transforms man. In a section of Chapter 3 we discussed Christ as redeemer and his universal act of cleansing from sin (Christ as lamb, redeemer, resurrection), and in Chapter 4 we indicated how Christ Jesus as the human model for imitation turns men, and the important place of virtue. But here we concentrate on the union of the higher spiritual nature or powers of man and Christ as Logos. Obviously all these aspects are of one person to Origen, but we discuss each separately in order to have a clearer view of how conversion in Origen, with respect to Christ, functions.

The image of Christ most useful for us in this chapter is Christ as mediator.[124]

We will divide the discussion into two subsections: The first will tend to stress how Christ as mediator is a revealer, enabling us to ascend to the highest heights of contemplation of God. The second will discuss how Christ as mediator is a restorer of life and right relationship. These two aspects are intimately related and will of necessity somewhat overlap.

1.

As we noted above, the roles of Christ involve not only the act of giving and enlightenment, but a veritable sharing of what Christ is. Wisdom is the goal men seek in their quest for knowledge.[125] But wisdom for Origen is not simply an inert group of revealed facts or speculation; it is Wisdom, one of the many aspects of Christ, the wisdom of the Father, that by which the "whole creation was enabled to exist."[126] Wisdom was created at the beginning, according to Prov. 8:22, and Origen does not hesitate to quote this text again and again.[127] To have wisdom, then, we must literally have Christ; we must in some sense share in him:

> Each of the sages, in proportion as he embraces wisdom, partakes to that extent of Christ, in that he is wisdom.[128]

Wisdom hence is created and personified by God. To be clear about Origen's view of revelation we need to keep this image before us. For how could one be wise without Christ who is wisdom? Christ encompasses, so to speak, the whole field of wisdom. There is no other way to attain wisdom about God than by entering that field of Christ's domain.[129]

In fact, not only does Christ encompass wisdom, he also encompasses all rational thought, as Origen clarifies in his distinction of Christ as Wisdom and Christ as Logos:

> With respect to the basic structure of the contemplation of the universe and of thoughts, Wisdom is understood, while with respect to the communication to rational beings of what has been contemplated, the Logos is understood. And it is no wonder if the Savior, who, as we have said before, is considered many good things, comprises in himself [goods of the] first and second and third [orders].[130]

For example, Christ, in different aspects, is Wisdom itself, that which communicates wisdom (Logos) and that which is able to receive wisdom (the power of *logos* in man). Christ then is not only an object of our contemplation and thought; he is not only the mode by which we know, think and contemplate; he is also the very substance or "structure" of that activity.

This interrelatedness of men and the divine by means of Wisdom or Logos, which lies at the foundation of much of Origen's thought, has a couple of implications that are especially pertinent to how we become Christians. For example, Origen believes firmly that our spiritual existence depends upon wisdom in at least two important ways: First, by wisdom we came to be, and, second, by seeking wisdom, we come to our true relationship with God, centered perfectly in Christ. The first is evident in Origen's discussion of Prov. 8:22 and Ps. 103:24. He writes:

> "God created me the beginning of his ways, in view of his works" (Prov. 8:22). By this creating act the whole creation was enabled to exist, not being unreceptive of the divine wisdom according to which it was brought into being. For God according to the prophet David (Ps. 103:24) made all things in wisdom.[131]

Man was made capable of receiving wisdom as well as being created by the power of wisdom. These statements indicate that from the beginning, wisdom, according to Origen, has been the source of man's existence. In a sense, revelation commenced from the moment of creation, for man is a kind of creative extension of God's wisdom, and God from the beginning erects a kind of bridge for man to Himself, so that man can turn to Him.

However, as a second aspect makes clear, being created in wisdom does not assure us of embracing wisdom. We need to "lay hold of it," as Origen states in the following sentences, not simply "share in" it.[132] And this laying hold of, and partaking of,[133] is the other dimension of spiritual growth, that is, the movement necessary to lay hold of wisdom. If we do not have wisdom (or life) by nature,[134] then we must become creatures who can at least "lay hold of" it. In other words, the more we contemplate, the more we receive the wisdom that is Christ and are converted. Essentially this idea is the point of Origen's commentary on the parable of the pearl in Matt. 13:45 and the pearls of Matt. 7:6ff. Origen stresses in this context again how the soul grows from that of a child to one who is mature. As one journeys down the road of change, one matures from the good pearls of the law and the prophets to the precious pearl of the knowledge of Christ incarnated in the gospel.[135] We need, he says, the exercise of those forms of knowledge in order to grasp the knowledge of Christ.[136] The great task of revelation, then, often occurs through Scripture, through the Logos who inspires and is behind every word of the text.[137] Christ as Logos turns men toward himself by means of himself.

For Origen, however, revelation happens on many levels. The level just described is the most subtle and essential level. By our very being and presence, our very essential natures as *logoi* or creatures, we are a continuing product of the revelation of Wisdom. Christ reveals himself as the object, as the mode, and as the substance of Wisdom, and incarnates himself as Logos in the biblical word. He guides us to a realization of what has been occurring all along by means of himself.

Another level is summarized in Origen's commentary on John 8:19: "You know neither me nor my Father; if you knew me, you would know my Father also."

> And as with respect to the temple there were steps by which one ascended to the holy of holies (cf. Acts 21:35, 40), so perhaps all our steps are the only begotten of God.... the first, at the bottom, is his humanity, from which when we rise above, we move

on to his next [aspects], to each way involved in the steps, so that we climb by means of him who is both angel and the rest of the powers.[138]

Here then is another level by which Christ turns us to himself. Each aspect of Christ, as well as each function of Christ,[139] is a transforming experience for us. Each leads to another, more high, aspect and role of Christ in his wish to bring all to the "top." Each step is part of the whole body of knowledge that is Christ, and that we must seek and acquire if we are to know him and the Father.[140] Each step is present as an example for us in our spiritual journey. We must know him as man, as door, as way, as angel, as pastor, and as all of his other aspects, which Origen details in Book 1 of his *Commentary on John*.[141] And if we combine this view of Christ and the first discussion on Christ as Wisdom and Logos, we may conclude that all steps of contemplation, all levels of spiritual thought, all forms of spiritual tasks, and all levels of rational being (from humanity to the angels and powers) are for Origen based in Christ and revealed by Christ. Moreover, all change involving these steps and levels will necessarily involve Christ. Christ is the absolute source for spiritual change in Origen's view. His purpose was to convert, as Origen writes in his interpretation of Rev. 22:13:

The saviour accordingly became, in a way much more divine than Paul, "all to all," in order that he might "win" or bring all to maturity (cf. 1 Cor. 9:22), and it is certain he became man for men and angel for angels.[142]

In this way, according to what follows in this passage, Origen supplies the reason why Christ says he is the "first and the last, the beginning and the end." He is all rational beings, whether they are first or last, at the beginning or the end of the rational order of being, to gain them, to turn them to a mature state. And viewed from the side of man, man gains and converts to Christ by following his example and coming to know all his aspects. As we noted in the prior section, truth itself can only arise for men through Christ,[143] for he is the means of knowledge.

These two dimensions tend to present Christ's work of conversion objectively. As Wisdom/Logos and as the supreme example for each movement of the upward journey through the chain of being, Christ converts, on first view, in a way external to the converted. But this view is only a part. There is another dimension of Christ as converter that is more subjective in that it involves his union with man— though this dimension cannot be separated from the foregoing. We find an interrelationship of Christ as the source and yet Christ as the inner agent of conversion in Origen's thought. Let us consider some examples.

A familiar way for Origen to clarify Christ's presence as an inner transforming power is in his discussions of the two comings, historical and spiritual, corporeal and intelligible, of Christ. In his role as prophet, for example, Christ once prophesied in the body, but now, "in power and in spirit," so as to "bring men to salvation."[144] But Origen does not intend that Jesus as the incarnate Christ should be seen in the image of a distant power or a faraway spiritual force. This nearness of God and the Son is noted by Origen in his interpretation of Jer. 23:23–24:

I am a God who is near, says the Lord, and not a distant God. If anyone hides himself in secret places, will I not see him? Do I not indeed fill heaven and earth? says the Lord.

Origen offers several scriptural texts (Wisd. 1:7; Acts 17:28; John 1:10; Matt. 18:20; Matt. 28:20) that support this idea both for God in general and for the Son in particular. The stress in these texts is that God/Son is in and with creation.[145] And this Son is not a different Son from the Incarnate Son or the Son who spoke to the prophets or the Son who is with each of the righteous. There is "one Christ, both then and now," Origen concludes in his interpretation of Jer. 11:1.[146] One of Origen's intentions in his presentation of this text is to indicate the continuity of influence from the same source, hence the continuity of the transforming agent.[147] And though this agent is outside or beyond the grasp of a single man, it is not, in fact, outside man.

For [Christ] was with Moses and he was with Isaiah and with each of the holy. How can they have spoken the word of God if the Logos of God did not dwell in them?[148]

In order to insure his meaning Origen offers the two views of how the Logos dwells among men: One is the bodily dwelling. But this bodily presence in the world, noted John 1:14, is only one dimension of Christ's coming and is insufficient for the needs of man "For what profit is it for me if the Logos has dwelt in the world, and I do not possess him?"[149] Hence, though Christ was incarnate and revealed the secrets of Scripture and the mysteries of God to his disciples, he is continually near man of all ages in an inward, spiritual way. Even the purification of the soul or the preparation of it for the heavenly is accomplished inwardly by Christ. For Origen, the proof of this task of Christ is evident in Jesus' purging of the temple. Christ clears away the unclean, the earthly and senseless to prepare the soul for the higher spiritual condition.[150]

A similar idea is found in his discussion of Christ as shepherd. Origen explicitly states that when Christ (or Jeremiah) speaks of a shepherd and sheep (in Jer. 3:24, John 10:1–16), he means he is a shepherd not only in an external sense, as one is an external guide or protector for believers:

For when the saviour says, "I am the good shepherd," I do not understand this only in the common sense, as all understand it, that he is the shepherd of believers—though this is also sound and true—but in my soul I also confess to have Christ within me . . . tending the irrational movements in me. . . . Now because of this, if the shepherd is in me, he rules my senses.[151]

If we can add a text given in Chapter 4,[152] we may present three inner spiritual activities of Christ, corresponding to the three modes:

First, as just quoted, Christ is one who spiritually guides the senses, so that they can be turned away from inordinate passion and desire. The faculty corresponding to Christ is the *logos* in man. Christ is within the soul enlightening it with respect to the self-control of the faculties of sense. Let us label this a revelation that helps to control the senses.

Second, in Chapter 4 we noted on several occasions how our works of virtue and virtue itself have a direct correspondence to Christ, who is said to be in everyone who is virtuous. This is not only an ideal union of Virtue with virtue, but a merging of identity between Christ and christs. It is a personal correspondence between that spiritual being and presence who is Christ and those who imitate him.[153] This is a revelation that opens up for the recipient the model of virtue that is Christ, so that he can be turned to higher levels of spiritual strength in moral practice.

Finally, for each revelation of virtue there opens up a revelation of the mysteries of divine knowledge.[154] In this same text that indicates this direction, Origen also writes:

> . . . [The text] "Repent, for the kingdom of heaven is at hand" (Matt. 3:2), is to be referred not to the time, but to deeds and dispositions; for Christ, who is all virtue, has come, and speaks, and on account of this "the kingdom of God" is "within" his disciples, and not "here or there." (Cf. Luke 17:21)[155]

Origen rejects the idea that Christ comes outside the inner spiritual lives of true disciples. The kingdom of God occurs from within by deed and by disposition, and leads ultimately, through Christ, to the higher spiritual dimension. At that dimension, as the remainder of the above text clarifies, the mysteries of divine knowledge are revealed. This text then indicates that the kingdom is brought about through the combined effort of the presence of Christ within his followers and their own dispositions. In other words, man must involve himself in Christ to share fully in Christ. Since man is by nature endowed with *logos*, he by nature can share in Christ. This, for Origen, is one of the points of John 1:9, "The true light who enlightens every person who comes into the world." But not all people try to benefit from or commit themselves to this participation. Hence the christ that is in them does not reveal or enlighten them. They do not receive him.

These conclusions arise in Origen's discussion of Jer. 15:10, ". . . my strength has failed among those who curse me."[156] In this section Origen directly relates the identity and revelation of Christ with the progress of man in drawing on the strength of Jesus.

> For it was not only with respect to himself that Jesus "progressed in wisdom and stature and grace with God and man" (Luke 2:52), but also in each of those who allow progress "in wisdom and stature and grace" Jesus progresses "in wisdom and stature and grace with God and men."[157]

In sum, in terms of the control of the faculties of sense, moral growth, and the struggle to know the mysteries, Jesus Christ, the Logos, holds the key. It is, in a sense, Christ who progresses in us, because all the powers that transform us—i.e., the *logos*—we do not own by nature, but share with Christ, who is their source. Man contributes the will—itself a gift of God—to commit himself to these powers. Insofar as he commits himself, he progresses along with the inner christ. The goal then, as we have noted previously, is to have no other intent but the intent of Christ, to be a "field," as Origen views 1 Cor. 3:9, in which God can uproot the bad and plant the good, or a "building" of which Christ is the "cornerstone" (cf. Eph. 2:20).

> . . . thus let us at last be able to merit a share with the Israelites in the inheritance of the holy land so that, after destroying and annihilating all our enemies, "not one remains from them who breathes in us" (Josh. 10:40), but the "spirit" (cf. Eph. 2:20) of Christ alone breathes in us through our works, our words and our spiritual understanding. . . .[158]

Christ is not required in the change only because a person is almost helpless against the mighty powers of evil. Nor is he merely a model for one's behavior. Equally important for Origen is the need for a mystical union of Christ with the person. Here and elsewhere the goal of revelation is that Christ alone must "breathe" in the person if the person is to be fully mature. We can conclude that the conquest of evil and the earthly, the imitation of Christ's way of life, are only movements toward and dimensions of a greater goal, namely, the creation of a christ who will be perfectly attuned to the Father as Christ himself is.

What, however, is the bond that links man with the Father and the Son, and that enables man to be transformed and obtain eternal life? Origen wrote an entire book on this subject, his *Commentary on the Song of Songs*. In his prologue, he clarifies two matters in the effort to distinguish between passionate love and charity. First, he identifies the bond between the Son, the Father, and the Holy Spirit, and the bond between man and God, as charity; and, second, he notes that the ultimate and absolute revelation and the foundation of any knowledge of God is charity. After quoting 1 Tim. 6:16, 1 John 4:8, and John 17:2–3, Origen writes:

> And for that reason we are told that the thing which in the first place and before all else is acceptable and pleasing to God is that a person should "love the Lord his God with all" his "heart and with all" his "soul and with all" his "powers" [Luke 10:27; Deut. 6:5]. And because "God is charity" (1 John 4:8), and the Son likewise, who is of God, is charity, he requires in us something like himself; so that through this charity which is in Christ Jesus, we may be allied to God who is charity in a sort of blood relationship as it were through this name of charity, even as he who was already united to him who said: "Who shall separate us from the charity of God which is in Christ Jesus our Lord?" (Rom. 8:35, 39)[159]

With respect to the connection of knowledge and charity, Origen includes in this bond of charity the Holy Spirit. After indicating that no one knows charity except the Son, he writes:

Further and in like manner, because he is called charity, it is the Holy Spirit alone "who proceeds from the Father" (John 15:26) and therefore knows what is in God just as the spirit of a person knows what is in the person (cf. 1 Cor. 2:10–12). Wherefore this "paraclete, the spirit of truth who proceeds from the Father" (John 15:26), goes about trying to find souls worthy and able to receive the greatness of this charity, that is "of God," that he desires to reveal to them. (Cf. 1 John 4.7)[160]

Though the charity indicated in these texts has its source only in God, it is directed to the neighbor also, so that charity is the substance of a grand and transforming relatedness between the trinity, the Son/Holy Spirit and man, and man with man.

Origen compares the effect of charity to the effect of passionate love. In fact, his language here describes being smitten by a "dart" (cf. Isa. 49:2) and receiving a saving wound that kindles a fire of love for the Logos. (cf. Song of Sol. 2:5).[161] The converting dart of love is discussed in more detail in a later section of the *Commentary* that interprets Song of Sol. 2:5. There Origen (1) gives some signs by which one can judge if he has been smitten by this spiritual love, (2) indicates that the wound of charity encompasses the other aspects of Christ, namely, wisdom, power, salvation, light, and justice, and (3) explains that these wounds restore health.[162] With respect to the first matter, the discussion revolves around the idea of complete commitment and loss of self to God, an idea we discussed above when we saw that the change resulting from revelation ultimately involves not only knowing something divine, but being someone who is a christ. The second matter clarifies for us that charity above all else is through Christ, the fundamental revealing agent of transformation. The final matter leads us to the next subsection, which concerns Christ as restorer and giver of life.

2.

Though one runs the risk of repeating himself unduly, let us recall and repeat that Christ as mediator in the spiritual transformation/conversion of mankind does not, for Origen, perform his work in parts or stages. His revelation is charity, as we have just discussed, but it is also a restorative and healing act. One follows from and is involved in the other. In simplest terms, the thought is described by Origen in one of his homilies on Josh. 19:49–50, which tells how the sons of Israel gave some of their land to Joshua (i.e., Jesus) son of Nave.

> If I am able to be good, I would give a place in me to the son of God, and when he received a place from me in my soul, the Lord Jesus would edify and adorn it, and make in it impregnable walls and lofty towers so that he would construct in me, if I merit, a mansion fit for himself and the Father, and thus adorn my soul so that he could create in it a capacity for his wisdom and knowledge and all of his holiness....[163]

The image of a house or building here, already familiar to us from prior texts, clarifies the restorative aspect of conversion. Man wills and does good; Christ enters and begins to make the soul strong and prepare it for the beauties of knowledge and holiness that are to come. Christ *enters* the soul; he does not perform his restoration outside the soul. He works from within, takes a place and builds it up. This building causes a change in the soul. Another spiritual step in growth has taken place.

Other images of restoration involve the idea of the lost being found, the part returned to the whole, the setting aright of what has fallen, and the giving of life to what was dead. Let us present texts that clarify the mediatorship of Christ. We shall see that in each image there rests a change from one condition to another, in every case a complete reversal, which Christ effects. Christ not only reveals; he also is instrumental in restoring.

Our first example is especially important because it provides an illustration of how all these aspects overlap in Origen's mind. In Jer. 27:17, it is written, "Israel is a wandering sheep." Origen connects this text with Luke 19:10 and Luke 15:3–5 / Matt. 18:12–14, all of which concern how Christ seeks out the sheep who has gone astray or become lost. Then Origen specifies why Christ seeks out the lost and with what force:

> "For we are all one body" (1 Cor. 10:7), and one "sheep" (Jer. 27:17). For someone is the feet, [someone] the head, another something else, and the shepherd who has come has brought together "bone" with "bone" and "joint" with "joint" (Ezek. 37:1–14), and, after uniting [them], has taken [them] up to his country. And the unity happens through love and truth and the choosing of good. Hence to his own Logos he has united all.[164]

The image here begins with a picture of fragmentation, disharmony, and alienation. Christ comes, brings the separated parts together into one body, unites them into a harmonious whole, and then takes what was once alienated to his country. Man is both a fragmented community and an alien without the restoring power of Christ.

Christ's method and materials are also clarified here. Christ unites through love, truth, and the power of free will. We have discussed each of these forces in the course of this and prior chapters. To stress the intimate nature of this restoration through the forces which Christ is absolutely, Origen adds that Christ unites not simply objectively—as a person might fit together the pieces of a puzzle—but he unites all to his own nature, which is, the Logos. We are only complete when we are in him. Let us note the restorative transformation away from the condition of fragmentation, alienation, and an enslaved will to the condition of community and freedom through love, truth, free choice, and unity with Christ's nature. Christ becomes our vehicle to the divine country. He is the mode of transition from one kind of disposition to another.[165]

To this restoration to wholeness and community, we can add a restoration to right relationship with God. Origen's interpretation of Jer. 10:12 explores this dimension. Jer. 10:12 says that the Lord "set right what is inhabited in his wisdom. . . ." Origen sees in this text an implication that there is a deserted soul and an inhabited soul. And the deserted soul is one that has not merged with God.

For if the soul does not have God, if it does not have Christ who said. "I and my Father will come to him and we will make ourselves one with him" (John 14:23); if it does not have the Holy Spirit, it is a desert.[166]

The soul then in its right condition is "inhabited" by the trinity. This event has been possible through the wisdom of God. Yet this inhabited soul's spiritual situation can vary:

For this inhabited [soul] has fallen whenever we have come to the place of corruption. This inhabited [soul] has fallen whenever "we have sinned, been impious and unjust" (Dan. 9:5), and there is need of a restoration. Thus God is "he who sets aright what is inhabited". . . . It is clear that each of those in the "inhabited" condition has fallen by sin and the Lord is he who "restores those who have collapsed" and "raised up all those who have fallen" (Ps. 145:14). "In Adam all die," and hence the inhabited has fallen and has need of a restoration in order that "all may come alive in Christ." (1 Cor. 15:22)[167]

Elsewhere in our discussions, we have noted Origen's use of the Pauline Adam-Christ contrast. Here as in other texts, he merges the fall of all men in Adam, and the fall of men through their individual sin. Christ is the inner spiritual force that brings the soul to life again. The movement from a fallen soul to an inhabited soul that has united, as in John 14:23, with Christ and the Father is a movement from death to life, a movement from being an adam to being a christ. There is no greater contrast than between life and death, and Origen is attracted to it in many ways, but specifically here in order to clarify the transformation process.

This image of movement between life and death is also illustrated through Origen's use of Paul's terms "flesh" and "spirit" (cf. Gal. 6:8).[168] The former he believes is implied in Jer. 12:11, "Through me all the earth in desolation was made desolate." Here again we find a radical division by Origen between what is of the flesh—corruption, immorality, impurity, idolatry, etc. (cf. Gal. 5:19-20)—and what is of the spirit—eternal life. And Origen points out that before Christ came there was no conflict between the flesh and spirit because men did not know what was of the flesh and what of the spirit. But Christ brought a "sword," which in Origen's opinion divided the two and made the difference very evident (cf. Matt. 10:34). Christ has made the path clear between what is attracted to the flesh and what is attracted to the spirit. For in the spiritual man, the flesh and all it implies has died; all is directed to the spirit in order to harvest eternal life.[169]

The soul in a sense is pulled away or lifted from its prior earthly concerns to a spiritual life based on, as we have shown above, union with Christ. Let us attend to the fact that again it is Christ's role, his "sword," that makes the spiritual life possible. Of course, as we have also seen, Christ is not only the means, he is the source of life itself, as Origen at one point simply repeats from the Jeremiah text, "Let them be written on the earth, for they have forsaken the source of life" (Jer. 17:13).[170]

As Origen clarifies in a fragment, however, the gift or sharing of life involves more than vivification or spirit. The text is John 1:4, "That which was made in him (that is, in the Logos) was life. And the life was the light of men."[171] Life, he writes, implies—besides vivification—virtue, illumination of the mind (light), and the knowledge of the truth, since it is centered in Christ. And the mediator of all these aspects is the Son of God. The Father, for Origen, is the source of life and the one who generates life, but not life itself. The Logos is life itself. As Origen states:

Just as God brought all things into existence, so also those who were brought forth to live were given life by his participation. Hence it is said fittingly, "And the Logos was the light of men." . . . This life, which intends to help those endowed with *logos*, undertakes a relation with them, so that they, by taking a share in [Life] by way of participation, are living. And not only "living" in the common sense is this said of them, but also according to virtue by which it happens that one lives well. This indeed results also from the text itself, for it says, "And the life was the light of men" (John 1:4). But that this is the [sense] here can also be confirmed from another [perspective]. The Son is the Logos of God, the Logos who "is God," is "with God," as it is said in the beginning (John 1:1), who also came to be with men, insofar as they can receive his presence. . . .[172] As the Logos then is "with God," and he is with those who were made (cf. John 1:1ff.), so he is the life who is with the Father, who brings life to those he visits, since there arises in him a life-giving relatedness which is harmonious with those who are vivified. But since in addition to the giving of life he also produces the knowledge of truth, by enlightening the intellect of the one who receives it, he is also called the "light" of men.[173]

The text has been given in length because it organizes nicely some central ideas concerning how Origen views Christ's role.[174] It is especially exemplified in his ideas on life.[175] Man's existence and life indeed do result from life, which is the Logos, the Son of God. But the Son is both with God as Life and with men as life, as the one through whom all men arose. To explain this mediatorship, Origen uses the word *schesis* (relation). There is a life that is united to the Father according to substance, and then there is the life that extends to or relates itself and participates in creaturely rational existence. And these ideas correspond to our earlier statements that man, for Origen, does not have spiritual life by nature, but only insofar as he shares in Christ. An analogy to the sun is useful: We can only receive light from the sun; we can create no such light of our own. And without the light of the sun, there is no life or light.

Also in this text, we note Origen's indication that this "life" implies a life of virtue. The implication is that the gift involves virtue. This connection between life and virtue is a result, in Origen's mind, of Christ as the light of men. Though he does not develop the matter here, he does consider the question in the body of his *Commentary on John* with respect to John 1:4. There he indicates that before life can enter the soul, there must be a "cleansing" and a movement away from "works of death."

> For the Logos, who cleanses the soul, must be present in the soul first, so that after him and the cleansing [that proceeds] from him, when all that is dead or weak in it has been taken away, the pure life emerges in every one who has made himself a fit dwelling for the Logos insofar as he is God.[176]

> . . . it is plain that he who is in the darkness of men is in death, and that he who works the works of death is nowhere but in darkness. But he who is mindful of God, if we consider what it is to be mindful of him, is not in death.[177]

The cleansing is a reference to the first mode discussed in Chapter 3, and the works of death, in contrast to the works of virtue, implies the second mode. The dependence of life and light, seen in the fragment text, is stated clearly in a later section of Book 2 of the *Commentary on John*, though still, however, concerned with John 1:4. There Origen states that participation in the divine life must come before enlightenment, even if "light" and "life" are the same.

> It would not be a good arrangement to speak of the illumination of one not yet conceived as living, and to make life come after the illumination.[178]

The reason for this logical priority is clarified in Origen's view of the "life" involved:

> . . . the life here spoken of is not that which is common to rational beings and to beings without reason, but that life which is added to us upon the fulfillment of *logos* in us, our share in that life, being derived from the first Logos.[179]

It has then become clear to us that the "life" about which Origen writes here is a spiritual life, a life beyond the earthly and the life of appearance, a life made possible by the Logos who is Christ. This is a life arising from an inner power from the Logos that we have presented many times. What then is the end of this journey of the soul—filled with death to the soul—in which *logos* is fully alive?

> And to the extent that we turn away from the life of appearance which is not [the life] of truth, and [to the extent that] we yearn to be filled with the true life, we first share in that [life] which arises in us, and it becomes a foundation of a light of knowledge.[180]

In sum, it is stated from the texts given that Christ as Logos, Life, and Light, and as other aspects, is involved in bringing the soul to spiritual maturity from first cleansing to the revelation of *gnosis*. It is logically and essentially impossible, in Origen's view, for Christ to be absent from the growth. Indeed Origen seems to enjoy exploring the numerous subtle ways in which God is at work in helping man change. And yet, as we have tried to stress in other parts of this inquiry, Origen also gives to man a role in his own growth. Especially in the texts just quoted the stress on participation and sharing of life is evident. Origen freely jumps from one dimension to the other, since he saw a cooperation rather than a domination of one side over the other. Nevertheless, man could not know or exist without Christ. There is no compromise on this point. In Origen's cosmos, the derived life and reason of man is free, free to choose even death and darkness, the antithesis to man's essential being.

Let us conclude with a text that summarizes the all-consuming mediatorship of Christ in the spiritual growth of man. It occurs in a context where Origen is replying to Celsus's charge that Christ was not unique, that others have done miraculous things and people did not think of them as gods. Origen replies that Celsus has considered the matter wrongly. It is not for the miracles themselves but for the enduring good to mankind, the continuous power to change, that Jesus is lauded.

We admire Jesus who changed our thoughts from considering all objects of sense, not only everything corruptible but also what will be corrupted, and who led us to honour the supreme God with upright conduct and prayers. And we offer these prayers to him who is, as it were, an intermediary between uncreated nature and that of all created things; and he brings to us the benefits of the Father, while as our high priest he conveys our prayers to the supreme God.[181]

What Is the Role of Faith?[182]

As we described in the first section of this chapter, with faith we begin the road of the spirit. The second and third sections of this chapter, one concerning the interface of the various dimensions and grace, the other concerning Christ, lay a foundation for what will be examined in the remainder of the chapter. The interface section enabled us to have an overview of the divine role in the spiritual journey with respect to several areas of Origen's philosophy. The section on Christ showed the centrality of Christ to this dimension.

The matter of faith will be discussed in two ways: A first subsection will explore how faith itself changes man. We will present its definition, its distinction from unbelief, its own growth patterns and its place in Christian life, according to Origen. Then a second subsection will consider how it relates to knowledge and wisdom in the process of becoming a Christian.

1.

There seems to be the following pattern in Origen's ideas on faith, a pattern we shall try to follow as closely as possible in this section.

First, of course, one is a nonbeliever, outside the faith, which, for Origen, means "outside" Christ and God. Second, there is the initial acceptance of Christ and Christian beliefs. Belief at this stage is very unstable, incomplete and uncertain, often slipping in and out of unbelief. However, third, with good ground, the initial seed of faith begins to grow and become more and more mature, confident and loyal to its roots until, fourth, it is fully mature. Baptism, repentance, and deeds are integral to the progress (and lapse) of faith. Also integral is the idea of faith as a gift of God.

In sum, we find four interrelated conditions with respect to faith: unbelief, immature belief, maturing belief, and mature belief. Let us now explore each in more detail.

As Origen points out in his discussion of Jer. 27:25, God has divided all men into "vessels," those like Pharoah and the Egyptians, and those like Paul and other believers.[183] The primary factor for entrance into the spiritual path would then appear to be belief. Concerning Jer. 11:9–10 and John 8:44, for example, Origen writes:

> Before we believe, we are so to speak sons of the devil, as the gospel word shows, "You are of your father the devil" (John 8:44), but when we have believed, we become "sons of God." (Rom. 8:14)[184]

Origen also connects conversion with believing and contrasts both to sin when he interprets Jer. 18:11–13. He writes:

> Let us compare the life of those who sin with the life of those who convert and believe. . . .[185]

Origen does not infer, however, that once we believe, we remain unconditionally sons of God. As we have noted previously, as soon as we sin, we become again sons of the devil. For Origen there is ontologically no "middle" between good and evil, no mixture that is in essence both good and evil, nor is there a friendship of any kind between God and devil.[186]

> For either we do sin or we do not do sin; there is no middle between doing sin and not doing sin. For if one does sin, he is of the devil, and if he does not do sin, he is begotten from God.[187]

Hence there is no mixture of unbelief and "faith," as we shall define it below, though Origen will state that one can believe in one aspect and not in another,[188] and, as we shall see below, there is a growth from faith to greater faith. Rather, in the initial stages, there is a leap from one condition to another, a leap so momentous for the person that Origen envisions a complete change of heart, a transformation akin to a change from death to life or, in biblical terms, the crossing of the Red Sea and the departure from Egypt, the land of idols and demons.

We speak in these matters concerning the faith of the heart, not the verbal profession that one might make. For Origen, a man may be in any public position in the Church, i.e., a member or a priest, and be at heart an unbeliever or one who is unconverted and requires faith and repentance. For this reason Origen can preach to his congregation as if some were unbelievers.

Before we offer textual proof of these ideas, let us first state a preliminary definition of faith. We will expand on this definition as we proceed, but it will help us if we have a point of departure. Origen offers one perspective when he interprets John 2:22, which states that the disciples "believed the scripture and the word which Jesus had spoken." The implication for Origen is that the disciples did not properly believe Jesus' statement, in John 2:19, prior to Christ's resurrection.

> For faith is properly with reference to the baptism of one who accepts with the whole soul what is believed. . . . For how can a person be said to believe properly the scripture who does not see in it the mind of the Holy Spirit, which God wants us to believe more than the will of the letter?[189]

We will see below that in this section Origen is speaking about two stages of faith, but for our present concern we view Origen's general definition of faith as the acceptance with the whole soul of the fundamentals of the religion as present in Scripture. This text concerns a passage of Scripture where Jesus states something and the disciples are said later to have believed it. The connection of Christ with the change from unbelief to faith is often present in Origen's discussions of faith. To accept the words of Christ through faith is to experience another plateau of spiritual growth.

For example, in his discussion of the reason for Jeremiah's mission, namely, to urge repentance before the captivity, Origen states again the dichotomy in choices noted above. We can either become captives or repent. If we sin, we become captives. But if we believe the words of the prophets and the apostles, we will be delivered.[190] Belief in the words of Christ, and in the words of those who precede and follow him, is an important factor in the choice between the captivity of sin and deliverance and mercy. Origen connects faith even more closely with Christ in his discussion of Jer. 15:10, a text that he applies to Christ. It is Christ who is "judged and at variance over all the earth."

> All those who do not fully believe sentence him; but all those who do not disbelieve but are doubtful about him "judge" him. Jesus suffers twice among men: by the unbelievers he is sentenced, but by the undecided he is judged.[191]

Again this text indicates some subtlety in Origen's view of faith. There is not only belief and faith, but also indecision. Though there still remain only two fundamental conditions in terms of ontology and ethics, as discussed above, there are different kinds of evil: One can disbelieve Christ or one can be doubtful. Origen recognizes the difference, but also recognizes that both cause Jesus to suffer. Faith is fully accepting Christ without doubt. The connection to Christ also implants in the minds of his listeners that belief is not only in terms of words or doctrine, but concerns the person of Christ. The one, the word (*logos*) of Christianity, is intimately linked with the other, the Logos.[192]

Nevertheless there is in Origen's thought an emphasis on the danger to belief of certain words and doctrines. In his description of the transformation of the Bride in Song of Sol. 1:6, in his *Commentary on the Song of Songs*, he notes that before her change of heart, she was taken by ". . . all the teachings which she had absorbed . . . from the false statements of the sophists. . . ."[193] Here conversion involves a working in the heart of the sons of the heavenly Jerusalem toward new teachings and books.

> Christ's apostles had, therefore, a great war to wage before they could cast down from the Bride all the towers of untruth and the walls of the wrong teaching, before they could overthrow the arguments of iniquity and overcome the evil spirits that wrought and kindled all these in her heart. And when they have thus routed from her all the dispositions of the old unbelief, they do not leave her idle, lest perchance through idleness the old things should creep back, and those that have been driven away return; but they give her a task to perform, they assign to her the charge of the vineyards. We may take the vineyards as meaning each and all the books of the Law and the Prophets; for every one of these was "as a plentiful field which the Lord hath blessed" (Gen. 27:27). . . . In the same way, we may take the evangelic writings and the apostles' letters as vineyards. . . .[194]

Unbelief then seems to concern, according to this text, a group of false beliefs that are both given by and attract evil spirits, based upon wrong teaching. The first change involves rooting out the old belief and then introducing new and better teachings and thoughts into the heart, namely, the books of the Law, Prophets, Gospels, and Apostolic Letters.[195]

Let us also attend to Origen's reference to the vacillating condition of the new believer, wherein through "idleness," the old ways can "creep back." This statement verifies again that belief can be a tenuous condition that requires support and growth. These are practical pastoral insights that Origen had acquired probably from his extensive experience as an advisor and priest to pagans, new believers, and the lapsed. One possible reference to Origen's own conversion is in the text from Eusebius concerning how he disposed of all his books. But we have no reason to doubt that he saw firsthand the remarkable change that can occur in those who fully accept in the heart Christ's teachings. Origen's rigorous separation of the states of evil (unbelief) and good (faith), and his refusal to acknowledge a middle condition arise perhaps not only from the Stoic milieu, but also from his pastoral experience. Becoming a Christian was being different from the world as he knew it. There was no possible integration of the two conditions. We are not to be surprised then when in his book on martyrdom, he will write:

> If we have passed "from death to life" by passing from unbelief to faith, let us not be surprised if "the world" hates us. (Cf. John 5:24, 15:18; 1 John 3:14)[196]

Death for him was a dark state without God, while life was the light of God.[197] Death and unbelief are not from God but conditions from the devil. Hence God, the source of all existence, shuns them, or as Origen comments in his views on Jer. 5:3:

> "Lord," he says, "your eyes are on faith." As "the eyes of the Lord are on the righteous" (Ps. 33[34]:16), for he turns them [the eyes] from the unrighteous, so the eyes of the Lord "are on faith," for he turns them from unbelief. . . . Thus if you want the rays

of the spiritual eyes of God to come to you, adopt virtues, and just as it is that "Lord, your eyes are on faith," so it will be that "Lord, your eyes are" on each of the good [virtues] which you acquire. And if you have grown to the point that the eyes of the Lord shine on you, you will say, "The light of your face, Lord, was marked upon us." (Ps. 4:7)[198]

So unbelief, a condition devoid of God's eyes and light, filled with sin, false teachings, death, and worldly concerns, is destroyed by God's servants working in the heart to make way for faith. Origen, who views all spiritual pilgrimages in terms of the Bible, summarizes this movement (or leap) in terms of the journey of the people of God from Egypt to the promised land. He states:

Let this be the first stage for us who wish to go out of Egypt. In it we left the adoration of idols and the worship of demons—not gods—and believed that Christ was born of the Virgin and from the Holy Spirit, and that the Logos made flesh came into this world. After this let us strive to go forward and to ascend one by one each of the steps of faith and the virtues.[199]

Now that we have reviewed the earliest point of faith, as it emerges after the leap from unbelief into the new realm of Christ, let us consider how belief grows. Essentially this part will cover the second and third dimensions noted above with respect to immature and maturing faith.

As we have already seen, Origen is quite aware that acceptance is never impervious to doubt and lapse until the power of faith overwhelms the whole heart. Believers are especially vulnerable in the early stages. In his discussion of Jer. 17:11, "The partridge cried out, she gathered what she did not lay," Origen sees the partridge as the devil, who gathers his followers from another and makes them his own.

But the voice of the "partridge" who "gathers what he does not lay" is in those who lead astray and deceive the naive among believers due to their innocence and lack of preparation.[200]

It is "innocence" and "lack of preparation" that can make the believer a prey for the devil and cause him to lapse into unbelief. The need for preparation and hard work in the beginning of belief is also evident in the way Origen views the "waistcloth" that clings to the hips of God in Jer. 13:11. Through the analogy to the waistcloth, which begins dark, the color of the earth, and through hard work becomes brighter and brighter, Origen tells the story of faith.

And all of us then have our beginning as the waistcloth of God, and since we have our beginning from the earth, we have need of much preparation so that we might appear yellow, so that we might be washed, so that we might discard the color of the earth. . . . For the color of the beginning of linen is darker, but [its color] becomes most bright from hard work. Thus some such process also happens to us who are at the beginning. We are dark due to our beginning in the act of believing, . . . then we are cleansed so that we may be brighter . . . and we become "pure white linen."[201]

Preparation and hard work, of course, require time and patience, and in this time there is the chance of lapsing. Many texts in Origen's work speak of the lapse of the faithful due to a faith that was only partial. Sometimes Origen intensifies the severity toward such faithful found in Scripture (cf. John 15:6; Matt. 3:10, 7:19; Luke 3:9) by saying that believers who sin gravely are thrown into the fire. But he sees the problem also as indicative of immaturity.[202] For example, in the passage that describes Jesus walking on the sea toward the disciples, Matt. 14:22–33, a passage that directly concerns faith, Origen points out that Peter is said to have a "little faith," and it was for this reason he doubted, for he still "had a tendency towards that which was opposed to [faith]."[203] A similar kind of doubt is found, according to Origen, in the servants of the official whose son was healed by Jesus in John 4:46–53. The official did not need to verify Jesus' statement, "your son will live," but "believed the word that Jesus spoke to him and went his way." Origen thus contrasts the "most mature" faith of the official, and those who believe in a way "more base and subordinate," since they thought the child would die.[204]

These passages display the weaknesses of the faithful, but they do not clarify directly the elements in faith that determine its growth or non-growth, concepts that concern spiritual movement. We have seen, so to speak, the negative way of viewing faith: Without experience, without preparation, without hard work, faith will be partial and tend to move toward unbelief and doubt. Obviously, positive aspects are recognizable here also. But does Origen specify the elements that turn faith from being immature to being mature? In fact, Origen does clarify these matters, but not all in one text. The primary elements involved are environment, stability (involving loyalty and courage), total acceptance of certain articles of Christianity and, most important, divine help. The endurance and growth of faith correspond to the extent to which a person fulfills these elements. Let us briefly offer texts that indicate Origen's view.

Earlier in this study we explored environment, or the context in which faith exists or will exist. We have seen numerous times how Origen stresses the importance of making the soul ready to receive what is good through a cleansing of earthly influences and good behavior. Faith, like all virtues, cannot grow in poor "soil," as Origen mentions when he includes faith in his thoughts on Matt. 13:18–23, 31–32, 17:20; Luke 8:8; Mark 4:8:

> For although faith is despised by men and appears to be something very little and contemptible, yet when it meets with "good soil," that is, the soul which is able fittingly to receive such seed, "it becomes a great tree" so that no one of those things which have no wings, but the "birds of heaven" which are spiritually winged, are able to lodge "in the branches" of such a faith.[205]

This preparation, as we have seen, is a cooperative effort between the gift of human free will and God's help.

With the respect to acceptance of the creed and stability, we find these clearly stated in Origen's discussion of John 13:19, "I tell you now, before this takes place, that when it does take place, you may believe that I am he." This statement might imply that the disciples had no faith at the time Jesus spoke. But Origen removes this impression by indicating that the disciples were not without faith, but without complete faith. For this reason, the disciples say elsewhere, "Increase our faith" (Luke 17:5).[206] Origen then proceeds to state that not only faith but all the virtues have levels of growth.[207] Having clarified this possible confusion from the scriptural text, Origen extends the matter one step further when he investigates the constitution of a mature faith.

> And if we want to know who is he who has all the faith, let us suppose for example that what principally saves the believer in believing adds up to, so to speak, the number hundred, and let us suppose that he who accepts without doubt the aforementioned hundred and believes in each of them firmly has all faith. But he who falls short in some number of what saves in believing falls short of having all the faith in firmness with respect to what is believed either in proportion to the number there is lacking, or insofar as he has drawn away from the firmness concerning either all or some of what is believed.[208]

Origen presents two aspects of the total faith that center about a hypothetical hundred elements. The first concerns the number of these hundred that the believer accepts, and the second concerns the firmness or stability of the believer's hold upon this number. With respect to the second, Origen points out two conditions. One involves a lack of firmness because there are lacking many elements of the hundred. Faith as a whole then is shaky. The second involves the idea of lapsing from a prior firmness, thus weakening the firmness of one's faith and its quest to be mature and complete. Accepting "without doubt" and believing "firmly" in all the elements that comprise faith become then the primary concerns of the believer as he moves from one level of growth to another.

However, not content with this clarification, Origen also specifies some of the matters that make up total faith, and the summary is not unlike a creedal formula.

> Believe first of all that there is one God, the creator and perfecter of all things, who has made out of nothing everything which has come to be. And it is necessary to believe that Jesus Christ is Lord, and to maintain all the truth concerning both his divinity and his humanity. It is also necessary to believe in the Holy Spirit and that we, being free, are punished for our own sins and are recompensed for what we do that is good. If anyone appears to believe in Jesus but does not believe that there is one God of the Law and the Gospel of whom the firmament shows his handiwork, being the product of his hands, this one is throwing aside a very important chapter of the faith; and again, if someone believes that he who was crucified under Pontius Pilate is a holy being and savior of the world, but not that he was born of the Virgin Mary, this one also lacks something necessary for holding the faith. Again, if one accepts his divinity, but finding difficulty in his humanity, should believe that his life had no human element and that he did not become a person, this one likewise falls short of the faith not an inconsiderable degree. If, on the other hand, he should accept the human element, but reject the hypostasis of the only begotten and first-born of all creation (cf. Col. 1:15), this one also could not say that he held all the faith.[209]

In this summary, Origen indicates how one might believe in one element of the faith, but not in another; to the extent he falls short, his faith is partial. However, the other aspect concerns the quality of faith, the degree of firmness (*bebaiotēs*) with which one holds his faith. The word *bebaiotēs* and its cognates are used five times in this chapter to stress that an erratic acceptance is insufficient to have faith; one must believe consistently and securely. It is clear that Origen connects faith not only with a sense of trust such as we have been discussing previously, but also with an acceptance and belief in certain specific ideas, i.e., those of the Trinity and Christology; and that one spiritually progresses according to the depth of one's convictions and trust as well as the number of elements one accepts. Origen, however, does not use the word *teleios* in these discussions, probably because he is mainly presenting the necessary articles of faith rather than faith alone. For this reason he begins with and continues to use the expression "all the faith," implying "all" the various articles in which one has faith.[210]

Also we might note the antiheretical tone of the summary. Origen realized that the specifics of what we believe are as important as blind albeit total acceptance. We have discussed in Chapters 2 and 3 that, according to Origen, the heretics and philosophers did not lack commitment and secure belief, but the content of their belief was erroneous. Hence while the reference to a number with respect to the articles one believes may seem a rather rigid or limiting idea, it was for Origen an essential consideration in the growth of faith and in the stability of one's spiritual progress. It is also with this standard that Origen severely judges the faithful of his own time. To his mind the faithful are those whose faith is worth every sacrifice, even death; they are those who are secure in their faith in every act.[211]

The final element of faith is the divine role. We have mentioned in Chapter 2 and elsewhere how Origen considered the relationship between the human will and divine power, and in this chapter especially we have stressed the importance of God's gift. We may now view how Origen applied this attitude to faith in his consideration of John 1:16, especially the phrase "grace upon grace." In this text, Origen offers another view of Luke 17:5 to explain "grace upon grace." The disciples say "Increase our faith," Origen states, because they recognize a dipolar view of faith.

> For the word "increase" indicates that they ask for the divine gift [to increase] what they have by free choice. And it is in this sense that Paul says in his letter that the gifts of the Spirit are given "in proportion to our faith" (Rom. 12:6) which each of us has in terms of his own power. "To one is given the faith," he says, "in the same Spirit" (1 Cor. 12:9). But if faith is given to someone in proportion to what he has of faith, it is evident that the faith sent by God joins to that which was achieved in us.[212]

Origen then continues by saying that since the virtue is a gift, and yet God's confirming gift is added to this virtue, the resulting event is "grace upon grace."

One need not interpret this text to mean that there are two kinds of faith, one developed by free will, one of God.[213] Rather, Origen seems to mean, especially in light of Luke 17:5, that God instills something into our faith, a gift for faith, which further empowers it. And this gift is given to those who have reached a certain level in their own efforts to develop the gift of faith. However, he does seem to indicate two different levels or dimensions of grace that help one along in one's journey to God. First are the gifts of virtues, one of which is faith, that man can freely develop and achieve note in his life. The second level is the confirming gift given by God after one has reached a certain level by his own use of the first level of gifts.[214]

The content of these two levels has been mentioned previously in our discussion of the meaning of grace. There Origen stated that we have in us what hopes, believes, and trusts, but "the principle of faith itself, both as knowledge and as mature understanding of things which we believe, is offered by God."[215] In our next subsection, we shall examine this matter again. For Origen, humans evidently have a certain capacity to develop virtue (itself a gift of God), a development that can include trust and belief, but advanced development or change involves an outside impetus and integral from God. Faith is not replaced by this impetus; it is given new potency and is transformed from being a blind faith into a faith of spiritual sight. So we note here two dimensions of growth in faith: the faith we develop and the change that occurs after God has bestowed a special potency to our faith. In both cases there is a continual movement.

Origen develops the relation of man and God with respect to faith in his discussion of Matt. 13:58, "He did not do there many mighty works because of their unbelief." For Origen this text indicates that unbelief hinders the cooperation of divine powers and faith. But it also brings to his mind the interdependence of both aspects. He offers two analogies to material processes in order to clarify the matter. The first analogy indicates that the presence of faith is a catalyst for healing and the working of wonders. For perhaps just as there is an attraction of iron to a magnet, he writes ". . . so it is with such faith toward the divine power," so that faith can move mountains, as in Matt. 17:20.[216] This catalytic magnetic capacity of faith offers, then, an explanation for how divine power comes to faith and lifts faith up onto another field of growth.

The other material process used by Origen is the process of organic growth itself. In order for the fruit to reach a state in which it can be harvested, two things contribute, the soil and the air. The soil must be tilled, and the air must contribute its powers, and vice versa. So just as these two elements cannot produce the harvested fruit without cooperation,

> . . . so also neither do the operations of the powers, apart from the faith of those who are being healed, exhibit the absolute work of healing; nor faith, however great it may be, apart from divine power.[217]

And lest someone perhaps interpret his statements to impute too much importance to the human contribution, Origen concludes this section with the following:

For that which is fit matter for glorying is not ours, but is the gift of God; the wisdom is from him, and the strength is from him; and so with the rest [of the virtues].[218]

Origen will on occasion extend this role of God even further. For example, in his interpretation of Rom. 4:4, 5.

But to the man who works the reward is not reckoned as of grace, but of debt. But to the man who does not work, but believes on him who justifies the ungodly, his faith is reckoned for righteousness.

Origen writes:

But when I consider the apparent meaning of the passage in which he says that recompense is given as of debt to him who works, I can scarcely persuade myself that there can be any work which can claim remuneration from God as a debt, since even the very ability to do, or think, or speak, comes to us from the generous gift of God.[219]

The attainment of faith, however, does bring certain rewards. Before we turn to the next subsection, let us consider a couple of examples of what powers faith brings. These powers in turn enable one to facilitate spiritual growth.

We have already seen on several occasions how Origen returns to the text on how faith can move mountains. However, the nature of these "mountains" has not been discussed. The mountains referred to in this text (Matt. 17:20) are actually seen as hostile powers in the soul. If the person who is converting has a powerful faith, according to Origen, then he will be capable of ridding unclean spirits and hostile powers from the soul.[220]

Another effect of belief is the capability to begin to grasp the meaning of Scripture. For example, we can turn to Origen's interpretations of Jer. 15:13 and John 4:13-14 among others. In the former text, Origen uses the distinction of those people God has turned away from and those people he has accepted because of their faith. And one of the treasures that God brought through Christ to his newly adopted believers is the gift of understanding of Scripture.[221] The other text indicates that before belief in Jesus, the Samaritan woman with many husbands could only pretend to interpret or understand the Scripture.[222]

Faith is often the quality in Origen that bridges the gap between two different conditions, one in which we are strangers, as is the pagan, and the other in which we, though still Gentiles, become the "good figs" (Jer. 24:1-3) because of our virtues.[223] Another view is found in the transition from God's being the God of the Jews to being also the God of Israel. The unifying element is faith.

For [he is] the same God of the Jews and the Gentiles, "since God is one and he will justify the circumcised on the ground of their faith and the uncircumcised through their faith" (Rom. 3:30). For we do not abolish the law through faith, but we uphold the law through it. (Cf. Rom. 3:31)[224]

Faith then acts as a power that can enable us under the law to attain justification. It bridges the condition under the law with the condition of salvation.

Faith also is not really faith, Origen says, unless it is practiced. In his commentary on John 8:24, "For you will die in your sins unless you believe that I am he," Origen understands the expression "die in your sins" as referring to sins that lead to death. These sins focus on not believing in the Christ and who the Christ is, that is, all the aspects that are united in him who is Christ. To believe in Christ is to begin to understand him and to act according to that understanding.

> For instance, he who believes what justice is, would not be unjust, and he who has believed in wisdom, having observed what wisdom is, would not say or do something foolish; moreover, he who believed in the "Logos who was in the beginning with God" (John 1:1), in comprehending him would do nothing against the Logos.[225]

Faith, then, by nature extends itself in works that reflect the object of faith, the Logos. Of course, this view of Origen follows from other statements we have offered on the impossible meeting in one thought or act of moral opposites. He makes this point very precise in his commentary on Rom. 4:1.

> For no part of faith exists together with lack of faith, nothing of justice has party with iniquity, just as there can be no fellowship of light with darkness (2 Cor. 6:14–15). For if "he who believes that Jesus is Christ, was born from God," and "he who was born from God, does no sin," it is evident that he who believes in Jesus Christ does not sin: because if he sins, it is certain that he does not believe in him. Hence it is a sign of true faith where no fault is present, just as vice versa where there is fault it indicates a lack of faith.[226]

The issue for Origen is that though faith is unseen and hidden in nature, such a faith is not separate from what a man does. Furthermore, good acts, as Paul states, do not justify us with God. Faith is the pivotal force. Without it no act has true goodness. God looks through the act to the heart and seeks for faith. The relation of faith with baptism and repentance can be seen more clearly if we do not have a chronological perspective. For all three—faith, repentance, baptism—are integral to each other. It is difficult for Origen to imagine one repenting without having the beginnings of faith, and repentance naturally encompasses the cleansing power of baptism.[227] However, we will discuss and document these ideas more fully in following sections.

2.

Before we can conclude the discussion of faith in how we become Christians, we need to clarify the relationship of faith to knowledge, reason, and wisdom as Origen states the matter. As we shall see, Origen no doubt felt compelled to define each condition in order to contrast his view (which he believed was the scriptural view) with the popular view, the views of critics of Christianity, and heretical views.

Because of Celsus's attacks on the intellectual sophistication of Christian thought and Christians themselves, Origen on several occasions sought to clarify the different dimensions of Christian understanding of theological matters. In his clarification emerges a subtle probing of faith as it relates to knowledge. The gist of this view is that the more mature condition is to "know" or to "see" what one has believed in faith. But this condition does not arise all at once at baptism or upon acceptance of Christianity. It evolves from a time of spiritual growth. And Origen often recognizes that some believers will not seek or desire knowledge (or sight); they are content with a simple faith. Let us then consider some texts that present his thought. It should be noted that the role of knowledge in the spiritual journey is the subject of a separate section.

The scriptural text that Origen seems to favor in this issue is 1 Cor. 12:8-9:

> For to one is given through the Spirit the word of wisdom; and to another the word of knowledge according to the same Spirit; and to another faith, in the same Spirit.

For Origen wisdom, knowledge, and faith in this text refer to fields of growth that indicate a person's progress. One context, for example, in the book *Against Celsus*, concerns Celsus's charge that Christians wish to convert only ignorant and uneducated folk. Origen denies this charge by a list of scriptural texts that laud wisdom. One of these is 1 Cor. 12:8-9. Origen writes:

> Moreover, Paul in the list of spiritual gifts given by God puts first the word of wisdom, and second, as inferior to that, the word of knowledge, and third, even lower, faith.[228]

The second text states that there are two kinds of wisdom, divine wisdom and human wisdom. The latter is only a preparation, Origen says, for the former. He writes:

> We maintain that human wisdom is a means of education for the soul, divine wisdom being the ultimate end.... So divine wisdom, which is not the same thing as faith, is first of what are called the spiritual gifts of God; the second place after it, for those who have an accurate understanding of these matters, is held by what is called knowledge; and faith stands in the third place, since salvation must be available also for the simple folk who advance in religion as far as they can. So Paul has it . . . [in 1 Cor. 12:8-9]. For this reason you would not find ordinary people partaking of divine wisdom, but those whose ability is superior and stands out among all those who are adherents of Christianity.[229]

Let us offer two more texts that use 1 Cor. 12:8-9 before we consider the content of those texts already given. The first context is John 8:19, "You know neither me nor my Father; if you knew me, you would know my Father also." At one point in his long discussion of this text, Origen is concerned to contrast one who believes in God and one who knows God. After offering texts that affirm that "to know the Father is not the same as to believe in him," Origen writes,

Knowing in addition to believing is much different from believing by itself.[230]

Then he quotes 1 Cor. 12:8–9.
Finally we find the text quoted in Origen's consideration of John 4:42:

It is no longer because of your words that we believe, for we have heard for ourselves, and we know that this is indeed the Saviour of the world.

Origen views in this text the comparison of those who "see" Christ firsthand, and those who simply believe. Origen states here that the heart itself is stirred differently in the former group. Then he writes:

And indeed it is better to walk by sight than by faith (cf. 2 Cor. 5:7). Hence those who in some sense walk by sight may be said to be with superior gifts, namely, with the "word of wisdom" "through the Spirit" of God and with the "word of knowledge according to the same Spirit." But those [who walk] by faith—if also faith is a gift according to the text "to another faith by the same Spirit"—are in rank after the preceding.[231]

These texts seem to affirm the same perspective, noted first in Scripture: Faith in rank comes third after wisdom and knowledge in terms of gifts and in terms of growth. One text pointed out that faith was "for the simple folk" who need salvation but do not have the desire to seek a superior dimension of their spiritual life. Wisdom is the supreme gift, exceeding even knowledge. Perhaps Origen differentiated between "knowing" theological matters, such as interpreting the Scriptures and explaining the meaning of creedal statements to the multitude, and a higher level of understanding, a gift that perhaps concerned only the great mysteries that Jesus told his disciples in secret. In any case, even among the "superior" there are plateaus of growth and continuing opportunities to change. In all of these statements, we see faith as a beginning state of mind that can be transcended, or, in one text, supplemented by knowledge. As we saw previously, true faith appears as a blind trust, absolutely loyal without proof, that is apparently confirmed and enriched by "sight" or knowing. One can believe without any knowledge of what one believes. Perhaps his own witness of such a basic belief encouraged Origen to see a real conversion of the heart when the dimension of "sight" emerged. It is in this sense that such a belief is inferior; it is inferior to the understanding and feelings that come with knowledge of what one believes. For example, Origen believes this difference lies behind Jesus' statement in Matt. 16:20, "Then he strictly charged the disciples to tell no one that he was the Christ." Before this time, the disciples only believed. Then they advanced until, this text indicates, at least one, Peter, knew him. Previous to this knowledge, Origen says, the belief that Jesus was the Christ was inferior to the knowledge of who he was.[232]

Hence, an accompanying image, also borrowed from Scripture, that Origen uses to explain this contrast of faith and knowledge is the one mentioned briefly above concerning walking by sight and walking by faith. Those who "see" God, he mentions in a fragment on John 12:44–45, are able, in some sense, to comprehend the Father. Such a comprehension is reserved not only for those who are pious believers, but for those who also are "pure in heart" (Matt. 5:8). Origen also indicates that Jesus intentionally distinguishes between believers who believe in the God of the universe but not in Christ, and those with vision who know the Son and the Father.[233] The implication is that the believer believes in a general way in his religion, with a simple but blind trust and instinct of God; but the one with sight comes to see in detail him who is Truth, Wisdom and the Logos. We thus can offer the analogy of the difference between the person whose view is blurred by poor eyes, and the person whose vision is clarified and precise, so that what was unclear or so general that he had to take the matter on trust has now become focused and understandable.[234]

Does it seem that faith and knowledge may be tied in some way? Perhaps the two of them are members of one process or development? These speculations seem to be verified in several texts. Origen never stresses the replacement of faith, but a new focus and vision comes with knowledge. Indeed in his *Commentary on Romans*, in a text already quoted, he writes:

> That faith certainly which hopes and believes and trusts without any doubt is in us; however, the principle of faith itself both as knowledge and as a mature understanding of things which we believe, is offered by God.[235]

Since this text is extant only in the Latin, we cannot be fully confident in the wording, but the meaning of the text is clear. The meaning centers on how we understand *ratio*. The interpretation offered here, noted in the translation as "principle," is that faith is weak not in itself—it is, after all, a gift of God, according to Origen—but in comparison to what it can become with grace. It is inferior to the power that God brings to it. This power clarifies what before was obscure, so that we do not move out of the field of faith, but we are converted from blind faith to a sighted faith. In light of this view, it is not unusual that Origen limits this condition to a few. To be worthy would require a rare commitment to the Logos. Origen notes this belief in his comments on John 8:30–32. He writes:

> "Many then believed in him," but not many knew him since among those who have believed in him, who "continue in his word," who "truly" become his "disciples," will "know the truth." But not many among his believers continue in his word, not many "truly" become his "disciples." Hence not many will know truth, and if truth "frees," they do not become free. For very few obtain this freedom.[236]

Origen does not specify here the meaning of Jesus' words "continue in my word," and the commentary on this text is not extant. However, from this context and many others in which he quotes John 8:31, we can offer a general view. Origen differentiates between different kinds of believers, especially between those who just believe and those who know, e.g., in this context, the different kinds of Jews in Jesus' audience who believed. There is a stress in Origen's thought on commitment to Jesus' intentions and meaning, and this commitment and seeking eventually determines who knows and who just believes. Origen connects the intention of abiding in his word as commitment to the substance of Christ's life and teaching.[237] We have already seen how stability affects faith. Here we see another dimension of stability: commitment to Jesus' teaching and, in a deeper sense, to the spirit of his words, their principle. In sum, knowledge is the clarity of what is present in faith, but of which faith can be blind and must accept on trust and without doubt.

There is a temptation upon reading one or two texts on faith in Origen to misinterpret his intentions. It might appear on first reading, or on examination of only a couple of texts, that he dismisses the role and importance of belief and faith as the Christian marches on. In fact, however, as we have seen, he considers it a seed that grows into knowledge, if the person has the desire to pursue the matter.

It is also a key element in how one chooses to change. In a debate about faith with Celsus, Origen indicates that not only Christians but all people base their initial philosophical choices on belief.

> As this matter of faith is so much talked of, I have to reply that we accept it as useful for the multitude, and we admittedly teach those who cannot abandon everything and follow in search of a doctrine to believe without thinking out their reasons. But, even if they do not admit it, in practice others do the same. . . . Even though they do not want to admit it, it is by an unreasoning impulse that people come to the practice of, say, Stoicism, [and] abandon the rest. . . .[238]

We notice here and also in other texts the contrast of a life based on "an unreasoning impulse" (*alogō tini*) and a life based in the *logos*. The former Origen connects directly with faith and belief, the latter with a later stage in one's spiritual growth. Origen does not indicate the source of this unreasoning impulse, but it seems quite possible that it might be similar to what is today labeled intuition. A person intuitively begins his spiritual journey by feeling a certain trust in one person or set of ideas over another. There is not necessarily a rational foundation for this choice, Origen admits; it is an intuitive feeling. The ultimate source, of course, is God.

In the next section, Origen carries his argument beyond the realm of philosophy to the feelings we have about the way of life itself. He points out that we must depend constantly on faith in the course of our lives, i.e., in taking voyages, sowing seeds in the earth, marrying, etc. The true believer trusts, however, not in processes and persons, but in God, and, on this account, Origen states, he believes "more reasonably" than others. For God created all of these things.[239]

Even if faith does mature into knowledge, however, it does not disappear. As we shall see in more detail in the section on knowledge, this thesis follows from Origen's view of man's limitations on earth. In order for faith to be replaced entirely, man would need to have come to know the answers to all the mysteries in faith. That event does not occur in this earthly life. To clarify this, Origen refers to an earthly and a heavenly faith, or a partial faith and a mature faith. For example, in his commentary on Matt. 16:8, he asks how the disciples could be called men "of little faith."

> But it is not difficult, I think, to say to this, that in relation to that which is "mature," on the coming of which "that which is in part shall be done away" (1 Cor. 13:9–10), all our faith here is "little faith," and in regard to that, we who know "in part" do not yet know nor remember, for we are not able to obtain a memory which is sufficient and able to attain to the magnitude of the nature of the speculations.[240]

The scriptural text 1 Cor. 13:10 is a favorite text of Origen to clarify this matter, with respect to both knowledge and faith.[241] Faith and knowledge admit of growth even beyond earthly life. In other words, even he who has progressed to a condition of knowledge still has other dimensions of growth in faith and in knowledge.

We may summarize our findings in this way: Origen in the broadest sense sees three areas of growth in knowledge: one tends to be linked to human culture, one is intuitive and non-rational, based on blind trust and acceptance without proof, and one is a contemplative inquiry into and understanding of the mysteries believed by the faithful.[242]

The first area is at best a preparation for the other areas. The second area is faith, a gift of God capable of realization by man's free choice. Faith to be faith is complete; that is, one must believe without doubt in all the elements of belief, and be secure in one's convictions. It also contains the germ of the third area, divine knowledge bestowed by God on those who are "free" and committed to the Logos and to inquiry into doctrine. Faith has four growth stages or spirals, each circle closer to the core of truth: Unbelief, nascent belief, maturing belief, and mature belief. "Faith" is the word Origen uses for the fourth level, but he recognizes the vacillating conditions that bring one to that level. Faith, let us repeat, is a spiritual gift, according to Origen. It is closely related to the Christian life of repentance and baptism, and gives support to those who are converting.

For Origen it is better to "see" and believe rather than to believe alone. However, Origen understood the combination of seeing and believing in the sense of faith preceding vision. This view corresponds to his belief that true faith does not need proof, and knowledge will not arise in those who doubt. Hence, though Origen realized that many people would never in this life move beyond faith, he also realized that wisdom cannot prosper without a solid conviction that needs no proof.

How Do Repentance and Prayer Contribute to Growth?

Becoming a Christian, of course, involves the question of how people change. We have not been so much concerned in this chapter with how one prepares his heart or what he says or does; our concern has been with the spiritual movement within the heart. After a general concern with purification and practice, we realize that the crux of the matter, as Origen stresses again and again, is in the development in the spiritual processes within the inner man.

In this same inquiry we come to the place of repentance and prayer in the process of change, and to both areas Origen gave considerable thought.[243] It may appear to some of us that repentance especially is the same as or similar to conversion. In fact, Origen clearly indicates that repentance is only one aspect of the larger movement of conversion. Basically it has two roles. First, it is involved in the early stages of change, and second, it is a critical return element when the Christian lapses. We shall consider these two roles together since the process is similar for both movements. The matter of prayer is a much more complex process that we are not able to discuss in detail. Origen himself devoted an entire book to the subject of prayer, but even he felt the matter was not treated thoroughly.

Our discussions concerning repentance will revolve around three matters: (1) clarification of the differences between conversion and repentance, (2) the factors that bring one to repentance, and (3) the general effect of repentance.

Then (4) we will conclude this section with a consideration of the role of prayer.

1.

While conversion concerns the whole process of returning to God, repentance basically always looks back to the past, and particularly the sins of the past.[244] It is for Origen fundamentally a negative process. When a person repents, he in effect does not change his soul from one condition to another; rather, he comes to recognize the actual state of his soul and expresses regret concerning it.[245] If we might offer a spatial analogy, repentance would be similar to swiveling 180 degrees on the same spot, but without moving forward. This spiritual realization, of course, is not without power with respect to one's relationship with God, but it is not the same process that causes new growth. Repentance thus breaks with the past, but it need not build for the future. Let us offer a few of many possible examples from Origen's works.

Origen defines repentance in one homily by the scriptural text Jer. 18:11, "Let each now turn away from his evil way, and amend your habits." Origen writes that men respond, according to Jer. 18:12, by following perverse and evil hearts.[246] But we should "turn away" from our old evil ways and "amend" our habits. By ways and habits Origen is not referring necessarily to external works and acts, but, as we shall see more clearly in texts to follow, to a change of spiritual direction. And "turning away" and amending imply no more than an end to the past inner history, and a new openness to the Lord's initiative to reform. Let us also take note of the context here. Origen is addressing primarily members of his congregation who are already members of the Church.[247] Hence repentance is a process of conversion that has a continuing role in reformation, wherever it may arise in the conversion journey. In light of this, Origen will stress that *now* this scriptural text refers "to us," meaning those who are listening to him in the service. This view also agrees with the scriptural context. For Jeremiah cries out to those who were once among the Lord's flock, but whom now the Lord threatens to destroy if they do not repent.

Repentance has two aspects: one in the initial stages of conversion, and one in the growth dimension of conversion, when the Christian may lapse. It does not directly cause growth; it opens up the possibility of growth. This perspective seems to be verified in a number of texts of Origen. For example, in his discussion of Jer. 18:7-10—a text that requires, in his opinion, a lengthy commentary because it seems to say that God can repent—Origen writes that this text, along with many others in Scripture, intentionally uses anthropomorphism. Origen then explains why God cannot repent. His explanation gives more clarity on how he understands repentance.

> For to repent seems to be reprehensible and unworthy not only of God but also of the sage. For I cannot conceive of a wise man repenting, but he who repents, in the customary sense, repents of not planning rightly. Yet God, one who foreknows future events, is unable to have planned wrongly, and beyond this to repent.[248]

Origen indicates in the phrase "in the customary sense" that the fundamental meaning of *metanoia* (repentance) is to change the direction of what one has morally decided or planned. God, and even the wise man, do not make such errors. They know the right course to take. It is inconceivable that they would need to change their minds about the course. Repenting, however, is not merely changing from a wrong course, but, more accurately, realizing one has planned wrongly and showing spiritually and in one's life a change of habit and mind. This fact will be more evident when we consider what brings one to repentance in the next discussion of repentance.

Often it appears that repentance is only an early stage of conversion, before one has fully turned and begun to progress. In his interpretation of Jer. 15:11, "Let it happen, Lord, if they go straight," Origen notes that one "turns" to the straight" path once one has repented.

> . . . let there be strength (which fails among my detractors) whenever, after speaking ill of me, they who have repented turn to the straight way and travel it.[249]

Here it seems that the sinner first shows signs that he has erred in the past and then turns to the way. Repentance is not a movement, but a static realization that allows one to change his spiritual direction and to exhibit the effects of this realization through confession, grief, shame, etc. It is a catalyst for movement and further, more substantial, change in one's life. For Origen there seems to be the awareness of the wrongful condition of one's life, the effect of this awareness in confession, grief, shame, acts of repentance, etc. (the fruits of repentance),[250] and then the growth movement of which repentance is an important, though not the only, catalyst.

Further examples of this view can be found in Origen's thoughts on the Song of Songs. In his commentary on 1:5(4), "I am dark and beautiful . . . ," Origen writes:

It can be said also of each individual soul that turns to repentance after many sins that she is "black" by reason of her sins, but "beautiful" through her repentance and the "fruits of her repentance." (Luke 3:8)[251]

The paradox inherent in the text (being black and beautiful) can be explained, Origen says, by the paradox of the moral condition of the soul. The soul has been made black through its sinful life. When repentance occurs, the soul remains black, because repentance makes no substantial effect on the soul itself; repentance, however, does open up the door to growth, and particularly the "fruits of repentance," which are good works.[252] The soul, once in sin, now is beautiful because the way is clear for further conversion. The other matter worthy of note in this text is that the soul "turns to repentance." Origen makes clear by this statement that repentance is within the conversion process, that there is even a process of turning to repentance. Moreover, this text indicates that repentance is not really a part of the actual turning. The turning, the actual conversion movement, brings the soul to the event of repentance, which, as we have seen, is a kind of realization of one's past errors and indirection, as well as the will to turn in another direction.

Hence there would appear to be spiritual movement prior to and after repentance. Repentance seems to be one of the bridges from the prior process to the latter process. A similar "turning to repentance" is also found in other texts of Origen.[253] We find also a similar commentary on this text in Origen's homily on the Song of Songs. He writes:

. . . but the question is, in what way is she black and how, if she lacks whiteness, is she fair? She has repented of her sins, beauty is the gift conversion has bestowed; that is the reason she is hymned as beautiful. She is called black, however, because she has not yet been purged of every stain of sin, she has not yet been washed for salvation; nevertheless she does not stay dark-hued, she is becoming white.[254]

Though repentance is involved in the conversion event, it is not part of the actual movement. We turn (or move) to repentance, or we repent and then we turn. In any case, repentance is very much integrated into conversion and is often the very earliest event of the one converting. In fact, the event is so early in spiritual growth that the soul is still "black" from sin.

Another text that indicates the role of repentance in the larger process of conversion concerns Origen's interpretation of John 15:1-2, 5-6 in conjunction with Ezek. 15:1-6. Both of these texts concern the parable of the vine, the branches, and the vinedresser who decides which branches need pruning and to be cast into the fire. For Origen, Scripture here is giving a warning which all should heed. For we are the branches that will be cast into the fire if we do not change.

> Truly we ourselves make sport among us and are deceived as well, and when we deceive ourselves we want to err with even more acts rather than be converted from the error, when we ought more to seek that which raises us up, which strengthens the fear of God, which calls us back to repentance, which leads to confession of our wicked acts, which helps us to know day and night what pleases the Lord, so that we might become fruitful "branches" on the "true vine" Christ Jesus and cling to its "root." (Rev. 22:16; Rom. 15:12; Rev. 5:5)[255]

This text, besides concerning repentance, offers several of the dimensions of becoming a Christian. First, Origen presents the general distinction of those who are in error and those who are converting from their error. Those who are in error are deceived and will be those who will be cut off by the vinedresser. Second, Origen lists some of the characteristic acts and attitudes of him who is converting: The one who is converting will seek (1) to raise himself up, (2) to augment in himself the fear of God, (3) to repent, (4) to confess his wickedness, and (5) to know what is pleasing to the Lord.[256] The order of events in this text may not be accidental. The first movement that describes conversion is the turning from the inferior position or direction to a superior position. This movement is spiritually a movement up. Second, after making the initial decision and movement upwards, the one converting then has a renewed image of God. For he begins to realize the power and magnificence of God, particularly God's power of judgment, and has a renewed respect. Then, third, after these initial movements in the heart, comes the clear recognition of one's past errors and the sense of regret as well as grief. This feeling expresses itself in confession and other fruits of repentance. The final event is the knowledge how to please God. Hence the cycle begins with God's certain displeasure and man's alienation and error, and ends with the knowledge how to please God. In the midst of this cycle is the event of repentance, which bridges the gap between the first steps away from sin and the full realization and knowledge of God's judgment and expectations.

2.

Now that we have set repentance in its place with respect to conversion, let us examine briefly the substance of repentance. Essentially we are here concerned to outline the elements of repentance that define it as an event. These elements center primarily around certain concrete deeds, a feeling of grief, a sense of shame, confession, and exercise of the rational faculty.[257] As in all matters concerning conversion, Origen is only concerned with the change within the heart. But he realizes that the change from a black to a white soul does not occur all at once or with a single realization. Repentance also is a period of suffering for the one converting because the change is extremely painful and difficult. The period of repentance is at the critical period of the process of conversion, as we have mentioned above. If the repentance is true, Origen writes in several texts, then salvation and further growth will follow.

What is then the true repentance? Origen clarifies repentance in his discussion of Jer. 20:9,

> And it arose in my heart as a burning fire, flaming in my bones, and I faced it from all sides and I could not bear it, for I heard the reproach of many who gathered around me.

The "fire" that Jeremiah describes in this text is a special fire, which Origen has already indicated in the prior section is kindled by Christ in those who hear him.[258] It is the fire of conscience and repentance. To illustrate the reality of this fire, Origen compares the way two different men respond to sin. The one is like the woman in Prov. 24:55 who, when she had done something wrong, washed herself and said she had done nothing. Then Origen describes the other man:

> See with me the other man who after the mistake is unable to hide his shame, but punishes the conscience, tortures the heart, is unable to eat and drink, who fasts not by a penalty but a sense of pain from repentance. I will describe him as a kind of man who appears sad all day long and who wears himself down with suffering and who goes wailing from the groaning of his heart, who sees his sin reproved before himself on account of all which happened before. And see that this sort of person is [this way] not only for one day or night, but who punishes himself for a long time. (Ps. 37:7, 9–10)[259]

Let us suggest that this whole series of attitudes and events defines the process of repentance within conversion. And the general theme of this process is the full realization of the reality of sin. Once the penitent feels the full consequences of his wrongdoing, he cannot help but react intensely, trying as it were to force a change upon himself in order to rid himself of the old person. His self-denial and suffering, as described by Origen, is very painful, but to the true penitent it is the complement to the realization of sin. The physical and emotional travails are metaphors of the inner spiritual struggles. They are signs of a deeper transformation. Hence the true repentance is a repentance that involves the whole person, that circumvents one's pattern of living and surfaces in an almost violent denial of every attitude and act that was customary. He is ashamed, conscience-stricken, sad, in mourning, unable to eat and drink, and continually groping, groaning and wailing about his mistakes. Origen lauds this repentance as a repentance resulting from the fire that Christ has initiated. It is the same fire that was in Jeremiah.

Hence in repentance as in so many areas of conversion Origen seeks a kind of revolution of spirit that bears no resemblance to the ordinary course of life. For example, the greatest act for Origen is not to give alms or care for the sick or feed the hungry, but to die for God, as his work *Exhortation to Martyrdom* verifies. And the greatest indication of inner movement is an almost frenzied kind of remorse and self-mortification, as if one was on fire internally, essentially reflecting the death of sin. There is no escaping the consequences of one's sins. For Origen sinning might be compared to dropping black ink into a glass of crystal-clear water; no part of the water escapes the influence of the ink. Hence to remove the ink every part of the water must be changed. Origen explains what the penitent endures not only to explain the true repentance, but also to indicate vividly how deeply sin hooks itself into man. Though he will admit there are both grave and lesser sins, not even the least sin, Origen writes, is forgotten at judgment.[260]

This vision of repentance is found in many other texts of Origen. Let us briefly summarize a few in order to present the diverse contexts in which he lays out his thought. A common way for Origen to note the difficulty involved in repentance is to stress God's patience with the sinner. For example, in his discussion of the texts in Jeremiah concerned with the period before the captivity, Origen points out that God gave Israel many opportunities to repent through the prophet's threats. The people have two choices:

> Become captives or repent! For if you repent, the conditions of the captivity will not arise, but the mercy of God will be known to you. . . . If we sin, we are about to become captives.[261]

In other words, God delays his judgment and punishment and waits for repentance. But repentance did not come and the captivity took place. The "captivity" for Origen is the captivity of sin. In other contexts, Origen will indicate how God was patiently awaiting repentance from the Ninevites, the people of Sodom and Gomorrah, the people of Jeremiah's time, and from the Jews after Christ's death.[262] But God's patience is limited, Origen notes in a fragment, as Scripture teaches with respect to the time of Noah, and in each of these cases the penalty for sin was inflicted.[263] Often God will use threats to try to guide man to repentance, treating humanity as a father treats his children through the use of fear.[264] Despite all this help from God, men nevertheless remained obstinate and failed to recognize the need for repentance. In this attitude they were deceived, according to Origen, for again and again Scripture presents the image of an extremely patient God who anxiously awaits change, but, seeing none, turns to punishment or turns away entirely. The pattern of God's way with repentance is to call for repentance, threaten to force repentance, and, if both fail, deliver the sinner to punishment and captivity of sin.[265] Repentance is evidently then, according to Origen's interpretation of Scripture, part of God's conversion plan, but recognizing man's obstinacy, God metes out punishment in small doses in order to encourage man to change.[266]

We may justifiably ask why God must be patient, why the process takes so long? The answer to these questions has to large extent been answered previously in our discussions. Repentance requires time because of the condition of man's soul before repentance. As we have seen in many texts, the state of man's soul, according to Origen, is effaced intrinsically by sin. Hence repenting is not simply a matter of a few alms, some good deeds, and a promise to change. Man has actually turned his soul upside down through the corruption from sin. As Origen states in one text concerning Jer. 6:9, reason itself is not working properly in the sinner.[267] The man of sin is, in fact, in light of Matt. 22:32, John 11:25 and Heb. 6:1, with respect to God, dead.[268] So the change from what is death to what is life is radical and requires a fundamental transformation of mind. Given the circumstances and environment of the sinner, an environment that tends to encourage sin rather than repentance, real change happens slowly. God, being cognizant of this fact more than anyone else, waits patiently and punishes intermittently.

The substance and difficulty of repenting is, of course, a matter of great concern. It might be worthwhile to consider a text offered by Origen on this subject. In the work *Against Celsus*, Origen quotes Celsus as saying that it is very difficult to change a man's nature completely. Origen senses in this opinion of Celsus an implicit limitation of God's power. So he offers this reply:

> We affirm that every rational soul is of the same nature, and deny that any wicked nature has been made by the Creator of the universe; but we think that many men have become evil by upbringing and by perversion and by environment, so that in some people evil has become second nature. We are convinced that for the divine Logos to change evil which has become second nature is not only not impossible, but is not even very difficult, if only a man admits that he must trust himself to the supreme God and do every action by reference to his good pleasure. . . . And if for some it is very hard to change, we must say that the cause lies in their will, which refuses to accept the fact that the supreme God is to each man a righteous judge of every past action done in this life. Determination and application can achieve much even with problems which appear very difficult, and, if I may exaggerate, which are all but impossible.[29]

Then Origen offers the example of the daring feats of the tightrope walker. If, he says, man can achieve this physical act with application and practice, why can a man, if he wishes, not become virtuous, even if he was very bad formerly? Then Origen more directly answers Celsus:

> Moreover, consider whether the man who asserts that it is impossible is not finding fault with the nature of the Creator of the rational being rather than with the creature, as if he had made human nature capable of doing very difficult things which are quite unprofitable, but incapable of attaining its own blessedness.[270]

Since this is a critical subject for anyone becoming a Christian, almost the entire section has been given. Some of what it concerns, such as the interplay of man's will and God's power, has been discussed previously. In brief, no creature endowed with *logos* is incapable of change, because God endowed each of them with the capacity to achieve "its own blessedness." That gift of *logos*, as we have discussed, is both from God and of God. Hence God shares in every step of growth.

However, the matter of most interest in the above text is the way in which Origen describes how one overcomes evil. Origen realizes that evil and the habits of evil are ingrained in some people. Four things can be done, he writes, to change this condition: (1) to admit that one must trust in God, (2) to do what would please God, (3) to have determination to change, and (4) to practice what would bring about change. The second and fourth elements are connected. Actually there are two dimensions of effecting change: the inner determination to change and the realization of one's relationship with God, and the extension of this inner attitude into actual applications. One helps the other. For example, doing virtuous acts can help strengthen one's confidence, but a firm resolve is necessary in order to attempt virtuous practice.

Another question remains. How does a man acquire the determination? What brings one to the need for spiritual growth in the first place? This question has been answered to a great extent previously. Constantly God is offering men opportunity to convert and change through Scripture, his messengers, wisdom, the sacraments, the work of the Church, and even by the wonders of his creation in nature. Hence the catalysts for change are offered by God and are always present. Variables do abound with respect to when men will respond to these catalysts. In any case, the differences among men in terms of growth and awareness present another need for God's patience.

Now that we have clarified the difficulty of repentance and God's patience, let us turn to a few of the aspects Origen mentions as key integrals of repentance. We have already noted that Origen expects a reversal in attitude and behavior in the penitent.

One element of this reversal is grief.[271] For example, let us consider Origen's interpretation of Jer. 51:34, "Those whom I will pull down, I will again build up." In fact, Origen produces one scriptural text after another to indicate that God first brings pain before he restores.[272] He concludes, however, with 2 Cor. 7:10, "For grief due to God produces a repentance that leads to salvation."[273] Moreover, in his commentary on John 11:41, Origen indicates that not everyone who has grief has a grief due to God, but only the one "who has done something worthy of such grief...."[274] The indication in this text is that, first, there is a preparation for grief through certain acts that God approves. The example offered by Origen is that of the tax collector in Luke 18:13 who would not raise his eyes, but simply beat his breast and begged for mercy.[275] We will return to these acts below.

The second matter to note is that God initiates this grief. Origen agrees with Scripture that it is a grief "due to God." In fact, it is worthwhile to mention that 2 Cor. 7:10 is concerned to distinguish grief due to God and "worldly grief." The latter does not lead to repentance. Hence spiritual grief will lead to repentance, as Origen verifies in his discussion of Isa. 6:5, "for I am conscience-stricken," a discussion in which he also again quotes 2 Cor. 7:10. Just as in the example

Origen offered above of the tax collector, Origen notes two aspects: humility and sincere weeping.[276] These are the signs of a true repentance, for they exhibit a sense of wrongdoing and of respect for God. In fact, the word "grief" may lead us astray to what is probably an inaccurate idea of grief for him. Spiritual grief seems to be closer to what we tend to call shame.

Proof of this is found in his discussion of Jer. 3:24, "But the shame has devoured all the labors of our fathers...." In this section of his homilies, he is concerned with how the Gentiles repented of their idolatry and worship of falsity. The "labors of the fathers" are devoured, that is, destroyed by shame. Then he writes:

The beginning of good is to find shame in some things of which one was not ashamed.[277]

There is a hint of repentance when one begins to have doubts about one's past attitudes and acts, but repentance happens when one responds concretely with grief or shame.

Another ingredient in the environment of repentance is confession. In his discussion of Ps. 73(74):19 and Jer. 12:9, "Go and assemble all the beasts of the field, and they came to eat it," Origen states that Christ makes this statement, that he relinquishes evil people to the beasts. Then he writes that we must pray not to be delivered and "...confess for transgressions when we repent, and let us not be delivered to the beasts...."[278] As we have seen in so many other matters of theology, Origen is led by scripture, and especially a connection he notes between Jer. 12:9 and Ps. 73(74):19. However, it is his addition of the concept of repentance to the idea of confession that interests us, as well as the reference to prayer. Confession also was connected to repentance in the section of homily five that was partially quoted above. After introducing the section as one that concerns repentance, Origen writes:

Then, when confessing concerning the sins in which both our fathers and we shared, when we were serving idols, we say: "But the shame has devoured all the labors of our fathers...."[279]

The connection between confession and repentance is so close in some texts that they often seem to coincide. An example of this similarity is found in Origen's views on Jer. 38:18–20. This entire fragment is concerned with repentance, shame, confession, and conversion in general, and, if we had the space, the whole fragment would be worth quoting. The story of Ephraim in this text is the story of one who turns to God after much pain and punishment, after realizing his error and feeling shame, after much lamenting for sin, and especially after confession of his sins. Ephraim erred, realized his error, lamented over his error, confessed his error, and repented. The core of his repentance also was his realization that he needed God, and that he needed to repent and be obedient in order to achieve spiritual growth. The entire scriptural text, however, is a confession, and, according to Origen and Jeremiah, when God hears the confession, he hastens to help him, for Ephraim has truly repented.[280]

Finally, we also find a preoccupation with confession as a foundation for repentance in Origen's views on Jer. 38:23-24. Origen writes:

> But if we are in him in the sense of "and you are in me" (John 14:20), we can build on "the righteous mountain." And a person does this when he is in Judea (which is translated as "she who has confessed"), he who has confessed to God his sins and who has given thanks. "For speak first of your licentiousness, so that you might become righteous." (Isa. 43:26)[281]

There is also another aspect of repentance that we have noticed in several of the texts above, namely, concrete acts that naturally emerge from repentance and that lead into repentance. With respect to the latter, Origen writes in his commentary on Song of Songs 1:5, 3 Kings 10:1-10 and Matt. 12:42 that the queen of Sheba, who is symbolically the Church, according to Origen, brings "good works," with "trained perceptions," and "rational habits of mind" when she "opens her heart to Christ, in confession, doubtless, and repentance for her past transgressions."[282]

We find this text interesting because it is evident that repentance can require extensive preparation of many aspects of a person's life. Evidently in Origen's mind a considerable amount of reflection as well as behavioral change can happen prior to the repentance event in the conversion process. One might state, however, that this text refers to the second or later events of repentance and not to the initial period of change. In Origen's view, while the details are different, the movement from sin to virtue, or from being out of favor with God to being in favor with God, is similar in one way. Even if a man's history had once been virtuous and pleasing to God, once he has fallen into sin, once he has crossed the gap into evil, all his good counts as nothing. He, like a novice, must begin again; he must be converted and repent. Origen's attitude follows logically from his belief, noted several times in this study, that there is no person who can be evil and good at the same time.

With respect to what emerges from repentance, let us turn to Origen's homily on Luke 3:8, "Bear fruits that befit repentance. . . ." Origen writes:

> And to you who come to baptism it is written, "Make then fruits worthy of repentance." Do you want to know what are the fruits worthy of repentance? Charity is a fruit of the spirit, joy is a fruit of the spirit; peace, patience, kindness, goodness, faith, gentleness, self-control and the rest in the same way. These are called the fruits of the spirit (cf. Gal. 5:22-23). If we have had all of them, we have made fruits worthy of repentance.[283]

A man who has truly repented will then produce the fruits mentioned above. Origen does not examine here the connection between the event of repentance and the various acts and attitudes mentioned in this text, which is based in Scripture. His concern is rather to indicate that the effect of repentance on the soul will be evident in the penitent life. True repentance results in a radical reversal.

3.

This last text leads us into our final concern with repentance, namely, the benefits of repentance in one's continuing growth in the conversion process. This text, for example, implied that repentance is necessary before baptism. In fact, not only is repentance necessary, but the "fruits" of repentance are required. Twice this conclusion is offered in Book 6 of the *Commentary on John*. For example, in discussing John's rebuke of the Pharisees in Matt. 3:10, Origen paraphrases John:

Since you have come to baptism without producing the fruit of repentance, you are a "tree" which does not "bring forth good fruit."[284]

Similarly on Matt. 3:11 Origen writes:

It is to be observed that while the four [gospels] represent John as declaring himself to have come to baptize with water, Matthew alone adds the words "for repentance," teaching that the benefit of baptism is connected with the intention of the baptized person; to him who repents it is salutary, but to him who comes to it without repentance it will turn to greater condemnation.[285]

Hence baptism to be salutary requires repentance.

The reason for this need for repentance lies very much in the connection with sin. Sin is what alienates one from God. Diminish the chance for sin and one diminishes the distance between himself and God. Hence before baptism the one converting seeks ways to please God, and to indicate by means of one's fruits that he has changed. A key element in the process of removing sin, however, is repentance.[286]

In fact, one of the benefits of repentance is the forgiveness and approval God offers. As we have shown, God is patient with man. However, he is also kind to those who repent.[287] Origen uses Luke 15:7 as a foundation:

There is more joy in heaven over one sinner who repents than over ninety-nine who need no repentance.[288]

In his discussions of the images that man can bear—the images of the earthly and the heavenly—Origen indicates that when one repents, one turns to the image of the heavenly away from the earthly, so that, it is implied, when one repents, he is in some way returning to the condition in which God "planted" the soul. This matter is discussed in Origen's consideration of Jer. 2:21, in which God says that he planted man as "choice vine," only to see man "turn to malice."

This text places repentance in the center of the critical shift from the image of the earthly to the image of the heavenly in the process of conversion. He writes:

> "We have borne," because we are sinners, "the image of the earthly"; let us bear, since we are repenting, the "image of the heavenly" (1 Cor. 15:49). In any case the creation arose in the image of the heavenly.[289]

Repentance, in a similar vein, also brings back what Origen calls the creation according to the image, first mentioned in Genesis. He raises this matter in his discussion of Jer. 22:24–26 and the meaning of the "seal" that is mentioned there.

> And every person who through repentance takes upon himself what is according to the image becomes a "seal," that is, a ring on the "right of God" (Jer. 22:24). For good works are understood as those acts on the "right of God," who places the sheep "at his right" (Matt. 25:33). The "father" gave this kind of "seal" to the profligate "son" who returned. (Luke 15:22)[290]

The story of the prodigal son in Luke 15 is the story of one who had strayed away and then returned (in the way of the Hebrew scriptures). The word Origen uses here, *epistrephein*, with respect to the son's action, is not found in the Luke text, but it suits the context of one who had once been near the Father, who had once had the image, had fallen, and became aware, through repentance, of his error, and desired "to return" to his former position. The text itself does mention, however, that the "son was dead and is now alive again" (Luke 15:24), and Origen in other contexts views this change in light of repentance.[291]

Another way in which Origen applies the concept of repentance is with respect to scriptural interpretation and understanding. As we have seen on many occasions, Origen views Scripture as a feast for the spirit. The deeper man pursues God in his life, the deeper will be both his understanding of Scripture and the way in which it affects him. Scripture is not only a kind of spiritual recipe book; it is also the living Logos for the person who comes to terms with it. And one way for this event to happen is through repentance.

These are Origen's conclusions in his commentary on Matt. 3:2, "Repent, for the kingdom of heaven is at hand." This text he believes, can be allegorically understood to mean that the scribes will repent of their own literal method of interpretation and come to learn the spiritual way of interpretation. Moreover, he continues, since the kingdom of heaven is where Christ is present, until one repents and makes a place for Christ, the kingdom of heaven will not arise. Repentance is a mode of allowing the word of God to enter the soul so that the kingdom of God can occur within the heart. Origen then adds:

> But if the kingdom of heaven and the kingdom of God are the same thing in reality, if not in idea, manifestly to those to whom it is said, "The kingdom of God is within you" (Luke 17:21), to them also might be said, "The kingdom of heaven is within you";

and most of all because of the repentance from the letter to the spirit; since "when one turns to the Lord, the veil over the letter is taken away. But the Lord is the Spirit." (2 Cor. 3:16–17)[292]

Repentance then not only opens up the heart to God and helps to initiate the kingdom of God; it also is a catalyst for leaping the gap between the letter and the spirit. Repentance can accomplish this feat because it is a process that brings the Logos into one's life. And the Logos, as we have discussed in other contexts, is for Origen automatically an agent of spiritual awareness. For the Logos is akin to the *logos* in man.

Therefore the great benefit and effect of repentance is the welcome one receives by the Father, as the father welcomed and had great joy in the return of the prodigal son. The effort to recognize one's sin and one's position vis-a-vis God is rewarded by enlightenment and forgiveness.

Nevertheless, the power of repentance cannot stand without qualification for Origen. Evidently each case must again be considered separately. What of those who have become Christians and have perverted, that is, who have repented and started on the road to becoming Christian and have lapsed? Suppose they should repent again; what will their repentance bring? Origen reflects on this situation in various contexts. His answer is the same: They will be generally welcome, but they will not be permitted to assume any position of responsibility or leadership in the Church. The rigor of Christian life and the selection process is proudly explained in reply to Celsus's claim that Christians take anyone and are particularly anxious to show off before those who are immature. In response Origen details how carefully the selection process of potential Christians is followed to ensure, as far as possible, sincere and worthwhile converts. With respect to those who once were faithful and have lapsed, Origen writes:

> But [Christians] mourn as dead men those who have been overcome with licentiousness or some outrageous sin because they have perished and died to God. They admit them some time later as though they had risen from the dead provided that they show a real change, though the period of probation is longer than that required of those who are joining the community for the first time. But they do not select those who have fallen . . . for any office or administration in the church of God, as it is called.[293]

Origen ends the discussion of this matter with the last quoted sentence. He does not pursue here the reasons why one kind of repentance, the repentance after one's first introduction to Christianity, is superior to another, the repentance of one who has lapsed. Repentance is not a magical event in itself that can each time transform the worst sinner and wipe away the blot of sin regardless how many times he had sinned. Repentance loses its full power, at least in terms of ecclesiastical positions, after the first time. In effect, there is one true repentance and one baptism. If one sins after repentance, and then sins again, God alone rather than anyone on earth can pardon the sin.[294]

In some contexts, Origen is even more demanding and exclusive. In his discussion of Jer. 15:5, "Who will spare you, Jerusalem?" he repeats with approval the severe text from Hebrews:

> Since we then know "it is impossible to restore again to repentance—if they commit apostasy—those who have once been enlightened, who have tasted the heavenly gift, and have become partakers of the Holy Spirit, and have tasted the goodness of the word of God and the powers of the age to come, since they crucify the Son of God on their own account and hold him up to contempt" (Heb. 6:4–6), let us do all lest it may also be said about us "who will spare you, Jerusalem? Who will feel sorry for you? Or who will turn back to plead for your peace?"[295]

In conclusion we may say that repentance has a tremendous effect on the soul of the one who is first turning to Christianity. This same effect happens to the one who repents after lapsing, but the Church community, according to Origen, is unwilling to entrust him with any official or clerical position. Moreover, Origen agrees with the above text from Hebrews that apostasy hinders true repentance for the one who was enlightened and had felt the goodness of God. This is particularly true for one who has blasphemed either the Son of God or the Holy Spirit. In sum, the greatest benefits accrue to the first repentance attached to baptism. And those benefits involve a new spiritual opportunity for the soul to begin to return to its original condition as the image of God and the image of the heavenly. Repentance for Origen is not a movement forward, but rather an about-face on the same spot. It turns one in the right direction in the conversion process, but other aspects of conversion draw one home to God.

4.

As mentioned at the beginning of this section, it is not possible to discuss in this subsection all the intricacies of prayer.[296] However, we shall try to consider those matters which are most relevant to our concern with the spiritual journey and conversion.

We are particularly concerned with the practical effects of prayer in terms of spiritual movement. Prayer is often indirectly involved in this movement, but nevertheless it is involved.[297] For example, Origen states in his work *On Prayer* that praying brings help from the Holy Spirit in overcoming certain problems, particularly in battling the forces of evil and turning from spiritual barrenness to "visions of truth." Origen writes:

> For souls that have become for the most part barren, when they perceive the sterility of their own hearts and the barrenness of their own mind, have conceived and given birth through persistent prayer from the Holy Spirit to saving words filled with visions of truth.[298]

Let us note especially in this text two conversion elements cooperating to bring about these "visions of truth." The first is very similar to the process of repentance we have just considered in the prior subsections, namely, the recognition of one's own spiritual sterility. Coupled with this, however, is "persistent prayer" and help from the Holy Spirit. Origen goes on to say in this section of this work that these elements are able to combat and overcome the forces of evil. For Origen the situation of the sinner is treacherous. Help is needed from self-reflection, prayer, and God in the person of the Holy Spirit.

Origen finds the images in Jeremiah 4 insightful with respect to this matter. There Scripture speaks of a lion who sets out to destroy us. The lion, according to Origen, is the devil, and we are his prey. Origen then offers this interpretation:

> Since then the lion has come up and the lion threatens you and wants to obliterate your earth, "gird yourself with sackcloth," cry out and mourn, implore God through prayers to eradicate this lion from you, and you may not fall into his pit.[299]

Again prayer is mentioned as one of the elements that can cause a change in the person, which can help him confront and destroy what seeks to destroy him. It is evident here and in previous texts offered that no person can underestimate the threat and danger of evil to the soul. To change one's course, a person must take several measures that are quite different from his previous life habits. For example, he must cover himself with sackcloth, cry out, mourn, and through prayer seek God.

Prayer too requires preparation and purification. In fact, Origen will write, concerning Jer. 51:21–22, that true prayers are those done from righteousness, that is, those arising from men who have clean hearts and behavior.[300] In Origen's view, the sinner needs prayer in order to change, but the sinner must first be transformed through preparation. Origen outlines some basic elements of this preparation in *On Prayer*. Preparation includes forgiveness of those who have sinned against him, so that no wrath remains, and concentration on nothing but the prayer, eliminating all distractions. In summary, he writes:

> For the eyes of the mind are lifted up from their preoccupation with earthly things and from their being filled with the impression of material things. And they are so exalted that they peer beyond the created order and arrive at the sheer contemplation of God and at conversing with him reverently and suitably as he listens. How would things so great fail to profit those eyes that gaze at the glory of the Lord with unveiled face and that are changed into his likeness from glory to glory (2 Cor. 3:18)? For then they partake of some divine and intelligible radiance, as is indicated in the words: "the light of your countenance, o Lord, was signed upon us" (Ps. 4:6). Moreover, when the soul is lifted up and follows the spirit and severs itself from the body—and not only follows the spirit but also dwells within it, as is indicated in the words: "Unto thee have I lifted up my soul" (Ps. 25:1)—it must needs be that in laying aside the nature of a soul it becomes spiritual.[301]

This description of prayer seems to us most complete. In no other work is there such a clear presentation, based in Scripture, of what Origen means fundamentally by prayer and by the transcendence to the spiritual level. And the immediate impression from his description is that prayer is a bridge between one state of mind/body, namely, that which concerns the earthly and material, and another, that which can see beyond the earthly and material. And not only is this process of prayer a way to see what is spiritual; it is also a way to merge with the spirit and dwell in the spirit. Prayer, then, transports one not only through knowledge but also through the full experience of being. We are changed not only in mind; we are completely transformed. In fact, Origen states that it is by putting aside its existence that the soul becomes spiritual. This view of prayer contrasts with a view that only sees prayer as a way for man to receive from, ask of, and thank God, but not to unite with him. Understood in Origen's view in this text, prayer is a mystical act and agent of conversion. Is it any wonder then that some preparation and purification is implict in his understanding?

By describing Origen's view of prayer in the above way, let us not conclude that we have exhausted his conception. Indeed we may assume that without the other side of prayer, the preparatory side, the mystical side would not arise. This preparatory side, however, is quite clear, at least with respect to conversion, and we need not dwell on it in depth.

In sum, this side involves several elements. The first and second were covered in prior chapters. Prayer plays a role in ridding us of sin, and prayer draws help and healing from the Holy Spirit. The other aspects are presented again in *On Prayer:* In his concluding paragraphs of this work, Origen sets down the four stages of prayer. The first aspect of prayer should be praise for God. Then one should offer thanks for the many things which have been given to one by God. Third, after praise and thanksgiving, one should show evidence of regret for the past sins by blaming himself and then ask for healing from the sins and for forgiveness. This stage of confession should be followed by requests for nonmaterial and spiritual gifts for oneself and for one's family and friends.[302]

These two sides of prayer, the preparatory and the mystical, are both connected to the process of transformation that is necessary for one who seeks God and salvation. Prayer, explained from another viewpoint on Origen's work, is community with God in which a relationship occurs, and that relationship has two basic rewards for the one converting: First, it brings God into one's earthly life for forgiveness, healing, and thanks; and, second, it enables one to journey to God for mystical union and loss of earthly ties. Prayer, then, seems to be a kind of pattern for the spiritual journey in Origen's thought. For to continue to be converted, man needs, first, to bring God into his life, and second, to transcend up to God through the spirit.

Why Does a Christian Need the Holy Spirit and Baptism?

1.

Throughout this study the role of the Spirit has been mentioned. In many texts the Spirit's power and importance has been evident, but the subsequent discussions of these matters have been kept at a minimum. In this section, however, we shall present an overview of the contribution of the Spirit to spiritual growth. In addition, we shall discuss the pivotal place of baptism in Origen's view of the Christian life.

Our consideration of the Spirit will be separated into four subsections: (1) an introduction explaining the distinct identity of the Spirit and the spiritual; (2) a discussion of how and why the Spirit comes to human nature, and of the gifts of the Spirit; (3) a summary of the role of baptism in spiritual growth; (4) a brief summary.

Origen's first aim in discussing the realm of the spirit is to distinguish between two ways of viewing reality.[303] One way is to see only the material reality. Those, for example, who interpret Scripture literally in those places where God is described as light and fire view reality through corporeal eyes only. The other view is to see the true reality, the reality that cannot be "seen" with physical eyes, but the with the eyes of the intellect. In this light Origen interprets John 4:23–24:

> But the hour is coming, and now is, when the true worshippers will worship the Father in spirit and truth, for such the Father seeks to worship him. God is spirit, and those who worship him must worship him in spirit and truth.

One person believes *pneuma* (spirit) is the physical "breath" of life that is common to all living things. He is thinking of that breath which gives existence to the "middle" (or earthly) level. But spirit has also another level of meaning with respect to its activity. Origen explains:

> For the spirit, according to scripture, is said to enliven, indicating that it enlivens not the middle [existence], but the more divine.... That which is deprived of the divine spirit becomes earthly, while he who makes himself capable of receiving it [the Spirit] and does receive it, will be recreated and, [when he has been recreated], will be saved.[304]

This text states that the presence of the spirit is necessary for participation in divine life.[305] Without it that life becomes earthly. Moreover, the spirit brings to life what is divine. The term used here is "re-created." The recreation then leads to salvation. In effect, the events seem to take this course:

Just as the physical spirit gives to us the capacity to maintain a corporeal existence and to enliven the body, so the divine spirit enlivens the soul so that it may share in the divine life. This sharing initiates a transformation and renewal of the soul's life to such an extent that it can now progress toward salvation.

In light of this view of the spirit, the place of conversion is quite clear. The role of the spirit stands at the very heart of the conversion movement and is the force that continues to move the soul closer and closer to God and the divine life. In fact, it is the element that effects the change from death to life, a transition we have discussed in other contexts, for the soul.

Accordingly Origen also distinguishes between the soul and the spirit. In his interpretation of John 13:21, which concerns how Jesus was "troubled in spirit," he informs his readers that we need to ask whether Scripture does not indeed contrast to some extent the soul and the spirit. What of, for example, John 12:27, where Jesus said, "my soul is troubled?" Why does Jesus not say here "my spirit is troubled," or I am "troubled in spirit"? Origen responds with the following:

> And with a measure of restraint I dare to inquire into these matters, noting in all of scripture a difference between soul and spirit and seeing that the soul is something in the middle and susceptible of virtue and vice, while the spirit which is in man cannot accept anything inferior. For the most noble fruits are said to be of the spirit, not, as one might suppose, of the Holy [Spirit], but of the human.[306]

In opposition to these fruits of the spirit, Origen continues in this section, are the works of the flesh (cf. Gal. 5:19). The soul, he says, stands to some extent indifferent, or susceptible, to either the influences of the spirit or the influences of the forces of evil, which can be either what Origen calls the flesh or external forces, especially the demons and wrongheaded teachers.[307]

If we merge these ideas with those thoughts given in the prior text and our discussions previously, we can offer an initial view of how Origen saw the environment of the soul with respect to the spirit. First of all, the environment is very flexible and vacillating. Movement toward the influence of the spirit or the influence of evil is not a determined or structured process. Numerous factors, many of which we have reviewed in other sections, have to be considered before a person shifts in one direction or another.

Second, the spirit is not integrated or mixed with anything inferior or what may be negative to spiritual progress. The spirit vivifies the soul with divine life, while the evil influences kill the soul spiritually. Hence the actual environment is, for Origen, well-defined. There is no obscure line or overlapping between divine reality and an existence tinged with evil, though a soul may vacillate from one to the other. Unlike certain Gnostics, however, Origen does not believe that a man is determined by nature to one of these levels.

Third, the participation in divine life seems to involve both the human spirit and the Holy Spirit. The actual relationship between these two forces is not made clear in the above discussions, but we will be returning to this matter in pages to follow.

With this introduction to the spirit in general and the significance of spirit to spiritual growth, let us briefly consider the person of the Holy Spirit. Since this study is not devoted to trinitarian questions, we will not be probing deeply into Origen's view of the Holy Spirit as a member of the Trinity. Our main concern is to understand the Holy Spirit insofar as the Spirit is involved in religious change. Two specific texts, both from Origen's early works but that do not seem to be contradicted by later texts, may be used as an overview of the Holy Spirit in Origen. The first occurs in Origen's interpretation of John 1:3, "All things were made through him." Origen inquires whether the "all" here also includes the

Holy Spirit. Was the Holy Spirit made through the Logos? After offering several possible answers to this question, Origen gives the following reply.

> Since we consider then that there are three hypostases, the Father and the Son and the Holy Spirit, and at the same time we believe nothing to be uncreated but the Father, we admit, as the more pious and true course, that "all things were made through" the Logos, the Holy Spirit being the most excellent and the first in order of all that was made by the Father through Christ. . . . The Only-begotten alone is by nature and from the beginning a son, and the Holy Spirit seems to have need of a son, to minister to [the Holy Spirit] his essence, so as to enable him not only to exist, but to be wise and reasonable and just, and all that we must think of him as being because he participates in the attributes of Christ which we have enumerated. And I consider that the Holy Spirit supplies to those who, through him and through participation in him, are called saints, the material of the gifts, which comes from God; so that the said material of the gifts is made powerful by God, is ministered by Christ, and owes its actual existence in men to the Holy Spirit.[308]

Origen points out that his view of the role of the Holy Spirit is supported by Paul in 1 Cor. 12:4–6, where Paul considers the diversites of gifts. In order to see the entire context and to present one of the very few discussions of the Holy Spirit extant in Origen's Greek works, the passage is quoted at length. However, of particular concern to us is the manner in which Origen describes the various functions of the Persons of the Trinity.[309] In this hierarchy of function (rather than of divinity), it appears that the Holy Spirit is the party who directly "supplies the material" that brings the converted to the opportunity for divine life. Though the participation is not altogether clear, Origen does say that the origin of the power for transformation is from God the Father; the agent who serves the Father in the cause of man is Christ, namely, he who is the power of transition from the Father to man; and finally, the force who actually instills that life made possible through Christ into human existence is the Holy Spirit.

Origen states a similar view of the Holy Spirit in his *On First Principles*, where there is an entire chapter on the Holy Spirit. Unfortunately, it is preserved in the Latin, and a couple of Greek and Latin fragments that may or may not be authentic, so that much of its detail is of uncertain quality.[310] However, the chapter as a whole verifies what we have just read from the *Commentary on John*. Origen more specifically says that the domain of the Father is all of creation, the domain of the Son is those beings with *logos*, and the work of the Holy Spirit is only in those "who are already turning to better things and walking in the ways of Jesus Christ, that is, who are engaged in good deeds and who abide in God."[311]

In any case, it is evident from these texts that Origen considered the Spirit to have a special role with respect to those who are converting (*convertunt*). As Origen continues to clarify in this chapter of *On First Principles*, the Spirit indeed is the very force that enables the converted to be spiritual and step into the divine life. Just as there are dimensions to the growth of a man on the path to God, so the Trinity itself may be seen as a series of conversion steps, with the Holy Spirit providing the catalyst to any further progress. In effect, this process, if we describe conversion from the view of the Trinity, seems to proceed, according to Origen, as follows: We obtain our existence from the Father, our rational nature from the Son, and our holiness from the Holy Spirit. Then, due to the sanctification by the Spirit, we can acquire wisdom from the Son and perfection and immortal life from the Father. Origen writes:

> Thus the working of the Father, which endows all with existence, is found to be more glorious and splendid, when each one, through participation in Christ in his character of wisdom and knowledge and sanctification, advances and comes to higher degrees of perfection; and when a man, by being sanctified through participation in the Holy Spirit, is made purer and holier, he becomes more worthy to receive the grace of wisdom and knowledge, in order that all stains of pollution and ignorance may be purged and removed and that he may make so great an advance in holiness and purity that the life which he received from God shall be such as is worthy of God, who gave it to be pure and perfect, and that that which exists shall be as worthy as he who caused it to exist.[312]

Now, Origen in many passages seems to discuss two kinds of spirit: The spirit of man and the Holy Spirit. Let us explore the relation of these two.[313] In his criticism of Heracleon's commentary on John 1:4, Origen points out that Heracleon's apparent use of man interchangeably with what is spiritual is faulty.

> For the spiritual person is more than a man, since a man is characterized as [being a man] either in soul or in body or in combination, but not also in spirit which is more divine than these; for the spiritual is so called according to the dominant share of [the spirit].[314]

This text indicates that a man by nature has a soul and a body, but the spirit, in the sense of spirit with which we are concerned, is something man shares with God, specifically with the Spirit. In other words, man becomes spiritual when he becomes more and more aligned with the Spirit. It should be noted that while Origen does not specifically mention the Spirit in the text quoted above, the context of the statement does concern the Spirit. In fact, in sentences preceding this text, Origen quotes 1 Cor. 2:14–15, a text that he in many other places uses to relate the Spirit and the spiritual man.[315] And the potential of man to change seems to depend on the share that he can acquire of the Spirit. In fact, Origen suggests that man is no longer "man" as he makes the transition to the spiritual condition. Man is totally changed to a being who can share in the Spirit. The implication of these thoughts is that in order for progress to occur, God and man must share in common. Man does not only move from being a "man" to being a creature who is more than soul and body. He moves to a condition in which he now shares with divinity in some sense. Moreover, as we shall see in more detail below, this transformed creature continues to change and convert under the tutelage of the Spirit and the Father and the Son, but now on the basis of a common kinship, spirit. It is spirit that becomes the agent of communication for man and God. This interrelationship between the converted and the spirit will be discussed in more detail in the following paragraphs.

2.

Often Origen states that the Spirit does not come to everyone. We have already seen that the Spirit for Origen literally gives spiritual life to those who receive him. The gift of the Holy Spirit is a gift of complete transformation and renewal. With respect to this involvement of the Spirit with man, two matters are of particular interest. The first refers to the condition of the one who receives the Spirit, and the second concerns the actual gifts of the Spirit. For Origen the Spirit cannot share space with what is wicked or sinful. Hence he will say that the Spirit is not found in those "who, though rational, still lie in wickedness and are not wholly converted to better things."[316] This is a remarkable statement in light of what we have discussed in prior chapters. This statement, in fact, clarifies that Origen was fully aware of the implications of other discussions made above, particularly those concerned with the relation between the Spirit and man in comparison to the relation of Christ and man or the Father and man. For Origen the Spirit is most intimately linked with the nature of humanity and its salvation on a personal basis. The Father and Son are to some degree in both saints and sinners,[317] but the Spirit is only involved in man's transformation and spiritual journey when he has already been "wholly converted to better things."

> Only in those who are already turning to better things and walking in the ways of Jesus Christ, that is, who are engaged in good deeds and who abide in God, is the work of the Holy Spirit, I think, to be found.[318]

Origen is so committed to this point of view, namely, that a person in the Spirit exists in a special relationship with God, that if someone who "partakes of the Holy Spirit" commits "apostasy," he is not "restored again to repentance." In his discussion of Jer. 15:5, in which the Lord says, "Who will spare you, O Jerusalem?" Origen views here a prophecy of doom for betrayers of Christ, and he quotes Heb. 6:4–6 in support, the full text of which we quoted in the previous section on repentance.[319]

Similarly, Origen in several different contexts will mention that one sign of a difference between the presence of the Holy Spirit with man and the presence of the Father or the Son with man is in the scriptural text Matt. 12:31–32, which explicitly states that one can be forgiven who speaks against Christ, but he who blasphemes the Holy Spirit will never be forgiven in any age.[320]

> What is the reason of this? Is it because the Holy Spirit has more honor than Christ that the sin against him cannot be forgiven? May it not rather be that all rational beings have part in Christ, and that forgiveness is extended to them when they repent of their sins, while only those have part in the Holy Spirit who have been found worthy of it,

and that there cannot well be any forgiveness for those who fall away to evil in spite of such great and powerful cooperation, and who defeat the counsels of the Spirit who is in them?[321]

Those then who receive the Spirit are expected to have achieved a mature plateau in their spiritual growth. When the Spirit finds them worthy, and they begin to share in the power of the Spirit, a return to those periods prior to reception of the Spirit (i.e., a sinful act, in terms of "ages") prevents spiritual growth with the Spirit. Sharing in the Spirit is clearly a level of excellence and virtue which, in Origen's thought, seems to allow no lapse. This achievement, however, does not hinder the need for further growth, as we shall discover in following discussions.

Spiritual growth involves the quest for all persons of the Trinity, each having a distinct role yet unified in the task of transforming man into a worthy friend of God. For example, returning to the text we have quoted above from the *Commentary on John* concerning the difference between Christ and the Holy Spirit, Origen also adds that the Father, the Son and the Holy Spirit all work together for the single task of man's salvation.[322] Also in his interpretation of Jer. 18:13–16, Origen views the three forms of water mentioned in the text as referring to the three persons of the Trinity. He then comments that we must thirst for all three persons of the Trinity if we are to know and experience God, not simply the Father in the way of the Jews or the God known from the New Testament in the way of certain heretics who deny the God of the Law and Prophets.[323] These facts must be taken into account when considering Origen's view of the role of the Trinity. Moreover, Origen sometimes overlaps the roles of Christ and the Holy Spirit. In texts above we have seen how the Holy Spirit enables one to be holy. In some contexts, however, Christ is said to be this force, especially when Origen is led by 1 Cor. 1:30, where it is written that Christ is our "sanctification." For example, he writes:

And when [you call him the power of] sanctification, [you mean the power] which enables those faithful and dedicated to God to become holy.[324]

...Christ is our "sanctification." "For he who sanctifies and those who are sanctified are all from one" (Heb. 2:11) .... And there can be no way to be just without Christ nor to be holy without him nor to endure without Christ, for he is the "endurance of Israel." (Jer. 17:12)[325]

This second text occurs in the context, as noted, of Jer. 17:12, in which the Lord is called our sanctification. However, there is no difficulty with these apparent paradoxes. First, we have already noted that the Spirit, according to Origen, is ministered to by Christ.[326] In fact, according to this text and others we have quoted above, Christ enables the Spirit to have all of his attributes, even his very existence, since all things, including the Spirit, were made through him. In light of this, holiness or spiritual knowledge does not originate with the Spirit. Second, the Son and the Spirit are said to cooperate together in reaching and transforming mankind.[327] Therefore, in these texts, Origen appears to be considering sanctification and holiness from its very root rather than from the mode in which we receive it. Indeed in these texts as well as in many others we need to consider the work of Christ and the Spirit not chronologically, spatially or hierarchically, but, as Origen himself insists, as the unified work of God to return man back.[328]

Therefore the condition of the one seeking to be a follower of Jesus is critical with respect to the acceptance of the Holy Spirit. For the Spirit cannot coexist with evil, as Origen mentions in a fragment:

> The Holy Spirit dwells in undefiled and pure souls, not remaining where there is sin.[329]

Origen sometimes makes the choice quite simple: He says that either a man chooses the flesh or he chooses the spirit,[330] yet the Spirit has no effect on this decision. For the Spirit enters one's life only after the choice has been made, or at least after the soul has become pure again. So in some sense, one first chooses what is of the Spirit without sharing in the Spirit. The Spirit enters the spiritual life when the soul is ready for renewal and spiritual growth, when it has been cleansed of sin. At this point one enters another dimension of spiritual life, the dimension we are discussing in this chapter.

This dimension of spiritual growth occurs primarily because of the gifts of the Spirit and the sharing of these gifts with the human spirit. Let us conclude this subsection with a brief overview of what these gifts include.

In his discussion of Joshua 13–14, Origen explores his view of revelation which involves the growth of knowledge from the Law and Prophets to the coming of Christ to the coming of the Holy Spirit. Hence revelation is tripartite, and in each stage the spiritual awareness is more complete. Origen views the history of the peoples of God as a history of transformation from inexperience and spiritual innocence to completion of both religious practice and spiritual knowledge. The Holy Spirit is the vehicle of maturity.

> For although repentence and conversion from evil to good is preached by means of the Lord and Savior, and remission of sins is given to all believers, and everything which leads to the maturity of the decade is fulfilled, nevertheless the completion and the consummation of all good consists in this: if after all these things, one can be worthy to receive the grace of the Holy Spirit.[331]

So, in the most general sense, the gift of the Holy Spirit is the gift of maturity (or completion), as we prefer to translate the Latin translation *perfectio* and the Greek original *teleiosis*. The Holy Spirit completes what had begun at the beginning of the history of revelation. Christ enables one to enter again into the grace of God by offering repentance and remission of sins, sins that repelled the Spirit. After Christ's pivotal act, the Holy Spirit comes to do the work of consummation. Of course, this role of the Spirit does not mean the Spirit was not involved in prior stages of revelation. In fact, the Spirit was the agent for revelation to the prophets,[332] a revelation that was essentially one concerning change from idolatrous and sinful ways.

What, however, are the gifts that effect completion? We may present two which seem particularly important. First, the Holy Spirit brings the possibility of acquiring spiritual knowledge and wisdom. As we have noted in other contexts, Origen, on the path of Paul, will contrast human wisdom and the spiritual wisdom of God. In his discussion of John 4:14, Origen distinguishes these two forms of wisdom. He concludes, however, by noting that it is the Spirit that brings the water which wells up to eternal life.[333] Similarly, in the chapter devoted to the Holy Spirit in *On First Principles*, Origen indicates that only through the Holy Spirit, who inspires the Scriptures, can man acquire knowledge about the Son of God.[334] At the end of this chapter also, Origen states how the Son, who is wisdom, and the Spirit work together to lead men on to maturity. Indeed, Origen points out, holiness and wisdom, purity and knowledge, lead into each other and are interdependent. Thus it is difficult for Origen to separate the work of the Father, Son and Holy Spirit, or to choose where sanctification ends and the grace of wisdom begins:[335]

> And those who have merited to reach this degree through the sanctification of the Holy Spirit obtain in addition the gift of wisdom by the power of the working of God's Spirit. And this is what I think Paul means when he says that "to some is given the word of wisdom, to others the word of knowledge, by the same Spirit." (1 Cor. 12:8)[336]

The second gift we have already discussed above. By participation in the Holy Spirit, we become holy and pure. This view is clarified especially in Origen's fragmentary discussion of John 3:5, where Jesus says, "Unless one is born of water and the Spirit, he cannot enter the kingdom of God." The water is viewed by Origen as an indication of the need for purification. To become a part of the kingdom of God, or to receive the Spirit, one must be purified of sin. For as we have discussed above, there can be no partnership between sin and the Spirit. Hence, after purification, the Spirit sanctifies and opens up the way for each to be a spiritual and holy being. For a man to change and receive the Spirit, he takes certain steps that basically involve purification. Then he is on the path for spiritual growth. That growth, Origen adds, is nurtured by an abundance of fruits.[337]

One of the most important lessons we learn from Origen's view of the Spirit in terms of change is that spiritual knowledge and holiness are indeed gifts and are not acquired by human study or individual human merit. Though Origen repeatedly encourages his readers and audience to do good works of all varieties, and to study the Scriptures especially, the final decision on one's incentive to turn to God is decided on much more subtle factors in one's heart. Constantly Origen juggles the condition of man's heart and the gifts of the Holy Spirit. Because so much is involved in the movement from one condition to another, he includes the roles of the Father and the Son, so that, in the end, the entire process of change becomes more and more mysterious. Each man has many divine forces affecting his choices, even inner forces, such as *logos* and spirit. After the initial stages of transformation, he begins again a new journey with new goals, gifts, rewards and, of course, new struggles. And it is here that the Spirit enlivens the soul and, in company with Christ and the Father, prepares and trains the one changing for more and more advanced levels of communion with God. The whole vision of Origen for the Spirit, when we take into account all we have discussed concerning the Holy Spirit, seems to be as an agent of divine communication, a vehicle between the risen Christ, the absolute Father and the reformed man. The Spirit brings the gift of life to man, and through the gifts of knowledge, holiness and scriptural inspiration, he transforms man into a spiritual being prepared to receive eternal life.[338]

3.

In his comments on Luke 3:16, in which Jesus baptizes "in the Holy Spirit and in fire," and in the context of Jer. 2:22, Origen states that there are two baptisms.[339] The first baptism is conferred on one who is holy and merits the Holy Spirit. The second baptism occurs when one believes, is found worthy of the Holy Spirit, but sins again. He will be given the judgment and punishment of the baptism of "fire." Blessed, says Origen, is the one who can keep the "baptism of the Holy Spirit," for he shares in the "first resurrection" (Rev. 20:6). The other man, the one who needs the baptism of fire, after enduring the tests of the fire will be "saved" by the second resurrection.[340] On earth there is only one baptism, according to Origen, the baptism which brings on the possibility of growth and new spiritual life, which changes a man from a creature only of earth to one worthy to share in the Spirit.

This theme of movement between life and death, which we have seen so often in Origen's understanding of spiritual life, is evident again in his understanding of baptism. The mention of resurrection with respect to baptism in the above text indicates that Origen believes one dies in the rite of baptism to be reborn as a new creature in Christ. This implication is more explicit in other contexts. For example, in his consideration of Jer. 1:10, Origen establishes a pattern to divine acts in which there arise unpleasant acts, and then, following them, the pleasant. For proof of this pattern, he mentions Jer. 1:10, Deut. 32:39, 2 Cor. 1:1 and, more applicable to our present concerns, Rom. 6:4. Origen writes:

> Yet do you not see in the scriptures the promise of the resurrection of the dead? Or do you not see that the resurrection of the dead is already foreshadowed in each individual? "We have been buried with Christ through baptism" (Rom. 6:4) and we rise with him. (Cf. Eph. 2:6)[342]

Baptism for Origen is a rite where there is movement, not stasis. In fact, the entire sacrament seems to involve, in Origen's mind, the most radical kind of changes.[342] Beside the movement from death to hope of life, there is the change, mentioned above, from the impure and unholy to purity and sanctity. For example, in his comments on Lev. 16:21, concerning the kind of sacrifices given to the Lord, Origen writes:

And you then are consecrated to the altars of God and you are made a clean animal through the grace of baptism.[343]

The implication in this text is that one comes to baptism impure and is purified in the actual rite of baptism.

In fact, however, this is not Origen's understanding of baptism. Baptism for Origen seems to have two levels of purification. One level is outside the control of man. This level, mentioned in the text above, enables the participant to achieve a spiritual purification produced wholly by divine means, assuming, we might add, that one's intentions are sincere. That matter was settled by Origen in his discussion of John 1:26, where he writes:

...the benefit of baptism is connected with the intention of the baptized person; to him who repents it is salutary but to him who comes to it [without repentance] it will turn to greater condemnation.[344]

This text implies another level of purification that involves the cooperation of man. One dimension of this purification is a sincere repentance. In fact, in many texts Origen speaks of a kind of preparation for baptism, a preparation that indeed purifies.

One great symbol of baptism and of the necessary preparation is the story of Israel crossing the Jordan.[345] Origen notes in his understanding of this event that before the actual cleansing that occurs in the baptismal event there is need that men prepare themselves "...so that they may be in a state to receive the spiritual word, brought home to them by the enlightenment of the Spirit."[346] This preparation is explained by Origen in terms of the biblical journey across the Jordan and the journey of the Israelites from Egypt to the promised land. First, he says, we must rid ourselves of the darknesses of idolatry and come to know something of the divine law. This dimension corresponds to the departure from Egypt. Second, we join the ranks of the catechumens and begin to obey the commandments of the Church. This process is analogous, Origen states, to the crossing of the Red Sea and the wilderness wanderings, when we hear the Law of God and contemplate the face of Moses, who has seen the glory of the Lord. Third, he continues:

But, if you will arrive at the spiritual source of baptism and, in the presence of the priestly and Levitical order, will be initiated to the highest and most sublime mysteries which only those who have the right to know do know, then, having crossed the Jordan thanks to the ministry of the priests, you will enter into the promised land, that land which Jesus, like Moses, upholds and he becomes the leader of a new journey for you.[347]

As this text amply illustrates, there are two journeys of change for the one becoming a Christian. There is the journey leading up to baptism, and there is the journey after one is baptized.[348] The above description was intended to clarify the first journey and to substantiate that each person coming to baptism for Origen has an extensive and, in accordance with the analogy of the Israelites' struggle to reach the promised land, arduous preparation. It is only after this struggle and these personal efforts that we come to the baptism that offers a divine cleansing and preparation. The above text, let us note, indicates that our leader after baptism is Christ himself.

Let us also repeat that, according to Origen, baptism is not the end but the beginning of a new journey. Origen stresses this view in this discussion of Jer. 27:16, Isa. 31:9 and Isa. 32:20, especially the latter. Origen states here that it is the baptismal water of rebirth in which one must "sow his seed" if he is to reach Zion, indicating that baptism effects a change which nurtures a new beginning.[349] It is in this frame of mind that Origen states that not everyone who comes to baptism is worthy of the Holy Spirit or the graces of the Holy Spirit.[350]

We have considered briefly some of the background and preparatory aspects of baptism as a vehicle for two kinds of purification and introduction to a new journey with Christ as leader. Let us now turn to the effects and expectations of baptism in terms of conversion.

One of the most evident gifts arising from baptism is forgiveness of sin. Origen lists this way of remission of sins first in his summary of seven ways one's sins can be remitted.[351] Without forgiveness of sins there can be no spiritual progress, for, as we have already discussed in the sections on the Spirit, the Spirit will not share quarters with sin. The gift of the Spirit himself is integrated with baptism. Origen summarizes the gifts quite clearly in a section comparing the baptisms of John the Baptism and Christ:

I, [John] says, baptize you with water unto repentance, purifying you, as it were, and turning you away from evil courses and calling you to repentance; for I am come to make ready for the Lord a people prepared for him, and by a baptism of repentance to prepare the ground for him who is to come after me, and who will thus benefit you much more effectively and powerfully than my strength could. For his baptism is not that of the body only; he fills the penitent with the Holy Spirit, and his diviner's fire does away with everything material and consumes everything that is earthly, not only from him who admits it to his life, but even from him who hears of it from those who have it.[352]

John's baptism has two sides: First, it cleans the body, thus symbolically representing a purification; and second, it is a powerful incentive of and seal for repentance. However, since it concerns the body only, it does not have the power of the baptism of Jesus. Jesus's baptism differs from John's, first, in the fact that it is spiritual; it fills the recipient with the Holy Spirit.[353] Second, the baptism of Jesus actually burns up whatever is material and earthly. Hence there seem to be three facets to the process: First, there is repentance and a symbolic cleansing (though this view is only implied in most texts of Origen, with the exception of the text above which contrasts the two baptisms). Second, there is a forgiveness of sins that we noted in the texts above. Third, there is the destruction of the unspiritual elements in order to make way for the Holy Spirit.[354] Without repentance, the cleansing, the forgiveness and the burning up by the divine fire, there is no baptism. All aspects are important.[355]

There is some indication in one text of Origen that baptism is a sacrament to gain converts, to make Christianity and spirituality accessible to those who would not in the normal course of things grasp the spiritual process that is occurring. This discussion appears at the beginning of the *Commentary on John* when Origen is clarifying the difference between the somatic and the spiritual gospels. Outwardly baptism appears in a certain form in order to be understood by and to reach those who would not ordinarily enter the spiritual realm. However, the matter is not altogether clear, so we cannot be certain this view of baptism is completely accurate.[356] If this view is one that Origen espoused, then the somatic baptism (and perhaps the sacraments in general) were meant in God's economy,[357] according to Origen, to be only a catalyst, without intrinsic importance outside of this fact. We might add, however, that baptism itself remains necessary, but only in terms of its spiritual dimension. The corporeal realm's importance lies in its role as an agent or bridge to the spiritual.[358] The one becoming a Christian is constantly moving from the more literal level of understanding and experience with respect to reality to the profound and subtle mysteries. Both dimensions are important, but the former has importance only in terms of the latter.

After baptism, each person, according to Origen, is expected to meet certain standards. He explains this view in his interpretation of Gen. 2:15, "And God put him in paradise..."

> Those who are reborn through divine baptism are placed in "paradise," that is, in the church, to work those spiritual works which are within. And they receive the commandment to love all as brothers and to eat through patience the growing fruit, as it is written, "From every tree which is in paradise you may eat." (Gen. 2:16)[359]

Baptism brings the responsibility of a Christian and church member to everyone who undergoes it. It is indicative of a change and Origen demands that the change be evident in one's attitudes and behavior. Two commandments are then mentioned as particularly important. The first is the supreme commandment to love one another. This statement covers the most important level of practice for the Christian. The second commandment for the one who is baptized and on his way in spiritual growth can only be understood if one is familiar with Genesis 2. God places man in paradise and commands him to eat of the fruit of every tree except one. If he eats of the forbidden tree, he will die. For Origen this mandate implies a commitment to pursue spiritual knowledge and wisdom only, as the text following what was quoted above substantiates. Indeed the goal of the one who has been renewed by baptism and is now being brought to spiritual knowledge and experience is to know and act in a new way, in a spiritual way.

But the path, as we have already seen above, is not easy. Baptism marks a transition point, a point where one can be reborn and start again. Lapse is possible, repentance is possible, but there is only one baptism in the earthly life of the Christian, and Origen stresses this fact in his interpretation, for example, of Eph. 4:4–6 and other texts.[360]

4.

Certainly the two subjects of this section are symbolic of the transition from being unconverted to being converted. It is assumed by Origen that if one has experienced a true and sincere baptism, then he will be growing spiritually. For the Spirit only comes for the Christian if one is spiritually pure, and this purification process occurs at baptism. Hence the connection between the Spirit and baptism is very intimate. Moreover, it is the Spirit who brings to man the power to grow and change. He is the messenger and carrier of the powers of the Father and the Son. Being spiritual, or being ruled by the spirit in one's heart, is not a human achievement or act; it is a sharing and participatory process that interacts with the Spirit. Indeed the process cannot occur without the Spirit. We may describe the process as communication. In act, this communication is perhaps the only communication man receives from divinity. As communication it has a common foundation, i.e., the Spirit. Thus, the Spirit is both the mode and the substance of this dimension of Christian transformation, and through baptism man is able to enter it.

What Are the Mysteries and How Can the Christian Know Them?[361]

Of all the areas regarding spiritual journey, the area of knowledge is the most obvious in Origen's thought. One could describe the progress of man in Origen's universe as a path from ignorance to knowledge, essentially an intellectual journey for the elite. It is possible to view all of Origen's philosophical theology around his epistemology. While this view may seem facile, Origen does give the one who probes into his works reason to trust this judgment to an extent. Yet, as this study has shown again and again in prior sections, the quest for and reception of knowledge is hardly the whole story of man's return to God. Nor are all of the other aspects of change merely a preparation for knowledge. Origen, as we have seen on several occasions, does not separate the dimensions by value judgments or levels of importance. The aspects tend to integrate in every text. So along with other dimensions, the elements associated with knowledge are present.

It is not possible to enter into all the discussions concerning Origen's view of knowledge, nor would it be desirable in a work on spiritual transformation and conversion. Our main concern will be to understand what Origen meant by knowledge and to relate this definition to the spiritual journey. Our task is divided, first of all, into two subsections. The first will consider the role of Scripture at this level. The second will briefly expand the discussion into Origen's general thoughts on the higher knowledge or mysteries for those able to attain such a level.

1.

We have already recorded a couple of modes of transformation with respect to Scripture. To summarize our prior discussions, we have seen that Origen, in the first place, sees basically two senses to Scripture, the literal and the spiritual, and basically two stages of spiritual growth associated with them. Then, in accordance with Scripture, Origen views these two levels as symbolic of those who are beginners, who "drink milk," and those who are advanced, who "eat solid food." Sometimes, we noted, he includes a third dimension for those who are progressing but are still not mature. In this dimension "vegetables" are eaten. It was clear from our discussions that Origen viewed Scripture, from one perspective, as a catalyst of transformation.

Our primary efforts in this subsection will be to document how the dimension of maturity has within it a kind of growth process, since there would appear to be no need to repeat the general process of scriptural movement noted above.[362] We recognize, however, that there are many complex interrelated aspects in this dimension, so that, according to Origen, no man in this life ever completely transcends the other modes in his studies and meditations. Nor is it possible, in light of what we have considered, for someone through human means suddenly to attain this third level. The need for growth, a preparatory period with the Scriptures, and a guide are self-evident elements in Origen's discussions and his interpretations of pertinent scriptural texts. In brief, it would seem, particularly in view of Origen's stand on the vacillating nature of most souls, that no one is completely spiritually mature. Some stability has been attained, of course, and this stability in part enables one to receive the benefits of this dimension.

Let us begin by repeating a fact that has been common in all of our various thoughts on Origen's theology. Regardless of one's spiritual level, Christ is needed for each person to attain and maintain the level. With respect to Scripture then, the revelation of Christ is assumed. We find this fact continuously in Origen's commentaries and homilies, where he himself will pray for Christ's help and indicate publicly that he is unable to proceed without external inspiration. Let us offer one text to illustrate this trait of his thought and his personal life:

> What then do these words mean? The struggle here is to present the plan of these writings, and yet on my own, I confess that I am not able to consider these words, but to need, as I have said before, the appearance of the power of Jesus, in the way that he is the

Wisdom, in the way that he is the Logos, in the way that he is the Truth, so that his coming may shed light on the countenance of my soul.[363]

Here Origen is considering the twentieth chapter of Jeremiah, which he finds beyond his individual capacity, and he confesses this to his congregation. Also in his commentaries he declares in the same manner. For example, in his exegesis of Matt. 18:24, he feels overwhelmed with mysteries. He writes:

> As for what the truth in these matters is, I declare that no one can interpret unless Jesus, who explained all things to his disciples privately, (cf. Mark 4:34) takes up his abode in the heart, and opens up all the treasures of the parable which are dark, hidden, unseen, and confirms by clear demonstrations the man whom he desires to illumine with the light of the knowledge of all things that are in this parable. (Cf. Col. 2:3)[364]

The implication of this text also indicates that in such matters no text can have a certain footing without the "demonstrations" of Jesus in the heart. Hence the understanding of such a person would seem to find full confidence in the surety gained from Jesus. This statement is especially important for Origen, for he was ever aware of the difficulties of grasping many passages in Scripture and the need for assistance. Even for those who have attained some level of spiritual maturity there is needed continual assistance from Christ.

By nature the Christian presumes the need for Christ, but we might probe a little deeper into Origen's motives. Two reasons are prominent for the role of Christ. First, Scripture is filled with mysterious ideas whose source lies outside human existence. These ideas are secret and only certain people are able to "hear" them, as Origen mentions in what he considers the scriptural distinction between "hear" akouō and "hearken" (enotizomai). He writes:

> And since among the ideas in scripture, some are more secret and mystical, and yet some are intended for those capable of apprehending them, I think, concerning those passages which are secret, that it is said "hear," and concerning those passages which are obviously useful which can also help the hearer without interpretation [I think it is said] "hearken."[365]

On the other hand, it is not only that we need help in understanding these mystical passages, but it is the job of the Logos, the word of divine wisdom, to reveal them to those ready to receive them. This view become quite clear when Origen attempts to expound the meaning of the temple in John 2:31 and the temple mentioned in the third book of Kings. He concludes:

> Persuaded especially by such texts which transcend human nature and which are in accord with the work of divine wisdom—the proper character of scripture, which God inspires and which makes known that mysterious wisdom, having remained hidden, which none of the rulers of this world knew—when comprehending we need the assistance of that excellent spirit of wisdom, as is fitting for such holy things, in order to understand them.[366]

Hence in at least two practical ways Christ is essential for this dimension of understanding: First, for those things that transcend human existence, that none could grasp without him, and, second, for the spiritually mature, in order to grow in spiritual wisdom.

Indeed, according to Origen, the soul in some sense reacts in psychological pain when it cannot grasp these hidden answers. For example, he approves of the lesson taught in Jer. 13:17, "But if you do not hear in a hidden way, your soul from the face of insult will cry out." Origen offers an example of what he believes Scripture to mean when it says to "hear in a hidden way."

> All of you who keep the Jewish fast so that you do not understand the day of sacrifice as the [celebration] for the coming of Jesus Christ, you do not understand the sacrifice in a hidden way, but only externally. For to understand the sacrifice in a hidden way is to "hear" how God put forward Jesus as an expiation for our sins and that "he is an expiation for our sins, but not for our [sins] alone, but also for the whole world" (1 John 2:2, cf. Rom. 3:25). And if the Gospel parables are read and the hearer is among those who are outside, he does not "hear" them "in a hidden way." But if the hearer is the apostle or among those who enter "into the house" of Jesus (Matt. 13:36), and he comes before Jesus, and he learns also about the obscurity of the parable and Jesus interprets it, then the hearer of the parables becomes one who "hears" it in a hidden way so that the soul does not "cry out."[367]

To hear in a hidden way, with respect to the Scriptures (or in any other aspect of Christianity), is, according to Origen, to hear in terms of God's plans for man, which is, of course, in terms of Jesus Christ.

Now that we have established the important place of Christ as one who enables us to transcend the more mundane interpretations and see the mysteries in Scripture, a movement that frees the soul from its "cries" and brings to it the wisdom of God, let us consider the human element in this dimension of spiritual growth insofar as it relates to Scripture.

One text that Origen uses on several occasions in this context is John 5:39, "Search the scriptures." The context for one of these uses concerns Origen's response to Celsus's comparison of Jesus with other figures who performed incredible acts. Origen indicates that these figures cannot be compared with Jesus because the lives of those who witnessed or knew about the acts were not changed. Thus, Christ's divinity, Origen says, is proven not only by what he did but by the effects of his acts and thought on others. Origen writes that the evidences of Jesus' divinity are found in:

> . . . the churches of people who have been helped, the prophecies spoken about him, the cures which are done in his name, the knowledge and wisdom in Christ, and *logos* which is to be found in those who know how to advance beyond mere faith, and how to search out the meaning of the divine scriptures. Jesus commanded this when he said "search the scriptures," and that was what Paul meant when he taught that we must "know how we ought to answer each one." (Col. 4:6)[368]

We have discussed above in another section the differences of faith and what transcends faith. It is clear Origen believes that searching the Scriptures for answers is a task for those who have "advanced beyond mere faith." Christ's divinity then seems to have the potential to affect people at many dimensions in their various religious journeys, but searching the Scriptures is placed last and given additional comments.

For Origen this task is not one that is accomplished quickly or easily. In another context of *Against Celsus*, he indicates that "those" who truly understand the teaching of the Church "devote their entire life, as Jesus commanded, to searching the scriptures . . . ," even more, he says, than Greek philosophers pursue their studies.[369] Ultimately one's inquiry would take him through the entire Bible. For, as Origen clarifies in his long discussion of the Scriptures in *On First Principles*, to understand all of the obscurities and difficulties of Holy Scripture demands that one trace out words and meanings that are similar or may have some relation throughout every book of the Bible, especially in texts where the literal meaning is impossible, unnatural, or disrespectful of divinity. He concludes his discussion, however, by stating that regardless of how advanced one becomes in his probing into the Scriptures, even if aided by grace,[370]

> . . . he will never be able to reach the final goal of his inquiries. For no created mind can by any means possess the capacity to understand all; but as soon as it has discovered a small fragment of what it is seeking, it again sees other things that must be sought for; and if in turn it comes to know these, he will again see arising out of them many more things that demand investigation.[371]

This task of scrutinizing and revealing the truths of Scripture is two-sided for the one who has reached the spiritual dimension. On the one hand, in order to know and share in the teachings and truths of the Spirit, he must continue to probe into the depths of Scripture, as we have just indicated. Indeed Origen explicitly states this view in his consideration of the purpose of Scripture. Origen claims that the purpose of the divine words of Scripture for those who probe deeply is to permit them to become privy to the teachings of the Spirit.[372] Then he points out that people "cannot reach maturity except through the rich and wise truth about God."[373]

On the other hand, as we have also noted above, no person can possibly comprehend everything that lies in Scripture. Thus the search is more exactly a way to continue to "perfect" one's soul than a search for an end. It is only in this sense that we use the word "perfect." A more appropriate word, as we have said previously, is "mature." The more the mature person finds, the more he knows of the teachings of the Spirit and comes closer to perfection. In sum, he seeks to know, and the knowledge brings him a share in the Spirit.

The seeking through Scripture is a movement of spiritual growth, for the knowledge given by the Spirit in all of Scripture continues to move one from a previous state of ignorance.[374] So there is the movement from the letter to the spirit, which we discussed in an earlier chapter,[375] and the movement in which more and more of the Spirit is known.

There is another way Origen expresses these thoughts. He indicates that there are those who partially believe, and these believe in the literal meaning of Scripture. Yet there are also those who believe the Scripture in the full sense: these see what they believe, and they see in Scripture the "mind of the Holy Spirit."

> He who is to be blessed must see in his mind the things which he believes. . . .[376]

The context of these statements concerns John 2:22, a text Origen views as an example of how the disciples changed from lack of understanding to "sight." Knowledge in this context is akin to be a belief in something that was always present but that one did not see. The body of the Scripture (or the words of Jesus), for example, is always present before man, but most people tend to grasp it only superficially, as if a veil was placed over its true meaning or over their eyes. Once this veil is taken off, as it was for the disciples in John 2:22, then knowledge becomes possible. Whereas before the disciples did not see the heavenly pattern in Jesus' words, now all becomes clear and they see in a new way.[377]

The mature person then views Scripture as a means to transcend to the Spirit. For such a person Scripture, according to Origen, does not seem to hold knowledge in the common sense of a group of facts or series of abstract principles. Rather, Scripture rewards the mature seeker with a new vision of reality. What he once had failed to see because of his blindness and the veil now can be seen. Knowledge is being able to see patterns and divine plans where before one could see only the history or the literal meaning of the words. Therefore, by this knowing, Origen sets before us a type of epistemological conversion from one kind of "knowing" to another.

2.

Yet even the kind of knowledge spread throughout the Scriptures is only partial. There are other dimensions of knowledge that Origen discusses in diverse contexts. Let us now investigate this dimension in terms of how it concerns the journey to become a Christian.

First, let us present a couple of texts that indicate the existence of this dimension of knowledge. One of these texts occurs in Origen's discussion of John 4:13–14. Here Jesus says.

> Everyone who drinks of this water will thirst again, but whoever drinks of the water that I shall give him will never thirst; the water that I shall give him will become in him a spring of water welling up to eternal life.

"This water" refers to the spring of Jacob from which the Samaritan woman was getting her water. Origen sees in this text a distinction made between the

Scriptures and what transcends the written word. He indicates that the Scriptures, in fact, comprise only the most basic principles and minimum introduction to the whole body of divine knowledge.[378] He clarifies that the spring of Jacob represents the knowledge from all the Scriptures,

> . . . but the water of Jesus is that "which exceeds what is written" (1 Cor. 4:6). For it is not possible for everyone to inquire into things which exceed what is written unless one has become akin to them, so that one is not reproved when hearing, "Seek not what is too difficult for you, nor investigate what is beyond your power." (Sir. 3:21)[379]

Origen quotes several other texts from Scripture in which Jesus, the disciples, and Paul indicate that they knew of matters which could not be expressed.[380] It is important to note that he does mention figures from New Testament times. The "Scriptures" here are not only those concerned with Jacob and the Jewish Scriptures in general, but the New Testament writings also. Does Origen, however, mean that these ineffable matters cannot be learned at all from Scripture, even with allegory, or does he mean that the ineffable thoughts can be drawn out by one who has studied them and has come to know some of the mind of Spirit, but that human words are incapable of expressing or explaining what Scripture is truly saying?

Though there is no clear answer to this question in this context, we do receive some help in his *Homilies on Joshua*, where he discusses the tribes and the lots given them in Joshua 13 and following. Near the end of his discussion of the various names of the tribes, he cautions his listeners about assuming these chapters of Joshua are without value:

> And thus let us point out to you, lest you read these matters with disdain and think that scripture holds something worthless because it is strewn with proper names: On the contrary, know that in these passages are contained some ineffable mysteries, greater than either a human can express or a mortal can hear, which, to explain completely and properly, I think, cannot be done, not only by me, who is "the least" (1 Cor. 15:9) but by those even who are much better than I. Moreover, I do not know if [these mysteries] were conveyed completely and clearly by the holy Apostles themselves. I do not say that they were not clearly understood, but that they were not clearly conveyed.[381]

This passage seems to indicate that the latter of the two alternatives is correct, namely, that Scripture does contain the mysteries but that mortals are unable to express them by human means. It is in this sense only that we can say that there is knowledge "which exceeds what is written" in scripture. For divine knowledge of this sort, according to Origen, cannot be "conveyed" or explained through words. Hence Paul and John knew of things they were unable to convey with verbal clarity.[382]

Now that we have clarified the existence of this knowledge, let us (a) define it in more detail and describe its source, (b) indicate how one acquires the knowledge, and (c) clarify the factors involved in the ascent from one degree of divine knowledge to another. Again our focal point is spiritual growth; it would not be possible to explore all the facets of this dimension of knowledge in Origen in one subsection of this chapter. Rather, we shall try to concentrate on how knowledge changes the soul and how the one who seeks God can move toward better and better relationships with God.

(a) We have already seen that the process of knowing for Origen is not knowledge in terms of the accumulation of facts or the comprehension of abstract theories. In fact, Origen bluntly states that human knowledge is distinct from this higher knowledge, though human knowledge is a preparation for it. For example, in *Against Celsus*, in a section in which Origen indicates that so-called education in terms of pagan religion is ignorance, he writes:

> But we also maintain that it is not possible for a man who has not been trained in human wisdom to receive the more divine, and hold that all human wisdom is foolishness in comparison with divine wisdom.[383]

Origen extends this view of human wisdom even more in his interpretation of Jer. 10:14, 1 Cor. 1:25, 1 Cor. 2:8 and 1 Cor. 3:19, all of which are concerned with clarifying the distinction of the realms of wisdom. He says:

> But even Paul, himself wise and with apostolic authority, has dared to say that every wisdom on earth, and the [wisdom] in him and in Peter and in the apostles, every kind of [wisdom] which dwells in the world is "the foolishness of God." (1 Cor. 1:25)[384]

In order to explain this view of Paul, he offers the analogy of an argument between an intelligent man and an ignorant man. Because of the superior training of the one, even foolish answers will suffice to overwhelm the other. So it is with what is knowledge with God and what is knowledge with man.[385]

Similarly we discussed above how knowledge is distinct from belief or faith. Origen summarizes the various levels in his discussion of Psalm 36, a discussion we mentioned previously but did not quote. Here is the text:

> Though the man we described above be untrained and without education, yet faithful and God-fearing, that little measure of faith is a better thing for this righteous man than the many riches of sins which compare with the wisdom of this age. But better than both of these is he who is rich in the word of God and the knowledge of truth, who, that is, in Paul's words, is rich in every word and in every knowledge and not the less is rich in good works. (1 Tim. 6:18)[386]

According to this text, the hierarchy is worldly wisdom, faith, and divine wisdom. Added to this knowledge, let us note, is also "good works." Here, as in other texts we discussed earlier in this chapter, Origen maintains a constant interdependence of contemplation and works. We might mention also that the above text offers its own form of epistemological growth from human knowledge to faith (which is continuous throughout the spiritual journey) to the higher knowledge. And, as we noted above, there is a certain amount of dependence of one level on another. Origen stated that one cannot attain divine knowledge without being trained in human knowledge.

This concern with a hierarchy introduces us to another matter that helps to define the meaning of knowledge and clarifies another aspect of knowledge as a catalyst of growth. In his commentary on Matt. 16:20, Origen enters into a discussion about the different ways in which God reveals himself and, in this context, why Jesus instructed the disciples to tell no one he was the Christ. In fact, according to Origen, Jesus did not want a more complete understanding of himself to be revealed until all the events, such as the crucifixion and resurrection, could enlighten the disciples and others. Origen sees here a progression of knowledge from belief without knowledge to more and more advanced levels of knowledge. Furthermore, because of the different comprehension of Christ by the various apostles as well as others, he also views different modes of knowing the same object. Origen writes:

> From the words in John, "If you abide in my word, you shall know the truth, and the truth shall make you free" (John 8:31, 32), it is plain that belief without knowledge is inferior to knowing; but that there is a difference in the knowledge of Jesus as Christ, as all who know him do not know him equally, is a fact self-evident to any one who gives even a very little consideration to the matter. . . . But it is not only in respect of the difference of knowing that those who know do not know alike, but also according to that which is the source of knowledge; so that according to this he who knows the Son by the revelation of the Father (Matt. 16:16), as Peter is testified to have known, has the highest beatitude. Now if these views of ours are sound, you will consider whether the Twelve formerly believed but did not know; but, after believing, they gained also the rudiments of knowledge and knew a few things about him; and afterwards they continued to advance in knowledge so that they were able to receive the knowledge from the Father who reveals the Son. . . .[387]

Knowledge, then, is not something one acquires all at once, for even the disciples had to advance from the rudiments after they had believed. It is also something quite individualistic; that is, the way and substance of knowledge varies with the person. Let us note this point with some emphasis. Each person comes to know differently, and the source of that knowing also varies. Such a view allows a great variety of routes and opportunities. In effect, there is no one way to know, nor is there but one source for the person.

Thus we have seen that knowledge is different from human wisdom and belief and that Origen believes that there are differences both in what each knows and the source of the knowledge.

In order to reach our second and third concerns, namely, what one needs to do to acquire knowledge and the actual process of knowledge, we need to understand more deeply how each of the above aspects gives to knowledge a place in the progress of the soul. Knowing itself, viewed philosophically, is defined by Origen in a manner similar to the Stoics. For example, in his commentary on John 8:43 and the significance of "understand" (or, in this context, know) and "hear" in the scriptural texts, Origen writes:

I think that to "hear" now means to comprehend what is said, yet to "know" [means] to assent to what one grasps, for one is enlightened with the light of knowledge concerning what is said. (Cf. Hos. 10:12 LXX)[388]

The key words here are "to grasp" and "to assent." Origen indicates that when we know something, we assent to what is stable and truthful because we have been enlightened. When we are enlightened, we know because the knowledge in what has been said is impressed upon us. If we combine this view with what we have been discussing above, the uniqueness of knowledge appears. Human "knowledge" is unstable and uncertain; it cannot be called or linked with truth. Similarly, belief can be based on assent without "seeing," as we noted above. Hence, without being founded in knowledge—which mature faith is—it too cannot be called truth or wisdom. Finally, before knowing the "language" of Jesus, one must be able to "hear" his word.[389] *Katalepsis*, which is the root of the verb Origen uses in this context, is, in Stoic epistemology, the criterion of truth, and hence is, in contrast to *doxa* (opinion), certain knowledge.[390] Therefore, before one can fully "grasp" the full meaning of Christ's language, one must be able, in a sense, to translate or understand his word. Comprehension describes the act of knowing; truth defines its substance. Indeed truth seems to be the best synonym for knowledge as we understand it in this fifth chapter. Let us explore this view of knowledge in more detail.

Above we reviewed a text that stated that one could not inquire into things that exceed what is written unless "one has become akin (*exomoioein*) to them." We have already reviewed the ancient idea to which Origen often subscribed, namely, like influencing and being able to share with like. The view also emerges in Origen's epistemology. If one is to know divinity, then one must in some way have divinity, or divinity must in some way be able to emerge. In the text just mentioned, Origen simply assumes his view. Let us quote a text that clarifies the matter more thoroughly. In his long discussion of John 8:19, a discussion we have quoted in the section concerned with the difference of believing and knowing, Origen offers another view of knowledge outside of his consideration of belief:

And see if the scriptures do not say, in another sense, that those who are mingled and unite with something know that with which they have been mingled and have formed a communion. Yet before such a union and communion (even if they comprehend the reasons), they do not know it. . . . "He who joins himself to a prostitute forms one body . . . ; and he who joins to the Lord forms one spirit" (1 Cor. 6:16, 17). So he who joins with the prostitute knows the prostitute, and he who joins with the spouse knows the spouse, and more important and holy than this, he who joins with the Lord knows the Lord.[391]

In addition to the aspects we have considered above, knowledge may also involve an element that is difficult to explain in common epistemological terms, and perhaps this element is what seals Origen's Christian vision.[392] To know in the fullest sense is not only to comprehend something about God, but to unite with

God, in the same sense that Paul says that we must join with God to form one spirit (1 Cor. 6:16–17).

However, how does union enable us to know God? The question is not answered in this section, but a clue to the answer is evident in Origen's use of 1 Cor. 6:16–17, particularly the formation of "one spirit." In our previous discussion of the Spirit, we indicated that man's direct bridge to God is through the Spirit. By the enlivening of the spirit in man, and the union with the Spirit, man is able to seek and relate with God. However, another bonus from the agency of the Spirit is divine knowing, as Origen states at the beginning of his work *On Prayer:*

> Moreover, just as no one "among men knows a man's thoughts except the spirit of the man which is in him, so also no one knows the thoughts of God except the Spirit of God" (1 Cor. 2:11). If no one knows the thoughts of God except the Spirit of God, it is impossible for a human being to know the thoughts of God. But now consider this—how it becomes possible. "Now we," he says, "have received not the spirit of the world, but the Spirit which is from God, that we might understand the gifts bestowed on us by God. And we impart this in words not taught by human wisdom but taught by the Spirit." (1 Cor. 2:12–13)[393]

In sum, knowledge is not only intellectual comprehension but also a union achieved through participation in the Spirit. Origen presents an overview of his position in his interpretation of John 1:47–50, which concerns the initial meeting of Nathanael and Jesus. Origen believes that Jesus' statements concerning Nathanael indicate that Nathanael was one who contemplated God. Origen says:

> And Jesus, who saw that Nathanael in bringing himself to contemplation was not only sauntering but was making progress, testifies to his eagerness for the understanding of truth and says to those with him: Do you see the one who approaches? There is an Israelite not only according to the senses and the flesh, but also according to the spirit and the understanding. For he has a mind which contemplates God. For there is a true rather than false Israelite, since, purified of every "guile," he is a friend of truth.[394]

We notice that Origen sees two sides to Jesus' comments about Nathanel. Nathanel contemplates "according to the spirit and the understanding," the two aspects we have been discussing above. Moreover, there is a stress in this text on Nathanel's truthfulness and quest for the truth. This position will remind us of our discussions above concerning how Origen considered certainty and truth the primary standards of knowledge. Truth especially is the benchmark for Origen in all considerations of knowledge and salvation.[395] Finally, let us note how Origen distinguishes one who "saunters" and one who truly progresses. His point here seems to be that Nathanael in his particular way of contemplating (and acting) is making progress toward God. All statements of spiritual "progress" concern spiritual growth, for they involve how a person changes from one condition to another.

The texts so far seem to indicate that knowledge is not a static event or fact, but rather a process, movement, or perhaps a progress from one state of relationship with God to another more intimate and more closely bonded one. The goal for the one experiencing the third mode is not knowledge itself, but the condition to which knowing brings one. We have seen how Origen attempts to describe this process through the scriptural images Paul offers of the union of man and woman. The image is powerful enough to eliminate a view of knowledge that is strictly intellectual or scientific. In order to know God, one must, in some sense, become like God so that some common bridge can be established. However, even if the bridge is established, it is only the beginning of a desire to grow closer and closer to the source of knowing.

(b) Now that we have presented a basic definition of knowledge according to Origen, let us consider briefly a couple of texts concerning the process of epistemological growth and what one needs in order to experience growth in knowledge. Since the patterns here are very similar to the other modes of change, we need only mention what overlaps with earlier considerations. These patterns are the following:

(1) First, that there are various kinds of knowledge, which Origen often describes as either partial or complete (mature) and sometimes as representative of different nourishments, depending on the capacity or preparation of the recipient. In these discussions, we view again the distinction of the one who is mature, one who is a beginner and the one who is progressing, or, in another context, the one who sees truly and the one who sees in a mirror.[396] Origen believes that all modes of change reflect the human condition rather than an abstract concept or ideal. By naming types or levels of knowledge, Origen does not mean that knowledge itself is ever partial, but that man's grasp of knowledge has various dimensions and interpretations, depending upon one's preparation and the grace of God. This view was also evident in our discussions about scripture. The level of knowledge, then, has at least two factors: how we prepare ourselves, and how we are nourished by God.

The other image of this hierarchical or multidimensional vision of growth is the image of ascent. This pattern is also abundant in many contexts. One is changed by the degree of ascent he has reached in his quest for all of wisdom. Hence the increase of wisdom brings one closer to the source of wisdom. Indeed this path upward in wisdom toward perfect knowledge continues even after one leaves the world, according to Origen, so that even in heaven, freed of the burden of the earthly body, we continue to be transformed by an ever-increasing growth in knowledge.[397] Yet even on earth, man may ascend a great distance. Thus, in a continuation of a text we offered in Chapter 3, Origen writes:

And when they have ascended from the created things of the world to the invisible things of God they do not stop there. But after exercising their minds sufficiently among them and understanding them, they ascend to the eternal power of God, and, in a word, to his divinity; for they know that out of love to man God manifested the truth and that which may be known of himself. (Cf. Rom. 1:8–20)[398]

Similarly, as we have noted previously, one can ascend by knowing aspects of Christ.[399] One of the most extensive discussions of this idea of knowledge as ascent or mystical journey is found in Origen's *Homilies on Numbers*. At the end of his description of each place and event in Num. 33:12–48 as allegorically comparable to a stage in one's spiritual journey, a journey that begins with the obtainment of spiritual "health" at Raphaca and ends at the Jordan, Origen summarizes the achievement and its significance:

> For when the soul has made its journey through all these virtues and has climbed the height of maturity,[400] it then "passes" (cf. Num. 33:47) from the world and "separates" from it, as it is written in Enoch, "And he was not found, because God had taken him across" (Gen. 5:24). Someone like this, even if he seems to be still in the world and to dwell in flesh, nonetheless will not "be found." Where will he not be found? In no worldly deed, in no fleshly act, in no vain conversation is he found. For God has taken him across from these pursuits and placed him in the realm of virtues. The last stage is east of Moab by the Jordan (Num. 33:48). For the whole journey takes place, the whole course is run, for the purpose of arriving at the river of God, so that we may be made neighbors of the flowing wisdom and may be watered by the waves of divine knowledge, and so that, purified by them all, we may be made worthy to enter the promised land.[401]

We have quoted this long passage in lieu of describing step by step the stages by which one arrives at the Jordan. Nevertheless, it is important to note that each of the steps of ascent is an aspect of conversion, of a process by which one who has achieved the spiritual level progresses step by step to the condition finally described above. In this long journey are discoveries of wisdom, temptations, lessons in endurance and patience, discipline of desires, understanding of Scripture, and acquiring the capacity to discern the heavenly. It is clear from the list that the same problems plague the mature as plague the beginner, but the mature is supposed to be able to manage them better.

(2) Second, another pattern which reappears in Origen's epistemology and which relates to the previous discussion of preparation is the need for good actions.[402] On several occasions in this study we have stressed the continual emphasis Origen places on the need for a union of so-called internal and external growth if one is to change and to reach God. In fact, God does not notice us without these acts. If we are to know God, in effect, God must also know us. "You must do many good acts so that God may begin to know you."[403]

(3) A third pattern that we have seen previously and that reappears in Origen's view of knowledge is his explanation of how humans can know God. Since we have already discussed this matter above in our presentation of a definition of knowledge, we need only summarize this view now. In brief, Origen believed that humans could know God only because they are, in some sense, similar to God, either by sharing in the spirit (as we mentioned above) or because they are

essentially akin to God through *logos* and the image. Indeed it is Origen's conviction that no one could have hope of finding God or of knowing God without having something within him which is like God. Moreover, God, of course, intentionally implanted in man this yearning and capacity.[404]

In a similar vein, Origen founds his epistemology in the idea of a correspondence also between objects, that is, that visible things have within them likenesses to heavenly things, so that "the human mind might mount to spiritual understanding and seek the grounds of things in heaven."[405] Thus, both by turning within himself to his inner gifts and by turning to and learning from the objects of the world, man is able to find and know God and divine truths.

(c) In addition to these familiar patterns, that we have discussed in other contexts as well as in respect of Origen's view of knowledge, there are three other factors that need to be included in our presentation. These are (1) the role of stability, (2) the contribution of man, and (3) the need for revelation.

(1) Because our concerns are with the process and movements by which one becomes a Christian, we have tended to stress factors that involve movement and progress. Becoming a Christian is primarily a matter of how one changes from one state of mind or action to another, but, as we have seen, this change includes many different aspects which are not necessarily concerned with movement or even change itself. Not only is there change from one condition to another, but there is also, at each spiritual plateau or condition, the attempt to maintain oneself without vacillating or lapsing or falling back. Origen considers this dimension of conversion under the idea of stability. In fact, we have already briefly discussed stability in another context, but here we are considering its importance to knowledge, which is intimately linked with the quest and reception of the truth. Origen raises the question in his interpretation of John 8:44, a passage in which Jesus describes the devil, in Origen's view, as one who has not "stood firm in truth." Origen expands on the nature of this stability:

> On the one hand, every single person who keeps in a secure way the sound teachings, and due to the stability of the teachings, is unshaken by his decisions in any situation, and under no condition or some bodily excuse (such as intolerable pains or intense sensual yearnings or some other such cause of being shaken) might be shifted from what is good, can be reasonably thought to have "stood firm in the truth". . . And the cause of his [the devil] not standing firm in truth is said this way: "Because there is no truth in him" (John 8:44). And "there is no truth in him" because he is deceived and admits to what is false.[406]

We see that Origen interconnects doctrine, judgment, bodily influences, and truth through the factor of stability. Knowing truth is again not simply an intellectual act, but an event that affects the degree to which one's life is stable or firmly affixed in doctrine, morality, and judgments. The knowledge of truth for Origen seems to imply the other factors, or the other factors seem to go hand in hand with the truth that is in one. If we have truth, then we are secure; if we do not have it, then we are somehow deceived. To be deceived, Origen writes, is to think falsely.

Origen continues in the next section of his commentary by noting that those without truth are those who do not have Christ, for Christ said, "I am the truth" (John 14:6). Not only do they share in truth, but truth itself is in them.[407] Thus, again Origen bases the entire foundation of knowledge and action on Christ rather than on only an abstract principle or group of teachings. Said another way, to have truth man must turn to Christ and without Christ, man's thoughts will be false. We must add, in accordance with prior discussions on Origen's view of the relation of non-Christian wisdom and the wisdom of Christ, that Origen is here speaking in an absolute sense. Other kinds of knowledge are not useless, but all must be viewed in the light of Scripture and the wisdom of Christ. If non-Christian wisdom is consonant with the wisdom of Scripture, then it too is truth and is inspired by the Logos.

Hence progress and achievement in knowledge growth cannot occur without also reaching some kind of stability in what one knows. One who is insecure, who vacillates and constantly lapses, does not, according to Origen, know truth. One who does not affix himself to the principles of good does not really have those principles. In sum, having the truth involves more than just thinking about some principle or teaching; it involves an allegiance that affects other aspects of one's life. In a word, it involves commitment.

(2) From the beginning of this chapter we have stated that the role of man in this mode of conversion is very limited. Both the agency and the substance of knowledge comes from God. Indeed it is this one-sided aspect of this mode that indicates the importance of the other modes in the process of growth. In the prior paragraphs, we discussed Origen's view of the place of stability in this mode, and we concluded by stating that security of conversion at any plateau is actually what we might label commitment. This commitment, however, emerges from man. How might it be described?

The answer to this question is not easily obtained for this dimension. However, Origen does offer a response in his interpretation of Matt. 16:21, where it is written: "From that time on Jesus began to show his disciples. . . ." We recall that prior to this text Jesus had asked his disciples, "Who do men say that the Son of man is?" and Peter responded with "You are the Christ, the Son of the Living God." Jesus replied, "Blessed are you, Simon Barjona! For flesh and blood has not revealed this to you, but my Father who is in heaven" (Matt. 16:13-17). For Origen the statement "from that time on" indicates that the disciples were now ready, due to the way they had responded to his question, for more advanced knowledge, and Jesus began to show them the meaning of the prior and future events in terms of God's plans. And, since he "began," Origen believes, it is assumed that Jesus also completed what he began. However, Jesus did not begin to present these matters until the disciples had reached a certain level of maturity. Origen writes:

For when anyone apprehends the mature knowledge from the Logos concerning these [mysteries], then it must be said that, from a rational exhibition in which the mind sees the things which are shown, the exhibition becomes complete for him who has the will and power to contemplate these things, and does contemplate them.[408]

The disciples, after an introduction by Christ, were now ready to contemplate greater matters. Apparently, according to Origen, the will and power of each of them had grown to a point where each was capable of knowing the mysteries that concern God's plan. Spiritual growth here occurs in the capacity and strength of the will and mind. These are background forces to knowledge itself, but they are nevertheless important to movement from one dimension of knowledge to another. They indicate that the level of knowledge is, according to Origen, dependent on the will and strength of one's attachment to the object of knowledge.

(3) The issue of attachment brings us to the question of deification, which concerns the event when man is assimilated, spiritually attached, to God. Since it is a final event rather than a process of conversion, we do not intend to explore the matter in depth.[409] Our main concern is how one attains the event. Origen offers at least a partial answer in his understanding of the word "glory" in John 13:31, Luke 9:29–31, and in other biblical passages. Three elements seems to be quite clear: First, the intellect, according to Origen, needs to be purified of any elements that cause it to focus on inferior or lower material or earthly objects. This purity enables the intellect to concentrate on its primary object, God. Second, separate from the matter of purity is the element of attention. In order for the intellect to be raised to such glory and deification it must achieve an extraordinary level of attention to the contemplation of God. The more the contemplator attends to the contemplation of God, the more he is drawn by God, transformed, and glorified. Again we see implied in this view the pattern of like becomes (or is assimilated to) like, which we have noted previously in our discussions. Of course, as noted above, in order to be assimilated to God one must become, in some sense, like God. This process brings us to the third aspect. Knowledge or knowing is of no consequence in itself. As we shall consider below, there is only one Knower in Origen's thought. And it is for this reason, namely, that knowledge is an agent of change, that we have treated it more thoroughly. The fact holds true also in the event of deification. The more one knows God, the more he is known by God. However, it is the Logos which supplies to us this food. Hence it is apparent that God in a sense knows himself in his knowledge of man, and that man quests for the food of the Logos so that God, who knows his Son, may know the Son in man. In other words, when Origen says we are made divine by the food of the Logos,[410] he means that God glorifies the Son who is in us. Hence the agency of Christ appears again in man's return to God. Origen writes:

But when the heavenly Father revealed to those who are from the world he revealed the knowledge of Jesus; then the Son of Man was glorified in those who knew him, and through such glory he was glorified in those who knew him, he obtained glory in those who knew him. For those who reflect the glory of the Lord in an unveiled face are transformed in the same image.[411]

Another indication that knowledge is more an agent than an end is the often-repeated statement by Origen that God is essentially unknowable. But an even more clear statement of this fact in Origen's thought is his stress on the need for revelation and an outside power before knowledge or truth emerges. Let us offer several texts that set these ideas in their contexts.

Two ideas seem to go hand in hand for Origen. The first is that God is essentially unknowable, that is, that no human can possibly take in all of the theory and knowledge about God. His viewpoint on this area occurs in his interpretation of the meaning of "darkness" in John 1:5, where he writes:

Indeed if one considers the multitude of speculation and knowledge about God, beyond the power of human nature to take in, beyond the power perhaps of all originated beings except Christ and the Holy Spirit, then one may know how God is surrounded with darkness.[412]

Hence, as this statement indicates, God is unknowable in a full sense to all but the Holy Spirit and Christ. The unknowable aspect of God is a result, as Origen notes elsewhere, of his transcendence.[413] Indeed, as we have shown elsewhere, man does not know anything about God except through the Logos, so divine knowledge is always given through the agent of the Logos who is the Image of the Father.

From the other side, man must continue to seek to know God. For, as Origen states in his discussion of John 8:47 and 1 Cor. 13:2 concerning "all in all," a man who has become a son of God in a mature way has come to know all the mysteries and all knowledge and completes every work of charity.[414] Though Origen does not specify, we may assume that all knowledge here indicates all knowledge a human is capable of acquiring as a son of God. In his interpretation of John 1:1 and Prov. 16:5, especially with respect to the meaning of "beginning" in these two texts, Origen clarifies also with respect to knowledge that it is the last stage of growth, the last activity that man has to accomplish in order to unite to God. Origen states that in the beginning man acts in a practical way by doing justice (Prov. 16:5), while the contemplative aspect comes later, after death, in the time of restoration.

For then but one activity will be left for those who have to come to God on account of the Logos which is with him (cf. John 1:1), that, namely, of thoroughly knowing God so that, being formed in the knowledge of the Father, they may all become exactly a son, as now no one but the Son knows the Father.[415]

Let us note that Origen describes knowing as an activity, a *praxis*, rather than a single finished event. In fact, he compares the two activities of doing justice and contemplation. Knowing is the final aspect of the process of spiritual growth in becoming a Christian, concluding even after death and the restoration of all things. It is the activity that finally seals man's potential to become a son of God. For no one, Origen says, has truly known until he "has become one, as the Father and the Son are one."[416] In sum, man by knowing is formed in the image of

God and grows to be like him to some extent, having a kind of kinship similar to that between the Father and Son. It is not, however, what man comes to know that creates the sonship, but what knowledge, as a catalyst, has done to transform man in God's image. The knowledge that God reveals through the Logos is thus an agent to draw man to sonship and deification.

Perhaps one of the most interesting aspects of Origen's view of knowledge is his understanding of knowledge as a process rather than a series of abstract principles, doctrines, or facts. Knowing for Origen is a kind of activity which is attracted to God's magnet and which, as it grows, transforms and unites man to God. Though man cannot fully know God in the way God knows himself, we need to know him in order to unite with him. Knowledge is a contemplative realm that brings one to God's realm. It, like other aspects we have mentioned, is a perfecting agent returning man to his proper place and depending not only on God's revelation, but also, in an indirect way, on man's will to know. Hence we must change in order to know, since we must stress in us what is akin to God, not what is earthly. And once we have willed to change in order to know, we undergo more and more change as the mysteries and wonders of the divine realm open up for us, and we ascend, step by step, into sonship. Knowledge is not an end in itself, but a way to God.

Summary

Chapter 5 has given an overview of the elements of the process of reaching the goal of maturity at a higher stage. We have discussed the role of repentance, baptism, and prayer in this level of transformation, and then, finally, we offered a brief analysis of the new knowledge of maturity.

Origen sets a high standard and a wondrous reward for those who can strain for the mysteries of maturity. In other words, it is one kind of accomplishment to be able to arrive at the dimension through a transformation of heart and conduct, but it is quite another, in Origen's opinion, to be changed and grow in one's maturity to higher and higher stations in God's sight within the dimension. We noted that the relation of the Spirit and the spirit of man is one of the key factors in this journey. In general, it is God's grace that initiates and enables the one becoming a Christian to make the climb upward through the Church, Christ and Scripture, and the Spirit, all of which take on different roles.

We have enveloped the chapter with epistemological explorations because ultimately it brings a knowledge that transforms and, according to several texts, allows one to transcend earthly concerns and even the body.

Hence we come full circle from the discussions about the body in the beginning. For then the body was a primary obstacle in man's growth. Finally, in this dimension, in the power of the spirit, through the enlivening grace of the Spirit, man can actually ascend spiritually without bodily burdens. And once there, he not only absorbs the grace of God's love, but also returns with renewed strength and understanding. It is no wonder then that Origen, in his teaching and preaching, constantly asks for revelation from God. For we can be assured that he knew the gifts of knowledge that await one who takes the climb.

We also learned in Chapter 5 that even the mature experience constant movement, that even the mature can lapse and even the mature cannot exhaust the well of divine knowledge. Hence, as we have noted previously, the spiritual process goes on beyond this life. The quest for a knowledge that transforms and brings one closer and closer to God's warmth does not end at any stage, but, as Origen wrote, the more one knows, the more one learns how much there is to know.

VI

Some Reflections

1.

Now that we have talked about the vast variety in Origen's attitudes toward change, let us probe a little into the quality of Origen's wisdom. Our purpose is not to summarize the preceding chapters, which we have already done at the end of each chapter, but to attempt to tie together the foregoing into a kind of unified statement of Origen's vision of change. We shall approach the task in two ways. First, we shall give a general overview of Origen's understanding. Then, second, we will probe deeper into his view in several ways by means of its form and structure.

As we stated at the beginning of this study, many ancient writers write or preach to influence and change their listeners or readers, but few consider the question of why and how people change from one condition to another. All had a particular bias or narrow understanding forced on them by circumstances (e.g., the challenge from the heretics). None of them directly addressed the question in an extant work, but each had the matter on his mind. For example, Socrates seeks to change minds and motivations by questioning presuppositions and attitudes. The prophets of the Hebrew Scriptures call their listeners back to repentance and God. The apostles offer the new way of Christ to pagans and Jews. No doubt all were primarily concerned about changing human minds and habits in a practical sense, because it is one of the key issues in the success or failure of a religion, philosophy, or way of life, depending on the meaning of change in that situation. If a religion such as Christianity is going to survive, it must attract committed followers. Hence it must change people from their present way of life to the way of Christ. Celsus knew this, and along the way he pointed to numerous reasons why, in his opinion, Christianity fails in this area. In fact, it was precisely this issue that encouraged him to write against the Christians and their way of life, namely, he saw the faith as lacking a true and lasting transformation worthy of replacing the old way of life. For him conversion was the crucial concern. And it was a concern for many ancient writers.

As we have seen verified throughout the study, how to become a christ is perhaps the key theme in Origen's thought, if we were asked to name one. But Origen not only calls for change to Christianity, he analyzes how that change would and should occur. In every context, the questions are before him: What transforms people, how are they transformed and what keeps them transformed? Origen gives a deep and yet far-reaching answer, and one of our tasks has been to reflect on the texts that offer it. It is deep because it is critical to the substance of his thought and offers an important contribution to the meaning of change. It is far-reaching because he believed that the answers affect many if not all areas of religious thought that he explored. Let us then present Origen's answers to these questions.

2.

What is the transforming agent? In a word, it is divine communication, or the creation of a kind of common base of divinity between God and man, based, in the mature, on spirit. God's plan is to establish a community with his rational creation in order to create an environment for transformation and to help man to transform himself, in order to bring him back to Himself. Origen's answer then is that only divinity working within men and women transforms people, and only humanity and God working together and freely on a common plane will return man back to God. Hence, if man is to change, he must have the power of divinity within himself. Obviously it is not the divinity of the Trinity, but Origen uses some common terms. For example, he calls the power in humans that sanctifies and gives divine life the "spirit." It is the same word as the Holy "Spirit." Similarly, the rational faculty is called "logos," the same word as Logos. And there are other terms used for the Trinity and man, such as "image" and "christ," which demonstrate his view of this common divine sense or force within man.

Origen's use of these terms is intentional. The way he describes these matters emerges from the way he saw the spiritual cosmos. For him all of God's rational creation—when it is functioning the way God intends—is a spiritual unity, all functioning together and intending to be linked and related. For Origen it can mean as much to say Logos and *logoi*, Spirit and spirit, as to say God and man, for in his essence man is *nous* (intellect), not *psyche* (soul); *pneuma* (spirit), not *sarx* (flesh). So this natural relationship with divinity is ultimately what transforms the entire rational creation. It is like cooperating with like, Spirit enlivening and renewing spirit. Without this mutual ground, no one can become a christ.

But, as we have seen, this view of man's inner transforming power comprises only a part of Origen's discussion of the spiritual journey. While he returns to the natural kinship of all spiritual beings again and again, his main concern is not with what transforms, but in *how* man is transformed! Evidently it is not enough that man has a kind of kinship with divinity. Man still sins. Man lapses. Man falls. Man even seems unaware of his kinship. Again and again Origen demonstrates man's blindness to his destiny and origin.

Indeed man seems to be attracted to another kind of kinship, namely, his kinship with all fallible things. For man is not only akin to the divine; he has also become a creature with a gross body, and the products of this other dimension of his nature often seem to be more attractive to him. In any case, in Origen's analysis, the other dimension takes control because of man's failure to make proper judgments on effects of his earthly creatureliness. And whenever man allows his creaturely self to grow in strength, he is ruled by what Origen calls passion. And passion drives man to sin and to disobey God's commands as they are written in Scripture.

3.

So what can be done? Origen believes that there are basically two contributions to the solution. First, from the view of man, in the midst of the two forces—the force of man's kinship with God and the force of his earthly creatureliness— there is a power, also a gift of God, which, used properly and with some divine support, can turn man in the right direction and enable him to control the potentially difficult forces of his creatureliness. This is the power of free will. Free will is truly free in Origen's thought; there is no divine tyranny. Not even his creator will interfere in the decisions of man. Man can freely turn to his higher being, the spirit and *logos*, and control the other forces which draw him down. He can freely change his thoughts, seek to imitate the best models, and quest for the mysteries of knowledge. Yet he can also freely turn away from his essential self and give way for the devil and his forces. The devil is the real tyrant in Origen's cosmos. But even the devil cannot resist a will that seeks God and his support.

Second, from the view of God, there is man's great supporter and savior, Christ, who never stops being the mediator, restorer, revealer, model, and, above all, converter. There is so much of Christ in the one converting that Origen even calls such a one a christ. Christ is found at every point in spiritual growth in some sense. As the great transformer, the prime converter, whose relationship with the Father hinges on his task and relationship with man and the need for man to be complete, Christ is the catalyst, the hope, for a true and perfect return, when "all is all" again. As Origen sees it, the universe is now out of balance because of the Fall and sin, and it is Christ's work to bring everything back to wholeness again, to complete the "harvest." And this task involves more than salvation, as we discussed briefly in one section. To Origen, Christ's work goes beyond salvation; all the rational creation must become *teleios*, spiritually mature or complete, and that task transcends this life and even this world. It goes beyond the ages.

How then does Christ accomplish this enormous task of transformation? Christ has many aspects, many of which Origen discusses in the early books of his *Commentary on John*. These aspects mean for Origen that at many dimensions of existence Christ is cooperating with man to guide him back to God. Christ not only works, for example, at the more evident levels, such as through the Church, Scripture, and good angels, but also through the more invisible dimensions, such as his kinship with the image and *logos* in man, his role as the model, and his work through the Holy Spirit. Of course, in effect, the whole task of Christ is a way to conform man to his model, the model of sonship, regardless which aspect is involved. Indeed this is the significance for Origen of the text, "I am the way." To change we need to get on the "way" of sonship, be conformed to his model, set up a community with the Logos and *logos*, search the Scriptures for mysteries of the Logos, seek Christ's baptism (which is the baptism of the Spirit), and await in contemplation the grace, revelation and spiritual gifts of God. In sum, Christ transforms from within and from without man. He transforms as God and as man, as Logos and as Jesus. He transforms through the Spirit, who enlivens the spirit in man. He transforms through his body, the Church. He transforms through the model of his soul. He transforms through his imitators, the disciples and saints. He transforms as the Redeemer when he dies and when he is resurrected. In discerning all these roles, Origen is led by Scripture.

But even salvation, repentance and forgiveness are not enough to bring some to maturity. Even the work of the Church and the Holy Spirit may be not enough on this earth. Because it transcends this earth and this age and can involve many lapses, the journey of man is a frustrating, insecure and painful transition which only the patience of God could manage. For this reason, Origen speaks about the importance of "stability" and "firmness" in one's spiritual growth. Man must not only turn; he must remain turned. In the study we discussed this important ingredient at some length. Although there are many divine aids to help man, fundamentally again it is man who must acquire the right habits, study the Scriptures, do good works, maintain a life of truth and virtue, and prepare himself to receive the Spirit if he is to succeed in reaching God.

In sum, we might use the word "revolution" when we consider spiritual change and growth in Origen. Man's *nous* (intellect) in Origen's cosmos is so crusted over with bad habits, sins, and poor judgments that a spiritual shock, akin to a kind of spiritual overthrow of the tyranny of the *sarx* (flesh), is continually necessary for man to change in order to find his destiny. It is a revolution that Origen incited incessantly throughout his life and his works.

4.

Having given an overview of Origen's view of becoming a christ, let us examine now in more detail the implications and involvement of spiritual change in Origen's thought. We have not had many opportunities to do this kind of reflection in the course of the main text due to the complexities of defining the content of the spiritual growth itself in Origen's thought, and especially because of the wish to reflect accurately Origen's thought by quoting texts and discussing it without anachronism.

Our discussion will center around some remarks on change and the structure of Origen's thought. Perhaps the word "structure" without qualification may be too strong a term to describe Origen's approach. We perhaps should add the adjective "contextual." Origen's method varies with the context. If the context is a scriptural commentary, he uses one approach; if the context is a homily, a defense, a letter, etc., he uses other kinds of approaches. Of course, in all situations he is in dialogue with his times, so there is always present, even if hidden by other issues, the cultural context. Hence his work balances on the contextual structure he uses to explore the subject.

We first need to note how this contextual structure reflects the culture and the age. We are able to discuss this matter from many points of view, but since our concern is only with the spiritual journey, we will focus on it. Origen knows and assumes—though he will rarely mention it—how the various sectors of the culture view change. The Roman culture, as we have noted in the introduction, did not think people changed when they entered a temple or religious area. A devotee went to complete his duty to the god and to show appreciation for the good. One did not repent of any moral wrong-doing or any problem of conscience. One did not go to become better or to await inspiration in any form. There was no scriptural catalyst to change. Hence we find built into Origen's viewpoint the stress on changing whenever a member approaches a sacred thing, i.e., Scripture, the sacred community, a priest, the Logos, Christ, good angels, the sacraments, etc.

The effect of this attitude yields a structure with two sides: On the one hand, Origen encourages his readers or listeners to recognize what is truly sacred; on the other hand, he points out that we also need to realize that the sacred, the religious person or thing, can indeed enable us to change. Religion is a transforming agent; it is not a ritual of duty in the sense that the Roman religion is. Even his own parishioners, whom we assume were not far removed in their instincts and habits from the ways of the Roman culture and of whom few were educated in philosophy, evidently needed constantly to be convinced of this new attitude toward change found in Christianity.

An extreme example of the clarity of vision of how Origen saw Christianity working in the culture of the Roman Empire can be viewed in his book on martyrdom, and the remarks we find elsewhere in his writing on persecution. Religion was not something which could be signed away on a piece of paper, or left outside the gate of the pagan temple. Religion transforms man. The Christian does not revere this god today, that god tomorrow. If we truly change into christs, we cannot practice a way of life that conflicts with truth, for, as we have seen Origen repeat in many ways, there is no compromise with evil, falsity or foolishness. The Spirit unites only in the pure heart. God builds his temple only on a good foundation. Hence it is better to die for Christ than live on in sin. It is better for the body to be whipped and tortured than the soul to be lost and perverted from its true course. In sum, he tells those who are in terror of pain and death, hold on; for you shall be changed. And for Origen, growth and change meant the spiritual return to God.

This attitude of Origen crucially affects every other aspect of his thought. For in his view nothing of the true religion lacks transforming power and nothing should be approached without purity of heart and preparation. Once we become members, we are committed to change as Scripture understands it; we are committed to spiritual growth, and that growth is integral to every atom of the religion. Hence we shall call this influence of conversion on the structure of Origen's thought the religious cultural context. It is a matter of considerable importance in understanding why conversion is discussed everywhere in Origen's writings and why it is more than a religious issue; it involves conversion from the culture.

The influence of conversion on Origen's contextual structure is also evident in the method of Origen's religious thought. Scholars have been probing into Origen's work for some time to uncover his method or design. However, as has just been noted, Origen did not have a single design or method that he applied to all works; rather he had a method for each genre in which he wrote or preached. But again even this method was not rigidly followed, and we need to be careful about categorizing Origen's approach. His mind is so fertile with possibilities and complexities that he will pursue what is required in the immediate paragraph and ignore any general system or structure.

This said, we can detect certain forms that are applicable to spiritual change and vice versa. One of these designs we have been pursuing throughout our discussions, namely, the tri-modal approach of what we have called *aisthesis*, conduct and spirit. But what kind of a form is this? It is one of the forms that indicates spiritual function.

For Origen there is only one agent of change within man: the *nous*. If man changes, he changes because the *nous* is enlivened and empowered to change, because there is a will to change. There is a unity, in other words, in the psychological agent of change. There is not one entity for *aisthesis*, one for conduct, and one for the spirit. All three modes arise from changes within the single entity, the soul, with its upper and lower parts. But in order to clarify the process of change and what actually occurs, Origen refers to the three dimensions of how the *nous* (with divine aid) transforms man. These three dimensions have three functions, which, in brief, are to turn the mind away from the distractions of the senses, to change conduct, and to turn to the higher life and mysteries. Origen, of course, did not originate these modes alone; he follows his interpretation of Scripture, as we have seen many times in the study, even though the dimensions may not be always explicitly articulated in Scripture.

The value of realizing this form of spiritual function is that it is precisely this form that Origen often uses in many areas, e.g., trinitarian thought, Christology, scriptural interpretation, thoughts on the beginning and the end, since, as we have noted, conversion involves many areas of his thought.

For example, in his approach to the trinity, we see again this form rather than technical trinitarian discussions, which would be anachronistic in Origen's age. God is one, but there are several functions within the Godhead that have for Origen, certain, specified tasks. These were discussed in the body of the study, and were all, we noted, directly concerned with conversion.

In his approach to Christology, we again see the form of spiritual function at work. Christ is one, but he is often described in terms of several functions rather than in terms of essence or substance. And again these functions are invaribly related to the Christ the Converter.

In his interpretation of Scripture, it is not the words themselves, but their function, the purpose they serve in changing men's hearts, that is the key factor. Each text may have several functions or one function, but the form is used. This form explains to some extent why allegory is for Origen a crucial technique. For every text needs a function. The literal words do not define the function; the function(s) transcend the letters on the page.

So too in his understanding of the beginning and the end, Origen seems to have this form in mind. It is spiritual function (or dysfunction) that determines man's condition. Origen follows Scripture in not discussing in any extant work why God created man. Genesis begins, "In the beginning, God created...." There is no discussion concerning God's motives. But Origen does speculate on the origin of man's predicament because that matter is discussed in Scripture. So Origen begins his anthropology with the causes of the Fall, and the environment before and after the Fall. Again it is function that seems to be a key principle. What is the spiritual function of man here? Is it not to exercise his free will in accordance with the *nous*? The universe was in harmony, all intellects worshipping the Father. The way in which free will is exercised determines the place of man. Man misuses his free will and follows the example of the devil. His spiritual function has a nemesis, a dysfunction, in which evil and passion cripple the soul from pursuing its function as God intended. Then another form of spiritual function arises, namely the form of conversion, which has three dimensions, as noted above. It should be also stated that we hear nothing of *aisthesis*, conduct, or pursuing the mysteries and spirit in Origen's discussions of the beginning. Thus, the form as it rules in conversion arises within, so-to-speak, the primary form of spiritual function in the beginning, namely, the free will's directives. Of course, the power of free will is not diminished, but it is crippled because of passion and rendered incapable of choosing the good. Finally, in the end, man again returns to his true spiritual function, and properly exercises his free will in using the spiritual energies of the *nous*.

No research has uncovered any extant works of Christian thinkers prior to Origen that probe into change and the form of spiritual function in the depth in which the works of Origen pursue the matter. We will not repeat the general views of conversion of writers such as the Apostolic Fathers, Justin, Irenaeus, Tertullian and Clement of Alexandria, which we offered in the introduction. In these thinkers we find a preocccupation with either heresies or a particular focus that narrowed their discussion to only one dimension of spiritual growth or a more general view of change. Origen not only responds to the practical questions of spiritual change, such as what preparation and commitment in acts, inner resolve, and purity are necessary for one joining the Church, but he also analyzes the complexities involved in all who must change from one way to another, and remain firm in that change. He rejects the idea of hereditary virtue, as well as the concepts of innate goodness or evil such as we find in the Gnostics. Man is created free to choose his own way. Thus, every man has the inner gifts to become a christ, a son of God. All are equal in the eyes of God, and God has given everyone the potential to achieve his own blessedness. Yet beyond this gift and the hope it engenders for every person, there is a greater hope, resulting from the gifts of Christ and the Spirit. Origen saw all the acts of God and the mysteries revealed by him as part of a grand plan for restoration, the great harvest to be reaped by Christ and the Spirit. The theology of Origen of Alexandria is, in the end, a theology of radical transformation and hope. In the end, it not only reminds us of our destiny, but offers, in light of the heart of Scripture, the way back to God.

Appendix A:
Origen's View of Fire in the *Homilies on Jeremiah*

The following is a synopsis of the uses of fire in the *Homilies on Jeremiah* (with a few additions from other works) to illustrate the variety of contexts.

The connection of the fire of punishment with conversion is evident right from the beginning, for Origen writes, in *Hom. 1.14 in Jer.*, that Jeremiah, unlike Isaiah, was not a sinner, was not converted, and therefore "did not have anything worthy of the fire." The fire is God's way to destroy evil elements, the "chaff", in the soul, (*Hom. 1.15–16 in Jer.*) and an alternative in the grouping of souls. Some go to heaven, some to the fire in *Fr. 22 in Jer.* In his exposition of Jer. 2:22, in *Hom. 2.2 in Jer.*, Origin argues that God purifies the soul with means compatible to the sickness. The worst condition is cleansed by the "spirit of burning" (cf. Isa. 4:4), though Origen admits, in *Comm. in Mt.* 13.30 that he does not know what happens to those who sin gravely. Cleansing the sinful soul, however, brings to his mind the baptism of Luke 3:16 and Heb. 12:29, and Origen states, in *Hom. 2.3 in Jer.*, that there are actually two baptisms, one in this life, in the Holy Spirit, the other in the fire in the next life for those who sin after the first. Origen also mentions here one of his favorite texts when considering this subject, 1 Cor. 3:11 ff., how the fire destroys the wood, hay and other unworthy stuff a lifetime of sinning has brought to the soul. Similarly, when considering Jer. 4:4, in *Hom. 5.15 in Jer.*, he states that "the fire has as its material the evil of your doings." On Jer. 5:18, Origen writes that earthly punishments as described in Scripture are copies of the true punishments after death (cf. *Hom. 7.1 in Jer.*). With respect to the length and severity of punishments, Origen indicates, in *Hom. 7.2 in Jer.*, in commenting on Lev. 26:21, that there are seven levels of punishments (i.e., seven plagues) comparable to the severity of sins. In *Hom. 12.3 in Jer.*, on Jer. 13:13–14, Origen provides a clear picture of what a punishment might be like. He states that God will punish some by separating people from their loved ones "so that once taught you may be saved." In cases involving punishment, God will not be merciful to one person for the sake of many, Origen writes in *Hom. 12.5 in Jer.* His punishment is the "eternal fire," "hell," and the "outer darkness." Yet in this text, as in all others mentioned above, there is given no indication that salvation is impossible. Punishment is necessary to encourage others to change in *Hom. 12.6 in Jer.* Forgiveness is not guaranteed to all in *Hom. 12.10 in Jer.*, on Jer. 13:16 and Matt. 12:32, particularly not guaranteed to those who curse the Holy Spirit. Origen quotes with approval 1 Cor. 3:15 again at *Hom. 16.7 in Jer.* Often the difficulty in these texts involves whether Origen is referring to simply one age in his description of punishment and the fire, or to the end of ends, the *apokatastasis*. For example, in *Hom. 18.1 in Jer.*, he says that we either enter the fire of the devil or the fire of God "after the present age" (cf. Deut. 4:24 and Heb. 12:29). From his other statements, we assume he is describing the fire of only one age, not the final time. Indeed there is a punishment even more grave, he writes in *Hom. 19.15 in Jer.*, than the hell of fire, but he does not depict it for us. Still he does not claim even for these persons that salvation is jeopardized. In *Hom. 20.8–9 in Jer.*, on Jer. 20:9, there is a fire other than the fire of God and the fire of devil, namely, the fire of the Logos in this life which is applied to those who are converting. Since we have mentioned the possibility of many ages in Origen's thought, we might also add that he rejects transmigration in *Comm. in Mt.* 13.1, *Cels.* 5.29 and 3.75. He does not give his view among several alternatives in *Jo.* 6.10–14.[1]

Appendix B:
Origen Scholarship and Textual Methodology

This appendix has been divided into four sections: First, we will briefly review the position of this study in terms of other major studies done on Origen and how it benefits from these studies. Our purpose here is not to review the whole literature on Origen, but to select certain foundational works to which any researcher, in our opinion, must first turn; second, we will connect the work to studies done on conversion and the spiritual journey in the ancient world; third, we will concisely state how the perspective of this study may help to view Origen's multifaceted thought; and fourth, we will discuss the various difficulties in researching Origen.

1.

There are very few studies of conversion in any of the ancient Christian thinkers, even though it was perhaps the time in the history of Christiantity when the most change and conversion was occurring.[1] Indeed Origen scholarship itself has tended to concentrate on traditional theological areas, such as anthropology, Christology, ecclesiology, sacramental theology, exegesis, and the milieu of and influences on Origen.[2] The result of this concentration on traditional areas of theological research has been that some areas of interest to the concept of change and spiritual growth are mentioned and discussed, but usually not in the fuller context of how one becomes a Christian, and never in terms of a complete, unified vision of change and reform. Our procedure is the reverse: many of the traditional theological areas of Origen's thought will be considered, but they will now be analyzed in terms of Origen's view of spiritual growth. In other words, Origen's vision of growth and change will be the vantage point for viewing all areas of his thought, a task which, as we will consider in more detail below, nicely clarifies areas of his thought. A secondary but equally important reason for the study is to try to give Origen his due. Other great theological figures, such as Tertullian, Augustine, and Thomas Aquinas have studies entirely devoted to their understanding of conversion.

In order to clarify this method in more detail, we will briefly consider several works in each of the above categories of research, and then give a synopsis of how each is applicable to our study. Two purposes stand behind this effort: First, it will give an overview of classic scholarship on Origen, and, second, it will indicate the studies whose themes overlap with ours but that fall short in presenting a unified vision of change and growth that draws on all areas of Origen's thought.

Becoming a Christian concerns how man turns from (or returns to) a condition different from his prior condition. Hence any element that enables man to accomplish this effort is in some sense of interest to us.

In light of these concerns, the major books on anthropology must command our attention in this study. A work on the "spirit" (*pneuma*) in man goes a long way toward clarifying the various terms Origen uses to describe man, especially *pneuma, nous, psyche, sarx,* and *soma*. We need this clarification in order to know in depth how change occurs in man and how man's spiritual life matures through the process of *pneuma* destroying sinful influence on the *psyche*.[3] This process of deification is also discussed in terms of the role of the Trinity in another major study on Origen.[4] A recent book on the journey of the soul through creation, fall, earthly existence and ascent not only gives an overview of a subject that concerns transformation on the cosmic level, but also offers a comparison with the thought of a contemporary, Plotinus.[5] The journey of the soul from fall to redemption is also considered in terms of the biblical history of the people of God, and how Origen interpreted the matter. Indeed this work focuses on how Origen uses the struggles of the people of God in Scripture as an analogue of man's spiritual struggles.[6] A study concerning the theme of light as a grace bestowing knowledge and thus transforming one's attitudes directly concerns a dimension of conversion.[7] The difference of and movement from ordinary to true life is a major dimension of this process, and it is handled thoroughly in a now-classic work.[8] Finally, two other books need to be mentioned. One work focuses entirely on the subject of man, and, while not directly concerned with our subject, does offer many insights on the progress of man and his moral life.[9] The other book considers the very complex issue of the meaning of the "image" in Origen. The author carefully dissects texts concerning how man journeys to God through the *psyche*'s power to receive grace. The movement from the image, given at creation, to the likeness, given to man when deified in the end, has important parallels to the process of transformation, even though this work is not concerned explicitly with the spiritual journey.[10]

All these works are applicable to our subject; they offer insights into Origen's view of man that can only be acquired through focusing on the texts concerned with specific areas of anthropology.

Change to Christianity involves the Church in many ways. For example, the sacraments are, for most ancient Christians, extremely powerful agents of transformation and enlightenment, agents that inspire believers to contemplate and commune with Christ. Moreover, since conversion occurs within a community, we need to understand something of the Christian community from which conversion arises, and how influential the Church is. Four recent studies give us some depth in these areas.[11]

Christ is the cornerstone for Origen's views on transformation. All three dimensions find him at their center. In light of this importance, our study needs the support of works on Origen's Christology. Unfortunately, Origen's Christology has never been treated in detail from all its aspects in one study. Hence in order to grasp his Christology in some depth, one must peruse several books, each with its own focus.

A work on the Logos and Origen's spirituality is one of the first to try to see Origen as one who belonged in the tradition of spirituality. It tended to stress Christ as Logos. The work mentioned above on the image of God in man probed more deeply into Christological questions, and remains an extremely useful sourcebook on such questions, as well as, of course, discussions about the role of Christ in man's spiritual life. Another study, however, has masterfully considered the relation of Christ/Logos to the rational creation, and needs to be consulted on all Christological and Trinitarian questions.[12]

Three works on the humanity and incarnate Word provide ample evidence of Origen's intense interest in this side of Christ's purpose and his attachment to the person of Jesus.[13] One of these works, though primarily a detailed study of Origen's attitude to the Incarnation, enables us to see how man is turned to knowledge of God through belief in the acts and works of the man Jesus and then enlightenment by the Logos. More important, it shows that Christ's revelation is not fulfilled in the historical reality, but that "his spirit and his power are still working in the whole world, until the end of the age." This point of view on the Incarnate Christ exposes clearly the importance of Christ in the work of returning God's people to him.[14] Both sides of Christ need to be understood if his role is to be clarified. Christ for Origen was not only the Logos; he was also the one whom we should imitate.

Though Origen was well-educated in philosophy and the culture of his age, his heart
was in Scripture. Indeed the more one probes into his scriptural reflections, the more one
discovers the extent of his union with what we might call a biblical perspective. It is at
times an extraordinarily original vision of Scripture that only one who had absorbed its
essence could generate. How Origen viewed Scripture has been well-researched, including
both his sources and his means of interpretation.[15] Of course, it is not only the literal
word or statement which concerns Origen. In fact, the mysteries behind the literal word
invite his searching analyses, many of which uncover ways in which man is transformed
by the powers of Scripture. Hence Scripture as the word of God is, like Christ, a key
catalyst in how man changes, though there has been no study which was devoted specifically
to the question of how Scripture converts man.[16]

Finally, let us conclude with a survey of studies on Origen's environment and those
who influenced him. There are ten books that would be a good basis for initial research.[17]
As we have already seen in Chapter 1 on Origen's milieu, the environment in which Origen
formed his thinking is significant to an understanding of his thought, regardless of the
subject. Fundamentally, these studies can be divided into two groups: those concerned
with the philosophical influences on Origen and his views of philosophy, and those
concerned with his Caesarean life.

The former subject has been the source of some controversy concerning Origen. It is
an old tradition in writing on Origen—almost from the time of Origen himself—to
emphasize him as a philosopher who was also a Christian rather than as a Christian
theologian based in Scripture who was conversant with contemporary philosophy and
sometimes addressed philosophical questions to convert the philosophers.[18] How does this
controversy concern us with respect to Origen's ideas on becoming a Christian? The
intention of this study is to try to see the Origen who exists in the extant texts, and to
try to portray his thought in all its complexity without necessarily categorizing him as
either a Christian mystic or a philosopher. His life and writings do witness that he was
at all times a committed Christian who sought to understand the mysteries of his faith
and to express them in the vocabulary of his age and training in terms of how he understood
Scripture and the Christian tradition. The best defender of Origen is Origen himself, and
we try to lay before the reader the texts themselves as often as possible.

The works on Origen's Caesarean life are particularly important to us, because, first,
the later life in Caesarea has, until now, been rather obscure and lacking concrete evidence,
and, second, many of the texts upon which this study are based were written while Origen
lived in Caesarea. Indeed the *Homilies on Jeremiah*, the heart of this study, were delivered
in Caesarea. These studies give a more accurate picture of Origen's relations with and
debt to the Jews, an updated description of his famous school, and a summary of the
general political, social, economic and religious climate of those years.

2.

Three general works directly concerning conversion and change demand our attention and
perusal. Each of these studies concerns both conversion, a turning from a position outside
the faith or philosophy to a new way of life and thought, and repentance, a change of
mind without growth usually occurring from within the faith. These two views, by the
way, are integrated by Origen in his ideas on conversion.

The first work uses a broad history-of-religions approach, and gives considerable detail
on how a pagan in the ancient world such as Celsus viewed Christianity. It is quite helpful
because it clearly presents the pagan/Christian contrasts and the general religious
environment in the first centuries. These elements are necessary for an understanding of
the psychological changes of the age in which Origen lived and how his view of change
compared to others.[19]

Another study on conversion explores the meaning of *epistrephein* and *epistrophe*, and one twenty page chapter of this work is devoted to Origen's use of these words.[20] Actually this book goes beyond being just a word-study, and offers many insights into the meaning of conversion. However, since it is primarily devoted to texts where these words appear, and only twenty pages in length, the broader vocabulary and the unified vision of conversion are not thoroughly uncovered.[21]

Finally, two general studies of the meaning of conversion and reform in the first centuries are foundational for understanding how Origen's view fits within the general context of Christian ideas on spiritual growth and transformation as viewed by other patristic thinkers. The author sees the desire for truth, salvation, deliverance from sin, and holiness as the great motifs of the Christian conversion in the first centuries.[22]

3.

As we have seen in the above discussion of scholarship on Origen, many different traditional areas of theological thought are involved in considering Origen's view of change. Indeed, it seems to this writer, how to become a Christian and grow spiritually is an idea that does more than concern these areas; it unites them into a synthesis. Conversion seems to be the thread that can weave through all of them without sacrificing the integrity of each area and without forcing a systematic perspective on any of the areas.[23] Origen's views on conversion are not an attempt to conform to some borrowed preconceived philosophical structure, nor does Origen have some massive theological structure in mind when he is writing, but his thoughts arise from the wish of a devotee to contemplate the way of his faith. It is also important to recall that Origen was pressed by others to write most of the extant works, and on several occasions he felt the task was either unnecessary, inappropriate, or incomplete. It is my opinion that the reason he probably never completed some of his more ambitious commentaries was that Scripture for Origen was an infinite well of spiritual life and mysteries. While he could have continued writing forever on the Bible, Origen, let us note, did not have a difficulty completing *Against Celsus* or *On First Principles*.

It is for this reason that it is difficult to confine Origen's views to some category. Origen was a man of the Church, an exegete, a speculative theologian, a practicing Christian/pastor and an intellectual who read widely and debated with the best minds of his time. With respect to the concept of spiritual growth, he was not one kind of person more than another, but all of them unite to project his vision of reality. The greatest harm done to Origen by present-day writers occurs, first, when they attempt to categorize his thought, and, second, when they read and judge his works through the eyes of later controversies and centuries. This study avoids whenever possible any evaluation of Origen's ideas with theological views after Origen's day.[24] Terms such as Donatist, semipelagian, Pelagian, Nestorian, Arian, subordinationist, etc., are not used because Origen himself did not know them. As is well known, Origen himself never consciously intended to exceed the rule of faith in his writings; on the contrary, he wished others to understand it through his writings. The key to Origen—if one insists on a single answer—is that he was a man who himself felt comfortable with his unified vision, and these various sides, which some writers separate today, were for him the product of a single, integrated, and, usually, a scripturally based theological conviction. And that conviction centers very often in the concept of how to become a christ.

4.

Now that we have briefly discussed the major scholarship that surrounds the study of Origen, let us clarify the textual method used to write this study. All scholars approach ancient texts with a method, even if they have never consciously thought it out. In Origen research if one's method is uncritical or lacking in thoroughness and caution, and especially if one is silent about how s/he is making decisions in handling texts, numerous inaccuracies can arise. So this section is an effort to clarify the methodology of the author.

Normally textual methodology encompasses the areas of (a) textual criticism, (b) use of modern language translations, (c) chronology of works, and (d) the manner of text selection, including (e) the use of works on scripture, (f) works on the theme of the book, and (g) the way the texts are used. We will conclude with (h) a summary of principles of methodology. Since the most difficult problems emerge in text selection, the first three areas of criticism, translations and chronology will be mentioned briefly while the subject of text selection will encompass most of the section.

(a) Concerns over textual criticism are beginning to lessen since the emergence of the parallel text editions of Origen's works in the *Sources Chrétiennes* (SC) series. Under the careful scholarship of Origen scholars, Origen's works are receiving proper attention. These texts are appearing steadily, replacing or at least offering an excellent alternative to the Greek or Latin only of the GCS series. The editors of the Origen volumes in the *Sources Chrétiennes* series tend to be theologians and those concerned with the religious dimension of Origen's work rather than philologists or literary specialists. One need only compare the text of *On First Principles* in the GCS series with that of the SC series to note the different presuppositions and editing methods. Many of the fragments inserted into the text by the GCS editors have been placed in an appendix or excised entirely as passages which are not from *On First Principles*, are quoted out of context, or have been changed in some way to discredit Origen. Moreover, in most of the *Sources Chrétiennes* works, there are extensive notes on the relation of the passage to Origen's thought. The above mentioned edition of *On First Principles* and the editions of *Against Celsus*, the *Commentary on John*, and the *Commentary on Matthew* are cases in point. These notes, plus the usual text references and source information, a parallel French translation, and detailed and useful introductions, make the job of text criticism at most secondary for writers on Origen.

In this study, whenever there was a question on the use of particular Greek or Latin manuscript, or on a different reading that substantially affects the meaning of the context, it has been duly noted. Whenever they were available to the writer, the editions of both the *Sources Chrétiennes* and the GCS series are noted, especially for the critical editions noted above. It should be remembered too that the translations are often translations of Latin translations or adaptations.

(b) All English translations have been checked beside the original Greek and Latin texts. When no name is given in the footnotes for translation, the reader may assume the translator was the author. Translations offered by the author are literal and are meant to be no more than guides to the original Greek or Latin. They make no other claims. When changes are made to an existing English translation, this is noted by an asterisk(*) after the translator's name.

(c) In general the problems of chronology are too complex to be the concern of this study. It is necessary to say at some point, however, what one's choice has been and to provide the rationale. For the sake of consistency, it seemed most prudent to follow the recent conclusions of Pierre Nautin.[25] Differences from his opinions will be noted. Except for *On First Principles* and Books i–v of the *Commentary on John*, all the works cited are from Origen's later, post-Egyptian period, from about 232 A.D. on. Later on in this section a list of approximate dates for the major extant works of Origen is offered. It should be noted that even *On First Principles* and the early books of the *Commentary on John* are from a time when most writers are considered mature.[26]

The later works, however, have the added dimension offered by Origen's experience as priest and preacher, and this dimension of his life is especially important for a discussion of any topic in Origen. They contrast nicely with works such as *On First Principles*, which is more explicit concerning certain subjects that are only implied in later works. Since these speculations include speculations on the beginning and the end, they are not without importance to our theme and are included in our considerations. But the main concern, with respect to chronology, is whether the conclusions evident in certain Greek fragments attributed to Origen and to a certain extent in the Latin translations remain Origen's hypotheses in his later career in Caesarea. Allusions and implications in the later works seem to support that he stood by his earlier opinions with respect to our topic. This fact will become more clear when we turn to the texts themselves.

(d) Origen's works survive in both the orginal Greek and Latin translations. Unfortunately, much of what survives is in Latin, and the Latin translations are usually not literal but are paraphrases. Obviously, since Origen wrote and preached in Greek, the most accurate presentation of his thoughts will be found in the surviving Greek texts, and the most accurate study of Origen's thought will rely primarily on these texts. Hence the first principle of the method followed in this study is to prefer the original Greek text whenever possible.

Let us quickly list what texts such a principle would include. In parenthesis will also be given the approximate date of composition, according to the most recent evidence.[27] It is not the task of this study to enter into the various problems concerned with the dating of Origen's works. It must suffice here to say that these dates are approximate and in some cases uncertain. Generally there is no problem in knowing whether the works come before or after Origen's Alexandrian period.

Among the works on Scripture in Greek, we possess twenty homilies on Jeremiah (242 or later),[28] one homily on 1 Kings (1 Samuel) (ca. 244), numerous fragments and selections from various homilies, eight books of the commentary on Matthew (244–249), eight books of the commentary on the Gospel of John, (Books I–V, before 228, remainder 235–238), and extensive Greek fragments from these and other commentaries, some of which are quite long.[29]

Other surviving Greek works include the apologetic work *Against Celsus* (244–249), a record of an informal inquiry into the Trinitarian opinions of a Bishop Heraclides entitled *Dialoque with Heraclides* (244–245), *On Prayer* (233/234), *Exhortation to Martyrdom* (235–238), a letter to Gregory Thaumaturgos in which Origen advises his former pupil on the use of Greek philosophy and the need to read Scripture (ca. 235–243??), a letter to Julius Africanus concerning the proper view and canonic position of Susanna (ca. 240), parts of *On Easter* (?), and large sections from several works of Origen, some of which we also possess in Latin, preserved in the *Philocalia* prepared by St. Basil and St. Gregory Nazianzen.[30]

These Greek works, then, are the core source material for an accurate understanding of Origen's thought.

Less reliable because they are translations—and every translation is an interpretation—are the edited but usually faithful translations of Jerome and some of the translations of Rufinus. The more "literal" translations of Rufinus include Origen's twenty-six homilies on Joshua (ca. 243), nine homilies on Judges (ca. 243) and the nine homilies on the Psalms (ca. 241). Jerome's translations include the two homilies on the Song of Songs (ca. 241)— which he himself claims are faithful, not ornate, in his prologue to the work—nine homilies on Isaiah (ca. 242), fourteen homilies on Ezekiel (ca. 242), two homilies on Jeremiah not in the Greek collection (ca. 242), thirty-nine homilies on Luke (ca. 242) and various fragments.

With respect to the other Latin translations of Rufinus, by his own admission he has paraphrased, lengthened, shortened when something needed explanation to his Latin readers, included passages from other works of Origen, and, in general, placed his own personality and interpretation between the reader and Origen's thought. In controversial passages that he thought would confuse the orthodox Christian readers of his Latin milieu, he has made alterations or sometimes excised them entirely.[31] According to most writers, he generally paraphrases accurately, but since we no longer have the original Greek for much of what he translated, we are not sure of the degree of his accuracy or even whether what he has left is complete.

Rufinus's surviving translations in this form include sixteen homilies on Genesis (ca. 243), thirteen homilies on Exodus (ca. 243), sixteen homilies on Leviticus (ca. 243), twenty-eight homilies on Numbers (ca. 243), ten books of the *Commentary on Romans* (ca. 244), four books of the *Commentary on the Song of Songs* (ca. 245), and the four books of *On First Principles* (ca. 229–230?), along with a group of fragments from lost works.[32]

In addition to the translations of Jerome and Rufinus, there is also extant a fifth-century translation of some books of the *Commentary on Matthew*. One scholar has indicated that it is relatively reliable.[33]

None of these translations comes up to modern critical standards. As one writer has said: "Les traducteurs anciens n'ont pas les scrupules des modernes."[34] When compared with the original Greek, both Rufinus and Jerome can miss the point and general direction of Origen's Greek and thought. Both tend to present Origen as a Latin writer of their own milieu and ecclesiastical environment. Still, for the general thrust of Origen's thought on uncontroversial issues, these translations may be trusted. Of course, they should be contrasted whenever possible with similar passages in Greek.

It is then not prudent to exclude the Latin translations from one's study of Origen, since they help to fill out three extremely important sides of Origen—his role as a preacher to a general audience, his spirituality, and his theoretical speculations and philosophical interests, which are not as commonly or sometimes as deeply exhibited in some of the extant Greek texts.

The following principle has been followed as a general rule in this study in referring to the Latin translations: If the Greek is unavailable to substantiate a Latin translation, then the more literal Latin translations are sought for support in the analysis. Naturally prudence and caution must be observed in the selection of supporting texts, especially with respect to controversial themes. In fact, Latin translations and Greek fragments will be avoided whenever possible concerning controversial subjects such as pre-existence, *apokatastasis*, trinitarian doctrine and Christology. By quoting several Latin translations from different books, with a careful consideration of context, we may avoid some inaccuracies. For the contexts of different passages in different works can lead us to Origen's view, whereas a single passage may be distorted. Of course, in matters concerning word studies, phraseology, style, and many other nuances of Origen's use of language, the Latin translations are almost useless. Translating Latin paraphrases back into Greek is an insurmountable task. Hence it must be the context that is quoted or noted, with respect to the Latin works, rather than the word or the sentence.

In sum, the Greek originals are the basic source material for this study. If Latin translations are used, they are used, first, to verify one another, second, by reference to the context, and, third, because no Greek text exists. One tries to avoid controversial subjects based on the Latin translations and very technical discussions in which Origen's language necessarily plays an important role. But in order to present a full view of the various sides of Origen, especially as found in the homilies and *On First Principles*, the Latin translations form an essential part of the Origen *corpus*, and hence will not be neglected.

(e) Of all the works which he completed, his favorite mode of communicating his ideas and the ideas found in Scripture was through homilies and biblical commentaries. The number alone of these works at Origen's death verifies this fact. Scripture was for him the source of many mysteries God intended in this life for man. With the proper preparation and the inspiration of the Spirit, the secrets of divine things would emerge from the pages. To unravel these mysteries, Origen is usually painstakingly detailed; he analyzes every nuance, even every significant word, and sees in each text a reflection of the whole Bible. In fact, the context of each passage was the whole Bible, because for Origen the Bible has spiritually only one author. All other knowledge, such as philosophy, geometry, astronomy and law, is preparation for the study of Scripture. These matters are made clear by Origen throughout his works, and particularly in his letter to Gregory.

In light of Origen's own preference and admiration for Scripture both as nourishment and as the subject of his thoughts, it seems likely that the most accurate expression of Origen's mind will be found in his works on Scripture.[35] Hence another principle for the selection of text in this study is to examine first Origen's scriptural works, that is, the homilies and the commentaries.

This decision does not diminish the importance of Origen's other works, especially *On First Principles* and *Against Celsus*, for an appreciation of his complexity. But these two works are written more with an intellectual than a religious tone due to the audience to which they are addressed and the genre in which Origen intentionally wrote. Indeed Origen in his preface to *Against Celsus* even resists writing the work. It was, in his own opinion, unnecessary. Again, this does not diminish the importance of such works, especially those preserved in Greek, but the circumstances and motives for the works have to be kept in mind. Some works, such as *On Prayer* and *Exhortation to Martyrdom*, are strictly occasional pieces; others, such as *Against Celsus*, reflect the milieu more than the man. Scripture, however, was the product of Origen's life-long contemplation, as is noted several times by Eusebius in Book vi of his *Ecclesiastical History*.

In sum, it is the method of this study to seek out first the scriptural homilies and commentaries of Origen. These would include, as noted above, the *Commentary on John*, the *Commentary on Matthew*, the *Homilies on Jeremiah*, the Greek fragments to these works plus the fragments extant of the *Commentary on Romans* and the *Homilies on 1 Corinthians*. Also valuable, within the guidelines mentioned in the previous section, are the Latin translations of various homilies and commentaries.

(f) Another consideration with respect to the selection of texts concerns the theme of this study: how does one become a Christian? It is possible to claim, in a general sense, that almost all of Origen's work is somehow connected to the effort to reorient his readers' or listeners' minds and lives. But three works are specifically directed toward this theme: *On First Principles*, the *Homilies on Jeremiah*, and *Against Celsus*.

With respect to *On First Principles*, writers have stated that one of its most important purposes is to convert the philosophers, since the problems discussed are problems interesting to philosophers.[36] Unfortunately, it survives complete only in the edited translation of Rufinus and was written prior to Origen's experiences as a presbyter in Caesarea. These later experiences would perhaps have given his ideas on conversion several added dimensions beyond what is said in *Peri Archon*.

Against Celsus, however, is one of Origen's latest surviving works, and it is extant in the Greek. In his preface, Origen explains that he wrote the book not for "true Christians," but for those either outside the faith or those weak in faith. Despite its general intellectual tone, directed toward educated readers, *Against Celsus* is very useful in the constant comparisons made between Christianity and other religions and philosophies. Equally important, the work is a defense of Christianity against the attack of a very able critic. Origen is forced to consider practically every issue of substance in the Christian faith, and this effort gives us clear, albeit often brief, answers in Greek to some questions that would otherwise be very difficult to uncover.

Yet the work most valuable for a study of the spiritual journey and spiritual transformation is the *Homilies on Jeremiah*.[37] It is extant in Greek, is among Origen's late writings when he was a pastor, and is, of course, one of Origen's studies on Scripture. Even more important, as noted earlier, it comments on a book of Scripture which is also concerned with conversion. Hence this study refers to the *Homilies* whenever possible. The *Homilies* also are a good source for a general understanding of the major themes in Origen's thought.[38] However, in order to reflect the different audiences to which Origen wrote, the contributions of other works will be presented.

(g) There has been an understandable tendency among some writers of books on Origen to cite many texts in the footnotes which are not, in fact, quoted in Greek or in translation, or analyzed in depth in the text. One reason for this tendency is probably to offset the uncertainty many feel about the Latin translations. Serious writers on Origen feel they need to overwhelm the reader with primary texts in order to assure the reader that the point made is indeed in Origen's thought, even if only in a Latin translation. Another reason is that it is believed that only many texts can validate a point in Origen's thought, since he discussed similar questions in many different contexts. The dean of Origen scholars, Henri Crouzel, in his work on knowledge, *Origène et la 'connaissance mystique'*, has pages with more than twenty texts cited per page, with no more than a phrase describing the text. In an article of less than twelve pages by the well-known and respected Origen scholar, Cécile Blanc, there are over two-hundred footnotes, almost all of which were references to texts. Such an approach, it seems to me, in less capable hands than that of Crouzel or Blanc, might have sacrificed analysis for erudition.

Thus, though we sympathize with the reasons mentioned above, the method used in this study concentrates less on the number of works cited than on the analysis and development of the critical texts which present the various sides of Origen. This method has made a longer work, but, let us hope, a work reflecting Origen's texts and thought. It strives to find a good text, in Greek whenever available, and to analyze it in as much detail as prudence allows.

(h) The criteria followed in this work for determining a "good" text will, in effect, summarize, with one addition, this section on textual methodology.

First, one seeks the original Greek text. If this is unavailable, a comparison between texts from several Latin translations, examined in their contexts and according to the context of the study, is considered. The more literal translations of Rufinus and Jerome are preferred, in general, to the freely edited versions of Rufinus. The results of this effort are then presented to the reader.

Second, one seeks a text(s) that can balance the various sides of Origen's personality, interests, and thought. Hence his views on a subject are to be compared from the speculative, apologetic, exegetical as well as practical points of view. Similarly, with respect to chronology, since all of Origen's major extant works stem from his maturity, the presentation here tries to balance what we can call his speculative writings with his writings as presbyter rather than balance so-called "early" writings with "late" writings. The "early" and "late" designations assume that Origen was perhaps young or immature in his thought in the "early" writings or that the two periods were many years apart.[39] In fact, this is not the case. It is much more functional and effective to consider Origen's writings in terms of genre rather than period.

Third, in these comparisons and efforts to present the various sides of Origen's writings, the works of biblical exegesis will be considered foundational. Scripture, in any case, nourished all sides of Origen's life and thought. He was a philosopher, but a philosopher of Scripture.

Fourth, the effort is made to analyze texts in as much detail as possible rather than simply cite a number of texts for the reader to track down.

Fifth, a text is considered "good" on a particular theme when Origen himself considers it to be the theme of the passage. In other words, the context of our exposition should be comparable to the context of the Origen text.

With respect to secondary sources, the text being used is the primary guide. If a scholar does not use the same text, in general—there are a few exceptions—he will be not cited at that point. With the rapid growth in Origen studies of the last generation, it is not possible, in any case, to cite all the work that has been done. Hence the present study relies primarily on the texts used.

Finally, it is important to discuss Origen's scriptural text. Though he did at times refer to the Hebrew,[40] his basic text for the Old Testament was in Greek.[41] When he found discrepancies, Origen compared his text with the Hebrew and other Greek texts. The touchstone for this study with respect to the Old Testament texts used will be the Septuagint. Origen, of course, also used a Greek text for the New Testament. With respect to the Latin Origen works, it has been shown that Rufinus did not use Origen's scriptural text for his translations, but an Old Latin version.[42] Hence we need to compare carefully the scriptural passages in the Latin version with the Greek before we can arrive at a text that will resemble in some way Origen's original.

Notes

Chapter I. Introduction:
How Was Spiritual Change Viewed in Origen's Day?

1. From the philosophical side it begins at least with Plato, whose dialogues influenced so many Christian writers, and whose work *The Republic* was written with the basic intention to guide man to a clearer vision of God, an expression of hope for man's transformation. See Plato, *Rep.* VI.508B–509C. W. Jaeger, *Early Christianity and Greek Paideia* (Oxford: Oxford University Press, 1961), p. 10, writes: "Even the word 'conversion' stems from Plato, for adopting a philosophy meant a change of life in the first place." Out of his thought emerge Philo, Clement of Alexandria and other early Christian writers, as well as Plotinus, all of whom were concerned with the question of how man would be reunited with the divine. See Philo, *De vita cont.* ii, Clement, *Str.* 7.40.1–2 and *Paed.* i.1. S. Lilla, *Clement of Alexandria—A Study in Christian Platonism and Gnosticism* (Oxford: Oxford U. Press, 1971), p. 165, finds a link in idea and terminology between Plato, Philo and Clement on the way the soul can turn from the sensible world to the intelligible world. For Plotinus, see *Enneads*, ed. and trans. A. Armstrong (Loeb ed.; Cambridge, Mass.: Harvard U. Press, 1966), I, xxv. H. Crouzel, "Origène et Plotin, élèves d'Ammonios Saccas," *BLE*, 57 (1956), 205, indicates that both men view the spiritual life as a path to bring man to a contemplation of God.

We should also note that the religious confusion was reflected in the political and economic climate also. See M. Rostovtzeff, *A History of the Ancient World*, 2nd corrected ed. (Oxford: Oxford U. Press, 1928), II.266–278. He claims that the Empire vacillated downward after the death of Marcus Aurelius (ca. 180 A.D.) in both political and economic areas. The crisis continued throughout the third century due to many factors, but Rostovtzeff notes two important ones: the increased power of the army, and the increased apathy of the people in working and using their resources. Instead they were preoccupied, Rostovtzeff writes, p. 271, with the "inner life of man, and especially with questions of religion." Furthermore, he claims, p. 291, that the cause of the fervent religious interests was the need for more personal and consoling faiths than what the people were experiencing in emperor worship. The general disorder and bankruptcy, power struggles and civil wars of the Empire in Origen's lifetime are discussed also in D. Dudley, *Roman Society* (Harmondsworth: Penguin, 1975), pp. 263–271. On the impersonal nature of emperor worship and its failure to satisfy the people, see also J. Ferguson, *The Religions of the Roman Empire* (Ithaca, N.Y.: Cornell U. Press, 1970), p. 99.

2. H. Jonas, *The Gnostic Religion* (2nd ed. rev.; Boston: Beacon Press, 1963), p. 31, writes: "At the beginning of the Christian era and progressively throughout the two following centuries, the eastern Mediterranean world was in profound spiritual ferment." A. Nock, *Conversion: The Old and New in Religion from Alexander the Great to Augustine of Hippo* (Oxford: Oxford U. Press, 1933), p. 99, points out for eastern cults, and on pp. 210–211 for Christianity, the reasons for their appeal to prospective converts. He also writes: "The success of Christianity is the success of an institution which united the sacramentalism and the philosophy of the time." Finally, F. Cumont, *Oriental Religions in Roman Paganism*, trans. G. Showerman (1911; rpt.; N.Y.: Dover, 1956), pp. 26–27, notes the "psychological crisis" involved in acceptance of the Oriental religions. The influence of the eastern cults on Roman paganism is especially important for an understanding of conversion in the era, for the destruction of the ancient religions by the Oriental religions prepared the way for conversion to Christianity. See Cumont, pp. xxiii–xxiv and p. 19.

3. Dates from P. Nautin, *Origène, sa vie et son oeuvre* (Paris: Beauchesne, 1977), pp. 409, 412.

4. For the life of Origen, written, it should be remembered, by an enthusiast, see Eusebius, *Ecclesiastical History* 6. For a critical analysis of that history, see Nautin's *Origène*.

5. The following works have been useful in preparing this section: A. Andrewes, *Greek Society* (Harmondsworth: Penguin, 1971), pp. 254–272; S. Angus, *The Mystery-Religions. A Study in*

the Religious Background of Early Christianity (1928; rpt.; N.Y.: Dover, 1975), especially pp. 1–38, 235–314; G. Bardy, *La conversion au christiansme durant les premiers siècles* (Paris: Aubier, 1949), pp. 9–45; J. Bayet, *Histoire politique et psychologique de la religion romaine*, 2nd rev. and corr. ed. (Paris: Payot, 1969), pp. 42–60; J. Behm, METANOIA METANOEO, *Theological Dictionary of the New Testament*, ed. G. Fiedrich, trans. G. Bromiley, IV: 975–980; J. Carcopino, *Daily Life in Ancient Rome. The People and the City at the Height of the Empire*, trans. E. O. Lorimer, ed. H. Rowell (Harmondsworth: Penguin, 1956), pp. 137–157; C. Cochrane, *Christianity and Classical Culture. A Study in Thought and Action from Augustus to Augustine* (Oxford: Oxford U. Press, 1944); F. Cumont, *The Mysteries of Mithra*, trans. T. McCormack, 2nd rev. ed. (1903; rpt.; N.Y.: Dover, 1956), pp. 175–208; *Oriental Religions in Roman Paganism*, trans G. Showerman, 2nd ed. (1911; rpt.; N.Y.: Dover, 1956); *Astrology and Religion among the Greeks and Romans* (1912; rpt.; N.Y.: Dover, 1960); E. R. Dodds, *Pagan and Christian in an Age of Anxiety. Some Aspects of Religious Experience from Marcus Aurelius to Constantine* (1965; rpt.; N.Y.: Norton, 1970); D. Dudley, *Roman Society*; J. Ferguson, *The Religions of the Roman Empire*; M. Hadas, *Hellenistic Culture. Fusion and Diffusion* (1959; rpt.; N.Y.: Norton, 1972), pp. 182–197; J. Harrison, *Prolegomena to the Study of Greek Religion*, 3rd ed. (1922; rpt.; N.Y.: World, 1959), pp. 1–31, 624–658; A. Hus, *Greek and Roman Religion*, trans. S. Tester (N.Y.: Hawthorn, 1962), pp. 141–153; H. Kitto, *The Greeks* rev. ed. (Harmondsworth: Penguin, 1957), pp. 194–204; M. Laistner, *Christianity and Pagan Culture in the Later Roman Empire* (Ithaca, N.Y.: Cornell U. Press, 1951), pp. 1–48; N. Lewis and M. Reinhold, eds., *Roman Civilization*. Sourcebook II: The Empire (1955; rpt.; N.Y.: Harper, 1966), pp. 419–489; M. Nilsson, *Greek Piety* trans. H. Rose (1948; rpt.; N.Y.: Norton, 1969); *A History of Greek Religion*, trans. F. Fielden, 2nd rev. ed. (1952; rpt.; N.Y.: Norton, 1964); A. Nock, *Conversion*; R. Ogilvie, *The Romans and their Gods in the Age of Augustus* (London: Chatto & Windus, 1969); W. Otto, *The Homeric Gods. The Spiritual Significance of Greek Religion*, trans. M. Hadas (1954; rpt.; London: Thames and Hudson, 1979), pp. 1–39, 231–260; H. Parker, *History of the Roman World A.D. 138–337*, 2nd ed. (London: Methuen, 1970); H. Rose, *Religion in Greece and Rome* (N.Y.: Harper, 1959); M. Rostovtzeff, *A History of the Ancient World*.

    6. Nock, *Conversion*, p. 14: "There was therefore in these rivals of Judaism and Christianity no possibility of anything which can be called conversion." The journey of Lucius in Apuleius's *Metamorphoses* he considers an "approximation." M. Green, *Evangelism in the Early Church* (London: Hodder and Stoughton, 1970), p. 382, n. 4, finds even this claim unfounded. Cf. also Bardy, *La conversion*, pp. 9, 18. The word *paganus*, in fact, involves a refusal to convert. Originally it meant one who wanted to stay at home and not become a soldier. But it came to mean one who would not become a soldier of Christ. See Rose, *Religion in Greece and Rome*, p. 292.

    These judgments on the subjective power of ancient pagan religions should not be exaggerated. As Angus, *The Mystery-Religions*, p. 142, writes, "It would run counter to our evidence and to what we know of human nature to deny that there were conversions and transformations of character among the members of the Mystery-brotherhoods." Nor should these judgments imply that there was never any element of personal feeling in traditions outside Judaism and Christianity. See Andrewes, *Greek Society* pp. 264–266, where he discusses the attachment which traditional Greeks had for their gods, as well as other personal tendencies.

    7. On *metanoia*, see Behm, 976–979, as well as Nock, *Conversion*, p. 180. For the sense of the word to the Jews and Christians, see following sections. Concerning *religio*, see Hus, *Greek and Roman Religion*, p. 105, Bayet, *Histoire*, p. 59, and Bardy, *La conversion*, pp. 18–19. In Greek, according to Nock, *Conversion*, p. 10, there is no word which defines religion as we use the word. The term *eusebeia*, the regular performance of due worship in the proper spirit, "approximates" it. Harrison, *Prolegomena*, p. 4, believes that the two Greek words *therapeia* and *deisidaimonia*, meaning respectively "service" to the gods and "fear of spirit-things" or fear of the supernatural, also express the meaning of religion in Greek. But in none of these words is conversion implied.

    8. Kitto, *The Greeks*, pp. 196–197, explains that, unlike the Romans, who respected the formal aspect of ritual with intensity, the Greeks would connect the idea of external purity to inward purity. Nock, *Conversion*, p. 15, points out that moral evil was put aside by the one sacrificing before approaching the holy. With respect to the role of duty, see Andrewes, *Greek Society*, pp. 264–265, and Rose, *Religion in Greece and Rome*, pp. 163ff., who discusses the ceremonies performed by the country folk in the Italian countryside, and the significance of the *numen* and *pietas* (divine power and piety).

9. Cf. Nilsson, *Greek Piety*, p. 193. Otto, *The Homeric Gods*, pp. 10–11, in a different context, points out that a "pious naturalism" was the great contribution of the Greek religion. Nilsson connects the Greek naturalism with the later stress on cosmology. In addition, on pp. 187–190, he states that the true conversion of the ancient world was from a worship of nature and the natural to a suspicion and even rejection of the "world" of nature, and from a societal collective piety to a religious collective piety. In this view, conversion involves the transformations of not only individuals, but of large communities, even nations over a span of many centuries. It approximates—though Nilsson does not mention the fact—the larger conversion plans implied in the economic conversion ideas of Irenaeus, the Logos conversion theologies of the Apologists and Clement of Alexandria, and the cosmic conversion ideas in Origen's thought.

On the cosmic positioning of man, see Ferguson, *The Religions*, pp. 77–87. A sense of powerlessness is also noted by Dodds, *Pagan and Christian*, pp. 7–9, who points out that eventually the powers of Fate were even considered a force opposing God. See pp. 13–15. "Fortune" too was considered a part of the necessity of things. See Cochrane, *Christianity and Classical Culture*, pp. 478–480. Both fortune and fate were deified by the ancients.

With respect to the place of sin, see Nock, *Conversion*, p. 15. Here again the chief refuge for ethics was not religion, but philosophy, especially, in the time of the Empire, Stoic thought.

10. As the religious syncretism of the Empire attests, the Romans were true polytheists and allowed gods from every source. See Ferguson, *The Religions* p. 211. The non-Roman gods were often renamed, however, and some of their objectionable aspects discouraged or rejected. See also Rose, *Religion in Greece and Rome*, pp. 272–293, who adds that the most reluctant group to give up the indigenous traditions and gods was the country folk. Cumont, *Oriental Religions*, pp. 28ff., notes that it was not necessarily Rome's receptivity which allowed oriental religions to grow, but the innate inferiority of the Greco-Roman religion.

11. Nock, *Conversion*, p. 12.

12. Rose, *Religion in Greece and Rome*, pp. 157–158.

13. Bardy, *La conversion*, p. 16. Hence the Roman seems to have been destined to follow the way of eclecticism in religion. This fact appears more clearly after considering one of the forces inhibiting conversion: the family. According to Hus, *Greek and Roman Religion*, pp. 99–100, ". . . each member of the family had his or her deity (*genius* or *juno*), divinities symbolizing the vital force of the individual. The genius of the *pater familias* ("father of the family") was the whole force of the ancestral gods. . ."

14. Bayet, *Histoire*, pp. 169–193.

15. Nock, *Conversion*, pp. 138–155; Angus, *The Mystery-Religions*, p. 142; Cumont, *Cumont, The Mysteries of Mithra*, pp. 150–164; G. Bertram, *epistrepho, Theological Dictionary of the New Testament*, VII.723 and note 3 confirms this view.

16. With respect to the mysteries of Mithra, Cumont, *Mysteries*, pp. 172–173, has said,

the gradual initiations kept alive in the heart of the neophyte the hopes of truth still more sublime, and the strange rites which accompanied them left in his ingenuous soul an ineffaceable impression. The converts believed they found, and, the suggestion being transformed into reality, actually did find, in the mystic ceremonies a stimulant and consolation. They believed themselves purified of their guilt by the ritual ablutions and this baptism lightened their conscience of the weight of their heavy responsibility.

17. In this section, the following works have been consulted: A. Armstrong, *An Introduction to Ancient Philosophy*, 3rd ed. (London: Methuen, 1957), pp. 114–167; Armstrong and R. A. Markus, *Christian Faith and Greek Philosophy* (London: Darton, Longman & Todd, 1960); Armstrong, "Introductory," "Plotinus," *The Cambridge History of Later Greek and Early Medieval Philosophy*, ed. A. Armstrong (Cambridge: University Press, 1967), pp. 1–9, 195–263; P. Aubin, *Le problème de la "conversion"* (Paris: Beauchesne, 1963), pp. 17–26, 49–68; Bardy, *La conversion au christianisme* pp. 46–89; H. Chadwick, "Philo," 137–157; F. Copleston, *A History of Philosophy*, rev. ed. (Garden City, N.Y.: Image, 1962), I, pt. II, 123–250; J. Dillon, *The Middle Platonists, A Study in Platonism: 80 B.C. to A.D. 220* (London: Duckworth, 1977); Dodds, *Pagan and Christian*; W. Jaeger, *Early Christian and Greek Paideia* (Oxford: University Press, 1961); A. Long, *Hellenistic Philosophy* (London: Duckworth, 1974); J. Marias, *History of Philosophy* trans. S. Appelbaum and C. Strowbridge, 22nd ed. (N.Y.: Dover, 1967); P. Merlan, "Greek Philosophy from Plato to Plotinus," *The Cambridge History*, pp. 14–132; A. Nock, *Conversion*; Nock, "Bekehrung," *Klauser's Reallexikon für Antike und Christentum* (1951), II: 105–118; J. Rist, *Eros and Psyche. Studies in Plato, Plotinus and Origen* (Toronto: University

Press, 1964); *Stoic Philosophy* (Cambridge: University Press, 1969); *Epicurus: An Introduction* (Cambridge: University Press, 1972); S. Sandmel, *Philo of Alexandria: An Introduction* (Oxford: University Press, 1979); D. Winston, "Introduction," *Philo of Alexandria—The Contemplative Life, The Giants, and Selections* (N.Y.: Paulist Press, 1981), pp. 1–37; E. Zeller, *Outlines of the History of Greek Philosophy*, 13th ed., trans. L. Palmer, rev. W. Nestle (1931; rpt.; N.Y.: Dover, 1980).

18. According to Nock, *Conversion*, pp. 164–186 and Bardy, *La conversion*, pp. 46–48, philosophy did offer a new set of values as well as a changed existence, and thus its understanding of conversion is comparable to the idea of conversion as a transformation of one's whole life. Nevertheless, Green, *Evangelism in the Early Church*, pp. 173–176, claims that this view of conversion is "utterly foreign" to everyone of the Greco-Roman world, except for the Jews and the Christians. Green offers three reasons: 1) First, "Hellenistic man did not regard belief as necessary for the cult"; 2) Second, ethics for Hellenistic man was not regarded as part of religion; 3) Third, the Greco-Roman man never turned "exclusively" to only one sect or philosophy; hence a complete change and reversal of allegiance did not occur. None of these reasons, however, militate against the view of conversion in philosophy as a break with the past, a renewed existence and a transformation from an unethical to an ethical person.

19. Nock, *Conversion*, p. 14.

20. According to Aubin, *Le problème*, pp. 55–59. With respect to the passage from the sensible to the intelligible, the best example is the cave myth presented in Book VII of *The Republic* of Plato (515D). In many senses, conversion in Epicureanism appears to be exactly the reverse of Platonic conversion. Epicurus rejects the Forms and bases all on sensation. As Cicero said, he places the criteria of reality (*judicia rerum*) in the senses. Hence Epicurus sees man's conversion journey as basically coming to appreciate the world as it is through sensation, and directing himself towards that which produces "pleasure." See Rist, *Epicurus*, pp. 14–31. Text and translation of Cicero also from Rist, p. 14. The converted person, according to Epicureans, frees himself from pain, necessity, death and fear of the gods.

Regarding the two dimensions of philosophic conversion and their appearance together in the philosophies of the Empire, see the discussion of Merlan, "Greek Philosophy," on the platonizing of the Later Stoa (Seneca, Epictetus, M. Aurelius, etc.), especially the borrowing from Plato's *Phaedo*, on p. 129. This interface particularly involves movement away from the senses. Rist, *Stoic Philosophy*, Chap. 14, also notes the use of Plato by Stoics, especially with respect to M. Aurelius.

In sum, in the three major traditions of Platonism, Stoicism and Epicureanism in the age of the Empire, we find the Platonists emphasizing the sensible-intelligible transition, the Epicureans committed to a view that is in direct contrast to the Platonists (though it remains a turning inward toward oneself), and the Stoics stressing self-conversion, but incorporating, notably in the later Stoa, the Platonic process in terms of movement away from the external.

21. Aubin, *Le problème*, p. 62.

22. On the mind's journey up through the hierarchy of "forms," see Armstrong, *An Introduction*, pp. 38–41, and Paul Shorey, "Introduction," II, ix–xxxvi. Shorey's discussion of the meaning of form, *idea* or *eidos*, is particularly useful. The journey is presented in the myth of the chariot in Plato's *Phaedrus*. In this myth, souls are placed in a hierarchy according to the degree they have seen the Forms in a previous existence. Sometimes man sees things that remind him of his previous existence, and this seeing stimulates the process of return to the realm of Forms. The process of conversion then in this myth is remembering what has been instilled in man. Things that are outside us are merely catalysts for the process of raising our thoughts. Hence the self-conversion is combined with the journey from the sensible to the intelligible. Cf. Marias, pp. 47–48.

23. On *logos* in Stoics, see Armstrong, *An Introduction*, p. 124; Copleston, *A History of Philosophy*, pp. 139–140; Zeller, *Outlines*, pp. 215–217. On the Stoic indifference to all things external, see Merlan, "Greek Philosophy," p. 125. The matter is discussed in many contexts in Rist, *Stoic Philosophy*. See, for example, pp. 22–36. Rist clarifies that the ideal for the Stoic is, according to Chrysippus, not *apatheia* (no emotion) but *eupatheia* (harmless emotion). Other Stoics, however, view the matter as a triumph of the *hegemonikon* (ruling judgment) over the *pathe* (emotions) as if the latter were different faculties in conflict with the former. See Zeller, p. 220.

24. "What led the founder of the Stoic system to philosophy was in the first instance the necessity of finding a firm support for his moral life." See Zeller, p. 210. Concerning the stress on ethics, see also Merlan, p. 125, Copleston, 145, and Marias, pp. 89–96. On the similar ethical goals— though their solutions were different—of the three schools, see Marias, pp. 89–96. The goal of Epicurean ethics is intellectual pleasure (in contrast to physical pleasure, which is fleeting), the goal

of the Stoics is *arete*, which is the perfection of one's self so that it is no longer swayed by fear, hope or any external motive (see D. Laertius VII.89–90), and the object of the Cynics is *autarkeia* (self-sufficiency). These are, of course, general assessments of the schools. A reading of Diogenes Laertius on any of the schools reveals numerous variations.

25. On several occasions, Rist, *Stoic Philosophy*, points out that the degrees of "more" or "less" really have little or no place in Stoic moral philosophy. The Stoics themselves use the example of the man coming up to the surface of the water. While under water—the condition of evil—he is never in a condition of being less drowned, though he may be closer to the surface—the realm of virtue. Hence, the Stoics see the change to good as sudden, while the movement away from evil as a matter of progress in condition without moral value. Good has no degrees. See Rist, pp. 13, 81–83, 90; Copleston, pp. 141–142.

26. Rist, *Epicurus*, pp. 100, 122–133.

27. The basic texts for Platonic conversion are found in the myths in *The Republic*, the *Phaedrus*, and the *Timaeus*. In these passages we find discussion of the need for conversion and the cause of conversion as well as the general pattern of the conversion process. On the importance of the present moral conduct to our future, see *Phaedo* 81Cff., 88AB and 107CD. On the fundamental epistemological basis of Plato's ethics, see Zeller, p. 135. On Platonic conversion in general, excluding Neo-Platonism, see Aubin, pp. 50–59 and Nock, "Bekehrung," 105–106. On the problem of free will for the Platonists, see Dillon, pp. 44–45. On demons in Platonism, see Dillon, pp. 46–47, Merlan, "Greek Philosophy," pp. 33–35. Rist, *Eros*, pp. 50–51, 68, and 110 notes the difficult demands made on man by Plato's idea of conversion. The fundamental dichotomy of the false (that which is based only on the senses) and the true (the Forms, the intelligible, the Real or Being), evident in the conversion process, has it source at least partly in Parmenides, *The Way of Truth*, Fr. 6, 8. Cf. Kirk and Raven, *The Pre-Socratic Philosophers*, pp. 266–278, Copleston, 65, and Marias, p. 23.

28. Dillon, p. 382.
The main themes of Middle Platonism revolve around three areas: Ethics, Physics and Logic. In our discussion, the main source is Dillon's *Middle Platonism*. We shall be concerned only with the first two. With respect to ethics, three dominant themes concerned the Platonists of this period: the purpose of life, the sufficiency of virtue for happiness, and the problem of free will and necessity. Regarding the first, two solutions were proposed: first, to live in accordance with nature, a solution also advocated by the Stoics and, second, to seek likeness to God. See Plato, *Theaetetus* 176B. The second solution became the distinctive Platonic definition of the end (*telos*). As for the second theme in ethics, two alternatives were offered: the first said that virtue was insufficient, that other "goods" were necessary for happiness; the second claimed virtue was sufficient for true happiness. The Platonists split over this issue, but Eudorus, Albinus, Atticus and Philo of Alexandria—along with the Stoics—stressed overall the sufficiency of virtue. With respect to free will, it has already been noted that the Middle Platonists failed to resolve the problem. Philo tries to balance both free will and providence and yet resist Stoic determinism, but his statements seem contradictory. See Dillon, pp. 43–45. On Philo, see pp. 146–148, 168.
The concerns of physics centered for the Middle Platonists in the supreme principle and the various other entities of the Platonic cosmos. The resulting schemes usually present a supreme principle, the One or God, and a force that is more or less in contrast or even opposite to it. Then there is an entity that is often responsible for contact with created life, a kind of intermediary for the One or at least a force that concerns itself with multiplicity. In the later Platonists it is often called Logos, and emerges in some of their writings as almost a second god. In Philo, however, a strong monotheist, the Logos belongs to God. Another figure, Sophia, is also present in Philo, though it is often equated with Logos. When Sophia is different from Logos, she is usually a kind of transcendent universal mother through which God generates Logos. In Platonic terms, she is comparable to the Dyad. Beside these three fundamental powers—the One, the Dyad and Logos— there are countless subordinate beings: demons, heroes and angels. These also are present to keep God from any ccontact with created things, especially matter. See Dillon, pp. 45–49. On the Logos and Sophia in Philo, see pp. 158–159, 163–164.

29. According to Armstrong, *Introduction*, p. 154, however, there are no true mystics in the Middle Platonic tradition, since their "religion" is more an intellectual than a religious journey. On the religious side of Middle Platonism, see Armstrong, p. 149, Copleston, pp. 195–200, and Zeller, p. 286, on direct revelation in Plutarch. On Middle Platonic views of the Forms, see Merlan, p. 55, Chadwick, "Philo," p. 142.

30. From *Didaskalikos* 28, trans. Dillon, p. 300.

31. According to Dillon, p. 300, regarding the path to virtue in Philo.

32. This discussion, except where noted, follows Chadwick, "Philo," pp. 145–150, and Winston, pp. 21–35.

With respect to the need for conversion, Philo adds a couple of possibilities to the solution offered in the *Phaedrus*, which he also approves. These are, in brief, that man is by nature finite, and that man lusted to be equal to God. The root of sin then is finitude and pride.

Like other Platonists, Philo sees the end to man's predicament in overcoming through spiritual self-discipline and training the problems posed by the body. The spiritual training involves total control of the senses; indeed an eventual renunciation of sense–reality entirely, and the complete release of oneself to that Power that lies outside one's soul in order to reach a state of contemplation in which one can experience the joy of God's presence.

The mind attains this mystical level by ascent through contemplation of God's designs, his rational creations, in the world in league with an ascetic pursuit of virtue in everyday life, a pursuit which should liken one to God. Philo's ideal is the total act of faith given by Abraham along with the strict control of the senses. Basically these steps describe the effort made by man using the gifts given him by God.

But this effort is, according to Philo, insufficient for conversion, which Philo seems to consider the way of salvation. According to the spiritual progress one has made, there is also revelation by God himself. In fact, only through revelation and grace is it possible for the soul actually to know God. "So at the very ascent of the climax of the long ascent of mental and moral discipline there stands a gift of grace which quite transcends it," writes Chadwick, "Philo," p. 150. The intermediary of this revelation and grace is the Logos, who accomplishes all of the supreme God's work with creation, who is "the idea of ideas, the first begotten Son of the uncreated Father and second God, the pattern and mediator of the uncreated Father and second God, the pattern and mediator of the creation, the archetype of human reason, and 'the man of God'." Again Chadwick, p. 143, and accompanying texts. Cf. also Winston, p. 26, where he discusses how for Philo man's mind is a fragment of the Logos.

Hence there are two ways to apprehend God: The first is indirect through inferential reasonings concerning God's designs in the created universe, and direct apprehension when the mind, being pure, realizes God by a kind of intuition, when it, as a portion of the Logos, is most in harmony with God's continuous revelation. Winston, p. 27, considers H. Wolfson's belief that revelation surpasses human reason "very unlikely" in Philo. Cf. H. Wolfson, *Philo*, 2 Vols. (Cambridge, Mass.: Harvard U. Press, 1947). Winston and Dillon both oppose Wolfson in his attempt to stress Philo's eclecticism. They tend to see Philo as a product of Alexandrian Platonism.

33. The main emphasis in this section is on Gnostic systems similar to Valentinian Gnosticism. However, it would not be possible, in any event, to detail all the different varieties of Gnosticism. The word "gnostic" itself has caused some confusion. The attempt has been made to follow R. Wilson, "Slippery Words II: Gnosis, Gnostic, Gnosticism," *Expository Times*, 89 (1978), 296–301. Wilson points out that "gnosticism" should be used for only the 2nd and 3rd century forms of the doctrine, since the line between orthodox and heresy was very faint up to the 2nd century.

The following works have been consulted for this section: Aubin, pp. 96–104; H. Chadwick, *The Early Church* (Harmondsworth: Penguin, 1967), pp. 33–41; J. Dillon, *The Middle Platonists*, pp. 384–389; R. Grant, *Gnosticism and Early Christianity*, 2nd ed. (N.Y.: Columbia U. Press, 1966); H. Jonas, *The Gnostic Religion*; J. Kelly, *Early Christian Doctrines*, 5th rev. ed. (N.Y.: Harper, 1978), pp. 22–28; Elaine Pagels, *The Gnostic Gospels* (N.Y.: Random House, 1979); J. Robinson, ed., *The Nag Hammadi Library* (N.Y.: Harper, 1977).

34. For those unfamiliar with Gnostic cosmology, here is an overview:

In order to keep the Unknown One from any contact with inferior things and offer an explanation for evil, Gnostic thinkers created an elaborate hierarchy of being. Before all else there was the Unbegotten One, the Unknown Father. Since he did not desire to remain alone, he produced two aeons, Mind and Truth. They produced World-Life and Man-Church. From these six aeons resulted twenty-two others. The last aeon generated by Man-Church was Wisdom who, in her sorrow at being so far from the Unbegotten Father, produced by herself Achamoth, whom the others rejected because its birth was unnatural. Sophia remained in sorrow. So Mind-Truth produced two other aeons, Christ and the Holy spirit, to help her. The resulting peace in the pleroma was so appreciated that the other aeons together created another aeon, Jesus. Meanwhile Achamoth produced her own offspring, Demiurge. From these two, Achamoth and Demiurge, arises matter, the creation of which was probably the reasons for this elaborate series of generation. Achamoth created the substance of matter, Demiurge gave it form and shape. Then, through Sophia's influence, Demiurge created three kinds of men: the *pneumatiki*, the spiritual elect, who receive spiritual knowledge and full salvation, the *psychiki*, who with good works receive a second-class redemption, and the *hyliki*, the mass of ordinary men who are irretrievably doomed. Sophia also caused Jesus to be born of the Virgin Mary. Jesus comes to reveal knowledge of the pleroma, but the Aeon Jesus is not crucified. Those who are able to receive the knowledge are the elect, as noted, and when they die will return to the pleroma. Eventually all material things will surrender to disorder and destruction. For this outline, cf. Kelly, pp. 23-24; Dillon, pp. 385-389; Jonas, *The Gnostic Religion*, pp. 179-197. Several Gnostic sects did not include such speculation in their beliefs. See, for example, the views of Marcion and his followers. For a summary of the kinds of Gnosticism alive in the Christian era, see Robinson, *Nag Hammadi*, pp. 6-10.

    35. *Teachings of Silvanus* 85, in Robinson, *Nag Hammadi*, p. 347.

    36. On the two sides of gnosis, see Jonas, p. 45. On necessity of a savior and revelation, see Chadwick, *The Early Church*, pp. 37-38, and Chadwick, "The Beginnings of Christian Philosophy: Justin: The Gnostics," *The Cambridge History of Later Greek and Early Medieval Philosophy*, pp. 166-167. A different perspective of gnosis and Gnosticism is offered in Pagels, *The Gnostic Gospels*, pp. 119-141. Pagels clarifies the subjective and individual aspects of gnosis in contrast to turning to the Church for knowledge of God. On the meaning of freedom for the Gnostics, see A. Orbe, *Antropologia de San Ireneo* (Madrid: BAC, 1969), pp. 164-165.

    In fact, since man has a very limited role in the process, it may be inaccurate to speak of conversion in Gnosticism. For both the cause of the spirit's entombment and its redemption by revelation are outside the person's own powers. The soul neither turned away nor does it, on its own or in partnership, turn toward God. All souls are captive to their predestined ends, although the *psychiki* are able, in some Gnostic texts, to earn salvation. Even the Gnostic asceticism is based on the knowledge that one is among the elect and can disdain mundane ties. In a few sects of Gnosticism, election became an excuse for libertinism.

    37. Indeed Irenaeus in his outline of Valentinian beliefs uses the word "conversion" to refer to Sophia and Achamoth. The conversion of Sophia concerns that point when she returned to herself after failing in her effort to comprehend the Father. In this view, conversion becomes in part a kind of stability of self resulting from a realization of impotence in comparison with the Father. The conversion of Achamoth occurs when the state of passion subsides and the desire to return to her source emerges. Again it appears to be more a movement of resignation and, in Achamoth, supplication than a movement toward the Father. The reception of gnosis is a separate matter. It is revealed from without. In sum, conversion as described above does not occur on the cosmic level prior to the generation of man. On the conversion of Sophia and Achamoth, see Irenaeus, *Adversus Haereses*, I.2.2-3; I.4.1,2,5; Aubin, *Le problème*, pp. 96-104.

    38. According to Irenaeus, *A.H.*, I.4.5; I.5.1,4.

    39. *Ibid.*, I.6.2,4.

    40. For the fate of the *psychiki* in the Tractate, see *Tractate* 118-119. Text suggested by M. A. Donovan, "Irenaeus' Teaching on the Unity of God and His Immediacy to the Material World in Relation to Valentinian Gnosticism," Diss. University of St. Michael's College, 1977, pp. 124-127. For conversion of Logos, see *Tractate* 81.

    41. The following works were useful in preparing this outline: Aubin, *Le problème*, pp. 33-47; G. Bertram, *epistrepho, epistrephe, TDNT*, VII: 723-725; Giblet, "Le sens," 79-92; M-F Lacan, "Conversion et grace dans l'Ancien Testament," *Lumière et vie*, No. 47 (1960), 5-24; Würthwein, *metanoia*, 980-989; Behm, *metanoia*, 989-999.

    42. By beginning with the prophets, we do not mean that spiritual turning did not exist before the prophets in the history of God's people. We are taking a broad historical view of conversion rather than a book by book approach. We find this historical model, however, in the conversion of many figures, before and after the prophets. We might note that this view is also how Origen approached conversion in the Hebrew scriptures.

    43. J. Giblet, "Le sens de la conversion dans l'Ancien Testament," *Maison Dieu*, No. 90 (1967), 86; E. Würthwein, *metanoeō/metanoia, Theological Dictionary of the New Testament*, IV: 984-985.

    44. Giblet, "Le sens de la conversion," 90.

    45. Cf. Test. XII, Sirach 17: 24ff., and Test. Abram 1:6.

    46. Lacan, "Conversion et grace," 9.

47. Bertram, *epistrepho*, 724 n.11.

48. Lacan, "Conversion et grace," 8, 18; Giblet, "Le sens," 89.

49. See the discussion of N. de Lange, *Origen and the Jews. Studies in Jewish-Christian Relations in the Third-Century Palestine* (Cambridge: University Press, 1976), p. 15.

50. The most important term for "conversion" in the Hebrew scriptures is *shub*. The Greek words to translate this single term are *epistrephein* and *metanoein*. In later Judaic literature *metanoein* becomes the common term for *shub* with respect to religious conversion, but *epistrephein* is more often used in pre-exilic scriptures. But even in the early period the two terms are religiously synonymous. See Behm, *metanoia*, 989.

51. Giblet, "Le sens," 80.

52. J. Dupont, "Repentir et conversion d'après les Acts des Apôtres," *Sciences ecclésiastigues*, 12 (1960), 138.

53. By Giblet, 86.

54. The noun "conversion" occurs once, Is. 30:15, according to Behm, 984.

55. Giblet, 81.

56. Cf. Jer. 8:6, Hos. 12:7, Is. 7:1ff.

57. Giblet, 87; Lacan, 16.

58. Lacan, 21; Behm, 985–986.

59. Aubin, pp. 71, 84.

60. J. Belche, "Die Bekehrung zum Christentum nach Augustins Büchlein De catechizandis rudibus," *Augustinus*, 27 (1977), 350–351.

61. Dupont, "La conversion dans les Actes des Apôtres," *Lumière et vie*, No. 47 (1960), 69; M. Green, p. 178; Dupont, "Repentir," 139. Paul, however, is also an important source, perhaps more important with respect to a writer such as Origen.

62. R. Michiels, "La conception lucanienne de la conversion," *Ephemerides theologicae Lovanienses*, 41 (1965), 49.

63. *Ibid.*, 45, 48, and 52; Dupont, "La conversion," 53. Though *metanoia* equals *epistrophe* sometimes, according to Michiels, 50–51. See Acts 11:18.

64. According to Bertram, 728, in Acts 11:21, 15:7.

65. Cf. Acts 26:17–18. See Michiels, 50; Dupont, "Repentir," 156–157.

66. Dupont, "La conversion," 58.

67. Dupont, "Repentir," 140, 144.

68. Dupont, "La conversion," 48, 58–60.

69. Dupont, "La conversion," 65, and "Repentir," 145. Dupont, 147, believes, however, that the idea of conversion should apply only to the third dimension—the total change in conduct. In contrast, Michiels, 49, views repentance as the first movement in the process of conversion. Green, p. 182, concurs with Michiels, and considers conversion in the New Testament to have the three elements of repentance, faith and baptism. The difference between Dupont and Michiels arises from whether one believes conversion is a single event or a process. Nevertheless, just because a word such as *epistrophe* can be defined does not mean the scope of conversion is defined.

70. Dupont, "La conversion," 67.

71. On the central place of grace, see Lacan, 41, Dupont, 162, 173; Behm, *metanoia*, 1001, and the texts given by Green, p. 179.

72. Lacan, "Conversion et royaume dans les Évangiles Synoptiques," *Lumière et vie*, No. 47 (1960), 27, 29. On John, see D. Mollat, "Ils regarderont celui qu'ils ont transpercé. La conversion chez saint Jean," *Lumière et vie*, No. 47 (1960), 95–114.

73. Lacan, "Conversion," 36–37, 41.

74. See Lacan, 42.

75. M. Boismard, "Conversion et vie nouvelle dans saint Paul," *Lumière et vie*, No. 47 (1960), 73, 75.

76. *Ibid.*, 93–94.

77. *Ibid.*, 74–75.

78. Mollat, "Ils regarderont," 95–114.

79. Before we begin the survey of other Christian writers, it is important to state that it has not been possible in any section to explore justly all of the complexities involved. The most that can be claimed—and this claim may itself be too extensive—is that we shall offer a summary of primary emphases. Especially when we turn to the Christian writers before Origen, the task becomes arduous because of the lack of scholarship in this area. With the exception of a recent work on

Tertullian, namely, J–C. Fredouille, *Tertullien et la conversion de la culture antique* (Paris: Études augustiniennes, 1972), there are no book-length studies of conversion on the separate figures, and almost no articles on what these Christian thinkers understood by conversion.

We have consulted the following studies on the idea of conversion prior to Origen: Aubin, *Le problème*; Bardy, *La conversion*; Belche, "Die Bekehrung;" S. Florez Folgado, "Sentido eclesial de la penitencia en el 'Pastor' de Hermas," *Ciudad Dios*, No. 191 (1978), 3–38; J. Fredouille, *Tertullien*; A. Harnack, *The Mission and Expansion of Christianity in the First Three Centuries*, trans. J. Moffatt (London: Williams & Norgate, 1908); G. B. Ladner, *The Idea of Reform. Its Impact on Christian Thought and Action in the Age of the Fathers* (Cambridge, Mass.: Harvard U. Press, 1959); A. Méhat, "Pour l'histoire du mot epistrophē: aux origines de l'idée de conversion," *Revue des études grecgues*, 68 (1975), ix; M. Merino, "La conversion cristiana. El concepto de epistrephein y metanoia en San Justino," *Studium legionense*, 20 (1979), 89–126; A. Nock, *Conversion*; O. Skarsaune, "Conversion of Justin Martyr," *Studia Theologica*, 30 (1976), 53–73.

This lack of secondary literatures forces one to rely on the works of the writers themselves and, wherever appropriate, general secondary literature.

80. The method of viewing the AF by area or schools is used by others. See, for example, J. L. González, *A History of Christian Thought* (Nashville, Tenn.: Abingdon, 1970), I.93–95.

81. Since no unique contributions were discovered in the Alexandrian view of conversion, Barnabas will not be discussed.

82. González, I.94.

83. II Clement 9.8 and 16.4.

84. Aubin, p. 80.

85. Cf. II Clement 3.1: 16.1–2; 17.1–2. See also Aubin, p. 84.

86. Aubin, pp. 85–87. Let us recall that Aubin's work is not a study of conversion, but of the Greek words for "conversion."

87. In Vis. I.3.1–2.

88. See, for example, Mand. IX.1,2,5; Vis. IV.2.4; Mand. X.

89. Cf. V. Corwin, *St. Ignatius and Christianity in Antioch* (New Haven, Conn.: Yale University Press, 1960), pp. 169, 227. Note Eph. 15.2–3, 11.1, 8.2; Mag. 13.

90. *Ibid.*, p. 235.

91. Eph. 20.3.2; Mag. 13; Smyrna 8.2.

92. Cf. Corwin, pp. 155, 234–235. See Eph. 14.1–2, 9.1.

93. Mag. 5.1–2. Cf. Corwin, pp. 170, 224.

94. J. Daniélou, *Gospel Message and Hellenistic Culture*, trans. J. Baker (London: Darton, Longman and Todd, 1964), p. 15.

95. E. Hardy, "Introduction," *The First Apology* of Justin, the Martyr, in C. Richardson, ed., *Early Christian Fathers* (Philadelphia: Westminster Press, 1970), p. 231, affirms the unique use of the logos idea, but wants to stress that Justin's approach, for example, is "primarily pastoral, biblical and traditionalist." R. Joly, *Christianisme et philosophie. Étude sur Justin et les Apologistes grecs du deuxième siècle* (Brussels: Presses Universitaires, 1973), pp. 85–154, sees the methods of the Apologists focused on a "rational" approach to Theology. L. Barnard, *Justin Martyr. His Life and Thought* (Cambridge: University Press, 1967), p. 85, views the Logos concept at work in apologetics, cosmology and soteriology. Cf. also E. Osborn, *Justin Martyr* (Tubingen: Mohr, 1973), p. 140.

96. Aubin, pp. 87–88, points out that Justin uses the terms "conversion" and "repentance" to show how the Jews failed to respond to the spiritual conversion, but knew only the conversion of the letter. Cf. also Osborn, p. 145. Joly, pp. 155ff. cautions that Justin and the other Apologists were not as tolerant of classical culture as many believe.

97. Cf. Aubin, p. 88, and Osborn, pp. 140ff. According to Justin, the entire world came into being through the Logos. On Logos, see I Apol. 44, 46; 2 Apol. 6 and Dial. 84.

98. I Apol. 46; 2 Apol. 8. See discussion of Osborn, p. 142.

99. 2 Apol. 10, 13.

100. 2 Apol. 6; Dial. 30.

101. Cf. 1 Apol. 28, 43; 2 Apol. 7.

102. Dial. 102.

103. 1 Apol. 61.

104. 1 Apol. 28.

105. On the issue of free will and grace in the Apologists, Osborn offers several insights. First, on pp. 142–143, he contrasts the pagan's logos and the Christian's logos. The pagan's logos is

limited by his own natural capabilities, whereas the Christian's logos is extended by grace. However, this divine help, Osborn claims, p. 152, does not limit free will or the natural capability. He writes, p. 150: "There is a necessity which governs things, but it is a necessity of choice."

106. On Irenaeus, see M. A. Donovan, "Irenaeus' Teaching on the Unity of God and His Immediacy to the Material World in Relation to Valentinian Gnosticism," Diss. University of St. Michael's College (Toronto), 1977.

107. Aubin, pp. 105-110.

108. *Ibid.*, p. 106. Cf. Haer. 3.42.2.

109. A. Benoit, *Saint Irénée. Introduction a l'étude de sa théologie* (Paris: Presses Universitaires, 1960), pp. 203ff. and 215, believes the theme most expressed is that of unity/oneness, i.e., the unity of God and Christ, and the unity of the Church. Conversion too must be informed by this theme. There can be for Irenaeus only one kind of conversion, the conversion to and within the true Church.

110. On the anti-Gnostic aspect of Irenaeus's anthropology, see Daniélou, *Gospel Message,* p. 414. Concerning uniqueness of Irenaeus's ideas on man as a maturing creature and the concept of progress, see Daniélou also, pp. 402-404, 408. Orbe, *Antropologia,* p. 6, views Irenaeus's anthropology as the pivot for his views on creation, paradise, original sin, Christology, eschatology, etc.

111. According to Benoit, *Saint Irénée,* pp. 219ff.

112. Orbe, *Antropologia,* p. 272, considers disobedience as the key to the Fall. Benoit, p. 230, notes that the Fall retards but does not change the plan of God in Irenaeus. In between the Fall and the Incarnation, God offers a series of covenants to guide man to Christ. The Law, for example, was given to retard sinfulness. See *Haer.* IV. 14-15.

113. According to Orbe, pp. 175ff. and Benoit, p. 229. See *Haer.* IV. 37.1ff.

114. Benoit, p. 230, succinctly presents a possible paradox in Irenaeus's theology which has implications for the role of sin in conversion: the idea of progress, so evident in Irenaeus's thought, may leave only a minor place for the notion of sin. Since Adam was not even created perfect, he would have to develop, one could legitimately speculate, even if the Fall never occurred. "In such a perspective, the remission of sins is only a preparatory step in the course of that great progression which leads men to perfection and divinisation." Benoit, p. 231, finds this view inconsistent with other aspects of Irenaeus's thought, but it, in fact, remains only a paradox since we lack sufficient textual evidence to support it.

115. With respect to Irenaeus, see Benoit, p. 230, where he considers Irenaeus's theology Christocentric. Like Ignatius, Irenaeus is native to Asia Minor. Though writers generally acknowledge Tertullian's legalism, recently T. D. Barnes, *Tertullian. A Historical and Literary Study* (Oxford: Clarendon Press, 1971), pp. 22-29, throws doubt on Tertullian the lawyer, and claims his "legalistic approach" does not issue from a legal background. Furthermore, J–C Fredouille, *Tertullien et la conversion de la culture antique* (Paris: Études augustiniennes, 1972), p. 245, believes that Tertullian's notion of law is "impregnated with Stoic thought."

116. Tertullian's view of Christ as saviour is often overshadowed, writes Kelly, *Early Christian Doctrines,* p. 177, by his view of Christ as illuminator, instructor and judge. However, it is likely that Tertullian believed that these latter aspects of Christ were part of Christ's saving work.

117. Cf. González, *A History,* p. 167. On Tertullian's Stoic view of the soul, see González, p. 188, Kelly, p. 175. Note *De anima* 19, 27.

118. *Contra Marcion* 2.5-7, 9.

119. *De poen.* 6.

120. On the power of baptism, see *De baptismo* 1. Cf. Kelly, p. 209.

121. See Fredouille, *Tertullien,* pp. 249, 435.

122. *Scorp.* 6; *De poen.* 5ff.

123. Tertullian saw *sacramentum* as an oath of fidelity in enlisting in the Christian militia.

124. *De poen.* 5-6.

125. *De poen.* 9.

126. H. Chadwick, *Early Christian Thought and the Classical Tradition. Studies in Justin, Clement and Origen* (Oxford: University Press, 1966), p. 33, points out Clement's worry about losing hearers to Gnosticism. Hence Clement's "gnostic" terminology may be deliberately confrontational.

127. Salvatore R. C. Lilla, *Clement of Alexandria: A Study in Christian Platonism and Gnosticism* (Oxford: University Press, 1971), pp. 118-226, considers the matter so important that he devotes a third of his book to the discussion. See also Daniélou, *Gospel Message,* pp. 305ff. and Chadwick, *Early Christian Thought,* p. 52, on complexities of faith in Clement.

128. Cf. *Protr.* 99, 115, 103, 122. See Chadwick, *Early Christian Thought,* p. 39.

129. See *Paed.* I.1.
130. Cf. C. Bigg, *The Christian Platonists of Alexandria*, 2nd ed. by F. E. Brightman (Oxford: University Press, 1913), p. 91, note 2.
131. For a thorough discussion of the various dimensions of *pistis* and *gnosis*, see Lilla, pp. 118–142, whose study is followed in this paragraph. There are three levels to faith. Two are epistemological, one religious.
132. *Strom.* VII. 10; ANF 2, col. A-B. Cf. also *Strom.* II.1–4; *ANF* 2, 347–351.
133. For a detailed discussion of Clement's ethics, see Lilla, pp. 60–117, especially pp. 84ff., in which Lilla indicates the Platonic influences, and O. Prunet, *La morale de Clément d'Alexandrie et le Nouveau Testament* (Paris: Presses Universitaires, 1966), pp. 68–117. Of course, the ethical life is divided into a higher and lower life also. See Lilla, pp. 92–106.
134. Bigg, *The Christian Platonists*, p. 105.
135. *Strom.* 4.8.59; 4.19.118–124.
136. *Strom.* VI.12
137. Cf. C. Mondésert, *Clément d'Alexandrie. Introduction à l'étude de sa pensée religieuse à partir de l'écriture* (Paris: Aubier, 1944), p. 195, note 2, and Bigg, pp. 109, 111.
138. *Strom.* V.1, VII.1. See Chadwick, *Early Christian Thought*, p. 63.
139. See Mondésert, *Clément*, p. 218, on the concept of unity.
140. Clement's tendency to see conversion at work in non-Christian settings may be a kind of compromise to his wish to appeal to educated (as well as uneducated) readers. See Chadwick, *Early Christian Thought*, p. 33. Mondésert, p. 231, note 6, points out that Clement saw other religions and philosophies not negatively, but as being inadequate or incomplete in some way.

Chapter II. The Beginning and the End:
What Happens before and after Earthly Life?

1. However, according to M. J. Dénis, *De la philosophie*, pp. 1–26, Origen is more interested in anthropology than in just a psychology of the present condition of the soul. As we shall note again below, this emphasis distinguishes Origen from some of his Platonic forebears. The purpose of the work, of course, is important. It has been noted by A. Monaci, "L'idea della preesistenza delle anime e l'esegesi di Rm 9, 9–21," in H. Crouzel and A. Quacquarelli, eds., *Origeniana Secunda*, Quaderni di "Vetera Christianorum", 15 (1980), pp. 77–78, that *On First Principles* especially seems more concerned with cosmic history than the stages of earthly Christian life. Origen's works written after ca. 231, on the other hand, ". . . sembra riflettere piu frequentemente sul significato salvifico dell'incarnazione, sul ruolo storico della chiesa, sul rapporto Vecchio-Nuovo Testamento." After 231, ". . . il tema della preesistenza della anima viene trattato raramente e sempre avanzato con circospezione e riticenza." While this statement is accurate as far as it goes, it requires some amplification. Since most of Origen's extant works after *On First Principles* were works which discussed books of scripture, the occasions for discussion of these topics were few. Even so, Origen often would point out, when preaching to a general audience, that there were deeper mysteries involved in the text—if it concerned, in his opinion, matters such as pre-existence, the resurrection and the restoration—so that those astute enough in the mysteries of divine scripture (matters such as discussed in *On First Principles*) would probe on. As we shall see in other sections, Origen believed with Paul that one should teach according to the level of one's listeners, that there was a time for "milk" and a time for "meat" when presenting the divine wisdom in scripture. The *Homilies on Jeremiah* are an excellent example of this method, and reflect more often Origen's approach than the adapted Latin homilies of Rufinus. See, for example, *Hom. 14.18 in Jer.*

References to Origen's works are abbreviated in accordance with *A Patristic Greek Lexicon*, ed. by G. W. Lampe (Oxford: University Press, 1961).

For a discussion of the textual methodology used in this book, please see Appendix B.

2. J. Laporte, "La chute chez Philo et Origène," in P. Granfield and J. Jungmann, eds., *Kyriakon—Festschrift Johannes Quasten* (Münster: Aschendorff, 1970), I, 321–322, seems to suggest Origen was having a dialog with philosophers. See also Appendix B, 4f, for articles claiming that Origen may be trying to convert philosophers, since he discusses problems interesting to philosophers.

3. As an example of Origen's method of questions/remedies, see *Princ.* 1.4.1. (5.63.10–29), where Origen uses the illustration of a doctor who loses interest in his studies and fails to exercise

his training not only to indicate how one has neglected his responsibilities and fallen from his previous position, but also, more importantly, how one can return to that position. For the doctor, if aroused soon enough from his previous negligence, is able to regain his knowledge and position. Origen writes, *Princ.* 1.4.1 (5.63.26–29), trans. G. Butterworth, p. 40, "Yet if, in the first stages of his fall, when the negligence which threatens to ruin him has not gone far, he is aroused and without delay returns to himself, it is certainly possible to recover that which had but recently been lost and to renew the knowledge which by that time had been only slightly erased [from his mind]."

This text is extant only in Latin. See the full discussion of textual methodology in the appendix. Because *On First Principles* is the best source for the subject in this section, we shall offer primarily texts from *On First Principles*. And since this work is only preserved in its entirety in Latin, we are compelled to use the Latin. Whenever possible, however, in line with the methodology, and particularly for controversial subjects, Greek texts which do seem to confirm, though perhaps less explicitly, the Latin adaptation will be offered.

Though the difficulties are not all resolved, there has been some agreement that Rufinus's Latin adaptation of *On First Principles* is usually faithful to the thought (though not the words) of Origen. On subjects such as the Trinity and the resurrected body, one is much less confident. See both J. Rist, "The Greek and Latin Texts of the Discussion on Free Will in De principiis, Book III," in H. Crouzel, et al, eds, *Origeniana* (Bari: Università di Bari, 1975), p. 111, and H. Crouzel, "Comparaisons precises entre les fragments du Peri Archôn selon la Philocalie et la traduction de Rufin," *Origeniana*, pp. 120–121.

4. *Hom. 8.1 in Jer.* (3.56.24–25). All translations, unless otherwise noted, are by the author. This is an ancient formula. See A. Van Eijk, "Only That can rise which has previously fallen: The History of a Formula," *JTS*, 22 (1971), 517–529.

5. We follow here the studies of J. Dupuis, *"L'esprit de l'homme": Étude sur l'anthropologie religieuse d'Origène* (Bruges: MLST, 1967) and H. Crouzel, "L'anthropologie d'Origène: de l'arche au telos," in U. Bianchi, ed., *Arche e telos. L'antropologia di Origene e di Gregorio de Nissa. Analisi storico-religiosa* (Milano: Università Cattolica de Sacro Cuore, 1981), pp. 37–42.

6. There are no adequate equivalent English translations of the terms for the upper part of the soul, though writers translate respectively "mind or intellect (*nous*)," "heart" (*hegemonikon*)," and "heart (*kardia*)." In the translation "intellect", we follow Corsini, Crouzel, Blanc, and Rius-Camps. The usual translation "mind" is much too vague. *nous* is similar to a pure soul without lower or earthly desires with a unique capacity to relate to and be influenced by spiritual understanding and the grace of God.

7. We use the term "man" here rather than "soul" to distinguish Origen from some Platonists whose anthropology concerns primarily the parts of the soul (*nous, thumos, epithumia*), whereas Origen's thought concerns man with the terminology outlined above. See Crouzel, *ibid.*, p. 36. See also *Jo.* 2.23 (4.79.27–28), trans. Menzies*, ANF, X, 336B, where Origen writes: ". . . for every being endowed with *logos* is man, since it is according to the image and likeness of God." (Gen. 1:26) The asterisk * after Menzies name indicates that I have slightly changed his translation. This text, according to Rius-Camps, *El dinamismo*, pp. 401–402, indicates that "man" is sometimes used by Origen to refer to the pre-existent creature.

8. Cf. *Jo.* 13.37 (4.262.14ff.), *Hom. 8.1 in Jer.* (3.56.18–30).

9. The stories, for example, of Jacob and Esau (Rom. 9:11–12), John the Baptist (Luke 1:41), and the texts of Eph. 1:4, Jer. 1:5 and possibly Jer. 4:4 imply for Origen a pre-existent state. Cf. *Princ.* 3.5.4 (5.273ff.), *Jo.* 6.14 (4.122ff.), *Jo.* 20.19 (4.351.24–30) on John 8.42, *Princ.* 1.7.4 (5.89ff.), *Jo.* 2.30–31 (5.86ff.), *Hom. 1.10 in Jer.* (3.9.23–27) and *Hom. 5.14 in Jer.* (3.44.3–16). On this last text, see Nautin, *Homélies sur Jérémie*, I.318, n.1. Concerning John the Baptist, see Corsini, *Commento al Vangelo di Giovanni di Origene*, p. 259, n. 56, and p. 261, n. 59. See also Monaci, "L'idea della preesistenza," pp. 70ff., for the various scriptural and Origen texts. It is this allegorical method used on scripture which Cadiou, *Introduction*, pp. 226, 275 sees as Origen's true source of divergence from later orthodoxy in *On First Principles*.

With respect to Origen's allegiance to the rule of faith, see *Princ.* 3.5.3 (5.273.1–3), trans. Butterworth, pp. 238–239: "We, however, will give a logical answer that preserves the rule of piety, by saying that God did not begin to work for the first time when he made the visible world. . . ."

For other texts concerning Origen's conscious effort to adhere to the rule of faith, see J. Armantage, "The Best of Both Worlds: Origen's Views on Religion and Resurrection," *Origeniana*, p. 346; R. Etcheverria, "Origenes y la regula fidei," *Origeniana*, p. 336, who referred me to the quoted text, and Crouzel, "Qu'a voulu faire Origène," *BLE* 76(1975), 175.

10. *Hom. 2.1 in Jer.* (3.17.22).

11. See Pseudo-Leont. Byz., *De sectis*, Act. X.5 (PG 86.1264–65), trans. Butterworth, *On First Principles* I.8.1, p. 67, where it is written: ". . . before the ages intellects were all pure, both demons and souls and angels, offering service to God and keeping his commandments. But the devil, who was one of them, since he possessed free-will, desired to resist God, and God drove him away. With him revolted all the other powers."

Though this text does arise from an unfriendly witness to Origen's thought, it is confirmed by Origen's other writings as noted. Crouzel and Simonetti, *Traité*, II, 114, n.5, do not include this fragment in their edition, nor the others which Koetschau added at this point. They believe all of them reflect a "flagrant simplification" of Origen's thought, and are not to be considered a part of *On First Principles*. Nor is it included in the edition of Görgemanns and Karpp, *Origenes—Vier Bücher von den Prinzipien* (Darmstadt: Wissenschaftliche Buchgesellschaft, 1976). Also, see *Cels.* 6.43–44 on the devil's role as instigator. Note that Origen views the fall not only in terms of the individual soul, but also as a group act. In *Comm. in Mt.* 14.17 (10.326.8–11), Origen writes that Christ left the Father above to join "with the" Church "his wife who had fallen down here . . ."

12. The role of free will in this event is explicit in his book *On First Principles*: "But the cause of the withdrawal will lie in this, that the movements of their souls* are not rightly or worthily directed. For the Creator granted to the intellects created by him the power of free and voluntary movement, in order that the good that was in them might become their own, since it was preserved by their own free will; but sloth and weariness of taking trouble to preserve the good, coupled with disregard and neglect of better things, began the process of withdrawal from the good." See *Princ.* 2.9.2 (I.354.39 ff./5.165.23–28), trans. Butterworth, p. 130.

*We note here that Butterworth has translated *anima* "mind" in order to accord with the following phrase which uses *mens*. As we have noted at the outset, we translate both *mens* and *nous* "intellect" along with many other writers on Origen. Crouzel and Simonetti, I, 355, also translate *anima* not by soul but "intelligences" here.

Other passages in Origen reiterate this view of the fall as a result of neglect. See, for example, *Cels.* 6.69 on the cause of the fall: neglect, evil, wickedness and ignorance; and *Hom. 18.3 in Jer.* (3.154.10–11) on Jer. 18:3–4, which concerns how the receptacle (man) falls from the potter's (God) hands from the negligence of man. For Origen, God alone is good; evil is non-being, and has no existence. The devil, for example, insofar as he is evil, is not the work of God, but as a created being, he is the work of God. In addition, see *Jo.* 2.13 (4.69.14–70.2), *Princ.* 2.1.1 and 2.1.3 (5.107.11–14; 109.1–4), and Justinian, *Ep. and Mennam* (Mansi IX.529).

On the discussion of individuality in other texts of Origen, see G. Christopher Stead, "Individual Personality in Origen," *Arché e Telos*, ed. U. Bianchi, pp. 184–187, and Crouzel's follow-up discussion on pp. 192–193, where he indicates the personality is the product of free will and conscience.

13. *Princ.* 1.2.13 (I.142.457–458, 462–465/5.48.1–2, 5–8), trans. Butterworth*, p. 28: ". . . the original goodness must be believed to reside in God the Father. . . . If then there are any other things called good in the scriptures, such as an angel, or a man, or a slave, or a treasure, or a good heart, or a good tree, all these are so called by an inexact use of the word, since the goodness contained in them is accidental and not substantial." On the goodness of the Father, see Crouzel and Simonetti, II, 53, n. 75.

This question is an important matter for Origen in his opposition to the Gnostics. For if good (or evil) resides in one by nature, then we are what we are by necessity rather than choice. For a development of this issue, see *Princ.* 1.5.3 (5.72.4–73.6). He writes: "We conclude then that the position of every created being is the result of his own work, and his own motives. . . ." For becoming good by choice rather than being good by nature, see also *Cels.* 6.44, a section in which Origen clarifies for Celsus the origin and role of the devil and evil in human affairs. One point made in this text is that God makes use of evil for conversion.

14. Another anti-Gnostic theme. Cf. *Jo.* 20.24 (4.357.32–358.5).

15. *Princ.* 2.9.6 (5.170.14), trans. Butterworth, p. 134.

16. This view arises in a context in which the matter is discussed with no reference to the devil: "And so each intellect, neglecting the good either more or less in proportion to its own movements, was drawn to the opposite of good, which undoubtedly is evil. From this source, it appears, the Creator of all things obtained certain seeds and causes of variety and diversity, in order that, according to the diversity of intellects, that is, of rational beings (which diversity they must have supposed to have produced from the causes stated above) he might create a world that was various and diverse." See *Princ.* 2.9.2 (I.356.49ff./5.166.3–10), trans. Butterworth, p. 130.

As Crouzel and Simonetti, II, 214, n. 9, state, here is one of the rare passages which indicates that *every* intellect fell. They point out, however, that certainly Origen meant to except the intellect of Christ, and that he is considering the matter after the fact. Hence he perhaps means "each intellect who fell. . . ."

17. *Princ.* 2.8.3 (I.346.154–157, 175–178/5.157.14–158.1; 158.22–159.2), trans. Butterworth*, pp. 124, 125. Brackets are mine. In *Princ.* 1.2.4 (5.31.9–16), the Fall is viewed also as a loss of or withdrawal from life. Crouzel and Simonetti, II, 206, n.27, offer several other texts which state this theme: *Mart.* 12, *Orat.* 9.2, and *Princ.* 2.11.7. See also their note, II, 204, n. 23 on Origen's understanding of the origin of the word soul.

18. *Princ.* 1.2.13 (47.5–8), trans. Butterworth, p. 28.

19. The *nous* concerns ". . . the intellect which is in them possessing the nature according to which the Creator made it. . ." *Fr. 121 in Luc.* (9.276.17–18). On the other hand, the other dimension, the body, is not light, but darkness: "If, then, the intellect of those untaught and ignorant, though by nature light, is found to be darkness, no doubt their whole body, i.e., the part of the soul connected with passion, that is, the irascible and concupiscent part, is to a much greater degree darkness." *Fr. 187 in Luc.* (9.307.8–10).

See also *Princ.* 2.8.3, quoted above. Rius-Camps, *El dinamismo*, p. 402, in commenting on *Jo.* 2.23 (4.79.27–28)—where Origen indicates that every being endowed with *logos* is man—points out how the rational substrate of man is the principle of divine life. An act of sin veils this principle, shields it, and thus obstructs the "interchange between God and man." These observations on Fr. 187 are made by H. Crouzel, F. Fournier and P. Périchon, eds., *Origène—Homélies sur s. Luc* (SC 87; Paris: Cerf, 1962), p. 536, n. 1.

The irrational and rational parts of the soul are discussed in more detail in J. Dupuis, *'L'esprit de L'homme.' Étude sur L'anthropologie religieuse d'Origène* (Paris: Desclée de Brouwer, 1967), p. 36, n. 53, where the above texts were also cited.

20. We have noted above that the devil is sometimes not included as the cause of the will's choices; rather Origen will simply consider "evil" as the cause without specifying. Concerning the meaning of evil for Origen, see *Jo.* 2.13 (4.69.25–31), trans. Menzies*, *ANF*, X, 331, where Origen discusses John 1:13, a text which tells how believers are born of God. In this text Origen precisely puts to rest any question what the nature of man is as God endowed it. If man is not good, he is ignoring his fundamental nature (the *nous*), and hence is living by something which has no existence. For only the good has being. Evil is without substance. Origen writes: "All then who share in him who is—and the saints share in him—may properly be called Beings; but those who have turned aside from their part in the Being, by depriving themselves of Being, have become non-beings. But we said when entering on this discussion, that non-being and nothing are synonymous, and hence those who are not Beings are nothing, and all evil is nothing, since it is non-being. . . ."

E. Früchtel, "Zur Interpretation der Freiheitsproblematik in Johanneskommentar des Origenes," *Zeitschrift für Religions—und Geistgeschichte*, 26 (1974), 314, comments on this passage, "With the intentional movement away from the *arche* of his being, man deprives himself of his deep root in the Logos and becomes as a result a child of the devil."

21. Cf. *Princ.* 2.8.3 (5.158.22–159.2). The mention of final return introduces the question of *apokatastasis*, which is discussed in the following sections.

22. Antipater of Bostra, *Adv. Orig.*, quoted Origen (in John of Damascus, *Sacra Parallela* ii.770B (PG 96, 501)): "God did not begin to create intellects . . ." (5.95.14), trans. Butterworth, *On First Principles*, p. 67. This may be taken to mean that God did not create intellects in time. One might also conclude from the fact, noted above, that God has essential goodness and being, while creatures receive their goodness and being accidentally, that intellects were not created from eternity. So reasons M. Simonetti, "Note sulla teologia trinitaria di Origene," *Vetera christianorum*, 8 (1971), 284–285.

23. According to C. Blanc, "L'angelologie d'Origène," *Studia Patistica*, 14 (1976), 84, n. 15, no text has been found which proves conclusively the fall of all of the angels. Texts such as *Princ.* 2.9.6 (5.170.10-12), which delineates how diversity arose, affirm only the instability of the beings and the possibility of progress.

24. *Princ.* 2.8.3, translated above.

25. *Jo.* 13.41 (4.267.23–27), where Origen is discussing how the "fruit" will be gathered for "harvest" in the "age to come", concerning John 4:34–38.

26. Studies of the restoration include: W. Breuning, "Zur Lehre der Apokatastasis," *Internationale katholische Zeitschrift*, 10 (1981), 19–31; H. Horn, "Ignis aeternus—une

interpretation morale du feu eternel chez Origène," *Revue des études grecques*, 82 (1969), 76–88; F. Kettler, "Neue Beobachtungen zur Apokatastasislehre des Origenes," in H. Crouzel and A. Quacquarelli, eds., *Origeniana Secunda*, pp. 339–348; P. Lebeau, "L'interpretation origénienne de Rm. 8, 19–22," in Granfield and Jungmann, eds., *Kyriakon—Festschrift Johannes Quasten* (Münster: Aschendorff, 1970), I.336–345; E. Lenz, "Apokatastasis," *Reallexikon für Antike und Christentum*, I (1954), 510–516; A. Méhat, "Apokatastase," *Vigiliae Christianae*, 10 (1956), 196–214; A. Monaci, "Apocalisse ed escatologia nell' opera de Origene," *Augustinianum*, 18 (1978), 139–159; G. Müller, "Origenes und die Apokatastasis," *Theologische Zeitschrift*, 14 (1958), 174–190; A. Oepke, *apokatastasis*, in G. Kittel, ed. *Theological Dictionary of the New Testament*, trans. G. Bromiley, I (1964). 389–393; B. Salmona, "Origene e Gregorio di Nissa salla resurrezione dei corpi e l'apocatastasi," *Augustianianum*, 18 (1978), 383–388; M.-B. Stritzky, "Die Bedeutung der Phaidrosinterpretation für die Apokatastasis des Origenes," *Vigiliae Christianae*, 31 (1977), 283–297; A. Turney, "Apokatastasis," *New Catholic Encyclopedia*, I (1967), 665; E. Corsini, *Commento al Vangelo di Giovanni di Origene* (Torino: UTET, 1968), p. 413, n. 27, p. 887, n. 62, P. 743, n. 8.

With respect to the history of the word itself and the concept before Origen, see especially the articles of Lenz, Oepke, and Turney, whose studies we follow in the discussion. In medicine and politics it refers to a kind of restoration to an earlier physical state and a reconstruction of the political order. Its astronomical use concerned the return of the constellation to its original position. Turning to the religious and philosophical usage, we find it rarely used in a soteriological sense. The Neo-Platonists relate it to reincarnation, the Stoics to astronomy and cosmic history and the Hermetics say the *dialusis* (dissolution) of the material body is called the *apokatastasis* of earthly beings. They point to the destruction of the world and the restitution afterwards of all good things and of nature. Cf. Sext. Emp. *Adv. astr.* 355, 105B, Iamblichus, *Myst.* I.10 and *Corp. herm.* III.64ff., VIII.4. With respect to biblical literature, the LXX, the Bible of Origen, does not use the word, and it is rare in Judaism in general. Philo of Alexandria thinks of redemption from Egypt, and links with it a mystical reference to the "restoration of the soul." See *Rer. Div. Her.*, 293.

27. Lenz, col. 513, points out a similar parallel of *apokathistemi* and *epistrephein* in Jer. 15:19. We consider and quote Origen's discussion of this text below.

28. Oepke, *apokatastasis*, *TDNT*, I.391–392, states that it does not concern the conversion of persons. However, Lenz, writing after Oepke, believes that Acts 3:17ff. concerns souls. He writes, col. 513: "Es handelt sich hier nicht um eine Apokatastasis des Kosmos, sondern der Seelen." Lenz also indicates that the use of the term in Acts 3:21 as "eine Wiederherstellung aller in ihren erstigen vollkommenen Zustand" is "eine neue, entscheidende Bedeutungsrichtung . . . " The idea of a common restoration (without *apokatastasis*) is found in Mt. 5:45, I Cor. 15:22, Rom. 5:18; 11:32, Phil. 2:10, etc. Oepke believes, with respect to the varied interpretations of the idea, there is a "strong tension throughout the New Testament, and, even if there is an underlying universalism, for reasons of admonition, the main emphasis falls on the fact few will be saved." He offers as evidence Matt. 22:14, 7:13ff., Luke 13:23ff., and 1 Cor. 9:24ff. He also adds that Paul knows judgment will have a two-fold outcome (Rom. 2:7ff., 2 Cor. 5:10), yet expects a powerful overthrow of all opposition (1 Cor. 15:22ff.). Lenz concludes by noting that the "dominant view" in the New Testament is that the judgment will separate men in the restoration.

29. *Str.* 6.9.75.2

30. Reported by Origen in *Jo.* 13.46 (4.272).

31. His use of this text is most evident in *Princ.* 3.6 (5.279–291), the chapter concentrating on the concept of the end. According to the editors of *Biblia Patristica*, it is quoted eleven times in this chapter, but cited in many other works.

32. Quoted four times in *Princ.* 3.6, once in *Princ.* 2.3.5 and found in other texts.

33. Cited eight times by Origen, according to *Biblia Patristica*, twice in *On First Principles* (2.3.5, 2.4.2), four times in the *Commentary on Matthew* (17.15, 17.16, 17.19 and in Frag. 55), and once each by the *Commentary on John* (1.16) and the *Homilies on Jeremiah* (14.18).

34. Oepke, *TDNT*, 1.392–393.

35. We know that the term was in use before Origen when Origen writes in his *Commentary on John* of the "so-called" *apokatastasis*. Cf. *Jo.* 1.16, quoted in the paragraph below.

36. Though as a concept (which includes the verbal form) it also had a general use. For example, it is used generally in *Hom. 14.18 in Jer.* (3.124.17–125.6), quoted in this section below.

37. *Jo.* 1.16 (4.20.11–12), trans. Menzies*, 305B.

38. *Princ.* 2.3.5 (I.262.196ff./5.120.17–23), trans. Butterworth*, p. 89.

39. For example, in the work *On First Principles*, three entire chapters are devoted to the events

and significance of the end (and ends), as well as sections of other chapters, (Cf. *Princ.* 2.10–11, 3.5–6).

40. *Princ.* 2.3.5 (5.120.19), 3.5.7 (5.278.22) and 3.6.9 (5.290.14).

41. *Cels.* 4.9 (II.206.7ff.), trans. Chadwick*, *Contra Celsum*, p. 189. Chadwick, p. 189, n. 4, notes a similar view made by Philo, *de Aetern.* 27. For Origen's care in working within the rule of faith, see this chapter, footnote 9.

42. This fact was clarified by the above quote from *Princ.* 2.3.5, a section which ends, by the way, with 1 Cor. 15:28, ". . . God is all in all."

43. *Hom. 14.18 in Jer.* (3.124.20–21). Origen realized he was considering deep matters. As was his habit, he wrote prior to this (3.124.19–20), "But for me there seems to be evident here a mystery in the 'I will restore you.'" Nautin, *Homélies sur Jérémie*, II, 108, n. 1, agrees that the word "restore" evoked for Origen his thoughts on the *apokatastasis*.

44. See especially *Princ.* 2.8.3.

45. *Princ.* 3.6.3 (III.240.68–69, 70–74, 78–80, 81–82, 85, 86–87/5.283.15–17, 18–21; 284.3–5, 6, 9–10), trans. Butterworth*, p. 248.

46. *Princ.* 3.6.6 (5.288.7–11), trans. Butterworth, p. 252.

47. *Princ.* 3.6.6 (5.287.24–26), trans. Butterworth, p. 251.

48. *Jo.* 32.3 (4.429.8–431.7). We follow here Corsini, *Commento*, p. 743, n. 8.

49. As Corsini notes, the subjection of these beings implies that ultimately they will be redeemed and included in the process of salvation. On the subjection and salvation of the devil, which we will discuss in more detail in another section, see Corsini, p. 741, n. 6. Other texts noting this subsection are *Jo.* 6.57 (4.166.6–18), 19.21 (4.323.16–19), and 20.26 (4.362.33–363.6).

50. It is discussed more thoroughly in the Latin adaptation of Origen's *Commentary on the Song of Songs*. We will have the opportunity to view these texts in more detail in later parts concerned with the church.

51. *Comm. in Mt.* 17.15 (10.628.13ff.). Origen gives a more extensive personal interpretation in *Comm. in Mt.* 17.17–24 (10.634–652).

52. Later works reiterate and confirm Origen's analysis as presented here in *On First Principles.*

53. Description and division from É. Junod, ed., *Origène—Philocalie 21–27* (SC 226; Paris: Cerf, 1976), pp. 18–20.

54. *Princ.* 3.1.14 (5.221.1), trans. Butterworth, p. 185.

55. *Princ.* 3.1.13 (III.80.371–373/5.218.9–11), trans. Butterworth, p. 182.

56. *Princ.* 3.1.13 (III.76.350–355/5.217.4–8), trans. Butterworth, p. 181.

57. Junod, *Philocalie*, pp. 279–280, note 4, in his commentary on *Philocalia* 27, notes the importance, in Origen's works, of the notion of God as physician and educator, and its source in Greek philosophy. Though Origen does often use the medical imagery, the image is also related to a biblical image, namely, the New Testament Father who raises his children with discipline and love.

58. Butterworth, *On First Principles*, p. 176, n. 2, referring to *Philocalia* 27, notes that, according to Origen, ". . . God, like a good physician, works for the salvation of all, though sometimes with painful remedies."

59. *Princ.* 3.1.14 (III.84.401ff./5.220.8–12), trans. Butterworth, p. 185. See the other texts mentioned by Crouzel and Simonetti, IV, 35, n. 77, on the ways God adapts to each person through different foods, even by means of the Incarnation.

60. Cf. Junod, *Philocalie*, p. 90.

61. According to H. Jackson, "Sources of Origen's Doctrine of Freedom," *Church History*, 35 (1966), 16.

62. *Princ.* 3.1.15 (III.88.425ff./5.222.1–7), trans. Butterworth, pp. 186–187. Junod, *Philocalie*, p. 20, points out that this reference to one who destroys free will may refer to the Gnostics. Früchtel, "Freiheit," 315, n. 27, agrees with other modern scholars that Origen did not appreciate the function of the free will in the "spiritual" class of the Gnostics. In reply to this, Origen might say that if all are not "free", then freedom does not exist for anyone. It is the selective process in Gnosticism which inhibits freedom from the outset. Moreover, see our discussion in Chapter I on the role of freedom in the Gnostic system.

63. *Princ.* 3.1.15 (III.92.442ff./5.222.16–223.1), trans. Butterworth, p. 187. There is also a sense of a community freedom in Origen. In *Princ.* 2.1.2 (5.107.28–108.10), trans. Butterworth, pp. 77–78, Origen states how in diverse ways every rational creature of God's "entire creation" (*universarum creaturarum*) exercises his free choice and works together to produce the "harmony of a single world." (*unius mundi consonantiam*)

We note that, in examining the last two texts, Origen has changed the divine agent from "God" to "the divine word." While we shall not enter here into a discussion of Origen's trinitarian thought, it is generally accepted by most writers that Origen's manner of distinguishing the work of the Father from the Son or the Word can border on what later was called subordinationism. But in Origen's thought the positions of the Trinity are based on a hierarchy of origin and of function in the economy of redemption, rather than a hierarchy of power. For more detail and other texts, see H. Crouzel, "Les personnes de la Trinité, sont-elles de puissance inégale selon Origène, Peri Archôn 1.3.5-8," *Gregorianum*, 57 (1976), 114.

64. Cf. Junod, *Philocalie*, p. 259, note 1, believes that this section is, in fact, a summary of the entire chapter.

65. *Princ.* 3.1.24 (III.148.779ff./5.243.10-12), trans. Butterworth, p. 210.

66. The question of divine foreknowledge and grace is a separate issue, and will be clarified in our discussion of *charis*. According to *Jo.* 6.36, God will grace someone with sufficiency whom he knows will be worthy, but God will not give someone worthiness, despite his foreknowledge of who will be worthy.

67. *Hom. 3.2 in Jer.* (3.50.1-3).

68. *Hom. 3.2 in Jer.* (3.50.6-10).

69. *Comm. in Mt.* 10.11 (10.12.16-17,24-25,26), trans. J. Patrick, ANF 10, 419AB. Origen discusses in this same section how men progress and regress by evident choice. Similarly, see *Comm. in Mt.* 13.26 (10.250.24-251.2). Another side of this is explored in *Hom. 18.3 in Jer.* (3.154.3-11), which comments on Jer. 18:3-4. In this text, the vessel of the potter falls from his hands. Origen indicates that the vessel (man) can only fall from the hands of the potter (God) on account of man's own choice; "no one" else can force us to fall or "snatch" us away from God.

70. *Jo.* 6.36(20) (4.145.20-22), trans. Menzies, 368B.

71. On the causes of the tension in Origen's thought, see the discussion of Junod, *Philocalie*, p. 90. Junod implicitly criticizes Origen for his interpretation of New Testament eschatology. But according to J. W. Hanson, *Universalism, the Prevailing Doctrine of the Christian Church during its First Five Hundred Years* (Boston and Chicago: Universalist Publishing House, 1899), p. 15, "The reticence of all the ancient formularies of faith concerning endless punishment at the same time that the great fathers were proclaiming universal salvation . . . is strong evidence that the former doctrine was not then accepted." For more on this issue of punishment and universality, see following sections.

Junod concludes, p. 90: "As an ardent champion of full human freedom and of the all-bracing goodness of God, he cannot bring himself to believe that the latter sets bounds for the former. . . . The work of Origen is inspired by the belief that all men, without exception, will choose finally to be known and loved by God."

72. *Hom. 20.2 in Jer.* (3.178.14-25). A similar idea is found in *Orat.* 29.15 (2.390.23ff.), where it is written, "For God does not wish that the good should come to someone by necessity but willingly . . ."

73. H. Crouzel, "L'exégèse origénienne de I Cor. 3, 11-15 et la purification eschatologique," in J. Fontaine and C. Kannengiesser, eds., *Epektasis—Mélanges patristiques offerts au Cardinal Jean Daniélou* (Paris: Beauchesne, 1972), pp. 273-283. See particularly p. 277. Crouzel recognizes that "sin unto death" involves as a consequence the death of the soul, but he refrains from a study of Origen's conception of hell. For Crouzel's view on hell, see "L'Hades et la Gehenne selon Origène," *Gregorianum*, 59 (1978), 291-331.

Crouzel does not enter here into what the "death of the soul" implies. As we have seen in II.1, the word "soul" for Origen refers to a fallen state. The *nous* is the pure created condition. Hence the "death of the soul" may imply the end or the extreme extent of the fallen condition, rather than the loss of salvation. There is no text which indicates that the *nous* dies or is detroyed by God. This view is confirmed by Origen himself in *Jo.* 13.60-61, where Origen, objecting to Heracleon's interpretation of John 4:46-53, notes that one of the weaknesses of Heracleon's position is his failure to understand the word "death." The soul, Origen continues, can die without being totally destroyed. Only the perishable parts are destroyed.

74. *Princ.* 2.10.4 (I.382.123-129,154-156/5.177.2-7, 178.13-14), trans. Butterworth, pp. 141-142.

75. *Princ.* 2.10.4 (5.178.8-9), trans. Butterworth, p. 142. In line with this view of the matter is *Jo.* 13.37 (4.263.7-13), where punishment is a way to prepare men for perfection by the Logos, though it is not clear whether these sufferings for sins occur before or during the endtimes.

76. *Princ.* 2.10.6 (5.179.20-21), trans. Butterworth, p. 143. H. Horn, "Ignis aeternus—une

interprétation morale du feu éternel chez Origène," *REG*, 82 (1969), 76–88, who comments on the above texts from *On First Principles*, states that the fire mentioned in *Princ*. 2.10.4 seems to offer two alternatives: either the sinner becomes aware of his sins and then he can be saved; or else he believes that he has nothing to blame himself for and then he is condemned. The second alternative is at best implied in the principal texts commented on by Horn. For there is no explicit mention of condemnation in *Princ*. 2.10.4 or 2.10.6. The emphasis in these two passages is on how man's conscience and God's remedies restore the soul to health.

77. Nautin, *Homélies sur Jérémie*, I, 177, claims that the *Homilies on Jeremiah* provide a better view of Origen's thought on the fire in store for sinners than does any of his other works. See Nautin, *Jérémie*, I. 172–179, for a summary of Origen's views on the end-times as reflected in texts from the *Homilies on Jeremiah*. Nautin sees four major themes: 1) All men in some way will experience the fire of purification, 2) this "fire" will be a spiritual rather than physical fire, 3) the fire will not be an eternal punishment, but will have an end, the length of punishment depending on the person, and 4) God himself is a "consuming fire" who will purify, but he purifies only those who are worthy and ready. Another stage of purification precedes the purification of God, which is reserved for those who have become elect. Separation from God is the most painful punishment of all, and when the soul senses this fire in conscience, it is being purified by God himself.

See an appendix of this book for a concise discussion on the view of fire in the homilies.

78. Cf. F. Ledegang, "Images of the Church in Origen: the girdle," *Studia Patristica*, 17 (1982), III. 907–911.

79. *Hom. 11.5 in Jer*. (3.83.15–18,22–84.1). There is a difficulty in this section of Homily 11 which is outside our present concerns. It involves the scriptural use of and Origen's understanding of the "body" of God, a Stoic idea which is repulsive to him in many texts. For a thorough discussion, see Erwin Schadel, *Origenes*, p. 291, n. 118.

80. *Hom. 16.5 in Jer*. (3.137.28–30).

81. *Hom. 16.5 in Jer*. (3.138.4–5).

82. *Hom. 16.5–6 in Jer*. (3.138.9–15).

83. *Hom. 16.6 in Jer*. (3.138.21–22).

84. Particularly with respect to blaspheming the Holy Spirit, Origen is quite severe in the extent of punishment.

85. See also *Cels*. 4.13 on Origen's interpretation of Deut. 4.24.

86. *Hom. 16.6 in Jer*. (3.138.27–29, 139.18–19).

87. *Cels*. 8.72 (IV.340.11ff.) trans. H. Chadwick*, p. 507. For some additional detail on this text, see H. Chadwick, "Origen, Celsus and the Stoa," *JTS*, 48 (1947), 34–49.

88. However, there are indications that Origen believed that evil could once again arise even after the *apokatastasis*. For example, in a context again concerned with the end, Origen writes: "But whether or not there is reason to suppose that after evil has disappeared it rises again, such a problem will be discussed in a book dealing primarily with this subject." Cf. *Cels*. 4.69 (II.354.14ff.), trans. Chadwick, p. 239. See Borret, *Celse*, II, 354, n. 4. He indicates that Origen neither denies nor affirms the event, but hesitates in the hope it will not happen. See texts cited by Borret. However, because freedom is never destroyed, it is a logical extension of Origen's thought. Also, in the next sentence after the above quotation, Origen writes: "But to teach whether or not the consequence is that it [evil] can under no circumstances be allowed any further existence, is not relevant to the present discussion."

89. This view is also noted by Nautin. *Jérémie*, I, 177, note 3. Cf. *Hom. 20.4 in Jer*. (3.183.5–10).

90. Cf. Nautin, *Jérémie*, I, 175–177. Nautin offers *Hom. 18.1 in Jer*. and *Hom. 7.2 in Jer*. as proof of this view.

91. Nautin, *Jérémie*, II, 269, note 3. The discovery by the so-called wise is not that there is not punishment, but that there is no corporeal punishment.

92. *Cels*. 5.16 (III.54.17ff.), trans. H. Chadwick, p. 276.

93. *Cels*. 8.48, p. 487.

94. Cf. Horn, "Ignis aeternus," 88, and Nautin, *Jérémie*, I, 176.

95. Mf. M-B. von Stritzky, "Die Bedeutung der Phaidrosinterpretation für die Apokatastasis des Origenes," *Vigiliae christianae*, 31 (1977), 294–295. For Plato, see T. Saunders, ed. and trans., *Plato–The Laws* (Leg. 716C) (Harmondsworth: Penguin, 1975), p. 175. These observations are made apropos of the following passage from Origen, *Princ*. 3.6.3 (5.284.3–10), trans. Butterworth, p. 248: "If then the end, having been repaired to the origin, and the issue of things,

having been made to resemble their beginning, returns to that condition which rational nature once enjoyed when it had no need to eat of the tree of knowledge of good and evil, so that all consciousness of evil had departed and given place to what is sincere and pure and he alone who is the one good God becomes "all things" to the soul and he himself is "all things" not in some few or in many things but in "all things," when there is nowhere any "death," nowhere any "sting" of death, nowhere any evil at all, then truly God will be "all in all."

Stritzky, "Die Bedeutung," 294, comments, "Es gibt dann keine Unterscheidung mehr zwischen Gut und Böse, weil das Böse nicht mehr da sein wird. Auf diese Weise kehrt das Ende zum Anfang zurück und der Ausgang fällt mit dem Urzustand zusammen."

96. *Cels.* 8.72. See section II.4.

97. M. Borret, ed., *Origène—Contre Celse* (Sources chrétiennes 136; Paris: Cerf, 1968), II, 435, note 2, also considers this passage a summary.

98. This point is made also by Borret, *ibid.*, 433, note 3, and Aubin, *Le problème*, p. 139.

99. *Cels.* 4.99 (1.373.9–13), trans. H. Chadwick*, p. 263.

100. *Jo.* 1.35 (4.45.13–18,30–32), trans. J. Patrick, 318B, 319A.

101. *Jo.* 13.37 (4.262.14–25).

102. *Jo.* 13.37 (4.263.6–7).

103. A similar conclusion is reached, based on this text, by H. Vogt, *Das Kirchenverständnis des Origenes* (Vienna: Böhlau, 1974), pp. 340–341. Vogt also adds other texts to show how Origen saw the beginning and the end as the only time worthy of the Father's knowledge. To the "inbetween times," imperfect and evil, the Father sends the Son, who is to return the rational creation to its original state. See also J. Rius–Camps, "La hipotesis origeniana sobre el fin ultimo (peri telous)," in *Arché e Telos*, pp. 78–85, and Henri Crouzel's response, based on the controversial letter of Origen to Friends of Alexandria, pp. 118–119.

104. *Hom. 8.1 in Jer.* (3.56.26–30).

105. Since the world *apokatastasis* means primarily restoration and need not imply universality, we might also distinguish between a "restoration," which is quite clear when the word *apokatastasis* is used, and a *universal* restoration, which need not be implied in extant Greek passages with *apokatastasis*. This is the the opinion of J. Dupuis, who writes, in *'L'esprit,'* p. 210, n. 199, "The idea of the universality of the restoration does not enter into the original meaning of the term apokatastasis, even as Origen understands it." Dupuis, p. 211, recognizes that in *On First Principles* Origen considered the possibility of a final conversion of the damned. But Dupuis, p. 212, regards this consideration as a working hypothesis which Origen gradually refined. Girod, *Commentaire*, I, 147, note 2, refers also to Dupuis's opinion.

This view is only one alternative, as we note in what follows in this section. The context in the end should determine the kind of restoration involved. In passages such as the one quoted above from *Jo.* 1.35, the context indicates that a universal restoration is implied.

106. *Comm. in Mt.* 10.2 (10.2.24–3.1), trans. Patrick, 414B.

107. See R. Girod, ed., *Origène—Commentaire sur Mathieu* (Sources chretiénnes 162; Paris: Cerf, 1970), I, 147, note 2.

108. So Dupuis, p. 212 and note 208.

109. We are assuming that the "end of things" implies the apokatastasis, but this may not necessarily be accurate. As we have mentioned previously, Origen believed the conversion of the world involved several ages.

110. Dupuis, p. 212 and note 208.

111. Cf. *Fr. 33 in Jer.* (3.215.25–216.4).

112. *Jo.* 19.14 (4.314.10–13).

113. *Orat.* 27.15 (374.13–18), trans. Rowan A. Greer, *Origen—An Exhortation to Martyrdom, Prayer, First Principles: Book IV, Prologue to the Commentary on the Song of Songs, Homily XXVII on Numbers* (New York: Paulist Press, 1979), p. 146.

114. *Hom. 20.9 in Jer.* (3.194.13–14).

115. *Fr. 7 in Jer.* (3.201.8–10).

116. The salvation of the devil, a corollary of universal restoration, is not denied by Origen, according to scholars, but is spoken about in an obscure way. Origen's enemies, all of whom claimed he taught the salvation of the devil, were, of course, quick to seize on these passages. H. Crouzel, M. Simonetti, eds., *Origène—Traité des Principes*, IV, 138, n. 26, concerning *Princ.* 3.6.5, write: "L'affirmation du salut du démon, telle qu'elle semble indiquée ici, reste donc dans la pensée

d'Origène problématique et non certaine, puisqu'on trouve dans le PArch. l'autre hypothèse, la malice se changeant en nature." What is clear for these writers is that all evil will end, and a corollary of this is that the devil will end because his will will no longer be evil. See texts quoted above, specifically *Hom. 1.16 in Jer.* and *Cels.* 8.72.

117. *Hom. 12.12 in Jer.* (3.99.4–14). Nautin, *Jérémie*, II, 43, n. 3, sees here also an indirect reference to a universal salvation.

118. *Jo.* 2.20 (4.77.12).

119. See *Hom. 14.18 in Jer.* (3.124.17–125.6).

120. *Jo.* 32.3 (4.429.27–431.7). Corsini, *Commento,* p. 741, n. 6, writes on this issue: "Senza pretesa di addentrarci in una questione cosi complessa e limitandoci all 'ambito del Commento a Giovanni, possiamo affermare che nelle parti giunte a noi tale dottrina non è mai affermata esplicitamente ma soltanto accennata dubitativamente." On p. 743, n. 8, Corsini writes that the subjection "implies" the concept of salvation and redemption of the demons and the devil, especially in light of Origen's belief that in the end all things will be similar to the beginning.

121. Cf. *Jo.* 2.13 (4.69.17–70.2).

122. See, for example, *Hom. 11.6 in Jer.* and *Orat.* 22.11.

123. This fact is noted also by Nautin, *Jérémie*, I, 293, n. 2, who believes it probably also includes indirectly the devil himself.

124. Grace is a subject we discuss in detail in chapter 5. In brief, God's grace awaits all men who show the slightest indication toward good, strengthening them toward spiritual maturity.

125. Horn, "Ignis aeternus," 84, note 35.

126. *Princ.* 2.2.2 (I.248.34ff./5.112.24–113.4), trans. Butterworth*, p. 81–82. On the quality of resurrected body, see Crouzel and Simonetti, II, 139, n. 7.

127. Justinian, *Ep. ad Mennam,* (Mansi IX 529). See *On First Principles* 2.3.3 (5.118.4–7), trans. Butterworth, pp. 86–87. This fragment is discussed by Crouzel and Simonetti, II, 145, n. 16, where they point out that the context is not offered.

128. *Princ.* 2.3.3 (I.256.125ff./5.118.7–11), trans. Butterworth, pp. 86–87.

129. *Ep. ad Avitum* 5.

130. For example, E. Schendel, *Herrschaft und Unterwerfung Christi* (Tübingen: J.C.B. Mohr, 1971), p. 171, offers the perspective of F. Kettler, *Der ursprüngliche Sinn der Dogmatik des Origenes* (Berlin: Töpelmann, 1966), pp. 21–31. Kettler notes three facts which point to a bodiless *apokatastasis*: First, the fragments of both Justinian and Jerome show that they thought this was Origen's teaching; second, a "considerable number of places" in surviving Greek passages seem to indicate a bodiless state; and third, this seems a likely conclusion from Origen's image of the soul returning to pure spirit. In a more recent discussion, "Neue Beobachtungen zur Apokatasislehre des Origenes," in H. Crouzel and A. Quacquarelli, eds., *Origeniana Secunda*, pp. 339–348, Kettler discusses 10 Greek texts which verify a bodiless existence in the apokatastasis. He states, p. 339: "Da sich alle diese Stelle im Einklang miteinander befinden, ist anzunehmen, dass Origenes von seiner Frühzeit bis ins Alter von der Körperlosigkeit der Apokatastasis überzeugt gewesen ist."

131. The opinion of H. Crouzel, "La doctrine origénienne du corps resuscité," *Gregorianum*, 53 (1972), 713. He writes that the context is clearly noted by Rufinus. The reference is to only one possibility among others. Moreover, Crouzel says, "Any of a number of Greek texts of Origen on the resurrection do not justify . . . the end of the body in the restoration."

132. *Princ.* 2.3.3 (I.258.130ff./5.118.12–119.3), trans. Butterworth, p. 87.

133. *Princ.* 2.3.7 (I.270.324ff./5.125.1–13, 16–17, 17–126.4), trans. Butterworth*, p. 93. This text is verified also by Jerome, *Ep. ad Avitum*, 5, 6. See English translation in Butterworth edition, p. 92, n. 7. Cf. Crouzel and Simonetti, II, 154, n. 43, for a comparison of the versions of Rufinus and Jerome on this passage.

134. Cf. Kettler, "Neue Beobachtungen," pp. 339–348. For texts mentioned by Kettler which seem to concern the corporeal body and the corporeal existence in general and do not deny the possibility of a spiritual body, see *Jo.* 1.17, 1.26, 13.14, 19.20, 19.22, *Mart.* 13, 44, *Comm. in Mt.* 16.4–5. For texts seemingly quoted out of context by Kettler, when Origen is actually concerned to inspire his readers to separate themselves from things of the gross body and material and do not concern the apokatastasis, see *Orat.* 9.2, *Mart.* 3, and *Jo.* 32.18.

We need to point out that Kettler discusses the issue as presented in *On First Principles* on pp. 342–343. Two clarifications are offered: First, he names an interesting distinction in Origen's thought with the terms exoteric and esoteric. The former level concerns those passages when Origen is addressing the common folk, or those who are only able at present to understand the literal and simple meaning of scripture and the Christian faith. The esoteric concerns the deep mysteries of the faith that require inspiration from the Spirit and spiritual understanding. The exoteric explanation of the body in the apokatastasis is that there will be a change from gross bodies to ethereal bodies suitable for a heavenly environment. The esoteric explanation is that body of any kind will cease to exist.

While this explanation is excellent for many issues in Origen's thought, none of the texts which Kettler presents indicates that Origen is using this distinction. Usually when Origen sees the deeper mystery concealed in the text, he boldly says so, with or without an explanation. See, for example, *Hom. 18.4-5 in Jer.* In none of the texts cited by Kettler is this the case. Moreover, *On First Principles* and *Against Celsus* are both works in which Origen addresses the deep mysteries and difficult scriptural texts of the faith. Third, the view which Kettler espouses implies that Origen views the body in a negative way. In fact, Origen sees the source of difficulty not in the body, but in the will. On Origen's view of the body, see Corsini, *Commento*, p. 146, n. 30.

Second, Kettler believes that there is an evolution of the body, even in the heavenly regions, toward the bodiless state, that the bodily resurrection is only the first step in a process toward the bodiless apokatastasis. While this evolutionary model is again evident in many areas of Origen's thought, it is presented in only a limited sense with respect to the future of the body, as we have seen in the above text from *Against Celsus*. No text explicitly carries the evolution of the body toward non-existence. While none of these arguments mean that the alternative of a bodiless apokatastasis is not viable, they do mean that it is not the only alternative in Origen's thought.

135. Cf. Armantage, "The Best of Both Worlds," *Origeniana*, p. 344.

136. *Hom. 18.4 in Jer.* (3. 154.26–155.1).

137. *Cels.* 7.32 (IV.84.5ff./2.182.23–24), trans. Chadwick, p. 420. See M. Borret, ed., *Origène—Contre Celse* (Sources chrétiennes 147; Paris: Cerf, 1969), III, 70–71, where he notes that Origen purposefully uses Stoic philosophical terminology in order to make the resurrection more intelligible to pagan readers.

138. *Cels.* 5.23 (III.68.4ff.), trans. Chadwick p. 281.

139. *Cels.* 7.32 (IV.86.12ff./2.182.29–183.5), trans. Chadwick, p. 420. As Chadwick notes, p. 420, n. 6, Origen discusses the resurrection in several other places in *Against Celsus*, all of which verify the above text. See 2.55–67, 5.18–20, 57–58. We would also add 5.21–24. Origen in 5.20 refers to his now lost work on the resurrection. This work preceded *On First Principles*, but Origen mentions and supports the discussion of the resurrection given there. Since *Against Celsus* was a very late work, this note offered by Origen himself indicates that his opinion stayed the same throughout his life on this subject, even if it did have several dimensions.

Another alternative similar to the above has recently been advanced by D. G. Bostock, "Quality and Corporeity," *Origeniana Secunda*, pp. 323–337. This view states that the body is transformed "through an interchange of qualities." See Bostock, pp. 330–334. However, the nature of the correspondence between the quality of the 'earthly body' and the quality of the 'spiritual body' is, according to Bostock, "far from clear." Bostock, pp. 335–337, does believe, however, that Origen thought that the body would cease to exist, because the body was a product of diversity, and because man is destined to be one with God, and this would not occur (unless God was corporeal). Still see Bostock's cautionary remark on this issue on p. 336. His supporting texts are *Princ.* 3.6.4 (286.3–9), 2.1.4 (109.9–10), 2.3.3 (118.1–4) and *Hom. 1.1. in Gen.* (2.17–19).

140. The latter text is quoted in *Cels.* 5.18–19.

Chapter III. Managing the Senses: How Does Man Acquire Self-Control and Restrain His Desires?

1. Origen believed that there was a great mystery in how the soul became bound to a body because the matter was not clarified in scripture or in the rule of faith. He also believed that such information should be offered to select people who are able to work out the doctrines. See *Cels.* 5.29. Origen, however, does exclude reincarnation.

2. For a concise overview of the "body" (*soma*), see H. Crouzel, "L'anthropologie d'Origène: de l'arche au telos," in *Arché e Telos* (Milan: Vita e Pensiero, 1981), pp. 41–42, and C. Blanc, "L'attitude d'Origène a l'égard du corps et de la chair," *Studia Patristica*, 17 (1982), III, 843–858, especially, 847ff. Blanc's article is also useful because she includes a discussion of the

attitude of the Greeks and the Jews to the body. Our main criterion in the consideration of other scholars is, as we have noted in the introduction, the texts which are cited.

3. Laporte, "La chute," 333–335, treats the problem of the fall and differentiation into angels and men. He suggests, 334, that there is a fall in differentiation and a second fall in flesh. But Laporte believes that one must distinguish the fall of angels from the fall of men. Although our main concern is anthropology, we need to note that all worldly things result from a fall. See, for example, *Jo.* 19.22 (4.324.4–25).

We should also distinguish in Origen's thought between the "body" and the "image of the earthly" which arises from sin and contrasts with the image of the heavenly. For a discussion using these terms and their meaning, see *Hom. 2.1 in Jer.* (3.17.7–16) and the discussion to follow in this part.

According to Rufinus's adaptation, Origen believes that only the Trinity can be without a body. Even minds, he says, had a kind of material body. *Princ.* 2.2.2 (I.248.31–32/5.112.21–22), trans. Butterworth, p. 81. Though Butterworth in his edition, p. 81, n. 1, claims Rufinus has altered this text, M. Alexandre, "Le statut des questions concernant la matière dans le peri archôn," *Origeniana*, p. 79, states, in light of the recurrence of this theme concerning God's bodiless and unchanging state, that it probably reflects Origen's thought. As we have discussed in the prior part, scripture led Origen to consider the possibility of a spiritual body, and probably the end of body. Hence when Origen says, as he does in *Jo.* 1.17, that the saints are incorporeal, he could mean either that they do not have gross, earthly bodies, or the body has ceased to exist. For the first alternative, see Blanc, "L'attitude d'Origène," 848,853, though her article concerns primarily the "flesh." For the second alternative, see the arguments of Bostock, *Origeniana Secunda*, pp. 334–337. He states that both matter and body, as products of diversity, will cease to exist. Crouzel and Simonetti, *Traité*, II, 139, notes 7, 9, point out that this section (2.2.2) has probably not been altered by Rufinus, that the first alternative is more probable.

What is certain is that Origen believed that the release from the influences of the earthly body were essential for conversion.

4. *Princ.* 2.2.2 (5.112.24–113.1), trans. Butterworth, pp. 81–82.

5. *Princ.* 3.4.5 (III.214.235–238/5.270.10–13), trans. Butterworth*, p. 236.

6. *Princ.* 4.4.8 (III.422.321ff./5.360.17–20), trans. Butterworth*, p. 325. It is worth mentioning, and perhaps even stressing, that God created the soul *and* the body. Moreover, according to *Hom. 3.2 in Jer.*, God created initially a healthy body. The body itself, as we shall discover in another section, is morally neutral.

7. "Unnatural" here is used in contrast to the pre-existent state before the fall which, I suggest, Origen hypothesizes is the "natural" state.

8. *Princ.* 1.8.4 (5.103.23–24/from Gregory of Nyssa), trans. G. Butterworth, p. 73.

9. On this section, see especially Dupuis, pp. 54–61, and, on the meaning of "matter" and "body," see D. G. Bostock, "Quality and Corporeity," *Origeniana Secunda*, 323–337. Bostock, p. 326, points out that "matter is distinct from body" in Origen, and that, p. 328, the four elements (earth, air, water, fire) were preceded and were produced from the qualities (heat, cold, dryness, wetness, hardness and softness). Matter is the substance underlying body. See *Princ.* 2.1.4 (110.1–4).

10. Cf. *Cels.* 7.38. Origen compares the intimacy of the soul with the body to the dependence of the soul on God. See *Fr. 18 in Jer.*

11. *Princ.* 3.1.3 (198.5–11/from Ch. 21 of the *Philocalia/Traité*, III, 24.47–54), trans. Butterworth, p. 160.

12. Many texts connect the control of passion with spiritual progress. In *Fr. 26 in Jer.*, man must destroy the forces of passion before they become mature. Passions are opposed to virtue in *Fr. 40 in Jer.*, and in *Jo.* 13.42, in order for anyone to raise up his eyes, he must not be tied to the passions and flesh. Finally, in *Fr. 11 in Jer.*, Origen states that man must restrain the body and irrational movements by rational impulses and the spirit. On the role of flesh in Origen, see Blanc, "L'attitude d'Origène a l'égard du corps et de la chair," *Studia Patristica*, 17(1982), II, 849–853.

13. For Origen, *Cels.* 3.42, the body is morally neutral, while the "flesh" includes a moral judgment. Origen, interpreting Jer. 13:1–4 and Ez. 1:27, will even refer to the body of God in *Hom. 11.5 in Jer.*, an interesting passage in light of Origen's views on the bodiless state of God. See Schadel's long discussion of this passage on p. 291, n. 118. He concludes concerning the expressions about the "body" of God: ". . . sie machen keine eigentliche Aussage über Gottes Wesen sondern sind a parte hominis zu verstehen."

The war then is not between the body and the spirit, but between the flesh and the spirit. See *Hom. 11.2 in Jer.*, and *Hom. 15.6 in Jer.*, where man establishes the fleshly while in the body. Dupuis, p. 55, goes one step further: "la vie terrestre n'est pas mauvaise: en elle-même, elle semble plutôt dénuée de connotation morale." On the body he quotes, p. 56, *Fr. in 1 Cor.* 30 (J.T.S., IX, 371, 1–2) to point out that the body is essentially an instrument of the soul, and depends for its moral value on the direction of the soul.

14. *Hom. 5.13 in Jer.*
15. *Hom. 5.9 in Jer.* (39.6–9).
16. *Cels.* 7.46 (198.6–17/IV.124.26–36)), trans. Chadwick, p. 434.

The use in this passage of the word *aisthesis* needs to be explored briefly, since it is an idea central to how the soul advances or lapses. Origen often uses the word *aisthetos* in contrast to the spiritual or intelligible, i.e., the five corporeal senses in contrast to the five spiritual senses. See, for example, *Jo.* 10.40 (218.6) and 13.9. On the use of the word, see H. Crouzel, *Origène et la 'connaissance mystique'* (Bruges: Desclée de Brouwer, 1961), pp. 230–232.

As we have already seen, the senses are good if they are kept under control by reason. *aisthetos* represents, in the neuter plural, the sensible realities in contrast to the intelligible realities. For example, in *Hom. 2.2–3 in Jer.*, Origen compares being washed in the sensuous "lye" (Jer. 2:22) and the washing of the spirits and Holy Spirit (Is. 4:4; Lk. 3:16). Only the latter purifies. In light of this definition, *aisthesis* is the mental process of receiving those sensible realities. Origen does not deny that there is knowledge from the senses, but this knowledge is only a starting point from which to ascend to a greater knowledge. Origen defines *aisthesis* in this light in the challenge by Celsus. See *Cels.* 7.36–39, especially 7.37.

In these texts it is clear how Origen on this issue separates himself from the Stoics who believed *all* knowledge arose from sense-perception and that reality is fundamentally material.

Confirming this definition is the epistemology of Origen's contemporaries, the Middle Platonists, especially Albinus. According to Albinus, there were two sources of knowledge: that which was received through sense-perception, and that which involved the "direct apprehension of intelligible reality," which is a perception in its pure form proper only to God. Albinus, in his book *didaskalikos* (154, 29ff.), defines sense-perception as "an affection produced in the soul by the body which presents the report, primarily, of the faculty affected." In these comments on Albinus, see the discussion and texts given by J. Dillon, *The Middle Platonists* (London: Duckworth, 1977), pp. 273–276.

aisthesis in itself then is dumb, that is, it cannot make judgments. It is the mind which does this. The mind receives impressions through the process of sense-perception, and then uses and directs them in accordance with its judgment and power.

17. *Cels.* 7.47 (IV.126.14–15/199.6–7), trans. Chadwick, p. 435.
18. *Princ.* 3.1.3 (198.5–11/from Ch. 21 of the *Philocalia*).
19. *Cels.* 3.47 (II.112.6–8, 14–20). See Borret, *Celse* II,114, n. 1, on this passage, to which he adds *Comm. in Rom.* 1.17.
20. *Cels.* 3.34 (II.80.19–22), trans. Chadwick. See also *Comm. in Rom.* 1.11–19 (PG 14:837–872). On comparison of Christianity and other religions with respect to the physical, see Origen's discussion of images in *Cels.* 8.17–18. There Origen stresses again that Christian images are in the mind, are intelligible and eternal, and images of virtue.
21. *Cels.* 7.46 (IV.124.36ff./198.15–17), trans. Chadwick, p. 434. Also in *Jo.* 1.26 (31.31–33), Origen states that what is sense, though not true, is not false, but serves as an analogy. Cf. Dupuis, pp. 58–59. See also *Cels.* 3.47.
22. On glorifying the senses and making physical things and externals into objects of worship, see *Hom. 5.2 in Jer., Hom. 7.3 in Jer.* and *Hom. 8.2 in Jer.*
23. *Princ.* 2.11.4 (I.400.100, 402.115–116/186.11–12, 23–24), trans. Butterworth, p. 149.
24. *Princ.* 2.11.4 (I.402.118–120/187.13–15), trans. Butterworth, p. 150.
25. *Princ.* 4.4.10 (IV.428.413–418/364.6–10), trans. Butterworth, pp. 327–328. As Crouzel and Simonetti, *Traitè*, IV, 275, n. 84, note, Prov. 2:5 is a justification for the doctrines of the five spiritual senses analogical to the five physical senses. See *Princ.* 1.1.9, *Cels.* 1.48, 7.34, and *Jo.* 20.43(33). It is based on Origen's reading in the LXX of *aisthesis* rather than *epignosin*.
26. J. C. McLelland, *God the Anonymous—A Study in Alexandrian Theology* (Philadelphia: Philadelphia Patristic Foundation, 1976), p. 99, writes that Origen "also presupposes such a degree of transcendence in God that He remains unknowable except to a mind set free from the senses." Though accurate as stated, this may lead readers astray. Origen would and does affirm

with Paul that God can be known through his visible creation. Thus, God can be known through the senses, but God cannot be known by one who is ruled by the senses.

27. *Cels.* 4.66 (II.348.8–12/336.27–30), trans. Chadwick, p. 237.

28. See *Jo.* 2.3 (I.220.SECT. 20ff.), 323Aff..

29. The following works need to be consulted on Origen's anthropology and psychology: Alcain, *Cautiverio v redencion*; Balas, "Participation," *Origeniana*; Benito y Duran, "El humanismo;" Bettencourt, *Doctrina*; U. Bianchi, ed. *Arché e Telos. L'antropologia di Origene e di Gregorio di Nissa. Analisis storico-religiosa*; Boada, "El pneuma en Origenes," *Estudios eclesiasticos* 46 (1971), 474–510; G. Bürke, "Des Origenes Lehre vom Urstand des Menschen," *Zeitschrift für katholische Theologie* 72(1950), 1–39; Dupuis, *'L'esprit de l'homme*; P. Faessler, *Der Hagiosbegriff bei Origenes* (Freiburg: University of Freiburg, 1928); G. Gruber, *ZOE: Wesen, Stufen und Mitteilung des Wahren Lebens bei Origenes* (München: M. Hueber, 1962); Kettler, *Der ursprüngliche Sinn*; H. Rahner, "Das Menschbild des Origenes," *Eranos Jahrbuch* 15 (1947), 197–248; G. Teichtweier, *Die Sundenlehre des Origenes* (Regensburg: F. Pustet, 1958); R. Trevijano Etcheverria, *En lucha contra las Potestades. Exegesis primitiva de Ef. 6, 11–17 hasta Origenes* (Victoriensia: Seminary of Victoria Press, 1968), pp. 151–373; A. Tripolitis, *The Doctrine of the Soul in the Thought of Plotinus and Origen* (Roslyn Heights, N.Y.: Libra, 1978); M. Van Parys, "Unification de l'homme dans le Nom. exégèse de Mt. 18:19–20," *Irenikon*, 50 (1977), 345–358.

30. See *Hom. 3.2 in Jer.*

31. Cf. *Fr. 12 in Jer.*, where Origen quotes I Cor. 3:9ff. See also, with respect to the building, *Fr. 13 in Jer.*

32. *Fr. 70 in Jer.*

33. The important terms, those which appear again and again in Origen's thought of the movements of the soul, are *eikon, nous, logos, sarx, hēgemonikon, pneuma, psyche, dianoetikon* and *soma. eikon* is discussed in the paragraphs to follow in the text. We have already introduced the terms *nous* and *logos*. Both of these terms are difficult to translate, but I have followed what seems the least perilous route, though not always the most helpful to the reader. On the definitions of these terms, I have followed the writings of Crouzel, Dupuis and Corsini. See Dupuis, pp. 64–76, Crouzel, *Connaissance*, pp. 41–45, Corisni, p. 163, n. 48 and p. 53. *Logos*— often translated "reason"—is the mode of participation with the *logos* in man. *nous*, often called "spiritual being" or "mind", I have translated "intellect." It refers to the original condition of all rational beings, man's essence and the fundamental power by which all rational beings spiritually know God.

The *hēgemonikon* is the superior ruling or higher part of the *psyche*; it is also the seat of the "heart" (*kardia*), a word often used as a translation. When it concerns the epistemological and intellectual activity, it is designated as *dianoetikon*. Corsini has indicated the closeness of this view to Stoic usage. See p. 167, n. 52 and p. 692, n. 4. For relevant texts with this usage, see *Jo.* 13.3, 1.25, 1.30, 2.36, 6.2, 6.38, sect. 189, 6.11, 20.36, sect. 333, 20.37, sect. 347, 28.4, sect. 24 and *Fr. 18 in Jo.* In *Hom. 1.14 in Jer.*, God sows the seeds on our "dominant parts." Also, see Blanc, *Commentaire*, I, 354, n. 3, on the connection of "heart" and *hegemonikon*.

The *psyche* is influenced by these powers, but is in itself neutral. Origen sees the *psyche* as midway between the *sarx* (flesh) which is, as we have noted, a condition in which the spiritual activity is negated, and the *pneuma* (spirit). The *pneuma* in man is the force of divine life and power in contrast to animal life, though this distinction is not always clear. See Corsini, p. 776, n. 35 and corresponding texts, especially *Jo.* 32.18. According to Dupuis, pp. 73ff., the spirit is a power which aids and influences the *nous*. See texts supplied in his notes. We will investigate the significance of the spirit in more detail in Chapter V. In *Hom. 20.7 in Jer.*, Origen indicates his accord with Paul that it is the "spirit" in man which "puts to death the deeds of the body." (Rom. 8:13)

Let us summarize Origen's view of the various dimensions of the soul by quoting a couple of statements on the same text, namely, John 1:23ff. In this interpretation, we see Origen using in one paragraph many of the terms we have discussed above.

"Among you stands one whom you do not know." (John 1:26) Giving testimony to the light (John 1:15), John in fact knew that he was the Logos who is God (John 1:1); as such he is present in every being endowed with the logos. And since some hold that the intellectual capacity is in the midst of us, which they call the dominant part, and the Logos by which we are rational beings is there [as well as] he who is the Image of

God by which man was made in the image of God, so John, by showing that the Logos of God is he who is about to come to be baptized by him, says, "Among you. . . ." See *Fr. 18 in Jo.* (497.18–498.1).

Or the words, "There stands among you," may be understood to say, 'In the midst of you men, because you are reasonable beings, stands He who is proved by Scripture to be the sovereign principle in the midst of every body, and so to be present in your heart'. See *Jo.* 6.38 (II.270. sect. 189), trans. A. Menzies, 369A. Cf. also *Jo.* 2.35.

As these texts indicate, terms used by Origen to explain his psychology and anthropology are interrelated and sometimes very close in meaning. In this one commentary, we noted that *logos, soma, eikon, kardia, hegemonikon* and *dianoetikon* are all used. And Origen has related biblical terms (*eikon, logos, kardia*) with philosophical terms (*hegemonikon, dianoetikon*).

34. *Fr. 22 in Jer.*

35. For good being accidental, see *Princ.* 1.6.2, 1.5.3, 1.2.4, *Jo.* 2.18 with Corsini's note, *Comm. in Mt.* 15.10 and *Cels.* 6.44. For evil being accidental, see *Jo.* 20.13.

36. For the classic study of the image in Origen, see Crouzel, *Théologie.* On p. 145, Crouzel gives a rough outline of the process as follows: Creation according to the Image, distortion of the image in the fall, progress of Christian life to bring the image again to resemblance, and final transformation in the glorious image of Christ.

37. Genesis 1:26,27; 5:3; 9:6.

38. According to Laporte, "La chute," 331, Origen often follows the thought of Philo on the image, but in Origen, the Logos is incarnated to restore the image and return it to likeness. For scriptural references, see the number of times Origen uses the scriptural imagery in his interpretations of Gen. 1:26–27 and I Cor. 15:49 in *Biblia Patristica* 3.

39. *Jo.* 20.22 (4.355.9–17). See Blanc, *Commentaire*, IV, 248, n.3 on the meaning of *eikon* here. This and many other texts are discussed in detail by Crouzel, *Théologie*, pp. 182–189.

40. Cf. *Jo.* 20.22, sect. 181, *Jo.* 20.25 sect. 229. See Corsini, p. 214, n. 14 on the meanings of "earthly" and "heavenly" in the *Commentary on John* and other works. Corsini refers to Crouzel's belief that Origen usually connects the image of the earthly not with Adam, but with the devil. Christ comes and replaces the image of the earthly with the image of heavenly. See Crouzel, *Théologie*, pp. 182 ff.

41. In *Hom. 2.1 in Jer.*, sinners have the image of the earthly, and those who have changed have the image of the heavenly. We should note that here as in many other texts the movement or lack of movement is entirely up to man. No one can snatch us away from God. For example, see *Hom. 18.3 in Jer.*

42. *Hom. 13.4 in Gen.* (6.119.26–27; 120.3–5). In *Hom. 5.14 in Jer.*, a similar image describes how we must circumcise the foreskin over the heart, a foreskin which is inborn because by nature we are now children of wrath. (Cf. Eph. 2:3, Jer. 4:4) Also in *Hom 11.6 in Jer.*, we begin as a dark waistcloth of the earth which must be purified. As Crouzel, *Théologie*, p. 106, n. 170, notes, man is also compared to the image of a statue in *Cels.* 8.17.

43. *Jo.* 20.22, sect. 181.

44. *Princ.* 3.6.1 (5.280.12–14), trans. Butterworth*, p. 245. See Crouzel and Simonetti, *Traité*, IV, 119–122 on this chapter. They note, 122, n.1, that Plato spoke of the idea of likeness to God in *Theatetus* 176b. It was a idea common among pagans, Jews and Christians, and accords with an idea which we will discuss in more detail below, that is, one can only know and become what one is akin to. On the whole idea of imitation, image and likeness, see the notes of Crouzel and Simonetti, *Traité*, IV, 122–124, notes 1–6.

45. *Jo.* 20.17 (4.349.27–31). See Crouzel, *Théologie*, p. 222.

46. *Sel. in Gen.* 1.26 (PG 12.96B). See Crouzel, *Théologie*, p. 223.

47. The discussion of imitation through acts of virtue is continued in more detail in chapter IV, which concerns the mode of conduct.

48. *Princ.* 2.11.4.

49. *Cels.* 4.85 (II.396.18ff./1.356.15–20), trans. Chadwick, p. 251.

50. See, for example, *Jo.* 1.37 and 2.15. We will be discussing the modes of the Logos below. Fundamental studies to consult include: L. Bargeliotes, "Origen's Dual Doctrine of God and Logos," *Theologia*, 43 (1972), 202–212; M. Harl, *Origène et la fonction révèlatrice du Verbe Incarné*; W. Kelber, *Die Logoslehre von Heraklit bis Origenes* (Stuttgart: Urachhaus, 1976); A. Lieske, *Die Theologie der Logosmystik bei Origenes* (Münster: Aschendorff, 1938); D. Pazzini, *In principio era la Logos. Origene e il prologo del vangelo di Giovanni* (Brescia: Paideia, 1983).

On participation with Logos, see particularly Crouzel, *Connaissance*, pp. 508–513, Dupuis, pp. 110–125, Balas's article in *Origeniana*, and Gruber, *Wesen*, pp. 306–322.

51. See *Fr. 19 in Jer.*, *Fr. 20 in Jer.* and *Jo.* 13.42. This latter text also indicates that the obstacle to this communication is passion.

52. *Princ.* 4.4.2 (III.406.77–79/5.352.2–3), trans. Butterworth, p. 316.

53. For example, Origen writes, according to *Hom. 5.6 in Jer.*, that Christ "rules my sense faculties." See also *Fr. 19 in Jer.*, where the Logos nourishes every rational movement.

54. Cf. *Hom. 5.6 in Jer.*, *Hom. 14.10 in Jer.*, *Jo.* 1.37, 2.3 and 19.6. See especially Corsini's notes, p. 209, n. 12 and p. 193, n. 83.

55. *Fr. 45 in Jo.* Indeed man can even be indifferent to it. See *Jo.* 20.39, 20.25.

56. Cf. *Jo.* 13.41 and 19.12, sect. 78.

57. In *Princ.* 3.1.3.

58. *Mart.* 47 (1.43.5–8), trans. J. O'Meara*, *Origen — Prayer/Exhortation to Martyrdom* (ACW 19; Westminster, Maryland: Newman, 1954), p. 191.

59. *Hom. 1.13 in Gen.* (6.15.7–8, 11–13).

60. *Fr. 14 in Jer.* (3.204.28–205.2).

61. A few of the basic studies useful in understanding redemption are: Alcain, *Cautiverio*; F. Bertrand, *Mystique de Jésus chez Origène* (Paris: Aubier, 1951); J. Papagno, "Flp. 2, 6–11 en la cristologia y soteriologia de Origenes," *Burgenese collectanea scientifica* (Burgos), 17, no. 1 (1976), 395–429; E. Schendel, *Herrschaft und Unterwerfung Christi* (Tübingen: Mohr, 1971).

62. For a discussion of the meaning of the *epinoia*, see Corsini, p. 173, n. 59, Dupuis, pp. 245–247, Gruber, pp. 241–267.

63. The Docetics were a group of early Christians who belived that Christ was never really human, but only "appeared" to be; hence the name "Docetic", which comes from the Greek "to appear."

64. *Jo.* 10.6 (II.396. sect. 23; 398. sect. 25, 26). Cf. also *Hom. 14.6 in Jer.* on the human dimension of Jesus. See studies by Bertrand, *Mystique de Jésus* (Paris: Aubier, 1951) and M. Eichinger, *Die Verklärung Christi bei Origenes* (Vienna: Herder, 1969).

65. *Hom. 14.6 in Jer.* (112.11–13).

66. In an interesting passage, Origen writes that actually the Holy Spirit was introduced for this task, but he could not endure it. So the Saviour was sent. See *Jo.* 2.11, 329B.

67. *Hom. 14.9 in Jer.* (114.10).

68. *Hom. 7.3 in Jer.* (54.28–31). Cf. also *Hom. 15.4 in Jer.*, where Origen says that Christ came for human life and took up a body on behalf of men.

69. *Hom. 14.5 in Jer.* (110.27–111.2).

70. *Jo.* 13.37 (III.158.13).

71. *Jo.* 13.37 (III.160.31–33).

72. Cf. *Jo.* 13.36, which discusses how the will of the Son and the will of the Father are one.

73. See Alcain's analysis of death, pp. 55–56, 101–112. Gruber, p. 24, points out that just as life, death has three aspects: good, bad, indifferent, and he cites *Comm. in Rom.* 6.6 (PG 14:1068A–1069A) to support this. Death is bad when the soul is far from God, the effect of sin and the work of the devil. Gruber's discussion of death is on pp. 24–33.

74. *Hom. 8.1 in Jer.* (56.28–30). For other texts on the Satan-Adam-Christ triangle, and the pattern of death to life, see *Jo.* 1.20, 20.35, 20.39, sect. 365, *Comm. in Mt.* 13.9.

75. Cf. *Jo.* 1.31 (I.170.sect.227), trans, Menzies*, 316A: "For since we were not helped by his pre-eminent life, sunk as we were in sin, he came down into our deadness in order that, he having died to sin—we, bearing about in our body the dying of Jesus—might then receive that life of his which spans the ages. For those who always carry about in their body the dying of Jesus shall obtain the life of Jesus also, manifested in their bodies."

In the translation of *proegoumenos* (pre-emiment), we follow Blanc rather than Menzies who has "original." Corsini has "principale."

76. The point of *Hom. 11.2 in Jer.* (79.12–80.5).

77. *Jo.* 1.32 (I.174,176. sect's 233–235), trans. Menzies*, 317A. We should note, in this text concerned with the sacrificial lamb, that Christ not only offers himself, but he also pleads with the Father on behalf of man, begging him to free us from the captivity of the devil. See *Hom. 14.11 in Jer.* On the ransom, see also *Fr. 58 in Jer.* See Alcain's discussion of the devil and Christ's sacrifice, as well as the effect on man, on pp. 257–280.

78. *Cels.* 4.3 (II.190.5–13), trans, Chadwick, p. 185. Cf. also *Cels.* 4.17.

79. For the views in this paragraph, see especially *Cels.* 4.15–16. The quote is found in *Cels.* 4.15 (II.218.3–4), trans. Chadwick, p. 193.

80. For Origen's teachings on evil and the devil, we have consulted primarily Hal Koch, *Pronoia und Paideusis. Studien über Origenes und sein Verhältnis zum Platonismus* (Berlin: W. De Gruyter, 1932), especially Chapter VII on theodicy: G. Teichtweier, *Die Sündenlehre des Origenes* (Regensburg:

F. Pustet, 1958), passim; J. Alcain, *Cautiverio y redencion del hombre en Origenes* (Bilbao: U. de Deusto, 1973), S. Bettencourt, *Doctrina ascetica Origenis* (Rome: Vatican Library, 1945), especially Chapter VI; E. Mühlenberg, "Das Verständnis des Bösen in neuplatonischen und frühchristilicher Sicht," *Kerygma und Dogma*, 15 (1969), 226–238; J. Gross, *Enstehungsgeschichte des Erbsundedogmas von der Bibel bis Augustinus*, 1, (Munich: Reinhardt, 1960). The main criterion has been, as we discuss in the section on textual methodology, the texts cited.

81. *Hom. 1.14 in Jer.* (13.14–18). Origen continues the comparison of the work of the devil and the work of God in *Hom. 1.15 in Jer.* There Origen uses the idea of a building, one built on sand, the other on rock (cf. Mt. 7:25–26). Similar are the images found in *Hom 1.16 in Jer.* and *Hom. 1.7 in Jer.* All of these texts find the devil's work preceding that of God, and God coming into the soul and uprooting the devil's work.

82. *Hom. 20.7 in Jer.* (188.17–22).

83. The terminology is actually used in *Fr. 30 in Jer.* (214.21–23).

84. Cf. *Fr. 18 in Jer.* (206.29–30).

85. *Hom. 20.3 in Jer.* (181.27–182.12).

86. *Princ.* 2.9.2 (I.354.45–47), trans. Butterworth, p. 130. Butterworth's translation of *effici* needs to be compared to Crouzel and Simonetti, "tomber," and Görgemanns and Karpp, *Origenes— Vier Bücher von den Prinzipien* (Darmstadt: Wissenschaftliche Buchgesellschaft, 1976), "geraten."

Crouzel and Simonetti write, II, 214, 8, "Cette conception platonicienne domine la cosmologie et l'anthropologie d'Origène." See also Koch, pp. 107–109, and his acccompanying texts. Blanc, *Commentaire*, I, 266, n. 2, writes: "Face au dualisme de la gnose, les écrivains ecclésiastiques garderont cette définition du mal."

87. *Jo.* 2.13 (I.270.SECT. 99), trans. Menzies*, 331A. I have followed Corsini's and Blanc's translation of *ouk on* (non-being) here. See particularly Corsini's useful note on this passage, p. 229, n. 26, in which he indicates the philosophical background to Origen's ideas. There he points out three fundamental ways Origen explains evil: as accidental, as a lacking in good, and as without subsistence. Origen, he adds, does not seem preoccupied with physical evil, but rather with moral evil. Also see Blanc, *Commentaire*, I, 266, notes 1 and 2, who also explores the philosophical background to Origen's views in this section.

88. Though God allows its earthly existence in order to manifest the greatness of virtue. See *Fr. 3 in Jo.*

89. *Jo.* 2.13.

90. *Cels.* 6.43 (III.286.38–40), trans. Chadwick, p. 360. Borret, III, 286, n. 1, sees have an allusion to Plato, *Phaedrus* 246bc. Note also the cosmic struggle and Antichrist image in *Cels.* 6.45.

91. *Cels.* 6.44 (III.286.6–7;288.13–14), trans. Chadwick, p. 361. See also *Princ.* 2.9.6 and *Cels.* 7.69.

92. *Cels.* 6.45 (III.290.13 ff.), trans. Chadwick, pp. 362–363. Borret, *Celse*, I, 353, n. 3, notes that the phrase *en to kata ton iesoun nooumeno anthropo* refers to a formula for Origen. He translates: ". . . dans l'homme que l'esprit discerne en Jésus. . ." in contrast to Chadwick's "in the human nature of Jesus".

93. Included also in the objective view of the devil and evil is how Christ ransomed us from the devil. It is mentioned, for example, in *Fr. 58 in Jer.* (226.28–29).

While this text provides one example of how Origen viewed the "extremes" of the good and evil, we need to point out that a fundamental dualism as it existed in Gnosticism and some contemporary philosophy is rejected constantly by Origen. See Teichtweier, pp. 37–39.

94. See *Fr. 29 in Jer.* (213.25–214.3) and *Cels.* 6.44.

95. There is a continual interchange and comparison in Origen's thought between the images of, and what concerns, the earthly, and images of the heavenly. For example, in his thoughts on Jer. 51:2–22, in *Fr. 68 in Jer.* (230.23–231.30), concerning the kind of incense the Lord accepts, Origen writes that evil beings swarm around *earthly* incense, "blood and sacrificial odors," while Christ seeks for incense of the mind, if we pray "from righteousness." Moreover, according to this fragment, God sometimes can no longer bear the "odor" of evil of those who offend him, those who will not change. See also *Jo.* 2.5 and 20.22, sect. 181.

96. Cf. *Jo.* 20.13–15, 22–23, for a complete picture of the polarity, in Origen's interpretation of John 8:41 ff., and *Hom. 15.5 in Jos.* (7.390.11–15). On the devil in general, see Corsini, p. 146. n. 30, particularly the important texts which he lists. Corsini mentions, with respect to the contribution of the *Commentary on John,* that the devil is sometimes seen there as one who is evil, not inherently, but because of his bad judgment, his poor use of his free choice. For the devil being prince over evil doctrines, see *Fr. 13 in Jer.* (204.14).

97. *Hom. 9.4 in Jer.* (70.8–10).

98. Origen uses many biblical images for evil and the devil, but he is especially fond of the kings of Assyria, Egypt and Babylon because of their parts in the captivities and slavery of God's people. Cf. *Fr. 28 in Jer., Fr. 36 in Jer., Fr. 58 in Jer.* Another common image for the devil is the "mountain." See *Fr. 41 in Jer.* (219.28–30). For an excellent study of these images, with accompanying texts, see Alcain, *Cautiverio*, Chapter 1.

99. *Hom. 12.4 in Num.* (7.104.88–22). According to M. Ruiz Jurado, "Le concept de 'Monde' chez Origène," *BLE*, 75 (1974), 5, there are a number of senses to *kosmos* in Origen. In this context, he writes, 18, to quit the world means to abandon sin, to purify one's thoughts and deeds.

100. We might add here a reference to Bettencourt's interesting note, p. 92, n. 15, on how the idea of participation, discussed above and to be discussed more in later sections, is applied to the relationship of man and the devil/evil. A soul in participation with the devil is in an irrational condition.

101. Cf. *Fr. 41 in Jer.* (219.28–30).

102. AS in *Hom. 16.9 in Jer.* (141.6–8).

103. *Hom. 12.4 in Num.*

104. *Hom. 17.4 in Jer.* (147.8–9). The text of "through his sinning" is not in all manuscripts, but is found in the Catena of the prophets, and Jerome's translation.

105. *Hom. 17.4 in Jer.* (148.2). Although there is also no middle between sinning and not sinning (cf. *Jo.* 20.13), there are basically, according to Origen, three different types of beings: good, bad and indifferent. See *Jo.* 20.25, sect. 224 and Corsini, p. 648, n. 39, who indicates that this is a Stoic distinction.

106. Jer. 4:7 I Pet. 5:8–9, Ps. 9:30, Ps. 103:20–21, Ps. 104: 20–21.

107. See *Hom. 5.16–17 in Jer.* – and *Fr. 28 in Jer.* In *Fr. 30 in Jer.* (214.9 ff.), the devil is a "hammer" (in line with Jer. 27:23) who pounds on us through varied temptations; and in *Fr. 54 in Jer.* (225.17–18), it is the devil who "drags us away."

108. *Hom. 17.2 in Jer.* (144.17–19).

109. A "demon," according to Origen, is one of those "who has fallen away from God." See *Cels.* 7.69.

110. On the demons and their powers, we have especially followed Teichweier, pp. 102–107; Bettencourt, *Doctrina*, passim; Blanc, "L'angélologie d'Origène," *Studia Patristica*, 14 (1976), 79–110, and Blanc, *Commentaire*, IV, 20–23. See *Hom. 1.6 in Jos.* (294.18–21, 22–23). A. Jaubert, ed., *Origène—Homélies sur Josué* (SC 71; Paris: Cerf, 1960), pp. 65–67, notes the exterior influence of demons, but she also points to an interior influence where demons work in man to nourish sin. The issue is for Origen is to be on guard for these impulses and passions. See *Jo.* 32.2, where the devil attacks those who do not guard their hearts.

111. *Fr. 40 in Jer.* (218.20–21).

112. Cf. *Hom. 5.2 in Jer.*

113. See also *Hom. 18.3 in Jer.*, where Origen explicitly states that we fall due to our own negligence.

114. *Hom. 2.1 in Jer.* (16.23–24).

115. *Ibid.*

116. Cf. *Fr. 25 in Jer.* (210.25–211.4).

117. *Princ.* 3.2.2 (III.158.94–97;160.118–121/247.7–9, 25–28; 132–134/248.2–4)), trans. Butterworth, pp. 213,214. Similarly, in *Hom. 5.7 in Jer.*, it is how our thoughts and acts are cultivated which determine their moral worth.

118. As mentioned above, in an extant fragment on Jer. 25:14–16, Origen lists the principal things which arouse the soul: desire, fear, pleasure and pain. Origen indicates that the Ailamites, who abandoned God, were influenced by these things. From this view, we may conclude that the devil especially encourages movements of any of these passions. For all excesses lead away from God and lead to the devil's captivity. On the four principal things, see *Fr. 25 in Jer.* (210.25–211.4).

119. *Hom. 12.4 in Num.* (105.15–16).

120. *Hom. 12.4 in Num.* (105.18). See Origen's essay on pride in *Hom. 12.7–8 in Jer.* and *Fr. 45 in Jer.*

121. *Fr. 37 in Jer.* (217.25–218.15).

122. *Hom. 1.3 in Jer.* (3.3–4).

123. *Hom. 1.4 in Jer.* (3.15–21). A paradox concerning the devil is that he is often used by God

to convert men, as in *Hom. 19.14 in Jer.* (171.1–10). According to Origen, this was Paul's view in I Tim. 1:20. Also see I Cor. 5:3–5 and Jer. 20:4.

124. *Hom. 4.5 in Jer.* (28.3–20). We see here that Origen considers also a corporate evil in the people of the ancient Jews. But he applies the same test to the Christians, and finds many of their assemblies (*ekklesia*) filled with evil. See *Hom. 14.15 in Jer.*

125. *Hom. 12.12 in Jer.* (99.12–15). See also *Fr. 25 in Jer.* We might note that Origen also calls the Lord Jesus the "mountain" (regarding Gen. 19:17) in *Hom. 13.3 in Jer.* In *Hom. 12.12 in Jer.* also, the angels, prophets and apostles are the bright mountains.

126. *Hom. 13.2 in Jer.* (104.11–18). See the section on repentance in Chapter V.

127. *Princ.* 3.2.5(253.19–21), trans. Butterworth, p. 219. The issue of free will, discussed in some detail in Chapter II, is evident in this text. Crouzel. *Virginité et mariage selon Origène* (Paris: Aubier, 1963), p. 174, in commenting on this text, notes that it and other passages have a semipelagian aspect to them, but other passages, such as *Hom. 13.4 in Gen.* (119.24 ff.) seem to counterbalance them by presenting man as the origin of evil impulses, and God as the author of all that is good. Früchtel, "Freiheitsproblematik," 316, sees such a passage as *Princ.* 3.2.5 as the true thinking of Origen. Without the help of God, the powers of evil would overcome man.

The extent of the help, it seems to me, is the concern here. Though man may need help, he also needs to contribute through his own will to overcome evil. The difficulty, as Crouzel notes, is that Origen's thought on major issues and especially areas which later became controversial needs to be considered as a whole and not through the eyes of only one passage. We must try not to judge Origen in light of the subsequent history of consideration of free will and grace in which he was not alive to participate or respond.

128. *Hom. 7.3 in Jer.* (54.26–31).

129. *Hom. 9.1 in Jer.* (65.12–16). In *Fr. 54 in Jer.* (225.19–21), Origen writes that through Christ, death will have no "sting." (Cf. I Cor. 15:55)

130. Actually there are three levels of embodiment for the Logos in the rational creation, namely, in the incarnation (Jesus Christ), in rational being, and in inspiration (scripture). These are the only true extensions of the Logos. All others are agents. See R. B. Williams, "Origen's Interpretation of the Gospel of John," Diss., University of Chicago, 1966, p. 57 ff.

We will not be discussing the Holy Spirit's role in this part, since the role of the Spirit in conversion will be considered in Chapter V. We might note, however, that the Holy Spirit for Origen is the source of sanctification and regeneration, and is connected especially with baptism and spiritual gifts. According to *Jo.* 2.18, the Holy Spirit receives instruction from the Logos. Particularly succinct sections on the nature and role of the Holy Spirit, beside the section devoted to him in *On First Principles*, are found in *Jo.* 2.10–11(6) and *Jo.* 6.33(17). On the functions of the Logos and Holy Spirit, see especially J. Rius–Camps, *El dinamismo trinitario en la divinizacion de los seres racionales segun Origenes* (Rome: Pontifical Institute of Oriental Studies, 1970), pp. 17–79, and Corsini, *Commento*, p. 222, n. 20.

131. Crouzel, *Théologie*, p. 211, clearly presents in a summary what we shall view as the three modes or dimensions of conversion. He writes: "D'abord pour Origène la purification de l'âme n'est que le début du progrès spirituel, qui s'accomplira d'une manière plus positive par la pratique des vertus. Ensuite et surtout, cette conversion est affaire de grâce, elle n'est possible que par la Rédemption du Christ, et son action qui se poursuit dans l'âme." Let us add to this summary that the interrelationship of the modes (purification, practice of virtues, grace) must be stressed.

132. Studies consulted on Origen's Logos teaching include: M. Harl, *Origène*; R. Gögler, *Zur Theologie des biblischen Wortes bei Origenes* (Düsseldorf; Patmos, 1963); J. 1963); J. Rius-Camps, *El dinamismo trinitario en la divinzacion de los seres racionales segun Origenes* (Rome: Pontifical Institute of Oriental Studies, 1970); H. De Lubac, *Histoire et esprit. L'intelligence de l'ecriture d'après Origène* (Paris: Aubier, 1950), Chapter VIII; A. Lieske, *Die Theologie der Logosmystik bei Origenes* (Münster: Aschendorff, 1938); W. Kelber, *Die Logoslehre von Heraklit bis Origenes* (Stuttgart: Urachhaus, 1958); H. Koch, *Pronoia und Paideusis. Studien üder Origenes und sein Verhältnis zum Platonismus* (Berlin: De Gruyter, 1932), Chapter IV. We are not including here those works which are primarily devoted to Origen's interpretation of scripture, such as the works of Caspary, Hanson, Caballero Cuesta and Daniélou. See bibliography.

133. For example, this is the finding of H. De Lubac, *Histoire*, p. 336. With respect to the distinction of the Spirit and the Logos in scripture, R. Gögler, *Zur Theologie des biblischen Wortes bei Origenes* (Düsseldorf: Patmos, 1963), p. 285, writes: "Der Logos als Ebenbild des Vaters vermittelt Gott, aber das Pneuma gibt den Zugang zum Logos frei und führt uns ein in seine hohen und tiefen

Geheimnisse." For scripture as an instrument of conversion, see also Aubin, *Le problème*, pp. 143–147. Aubin, basing his view partly on *Cels*. 4.53 (326.2–20), writes, p. 144, "Bref, les Ecritures sont le grand instrument par lequel se fait la conversion." As Aubin continues, this view is accurate as long as we understand that the Logos and Christ are assumed to be the key instruments of scripture.

134. *Cant*. 3.12 (212.1–5), trans. R. P. Lawson*, *Origen—The Song of Songs* (ACW 26; Westminster, Maryland: Newman, 1957), p. 223. The connection of the Logos and scripture is commonplace in Origen's thought. For examples, however, see *Hom*. *5.15–16 in Jer*. and also *Hom*. *10.1 in Jer*., where Origen preaches that God teaches through the scripture. See Gögler, pp. 160–164, on the workings of the Logos in scripture. *Cant*. 3.12 is also used by Gögler in this context.

135. See above in the section "On the Meaning of the Body."

136. *Philoc*. 6.1 (from *Comm. in Mt*. 2) (308.11 ff./12.5.10–14), trans. Patrick*, 413A. See the interpretation of these texts by M. Harl, *Origène—Philocalie, 1-20 sur les Écritures* (SC 302; Paris: Cerf, 1983), pp. 313 ff, and on Origen's view of Ecclesiastes, see Sandro Leanza, *L'esegei di Origene al libro dell'Ecclesiaste* (Reggio Calbria: Edizioni Parallelo, 1975), especially pp. 48, 71, 89, 102, 103, 107, 109.

137. *Philoc*. 6.2 (from *Comm. in Mt*. 2) (310.17–21/12.5.27–30), trans. Patrick*, 413B.

138. Although we will be discussing the role of the teacher in more detail in Chapter IV, it is worthwhile to note here that the power of scripture is also, according to Origen, dependent on the interpreter. The Logos works through the "fishermen" who throw out upon believers their tightly woven net, the books of scripture. See *Hom. 16.1 in Jer*.

139. Cf. K. Pichler, *Streit um das Christentum. Der Angriff des Kelsos und die Antwort des Origenes* (Frankfurt: P. Lang, 1980), pp. 236 ff., and Borret, *Celse*, V, 207ff.

140. *Hom. 4.6 in Jer*. (29.22–28). A similar passage is found at the end of *Hom. 4.5 in Jer*. In the same light, see *Jo*. 13.5–6, where Origen indicates that scripture is fundamentally an introduction and holds the basic principles to lead one to Jesus.

One word about the context of the quoted text and the translation "the true conversion" (*he alethōs epistrophē*): The homily concerns fundamentally the relationship between ourselves and Judah, in accordance with the scripture, Jer. 3:6–11, and how Israel and Judah refused to convert even after being exhorted. In this homily then Origen asks: Are we like Judah? In 4.1 he clarifies that Judah did not turn to God with a whole heart, in falseness, in a pretense. Due to their apostasy, 4.2 concerns how Israel was given a bill of divorce and the Gentiles were offered salvation. 4.3 indicates that we have become like sinful Judah (who followed Israel in her sinning), and that many of us may lose election. Hence, in 4.4–5, Origen, like Jeremiah, exhorts us to repent and convert, especially stating that we need to have at the forefront of our minds what happened in those old times so that it does not happen to us again. Then in 4.6, Origen summarizes the point of his exposition by stating that we not only need to turn, but to turn fully and not in pretense as Judah did. Hence, when Origen uses the word *alethōs* here, he is contrasting the pretense of Judah's conversion and a conversion with a full and sincere heart.

141. *Hom. 5.8 in Jer*.

142. *Hom. 5.9 in Jer*. (38.32–34, 39.7–9).

143. See *Princ*. 1.1.2 (I.94.58–62). For other texts on this theme, see Crouzel and Simonetti, *Traité*, II, 22, n. 9.

144. We have, of course, discussed the issue of free will in Part II, in our discussion of apokatastasis. We need always to be cautious in our understanding of freedom in Origen. Freedom is so tightly built into his viewpoint as a gift of God that not even the machinery of God himself wishes to undo it.

Früchtel, "Freiheitsproblematik," 317, believes that the cooperation lies in the fact that grace enables the interior man to exercise his freedom, and reach perfection. A writer who finds Origen's idea of God's plan more deterministic is H. Holz, "Über den Begriff des Willens und der Freiheit bei Origenes," *Neue Zeitschrift für systematische Theologie*, 12 (1970), 81–84. In light of *Princ*. 3.2.3 and *Princ*. 3.2.7, Holz believes that God controls the direction of all things, even the degree to which one is tempted. Holz also believes that the nature of Origen's concept of God logically demands that God control all things toward a certain end, which he alone knows.

Since such a viewpoint without qualification would perhaps make conversion also deterministic—in which case conversion has little or no meaning (i.e. the Gnostic systems)—we need to clarify these texts as we understand them. While 3.2.3 does state that God controls the extent each is tempted,

3.2.3 also states that we must choose through our free will whether we will use the strength given us by God to conquer the temptations. 3.2.7 does not state that all things happen under God's *active* control, but that nothing happens without God's knowledge and permission. In this sense, as *Princ.* 3.1.24 states, while we can do nothing outside God's knowledge, God's knowledge does not compel us.

145. *Cels.* 8.72 (IV.340.18ff./289.4-9), trans. Chadwick*, p. 507. We see here another implication of universal salvation.

146. Crouzel, *Connaissance*, p. 404, based on several texts (i.e. *Philocalia* 10.2 [368.7ff./197.15,30]), writes, "Tout cela est fort laborieux: comprendre l'Écriture selon le sens de l'Esprit, comparer les réalités spirituelles entre elles, discuter la lettre dans le moindre détail, interpréter la Bible de facon digne de Dieu." Similarly, in *Philoc.* 10.2 (370.22ff.), Origen exhorts his people to blame themselves, not the scripture, if the text is difficult. See Harl, *Philocalie*, pp. 374-376. With respect to the need for help, Origen requests help for himself in *Jo.* 10.39.

147. *Hom. 18.4 in Jer.* (154.14). However, every soul comes to the worship of God in scripture through the bodily sense, and then, with the help of the Logos, moves to the spiritual. See *Jo.* 13.9 on John 4:17.

148. *Philoc.* 1.11 (from *Princ.* 4.2.4) (III.310.111-115; 312.121-122/312.7-11; 15-313.1), trans. Butterworth*, pp. 275-276. See the note by Crouzel and Simonetti, IV, 181, n. 33 on these different levels. They point out, in accordance with *Hom. 5.1 in Lev.* that Origen sometimes says the spiritual sense is also for those who are making some progress toward maturity.

Some, like the ancient Jews, are unable to see the "hidden" message in scripture. See *Hom. 12.13 in Jer.* For an excellent example of what Origen means by an allegorical interpretation, see *Jo.* 10.28 on Mt. 21: 1-13. For the three senses of scripture, see Hanson, pp. 235-258, though Hanson is not sympathetic to Origen's method or intentions. He writes, p. 258, Origen's scriptural method ". . . was largely a facade or a rationalization whereby he was able to read into the Bible what he wanted to find there." A contrasting viewpoint is expressed by H. de Lubac, *Histoire et esprit*, pp. 92-194, who basically discusses two senses, the historical and the spiritual. See especially his conclusions, pp. 377-379, where he states that Origen's approach developed from an inspired and pious Christian who took seriously that man's spiritual life was always at stake. See also Daniélou, *Origen*, pp. 133-199, and his later article, "Origène comme Exégète de la Bible," *Studia Patristica*, 1 (1958), 280ff., as well as M. Wiles, "Origen as Biblical Scholar," in *The Cambridge History of the Bible*, Vol. 1 (1970), 454ff.

149. *Philoc.* 1.11 (from *Princ.* 4.2.4) (III.312.122-125/313.1-4), trans. Butterworth, p. 276.

150 Cf. *Jo.* 13.9, which indicates that all begin with the bodily sense.

151. *Philoc.* 1.15 (from *Princ.* 4.2.8) (III.334.259-262/320.15-321.2), trans. Butterworth, p. 285. Origen recognizes, as evident in *Philoc. 1.20 (from Princ.* 4.2.5) (314.6-7), that not every scriptural passage has a believable bodily interpretation.

152. *Hom. 5.1 in Lev.* (334.4-7).

153. As M. Wiles, "Origen as Biblical Scholar," in *The Cambridge History of the Bible*, I, 469, mentions, Origen does not always limit himself to three dimensions, but recognizes that "growth in Christian maturity is not a matter of two, or even three, stages." Nevertheless, Origen himself generally only uses two dimensions, the literal and the allegorical (spiritual/figurative). For example, see *Hom. 1.7 in Jer.* In *Hom. 12.7 in Jer.,* on Jer. 13:15, Origen points out that there are two levels: one which requires interpretation and one which is obvious and requires no interpretation. On the use of two levels, see R. B. Williams, "Origen's Interpretation of the Gospel of John," pp. 30, 41, 44-45. He believes it is by far the most important model for Origen. Crouzel and Simonetti, *Traité*, also note, III, 182, n. 34, that the use of the three senses is more theoretical than practical for Origen.

154. For a discussion of this kinship, see above in this chapter. See also, for example, *Hom. 5.6 in Jer.*.

155. *Cels.* 6.67 (III.346.14-21/137.15-21), trans. Chadwick, p. 382.

156. We considered how the willingness of man and his use of the rational faculty determine, to a great extent, his success in the control of the effects and distraction of *aisthesis* and the control of the images which the senses engender. Earlier in this section, it was noted that the understanding and power of scripture is also, to an extent, dependent on these factors.

157. *Hom. 9.6 in Lev.* (428.15-18, 20-26).

158. *Hom. 2.2 in Jer.* (18.9-12).

159. *Hom. 9.6 in Lev.* (428.28-429.3).

160. *Philoc.* 12.1 (from *Hom. 20.1 in Jesu Nave*) (388.11–390.21; 24–28/416.21–417.23, 26–29), trans. G. Lewis*, *The Philocalia of Origen* (Edinburgh: T & T Clark, 1911), p. 55. On the divine power of words in general, for those who have destroyed the evil elements and have faith, see *Hom. 1.16 in Jer.*

161. *Philoc.* 12.2 (from *Hom. 20.3 in Jesu Nave*) (329.23–26/420.26–30), trans. Lewis*, p. 56. In *Hom. 1.4 in Jer.*, "hearing" the message of repentance and conversion in the words of the prophetic law, Apostles and Jesus can save us from a captivity to the devil. In *Hom. 18.8 in Jer.*, responding to the words of the prophet (Jer. 18:11) can convert us.

162. We should note that the role of the teacher/priest in the church is discussed in Chapter IV. Origen also believes that the Logos and the Holy Spirit dwell in the *true* priest and teacher of the church. For example, see *Hom. 10.1 in Jer.*
Studies consulted on the church include: G. Bardy, *La théologie de l'eglise de saint Irénée au concile de Nicée* (Paris: Cerf, 1947); J. Chênevert, *Léglise dans le commentaire d'Origène sur le Cantique des Cantiques* (Paris: Desclée, 1969); H. Vogt, *Das Kirchenverständnis des Origenes* (Vienna: Böhlau, 1974); J. Rius-Camps, *op. cit.*; H. Crouzel, *Virginité et mariage selon Origène* (Paris: Desclée, 1963), pp. 15–46; G. Sgherri, *Chiesa e sinagoga nelle opere di Origene* (Milano: Università Cattolica del Sacro Cuore, 1982); J. Losada, "La Iglesia kosmos en Origenes," *Miscellanea Commillas*, 51 (1959), 33–112.

163. Vogt, *Das Kirchenverständnis*, p. 271, commenting on *Princ.* 4.2.4 (312.5ff.), where Origen clarifies how each level of scripture applies to different condition of the churchgoers, writes, "Die Kirche findet alles, was sie sucht, in der Schrift. Die heiligen Schriften ihrerseits sind zum Zweck der Erbauung der Kirche geschrieben."

164. *Cant.* 2.8 (157.13–16), trans. Lawson, p. 149. Cf. Chênevert, p. 160 on this text.

165. For the fall of the church, see *Comm. in Mt.* 14.17. Vogt, *Das Kirchenverständnis*, pp. 205–207, on the basis of *Cant.* 2.8, also draws the connection between the church and the pre-existent community. On p. 207 he writes: "Die Kirche ist also nichts anderes als die auf dem Wege zur ursprünglichen Einheit voranschreitende Menschheit." Vogt also notes, p. 206, n. 67, that the view of G. Bardy, *La théologie de l'église*, II, 146, that the earthly church is an image of the heavenly church is "gute moderne Theologie," not the thought of Origen. According to Chênevert, p. 160, the fact that the Church becomes the body of Christ on earth is a new element.

166. Aubin, *Le problème*, basing his argument on *Hom. 4.6 in Jer.* and *Mart.* 9, also notes such a reciprocal conversion in Origen. On p. 146, he connects the communal aspect of conversion with the practice of virtue required for understanding the spiritual sense of scripture. See p. 138 for his discussion of reciprocal conversion.

167. In *Jo.* 6.59, to be discussed below, this is affirmed.

168. *Cant.* 3.13 (218.28–219.1), trans. Lawson, p. 232. In his commentary on this text, Chênevert, *L'Église*, p. 245, also notes that the church is considered distributively. With respect to the church as the "souls of believers," Chênevert points out that the key to salvation of the church, as in *Cant.* 2.8 (142.22–25), lies in the way each of the individual souls knows itself. For then it will realize the beauty and blessedness of its original pre-existent state. Finally, in passages concerned with the church, such as *Cels.* 8.19 (237.1–2), Chênevert notes, pp. 9–10, that Origen seems to be more interested in the individual soul's relationship to the Logos than in "ecclesiology."

169. *Cels.* 6.48 (III.300.14–21/119.27–120.5), trans. Chadwick*, p. 365. Cf. also *Jo.* 10.35 where Origen writes, following I Pet. 2:5 and Ephes. 2:20, that the church is like a structure, built up by the saints and based on the foundation of the Apostles and prophets, with Christ as the cornerstone. See also *Jo.* 10.39 on how the church is the body of Christ and we are assigned a place according to our work here on earth.

170. *Comm. in Mt.* 14.17 (325.27–326.15, 18–27), trans. Patrick, 506B–507A.

171. Vogt, *Das Kirchenverständnis*, pp. 245ff., discusses the meaning of the "temple of God" in Origen in much detail. On the basis of *Cels.* 8.19 (236.19ff.) and other texts, he notes, pp. 246–247, the link between the earthly body and the life of Christ as the temple, the house of God which the believer helps build, and that place where he can experience the goodness of God. Vogt also indicates that Origen implies there is a difference between the house and the temple of God, but the final decision on this point is left to the reader or hearer. Cf. also Sgherri, pp. 414–419, on Church as the temple, house and tabernacle.

172. Cf. *Cels.* 7.66 (216.9–10). Other texts showing the connection between the Logos and the development of virtues are given by Crouzel, *Théologie*, p. 158, and in Chapter IV of this work, where the role of conduct and virtue is discussed in detail.

173. *Cant.* 3.15 (232.25-28), trans. Lawson, p. 251. See also Origen's view of the degeneration of the church in *Jo.* 10.23.

174. *Cant.* 3.15 (232.18-19), trans. Lawson, p. 251.

175. *Comm. in Mt.* 12.10 (86.1-12), trans. based in part on Patrick, 456A. It is clear Origen has based his interpretation of this text on the relationship between Peter and rock in Greek.

We should note also that the world *teleios*, here translated "mature" (though commonly and more loosely translated "perfect"), means for Origen the spiritually mature, those who have "completed" the initial studies in the scripture, are virtuous, and are now contemplating the divine mysteries. Please see Chapter V for a more detailed discussion of this group of Christians, and Crouzel, *Connaissance*, pp. 482-486, where he quotes the text from *Comm. in Rom.* 10.10 (PG 14:1266BC).There Origen sees Paul (Phil. 3:12,15) using the word in two senses: heavenly "perfection" and human "perfection." (Crouzel's translation) However, with respect to conversion—and we consider "maturity" a key member of Origen's conversion vocabulary—we would state that, according to Origen, there are levels of maturity rather than two different "perfects," one level we reach on earth, another in heaven. For all practical purposes in a study devoted to conversion, the word "perfect" implies a state which to Origen only the Father or the Logos possesses. The word "maturity" more accurately allows for the vacillating process of conversion and spiritual growth.

176. *Hom. 5.16, in Jer.* For those outside the church are destroyed by the "lion."

177. *Cant.* 2.6 (153.14-21), trans. Lawson*, p. 143. With respect to the accuracy of the view expressed here on the pattern, we are assuming the fidelity of Rufinus's translation. See Chênevert, pp. 235, n. 2, and 285.

178. The role of the imitation of Christ is considered in some detail in the next dimension in Chapter IV. However, Vogt, *Kirchenverständnis*, p. 220, writes: "Diese eine Seele vermittelt das Leben des Logos an alle Seelen, welche die Kirche bilden. Trotzdem hält Origenes daran fest, dass es sich dabei nicht um rein innerlich-seelische Vorgänge handelt. Sie sind vielmehr durch das Äussere vermittelt, und zwar in doppelter Weise, zunächst durch das Fleisch des Menschgewordenen und dann durch die Tätigkeit der Diener Gottes, d.h. der Glaubensboten."

179. Cf. *Hom. 9.2 in Jer.*

180. *Hom. 1.5 in Gen.* (7.16-19).

181. *Hom. 1.5 in Gen.* (7.11-15). Vogt, *Das Kirchenverständnis*, p. 219, notes that enlightenment by Christ yields different degrees, depending on the individual. This was noted also above.

182. This appears to be the interpretation of Chênevert, *L'Église*, pp. 150-151. See especially p. 151, n. 1, in his commentary on *Cant.* 2.2 (127.6-9). In this context, Origen is discussing the sinful condition of the Ethiopian woman who became Moses' wife. As the text summarizes, the "sun has looked askance at me by reason of my unbelief and disobedience." See *Cant.* 2.2 (127.1-2), trans. Lawson, p. 109.

183. *Cels.* 4.99 (II.434.22-25/373.8-13), trans. Chadwick*, p. 263. Most of the words in this quotation are from Celsus, but turned to Origen's favour. Aubin, *Le problème*, p. 139, sees Origen referring here to the turning back of the All, and not only man, whom, Aubin believes, is more often the object of divine providence in Origen's thought. Indeed the point of this section (4.99) is that God's primary object is man.

184. *Hom. 3.5 in Jesu Nave* (307.9). In *Hom. 5.14 in Jer.*, with respect to the practice of circumcision, Origen notes that no virtue, no self control, or no circumcision is true outside the "rule" and "word" of the church. For, outside the church, these occur for false reasons. Moreover, in *Hom. 7.3 in Jer.*, Origen mentions that anyone who is fettered by the passions, such as greed or gluttony, is outside the church.

185. Cf. *Hom. 3.5 in Jesu nave* (306.26-307.8).

186. *Comm. in Mt.* 10.12 (14.24ff.). Vogt, *Das Kirchenverständnis*, p. 339, interprets the "net" also as the church. He comments on this passage, "Die Geschichte der Kirche währt so lange, bis alle Völker die Bekehrungsmöglichkeit hatten." Cf. also *Fr. 31 in Jer.*, which also concerns a time of selection, but here the vessels of anger (Jer. 27:25) are thrown out in the judgment time. Cf. Sgherri, *Chiesa*, pp. 429-444 on the church and the end-time. Sgherri believes, pp. 442-444, that we must be careful to distinguish in Origen texts which refer to the end of the present age, and those texts which refer to the end of the ages. The question of universality remains open, according to his reading of the texts.

187. *Jo.* 6.59 (II.362.20–29/167.32–168.6), trans. Menzies*, 380A.
188. See Chapter II. Apokatastasis for Origen meant a return to the primitive state, and the terrestrial life is a process of purificiation back toward that state, according to Nautin, *Homélies sur Jérèmie*, I, 160 and II, 108–109, n. 1.
189. More detailed analyses of Origen's angelology can be found in S. T. Bettencourt, *Doctrina ascetica Origenis* (Rome: Libreria Vaticana, 1945), pp. 12–34; C. Blanc, "L'angélologie d'Origène," *Studia Patristica*, 14 (1976), 79–110; Daniélou, *Origen*, pp. 220–245; Daniélou, "The Demonology of Origen," in *Gospel Message and Hellenistic Culture*, trans. J. A. Baker (London: Longman and Todd, 1973), pp. 434–441; Anton Engloff, "Die Engellehre bei Origenes," Diss. Pontificia Universitas Gregoriana, 1941: M. Simonetti, "Due note sull'angelologia origeniana," *Rivista di cultura classica e medioevale*, 4 (1962), 165–208.
190. Angels also influence the spiritual health of the church. See *Jo.* 10.39.
191. *Hom. 13.7 in Num.* (117.15–17). Cf. Also *Hom. 1.6 in Jesu Nave* (294.18–21, 22–23). The angels are not sufficient alone to save man in this struggle with the demons. As Früchtel, "Freiheitsproblematik," 316, points out, grace is the key element.
192. Cf. *Cels.* 5.4 (4.23–26) and *Jo.* 2.23(17) (I.302. *sect.* 145).
193. *Hom. 10.6 in Jer.* (76.19–22). Nautin, *Jérémie*, I, 410, n. 1, points out that Origen, like most of his contemporaries, believed that the stars were living, and that their life came from the presence of an angel in them. See the texts which are offered.
194. See *Jo.* 13.50 (III.212), and Blanc, "Angélologie," II, Part II. Also *Hom. 10.8 in Jer.* and *Hom. 10.6 in Jer.*
195. *Cant.* 3.15 (235.21–236.4), trans. Lawson*. p. 235.
196. Cf. *Jo.* 10.28 (II.490. *sect.* 176ff).
197. See particularly Part II.
198. *Princ.* 3.2.4 (III.170.268–273/251.16–19), trans. Butterworth, p. 217. On the role of free will, grace and foreknowledge in this text and others, see *Jo.* 6.36 (20), SECT. 180–183, which is discussed by Blanc, *Commentaire*, II, 43–45.
199. *Comm. in Mt.* 14.13 (308.20–314.17).
200. Origen says in *Comm. in Rom.* 10.14 (PG 14.1275B/C):

Ego autem per hujusmodi ministerium etiam illud advertendum puto quod est in Psalmis: "Qui facit angelos suos spiritus, et ministros suos flammam ignis," (Ps. 103:4) ut scilicet angelos bonos, spiritus appellaverit tanquam spiritales, eos vero qui praesunt ministeriis poenarum, et flammas peccatoribus parant, ministros flammae ardentis nominaverit.

Text suggested by Blanc, "L'angélologie," 106, n. 13.
201. According to Blanc, 106.
202. *Comm. in Mt.* 14.21 (334.18–32), trans. Patrick, 509A.
203. *Fr. 37 in Jer.* (217.23–28). The word *aniatos* (incurable) does not necessarily mean that the sick one is eternally or permanently incurable, only that he cannot be cured by God's agents. As we have noted above, no evil or sickness, according to Origen, is beyond the healing powers of God himself, even that of the devil. Cf. also *Hom. 13.1 in Jer.*
204. Blanc, "L'angélologie," 106, points out that Origen's treatment of the angels is incomplete. For example, he does not clearly distinguish the roles of the angels now and the roles of the angels in the final days.

Chapter IV.
Developing Good Conduct:
How Does One Come to Act as a Christian?

1. *Hom. 5.2 in Jer.* (32.25–27).
2. Cf. *Hom. 18.1 in Jer.*
3. See, for example, the use of the terms, *poiein, praxis* and *ergon* in *Hom. 12.2 in Jer.*
4. In this light too we might remind ourselves of the statement of Origen quoted above, from *Hom. 9.4 in Jer.*, that Christ generates us in himself according to both thought and deeds.
5. *Hom. 5.7 in Jer.* (37.9–10).

6. *Hom. 5.8 in Jer.* (38.15–19).

7. We need to mention also that both *ergon* and *praxis* can also be used in a negative way. See *Hom. 8.1 in Jer.* and *Hom. 11.2 in Jer.*

8. *Hom. 8.2 in Jer.* (58.8–10).

9. *Fr. 61 in Jer.*

10. See *Jo.* 32.11, *sect.* 127 and *Jo.* 1.37, *sect.* 267.

11. See *Jo.* 32.15, *sect.* 178–179 and *Jo.* 20.13, *sect.* 106.

12. *Hom. 2.3 in Jer., Hom. 12.2 in Jer., Hom. 1.10 in Jer.* and *Hom. 12.11 in Jer.* See also *Hom. 16.5–6 in Jer, Hom. 20.3 in Jer.* and *Hom. 20.9 in Jer.*

13. Aubin, *Le problème,* pp. 153–154, also notes the ethical character of *Against Celsus,* and the influence of Epictetus. However, Aubin notes, "L'argumentation du *Contra Celsum* porte moins sur l'analyse précise de ce qu'entraîne la conversion chrétienne que sur son pouvoir de s'étendre à un grand nombre d'hommes." This dimension is present in *Against Celsus* because of the nature of Origen's task in that work. He is constantly trying to refute Celsus and demonstrate his facts, as Borret, *Celse,* V, 201–245, has so well shown us in his introduction to the work; and what better way than through the morality of the great sages and saints of scripture and the church?

14. *Jo.* 13.33 (III.144.6–7).

15. *Hom. 18.1 in Jer.*

16. See *Hom. 17.2 in Jer.* (II.162.19).

17. From *Cels.* 4.64.

18. *Cels.* 4.64 (II.344.5–12/334.34–335.5), trans. H. Chadwick, p. 235. The word here translated as "perfection" means spiritual maturity. This wavering nature of conversion is stated in a simpler way by Origen in one of his homilies. He writes that just as a wound takes time to heal, so a complete and pure conversion to God also takes time. See *Hom. 5.10 in Jer.* (I.304.27–30).

19. *Hom. 5.7 in Jer.* (37.9–10). See also *Fr. 48 in Jer.* on Jer. 36:4–6, where righteousness generates the children: thoughts and practices. On using the human family in this way, see Schadel, p. 261, n. 41.

20. Though we have continued to discuss the role of freedom at every opportunity, and have assumed that these discussions apply to all areas of spiritual growth and conversion, let us note again that our conduct too is dependent on our own choices. If we turn or fall away in the way we act or in our inner sense of conduct, it is our own negligence of what is good. Cf. *Hom. 18.3 in Jer.*

21. *Jo.* 6.19 (II.206. *sect.* 103/127.29–32), trans. Menzies*, 360A. See Blanc, *Commentaire,* II, 206, n. 4, on this text. She notes that while in some texts (*Jo.* 1.16, *sect.* 91 and 2.36, *sect.* 219) the active life seems to precede the contemplative, it is in contemplation that one receives the power not to sin. (Cf. *Jo.* 20.14, *sect.* 110) Hence, she says, contemplation and action are inseparable in Origen. For W. Völker, *Das Vollkommenheitsideal,* pp. 193–196 and Dupuis, *L'esprit,* p. 163, n. 9, there is also a mutual dependence and inseparability of action and contemplation. Crouzel, *Connaisance,* pp. 375–376, believes that there are two general uses of *theoria* by Origen: as the act itself which is separate from *praxis,* and as the activity resulting from it. The former use, because of its stress upon the contemplative, is more indicative of the third mode. Crouzel also indicates, p. 437, that the action is determined by the contemplation of what one is to do. Such a harmony of action and contemplation is the basic intent of this mode.

22. *Jo.* 1.16 (I.108. *sect.* 94/20.26–21.2), trans. Menzies*, 306A.

23. See footnote 21 above.

24. *Fr. 171 in Lc.* (298.1–4). Text suggested by Blanc.

25. *Cels.* 4.64.

26. *Hom. 2.1 in Ex.* (155.15–18).

27. *Hom. 2.1 in Ex.* (155.28–156.6).

28. Dating according to Borret, *Contre Celse* (SC 227; Paris: Cerf, 1976), V, 129.

29. *Cels.* 3.49 (II.118.15ff./245.22–25, 27–246.2), trans. Chadwick, p. 162. Borret, II.119, uses the word "cultiver" to translate *paideuein* in this text.

30. Cf. also *Fr. 61 in Jer.*

31. *Cels.* 3.51 (II.120.5ff./247.5–9), trans. Chadwick, p. 163. Borret, II, 121, n. 2, offers the following works on Christian initiation to clarify in more detail this passage: K. Rahner, "La doctrine d'Origène sur la Pénitence," *RSR* 37 (1950), 47–97, 252–296, 422–456, especially 422–436, and M. DuJarier, *Les parrainage des adultes aux trois premiers siècles de l'Élise* (Paris: Cerf, 1962), pp. 270–290 on Origen.

32. *Cels.* 3.51 (247.9–12).

33. Borret, III, 186, n. 1, writes: "La conduite qui est un désaveu pratique de la pensée philosophique est souvent blâmée par Origène." Borret offers *Cels.* 6.4, 5.35, and 7.44 as texts which present this view.

34. *Cels.* 6.4 (III.186.4ff./73.17–21), trans. Chadwick, p. 318. The reference to Ascelpius, as Migne noted, is from *Phaedo* 118a. On the comparison of Christianity with Greek philosophy, see H. Crouzel, *Origène et la philosophie* (Paris: Aubier, 1962), especially Chapter 1. For this passage and others similar to it, see Crouzel, p. 97. See also M. Harl, *Origène et la fonction révélatrice du Verbe Incarné* (Paris: Seuil, 1958), pp. 316–318. On p. 317, with *Cels.* 7.46 (198.21–27) as her text, she writes: "Malgré leurs belles proclamations sur Dieu, les philosophes grecs sont restés, par leurs actes, dans la même impiété que leurs contemporains. Ils ont, selon les termes de Paul, 'tenu la vérité captive dans l'injustice.' "

35. *Cels.* 4.26 (II.246.23ff./295.16–25), trans. Chadwick, p. 202.

36. As Origen writes in *Fr. 21 in Jer.*

37. *Cels.* 7.66 (IV.166.1ff./215.18–20, 22–23), trans. Chadwick, p. 449. Crouzel, *Origène et la philosophie* (Paris: Aubier, 1962), p. 100, sums up: "Sur l'idéal moral et religieux du philosophe— l'intellectuel en est une conséquence—la critique d'Origène ne concerne pas tant la moralité ou matérielle, les actes eux-même, que la moralité subjective ou formelle, l'intention qui y préside."

38. *Cels.* 6.2 (II.182.25ff./71.26–72.3, 6–13), trans. Chadwick, p. 317. Gögler, *Zur Theologie*, p. 274, comments on this passage that Origen wants to clarify the source of power of scripture. The power of scripture comes from the spirit of God within the words, not the words themselves. Both Daniélou, *Origen*, pp. 103–104, and Crouzel, *Philosophie*, p. 133, point out the importance of the divine gift in the efficacy of conversion. Grace will be considered in more detail in chapter V.

39. *Cels.* 1.9 (I.100.38ff./62.14–22), trans. Chadwick*, pp. 12–13.

40. As Daniélou, *Origen*, p. 103, writes: "In Origen's view, Christianity is not so much a set of doctrines as a divine force changing men's hearts."

41. *Cels.* 7.54 (IV.142.24ff./204.22–27), trans. Chadwick, p. 44.

42. *Cels.* 6.2.

43. Cf. *Cels.* 4.64.

44. *Comm. in Mt.* 11.5 (I.290.44ff./41.34–42.3), trans. Patrick*, 434–435.

45. *Comm. in Mt.* 11.5 (I.290.65ff./42.17–27), trans. Patrick*, 435A. As R. Girod, ed., *Origène — Commentaire sur L'Évangile selon Matthieu* (Paris: Cerf, 1970), I, 71, writes, with respect to the limits of the disciples, "Pourtant la supériorité des disciples sur la foule, n'est pas un privilège, mais une mission."

46. *Comm. in Mt.* 11.6 (I.294.3–9/43.7–12), trans. Patrick, 435B.

47. *Comm. in Mt.* 11.6 (I.296.30–38, 39–41, 47–48/43.29–44.5, 6–8, 12–14), trans. Patrick*, 435–436.

48. *Comm. in Mt.* 11.6 (44.19), trans. Patrick*, 436A.

49. See on Peter, B. Schultz, "Origenes über Bekenntnis und Fall des Petrus," *Orientalis Christiana*, 40 (1974), 286–313.

50. *Comm. in Mt.* 11.6 (I.298.67–69/44.29–31), trans. Patrick, 436A.

51. *Cels.* 4.64.

52. Celsus, according to Borret, IV, 296, n. 1, was typical in his views of Christians with respect to martyrdom and the Christian's response to torture. He saw them as fanatics without rational motivation in their acts. So too Epictetus (*Discourses* IV, 7, 6) and Marcus Aurelius (*Meditations* 11, 3). Origen attempts in this section of his work to respond to such misconceptions.

53. *Cels.* 8.54 (IV.296.38–45/271.5–10), trans. Chadwick, p. 493.

54. Cf. *Cels.* 8.55 (272.6–7).

55. *Cels.* 6.3 (72.19), trans. Chadwick, p. 317. Celsus quotes Plato, *Epist.* vii, 341C.

56. *Cels.* 6.5 (III.188.1–8/74.22–75.1), trans. Chadwick, p. 319.

57. According to Blanc, *Commentaire sur Jean* (SC 222; Paris: Cerf, 1975), III.285, the origin of the principle of like with like is Plato, who used it to demonstrate the incorporeity of the soul.

58. Cf. *Hom. 19.14 in Jer., Hom. 18.8 in Jer., Hom. 20.7 in Jer.*, etc. In *Hom. 17.6 in Jer.*, Origen asks his audience to choose between the day of resurrection and the day of man. On the other hand, in the same section, he proclaims that there is no hardship in following Jesus. In *Hom. 17.4 in Jer.*, he says that one cannot seek things on earth and things in heaven simultaneously. However, in *Hom. 14.16 in Jer.*, quoting Mt. 7:14, he notes that there is "nothing sweet" for the Christian. "Or did you not know that your feast comes with bitter herbs?" This entire section is devoted to the discussion of the hardships of Christian life by using the example of the apostles, especially Paul.

59. *Hom. 11.3 in Ex.* (254.25–27).
60. For Origen, there are heavenly regions which are only places of passage for the mature and holy ones. See *Hom. 21.1 in Num.* and A. Jaubert, ed., *Origène — Homélies sur Josué* (Paris: Cerf, 1960), pp. 51–56, and the texts which she offers on this subject. She writes, p. 54, "Il existe donc une certaine correspondance entre le lieu spirituel de l'âme et le lieu qui lui sera assigné dans la Terre céleste." Hence stages of conversion are occurring even after this earthly life.
61. *Hom. 10.1 in Jesu Nave* (358.4–5).
We might also note that we have no reason to distrust the Latin translation for what follows. First, the homilies on Joshua, as we note in the appendix on textual methodology, were more literal translations than some of Rufinus's other work. Second, the subject is not particularly controversial.
62. *Hom. 10.1 in Jesu Nave* (358.13–24).
63. *Hom. 10.2 in Jesu Nave* (360.1–8).
64. Cf. *Hom. 13.7 in Ex.* (278.24–28), where Origen says: "Actions therefore are associated with reason and reason with actions in order that there may be harmony in both."
— 65. *Hom. 10.3 in Jesu Nave* (361.22–25).
66. Faith will be considered in detail in Part V.
67. *Hom. 14.14 in Jer.* (120.19–22).
68. *Hom. 15.2 in Jer.* (126.11–12).
69. According to Ladner, *The Idea of Reform*, p. 86, n. 13, *mimesis* (imitation) in Patristic thought has its source in Paul (I Cor. 11:1; Eph. 5:1) and various texts from Philo (*De congressu* 69–70, Winston, *Philo*, p. 215).
We will not be considering in any depth the role of the apostolic life in Origen's views on conduct. For a discussion of this aspect, see Vogt, *Kirchenverständnis*, pp. 17–22. It might be noted, however, that, according to Vogt, pp. 17–18, Origen considers the apostles in a similar way and often together with the prophets. Hence, in terms of conduct, we can rightfully assume that the comments on the prophetic life can be applied also to the apostolic life. The difference, Vogt observes, lies in the closeness of the apostles to the Logos and the accompanying enlightenment, but this epistemological difference is not our concern in this section on conduct.
Two articles by K. Suso Frank are also useful. See "Vita Apostolica. Ansätze zur apostolischen Lebensform in der alten Kirche," *Zeitschrift für Kirchengeschichte*, 82 (1971), 145–166, and "Vita Apostolica als Lebensnorm in der alten Kirche," *Internationale katholische Zeitschrift*, 8 (1979), 106–120, In the latter article, pp. 108–110, Frank points out that in Origen there are three ways of imitation of the apostles: the martyrs, the perfect and being among the true apostolic church.
70. *Hom. 14.16 in Jer.* (122.14–18). Vogt, p. 31, sees in this text a goal for clergy also.
71. *Hom. 14.14 in Jer.* (120.22–25). On imitating the prophets, see also *Hom. 15.1 in Jer.* (125.11–17) and *Hom. 20.7 in Jer.* (189.3–5) among many other texts.
72. *Hom. 14.14 in Jer.* (119.10, 14–15).
Origen does not specify in this context why such imitation will turn us, but as we continue on in our discussion of this crucial concept we will learn that imitation of the prophetic and apostolic models is imitating Christ, and when we imitate Christ in any way we have Christ in us.
73. The word *hagios* (holy), its cognates and the words with which it is used are exhaustively considered in P. F. Faessler, *Der Hagiosbegriff bei Origenes* (Freiburg: University Press, 1958). The prophets and other Old Testament figures are often call *hagios*. Faessler, p. 72, writes: "Die Propheten sind *hagioi* als Empfänger, Vermittler und Repräsentanten der göttlichen Offenbarung." Faessler points out on a couple of occasions in his book that Origen makes no distinction between the *hagioi* of the Old Testament and those of the New Testament. See, for example, pp. 62–63, 73. For a more detailed discussion of *hagioi* as referring to the martyrs and others, see Faessler, pp. 78–112. For martyrs, see especially pp. 108ff. In general, Faessler states, pp. 107–108, that the *hagioi* refer to the perfected, spiritual ones, those who have attained a certain moral level of distinction, and belong in a special way to God, participating in him through the Holy Spirit and/or the Logos.
74. Cf. *Hom. 4.2–3 in Jer.*
75. *Hom. 4.3 in Jer.* (25.18–24).
76. Martyrdom, according to Bettencourt, *Doctrina*, p. 119, is prized very highly by Origen. It is equal to *teleiotes* (spiritual maturity), which is the highest goal of every Christian. Moreover, the soul of the martyrs attains the same state as the souls of the angels. Bettencourt in his notes supplies the following texts: *Mart.* 11 (11.8), 50 (46.27–47.2), and 3(4.20ff).
77. Origen himself was later nicknamed Adamantius for this reason.
78. *Fr. 30 in Jer.* (214.13–19). Since a parallel passage exists in the Latin (GCS

8.304.16–305.2), Faessler's doubts, p. 122, n. 2, on this fragment are probably unfounded. Nautin, *Jérémie*, II, 300ff., includes it in his edition.

79. *Hom. 10.1 in Jer.* (71.5–14). On this text, Schadel, *Jeremiahomilien*, p. 285, n. 100, adds the observation that these different agents do not fragment the unity of knowledge which is all of one source. There is one teaching as well as one true teacher.

✓ 80. *Hom. 17.5 in Jer.* (149.6–8).

81. *Hom. 6.2 in Jer.* (49.31–50.10).

82. These matters are precisely clarified in Origen's discussion of Ezek. 11: 19,20: "I will take away their stony hearts and I will put in the hearts of flesh..." See *Princ.* 3.1.15 (90.434–438; 92.442–445), trans. Butterworth*, p. 187.

83. See Daniélou, *Origène*, pp. 235–242, on the moral work of the angels.

84. *Cant.* 2 (133.29–134.8), trans. Lawson, p. 118.

85. *Cant.* 2 (133.29–134.8), trans. Lawson*, p. 117. Lawson, *Origen — The Song of Songs. Commentary and Homilies*, p. 332, n. 85, points out that the idea of a guardian angel is based principally on scripture. See Gen. 48:16, Tob. 3:25, Mt. 18:10 and Acts 12:15. It is later present in *Ps-Barnabas*, the *Shepherd* and Clement of Alexandria. Everyone, whether beginner or perfect, has, according to Origen, a guardian. See *Princ.* 2.20.7 (181.20–22).

86. *Jo.* 13.52 (281.2–7).

87. *Jo.* 13.53 (281.32–282.3).

88. Though Origen stresses the key importance of God in teaching and salvation, he also exalts the role and behaviour of the teacher and other workers of the church. In fact, he insists on rigorous moral standard for teachers and church leaders, as well as lay folk. The basis of this high standard of conduct is in the concept of example, which we shall present in its various dimensions in the remainder of this chapter.

89. *Hom. 14.5 in Jer.* (110.23–24).

90. *Hom. 14.7 in Jer.* (112.15–18).

As Bettencourt, pp. 112–113, notes on this and other passages, martyrdom for Origen is especially related to the passion of Christ and his supreme sacrifice. Everyone who suffers — and especially is martyred — for truth is victorious over evil. Christ, by virtue of being the Logos who assumed flesh, an event which touched all, is in him, and when a Christian suffers, it is Christ who suffers with him. Bettencourt says that the body as well as the soul is assumed by the Logos, so that Christ shares in the sufferings of both. His texts are *Cant.* 3 (222.9–17), *Hom. 2.12 in Cant.* (58.8–18), *Hom. 2.3 in Ex.* (158.10–21).

91. As a note above just indicated, the saints become such, according to Faessler, by participating in the Logos.

92. *Comm. in Mt.* 10.15 (19.25–27), trans. Patrick*, 423A. Girod, *Matthieu*, I, 206, n. 2, comments on this text that just as Christ is an intermediary between God and man, so the teacher, as an imitator of Christ, is a mediator between Christ and the one whom he teaches. Of course, as Origen states elsewhere (*Jo.* 2.6 (61.1–3)), no one can actually attain Christ's level.

93. The role of the resurrection, with respect to imitation, will not be considered in this section. According to Chênevert, *L'Église*, p. 155, in both the intellectual and moral realms of Christian life, training and models are necessary. "Bien plus, la pratique des vertus reste toujours en-decà de la perfection réalisée dans le Christ, qui lui sert de modèle." One is not automatically confirmed in virtue by baptism. Numerous steps must be taken to reach the ultimate goal, and one will need to follow Christ for a long time. Hence there is a time of renewal and progress between baptism/repentance and salvation in which the "bride" who begins "black" slowly becomes white. (Cf. Song of Songs 1:25 and 8:5/LXX) The principle of this change is the various dimensions involved in the imitation of Christ. Chênevert's texts are *Cant.* 3 (178.15–19), pp. 177–178, 2 (126.1–6), p. 107, 1 (101.13–102.8), pp. 74–75 and *Hom. 1.6 in Cant.* (36.3–16), p. 276.

According to Ladner, *Reform*, p. 86, there is an emphasis upon imitation of Christ rather than of God in Origen, in contrast to Clement in whom the process is of God or of Christ. Ladner, in fact, in agreement with Völker, *Vollkommenheitsideal*, pp. 215ff., writes that Origen stressed a Christ-mediated piety, first, by his idea of the bridal union of the soul and Christ, and, second, by his views on the birth and growth of Christ in the heart of man. We have already seen in Chapter III how Christ the redeemer plays a key role in the process involving *aisthesis*. Here we shall view his decisive part in the mode of conduct. Ladner, p. 89, also points out that though man cannot become similar to God solely by his own power, he creates the conditions for such an assimilation in the imitation of Christ. His text is *Hom. 8 in Luc.* (9^2.48.8–49.9).

94. *Comm. in Rom.* 5.1 (PG 14:1010AB).

95. *Philoc.* 25.2 (PG 14:842A)/*Comm. in Rom.* 1.3, p. 210. According to Harl, *Origène*, p. 281, this text is the only extant, certain and explicit reference in Origen of the concrete example of Jesus as man. She does offer on p. 281, n. 55, several texts on the inner imitation: *Hom. 8 in Luc.* (56.23ff.), *Fr. 14 in Jer.* (205.1ff.), *Hom. 24.2 in Num.* (227–228), *Cels.* 6.63 (134.3ff.) and *Or.* 22.4 (348.28–349.3). According to Crouzel, *Théologie*, p. 224, imitating Christ bolsters the 'creation according to the image' in us. Crouzel summarizes, p. 232, the connection with the practice of virtue: "Les vertus ont donc bien leur rôle notre assimilation au Christ, dans le renforcement du selon-l'image qui aboutit à la ressemblance." He quotes from *Sel. in Ps.* 4.7 (PG 12:1164–1165), which indicates virtue brings us closer to God and distinguishes us. Teichtweier, *Sundenlehre*, p. 55, observes, however, that it is the Logos in Christ which can free us from the weaknesses of the soul. Christ's presence then as Logos opens up the way for us to follow the model of Jesus's soul.

96. On the theme of imitation, cf. Crouzel, *Théologie*, pp. 222–232. On following Jesus, see Bertrand, *Mystique*, pp. 106–120. Bertrand writes, p. 109, that one follows behind Jesus because Jesus leads to the Father. Bertrand connects the idea of following Jesus with his general perspective of the mystical dimensions to Origen's understanding of Jesus. Following Jesus for Origen was following a mystical path to God. According to *Jo.* 6.40 (149.12–17), Origen traced this path personally, historically and spiritually.

97. Cf. Teichtweier, *Sundenlehre*, pp. 54–56, tripartite discussion, "Nachfolge Christi": 1) In der Affektlosigkeit, 2) in der Lebensgestaltung and 3) im 'neuen' Leben.

98. *Fr. 12 in Jer.* (203.13–20).

99. *Hom. 17.4 in Jer.* (147.2–5). On the text, Schadel, *Jeremiahomilien*, p. 315, n. 186, points out that these absolutes are not unconnected or separate events, but essentially the result of an absolute divine unity. For other texts which define Christ in terms of various absolutes, see Nautin, *Jérémie*, II, 167, n. 3, and Crouzel, *Théologie*, pp. 227, 230–231. For its application to redemption, see Alcain, *Cautiverio*, pp. 197–198. On the use of *auto-*, see Corsini, p. 133, n. 17, where he cites Gruber, pp. 104ff.

100. *Jo.* 32.11 (444.3). See Corsini, *Giovanni*, p. 760, n. 22, on the Stoic and Philonic precedents to this idea.

101. *Hom. 17.4 in Jer.* (147.8–9). Words in brackets are not found in all texts, only in the Catena and Jerome's translation.

102. *Comm. in Rom.* 6.3 (PG 14:1061D ff.). A similar thought is found in *Or.* 11.2, where virtues are to be perfected in a future life. See Crouzel, *Théologie*, p. 231. Both texts are comments on I Cor. 13:12.

103. *Fr. 13 in Jer.* (204.16–17). We will consider the connection of doing and knowing in more detail in the next Part.

104. *Hom. 15.6 in Jer.* (130.18–24, 25–28).

105. Cf. *Hom. 9.1 in Jer.* (63.17–20; 64.7–8; 65.12–19). This section of the homilies is especially addressed to how we are in Christ and Christ is in us. See also *Jo.* 1.27.

106. *Hom. 9.3 in Jer.* (67.24–68.9).

107. See also *Hom. 20.7 in Jer.* (187.19–23) on being delivered from the body of death, in light of Rom. 7:24.

Gruber, pp. 37–38, stresses, concerning this text and others, that the life referred to here is a unique one, a life of fulfillment made possible by the relation of Christ and God, a relation the pagans and sinners do not experience, though they are God's creations. Cf. also Gruber, pp. 200–203, concerning Christ as the life of the soul.

108. *Hom. 9.4 in Jer.* (69.19–20).

109. Origen offers, in *Hom. 9.4 in Jer.* (69.19–70.9), the following scriptural supports: John 8:44, Rom. 8:14, I John 3:8 and Ps. 44:11 (45:10).

110. *Hom. 9.4 in Jer.* (70.9–10).

111. *Hom. 9.4 in Jer.* (70.11–16, 24–27). Schadel, *Jeremiahomilien*, p. 281, n. 96, has a long note on this passage regarding the nature of the process of generation of Christ and the righteous. He relies particularly upon *Princ.* 1.2.6 (35.16–36.2) in which the Son is said to be begotten "as the will proceeds from the mind (*sicut voluntas procedit e mente*)" and *Princ.* 4.4.1 (349.11) in which he says that "the Son was begotten from the will of the Father." This latter text derives from Justinian, no friend of Origen, and must be read in this light. It is absent from Rufinus's Latin text, but in this same section, the Latin views him as the Son of God's will. Schadel notes that Origen's understanding of the procession and generation of the Son, involving mind and will,

is also applicable to the generation of the righteous. The righteous are those whose mind and will work together to cause to arise a "good act." This good act has then two elements totally interrelated: the *ergon*, which is the outer aspect, and the *dianoema*, which is the inner dimension. So the inner unity and harmony of the Mind and Will in the Trinity is, according to Schadel's interpretation, reflected in the mind and will of the righteous, so that a son of God is begotten in the good act which is the result.

Bardy, *La théologie*, p. 156 and note 1, makes an apt comment on this text. To become, he says, a son of God, as far as Origen is concerned, gnosis is insufficient; one must also do the works of God. "...et la grâce d'adoption n'est pas seulement une grâce de connaissance, mais aussi une grâce d'action."

A more detailed discussion, but along similar lines, of the meaning of "father" for Origen is found in *Jo.* 20.13 (342.31–344.19).

112. *Cels.* 1.57 (108.5–10). The phrase "source and origin" comes from Plato, according to Chadwick, *Contra Celsum*, p. 52, n. 2, and is also found in Philo. See *Phaedrus* 245C and *De mutatione nominum* 58. Borret, *Celse*, I, 231, n. 3, notes on this text that "la filiation divine au sens plein est l'apanage du Christ; mais il nous la communique en nous faisant participer à sa nature divine." He refers also to *Cels.* 8.17 (234.24–235.3) where all the virtues are *mimemata* and *paradeigmata* of the first-born of all creation. The list of virtues includes prudence, righteousness, courage, wisdom and piety. See also Crouzel's discussion in *Théologie*, p. 88, n. 68.

113. *Jo.* 20.33–34 (370.5–373.19) whose general context is John 8:47, and *Comm. in Mt.* 13.26 (253.4–14) on Rom. 8:15 and Mt. 18:10.

114. *Fr. 401 in Mt.* (169).

115. *Jo.* 20.33 (370.23–29). Concerning this section, Alcain, *Cautiverio*, p. 160, points out that the sons are those who have reached adulthood in the spiritual life. They have advanced their simple faith to spiritual knowledge. It is important to distinguish the slaves from the servants of God. The matter of servitude, as Alcain, *Cautiverio*, pp. 158–162 and n. 74, has shown us, is a profound issue in Origen. For only those who accept God as Lord can be among his people, in his service, and within the church. No other god or lord can be included. Hence, as Alcain notes, p. 161, man's choice is between being a servant to God and virtue, or a slave to the devil and sin; in light of the above texts, we would also add a slave to fear. In any case, servitude is man's natural condition with respect to religion; man simply passes from one form to another. Paradoxically, however, being a servant of God is better than any freedom. So Origen writes, with respect to Paul calling himself a servant, in *Comm. in Rom.* 1.1 (PG 14: 837C), "He serves Christ, not in a spirit of servitude, but in a spirit of adoption, for it is more noble to be a servant to Christ than every liberty." The choice is between a culpable freedom or a praiseworthy servitude. See *Comm. in Rom.* 6.5 (PG 14:1064B). Even more paradoxical, according to Alcain, p. 162, based on *Comm. in Mt.* 12.41 (164.5–9), is that those who are true servants of God are slaves to all others. Finally, Alcain notes, p. 162, that the contrast of those who are slaves and those who are free is not absolute: "El hombre, en cuanto ser responsable que camina de la imperfeccion a la perfeccion, puede alcanzar la libertad en determinados campos de la virtud, a pesar de seguir siendo esclavo en otros. El cambio no es instantanes sino sucessivo y lento." This quotation is based primarily on *Comm. in Rom.* 6.11 (PG 14:1092AB). Only the perfect one is totally free, and even this freedom must be understood only in terms of the world. Absolute freedom exists only in the heavenly Jerusalem.

116. *Jo.* 20.33 (370.29–371.14). The contrast of the roles of love and fear in one's spiritual journey, and especially the ultimate conquest of love over fear, is found in *Comm. in Mt.* 13.26 (253.4–14).

117. *Princ.* 4.4.2 (406.77–79), trans. Butterworth, p. 316. This vacillating relation to Christ, dependent on one's spiritual condition, is also applicable to sonship, and to all aspects of the Son. See Crouzel and Simonetti, *Traité*, 4, 248, n. 20 for other texts which explore this idea.

118. *Hom. 12.13 in Jer.* (101.21–22).

119. *Jo.* 6.6(3) (115.16–19), trans. Menzies*, p. 353B. Bettencourt, *Doctrina*, pp. 29–30, sees in this text and others a reflection of Origen's doctrine of the matrimonial union of the soul and Christ. Hence the imitation does not maintain two separate entities, but creates one. Elsewhere Bettencourt, p. 92, agrees with Cadiou, *Jeunesse*, p. 404, that these patterns and models and interrelationships leading to union are based in a very ancient Greek philosophical concept, namely, participation. With respect to conversion, this notion is critical and is discussed in several sections of this study. For a concise overview of the concept in Origen, see D. Balas, "The Idea of Participation in the Structure of Origen's Thought," *Origeniana*, pp. 257–275. Teachers are called christs in

310 NOTES

Cels. 6.79, and in his interpretation of Song of Songs 2:1, Origen claims that all who draw near the "Lily" become "lilies." See *Cant.* 3 (178.13–19), p. 177. Chênevert notes on this text, p. 170, that it may also refer to the church: When the church imitates Christ, she is assimilated to Christ.
120. *Hom. 6.9 in Ezech.* (387.22). Text suggested by Teichtweier, *Sundenlehre*, p. 55. The scriptural context here is Ezek. 16:8–9. In this chapter, God tells of how he transformed Jerusalem from the deformed to the beautiful.
121. To these discussions must also be added prior considerations of imitation with respect to the image.
122. "Up," "below," "ahead," and "behind" are just four of several words of time, place and movement used by Origen to designate theological and conversion matters. Two other important pairs are what is "above" (heaven/divine) (Cf. *Jo.* 19.20 (321.27) and 19.22 (323.31–34)) and what is "below" (earthly/corruptible), and the "inner" and the "outer" man. (Cf. *Comm. in Mt.* 10.1 (1.4ff.) and *Cels.* 3.21 (217.22ff.)) Origen is usually basing his use of such words in scripture. For the theological use of these terms by Origen, and particularly *kato* (below) and *ano* (above), see Eichinger, *Verklärung*, pp. 26–29. He notes, p. 29, that these terms do not reflect a natural or fundamental dualism in Origen, for the universe begins as only a spiritual cosmos. Furthermore, in agreement with Teichtweier, *Sundenlehre*, pp. 95ff., Eichinger states that there is no natural necessity for sin in Origen's cosmos.
123. For other texts on the new life which results from following Christ, see Teichtweier, *Sundenlehre*, p. 56.
124. *Hom. 16.1 in Jer.* (132.15–19). See Crouzel, *Théologie*, p. 195, n. 125 on the biblical use of the sea as a place of evil and demons. The word *kosmos* (world) used in this passage is defined in depth by Origen in *Princ.* 2.3.6, 2.9.3 and *Comm. in Mt.* 13.20–21. For him, it can mean 1) ornament, 2) our earth and its inhabitants, 3) the entire universe (earth and heavens), 4) all those who dwell above the heavens, in the heavens, on the earth and in hell and 5) those who live on earth and love earthly things.
These texts were suggested by M. Ruiz Jurado, "Le monde chez Origène," *BLE*, 75 (1974), 5, n. 4. Ruiz Jurado's own list of uses includes 1) a spatial use, 2) a temporal use, 3) a spiritual use, 4) a negative moral/spiritual use, 5) the anthropological use, as referring to the human race as a group and all its institutions and occupations, and to man as a microcosmos, and 6) the ecclesiastical use in which the church is the world in the eyes of God.
The use of the word in this text and in those which we will discuss below is 5) in Origen's own list and 4) in Ruiz Jurado's survey of all of Origen's extant writings. Dying to the world then is being crucified to the world, being not among those who care for the things of the terrestrial life only. Ruiz Jurado writes that the cross of Christ implies "une forme spéciale de vie," a wisdom which triumphs over the wisdom of the world. It is a life in Christ who guides and is the light and the life. Ruiz Jurado then indicates that this passage from one life to another involves many steps and struggles. For Origen's understanding of dying and being crucified to the world, see Ruiz Jurado, 13–17. For the discussion of the steps involved in passage from this world, see 17–22.
It is worthwhile to note here, with respect to the "giving of life" by the Logos, that the "spirit" (*pneuma*) is a gift of God to teach the soul. *Comm. in Rom.* 2.9 (PG 14:893B) considers it a kind of moral conscience. On the dual contemplative and moral function of the spirit, see Crouzel, "L'anthropologie," 367. For a detailed study of the spirit, see J. Boada, "El pneuma en Origenes," *Estudios eclesiasticos*, 46 (1971), 475–510, and J. Dupuis's study, *L'esprit de l'homme*, both of which we shall consider more often in the next Chapter. According to Dupuis, p. 109, and Crouzel, *Théologie*, p. 131, this spirit should be distinguished from the Holy Spirit. For our concerns here, it is important to note that the spirit in man brings life to the soul when one become dead to sin. See, for example, *Comm. in Rom.* 6.13 (PG 14:1099B). So the background of the new life is the death of sin and the revivifying power of the *pneuma*. See Boada, 500–510 and accompanying texts. This involvement of the spirit in conduct is but another indication of the interrelationship of the modes.
125. *Hom. 16.1 in Jer.* (133.7–9). Gruber, p. 169, comments on this passage: "Dieser Seelenhylemorphismus ist der Grundvoraussetzung aller Bekehrungsmöglichkeit und daher die Voraussetzung der christlichen Busspredigt, die ja in der Gnosis wenig Sinn hat. Origenes schildert seinen Hören immer wieder diesen übergang der Seele von der Sünde zum wahren Leben."
126. *Hom. 16.1 in Jer.* (133.13–16).
127. *Hom. 16.2 in Jer.* (133.24–28). Cf. Origen's comments on the transfiguration in *Comm. in Mt.* 12.36–39 (150.15–157.8), and especially *Comm. in Mt.* 12.37 (153.8–25), where Origen

writes that those who go up on the mount with Jesus and see his transfiguration receive wisdom and know his divinity. To those "below", he is known only after the flesh which is, according to the parallel anonymous Latin translation, "living in the earthly way of life." On this text, see Eichinger, *Verklärung*, pp. 23–24, 48–59, 163–168, *passim*. He does not refer on pp. 23, 31, and 48–49, to the Latin translation. He concludes, p. 196, that Origen stressed that the transfiguration was an agent for spiritual ascent.

Cf. also *Cant.* 3 (205.5–206.14), pp. 214–216, for a similar discussion.

128. *Hom. 13.1 in Jer.* (102.19–20) and *Hom. 13.2 in Jer.* (103.15–18; 22–26).

129. *Hom. 13.3 in Jer.* (104.28–105.6).

130. Bertrand, *Mystique*, pp. 113–119, perhaps presents a parallel here in his consideration of *Comm. in Mt.* 14.15 (317.26–318.17), regarding the disciples leaving all and following Jesus, and *Comm. in Mt.* 15.21 (410.26–411.10), in which Peter leaves behind all which could be an occasion for sin. See Schultz, "Bekenntnis," 286–313.

131. *Hom. 13.3 in Jer.* (105.20–24).

132. *Hom. 17.6 in Jer.* (150.4–13).

133. *Hom. 17.6 in Jer.* (149.18–29). Origen's scriptural support is Mt. 11:28.

134. *Hom. 18.2 in Jer.* (152.6–34). Schadel, *Jeremiahomilien*, p. 317, notes 193 and 194, and pp. 241–242, notes 11 and 12, discusses the ontological significance of *kato* and *ekei* for Origen, with respect to this and other texts. He also points to a possible Platonic source for Origen's view, but this supposition will need to be tempered with the powerful scriptural imagery which is so evident in these discussions.

See especially *Hom. 18.2 in Jer.* (152.26–153.25).

135. On translating *nous* as "intellect" or "mind" rather than "spirit," see Corsini, *Giovanni*, p. 163, n. 48. Schadel uses "Geist," Nautin/Husson "intelligence," and Corsini himself "intellecto." See also Crouzel, *Connaissance*, pp. 41–43. It is distinct from *pneuma*. Crouzel, "L'anthropologie," 365, believes *nous* should be translated in French "intelligence," and *pneuma* "esprit," for the *psyche* in the pre-existent state is a *nous* which lives according to the *pneuma*. See the discussion of terms in Chapter III.

136. *Hom. 18.2 in Jer.* (153.2–6). In a fragment of homily 18 (GCS 3, p. 165, apparatus; SC 238, 214, n. 1), Origen distinguishes him who follows Jesus, the eternal way, and him who seeks what is below, the worldly, temporal way.

137. *Comm. in Mt.* 12.24–27 (122.24–130.32).

138. *Comm. in Mt.* 13.20–21 (234.4–239.32). See note above on the meaning of "world" in Origen's thought.

139. Ruiz Jurado, "Le monde," 9–10, 15, specifies that neither matter nor the world is intrinsically evil for Origen. His texts are *Princ.* 1.5.5, *Cels.* 3.42, 4.66, 8.56, and others.

140. Klostermann's addition in light of the Latin *spiret*.

141. Diehl's addition in light of the Latin *atque confessionem*.

142. *Comm. in Mt.* 12.24 (124.22–125.1), trans. Patrick*, 464A. The translations "consideration" and "thought" are uncertain here. Patrick translates "thought" and "purpose," Bertrand, *Mystique*, p. 110, "tout ce qui est raisonnement." The parallel Latin has *cogitatio* and *intellectus* respectively. On Origen's use of *noema* ("thought"), see Crouzel, *Connaissance*, pp. 384–385. Crouzel translates it "pensée." In terms of the Platonic tradition, which we may assume has had some influence in the use of these words, we may note the following: By the time of Origen, intellectual activity was defined by the Platonic and Aristotelian traditions as having two different dimensions, one intuitive, *noesis*, and the other discursive, called by several names, i.e., *dianoia* and *logismos*. The latter is intrinsically dependent on the former. See F. E. Peters, *Greek Philosophical Terms*, "noesis," pp. 121–128, and Copleston, *A History of Philosophy*, I.i.173–180 on Plato's thought. The "perfect" are the spiritually mature.

143. *Comm. in Mt.* 12.27 (129.31–130.24), trans. Patrick*, 465A.

144. It should be mentioned, in our consideration of the imitation of Christ, that there is a connection in Origen between the concept of Christ as the High Priest and our own priesthood. Christ on a higher level has a priesthood which has a mediating role to transmit benefits of the Father and to carry up our prayers and our sacrifices. See the texts given by Lécuyer, "Sacerdoce des fidèles et sacerdoce ministériel chez Origène," *Vetera christianorum*, 7 (1970), 255. Let us take note especially of *Cels.* 8.13 (230), where Christ offers our sacrifices. These sacrifices, as Origen explains elsewhere (*Fr. 4 in Jer.* (200), *Hom. 9.13 in Ex.* (241.9 ff.)), are spiritual, not material sacrifices. They include both interior acts (charity, joy, peace, patience, etc.) (*Hom. 11.8 in Num.*

(91.14–25)) and exterior acts (mercy, praise of God, prayer and penitence) (*Hom. 11.9 in Num.* (92.16–93.10), *Hom. 23.3 in Num.* (214.4–215.16) and *Hom. 9.8 in Lev.* (434.20 ff.)). On our sacrifices, see Lécuyer, 256. Hence, though we imitate Christ's sacrifice, he as High Priest carries our acts in offering to the Father.

145. *Fr. 109B in Mt..* (60).

146. For an extensive list of text citations concerning Jesus's terrestrial life as model, see Crouzel, *Théologie*, p. 225. The humanity of Jesus for Origen has many meanings for us, as Eichinger particularly has shown in his study *Die Verklärung Christi bei Origenes*. Besides the earthly model which is being discussed here, which is expressed openly in conduct, there is the more profound level of example which concerns our spiritual growth. Eichinger, p. 35, writes: "Die Menschheit Jesu ist die erste Stufe, oder wie Origenes an einer anderen Stelle sagt, die Einführung nach dem Fleische bei dem Aufstieg zur Erkenntnis des Logos." Eichinger offers *Cels.* 6.68 (138.15) and *Jo.* 19.6 (305.17ff.) to substantiate his view. There is also a mystery to the humanity or presence of Jesus which transcends his body. This fact is evident in *Cels.* 7.43 (194.10ff.) which indicates that divinity can be seen in Jesus. Cf. Eichinger's commentary on these and other texts on pp. 35–47. The sinful man, Eichinger, p. 47, notes, attaches himself to the humanity of Jesus as an end, whereas the believer sees it as a step and analogy to the spiritual, the Logos.

147. *Comm. in Mt.* 16.1 (462.8–463.18). On the high place of Paul in Origen, see Karl Frank, "Vita Apostolica," *ZFK*, 82 (1971), 160–161.

148. *Hom. 12.8 in Jer.* (95.21-22).

149. *Hom. 12.7 in Jer.* (94.9–12). Mt. 11:29 is also quoted in Origen's exposition of the feet washing episode (John 13:1-20; *Jo.* 32.4 (431.30–432.1), a example for Origen of Jesus's humility. Cf. Bertrand, *Mystique*, pp. 117–118.

150. *Comm. in Mt.* 13.16 (219.23–222.31). Origen here offers a simple interpretation. However, another interpretation is given in *Comm. in Mt.* 13.18 (226.18ff.).

151. *Hom. 6.1 in Is.* (269.18–19; 270.7–10). Vogt, *Kirchenverständnis*, p. 30, views also in these texts the model of humility which is presented to the people by the bishop.

152. Cf. the sections of Vogt, *Kirchenverständnis*: "Amtsaufgaben der Kleriker," pp. 29–44, on Origen's understanding of the work of the priest, and pp. 320–330 on Christ and the Church. Those who have the office of the clergy, Vogt says, must be constantly self-critical and worthy of being judged by the people.

153. Cf. Schultz, *op. cit.*, on Origen's view of Peter.

154. *Comm. in Mt.* 12.11 (88.15–19), trans. Patrick*, 456B.

155. *Comm. in Mt.* 12.10 (86.4–12), trans. Patrick*, 456A. *Jo.* 10.39 (23) (215.31–216.14) also sees the Church, regarding I Pet. 2.5, as a construction built upon living rocks, the quality of which depends upon the deeds and thoughts of each.

156. See Crouzel, *Virginité*, p. 15, n. 2, for the sources of the idea of the mystical marriage. The idea is found in varying forms in the Hebrew scriptures (union of Yahweh with Israel), the New Testament (Mt. 25:1-13), Philo (*De cherubim* 42ff. and *Legum allegoriae* 3.180–181), the mysteries, and the *Corpus Hermeticum*, 9.3–4. For Christ's union with the Church in Origen, see *Virginité*, pp. 15–44.

157. *Cant.* 2 (155.3–6, 24–156.19), trans. Lawson, pp. 146, 147.

158. *Cant.* 2 (156.19–21), trans. Lawson*, p. 147. Crouzel, *Virginité*, p. 25, notes in this context that the chastity of the members and the virginity of the Church is intimately tied to their union with Christ. Virginity is the true circumcision of the flesh, and is the sign of the second covenant between God and his people. The circumcision of the Jews was the sign of the first covenant.

159. For this analysis, see Chênevert, *L'Église*, p. 221. See pp. 218–223 especially on the mystery inherent for Origen in the concept of the Church as the body of Christ. Chênevert also considers *Cant.* 3 (176.18–21), p. 174, which indicates that we have a share in and can partake of the Logos because the Church is the body. Cf. also *Cels.* 6.79 (151.1-3), where Church and Christ are referred to as one body. On *Cels.* 6.79 , Vogt, *Kirchenverständnis*, p. 325, points out that those who serve Christ, who strive for the salvation of men, who preach the word of Jesus through their just lives become christs. And this is possible only if the Church is the body of Christ. See also *Cant.* 2 (154.24-27), trans. Lawson*, p. 145.

160. *Cant.* 3 (174.11–13), trans. Lawson, p. 171. Concerning the Church in the age to come, see Chênevert, pp. 258–270.

161. Chênevert, *L'Église*, p. 191, comes to a similar conclusion. He here sees the imitation of Christ as the focus in Origen's thought of what man must do to enter into communion with God: 'Ainsi, toute la spiritualité qu' Origène dégage à partir du mystère de l'Incarnation et de kénose

du Verbe vient se condenser dans cet idéal d'imitation... qui est fondamentalement l'épanouissement progressif, dans l'espace intérieur de la liberté personnelle, d'un dynamisme ontologique, d'une puissance de participation communiquée au croyant par le sacrement, bien plus, qui est l'action même du Christ, rendu présent dans le croyant par sa foi."

162. Cf. Crouzel, *Théologie*, p. 227: "Le Verbe n'est pas seulement le modèle, mais l'agent de cette formation."

163. Cf. Crouzel, *Théologie*, p. 232, and Völker, p. 100.

164. *Hom. 12.4 in Lev.* (462.1–5).

165. *Hom. 9.2 in Jer.* (65.19–21).

166. *Hom. 9.2 in Jer.* (66.26–30).

167. *Hom. 9.3 in Jer.* (67.16–68.6).

168. *Hom. 9.4 in Jer.* (68.28–69.6). Alcain, *Cautiverio*, pp. 90–97, considers how Origen views the biblical images of "chains" and "bonds" seen in Is. 49:9, Ps. 2:3 and Jer. 11:9. According to Alcain, Origen interprets the chains of Is. 49:9 as either the sins of the Gentiles or the sins of the whole human race (as far as it is bonded to sin) or the chains which keep us tied to Satan. Similarly, with respect to Ps. 2:3, Origen understands the chains as the oppressive powers—kings of the earth, princes of the age—whose bonds we can break when we are in Christ. Such bonds are also interpreted as sins or passions.

169. *Hom. 9.3 in Jer.* (68.3–9).

170. Cf. *Hom. 16.5–6 in Jer.* (137.2–139.19).

171. *Hom. 16.7 in Jer.* (139.24–29).

172. A common symbolic reference for Origen. See *Hom. 1.3 in Jer., Hom. 9.2 in Jer., Hom. 18.14 in Jer.* and *Fr. 48 in Jer.*

173. *Fr. 11 in Jer.* (202.12–14, 15–20).

174. Cf. *Fr. 11 in Jer.* (202.20–203.11).

175. As Chadwick, *Contra Celsus*, p. 147, n. 1, notes, the use of *ekklesia* in this sentence is difficult to render into English. Though both are *ekklesiai*, only one is *tou theou* (of God).

176. *Cels.* 3.29 (227.7–12/11.70), trans. Crombie and Cairns*, ANF, 476A. This text is part of the discussion raised by H. Gamble, "Euphemism and Christology in Origen: Contra Celsum III, 22–43," *Vigiliae Christianae*, 33 (1979), 12–29. Origen lifts Jesus's status as God above pagan deities because of the "benefaction" resulting from his work. This benefaction comes from his power to convert and reform men and make them devoted to God. The proof can be seen in the Christian "assembly" compared with the secular. In effect, Jesus is God because he can fully convert men and change their lives. See Gamble, 24.

177. *Jo.* 10.39(23) (215.31–32), trans. Menzies, 404A. Cf. I Pet. 2:5.

178. *Jo.* 10.39(23) (216.9–10), trans. Menzies*, 404A. For an extensive discussion of the Church as the body of Christ and temple of God in Origen, see Vogt, *Kirchenverständnis*, pp. 235–249. On p. 239, where he considers this text, Vogt writes, "Sie ist nicht Haus Gottes, das ein für alle Male dasteht, sondern Haus Gottes, das während der ganzen Geschichte der Menschheit weitergebaut wird, ja die Inkarnation scheint nur geschehen zu sein, damit der Leib Christi, die Kirche, zum geistlichen Haus und Tempel Gottes erbaut werden kann." Vogt also adds *Jo.* 10.41 (218.28–219.10) to confirm this view. Vogt notes here the incarnation as primarily a vehicle of conversion.

179. *Jo.* 10.40(24) (217.31–34).

180. *Hom. 7.3 in Jer.* (53.34), *Jo.* 10.23 (195.16) and *Jo.* 10.41 (219.5–6).

181. Concerning this subject, see Teichtweier, *Sundenlehre*, pp. 58–67, 309–328 and 336–342. His basic point, noted on p. 61 and referred to above in a note by Vogt, is that the Church for Origen in this age is on the way to perfection, not perfect. Nevertheless, Teichtweier, p. 59, also confirms the existence in Origen of a heavenly church whose members are holy ones. See *Princ.* 4.2.2 (308.16). For another discussion of what sin does to the Church, based on different texts, but with similar conclusions, see Bardy, *La théologie*, pp. 138–139. According to *Hom. 21.2 in Jos.* (428.15–16): "Neque enim possibile est ad liquidum purgari ecclesiam, dum in terris est..." This is confirmed in a Greek summary of the passage (429.20–23). Cf. also *Comm. in Mt.* 16.24 (557.2–8). Passage suggested by Teichweier, *Sundenlehre*, p. 60.

182. *Fr. 31 in Jer.* (215.7–14/II.318).

183. *Hom III.3 in Jer.* (Lat.) (8.309.18–313.13/II.316–326) and *Fr. 31 in Jer.* (215.14–15/II.320). The reader should compare this discussion with the Gnostic hierarchy of salvation discussed in Chapter I.

184. *Hom. 15.3 in Jer.* (127.31–128.6).

314 NOTES

185. *Comm. in Rom.* 5.10 (PG 14:1052C–1053A). Cf. Is. 14:12 and Ezekiel 28:14–17.
186. *Hom. 10.1 in Num.* (68.17–71.1). See A. Méhat, *Nombres*, p. 189, n. 2 on this text. See Chapter V for more detail on repentance.
187. *Fr. 48 in Jer.* (222.16–17). Similarly, in *Hom. 7.3 in Jer.* (53.34–54.3), he specifies, in light of Jer. 5:19, that one who worships other gods, such as money and food, is exiled to an alien country, outside the land of God. Also, *Hom. 12.6 in Lev.* (465.1–4), concerning Lev. 21:13–14, points out that even if one is not rejected by the bishop, he is rejected in conscience. Cf. Vogt, *Kirchenverständnis*, pp. 133–134, on use of *ekballein* ("cast out"), here and elsewhere, for excommunication. See also the similar comments of Vogt, p. 137, on this fragment.
188. *Noemata* as sons and *erga* and *praxeis* as daughters are noted also, in light of Jer. 3:4, in *Hom. 5.7 in Jer.* (37.9–10). All are children of the soul. This text indicates, as Vogt, *Kirchenverständnis*, p. 169, n. 90, verifies, that there apparently was the opportunity for readmittance to the Church after excommunication. Vogt offers also *Comm. in Rom.* Pref. (PG 14:834BC). See also Vogt, p. 182, on the need for "sons" and "daughters" which Fragment 48 noted.
189. *Hom. 12.5 in Jer.* (91.26). This entire section (12.5) needs to be read for an understanding of Origen's views on the matter. Vogt, *Kirchenverständnis*, pp. 34, 37–38, on this text and others, sees here one of the primary functions, according to Origen, of the early Christian bishop, namely, to care for souls and be vigilant about the conduct of the community. The whole community must be considered. There is a sense also in this text, and in Frag. 48 quoted above, of having to prove one's sincerity by an extended time of penitence before a return to the community can be allowed. See Chapter V for a more detailed discussion of repentance.
190. With respect to a member soiling the church, see *Hom. 5.6 in Jos.* (320.8–13), which concludes by saying,"...*quia per unum membrum macula in omne corpus diffunditur.*" This text appears in the general context of Jos. 5:9 concerning the remittance of sins. The specific scriptural context for this text is 1 Cor. 3:17 and 1 Cor. 6:18.
191. The idea of return to the community after rehabilitation is similar to the idea of conversion in the Hebrew scriptures. See Chapter I. For a more detailed discussion of repentance, see the section in Chapter V.
192. Cf. again *Hom. 12.5 in Jer.* (92.25–93.2). That Origen leaves open the chance for a return or a remission is clear in many texts, even for that nature which has become "very bad," as *Cels.* 3.69 states. However, men can reach a stage where their lives and sins are irremediable by other men or by the earthly Church. In such a case, Origen recommends rejection for the sake of the community. See *Hom. 7.6 in Jos.* (332.21–334.20). See the discussion in Chapter V on repentance and Karl Rahner, "La doctrine d'Origène sur la pénitance," *Recherches de science religieuse* 37 (1950), 47–97, 252–286, 422–456.
193. *Hom. 12.6 in Jer.* (93.11–13).
194. *Fr. 64 in Jer.* (229.26–29). Cf. Vogt, *Kirchenverständnis*, p. 141, who states that the view expressed in this text may refer to cases where no formal ruling by the bishop has been given.
195. *Fr. 13 in Jer.* (204.19–21). Cf. also Jer. 9:3,5,8.
196. Cf. Teichtweier, *Sundenlehre*, pp. 339–342.
197. On these demands, as well as the failure of leaders to achieve them, see Bardy, *La théologie*, pp. 133–144. On the whole subject of the priesthood in Origen, we now have a complete book devoted to this subject: Theo Schafer, *Das Priester-Bild im Leben und Werk des Origenes* (Frankfurt: P. Lang, 1977).
198. *Kleros*, translated "Amt" by Schadel, "fonction" by Nautin/Husson.
199. *Hom. 11.3 in Jer.* (80.20–81.7). The "chief [office]" refers, according to Vogt, p. 4, to the bishop. Schadel translates this office as "das oberste Kirchenamt," while Nautin/Husson "le commandement ecclésiastique."
There is in Origen the idea of a priesthood of believers, within which is the lay priesthood and the ministerial priesthood. Each has its own demands, but each is separate from the other. The ministerial order, as Origen clarifies here and in what is to follow, requires even more from priests. On the lay priesthood, see Joseph Lécuyer, "Sacerdoce des fideles et sacerdoce ministériel chez Origène," *Vetera christianorum*, 7 (1970), 256–259. The ministerial priesthood, Lécuyer writes, p. 259, is at the interior of the general priesthood of believers. A special ministerial role is required for the eucharist celebration. See Lécuyer, p. 261. In brief, its uniqueness arises because of Origen's image of a heavenly priesthood and celebration of which this earthly celebration and its participants are shadows and symbols. Cf. Heb. 10:1 for the probable background of this idea. Lécuyer's texts are *Hom. 38(1).1 in Ps.* (PG 12:1391BC) and *Hom. 38(2).2 in Ps.* (PG 12:1402–1403).

200. *Comm. in Mt.* 12.14 (98.28–99.15) and 13.31 (268.26–271.1). These texts are also suggested by Teichtweier, *Sundenlehre*, p. 340. Cf. also Schultz, "Bekenntnis," 286–313. Vogt, *Kirchenverständnis*, pp. 143–169, devotes an entire section of his study to the issues surrounding Matt 16:18ff., Matt 18:18 and John 11:44, with particular attention to what is "bound" and "loosed" in heaven. In addition to what we have already discussed, Vogt believes, p. 151, that there is in Origen no Donatist attitude, "sondern dass er nur seinem Grundsatz treu bleibt, nämlich dem, dass nicht nur die Amtsträger der Kirche Apostelerben sind, sondern dass die grösseren Verheissungen auf die Vollkommenen übergegangen sind."

201. See, for example, *Hom. 19.14 in Jer.* (171.1–12).

202. *Fr. 50 in Jer.* (223.21–23).

203. For other texts verifying the necessary eminence of Church leaders, see Vogt, *Kirchenverständnis*, pp. 7–13. Vogt, p. 7, notes that the holy nature of the event requires one who is in holiness worthy of it.

204. *Comm. in Mt.* 11.15 (59.11–14, 16–17, 18–20), trans. Patrick*, 444B. Text suggested by Nautin, *Jérémie*, I, 421, n. 1.

205. *Comm. in Mt.* 16.8 (497.19–32). Scriptural context is Matt. 20:25–28.

206. *Comm. in Mt.* 16.8 (493.24–494.4), *Comm. in Mt.,* ser. 12 (22.23–31), and *Comm. in Mt.* 16.22 (549.22–550.1). Scriptural contexts for these texts are Matt. 20:25–28, and 23:6–7.

207. *Hom. 6.3 in Lev.* (362.26–363.5). Lécuyer, "Sacerdoce," 263, adds also to this text *Hom. 22.4 in Num.* (208–209) in which Origen indicates that no bishop may be ordained if the people and the priests have not prayed to receive the light of God.

208. This word (*mobilia*) is used earlier in this same text in a translation of Deut. 11:18. See *Comm. in Mt.,* ser. 11 (21.22). Fortunately, a Greek fragment survives which indicates that Origen reproduced the LXX *asaleutos*, which refers to something unmoved or unshaken, according to Liddell-Scott-Jones. Klostermann, p. 21, notes in his critical apparatus that one Greek text has *saleuta*. The Hebrew has "totaphoth" which Brown-Driver-Briggs translates "bands" or "frontlet bands." The word is also used in Ex. 13:16, in both cases translated *asaleutos* by the LXX translators. These texts are not cited, according to the indices of the GCS edition, in the Latin Origen. The Vulgate translates the word differently in each passage. It is probable the Latin translator of Origen had a defective text here.

209. *Comm. in Mt.,* ser. 11 (22.13–18).

210. This point of view of conversion would be very much the thrust of Hal Koch's work, *Pronoia und Paideusis*, a study whose primary purpose, let us recall, was to show the influence of Platonism on Origen. See especially pp. 79–81, 305ff., 310–311. For example, he writes, p. 81: "Die Aufgabe der Kirche ist, kurz gesagt, die Pädagogie zu verwicklichen, welche der Logos bringt, d.h. alles für alle zu sein." Also, Koch writes, p. 79, "Für Origenes war die Kirche, was die philosophischen Schulen für andere Gelehrte seiner Zeit waren." Because of the theme of his study, Koch tends to stress the role of education in conversion, especially in terms of philosophical models. And certainly, like Augustine, Meister Eckert, and Thomas Aquinas, Origen was interested in philosophical problems, argumentation and approaches. But the center of Origen's attention was not Plato but the Christ and the church, which we have demonstrated many times already, and the focus of his meditation was not on Plato's books but on scriptural books. Hence all concerns with education in Origen, especially with respect to conversion, need to reckon with these facts. Furthermore, as we have already seen, the Church was not only a group of students and teachers, but the Body of Christ and partner with God in his economy.

211. Cf. Vogt, *Kirchverständnis*, pp. 58–70, and G. Lomiento, "Cristo Didaskalos," 25–54, especially 25–32. Pages 32–51 are taken up with a discussion or *Comm. in Mt.* 10.1–12 with the focus on the title issue.

212. Cf. *Jo.* 32.10 (443.14–15). See Vogt, *Kirchenverständnis*, pp. 58–64 on the pre-eminent place of the teacher in the contemporary church of Origen. See especially pp. 59–60 concerning Eph. 4:12 and I Cor. 12:28. The text is cited in *Comm. in Mt.* 11.15 (59.7–11) on Matt. 15:14–20, *Fr. 446 in Mt.* (186) on Matt. 23:8 and *Jo.* 32.10, discussed above.

213. *Jo.* 32.10 (441.29–443.14). This passage indicates, as Vogt, *Kirchenverständnis*, pp. 69–70, has noted on this text, that the teacher not only enlightens and is a means for knowledge, but is one who aids in purification also. Hence he is one who helps to build the church. Vogt views the teacher as having an "outer" and an "inner" purpose. The outer purpose is the apologetic task to change pagans and heretics. The inner purpose concerns those of the Church. The teacher builds up believers, brings them along in understanding through the Logos, and is, as we noted

initially, an ambassador for scripture and the truth, as well as a moral inspiration. See Vogt, p. 68. Obviously both of these tasks apply to conversion, and will have an effect on conduct. In this section, the object is to bring into relief the more explicit role of the teaching/teacher in turning one to better conduct.

Lomiento, "Cristos Didaskalos," 37, perhaps offers the critical agent in conversion by purification when he discusses the role of love in the relation of Christ and his hearers. God's love is the force which keeps us near God, and yet it is also a force which attracts (turns) men to God because it moves us away from earthly things. He writes, "Il particolare affinamento dell'udito consente di avvertire uno degli effetti dell'amore a Dio, nei discepoli intimi di Cristo. Questo amore penetrando lo spirito va in profondità e divide, distacca l'anima dalla terra, scrosta ogni affectus, che dà subito un suono nuovo."

See also Bertrand, *Mystique*, pp. 116–117, concerning *Jo.* 32.7 (436.30–437.22).

214. *Hom. 6.6 in Lev.* (367.29–368.3, 5–7). Vogt, *Kirchenverstandnis*, p. 61, points out that in the homilies on Numbers and Leviticus, the offices of the teacher and priest are often combined, whereas in the homilies on Ezekiel, there are two separate offices. Cf. *Hom. 6.6 in Lev.* (368.30ff.), *Hom. 2.1 in Num.* (9.22ff.) and *Hom. 3.7 in Ezech.* (354.15ff.). As Vogt notes, there is no need to view here a development in Origen's attitude. In fact, the two modes can co-exist. In the above text, Origen does not discuss two different offices, but two different aspects which some priests have polarized.

215. *Hom. 5.16 in Jer.* (45.21–24). Bettencourt, *Doctrina*, pp. 35–36 and note 8 on this text and *Hom. 3.3 in Ex.* (169.19–27) writes that before the Word is preached by the teacher, there is no real movement in the soul. The Word, given through the agency of the preacher, begins the war against evil. Gögler, *Theologie*, p. 265, points out that the Logos is always the agent of what is spiritual rather than what is formal. The Logos is like a trumpet not because of his Lautstärke, "sondern ob seiner erhabenen Bedeutung, die den Hörer wecht und bereit macht."

216. *Hom 5.16 in Jer.* (45.30–46.2). Klostermann notes in his apparatus that there is some uncertainty concerning the interpretation of Psalm 17 in this text. While God is called a fortification in this text, in *Sel. in Ps.* 17.30 (PG 12:1236B) Origen considers it a fortification of sin. Though the authenticity of this latter text has been questioned, it is probable that Origen considered the idea of fortification applicable to both. Both Schadel and Nautin are silent here.

217. *Hom. 5.16 in Jer.* (46.10–15).

218. *Hom. 5.17 in Jer.* (47.10–13).

219. *Comm. in Mt.* 11.14 (56.15–23), 442B.

220. *Hom. 4.4 in Jer.* (27.10–13).

221. *Hom. 3.3 in Ezech.* (351.22–27), trans. Tollinton*, p. 176.

222. I will discuss these in more detail below.

223. *Fr. 21 in Jer.* (208.7–10).

224. *Fr. 13 in Jer.* (204.2–16).

225. *Hom. 38 in Luc.* (218.1–8). As Crouzel, Fournier and Perichon, *S. Luc.*, p. 446, n. 2, point out in their edition, Origen also views the parallel passage (Mt. 21:12–13) as referring to bishops, presbyters and deacons who sell their office for personal favors. Cf. *Comm. in Mt.* 16.22 (549.22–550.1).

226. Pretense and hypocrisy apply not only to teachers, but to bishops, presbyters, deacons and even martyrs (heretics who die for false teachings). Cf. *Comm. in Mt.*, ser. 24 (40.19–22). Text suggested by Bardy, *Théologie*, p. 143.

227. Sometimes the matter of pretense is quite subtle. Cf. *Hom. 10.5 in Jer.* (75.24–76.1) with respect to the heretics.

228. *Hom. 7.3–4 in Ezech.* (392.24–393.1, 395.1–10).

229. *Hom. 7.3 in Ezech.* (394.1–6). As is evident, I have paraphrased some of the translation in order to clarify the point, but, as it stands in the Latin, it has probably been abridged.

230. *Comm. in Mt.* 10.15 (18.30–32), 422B.

231. *Comm. in Rom.* 7.17 (PG 14: 1148A).

232. *Hom. 4.5 in Jer.* (29.5–8).

233. *Hom. 4.6 in Jer.* (29.16–17).

234. The word *alethos* is used to stress what is real rather than what is just appearance. Judah's conversion was just appearance and pretense. She turned half-heartedly. Hence I (as well as Nautin/Husson and Schadel) can translate "true" in contrast to what is insincere. Origen is fully aware of the complexities in the movements of the heart.

With respect to the translation of *epistrophe* as "conversion," a translation which Nautin/Husson, Aubin, Chadwick and Corsini, as well as many others, accept, we need to add a note of concern. Schadel uses the terms Rückkehr and Umkehr rather than Bekehrung or Verwandlung throughout his translation in order to reflect the more fundamental sense of the word, as well as perhaps the philosophical usage. With his German terms, the translation would then be "turning back," or a "return."

There are several implications involved in how one translates the word. First, the word "return" or a "turning back or about" involves direction, whereas the word "conversion" lacks this dimension. Second, the word "return" and a "turning back" more strongly suggest a process rather than an event. Third, the word "conversion" in English and comparable words in French, Italian, Spanish and German mean primarily a transformation or a kind of change, whereas *epistrophe* primarily refers to a return to the place where one was, or at least a turning back toward that direction. So also *conversio* in the time of Origen and several centuries after him. However, the words "return" and a "turning back" lack the religious connotations which are so often involved in these texts, namely, that the turn is a turn back to God and a more godly life. Finally, fifth, all these translations somehow fail to communicate the moral dimension of the word, namely, the sense of repenting from error.

235. *Hom. 4.6 in Jer.* (29.22–27). Origen's discussion of conversion in this text must be understood, it seems to me, within the context of the homily. The definition was not intended to be an all-encompassing summary of his view on conversion. Rather it is the culmination of the points discussed within the homily, particularly, the failure of the Jews to turn properly to the Lord.

236. Cf. Schadel, p. 252, n. 29 on this "library."

237. *Hom. 16.1 in Jer.* (132.5–19, 23–133.4). This is partially translated above. For the development of Origen's thought on the allegory of heaven, the firmament and the waters, See J. Pépin, *Théologie cosmique et théologie chrétienne* (PUF: Paris, 1964), pp. 390–417. Reference given by L. Doutreleau, *Genèse*, p. 28, n. 1.

Crouzel, *Théologie*, p. 234, points to this text, along with several others, which refer to Origen's attitude about this life and the evils of the world as a kind of veil which needs to be removed, partially on earth, but fully in the resurrection. Origen does quote 2 Cor. 3:18.

238. *Hom. 3.3 in Ezech.* (350.24–30).

239. *Hom. 3.3 in Ezech.* (350.30–351.4), trans. Tollinton, p. 175.

240. *Hom. 5.8 in Lev.* (348.26–349.4), trans. Tollinton*, p. 178.

241. The Logos has already adapted himself in the incarnation and in scripture to people for their conversion and salvation. See Gögler, *Theologie*, pp. 307–319 and p. 318, n. 69 on the ancient origins of this idea of adaptation. As an agent of the Logos, the teacher is still at another level of the process of adapting according to the condition of people and their needs.

242. Cf. Lomiento, "Cristo Didaskalos," 32–51, on *Comm. in Mt.* 10.1–2, concerning how Christ himself is careful in both his method and in what he teaches to different hearers. To the multitudes he gives his parables; to his disciples, who come in to his "house," he explains the deeper meanings. To the crowd Christ exhibits his humanity, but to his disciples his divinity.

243. *Hom. 5.10 in Jer.* (39.33–40.2). Cf. also *Hom. 5.11 in Jer.* (40.3–6).

244. *Hom. 20.5 in Jer.* (184.12–20, 31–185.5) concerning Jer. 20:7–9.

245. *Hom. 11.3 in Num.* (82.2–4), suggested by Nautin, *Jérémie*, I, 311, n. 3.

246. Cf. Lomiento, *Vangelo di Luca*, pp. 18, 62, and *Fr. 5 in Jer.* (200.21–25), concerning Jer. 8:7, on the image of the untilled field.

According to *Fr. 294 in Mt.* (131.1–10), however, it is the individual himself who determines whether thorns are to be produced and the land is ploughed up. So also *Fr. 157 in Lc.* (289), on Luke 9:62, where he uses scripture to plough. Cf. also *Hom. 23.8 in Num.* (220.2–6).

247. Nautin/Husson translate *hegemonikon* "raison," Schadel "Geistgrund." See notes above on this subject, and Corsini, *Giovanni*, p. 167, n. 52 and p. 176, n. 62, where it means "heart." Rufinus often translates *principale cordis*.

248. Nautin/Husson translate *logos* here "doctrine," Schadel "Wort." Cf. Mark 4:14 and subsequent text.

249. See Schadel, p. 265, n. 56, on the meaning of *anapausis* (repose), a word used often in the *Homilies on Jeremiah*. The repose is from the "world;" all activity is now directed toward the contemplation of God. *Mart.* 47 confirms this view.

250. *Hom. 5.13 in Jer.* (42.6–13). Similar thoughts are in *Hom. 23.6 in Num.* (218.21–25).

251. *Hom. 12.5 in Lev.* (464.24–27).

252. *Hom. 12.7 in Lev.* (466.12–23). This idea of not rashly committing secrets of wisdom to just anyone is also found in *Hom. 4.3 in Num.* (23.1–8) among other texts. The image of the different lovers who yearn for the soul's beauty is found also in *Hom. 7.6 in Ezech.* (396.10–22).

253. *Cels.* 3.52 (248.15–23/II, 124). Words in quotations are used by Celsus. For *phronimos* (sensible), Chadwick has "intelligent," Crombie has "wise," Borret has "prudent," and Nautin/Husson use "sensée" in *Hom. 12.6 and 17.3 in Jer.* (93.7 and 145.14), where it is used in contrast to *aphron*. This contrast would seem to apply here also. Celsus refers to boys, fools and slaves.

254. *Hom. 1.4 in Lev.* (285.24–25; 286.6–9).

255. *Hom. 1.4 in Lev.* (286.12–15).

256. *Hom. 27.1 in Num.* (255.25–256.4). In *Jo.* 13.33 (258.5–11), Origen specifies that, in both the physical and spiritual realms, it is the *poiotes* of what nourishes which varies with every soul.

257. *Hom. 27.1 in Num.* (256.8–257.12).

258. *Hom. 27.1 in Num.* (257.26–258.2). *Philoc.* 10.2 (197.15–198.3), a fragment from a missing homily on Jeremiah, refers to the scripture as a group of herbs, and the saint a kind of expert botanist and spiritual herbalist. If we do not understand a point, it is perhaps due to spiritual inexperience.

259. In *Hom. 4.3 in Num.* (23.9–24.18), Origen also seems to consider four orders: Sons of Aaron, Caathites, Gersonites and Merarites. See Méhat, *Nombres*, p. 108, n. 1.

260. *Hom. 9.9 in Jos.* (354.25–355.14). On the different nourishments, see also *Jo.* 13.33–34 (257.22–260.13) and *Hom. 23.6 in Num.* (218.15–28). Though the idea of different orders of men and different kinds of nourishment is present in Scripture, Philo, *De agricultura* 159–162, also presents three levels of moral development: beginners, those advancing and the mature. On the different levels of nourishment, see also Philo, *De congr. erud gr.* 19. Text supplied by Méhat, *Nombres*, p. 512, n. 1.

Origen's reference here to women who are "weak" needs further comment. Though Origen presents many women of scripture favorably, i.e., Sarah, Deborah, Rebecca, Elizabeth and the Virgin Mary, the feminine image in general for him is one of weakness, subjection, dependence and works of flesh. However, this image is only an allegorical device. Origen, for example, refers to men with feminine souls, and vice versa. Hence he states, in *Hom. 9.9 in Jos.* (356.3–5): "For the divine scripture does not make a separation according to sex of men and women. Indeed sex with God is not a criterion, but according to differences in the soul one is designated either a man or a woman." For the meaning of "woman" to Origen, see Crouzel, *Virginité*, pp. 134–142. This text was suggested by Crouzel's study.

261. Of course, the teacher himself must be capable of searching the scripture for the spiritual sense. Vogt, *Kirchenverständnis*, pp. 66–68, considers the exegetical expertise needed by the teacher to be truly a teacher and to counter false teachers. Vogt's texts are *Jo.* 5.8 (105.4ff.), 348B, *Cels.* 6.37 (106.24ff.), *Comm. in Mt.*, ser. 15 and 18 (28.14ff. and 53.1ff.), and *Hom. 7.4 in Lev.* (382.30ff.).

262. *Jo.* 1.18(20) (22.32–23.8), 307A. Christ is both wisdom itself and wisdom incarnate. He is the first-born of all creation and, Origen states in this section, Man himself, "Adam."

263. A brief summary of Origen's understanding of the use of non-Christian material in preparatory education and how this material can lead to the "exalted height" of Christian doctrine is found in *Cels.* Pref. 5 and 3.58. Origen's main requirement is that the material benefit and improve the hearer. Texts suggested by Angel Benito y Duran, "El humanismo cristiano de Origenes," 133. This article is devoted to an analysis of selected texts of *Contra Celsum* which indicate Origen's "humanism," a humanism which he describes as a view of man and his world resulting from the image of God as a beneficent administrator who loves and cares for all he has created, and who created all with a purpose. Man is a rational creation with an intelligence to be used in many studies and fields of interest. It is part of God's providence that man exercise his rational power in many directions. Cf. *Cels.* 4.74–78.

264. *Hom. 11.6 in Ex.* (260.7–17).

265. The identity of this student is unclear. Though traditionally also ascribed to Gregory, Nautin in his recent *Origène* has questioned whether this attribution is documented adequately.

266. For such detail, see the following studies: F. Cavallera, "Origène éducateur," *BLE* (1943), 61–75; H. Crouzel, "Le 'Remerciement à Origène' de saint Gregorire le Thaumaturge: Son

contenu doctrinal," *Sciences ecclésiastigues*, 16 (1964), 59–91; A. Knauber, "Das Anliegen der Schule des Origenes zu Cäsarea," *Münchener theologische Zeitschrift*, 19 (1968), 182–203; H. Crouzel, *Gregorire le Thaumaturge*... (SC 148; Paris: Cerf, 1969).

267. *In Origenem oratio panegyrica* (PG 10:1051–1104). See the translation by S. Salmond in *ANF* 6, 21–39.

268. The teacher as physician is a scriptural image (Matt. 9:11–12). But Borret, *Celse*, II, 168, n. 1, also indicates that it was a traditional view of the philosopher and philosophy, as Origen himself confirms in *Cels*. 7.60. See also *Cels*. 3.74–75 (265.14–268.3).

269. *Hom. 14.1 in Jer*. (106.13–107.3).

270. *Hom. 14.2 in Jer*. (107.4–9).

271. Words in brackets added due to the Jerome translation.

272. *Hom. 14.3 in Jer*. (108.4–10).

273. *Hom. 14.3 in Jer*. (108.10–20).

274. *Hom. 14.4 in Jer*. (109.6–14).

275. *Hom. 5.5 in Ex*. (376.7–11).

276. Hamilton, "The Church," 488, along with Jaeger and Marrou, believe that Origen and Clement use this image of the teacher and doctrine to attract pagans.

277. *Hom. 6.3 in Jer*. (50.27–29).

278. *Hom. 6.3 in Jer*. (50.33–51.1).

279. *Hom. 6.3 in Jer*. (51.6–7).

280. Cf. Philo, *De congressu eruditionis gratia* 69–70, where the beginner listens to words, but the one who practices imitates life and is not a listener to words only.

281. *Fr. 23 in Jer*. (209.24–28).

282. *Fr. 27 in Jer*. (212.11–16).

283. A pure heart leads to good practice, just as the end of *theoria* is practice. Cf. *Hom. 1 in Luc*. (8.13). For, as Lomiento, "Cristo Didaskalos," 28ff., writes, one is not able to love the good of the kingdom and not communicate it.

284. Bettenson translates *dogma* throughout this text "belief." Lawson often translates "teaching," Vogt, *Kirchenverständnis*, p. 283, with the German "Dogma," and Crouzel, *Virginité*, p. 93, uses "doctrine" and sometimes "opinion."

285. According to the Latin translator of the *Commentary on Matthew* of that portion which is extant in Greek, *sermo*, though used for several words (*lexis, phone, deixis*), is most often a translation of *logos*. See *GCS* 12/3.413.

286. *Comm. in Mt.*, ser. 33 (61.14–26, 32–62.6), trans. Bettenson* (in part), p. 260. It is worth noting how Origen, in this text, clarifies what he is sometimes denounced for, namely, his intellectualism. Correct thinking is inseparable from correct living. And one cannot really be living correctly if his heart is impure; nor can the heart be pure if it does not extend to acts of innocence. Bettencourt, pp. 106–107, may have underestimated the point of this text. Doctrine is not sufficient to distinguish Christians and heretics and others. Even their "distinguished" actions are in essence without basis. What distinguishes is the whole activity and life of the soul, all its "sons" and "daughters."

287. So *Hom. 10.1 in Num*. (70.6–7), concerning which Stelzenberger, *Syneidesis*, pp. 24–25, says that Origen here follows Paul, namely, that the more serious problem of the sinner is in matters of faith rather than moral crimes. The source of the problem, in other words, is inward. Stelzenberger is considering the use of *suneidesis* as an inner concern of faith/belief rather than a moral offense (as it is so often in the West (*conscientia*)).

Chênevert, *L'église*, p. 154, notes also that whenever conversion of the pagans is mentioned in the *Commentary on the Song of Songs*, the intellectual and moral aspects are always paired together. Similarly, he mentions that there is no conflict of faith and works in Origen, even if the faith must take precedent. Origen assumes, as we have noted, that a true faith will extend to virtue and good morals. Crouzel, *Virginité*, p. 94, has a similar opinion on this text. But see the other texts which Crouzel, pp. 94–98, supplies on Origen's criticism of philosophers, heretics, pagans and Jews regarding how their conduct is soiled by their beliefs and salvation is compromised.

In fact, Crouzel, pp. 93–94, believes this text (*Comm. in Mt.*, ser. 33) may indicate Origen's opposition to universality of the apokatastasis. However, as we have already discussed in Chapter II, the apokatastasis must be understood in light of many other themes in Origen's thought (i.e., succession of worlds, the punishment and pre-existence) most of which Origen recognized as speculative and hence only tentative.

288. *Jo.* 13.29 (253.23–28).

Chapter V.
Becoming a Christian:
How Does a Christian Come to Know the Way of God?

1. Many studies have been useful for the preparation of this Chapter. See especially R. Arnou, "Le thème neoplatonicien de la contemplation créatrice chez Origène et chez s. Augustin," *Gregorianum*, 13 (1932), 124–136; F. Bertrand, *Mystigue de Jèsus chez Origène*; J. Boada, "El pneuma en Origenes"; N. Brox, "Spiritualität und Orthodoxie zum Konflikt des Origenes mit der Geschichte des Dogmas," *Jahrbuch für Antike und Christentum*, 8 suppl. (1980), 140–154; Crouzel, *Théologie* and *Connaissance*; J. Dupuis, *L'esprit de l'homme*; P. Faessler, *Der Hagiosbegriff*; G. Gruber, *ZOE*; W. Hauschild, *Gottes Geist und der Mensch*; A. Lieske, *Losgosmystik bei Origenes*; H. de Lubac, *Histoire et esprit;* H. Rahner, "Taufe und geistliches Leben bei Origenes"; J. Rius-Camps, *El dinamismo*, and Völker, *Der Vollkommenheitsidenl*, all cited previously, and listed in full in bibliography.

2. Cf. *Hom. 16.2 and 19.13 in Jer.*
3. *Jo.* 13.14 (238.17–24). Cf. Rius-Camps, pp. 432–433, where he comments on this text.
4. *Comm. in Mt.* 13.26 (251.12–29).
5. *Hom. 1.7 in Jer.* (6.23–24).
6. See, for example, *Hom. 18.6 and 19.15 in Jer.* on the use of *teleios* contrasted with *paidion* and *brephos.*
7. *Hom. 4.1 in Jer.* (23.29–31).
8. Hence we shall also translate the words *teleiōs, teleios* and words from these roots in this context with the English "complete," or "completely," with the understanding, of course, of the idea of "mature" being involved.
9. *Hom. 5.2 in Jer.* (31.29–32).
10. *Hom. 5.2 in Jer.* (31.32–32.14).
11. *Hom. 5.2 in Jer.* (32.18–25).
12. *Hom. 5.2 in Jer.* (32.25–27).
13. *Hom. 5.2 in Jer.* (32.27–33.3).
14. *Hom. 5.2 in Jer.* (33.3–6). With respect to the translation of *artaō* (depend), see *Fr. 1 in Jo.* Schadel and Nautin/Husson have variants.
15. *Hom. 5.10 in Jer.* (40.1–2).
16. *Hom. 12.13 in Jer.* (101.18–22).
17. *Jo.* 13.24 (III.108.18–24/248.2–8). Blanc adds *echontas.*
18. *Jo.* 13.37 (262.9).
19. Cf. *Jo.* 13.47.
20. *Jo.* 13.37 (262.19–22). Cf. Rius-Camps, p. 366.
21. *Jo.* 13.37 (262.24–25).
22. See Rius-Camps, p. 364, n. 33, where he cites all the principal texts which discuss Heb. 5:14. Also Crouzel, *Connaissance*, pp. 486ff., and *Studia Patristica*, Volume III, which is completely devoted to Origen.
23. *Fr. 51 in Jer.* (224).
24. *Orat.* 27.1–2.
25. *Cf.* Crouzel, *Connaissance*, pp. 458ff.
26. *Jo.* 6.51 (160.23–26).
27. *Jo.* 6.52 (161.12–18), trans. Menzies*, 376B–377A.
28. *Fr. 93 in Jo.* (556.14–16).
29. *Comm. in Mt.* 10.9–10 (I.172ff.).
30. *Comm. in Mt.* 10.10 (11.25–27), trans. Patrick, 419A.
31. Cf. *Princ.* 1.1.7 (I.104.232ff.), p. 12–13, which is directed to this theme.
32. *Comm. in Mt.* 17.15 (629.2–12).

33. *Jo.* 13.53 (282.7–11).

34. *Jo.* 13.53 (282.7–283.14).

35. *Orat.* 9.2 (318.26–319.8), trans. Greer, p. 99. E. C. Jay, *Origen's Treatise on Prayer* (London: SPCK, 1954) p. 108, n. 1, also refers to *Princ.* 3.4.2 as a parallel text.

36. *Orat.* 25.2 (358.12–21), trans. Greer*, p. 133. See Rius-Camps, pp. 338–339, 438–439.

37. *Hom. 17.2 in Jos.*

38. *Jo.* 13.16, 18 (240.9–22, 242.10–243.11).

39. *Jo.* 13.30 (254.12–13).

40. *Jo.* 13.59 (290.20–22).

41. *Jo.* 13.58 (289.16–22).

42. *Jo.* 13.59 (290.10–13).

43. We will return to the meaning of faith in a later section.

44. For a discussion with texts on Origen's definition of grace, see Drewery, pp. 18–65, and his summary on pp. 47–48. Drewery, p. 49, points out that "Origen was not conscious of a technical theological problem in *charis*, and did not therefore feel it necessary to guard himself by definition, etc., in his use of it..."

45. *Hom. 1.7 in Jer.* (5.17–19).

46. *Hom. 1.7 in Jer.* (5.22–23).

47. *Hom. 1.12 in Jer.* (10.22–27).

48. *Hom. 20.3 in Jer.* (182.8–12).

49. *Hom. 20.3 in Jer.* (182.13–14).

50. *Fr. 19 in Jer.* (207.16–17).

51. Cf. Drewery, p. 48: "In general Origen seems to link grace rather with divine power than with the other attributes." See supporting texts in note 42.

52. *Hom. 4.2–4 in Jer.*

53. *Hom. 3.2 in Jer.* (21.12–15).

54. *Jo.* 6.6 (II.156.39–40), trans. Menzies, 353A.

55. *Comm. in Rom.* 4.8 (PG 14:990). By Rufinus's own admission, his translation of the *Commentary on Romans* is a paraphrase. However, since this subject created no difficulties for the orthodoxy of Rufinus's time, we have no reason to suspect the general thrust of the argument here. Of course, as we discuss in the Appendix on textual methodology, it is likely that the key words of Origen are probably preserved.

56. *Comm. in Rom.* 5.2 (PG 14:1021B–1026A). Cf. Rius-Camps, p. 196, on the influence of Adam's sin on descendents.

57. *Comm. in Rom.* 5.6 (PG 14:1033D–1035A).

58. On the lists of virtues, see Rius-Camps, pp. 323–324.

59. See Corsini, p. 255, n. 53, on this idea, and how it differs from other attitudes of Origen's day, particularly those of the Neoplatonists and Middle Platonists.

60. *Jo.* 2.28 (85.4–20).

61. *Jo.* 2.28 (85.20–25), trans, Menzies*, 339B.

62. *Orat.* 1.1 (297.1–6), trans. Greer, p. 81.

63. *Jo.* 2.10 (65.26–31), trans. Menzies, 329A. A similar thought is found in Greek in *Princ.* 1.3.5 (55.4ff.). Cf. Rius-Camps, pp. 23–31 on the Holy Spirit. He writes on this passage: "Es la unica ocasion—que sepamos—en que se nos habla explicitamente de una 'materia' de origen divino: la Materia subyacente en los carismas que nos vienen de Dios. Origenes relaciona esa Materia divina con la formacion y substantivacion del Espriritu santo." Also see Harl, *Origène*, p. 107.
For an overview of the functions in Origen's Trinity, see Blanc, *Commentaire*, I, 252, n. 1, in which she offers the distinctions as *ex ipso* (Father), *per ipsum* (Son) and *in ipso* (the Holy Spirit).

64. See Corsini, p. 222, n. 20.

65. Again, see Blanc, *Commentaire*, I, 252, n. 1 on the functions within Origen's trinity.

66. Cf. *Hom. 3.2 in Jos.*

67. *Jo.* 6.36 (145.7–12), trans. Menzies*, 368B.

68. *Jo.* 6.36 (145.12–22).

67. *Jo.* 6.35 (144.16–21), 368A.

70. Several scholars have been puzzled by the implications of *Jo.* 6.36 on grace. See Völker, p. 40, Gruber, p. 229–240, and Blanc, *Commentaire*, II, 43–45, where she summarizes the arguments. The text, which states that God foreknows and assigns worth to certain souls *by nature* and that souls thus conform to a prevenient knowledge, seems to contradict other passages in Origen

which state that human nature cannot have the worth to do good in itself; it must receive its good through Christ. Only God gives the possibility in each situation of doing good. See texts given by Blanc, and her other discussion of this issue in I, 402, n. 10 on *Jo.* 2.31 (I.336. sect. 192).

But see also Crouzel, *Théologie*, p. 243, who believes this text has an "antipelagian" character which balances other Origen texts which stress more the human initiative. Corsini, who referred me to Crouzel's thought on this text, correctly notes, p. 826, n. 15, on *Fr. XI in Jo.*, that the above discussions are anachronistic. "L'accento messo da Origene sull'iniziativa umana è da inquadrare nella sua intenzione polemica verso lo gnosticismo e, in particolare, contro un certo tipo di predestinazione divulgato da Marcione e dai suoi seguaci."

71. *Hom. 1.8 and 1.10 in Jer.*
72. *Hom. 8.2 in Jer.*
73. *Hom. 8.6 in Jer.*
74. *Hom. 11.6 in Jer.*
75. *Hom. 12.6 in Jer.*
76. *Hom. 14.5 in Jer.*
77. *Hom. 16.5 in Jer.*
78. *Hom. 20.9 in Jer.*
79. *Jo.* 19.3 (301.22–26).
80. *Commentary on Romans* 4.5.
81. *Comm. in Rom.* 4.5 (PG 14:975A). *perfecta* is assumed to be a translation of *teleios*.
82. *Comm. in Rom.* 9.2 (PG 14:1213A–1215C).
83. *Comm. in Rom.* 9.2 (PG 14:1214B). *ratio* (principle), we assume, is a translation of *logos*. For a similar translation in the Latin *Commentary on Matthew*, see GCS XII, p. 409.
84. *Cels.* 6.13 (III.210.10–11).
85. *Cels.* 3.47 (II.112.14ff.), p. 161. Cf. also *Cels.* 6.13.
86. One of the best examples of how Origen explores the three dimensions is found in *Com. in Mt. 13.14–18* (10.213–230), but unfortunately its explication would require too many pages. It concerns Matt. 18: 1–6.
87. *Hom. 22.2 in Jesu Nave* (433.17–434.2). This text and the two following are summarized in an extant Greek fragment. See GCS, p. 433, 27ff.
88. *Hom. 22.2 in Jesu Nave* (434.2–5).
89. *Hom. 22.2 in Jesu Nave* (434.5–11).
90. A glance through the scriptural indices of Origen's works indicates the remarkable number of times he refers to these texts. See *Biblia Patristica*, Volume 3.
91. *Hom. 6.1 in Jesu Nave* (323.3–20).
92. *Jo.* 13.33 (257.26–258.1).
93. *Jo.* 13.33 (258.9–11). See Blanc, *Commentaire*, III, 144, n. 3, on translating this difficult passage. Gögler, Crouzel, Corsini and she have all translated it differently. I have dropped the *te* which she adds after *praxeon*.
94. *Jo.* 13.34 (III.152.46–49/260.10–12).
95. *Hom. 8.3 in Jer.* (58.17; 59.5).
96. *Hom. 8.4 in Jer.* (59.28–33).
97. *Comm. in Mt.* 13.26 (250.24–251.2; 251.24–29), trans. Patrick, 490A. Patrick translates the motivating power for this change as "free will." The Greek, however, has *to eph' hemin* which is comparable spiritually, for Origen, to the physical *tous spermatikous logous* which determine why one is short or tall.
98. *Hom. 16.4 in Jer.* (136.18–20).
99. *Hom. 16.4 in Jer.* (136.15–16).
100. *Hom. 16.2 in Jer.* (133.26).
101. *Cels.* 4.7 (II.202.8ff.), trans. Chadwick*, p. 188.
102. On the word "heart," see Crouzel and Simonetti, *Traité*, II, 30, n. 40. They write that "heart" in the ancient world was more intuitive than discursive, an equivalent, as we have noted previously, of *nous* and *hegemonikon*. It was not directly concerned with love or affection.
103. Cf. *Comm. in Mt.* 16.11, *Jo.* 19.3, sect. 17, 19.22, sect. 146, *Cels.* 6.69, 7.33, *Princ.* 1.1.7, 9, etc. For a detailed list, see *Biblia Patristica*, III, 230–231.
104. As we have noted above, in our discussions in Chapter III on Origen's anthropology, "intellect" (sometimes translated as "mind" by English translators) or *nous*, and "heart" or *hegemonikon/kardia*, are interchangeable in Origen.

105. *Princ.* 1.1.7 (I.106.253–256), p. 12.
106. *Princ.* 1.1.9 (I.110.311–312), trans. Butterworth, p. 14.
107. *Jo.* 32.27 (472.29–34). See note in Corsini, p. 799.
108. Cf. Corsini, p. 167, n. 52.
109. *Comm. in Mt.* 16.11 (509.1–14).
110. *Cels.* 7.33 (IV.88.11ff.), trans. Chadwick, p. 421.
111. For this viewpoint, see *Jo.* 6.19, *Hom. 1 in Luc.*, *Hom. 10.1 in Jer.*, *Fr. 61 in Jer.*, *Comm. in Rom.* 5.2 (1025BC), *Comm. in Rom.* 8.7 (1178B–1179A).
112. See *Jo.* 1.16, 2.36, *Fr. 21 in Jo.*, *Comm. in Mt.* 16.7.
113. For this view, see *Jo.* 1.27, 20.34, *Fr. 39 in Luc.*, *Comm. in Mt.* 12.14.
114. *Fr. 171 in Luc.*.
115. *Comm. in Mt.* 12.14 (96.33–97.1), trans. Patrick, 458B.
116. *Comm. in Mt.* 12.14 (97.13–21), trans. Patrick, 458B.
117. *Fr. 61 in Jer.*, *Hom. 10.1 in Jer.* and *Comm. in Rom.* 5.2.
118. Cf. *Hom. 1 in Luc.*
119. Cf. *Comm. in Mt.* 16.7 (487.22–488.15).
120. *Comm. in Rom.* 8.7.
121. See P. G. Alves-de-Sousa, "A presenza de cristo nos comentarios de Origenesa Jo. 6, 55–57," *Theologica*, 11 (1976), 313–334; L. W. Barnard, "Origen's Christology and Eschatology," *Anglican Theological Review*, 46 (1964), 314–319; F. Bertrand, *Mystique de Jésus chez Origène*; C. Blanc, "Qui est Jésus Christ? La response d'Origène," *BLE*, 80 (1979), 241–256; H. Crouzel, *Théologie*; M. Eichinger, *Die Verklärung Christi bei Origenes* (Vienna: Herder, 1969); R. Gögler, *Zur Theologie des biblischen Wortes bei Origenes* (Düsseldorf: Patmos, 1963); M. Harl, *Origène*; A. Lieske, *Die Theologie der Logosmystik bei Origenes* (Münster: Aschendorff, 1938); J. A. Lyons, *The Cosmic Christ in Origen and Teilhard de Chardin* (Oxford: University Press, 1982); J. C. McLelland, *God the Anonymous — A Study in Alexandrian Theology* (Philadelphia, Pa.: Patristic Foundation, 1976); D. Pazzini, *In principio era il Logos. Origene e il prologo del vandelo di Giovanni* (Brescia: Paideia, 1983); J. Rius-Camps, *El dinamismo trinitario*; E. Schendel, *Herrschaft und Unterwerfung Christi* (Tübingen: Mohr, 1971); B. Studer, "La résurrection de Jésus d'après le Peri Archon d'Origène," *Augustinianum*, 18 (1978), 279–309.
122. For a discussion of these, see H. Crouzel, "Le contenu spirituel des dénominations du Christ selon le Livre I du *Commentaire sur Jean* d'Origène," *Origeniana Secunda*, pp. 131–150. According to Crouzel, p. 149, rational creatures participate only in the aspect of the Image. The list includes: Christ as the Beginning, Wisdom, Light, Resurrection, the Way, the Truth, the Life, the Door, the Shepherd, the Anointed, Teacher, Son, Bread, Vine, Sword, Servant, Living and the Dead, First, End, Lamb, Paraclete, Power, Sanctification, Redemption, Righteousness, Demiurge, High Priest, Image, etc.
123. Cf. *Jo.* 1.37.
124. Lyons, *The Cosmic Christ*, p. 130, writes, "The doctrine on mediation, which we have been considering, forms the starting-point of Origen's conception of the cosmic Christ." For the use of mediator (*mesites*) and to mediate (*mesiteuein*) with reference to Christ, see especially *Jo.* 1.16. sect. 92; 2.8. sect. 61; 2.34; 6.15; *Fr. 140 in Jo.* and *Or.* 10.2. On the meaning of mediatorship in Origen in the *Commentary on John*, see Corsini, p. 611, n. 7, where he discusses the views of various scholars on the mediatorship of Christ. In brief, writers divide on whether, according to Origen, there is a permanent role for Christ in contemplation. On the one hand, De Faye, *Origène*, pp. 245–246, believes that the role of Christ is ultimately passed over in favor of the Father. De Faye essentially believes that Origen and Plotinus are alike in this issue. Völker, *Das Vollkommenheitsideal*, p. 110, on the other hand, states that the mystical contemplation of Christ is a means, or instrument, to reach the Father, but it is integrated rather than negated in the ultimate process of contemplation. Crouzel, *Théologie*, pp. 82ff., agrees with this analysis, but adds that the soul is assimilated to the Son and sees the Father in the same way through the Son. Hence, for Crouzel, Christ is not a stage which we need to pass over. However, Crouzel, "Les Dénominations du Christ," p. 150, does say that the Origenist doctrine of virtues with its four steps, God-Son-Soul of Son-souls is parallel to Plotinus's One-Nous-Soul of World-soul. Most recently, Lyons, *The Cosmic Christ*, pp. 115, has no qualms discussing Christ's role as a mediator in Origen in the work of creating, prayer, and the divinization of rational creatures. He writes, p. 124, "What emerges in Origen's teaching is a type of mediation which is neither strictly emanationist nor entirely subordinationist. Rather, it is a kind of mediation which is co-operative, with an element of

subordinationism." Cf. also Blanc, *Commentaire*, I, 180, n. 3, where she discusses how Christ is *metaxu* between the *agenetos* and *genetos* (*Cels*. 3.34).

125. See *Jo*. 2.24 for the difference of knowledge and wisdom, and *Hom. 8.2 in Jer*. on the definition of wisdom.

126. *Jo*. 1.34 (43.24ff.), trans. Menzies, 317B.

127. For example, it is quoted six times in Book I of the *Commentary on John*. See *Biblia Patristica*, III, 203, for other texts of Origen which use it.

128. *Jo*. 1.34 (I.182. sect. 246), trans. Menzies, 318A.

129. Cf. Blanc, *Commentaire*, I, 180, n. 1.

130. *Jo*. 1.19 (I.118. sect. 111-112). See Blanc, I.120. n. 1, on the difficulty of this Greek, and the various translations which scholars have offered. Corsini translates *sustasin* "sussistere" while Blanc offers "formation," and Crouzel "organization." On this entire section, see the notes by Corsini, pp. 151-153, notes 38 and 40, who explores the possible philosophical foundations of Origen's definitions, and offers some parallel texts in Origen's thought. See also Rius-Camps, *El dinamismo*, pp. 131-139 on Wisdom and Logos.

131. *Jo*. 1.34 (I.180. sect. 244), trans. Menzies, 317A.

132. *Jo*. 1.34 (I.180. sect. 245/43.26-30), trans. Menzies*, 317-318.

133. See text quoted at the beginning of this subsection.

134. Cf. *Jo*. 2.17.

135. We are using the word "knowledge" here interchangeably with "contemplation." According to Crouzel, *Connaissance*, p. 375, n. 1, 397-398 and Cadiou, *La jeunesse*, p. 96, n. 1, there is a close intimacy in Origen's thought between *gnosis* and *theoria*. Cadiou states that *gnosis* leads to *theoria*, while Crouzel believes they are generally interchangeable.

136. *Comm. in Mt*. 10.9-10 (10.17-11.27).

137. This aspect of the Logos was discussed in Chapter III.

138. *Jo*. 19.6 (IV.68. sect. 38/305.17-25). Blanc, IV, 69, n. 6, writes: "A plusieurs reprises Origène a lié, comme ici, le progrès spirituel a la connaissance de ces titres et à la participation au Christ selon ces différents aspects." See the other parallel texts which Blanc offers.

139. See *Jo*. 19.6 (305.25-33).

140. Just as we must also seek Christ. Witness Origen's continual request for knowledge from Christ in profound passages, i.e., *Hom. 19.11 in Jer*. (166.35-167.5). Cf. also *Hom. 18.2 in Jer*. (152.29-153.6), in which Origen states that the Logos encompasses all levels of knowledge.

141. And in *Jo*. 19.6.

142. *Jo*. 1.31 (34) (I.166. sect. 217/38.30-33), trans. Menzies*, 315A.

143. Cf. *Jo*. 6.6.

144. *Hom. 1.12 in Jer*. (10.22-27).

145. *Fr. 17 in Jer*. (206.12-24). On nearness of God, see *Hom. 18.9 in Jer*.

146. *Hom. 9.1 in Jer*. (64.23-24).

147. The other intention is to confront those who radically separate the divine source of the Hebrew from the Greek scriptures. See See *Hom. 9.1 in Jer*. (64.20-23).

148. *Hom. 9.1 in Jer*. (64.14-17).

149. *Hom. 9.1 in Jer*. (64.7-8).

150. Cf. *Jo*. 10.24 (196.20-197.2), 394.

151. *Hom. 5.6 in Jer*. (36.18-23, 25-26).

152. *Comm. in Mt*. 12.14.

153. See, for example, *Jo*. 6.6 and *Hom. 6.9 in Ezech*.

154. Cf. *Comm. in Mt*. 12.14.

155. *Comm. in Mt*. 12.14 (97.18-30), trans. Patrick*, 458B.

156. *Hom. 14.10 in Jer*. (114.16-115.10).

157. *Hom. 14.10 in Jer*. (114.27-115.1).

158. *Hom. 13.4 in Jesu Nave* (374.20-24).

159. *Cant*. Prol. (70.9-17), trans. Lawson, p. 33.

160. *Cant*. Prol. (74.24-30), trans. Lawson*, p. 39.

161. *Cant*. Prol. (67.7-16), pp. 29-30. The "wound of love," Lawson notes, p. 369, n. 64, is referred to again in the third book of this commentary and in the second homily on the Canticle.

162. *Cant*. III (194.3-195.5), pp. 198-199.

163. *Hom. 24.3 in Jesu Nave* (451.4-9).

164. *Fr. 28 in Jer*. (212.24-213.1).

165. As we have stated throughout the discussion, the restoration process is not accomplished by Christ alone. As Origen states concerning the two kings of evil (kings of Assyria and Babylon) in Jer. 27:17–19, man does contribute. See *Fr. 29 in Jer.* (213.29–31). We note, for example in this text that Origen does mention "the choosing of good."

166. *Hom. 8.1 in Jer.* (55.22–25).

167. *Hom. 8.1 in Jer.* (56.15–18, 26–30). With respect to the first sentence of this text, see Schadel's note, p. 268, n. 69, and also Nautin, *Jérémie*, I, 356, n. 1, who claim this passage is an allusion to the fall of souls.

168. We introduced these terms and their implications in Chapter III in our discussion of Origen's anthropology.

169. *Hom. 11.2 in Jer.* (79.12–80.5).

170. *Hom. 17.4 in Jer.* (148.8–16).

171. Variant and parenthesis by Origen.

172. Here Origen offers several scriptural texts, which, because this is a long quotation already, we will not offer. They are Hos. 1:1, Jer. 1:4, and John 10:35.

173. *Fr. 2 in Jo.* (485.25–27, 486.7–16, 18–24). On this text, see Rius-Camps, pp. 142–146. De Faye doubts the authenticity of this fragment because it does not exactly correspond to the text preserved in the Commentary. But Corsini, p. 816, n. 6 and Gruber, *ZOE*, p. 287, n. 36, disagree. See the discussion of the varying points in those notes. It is not listed as spurious in the *Biblia Patristica*. See also the translations of Corsini, Rius-Camps, pp. 143–145, and Gruber, pp. 285–286. Gruber concludes, p. 287, n. 36, that the fragment accords with what is written in the main body of the work. "Was das Fragment an Neuem bringt, ist das, da, das ewige Leben und das gewordene Leben nebeneinandergestellt und letzteres als angenommene *schesis* des erstenen erklärt wird; sollte dieses Fragment nicht (wenigstens auszugsweise) Origenes' Meinung wiedergeben, so formuliert es doch nur das, was aus Buch II und den Vergleichsstellen und unmittelbar folgt."

174. See a similar view on wisdom in *Fr. 1 in Jo.* (485.4–16), and Rius-Camps, pp. 135–139. Since this study concerns conversion, I, of course, do not claim to present Origen's Christology in any thoroughness. Origen himself in large part does this in Book I of his *Commentary on John*. For a summary, see the conclusions to chapters 1–3 in Rius-Camps, *El dinamismo trinitario*, pp. 75–79, 163–168 and 218–221.

175. Cf. Gruber, *ZOE*, pp. 112, 285–287 on the meaning of "Life" in this fragment. We follow Gruber's comprehensive discussion of "life" in Origen in the texts following.

176. *Jo.* 2.18 (12) (I.292. sect. 129/76.4–8), trans. Menzies*, 334B. See Gruber, *ZOE*, pp. 318ff. for a German translation and a more detailed discussion of this text and other similar texts.

177. *Jo.* 2.20 (14) (I.296. sect. 133/76.33–77.2), trans. Menzies*, 335A. Origen quotes Ps. 6:6 and Eph. 5:8 to clarify the source of his ideas.

178. *Jo.* 2.23 (18) (80.28–30), trans. Menzies, 337A.

179. *Jo.* 2.24 (19) (81.12–15), trans. Menzies*, 337A. See Gruber, p. 306–307.

180. *Jo.* 2.24 (I.310. sect. 156/81.15–18), 337AB.

181. *Cels.* 3.34 (II.80. 19FF.), trans. Chadwick*, p. 151. Chadwick has "midway" for the Greek *dia metaxu*, which seems to imply a less relational role for Christ than "intermediary." See discussions above on how Christ is *metaxu*.

182. To my knowledge, no study devoted only to faith in Origen has been published. A. C. Outler, "Faith and Reason in the Theology of Origen," (Diss.; Yale University, 1938) is the only major work on the subject, and J. C. Van Winden, "Le christianisme et la philosophie. Le commencement du dialogue entre foi et la raison," in *Kyriakon, Festschrift J. Quasten* (Münster: Aschendorff, 1970), I, 205–213 is the only recent general article. However, many writers have defined and discussed the subject of faith in the course of their individual themes. See under "foi" in Crouzel's *Bibliographie critique d'Origène* and his recent publications. Most writers on Origen who discuss the *Contra Celsum* will study the meaning of faith in Origen, since Celsus' attacks on faith force Origen to consider the issue. See Borret, *Celse*, I, 102, n. 1, and his Greek index, i.e. *pistis*, V, 468, for the use of the word in *Against Celsus*; Crouzel, *Origène et la philosophie* (Paris: Aubier, 1962), pp. 117–119, and Blanc, *Commentaire*, II, 101–105.

183. *Fr. 31 in Jer.* (215.5–6).

184. *Hom. 9.4 in Jer.* (69.19–22).

185. *Hom. 18.8 in Jer.* (162.15–16).

186. For example, see *Hom. 20.7 in Jer.* (188.17–22).

187. *Jo.* 20.13 (IV.212. sect. 107/344.16–19). Corsini, p. 624, n. 18, and Blanc, IV, 213, n. 2,

note that this is also a Stoic conception. For more detail see Teichtweier, *Die Sündenlehre*, pp. 180ff.
188. *Jo.* 20.30 (367.14–32).
189. *Jo.* 10.43 (II.566. sect. 298, 300/221.15–16, 23–26), 406B, 407A.
190. *Hom. 1.4 in Jer.* (3.20–24).
191. *Hom. 14.8 in Jer.* (113.18–21).
192. Cf. *Hom. 14.8 in Jer.* (113.5–17).
193. *Cant.* II (131.22–23), trans. Lawson, p. 115.
194. *Cant.* II (131.23–132.6, 8–10), trans. Lawson, p. 115.
195. For a more thorough discussion of the role of teaching, see Part IV.
196. *Mart.* 41 (38.21–23), trans. Greer, p. 72.
197. *Ibid.*
198. *Hom. 6.1 in Jer.* (47.23–26, 48.7–13).
199. *Hom. 27.3 in Num.* (260.19–24), trans. Greer, p. 250.
200. *Hom. 17.2 in Jer.* (144.17–19).
201. *Hom. 11.6 in Jer.* (84.17–20, 21–24, 26–27, 85.1–2).
202. See *Fr. 23 in Jer.* (210.2–4), and *Hom. 2.3 in Jer.* (19.9–21), where he relies on Luke. 3:16, Heb. 12:29. See also parallel texts given by Klostermann, p. 19, notes, and notes by Nautin, pp. 224–246.
The Logos can cleanse the soul of minor sins, but grave sins require the fire for purification. See *Hom. 2.2 in Jer.*
203. *Comm. in Mt.* 11.6 (I.298.67ff./44.29–31), trans. Patrick, 436A.
204. *Jo.* 13.59 (III.258.18–19, 29/290.10–22). However, as Blanc, III, 258, n. 1, notes, those with a more base and subordinate faith still can grow and become sons, as Origen states elsewhere in his *Commentary*. See Blanc, *Commentaire*, II, 102–103, and the texts cited.
205. *Comm. in Mt.* 13.5 (192.24–34), trans. Patrick*, 478A.
206. *Jo.* 32.15 (450.1–5).
207. *Jo.* 32.15 (450.15–28).
208. *Jo.* 32.16 (450.32–451.6).
209. *Jo.* 32.16 (451.26–452.13), trans. A. C. Outler*, "Origen and the Regulae Fidei," *Church History* 8 (1939), 215–216.
210. Corsini, p. 733, n. 3, suggests the aspect of stability is what distinguishes simple and mature faith, but before we can be certain of this, we need to know how *pasa hē pistis* (all the faith) is connected to *teleiē pistis* (mature faith).
211. Cf. *Hom. 4.3 in Jer.* (25.18–26).
212. *Fr. 11 in Jo.* (493.23–29). Cf. *Comm. in Rom.* 4.5 (PG 14:975A), also on Lk. 17:5, and quoted in 5.1B. See Crouzel, *Théologie*, pp. 241–242, on this text and his translation.
213. Crouzel, *Théologie*, p. 242, finds Origen's expressions in this fragment "maladroit." He writes, pp. 242–243: "Il veut seulement affirmer les deux éléments en présence dans le progrès spirituel, mais il les exprime mal." Crouzel believes that his expressions might lead one to believe that the beginning of faith is initiated by man's free will, whereas Crouzel has tried to show that in Origen the initiative of faith is with God. Faith, as one of the virtues, is a gift of God. In fact, in *Comm. in Rom.* 4.5 (PG 14:975A), Origen concludes his discussion of Luke 17:5 with: "... for the faith itself by which we seem to believe in God is based on a gift of grace in us."
214. This issue is separate from that discussed above, on John 1:26, concerning God's freedom to bestow the second level prior to achievement in the first. See also on faith as a gift confirmed by grace, *Comm. in Rom.* 4.5 (PG 14:974C–975A), partially translated in Bettenson, p. 201, and Crouzel, *Théologie*, pp. 239–244.
215. *Comm. in Rom.* 9.2 (PG 14: 1214B). See p.166 for this discussion.
216. *Comm. in Mt.* 10.19 (I.230.22ff./25.28–26.1), trans. Patrick*, 426B.
217. *Comm. in Mt.* 10.19 (I.232.43ff./26.16–19), trans. Patrick, 427A.
218. *Comm. in Mt.* 10.19 (I.234.57ff./26.27–28), trans. Patrick, 427A. In section 10.19, as Girod, *Commentaire*, I, 234, n. 2, notes, Origen balances the roles of God and man. Man continues to will freely his own desires, but he cannot move toward salvation without God's help.
219. *Comm. in Rom.* 4.1 (PG 14:963D–964A), trans. Bettenson, p. 201.
220. *Comm. in Mt.* 13.7 (197.11–198.4). Similar exegesis is in *Hom. 12.12 in Jer.* (98.15–24) and in *Fr. 41 in Jer.* (219.26–30).
221. *Hom. 14.12 in Jer.* (116.24–117.16).
222. *Jo.* 13.6 (231.9–20).
223. *Fr. 22 in Jer.* (208.22–209.19).

224. *Jo.* 13.17 (III.88. sect. 108/242.4–7).
225. *Jo.* 19.23 (IV.142. *sect.* 155/325.17–21).
226. *Comm. in Rom.* 4.1 (PG 14:961B).
227. Cf. *Jo.* 6.33.
228. *Cels.* 3.46 (II.110.11ff.), trans. Chadwick*, p. 160.
229. *Cels.* 6.13 (III.210.10ff., 23ff.), trans. Chadwick*, p. 326, 327.
230. *Jo.* 19.3 (IV.56. *sect.* 20/302.6–7). Blanc, IV, 57, n. 3, adds *Jo.* 10.37 (II.526. sect. 241), plus 10.43–44 (II.566–576. sect. 298ff.) concerning the knowledge added to faith, and the difference between complete and incomplete faith. See also Blanc, II, 101–105.
231. *Jo.* 13.53 (III.228. sect. 353–354/282.6–11). See Blanc, *Commentaire*, III, 230, n. 1 on this text. She indicates that sometimes Origen considers the word of knowledge the greatest of gifts, but more often it is the word of wisdom. Agreeing with Crouzel, *Connaissance*, p. 459, she writes that while Origen seems to have sensed a difference, it is difficult to find a difference between wisdom and knowledge in explicit terms.
232. *Comm. in Mt.* 12.15 (101.4–105.33).
233. *Fr. 93 in Jo.* (556.13–557.16).
234. A similar preference for sight over belief is found in *Jo.* 10.43 (221.35–222.23).
235. *Comm. in Rom.* 9.2 (PG 14:1214B). We translate *perfectus* as "mature" in the assumption that the Greek had *teleios.*
236. *Jo.* 19.11 (IV.88. sect. 66–67/310.21–28). Corsini translates *menein perseverano.* Blanc translates *chorousi* "sont capables de." Cf. also *Hom. 4.3 in Jer.*
237. Cf. also *Comm. in Mt.* 12.15, *Jo.* 20.13, 20.16.
238. *Cels.* 1.10 (I.102.1–6, 14–16), trans. Chadwick*, p. 13. Borret, *Celse,* I, 102, n. 1, notes, "La foi ne va pas sans raison, mais comporte des degrés. La foi raisonnée ou réfléchie est supérieure, Origène le rappelle ici et in 11, 1 s., et deux passages l'affirment, 9, 13–23 et 13, 23–31, encadrant la discussion sur la foi simple. Celle-ci n'est pas l'apanage de l'élite, mais le lot de tous." See also the remainder of this note, and Blanc, II, 102–103.
239. *Cels.* 1.11 (I.104.1–24).
240. *Comm. in Mt.* 12.6 (78.3–8), trans. Patrick, 454A.
241. Cf. *Jo.* 10.43 (222.14–23), 20.24, sect. 306–307.
242. These areas are actually mentioned in *Hom. 3.6 in Ps.* (PG 12:1342B).
243. Latko, *Origen's Doctrine of Penance* (Quebec: Université Laval, 1949), p. viii, on Origen's understanding of penance: "Origen can unequivocally be called the Father of Church Penance."
244. Studies to consult initially include: Bardy, *La théologie de l'église;* Chênevert, *L'église dans le Commentaire d'Origène sur le Cantique des Cantiques,* especially, pp. 154–158; E. F. Latko, *Origen's Doctrine of Penance* (Quebec: Université Laval, 1949); B. Poschmann, *Paenitentia secunda. Die kirchliche Busse im ältesten Christentum bis Cyprian und Origenes* (Bonn: Hanstein, 1940); B. Poschmann, *Penance and the Anointing of the Sick,* trans. F. Courtney (Freiburg: Herder, 1964), a translation of *Busse und Letzte Ülung* (1951); K. Rahner, "La doctrine d'Origène sur la pénitence," *Recherches de science religieuse,* 37 (1950), 47–97, 252–286, 422–456; G. Teichtweier, *Die Sündenlehre des Origenes,* Chapter 6; F. Van de Paverd, "Disciplinarian Procedures in the Early Church," *Augustinanum,* 21 (1981), 291–316; H. Vogt, *Das Kirchenverständnis des Origenes,* especially pp. 169–187. For a more detailed list, see works cited by Rahner at the beginning of his study, and by Latko in his bibliography. Rahner states, 47, n. 1, that Latko's work makes no progress over the work of B. Poschmann cited above.

In what follows on the technical discussions of repentance, outside its relation to conversion and its place in the spiritual journey, I follow the studies of Poschmann, Latko and Rahner.

Latko, p. 3: "Origen defines penance as a sorrow for sins, inasmuch as they are an offense of God, with the intention of expiating them. It embraces the following acts: first, sorrow for sins; secondly, an avowal of guilt; and thirdly, satisfaction for all sins."
245. Cf. Rahner, 79ff. on "le feu de la penitence."
246. *Hom. 18.8 in Jer.* (161.14–21).
247. However, in the ancient Christian churches, a location was available to outsiders for those who would stand. These were not members, but catechumens or even pagans. No doubt many pagans listened to Origen's sermons.
248. *Hom. 18.6 in Jer.* (157.29–34).
249. *Hom. 14.11 in Jer.* (115.14–16). *metanoesantes* is not in all the manuscripts. It is present in Jerome's translation: *ad poenitentiam conversi.*
250. For detail on the acts which surround repentance, see the next subsection.

251. *Cant.* II (125.6–9), trans. Lawson, pp. 106.
252. See Chênevert, pp. 157–158.
253. *Hom. 3.2 in Jer.* (Latin) (309.11–13).
254. *Hom. 1.6 in Cant.* (36.1–5), trans. Lawson, p. 276.
255. *Hom. 5.5 in Ezek.* (377.21–27).
256. This contrasts, we might note, with Latko's observations given at the beginning of this section. Here repentance does not include in itself the fear of God or confession, but is one element of the growth process. See Latko, pp. 4–18 for his interpretation.
257. For the role of the church in repentance, see the thorough discussion of Rahner, Part II. Unfortunately, we do not have the space to clarify this side of Origen's thought. Our discussions concern primarily the penitence of man himself, which is Part I of the studies of Rahner and Latko.
258. *Hom. 20.8 in Jer.* (191.8–12). See Rahner, 79–97, on the fire.
259. *Hom. 20.9 in Jer.* (191.23–31).
260. *Hom. 20.3 in Jer.* (181.13–21). The issue of grave and lesser sins, when and how they are forgiven, is a matter which is discussed in detail by both Rahner and Latko throughout their works. See Rahner, 53–79, 252ff. and 422ff., and Latko, pp. 69ff. See also Poschmann, *Paenitentia*, pp. 427ff. and *Penance and the Anointing of the Sick*, pp. 66–74. Poschmann states in the last work, p. 67: "Not even the gravest offences are excluded from forgiveness."
261. *Hom. 1.3 in Jer.* (2.31–33, 3.3–4).
262. *Hom. 1.1–2 in Jer.* (1.9–2.5); *Hom. 14.13 in Jer.* (118.17–22); *Hom. 18.5 in Jer.* (155.25–156.17).
263. *Fr. 68 in Jer.* (231.27–30).
264. *Hom. 19.15 in Jer.* (173.34–174.29).
265. *Hom. 15.15 in Jer.* is completely concerned with this matter.
266. *Hom. 7.1 in Jer.* (51.18–19, 52.1–3), on Jer. 5:18.
267. *Hom. 9.4 in Jer.* (68.28–69.2).
268. *Hom. 9.3 in Jer.* (67.24–68.3).
269. *Cels.* 3.69 (II.156.2–11/261.12ff.), trans. Chadwick, p. 174. Borret, *Celse*, II, 156, n. 3, points out that by affirming that education can change a person's direction, Origen aligns himself with those who oppose the old idea, still common in his time, that virtue is hereditary.
270. *Cels.* 3.69 (II.158.26ff.), trans. Chadwick, pp. 174–175.
271. Cf. Latko, pp. 4–6.
272. Job 5:18; Sir. 40:16; Mt. 15:13; Ps. 79:9, 13; Heb. 12.6.
273. *Fr. 70 in Jer.* (232.21–22).
274. *Jo.* 28.4 (393.9–10).
275. *Jo.* 28.4 (393.5–7).
276. *Hom 4.3 in Is.* (260.15–17, 26–29, 31–32).
277. *Hom 5.5 in Jer.* (36.7–8).
278. *Hom 10.8 in Jer.* (78.17–22).
279. *Hom. 5.5 in Jer.* (35.22–25).
280. *Fr. 57 in Jer.* (226.9–26).
281. *Fr. 58 in Jer.* (227.3–7).
282. *Cant.* II (119.5–16), trans. Lawson, pp. 98–99.
283. *Hom. 22 in Lk.* (136.26–137.10).
284. *Jo.* 6.22 (II.224. *sect.* 122/132.30–32), trans. Menzies*, 362A.
285. *Jo.* 6.33 (II.254. *sect.* 165/142.18–23), trans. Menzies*, 367A.
286. See the text quoted above from *Hom. 1.4 in Jer.*
287. *Hom. 4.4 in Jer.* (26.20–23).
288. *Hom. 15.4 in Jer.* (128.22–23).
289. *Hom. 2.1 in Jer.* (17.14–16).
290. *Fr. 14 in Jer.* (204.28–205.4).
291. *Comm. in Rom.* 2.8 (PG 14:891A); *Comm. in Mt.* 14.1 (271.30–272.5), 494A.
292. *Comm. in Mt.* 10.14 (I.200.67ff./17.32–18.3).
293. *Cels.* 3.51 (II.122.25ff.), trans. Chadwick, pp. 163–164. Of course, Origen was not alone in this kind of exclusion in the ancient church. As Chadwick notes in his edition, p. 164, see, among others, Cyprian, *Ep.* 67.6; 72.2, Peter of Alexandria, *Ep. Canon* 10.
294. Though we do not have the space to support this discussion textually, we might add, based on the studies of Latko, Poschmann and Rahner, that all sins can be "forgiven" by penance, but after one has been baptized, no sin can be pardoned. Poschmann writes, *Penance*, p. 66: "The taking away sins is in direct contrast with the reception of forgiveness of sins in baptism..."
295. *Hom. 13.2 in Jer.* (104.11–18).

296. See H. Crouzel, "Les deux commentaire les plus anciens du Notre Père," *Studia Missionalia*, 24 (1975), 293–309; W. Gessel, *Die Theologie des Gebetes nach 'De Oratione' von Origenes* (Munich: Schöningh, 1975), and the introductions to the various translations of *On Prayer* listed in the bibliography.

297. See Gessel, pp. 218ff., and accompanying texts, who points out that one of the key factors of such movement is that prayer sets up a relationship, a community, between the one praying and God which can help the worshipper toward maturity.

298. *Orat.* 13.3 (327.6–10), trans. Greer, p. 106.

299. *Hom. 5.17 in Jer.* (47.5–9).

300. *Fr. 68 in Jer.* (230.23–231.30).

301. *Orat.* 9.2 (318.26FF.), trans. Greer, p. 99; Oulton, p. 256.

302. *Orat.* 33.1.

303. In our discussions of the spirit, we have consulted the following studies: J. Boada, "El pneuma en Origenes," *Estudios eclesiasticos*, 46 (1971), 474–510; H. Crouzel, *Origène et la "connaissance mystique"* (Paris: Desclée de Brouwer, 1961), especially pp. 124ff., 142ff., passim; J. Dupuis, *'L'esprit de l'homme.' Étude sur l'anthropologie religieuse d'Origène* (Paris: Desclée de Brouwer, 1967), Chapter VI, pp. 221ff.; G. Gruber, *ZOE: Wesen, Stufen und Mitteilung des Wahren Lebens bei Origenes* (Münich: Hueber, 1962), Chapter VI, pp. 176ff.; W. Hauschild, *Gottes Geist und der Mensch: Studien zur früh-christlichen Pneumatologie* (Münich: Kaiser, 1972); J. Rius-Camsp, *El dinamismo trinitario en la divinizacion de los seres racionales segun Origenes* (Rome: Pontifical Institute of Oriental Studies, 1970), passim.

304. *Jo.* 13.23, 24 (III.106. sect. 140, 141/247.16–17, 25–28). The phrase "when he has been recreated" is an addition by the editor. Cf. Rius-Camps, p. 48. Dupuis, p. 4, believes that this text has a fundamental importance for understanding how God is spirit and what spirit is in Origen. The emphasis, Dupuis points out, is on the communication of the divine life. This is the function of the spirit. See also p. 31.

305. We have discussed Origen's view of man, and the place of the spirit, in Chapters II and III. Essentially, the spirit is one aspect of the *nous*, the spiritual *soma* being the other. The spirit brings to the soul divine life, while the flesh draws it down to the earthly. For more detail, see our discussions as cited, and Dupuis, chapter 1, especially pp. 29–42.

306. *Jo.* 32.18 (455.17–22). See Corsini's note on the philosophical background to the distinction of the soul and the spirit.

307. *Jo.* 32.18 (455.22ff.).

308. *Jo.* 2.10 (I.254. sect. 75ff./65.15–21, 22–25, 26–31), trans. Menzies*, 328B, 329A. For the meaning of "hypostases" here, see Blanc, *Commentaire*, I, 401, n. 9. The word has, she writes, "le sens qui demeurera après Nicée, celui d'existence distincte, de réalité individuelle." It is most precisely offered, she says, in *Cels.* 8.12.

309. We might repeat here that our discussions of the Trinity are only an overview. For thorough discussions see the texts cited in our original note for this subsection, and also H. Crouzel, "Les personnes de la Trinité sont-elles de puissance inégale selon Origène, *Peri Archon* I, 3, 5–8?" *Gregorianum* 57 (1976), 109–125, and the notes (and other references) supplied to the chapter on the Holy Spirit in *On First Principles* (I.3) by Crouzel and Simonetti in Volume II of their critical edition.

310. Cf. See the comments of Crouzel and Simonetti, *Traité*, II, on the various fragments, especially, pp. 64–70, notes 20, 23, and 29.

311. *Princ.* 1.3.5 (I.154.152–154), trans. Butterworth, p. 34. See also 1.3.6 on the roles of the Father and the Son.

312. *Princ.* 1.3.8 (I.162.292ff.), trans. Butterworth, pp. 38–39. See the parallel passages in Greek offered by Crouzel and Simonetti, *Traité*, II. 76, notes 49 and 50.

313. For detail on the spirit of man, see Dupuis, pp. 90–125. For discussion of how the spirit of man participates with the Holy Spirit, see pp. 98–109, and accompanying texts. While Dupuis's book begins with man and moves up to the Trinity, Rius-Camps' work begins with the Trinity, and discusses the participatory and divinization aspects for man. See Rius-Camps, pp. 368ff. on the spiritual ones.

314. *Jo.* 2.21 (I.298. *sect.* 138/78.2–5), 335A. Both Corsini and Blanc add "the Spirit" to their translations, but the context seems to refer to the inner man rather than the divine person.

315. See, for example, *Cels.* 6.70–72, pp. 384–386, in which Origen refutes what he believes is Celsus's material view of *pneuma*, and *Princ.* 2.8.2, pp. 121–122, in which Origen interprets Paul's statement as indicating that the human spirit is akin to the Holy Spirit. Also, in *Princ.* 3.6.6, pp. 252–253, man becomes spiritual by coming to understand the things of the Spirit of God. See also *Hom. 7.2 in Gen.* (72.23–73.16).

316. *Princ.* 1.3.5 (I.152.149–151), p. 34.
317. *Princ.* 1.3.6, p. 34.
318. *Princ.* 1.3.5 (I.152.151ff.), trans. Butterworth, p. 34.
319. *Hom. 13.2 in Jer.* (104.11–18).
320. Cf. *Princ.* 1.3.2, p. 30, 1.3.7, p. 37, *Jo.* 2.10, sect. 74, 328B, *Jo.* 19.14, sect. 88, etc.
321. *Jo.* 2.11 (I.258. sect. 80), 329A. See Blanc, *Commentaire*, I, 258, n. 3, where she discusses the significance of this text in Origen's theology. She notes that in Origen, while all of the activity of the Father and the Son extends to all creatures, only the holy participate in the Holy Spirit, and Origen unites the holy with the spiritual in agreement with Paul (Cor. 2:15, 3:1; Gal. 6:1). When someone sins, the Spirit withdraws from him.
322. *Jo.* 2.11 (I.260. sect. 83), 329B. Blanc, I, 259, n. 4, indicates that Origen probably changed his mind on how they work together. In *Cels.* 1.46, Origen indicates that the Father sends both the Son and the Holy Spirit, rather than the Father and the Holy Spirit sending the Son, as it is in this text.
323. *Hom. 18.9 in Jer.* (162.27–163.19). See also *Hom. 8.1 in Jer.* (55.21–56.8), where Origen indicates that the soul needs all of the Trinity.
324. *Hom. 8.2 in Jer.* (57.13–15).
325. *Hom. 17.4 in Jer.* (147.1–2, 3–5).
326. See the quote above from *Jo.* 2.10.
327. See *Jo.* 2.11, 329B.
328. In *Fr. 20 in Jo.* (501.18–24), in fact, Origen says the Holy Spirit cannot be separated from Christ. See also *Princ.* 1.3.8 on unity of work of the Trinity.
329. *Fr. 20 in Jo.* (501.8–9).
330. *Jo.* 13.13 and 13.43.
331. *Hom. 3.2 in Jos.* (303.18–23) Cf. Jaubert, p. 132.
332. *Jo.* 13.49 (III.210. sect. 321).
333. *Jo.* 13.6 (III.50. sect. 36).
334. *Princ.* 1.3.1. (I.144.11ff.), p. 29.
335. *Princ.* 1.3.8 (I.162.292ff.), pp. 38–39, quoted above.
336. *Princ.* 1.3.8 (I.162.283ff.), trans. Butterworth*, p. 38.
337. *Fr. 36 in Jo.* (511.13–31).
338. Origen discusses the seven gifts of the Spirit in several texts. These gifts are good spirits in the form of wisdom, intellect, counsel, power, knowledge, piety and fear, some of which we have mentioned. The agency of these in conversion, however, is similar to the gifts we have discussed above, that is, they depend on the person's behavior and thoughts, they arise inwardly to support one in the war with the evil spirits and to enable one to grow in the various areas of the gifts. Only Jesus, however, has the full complement of these gifts. See, for example, *Hom. 8.11 in Lev.*, *Hom. 6.3 in Num.*, the third homily on Isaiah, *Princ.* 1.1.3, 3.3.4, and, the spirits mediated by Christ, in *Comm. in Mt.* 13.2. There are ten gifts of the Spirit (Origen adds energy, love and prudence) in a Greek fragment from the *Commentary on Jeremiah* (PG 13: 549AB). For a brief discussion of Origen's view of these spiritual gifts and the texts mentioned above, see *Dictionnnaire de spiritualité ascétique et mystique*, III (1957), 1582ff.
339. Studies initially to consult on baptism include: C. Blanc, "Le bapteme d'après Origène," *Studia Patristica*, 11 (1972), 113–124; H. Crouzel, "Origène et la structure du sacrement," *BLE*, 63 (1962), 83–92; H. Rahner, "Taufe und geistliches Leben bei Origenes," *Zeitschrift für Aszese und Mystik*, 7 (1932), 205–223; J. Trigg, "A Fresh Look at Origen's Understanding of Baptism," *Studia Patristica*, 17 (1982), 959–965. Trigg was unaware of the articles of Crouzel or Blanc, since he claims Rahner is the principal work published on the subject. Hence he contrasts his views only with those of Rahner.

According to Blanc, 116, Book VI of the *Commentary on John* considers the "principaux éléments du bapteme chrétien..."

The purpose of this subsection is only to clarify the role of baptism in the spiritual journey as Origen understands it. For detail on baptism, see above studies.

We should note that the agency of change in other sacraments is not as clearly outlined as in baptism, and it is for this reason we have not included any detail on them. However, in general, we can apply what is mentioned in this section, with respect to conversion, certainly to the eucharist, and, to some extent, to penance. See, however, the discussion of repentance above.

We should note that there are several other categories of baptism mentioned in Origen's works, i.e., the baptism of water, the baptism of blood, the baptism of John, the baptism of Jesus, the baptism of Moses. See Blanc, 113–114 for the kinds of baptism in Origen. On the baptism of blood, the martyr's baptism, see Blanc, 122ff. Though we will not be discussing all of these baptisms, it should be noted that each has a power to turn and change the one affected, so that a new direction begins. We provide in this section some examples of how baptism can function in conversion.

340. *Hom. 2.3 in Jer.* (19.9–20.3).

341. *Hom. 1.16 in Jer.* (15.4–7). Cf. also *Hom. 19.14 in Jer.*

342. Cf. Blanc, 118: "L'eau du baptème régénère, au sens propre du terme: elle permet de devenir enfants de Dieu; comme Adam fut le père de notre vie terrestre, le Christ y est pour nous début d'une vie nouvelle; c'est une nouvelle naissance de Dieu, une participation à la nature divine de l'amour." See accompanying texts for her view. Also, see Trigg, 959, with reference to Origen's reminders to his congregation not to sin: "An understanding of baptism as marking a radical change in the Christian's manner of life is explicitly his basis for such exhortations."

343. *Hom. 9.4 in Lev.* (424.5–7).

344. *Jo.* 6.33 (II.254. *sect.* 165/142.20–23), trans. Menzies*, 367A. See Blanc's discussion and texts, 117–118, on the need for sincerity and the right disposition for baptism.

345. Cf. Blanc, pp. 114–115. She also discusses the baptism in the Jordan.

346. *Jo.* 6.43 (II.300. *sect.* 225/152.30–31), trans. Menzies, 372A.

347. *Hom. 4.1 in Jos.* (309.7–127).

348. Cf. Trigg, 960, who believes Origen saw baptism as the beginning of a journey within the purifying powers of the church.

349. *Fr. 26 in Jer.* (211.23–212.9).

350. *Hom. 3.1 in Num.* (14.1–8).

351. *Hom. 2.4 in Lev.* (295.25–296.22).

352. *Jo.* 6.32 (II.252.SECT.162/141.22–31), trans. Menzies*, 367B,

353. Being filled with the Holy Spirit does not necessitate being filled with higher knowledge and mysteries. For, as we have seen in many other contexts, and have also mentioned in this section, wisdom and access to the mysteries is a process of growth. Baptism is an opportunity for the Christian; it is not, as in the rites of the contemporary mystery religions, a gift of secret knowledge.

354. Trigg, 962–963, believes that Origen viewed two separate baptisms, one for the lay folk of the church, and one for the spiritual one. The first is corporeal, given through the traditional rite of baptism, the second spiritual. The implication of this statement may be that lay folk are "lay folk" because of a ritual or level of maturity. However, Origen believed that no one by nature is destined for one baptism or the other, and that anyone can be "spiritual." This view, in fact, accords with a form which appears in many ways in Origen's thought, namely, that some are more mature than others by choice, and thus appreciate a more spiritual baptism, regardless of their official position in the church. As Origen teaches us in his discussion of Jacob and Esau, a soul is judged by its entire history and the choices it has made, not by its present status. Trigg's texts are *Jo.* 32.2. 32.4, 6.32–33. These texts support that there is a kind of spiritual growth—a conversion, if you will—needed for baptism, when baptism is complete, and not everyone has the right intentions to progress and receive the mature gifts of baptism. Many receive only what is similar to John's baptism, but others receive regeneration and the gift of the Spirit, and it comes only to those who have the proper disposition.

355. According to *Jo.* 6.54, even Christ must wash before the "great baptism."

356. See *Jo.* 1.7 (12.8–13.10), 301B–302A. If one is relying on the English translation in ANF 10, it needs to be checked carefully with the Greek.

357. This term *(oikonomia)* is used in the text mentioned in the previous note with respect to God's plan of salvation through the apostles.

358. The comparison between the corporeal and the spiritual, or the earthly and the heavenly, is found in many areas of Origen's thought, many of which we have noted in other sections.

359. *Selecta in Genesim* 2.15 (PG 12:100B).

360. Cf. *Hom. 11.7 in Ex.* and *Hom. 7.7 in Jud.* on the need to guard the purity one has received from baptism with great care. Texts suggested by Blanc, 118.

The other baptism, as we noted at the beginning of this subsection, concerns the baptism of fire which arises for some in this life, for others after this earthly life. See Blanc, 120 ff.

361. On the role of knowledge/wisdom in Origen's thought, consult studies given in the first

section, especially H. Crouzel, *Origène et la 'connaissance mystique'* (Paris: Desclée de Brouwer, 1961) and R. Gögler, *Zur Theologie des biblischen Wortes bei Origenes* (Düsseldorf: Patmos, 1963).
362. Cf. Crouzel, *Connaissance*, pp. 280 ff., 324 ff., 400–409, and Gögler, pp. 365 ff.
363. *Hom. 19.11 in Jer.* (166.35–167.5).
364. *Comm. in Mt.* 14.11 (302.17–29), trans. Patrick*, 501B.
365. *Hom. 12.7 in Jer.* (94.1–5).
366. *Jo.* 10.39 (II.544. *sect.* 266). For the vocabulary of knowledge as used by Origen, see Crouzel, *Connaissance*, the sections on vocabulary.
367. *Hom. 12.13 in Jer.* (100.15–27).
368. *Cels.* 3.33 (II.78.10–18), trans. Chadwick, p. 150.
369. *Cels.* 6.37 (III.268.22–27), trans. Chadwick, p. 353.
370. See Crouzel and Simonetti, *Traité*, IV, 232, n. 86, on the necessity of divine enlightenment in order to understand scripture, and the texts offered by them.
371. *Princ.* 4.3.14 (III.392.432 ff.), trans. Butterworth, p. 311. Cf. *Hom. 17.4 in Num.* on this same theme. Text suggested by Crouzel and Simonetti, IV, 233, n. 87.
372. Cf. also *Jo.* 10.43.
373. *Princ.* 4.2.7 (III.328.227–229), trans. Butterworth, p. 283.
374. *Jo.* 10.18 (189.9–13), 390A.
375. See, for example *Comm. in Mt.* 10.14 (17.18–20), 422A.
376. *Jo.* 10.43 (II.568. *sect.* 302/221.35–222.1), trans. Menzies, 407A.
377. Cf. *Jo.* 10.43, *sect.* 299, 407A.
378. *Jo.* 13.5 (III.48. *sect.* 30/230.13–15).
379. *Jo.* 13.5 (III.48. *sect.* 31–32/230.19–22). See Blanc, *Commentaire,* III, 285–286 on the meaning here of "unless one has become akin to them." We have discussed the ancient belief in like being attracted to and knowing like in Chapter III.
380. Origen quotes John 21.25, Apoc. 10:4, 1 Cor. 6:12 and 2 Cor. 12:4 in the section (13.5) under discussion. In the following section of his commentary (13.6), he explores again how Paul and John explicitly mention the inexpressible things which they knew.
381. *Hom. 23.4 in Jesu Nave* (446.17–25).
382. Again in this text Origen offers several scriptural texts to support his view. He mentions 2 Cor. 12:2 and II Tim. 2:2. Both of these texts indicate for Origen that Paul himself realized he knew of mysteries he could not express. According to Jaubert, p. 468, n. 1, this text does not mean that Origen believed in a secret apostolic tradition.
383. *Cels.* 6.14 (III.212.14–17), trans. Chadwick, p. 327.
384. *Hom. 8.8 in Jer.* (62.7–10).
385. *Hom 8.9 in Jer.* (62.27–63.6).
386. *Hom. 3.6 in Ps.* (PG 12:1342B), trans. Harris*, pp. 231–232. On Origen's interpretation of the Psalms, see Karen J. Torjesen, "Origen's Interpretation of the Psalms," *Studia Patristica*, 17 (1983), 944–958.
367. *Comm. in Mt.* 12.15 (103.29–104.6;104.34–105.16), trans. Patrick, 459–460.
388. *Jo.* 20.20 (IV.238. *sect.* 167/352.17–19). Corsini, p. 634, n. 22, indicates that this view of knowledge combines the Stoic *episteme* and *sophia,* and is meant to contrast with *doxa* which is not certain knowledge.
389. *Jo.* 20.20 (351.33–352.8).
390. Cf. F. E. Peters, *Greek Philosophical Terms* (N.T.: NYU Press, 1967), p. 97. Origen's use of Stoic terminology is indicated by Corsini, p. 634, n. 22.
391. *Jo.* 19.4 (IV.58. *sect.* 22,23–24/302.17–20, 28–32). See Blanc, *Commentaire,* IV, 363–364 on Origen's use of 1 Cor. 6:16,17. Here she says that Origen wishes "pour exprimer l'intimité requise par la connaissance de Dieu."
392. We say "may" because Origen himself indicates that it is one of two alternatives, though there seems to be little doubt that both views are possible and compatible with Origen's theology.
393. *Orat.* Pref. 1 (298.8–17), trans. Greer, p. 82.
394. *Fr. 27 in Jo.* (504.27–505.5).
395. See, for example, on the critical importance of truth to salvation in *Jo.* 13.18, concerning Origen's interpretation of John 4:23.
396. Texts which indicate these patterns include: *Jo.* 13.10 (the complete and the partial knowledge), *Jo.* 13.33 (the need for different nourishments in order to know), *Hom. 8.7 in Jer.* (partial and mature knowledge), *Comm. 11.4 in Mt.* ("disciples" are more mature than the multitude),

Jo. 32.2 (the perfect and the ordinary man), *Hom. 9.9 in Jos.* (different foods), *Hom. 6.1 in Jos.* (three degrees of knowledge), *Jo.* 13.18 (seeing with and without a mirror), *Cels.* 6.13 (two kinds of wisdom, human and divine), *Hom. 18.2 in Jer.* (three wisdoms comparable to a three–layer cosmos), *Cels.* 6.14 (no divine wisdom without human wisdom).

397. *Princ.* 2.11.7, p. 153.

398. *Cels.* 7.46 (IV.126.39ff.), trans. Chadwick, pp. 434–435.

399. See *Jo.* 19.6, quoted above.

400. We translate the Latin *perfectio* "maturity" assuming the original Greek had *teleiosis* or its derivatives.

401. *Hom. 27.12 in Num.* (279.3–15), trans. Greer, p. 268.

402. Origen writes, in *Hom. 12.11 in Jer.* (97.15–16), "...he who gives glory to the Lord God gives glory to him in actions."

403. *Hom. 1.10 in Jer.* (9.22–23). Nautin, I, 219, n. 4, also adds *Fr. 71 in Jo.* (539.27–28): "But after the introduction, it is necessary for progress that one may be seen and known by God."

404. Though we find this view everywhere implicit, it is explicit in *Mart.* 47 and *Princ.* 4.4.9–10, pp. 326–327. As we mentioned above, Origen's *Commentary on the Song of Songs* is continually working with this commonality of God and man.

Indeed there is in Origen's thought the idea that, in some sense, there is only godness, and one cosmic aspect of conversion is to return what was generated and freed back to its source. See, in the context of corporeity, Bostock's discussion in *Origeniana Secunda*, pp. 335–337.

405. *Cant.* 3 (208.5–210.4/quotation: 210.1–3), trans. Lawson, pp. 218–221.

406. *Jo.* 20.27 (IV.274. *sect.* 237; 278. *sect.* 243–244/363.8–14, 364.7–10).

407. *Jo.* 20.28 (364.14–18).

408. *Comm. in Mt.* 12.20 (113.17–24), trans. Patrick*, 462A. "Mysteries" is in the anonymous parallel Latin text.

409. See Crouzel, *La théologie de l'image*, pp. 232 ff., and Rius-Camps, *El dinamismo*, chapter six.

410. *Orat.* 27.13 (372.2).

411. *Jo.* 32.28 (474.23–28). For the discussions of glory, purity and contemplation, see the prior sections of the *Commentary*, i.e., 32.25ff., especially 32.27.

412. *Jo.* 2.28 (I.322. *sect.* 172/85.4–7), trans. Patrick, 339A. Compare also *Jo.* 32.28, in which Origen indicates that God knows more than any being can know.

413. Cf. *Princ.* 1.1.5 (20.5ff), pp. 9–10. See Corsini, p. 255, n. 53 for other texts and an extended discussion of God's unknowable nature. Corsini indicates that Origen differs from Plotinus and Pseudo-Dionyius in that God is not unknowable to himself, nor is he without any positive quality, since Origen defines him clearly as the Good. However, Corsini notes that Origen more often stresses not the unknowable nature of God but the weakness of the human mind, another indication of the importance of conversion in his thought.

414. *Jo.* 20.34, sections 304–305.

415. *Jo.* 1.16 (I.108. *sect.* 92/20.15–18), trans. Menzies*, 305B–306A. Preuschen suggests there is probably a lacuna in this text. See the solutions of Corsini, p. 144, n. 28, and Crouzel, *La connaisance*, p. 497, n. 9. The translation above is uncertain. For the meaning of *apokatastasis*, see our Chapter II, and Corsini, p. 143, n. 27.

416. *Jo.* 1.16 (20.18–22), trans. Menzies*, 306A.

Appendix A: Origen's View of Fire in the *Homilies on Jeremiah*

1. Corsini, *Commento*, p. 306, n. 13, has pointed out that Origen may have disapproved only of Pythagorean reincarnation.

Appendix B: Origen Scholarship and Textual Methodology

1. Cf. H. Crouzel, *Bibliographie critique d'Origène* (The Hague: M. Nijhoff, 1971), p. 627. Before Origen, only the work on Tertullian, referred to in section I.1, exists at present. The books by Aubin, Ladner and Bardy, noted many times above, are general works. See discussion below of these works.

2. Beside Henri Crouzel's *Bibliographie critique d'Origène*, which summarizes the entire field

of Origen research up to 1980, there have been five attempts to review Origen scholarship: H. Mururilio, "The Recent Revival of Origen Studies," *Theological Studies*, 24 (1963), 250–263; Étienne Cornélis, "Origenes als Theoloog: recente interpretaties," *Tijdschrift voor theologie* 4 (1964), 416–424, devoted primarily to Crouzel and Gögler; R. Daly, "Origen Studies and Pierre Nautin's Origène," *Theological Studies*, 39 (1978), 508–519; L. Lies, "Zum Stand heutiger Origenesforschung," *Zeitschrift für katholische Theologie*, 102 (1980), 190–205; J. Trigg, "A Decade of Origen Studies," *Religious Studies Review*, 7 (1981), 21–27; Also useful are the reviews on recent works in the *Bulletin de littérature ecclésiastique* and the *Journal of Theological Studies*.

3. See J. Dupuis, '*L'esprit de l'homme.' Étude sur l'anthropologie religeuse d'Origène* (Paris: Desclée de Brouwer, 1967).

4. J. Rius-Camps, *El dinamismo trinitario en la divinizacion de los seres racionales segun Origenes* (Rome: Pont. Institutum Orientalium Studiorum. 1970).

5. A. Tripolitis, *The Doctrine of the Soul in the Thought of Plotinus and Origen* (Roslyn Heights, N.Y.: Libra, 1978).

6. J. Alcain, *Cautiverio y redencion del hombre en Origenes* (Bilbao: Universidad de Deusto, 1973), p. 87, for example summarizes the symbolic significance of Egypt and Babylonia: "If Egypt can be considered, in a certain sense, the point of departure (for captivity), it is to Babylonia alone that one arrives as a punishment for one's own infidelity to God and as a means of instruction towards conversion."

7. M. Martinez Pastor, *Teologia de la luz en Origenes* (Santander: Universidad Pontificia, 1962).

8. G. Gruber, *ZOE: Wesen, Stufen und Mitteilung des wahren Lebens bei Origenes* (Münich: Hüber, 1962).

9. G. Teichtweier, *Das Sein des Menschen* (Regensburg, 1953).

10. H. Crouzel, *Théologie de l'Image chez Origène* (Paris: Aubier, 1956), p. 145.

11. J. Chênevert, *L'Église et l'âme dans le commentaire du Cantigue des Cantigues* (Paris: Desclée de Brouwer, 1969); H. Vogt, *Das Kirchenverständnis des Origenes* (Vienna: Böulau, 1974); L. Lies, *Wort und Eucharistie bei Origenes. Zur Spiritualisierungsteinenz des Eucharistieverständnisses* (Innsbruck: Tyrolia, 1978); G. Sgherri, *Chiesa e Sinagoga nelle opera di Origene* (Milan: Vita e Pensiero, 1982).

12. A. Lieske, *Die Theologie der Logos-Mystik bei Origenes* (Münster: Aschendorff, 1938); H. Crouzel, *Théologie de l'Image chez Origène*; J. Rius-Camps, *El dinamismo trinitario en la divinizacion de los seres racionales segun Origenes* (Rome: Pontifical Institute of Oriental Studies, 1970).

13. Frédéric Bertrand, *Mystique de Jésus chez Origène* (Paris: Aubier, 1951); M. Harl, *Origène et la fonction révélatrice du Verbe Incarné* (Paris: Seuil, 1958); M. Eichinger, *Die Verklärung Christi bei Origenes* (Vienna: Herder, 1969).

14. Cf. Harl, p. 338. See review by R. Hanson, *JTS*, n.s., 10(1959), 384–386.

15. H. de Lubac, *Histoire et esprit* (Paris: Aubier, 1950); J. Daniélou, "Origène comme exégète de la Bible," *Studia Patristica* (1957), 280–290; R. Hanson, *Allegory and Event: A Study of the Sources and Significance of Origen's Interpretation of Scripture* (London: SCM, 1959); R. Grant, *The Earliest Lives of Jesus* (1961), R. Gögler, *Zur Theologie des biblischen Wortes bei Origenes* (Düsseldorf: Patmos, 1963); M. Wiles, "Origen as Biblical Scholar," *The Cambridge History of the Bible*, I (1970), 454–489; G. Caspary, *Politics and Exegesis: Origen and the Two Swords* (Berkeley, Ca.: University Press, 1979). According to Crouzel, *Bibliographie*, p. 530, the work by Gögler is a "livre nécessaire pour une compréhension sérieuse de l'exégèse, de la théologie et de la spiritualité d'Origène." To some extent, however, the first part repeats the work of Hanson on the influences and sources of Origen's view of scripture, but in the second part he explores intensely how Origen viewed the word as a "mediator of the divine revelation and presence." This subject is of critical concern to the perspective of conversion.

16. However, anyone who works on conversion will owe a debt if he reads Gögler's study.

17. Hal Koch, *Pronoia und Paideusis: Studien über Origenes und sein Verhältnis zum Platonismus* (Berlin: De Gruyter, 1932); H. Crouzel, *Origène et la philosophie* (Paris: Aubier, 1962); J. Rist, *Eros and Psyche* (Toronto: University Press, 1964), H. Chadwick, *Early Christian Thought and the Classical Tradition* (Oxford: University Press, 1966); P. Kübel, *Schuld und Schicksal bei Origenes, Gnostikern und Platonikern* (Stuttgart: Calwer, 1973); J. McClelland, *God the Anonymous — A Study in Alexandria Theology* (Philadelphia: Patristics Foundation, 1976); H. Bietenhard, *Caesarea, Origenes und die Juden* (Stuttgart: Kohlhammer, 1974); N. De Lange, *Origen and the*

Jews (Cambridge: University Press, 1976); L. Levine, *Caesarea under Roman Rule* (Leiden: Brill, 1975); J. Ringel, *Césarée de Palestine. Étude historique et archéologigue* (1975); J. Trigg, *Origen. The Bible and Philosophy in the Third Century Church* (Atlanta: John Knox Press, 1983).

18. Crouzel, in his many articles and books, presents the origin of the two groups, groups which seem to separate into Protestant and Catholic camps. He sees the origin of the attitude in modern times beginning probably in Harnack, and continuing on in works on Origen by De Faye, Jonas and Koch. See his introduction to *Connaissance*. De Faye, pp. 174–176, sees a just equilibrium of Origen's thought between the gospel and philosophy. Koch states from the start that he will analyze only one aspect of Origen's thought. On this controversy, see also, Daly, "Origen Studies," 510–512; Trigg, "A Decade of Origen Studies," 22; Corsini, *Origene — Commento al Vangelo di Giovanni* (Torino: U.T.E.T, 1968) pp. 22–27. Harnack, De Faye, Koch and others do tend to center their views of Origen on philosophical issues and contexts, and to see Origen sometimes thrusting on Christian doctrine ideas of non–Christian (Platonic, Stoic, Gnostic) origin; whereas other scholars begin with the scriptural context and Origen's roots in scripture. Philosophy, they would say, is not recommended as a way of life; it is only a means to the true life found in the way of Christ. Trigg, *Origen*, p. 75, writes: "We should never pretend that Origen's philosophical concerns and his mysticism were two separable and perhaps even incompatible sides of his character: they were one and the same." However, I would add that philosophical concerns were subordinate to the mystical.

19. Cf. A. Nock, *Conversion*. Nock's basic approach is to try to understand, from the point of view of the pagan, the psychological factors which drew the pagans to the oriental cults and to Christianity. See, for example, *Conversion*, p. 10. The views of E. R. Dodds on ancient Christian conversion are summarized in *Pagan and Christian*, pp. 74–78. There he describes the process as an "actual change or crisis of identity," a "regeneration," an act where the God comes into the man, where one is divinized through ritual, grace or a combination of both. Dodds's point of departure is outlined on p. 2.

20. P. Aubin, *Le problème*, pp. 137–157.

21. A more thorough study of Origen's vocabulary in describing the history of the soul is found in R. Cadiou, *Introduction au système d'Origène* (Paris: Les Belles Lettres, 1932), pp. 108ff.

22. G. Bardy, *La conversion au christianisme durant les premiers siècles* (Paris: Aubier, 1949), p. 157. Also see Gerhart B. Ladner, *The Idea of Reform. Its Impact on Christian Thought and Action in the Age of the Fathers* (Cambridge, Mass.: Harvard University Press, 1959). However, long before these works, C. Merivale, *The Conversion of the Roman Empire* (New York: D. Appleton, 1865), pp. 8–16, lists four causes of conversion to Christianity: 1) external evidence through fulfilled prophecies and miracles, 2) internal evidence in the need for a sanctifier and redeemer, 3) the testimonies of primitive believers, and 4) the continual success of Christianity.

23. One writer has said that Origen's scattered comments on conversion defy any systematic approach. See Chênevert, *L'Église*, p. 141. Chênevert claims the support of Paul Aubin. In fact, Aubin does not speak of a systematic perspective. However, he does say that a "synthèse" is possible. See Aubin, *Le problème*, p. 137. While the word "systematic" is difficult to define here, there is truth to Chênevert's view, as we mention in the text.

24. However, it would be a worthy project, in our view, to know how Origen influenced those who followed. Unfortunately, we do not have the space to consider how Origen's views on conversion may have influenced the succeeding generations.

25. Nautin, *Origène*, Chapter X.

26. Origen would be around 47 years old, if he was born ca. 185 and finished these works, as we suspect, about 232 A.D.

27. See Nautin, *Origène*, pp. 409–412, for a recapitulation of chronology.

28. Peri, p. 127, n. 68, claims that the date of these homilies may be as late as 249, but certainly after 246/7. But Schadel, p. 6, says no later than 245.

29. With respect to the Greek fragments, since we very often lack the context, caution must be exercised, especially concerning those fragments obtained from Origen's detractors. Regarding the fragments from the catenas, a definitive judgment can probably never be offered. There is evidence that a kind of condensation has been often the method by the compilers, but, in general, no tampering with the essence of Origen's ideas seems to have occurred. Again the context must decide. See Lawson, p. 5, and Völker, pp. 18–20.

30. See Crouzel, *Bibliographie*, pp. 581–584 for a list of the works included in the Philocalia.

31. Cf. Rufinus, *Ad Heraclium* (PG 14: 1292–1294); *De principiis*, Preface. In this method he

336 NOTES

claims to be following Jerome's lead in his translation of the homilies. Crouzel, generally favorable to Rufinus, has found errors of translation even in non-controversial passages of *De principiis*. See Crouzel, "Comparaisons precises," *Origeniana*, p. 121. J. M. Rist compared the section on free will in *De principiis* in the Greek and Rufinus's Latin, and evaluated Rufinus's work by the phrase "approximately satisfactory authority." He excused him as an unfortunate victim of his own Latin mentality. See Rist, "The Greek and Latin Texts," *Origeniana*, p. 111: Rufinus, he says, was "largely ignorant" of Origen's world. De Faye writes, pp. 34–35, "...very often he clearly does not understand the author's meaning." Cf. also Lawson, *Song of Songs*, p. 5 concerning the translation of this work.

32. For a handy summary of Origen's works and where they can be found, see E. Schadel, ed. and trans., *Origenes — Die griechisch erhaltenen Jeremiahomilien* (Stuttgart: Hiersemann, 1980), pp. 339–355. This list also includes locations for the many fragments.

33. R. Girod, "La traduction latine anonyme du Commentaire sur Matthieu," *Origeniana*, pp. 132–137. "The essence of Origen's thought is probably preserved."

34. *Ibid.*, p. 132.

35. Cf. Bigg, p. 127, who states that Origen's works on the Bible give sufficient material to judge both the method and the substance of his teaching.

36. C. Richardson, "The Condemnation of Origen," *Church History*, 6 (1937), 50–64, and Crouzel, "Qu'a voulu faire Origène en composant le Traité des Principes?," *BLE*, 76 (1975), 168.

37. For excellent introductions to this work, see P. Nautin, *Origène — Homélies sur Jérémie* (SC 232; Paris: Cerf, 1976), I, 15–191, and E. Schadel, *Origenes — Die griechisch erhaltenen Jeremiahomilien* (Stuttgart: Hiersemann, 1980), 1–50.

38. See Nautin, *Homélies sur Jérémie*, I, 151–183.

39. Redepenning, *Origenes*, separated his study into 2 volumes, one devoted to Origen's Alexandrian period, the other to his Caesarean period.

40. The amount of Hebrew Origen knew is a contested issue. For a summary of different assessments, see De Lange, *Origen and the Jews*, pp. 21–23, 153, n. 61.

41. *Ibid.*, p. 15.

42. Cf. Caspary, *Politics and Exegesis*, pp. 33, n. 75, p. 34, n. 80, p. 36, n. 83, and p. 147, n. 58.

Bibliography

This bibliography includes all of those works mentioned in the text, several others which have proved useful but were not cited, a few on special topics, though not all were available to me, and several after the work was written. Unfortunately, in the latter categories I have to include recent books by Bammel, Berchman, Castagno, Crouzel, Gorday, Hällström; Heine's translation of the *Commentary on John*; Neuschäfer, Rowe, Torjesen, and several recent critical editions and translations, all of which were unavailable to me at the time I finished the book. I also did not have access to the fourth and fifth volumes of *Origeniana*. I have not attempted to mention all of the books and articles published on Origen, even since the bibliography, published in 1971 and 1982, by Henri Crouzel. The major books are reviewed in the *BLE* and the *JTS*, but there are now appearing many other books, dissertations and articles which are too numerous to include, obtain or read. I have tried to include everything which offers an important contribution to the subject of the book and to a foundation in Origen studies. The major focus of this work is on the texts of Origen, not on the secondary literature. As I note in the appendix on textual methodology, it is the texts which led me to the scholarship.

1. Critical Texts

Die griechschen christlichen Schriftsteller der ersten drei Jahrhunderte (GCS) series. Leipzig: Hinrichs, 1899ff. Arranged by editor.

Origenes Adamantius. *In Genesim, Exodum et Leviticum homiliae*. Ed. W. Baehrens. VI, 1920.

_____. *In Numeros, Jesu Nave et Judicum homiliae*. Ed. W. Baehrens. VII, 1921.

_____. *In Canticum canticorum*. Ed. W. Baehrens. VIII, 1925.

_____. *In Canticum canticorum homiliae*. Ed. W. Baehrens. VIII, 1925.

_____. *In librum Regnorum, Isaiam et Ezekielem homiliae*. Ed. W. Baehrens. VIII, 1925.

_____. *In Matthaeum*. Ed. E. Benz and E. Klostermann. X-XII, 1933, 1935, 1941, 1955.

_____. *In Jeremiam homiliae*. Ed. E. Klostermann. III, with corrections by P. Nautin, 1983.

_____. *Exhortatio ad martyrum*. Ed. P. Koetschau. I, 1899.

_____. *Contra Celsum*. Ed. P. Koetschau. I–II, 1899.

_____. *De oratione*. Ed. P. Koetschau. II, 1899.

_____. *De principiis*. Ed. P. Koetschau. V, 1913.

_____. *In Joannem*. Ed. E. Preuschen. IV, 1903.

_____. *In Lucam homiliae et fragmenta*. Ed. M. Rauer. IX, 1959 [2nd ed.].

2. Critical Texts

Sources chrétiennes series, including text and French translation. Paris: Cerf, 1960ff. Arranged by editor.

Origenes Adamantius. *Commentaire sur saint Jean.* Ed. C. Blanc. SC 120, 157, 222, 290; 1966, 1970, 1975, and 1980. Books I, II, VI, XIII, XIX and XX.

_____. *Contre Celse.* Ed. M. Borret. SC 132, 136, 147, 150 and 227; 1967, 1968, 1969 [2] and 1976.

_____. *Homélies sur le Levitique.* ed. M. Borret. SC 286–287, 1981.

_____. *Homélies sur l'Exode.* ed. M. Borret. SC 321, 1985.

_____. *Homélies sur s. Luc.* Ed. H. Crouzel, F. Fournier, and P. Perichon. SC 87, 1962.

_____. *Traité des principes.* 5 volumes. Ed. H. Crouzel and M. Simonetti. SC 252, 253, 268, 269, 312; 1978(2), 1980(2), 1984.

_____. *Grégoire le Thaumaturge: Remerciement à Origène. Suivi de la Lettre d'Origène à Grégoire.* ed. H. Crouzel. SC 148, 1969.

_____. *Homélies sur la Génèse.* Ed. L. Doutreleau. SC 7, 1976 [2nd edition].

_____. *Homélies sur l'Exode.* [Translation only.] Ed. P. Fortier. SC 16, 1947.

_____. *Commentaire sur l'Évangile selon Matthieu.* Ed. R. Girod. Books X, XI SC 162, 1970.

_____. *Philocalie 1–20, Sur les Écritures.* Ed. M. Harl. SC 302, 1983.

_____. *Homélies sur Josue.* Ed. A. Jaubert. SC 71, 1960.

_____. *Philocalie 21–27 sur le libre arbitre.* Ed. E. Junod. SC 226, 1976.

_____. *La lettre à Africanus sur l'histoire de Suzanne.* ed. N. de Lange. SC 302, 1983.

_____. *Homélies sur le Nombres.* Ed. A. Mehat. SC 29, 1951.

_____. *Homélies sur Jérémie.* Ed. P. Nautin and P. Husson. SC 232 and 238; 1976 and 1977.

_____. *Homélies sur Samuel.* ed. P. and M. Nautin. SC 328, 1986.

_____. *Homélies sur le Cantique des Cantiques.* Ed. O. Rousseau. SC 37; 1966.

_____. *Entretien d'Origène avec Héraclide.* Ed. J. Scherer. SC 67, 1960.

3. Critical Texts

Other. Arranged by editor.

_____. Fragments in: *Analecta sacra, spicilegio Solesmiensi parata.* Tomus Secundus et Tertius. Tusculum and Paris: Roger et Chernowitz, 1883–1884.

_____. *Der Scholien-Kommentar des Origenes zur Apokalypse Johannis,* eds. C. Diobounitis and C. Harnack. Leipzig: Hinrichs, 1911.

_____. *Vier Bücher von der Prinzipien.* Trans. and ed. H. Görgemanns and H. Karpp. Darmstadt: Wissenschaftliche Buchgesellschaft, 1976.

_____. Fragments from the *Commentary on Ephesians.* Ed. J. A. Gregg. In *Journal of Theological Studies,* 3(1901–1902), 233–244, 398–420 and 554–576.

_____. *Le chaîne palestinienne sur le Psaume 118.* Eds. M. Harl and G. Dorival. 2 Vols. SC 189–190. Paris: Cerf, 1972.

_____. Origen on I Corinthians. Eds. C. Jenkins and C. Turner. In *Journal of Theological Studies*, 9(1908), 231–247, 353–372, and 500–514; 10 (1909), 29–51.

_____. *Origenis Opera Omnia*. Ed. C. and C. V. Delarue. Reprinted in J. Migne, ed. *Patrologia Graeca* (PG), Vols. 11–17 (1857).

_____. *Origène sur le Pâgue* : Traité inédit publié d'après un papyrus de Toura. Ed. P. Nautin and O. Guéraud. Paris: Beauchesne, 1979.

_____. Fragments from the *Commentary on Romans*. Ed. A. Rambotton. In *Journal of Theological Studies*, 13 (1911–1912), 209–224, 357–368; 14 (1912–1913), 10–22.

_____. *The Philocalia of Origen*. Ed. J. Robinson. Cambridge: Cambridge University Press, 1893.

_____. *Le Commentaire d'Origène sur Rom. III, 5–V, 7*. Ed. J. Scherer. Le Caire: Institute français d'archéologie orientale, 1957.

_____. K. Staab, ed., "Neue Fragmente aus dem Kommentar des Origenes zum Römerbrief." *Biblische Zeitschrift*, 18 (1927–29), 72–83.

4. English Translations. Arranged by translator.

Origenes Adamantius. Selections in: *The Early Christian Fathers*. Trans. H. Bettenson. Oxford: Oxford University Press, 1956. Pages 185–262.

_____. *On First Principles*. Trans. G. W. Butterworth. 1936; rpt; New York: Harper, 1973.

_____. *Contra Celsum*. Revised edition. Trans. and ed. H. Chadwick. Cambridge: Cambridge University Press, 1980. Original Edition published 1953.

_____. *On Prayer, Exhortation to Martyrdom, Dialogue qith Heraclides*. Trans. H. Chadwick. In: *Alexandrian Christianity. Selections from Clement and Origen*. Philadelphia: Westminster Press, 1954.

_____. *Contra Celsum. De Principiis. Letter from Africanus. Letter to Africanus. Letter to Gregory*. Trans. F. Crombie and W. H. Cairns. Ante-Nicene Christian Library, Volumes X, XXIII. Edinburgh: T. & T. Clark, 1869, 1882.

_____. Selections: *Spirit and Fire*, translation of H. urs von Balthasar, *Geist und Feuer* (Leipzig: Müller, 1952). Trans. R. J. Daly. Washington: CUA Press, 1984.

_____. Selections: *Origen and the Doctrine of Grace*. Trans. B. Drewery. London: Epworth, 1960.

_____. *An Exhortation to Martyrdom, Prayer, First Principles* : Book IV, Prologue to the *Commentary on the Song the Songs, Homily 27 on Numbers*. Trans. R. Greer. New York: Paulist Press, 1979.

_____. *Homilies on Genesis and Exodus*. Trans. R. E. Heine. The Fathers of the Church, Vol. 71. Washington, D.C.: the Catholic University of America Press, 1982.

_____. *Commentary on the Gospel according to John, Books 1–10*. Trans. R.E. Heine. The Fathers of the Church, Volume 80. Washington: CUA Press, 1989.

_____. *Origen's Treatise on Prayer*. Trans. with notes by E. C. Jay. London: SPCK, 1954.

_____. Selections: *The Faith of the Early Fathers*. Trans. W. Jurgens. Collegeville, Minn.: The Liturgical Press, 1970. Pages 189–215.

_____. *The Song of Songs, Commentary and Homilies*. Trans. R. Lawson. Westminster, Maryland: Newman Press, 1957.

_____. *The Philocalia of Origen*. Trans. G. Lewis. Edinburgh: T & T Clark, 1911.

_____. *Commentary on the Gospel of John*. Trans. A. Menzies. *The Ante-Nicene Fathers*, X. Books I–X only.

_____. *Origen's "Commentary on John"*, Book XIII. Trans. Carl Michael Moss. Diss. Southern Baptist Theological Seminary, 1982.

_____. *Prayer/Exhortation to Martyrdom*. Trans. J. O'Meara. ACW 19. Westminster, Maryland: Newman, 1954.

_____. *Commentary on the Gospel of Matthew*. Trans. J. Patrick. *The Ante-Nicene Fathers*, X. Books II–XIV only.

_____. *Homilies on Jeremiah and I Samuel 28*. Trans. John Clark Smith. The Fathers of the Church series. Washington: CUA Press (forthcoming).

_____. *Selections from the Commentaries and Homilies of Origen*. Trans. R. Tollinton. London: S.P.C.K., 1929.

5. Other Translations. Arranged by translator.

Origenes Adamantius. *Da la Prière. Exhortation au Martyre*. Trans. G. Bardy. Paris: Lecoffre-Gabalda, 1932.

_____. *Commento alla Lettera ai Romani*. Trans. F. Cocchini. 2 Volumes. Casale Monferrato: Marietti, 1985–1986.

_____. *Commento al Vangelo di Giovanni di Origene*. Trans. Eugenio Corsini. Torino: Unione tipografico-editrice torinese, 1968.

_____. *Origène et les grands thèmes de l'Épître auz Ephésiens*. Trans. F. Deniau. Diss. Universitas a S. Thoma Aquinate in Urbe, 1963. Volume II.

_____. *Das Gesprach mit Herakleides und dessen Bishofs-kollegen über Vater, Sohn und Seele. Die Aufforderung zum Martyrium*. Trans. E. Früchtel. Stuttgart: Hiersemann, 1974.

_____. *Das Evangelium nach Johannes*. Trans. R. Gögler. Einsiedeln: Benziger, 1959.

_____. *Traité des Principes*. Trans. and ed. M. Harl, G. Dorival, and A. le Baulluec. Paris: Études Augustiennes, 1976.

_____. *Die Origenes Schriften vom Gebet und Ermähnung zum Martyrium. Des Origenes acht Bücher gegen Celsus*. Trans. P. Koetschau. Munich: BKV, 1926–27.

_____. *Contra Celso*. Trans. D. Ruiz Bueno. Madrid: BAC, 1967.

_____. *Die griechischen erhaltenen Jeremiahomilien*. Trans. Erwin Schadel. Stuttgart: Hiersmann, 1980.

_____. *Il dialogo di Origene con Eraclide ed i vescovi suoi colleghi sul Padre, il Figlio e l'anima*. Trans. M. Simonetti. Quaderni di Vetera Christianorum. Bari, 1971.

_____. *I principi di Origene*. Trans. M. Simonetti. Torino: Unione tipografico-editrice torinese, 1968.

_____. *I principi-Contra Celsum e altri scritti filosofici*. Trans. M. Simonetti. Firenze: Samsoni, 1975.

_____. *Der Kommentar zur Evangelium nach Mattaus*. Ed. and Trans. H. J. Vogt. Stuttgart: A. Hiersemann, 1983.

6. The Third Century, Origen and Patristics

Alcain, J. *Cautiverio y redencion del hombre en Origenes.* Bilbao: Universidad de Deusto, 1973.

Alexandre, M. "Le statut des questions concernant la matière dans le peri archon." In *Origeniana* (see Crouzel below), pp. 63–81.

Allenbach, J., Benoit, A., Bertrand, D. A., Hanriot-Coustet, A., Junod, E., Maravel, P., Pautler, A., Prigent, P., eds. *Biblia Patristica.* 3. Origène. Paris: Centre d'analyse et de documentation patristique, 1980.

Altaner, B. *Patrology.* Trans. H. Graef. New York: Herder, 1960.

Alves-de-Sousa, P. G. "A presença de Cristo nos comentarios de Origenesa Jo. 6, 55–57." *Theologica,* 11 (1976), 313–334.

Andresen, C. *Logos und Nomos: Die polemik des Kelsos wider das Christentum.* Berlin: De Gruyter, 1955.

Andrewes, A. *Greek Society.* Harmondsworth: Penguin, 1971.

Angus, S. *The Mystery-Religions. A Study in the Religious Background of Early Christianity.* 1928; Reprint; New York: Dover, 1975.

Armantage, J. "The Best of Both Worlds: Origen's Views on Religion and Resurrection." In *Origeniana* (see Crouzel below), pp. 339–347.

Armstrong, A. H. *An Introduction to Ancient Philosophy.* 3rd ed. London: Methuen, 1957.

_____. and Markus, R. A. *Christian Faith and Greek Philosophy.* London: Darton, Longman & Todd, 1960.

_____. "Introductory," "Plotinus," in *The Cambridge History of Later Greek and Early Medieval Philosophy,* ed. A. H. Armstrong (Cambridge: University Press, 1967).

Arnaldez, R. "Philo Judaeus." In *New Catholic Encyclopedia,* 11 (1967), 287.

Arnou, R. "Le thème neoplatonicien de la contemplation créatrice chez Origène et chez S. Augustin." *Gregorianum,* 13 (1932), 124–136.

Aubin, P. *Le problème de la "conversion." Étude sur un terme commun à l'hellénisme et au christianisme des trois premiers siècles.* Paris: Beauchesne, 1963.

Balas, D. "The Idea of Participation in the Structure of Origen's Thought." In *Origeniana* (See Crouzel below), pp. 257–275.

Balthasar, Hans Urs von. *Parole et Mystère chez Origène.* Paris: Cerf, 1957.

Bammel, Caroline Hammond. *Der Römerbrief — Kommentar und seine Origeneübersetzung.* Freiburg: Herder, 1985.

Bardy, G. "Origène." *Dictionnaire de théologie catholigue,* 11 (1932), 1489–1565.

_____. *La théologie de l'église de saint Irénée au concile de Nicée.* Paris: Cerf, 1947.

_____. *La conversion au christianisme durant les premier siècles.* Paris: Aubier, 1949.

Bargeliotes, L. "Origen's Daul Doctrine of God and Logos." *Theologia,* 43 (1972), 202–212.

Barnard, L. W. "Origen's Christology and Eschatology." *Anglican Theological Review,* 46 (1964), 314–319.

_____. *Justin Martyr. His Life and Thought.* Cambridge: University Press, 1967.

Barnes, T. D. *Tertullian. A Historical and Literary Study*. Oxford: Clarendon Press, 1971.

Bauer, Walter. *Orthodoxy and Heresy in Earliest Christianity*. Trans. and ed. R. Kraft and G. Krodel. 1934; rpt.; Philadelphia: Fortress, 1971.

Baus, Karl. *From the Apostolic Community to Constantine*. Translator unnamed. London: Burns and Oates, 1965.

Baud, R. C. "Les 'regles' de la théologie d'Origène." *Recherches de science religieuse*, 55 (1967), 161–208.

Baumeister, T. "Gottesglaube und Staatsauffassung: ihre Interdependenz bei Celsus und Origenes." *Theologie und Philosophie*, 53 (1978), 161–178.

Bayet, J. *Histoire politigue et psychologigue de la religion romaine*. 2nd rev. and corr. ed. Paris: Payot, 1969.

Behm, J. *metanoia, metanoeō*. *Theological Dictionary of the New Testament*, IV, 975–980.

Belche, J. "Die Bekehrung zum Christentum nach Augustins Büchlein De catechizandis rudibus." *Augustiniana*, 27 (1977), 333–363.

Benito y Duran, A. "El humanismo cristiano de Origenes." *Augustinus*. 16 (1971), 123–148.

Benoit, A. *Saint Irénéee. Introduction à l'étude de sa théologie*. Paris: Presses Universitaires, 1960.

Berchman, R.M. *From Philo to Origen: Middle Platonism in Transition*. Chico, Ca.: Scholars Press, 1984.

Berlinski, Romanus. *Praeexistentia spiritum in systemate theologico Origenis*. Rome: Pontificia Universitas Gregoriana, 1936.

Bertram, G. *epistrephō/epistrophē*. *Theological Dictionary of the New Testament*. VII, 723–725.

Bertrand, F. *Mystique de Jésus chez Origène*. Paris: Aubier, 1951.

Bettencourt, S. T. *Doctrina ascetica Origenis*. Rome: Vatican Library, 1945.

Bianchi, U. and Crouzel, H., eds. *Arche e Telos. L'antropologia di Origene e di Gregorio di Nissa. Analisi storico-religiosa*. Milan: Catholic University of the Sacred Heart, 1981.

Bietenhard, Hans. *Caesarea, Origenes und die Juden*. Stuttgart: Kohlhammer, 1974.

Bigg, C. *The Christian Platonists of Alexandria*. 2nd ed. F. E. Brightman. Oxford: University Press, 1913.

Blanc, Cécile. "Le bapteme d'après Origène." *Studia Patristica*, 11 (1972).

———. "L'angélologie d'Origène." *Studia Patristica*, 14 (1976), 79–110.

———. "Les nourritures spirituelles d'après Origène." *Didaskalia*, 6 (1976), 3–19.

———. "Qui est Jésus-Christ? La response d'Origène." *BLE* 80 (1979), 241–256.

Boada, J. "El pneuma en Origenes." *Estudios eclesiasticos*, 46 (1971), 474–510.

Boismard, M. "Conversion et vie nouvelle dans saint Paul," *Lumière et vie*, No. 47 (1960), 73ff.

Boman, Thorleif. *Hebrew Thought Compared with Greek*. Trans. J. Moreau. New York: Norton, 1960.

Borriello, L. "Note sulla mistagogia o dell' introduzione all' esperienza di Dio." *Ephem. carmel*. 32 (1981), 35–89.

Borst, Joseph. *Beitrage zur sprachlich-stylistischen Wurdigung des Origenes*. Freising: Datterer, 1913.

Bouilleuc, Alain le. "De la croissance selon les Stoîcienes à la résurrection selon Origène." *Revue des études grecgues*, 88 (1975–1976), 143–155.

Bostock, D. G. "Egyptian Influence on Origen." In *Origeniana* (see Crouzel below), pp. 243–256.

Bouyer, Louis. *The Spirituality of the New Testament and the Fathers*. Trans. M. Ryan. In *A History of Christian Spirituality*. Paris: Desclée, 1960.

Boyd, W. J. C. "Origen on Pharaoh's Hardened Heart. A Study of Justification and Election in St. Paul and Origen." *Studia Patristica*, VII (1966), 434–442.

Bréhier, Emile. *The Philosophy of Plotinus*. 1928; rpt. Chicago: University Press, 1958.

Breuning, W. "Zur Lehre de Apokatastasis." *Internationale Katholische Zeitschrift* 10 (1981), 19–31.

Brox, N. "Spiritualität und Orthodoxie zum Konflikt des Origenes mit der Geschichte des Dogmas." *Jahrbuch für Antike und Christentum*, P. Vol. Suppl. 8 (1980), 140–154.

Bürke, G. "Des Origenes Lehre vom Urstand des Menschen." *Zeitschrift für katholische Theologie*, 72 (1950), 1–39.

Cabellero Cuesta, Jose Maria. *Origenes interprete de la Sagrada Escritura*. Bargos: Seminario Metropolitano, 1956.

Cadiou, René. *Introduction au systeme d'Origène*. Paris: Les Belles Lettres, 1932.

_____. *La jeunesse d'Origène*. Paris: Beauchesne, 1936. In English: *Origen: His Life at Alexandria*. Trans. J. Southwell. London: Herder, 1944.

Cantalamessa, R. "Origene e Filone: a proposito de C. Celsum IV, 19." *Aevum*, 48 (1974), 132–133.

Carcopino, J. *Daily Life in Ancient Rome*. Trans. E. Lorimer. Harmondsworth: Penguin, 1956.

Caspary, Gerard E. *Politics and Exegesis: Origen and the Two Swords*. Berkeley: University of California Press, 1979.

Castagno, Adele Monaci. *Origene predicatore e il suo pubblico*. Milan: F. Angeli, 1987.

Cataudella, Quintino. "Celso e gli apologeti cristiani." *Nuovo Didaskaleion*, 1 (1947), 28–34.

Chadwick, Henry. "The Evidences of Christianity in the Apologetic of Origen." *Studia Patristica*, 2 (1957), 331–339.

_____. "Origen, Celsus and the Stoa." *JTS*, 48 (1947), 34–49.

_____. *Early Christian Thought and the Classical Tradition*. Oxford: University Press, 1966.

_____. "Philo and the Beginnings of Christian Thought." *The Cambridge History of Later Greek and Early Medieval Philosophy*. A. H. Armstrong, ed. Cambridge: University Press, 1967. pp. 137–192.

Chênevert, Jacques. *L'Église dans le commentaire d'Origène sur le Cantique des Cantiques*. Paris: Desclée, 1969.

Cocchini, Francesca. *Origene — Commento alla Lettera ai Romani: Annuncio pasguale, Polemica antieretica*. L'Aquila: Japadre, 1979.

Cochrane, Charles. *Christianity and Classical Culture*. Oxford: University Press, 1944.

Coman, I. C. "Le Logos, l'Église et l'Âme dans le commentaire du Cantique des Cantiques d'Origène." *Studii Teologice* [Romanian], 25 (1973), 165–172.

Conlon, S. "A Select Bibliography of Modern Studies (1850–1977) on Eschatology in the Western Church of the First Four Centuries." *Ephem. Carmel.* 28 (1977), 351–372.

Copleston, F. *A History of Philosophy.* Volume I. Rev. ed. Garden City, N.Y.: Image, 1962.

Corbett, T. "Origen's Doctrine on the Resurrection." *Irish Theological Quarterly*, 46 (1979), 276–290.

Cornélis, E. "Origenes als Theoloog: recente interpretaties," *Ti jdschrift voor theologie*, 4 (1964), 416–424.

Cornélis, H. *Les fondements cosmologiques de l'eschatologie d'Origène.* Paris: Vrin, 1959.

Corwin, V. *St. Ignatius and Christianity in Antioch.* New Haven, Conn.: Yale University Press, 1960.

Cox, D. " 'In my Father's House are many Dwelling places,' ktisma in Origen's De principiis." *Anglican Theological Review*, 62 (1980), 322–337.

Crouzel, Henri. "L'anthropologie d'Origène dans la perspective du combat spirtuel." *Revue d'ascétique et de mystique*, 31 (1955), 364–385.

_____. "Origène et Plotin, élèves d'Ammonios Saccas." *BLE*, 57 (1956), 205.

_____. *Théologie de l'Image de Dieu chez Origène.* Paris: Aubier, 1956.

_____. *Origène et la 'connaissance mystique.'* Bruges: Desclée de Brouwer, 1961.

_____. *Origène et la philosophie.* Paris: Aubier, 1962.

_____. "Origène et la structure du sacrement." *BLE* 63 (1962), 81–104.

_____. *Virginité et mariage selon Origène.* Paris: Aubier, 1963.

_____. "La distinction de la 'typologie' et de l'allegorie.' " *BLE*, 65 (1964), 161–174.

_____. "Origen and Origenism." *New Catholic Encyclopedia*, 10 (1967), 767–774.

_____. "Un nouveau plaidoyer pour un Origène systematique." *BLE*, 68 (1967), 128–131.

_____. "La lettre du P. Harr. 107 et la théologie d'Origène." *Aegyptus*, 49 (1969), 138–143.

_____. "Origène et le sens littéral dans ses 'Homélies sur l'hexateuque.' " *BLE*, 70 (1969), 241–263.

_____. "Chronique origénienne." *BLE*, 71 (1970).

_____. "Origines patristiques d'un thème mystique: le trait et la blessure d'amour chez Origène." In *Kyriakon*, Festschrift J. Quasten, Vol. I. Münster: Aschendorff, 1970. 309–319.

_____. "L'École d'Origène à Césarée." *BLE*, 71 (1970), 15–27.

_____. *Bibliographie critique d'Origène.* The Hague: Nijhoff, 1971. Supplement I, 1982.

_____. "L'exégèse origénienne de 1 Cor. 3, 11–15 et la purification eschatologique." In *Epektasis — mélanges patristigues offerts au Cardinal Jean Daniélou.* Eds. J. Fontaine and C. Kannengresser. Paris: Beauchesne, 1972. 273–283.

_____. G. Lomiento and J. Rius-Camps, eds. *Origeniana.* Bari: Insituto di letteratura cristiana antica, 1975.

_____. "Comparaisons precises entre les fragments du Péri Archôn selon la Philocalia et la traduction de Rufin." In *Origeniana*, pp. 113–121.

_____. "Qu'a voulu faire Origène en composant le Traité des Principes?" *BLE*, 76 (1975), 241–260.

_____. "Les deux commentaire les plus anciens du Notre Pere." *Studia Missionalia*, 24 (1975), 293–309.

_____. "Les personnes de la Trinité, sont-elles de puissance inegale selon Origène, Peri Archôn 1.3.5–8." *Gregorianum*, 57 (1976), 109–125.

_____. "Conviction intérieure et aspects extérieurs de la religion chez Celse et Origène." *BLE*, 77 (1976), 81–98.

_____. "Le thème du mariage mystique chez Origène et ses sources." *Studia Missionalia*, 26 (1977), 37–57.

_____. "Le thème platonicien du 'venicule de l'âme' chez Origène." *Didaskalia*, 7 (1977), 225–237.

_____. "Mort et immortalité selon Origène." *BLE*, 79 (1978), 19–38, 81–96.

_____. "L'Hades et la Gehenne selon Origène." *Gregorianum*, 59 (1978), 291–331.

_____. "Origène est-il la source du catharisme?" *BLE*, 80 (1979), 3–28.

_____. "La doctrine origénienne du corps ressuscité." *BLE*, 81 (1980), 175–200 and 241–266.

_____. "Actualité d'Origéne. Rapports de la foi et des cultures. Une théologie en recherche." *Nouvelle revue théologie*, 102 (1980), 386–399.

_____. and Quacquarelli, A. eds. *Origeniana Secunda*. Rome: Edizioni dell'ateneo, 1980.

Crouzel, Henri. *Origène*. Paris: Lethielleux, 1985.

_____. and Richard Hanson, eds. *Origeniana Tertia*. Rome: Edizioni dell'ateneo, 1985.

Cumont, Franz. *The Mysteries of Mithra*. Trans. T. McCormack. 1903; rpt.; New York: Dover, 1956.

_____. *Oriental Religions in Roman Paganism*. Trans. G. Showerman. 1911; rpt.; New York: Dover, 1956.

_____. *Astrology and Religion among the Greeks and Romans*. Trans. J. Baker. 1912; rpt.; New York: Dover, 1960.

Daly, Robert J. "Origen Studies and Pierre Nautin's Origène." *Theological Studies*, 9 (1978), 508–519.

Dando, M. "D'Origène aux Cathares." *Cahiers d'études Cathes*, 29 (1978), no. 79, 3–22.

Daniélou, Jean. *Origen*. Trans. W. Mitchell. New York: Sheed and Ward, 1955.

_____. "Origène comme exégète de la Bible." *Studia Patristica* 1 (1957), 280–290.

_____. *Gospel Message and Hellentistic Culture*. Trans. J. Baker. 1961; London: Longman and Todd, 1973.

_____. and Marrou, Henri. *The Christian Centuries*. Trans. V. Cronin. London: Longman and Todd, 1964.

_____. "Recherche et tradition chez les Pères du IIe et due IIIe siècles." *Nouvelle revue théologigue*, 94 (1972), 440–461.

De Andrés Hernansanz, Teodoro. "Aspectos biograficos, metodologicos y doctrinales de Origenes como filosofo." *Pensamiento*, 34 (1978), 409–436.

Dechow, Jon. *Dogma and Myserium in Early Christianity: Epiphanius of Cyprus and the Legacy of Origen*. Atlanta: Mercer University, 1989.

Denis, J. *De la philosophie d'Origène*. Paris: Imprimerie nationale, 1884.

Dillon, J. *The Middle Platonists*. London: Duckworth, 1977.

Dodds, E. R. *The Greeks and the Irrational*. Berkeley: University of California Press, 1951.

_____. *Pagan and Christian in an Age of Anxiety*. New York: Norton, 1965.

Donovan, M. A. "Irenaeus' Teaching on the Unity of God and His Immediacy to the Material World in Relation to Valentinian Gnosticism." Diss. University of St. Michael's College, 1977.

Doutreleau, L. "Le fragment grec de l'Homélie II de Origène sur la Genese. Critique du texte." *Revue d'Histoire des Textes*, 5 (1975-1976), 13-44.

Drewery, Benjamin. *Origen and the Doctrine of Grace*. London: Epworth, 1960.

Dudley, D. *Roman Society*. Harmondsworth: Penguin, 1975.

Dupont, J. "Conversion et repentir d'après les Actes des Apôtres." *Sciences ecclésiastiques*, 12 (1960), 137-173.

Dupuis, Jacques. *'L'esprit de l'homme.' Étude sur l'anthropologie religieuse d'Origène*. Paris: Desclée de Brouwer, 1967.

Edwards, A. "Vida y muerte. La unidad del lenguaje total segun Origenes." *Stromata* (San Miguel, Argentina), 35 (?), nos. 3-4, 147-166.

Egloff, Anton. "Die Engellehre bei Origenes." Diss. Gregorian Pontifical University. Rome, 1941.

Eichinger, M. *Die Verklärung Christi bei Origenes*. Vienna: Herder, 1969.

Elorduy, E. "El influjo estoico en Origenes." In *Origeniana* (see Crouzel above), pp. 227-288.

Eno, R.B. "Origen and the Church of Rome." *American Ecclesiastical Review*, 167 (1973), 41-50.

Eusebius. *Ecclesiastical History*. Trans. K. Lake and J. Oulton. 2 Vols. Loeb Classical Library. Cambridge, Mass.: Harvard University Press, 1926 and 1932.

Faessler, P. Franz. *Der Hagiosbegriff bei Origenes*. Freiburg: University of Freiburg, 1958.

Fairweather, W. *Origen and Greek Patristic Theology*. Edinburgh: T & T Clark, 1901.

Faye, Eugene de. *Origène, sa vie, son oeuvre, sa pensee*. 3 Vols. Paris: E. Laroux, a 1928.

_____. *Origen and His Work*. Trans. of Vol. I of *Origène* by F. Rothwell. London: Allen and Unwin, 1926.

Fee, G. D. "The Lemma of Origen's Commentary on John, Book X: An Independent Witness to the Egyptian Textual Tradition." *New Testament Studies*, 20 (1973), 78-81.

Ferguson, E. "Origen and the Election of Bishops." *Church History*, 43 (1974), 26-33.

Ferguson, J. *The Religions of the Roman Empire*. Ithaca, N.Y.: Cornell University Press, 1970.

Fernandez, Ardanaz S. "El problema del dinamismo trinitario en Origenes." *Angelicum*, 49 (1972), 67-98.

Folgado Florez, S. "Sentido eclesial de la penitencia en el 'Pastor' de Hermas." *Ciudad Dios*, 191 (1978), 3-38.

Frank, K.S. "Vita Apostolica. Ansätze zur apostolischen Lebensform in der alten Kirche." *Zeitschrift für Kirchengeschichte*, 82 (1971), 145-166.

_____. "Maleachi 1, 10ff. in der frühen Vater deutung. Ein Beitrag zu Opferterminologie und Opferverstandnis in der alten Kirche." *Theologie und Philosophie*, 53 (1978), no. 1, 70-78.

Fredouille, Jean-Claude. *Tertullien et la conversion de la culture antique*. Paris: Études augustiniennes, 1972.

Frend, W. H. C. *Martyrdom and Persecution in the Early Church*. Oxford: Blackwell, 1965.

Früchtel, E. "Zur Interpretation der Freiheitsproblematik in Johannes-kommentar Origenes." *Zeitschrift für Religions—und Geistesgeschichte*, 26 (1974), 310–317.

Gallagher, E.V. *Divine Man or Magician? Celsus and Origen on Jesus*. Chico, Ca.: Scholars Press, 1982.

Gamble, H. Y. "Euphemism and Christology in Origen. Contra Celsus III, 22–43." *Vigiliae Christianae*, 33 (1979), 12–29.

Garijo, M. "Vocabulario origeniano sobre el Espiritu Divino." *Scriptorium Victoriense*, 10 (1964), 320–358.

Geerard, M. ed. *Clavis patrum graecorum*. Volume I. Turnhout, Belgium: Brepols, 1983.

Gessel, Wilhelm. *Die Theologie des Gebetes von Origenes*. Munich: F. Schöningh, 1975.

_____. "Der origenische Gebetslogos und die Theologie der Mystik des Gebetes." *Münchener Theologische Zeitschrift* 28 (1977), 397–407.

Giblet, J. "Le sens de la conversion dans l'Ancien Testament." *Maison Dieu*, 90 (1967), 79–92.

Gögler, Rolf. *Zur Theologie des biblischen Wortes bei Origenes*. Düsseldorf: Patmos, 1963.

Gonzalez, Justo L. *A History of Christian Thought*. Vol. I. Nashville: Abingdon, 1970.

Gorday, Peter. *Principles of Patristic Exegesis: Romans 9–11 in Origen, John Chrysostom and Augustine*. New York: Edwin Mallen, 1983.

Goulet, Richard."Porphyre, Ammonius, les deux Origène et les autres." *Revue d'histoire et de philosophie religieuse*, 57 (1977), 471–496.

Grant, Robert. *The Letter and the Spirit*. London: SPCK, 1957.

_____. *Gnosticism and Early Christianity*. 2nd ed. New York: Columbia University Press, 1966.

_____. *Augustus to Constantine. The Thrust of the Christian Movement into the Roman World*. London: Collins, 1971.

_____. "The Stromateis of Origen." in *Epektasis; mélanges patristiques offert au card. J. Daniélou*. Paris: Beauchesne, 1972. pp. 327–334.

_____. "Early Alexandrian Christianity." *Church History*, 40 (1971), 133–144.

Green, Michael. *Evangelism in the Early Church*. London: Hodder and Stoughton, 1970.

Gregory Thaumaturgus. *The Oration and Panegyric*. Trans. S. Salmond. ANF VI, 1871.

Grillmeier, Aloys. *Christ in Christian Tradition*. 2nd rev. ed. Vol. I. London: Mowbrays, 1975.

Gross, J. *Enstehungsqeschichte des Erbsundedogmas von der übel bis Augustinus*. Vol. 1. Munich: Reinhardt, 1960.

_____. *La divinization des chrétiens d'après les pères grecs*. 1938.

Gruber, Gerhard. *ZŌĒ: Wesen, Stufen und Mitteilung des Warhren Lebenes bei Origenes*. Münich: M. Hüber, 1962.

Hadas, Moses. *Hellenistic Culture, Fusion and Diffusion*. 1959; rpt.; New York: Norton, 1972.

Hadot, P. "Epistrophē et metanoia dans l'histoire de la philosophie." *Acts of the XIth International Congress of Philosophy*, 12 (1953), 31–36.

Hällström, Gunnar. *Fides simpliciorum according to Origen of Alexandria*. Helsinki: Societas Scientiarum Fennica, 1984.

Hällström, Gunnar. *Charismatic Succession: A Study in Origen's Concept of Prophecy*. Helsinki: Enroth, 1985.

Hamilton, J. D. B. "The Church and the Language of Mystery: The First Four Centuries." *Ephemerides theologicae lovanienses*, 53 (1977), 479–494.

Hammond, C.P. "Some Textual Points in Origen's Commentary on Matthew." *Journal of Theological Studies*, 24 (1973), 380–404.

_____. "Philocalia IX, Jerome, Epistle 121 and Origen's Exposition of Romans VII." *Journal of Theological Studies* 32 (1981), 50–81.

Hanson, J. W. *Universalism, the Prevailing Doctrine of the Christian Church during its First Five Hundred Years*. Boston and Chicago: Universalist Publishing House, 1899.

Hanson, R. P. C. *Origen's Doctrine of Tradition*. London: S.P.C.K., 1954.

_____. *Allegory and Event*. London: SCM, 1959.

_____. "Did Origen Apply the Word Homoousios to the Son?" in *Epektasis; mélanges patristiques offert au card. J. Daniélou*. Paris: Beauchesne, 1972. pp. 327–334.

_____. Review of Nautin's *Origène*. JTHS, 28 (1978), 556–558.

Harl, Marguerite. *Origène et la fonction révélatrice du Verbe Incarné*. Paris: Seuil, 1958.

_____. "Recherches sur l'origénisme d'Origène: la satiété de la contemplation comme motif de la chute des âme." *Studia Patristica*, 8 (1966), 373–405.

_____. "Origène et l'interprétaton de l'Epitre aux Romains. Étude du chapitre IX de la Philocalie." in *Epektasis* (see Hanson above), pp. 305–316.

_____. "Origène et la sémantique du langage biblique." *Vigiliae Christianae*, 26 (1972), 161–187.

_____. "Qu'est-ce que 'la Bible' pour l'Église ancienne? Le témoignage d'Origène." *Quatre fleuves*, 7 (1977), 82–90.

_____. "Le langage de l'expérience religieuse chez les Pères Grecs." *Revista di storia e letteratura*, 13 (1977), 5–34.

Harris, Carl V. "Origen of Alexandria's Interpretation of the Teacher's Function in the Early Christian Hierarchy and Community." Diss. Duke University 1952.

Harrison, Jane. *Prolegomena to the Study of Greek Religion*. 3rd ed. (1922) New York: World, 1959.

Harnack, Adolf. *History of Dogma*. Trans. N. Buchanan. Vol. II. 1896; rpt.; New York: Dover, 1958.

_____. *The Mission and Expansion of Christianity in the First Three Centuries*. Trans. J. Moffatt. London: Williams and Norgate, 1908.

Hauschild, Wolf-Dieter. *Gottes Geist und der Mensch: Studien zur früh-christlichen Pneumatologie*. München: Chr. Kaiser, 1972.

Hein, Kenneth. *Eucharist and Excommunication. A Study in Early Christian Doctrine and Discipline*. Frankfurt: Peter Lang, 1973.

Heitmann, A. *Imitatio Dei: Die ethische Nachahmung Gottes nach der Väterlehre der zwei ersten Jahrhunderte*. Rome, 1940.

Holdcraft, I. T. "The Parable of the Pounds and Origen's Doctrine of Grace." *JTHS*, 24 (1973), 3–504.

Holz, H. "Über den Begriff des Willens und der Freiheit bei Origenes." *Neue Zeitschrift für systematische Theologie*, 12 (1970), 63–84.

Horn, H. J. "Die Hölle als Krankneit der Seele in einer Deutung des Origenes." *Jahrbuch für Antike und Christentum.* 11/12 (1968/69), 55–64.

_____. "Ignis aeternus—une interpretation morale du feu eternel chez Origène." *Revue des études grecques,* 82 (1969), 76–88.

Hornschuh, Manfred. "Das Leben der Origenes und die Entstehung der alexandrinischen Schule." *Zeitschift für Kirchengeschichte,* 71 (1960), 1–25, 193–214.

Horsley, R. A. "Spiritual Marriage with Sophia." *Vigiliae Christianae,* 33 (1979), 30–74.

Hulsbosch, A. *The Bible on Conversion.* Trans. F. Vander Heijden. De Pere, Wisconsin: St. Norbert Abbey Press, 1966.

Hus, A. *Greek and Roman Religion.* Trans. S. Tester. New York: Hawthorn, 1962.

Ivanka, Endre V. *Plato Christianus. Übernahme und Umgestaltung des Platonismus durch die Väter.* Einsiedeln: Johannes Verlag, 1970.

Jackson, H. "Sources of Origen's Doctrine of Freedom." *Church History,* 35 (1966), 13–33.

Jaeger, Werner. *Early Christianity and Greek Paideia.* Oxford: University Press, 1961.

Joly, Robert. "Patristique et libre examen." *Revue de l'Université de Bruxelles,* 18 (1966), 218–237.

_____. *Christianisme et philosophie.* Brussels: University Press, 1973.

Jonas, Hans. *The Gnostic Religion.* 2nd rev. ed. Boston: Beacon, 1963.

_____. "The Soul in Gnosticism and Plotinus." In *Le Néoplatonisme.* Eds. P. M. Schuhl and P. Hadot. Paris: Editions du Centre National de la recherche scientifique, 1971. pp. 45–53.

Judant, D. "A propos de la destinée d'Israel. Remarques concernant un verset de l'épitre aux Romains XI, 31." *Divinitas,* 23 (1979), 108–125.

Junod, E. "Entre deux éditions du De principiis d'Origène." *BLE,* 78 (1977), 207–220.

_____. "Smaragde de Saint-Michiel cite-t-il des textes d'Origène non transmis par ailleurs." *BLE* 82 (1981), 57–59.

Karpp, H. *Die Busse. Quellen zur Entstehung des altkirchlichen Busswesens.* Zurich, 1969.

Kelber, Wilhelm. *Die Logoslehre von Heraklit bis Origenes.* 2nd ed. Stuttgart: Urachhaus, 1976.

Kelly, J. N. D. *Early Christian Doctrines.* Rev. 5th ed. New York: Harper, 1978.

Kettler, F. H. *Der ursprüngliche Sinn der Dogmatik des Origenes.* Berlin: Töpelmann, 1966.

_____. "War Origenes Schüler des Ammonios Sakkas?" In *Epektasis* (see Hanson above), pp. 327–334.

_____. "Funktion und Tragweite der historischen Kritik des Origenes an den Evangelien." *Kairos,* 15 (1973), 36–49.

Kimelman, R. "Rabbi Yohanan and Origen on the Song of Songs: A Third Century Jewish-Christian Disputation." *Harvard Theological Review* 73 (1980), 567–585.

Kitto, H. *The Greeks.* Rev. Ed. Harmondsworth: Penguin, 1957.

Klostermann, E. "Überkommene Definitionen im Werke des Origenes." *Zeitschrift für die neutestamentliche Wissenschaft und die Kunde der älteren Kirche,* 37 (1938), 54–61.

Koch, Hal. *Pronoia und Paideusis; Studien über Origenes und sein Verhältnis zum Platonismus.* Berlin: W. de Gruyter, 1932.

Kraemer, H. J. *Aretē bei Platon und Aristoteles*. Heidelberg, 1959.

Kübel, Paul. "Zum Aufbau von Origenes' De principiis." *Vigiliae Christianae*, 25 (1971), 31–39.

_____. *Schuld and Schicksal bei Origenes, Gnostikern und Platonikern*. Stuttgart: Calwer, 1973.

Lacan, M-F. "Conversion et grace dans l'Ancien Testament." *Lumière et vie*. No. 47 (1960), 5–24.

_____. "Conversion et royaume dans le Évangiles Synoptiques." *Lumière et vie*, No. 47 (1960), 27ff.

Ladner, Gerhart B. *The Idea of Reform. Its Impact on Christian Thought and Action in the Age of the Fathers*. Cambridge, Mass.: Harvard University Press, 1959.

Laistner, M. L. W. *Christianity and Pagan Culture in the Later Roman Empire*. Ithaca: Cornell University Press, 1951.

Lampe, George, ed. *A Patristic Greek Lexicon*. Oxford: University Press, 1961.

Lange, N. R. M. de. "Origen and Jewish Bible Exegesis." *Journal of Jewish Studies*, 22 (1971), 31–52.

_____. *Origen and the Jews*. Cambridge: University Press, 1976.

Laporte, Jean. "La chute chez Philo et Origène." in *Kyriakon*, P. Granfield and J. Jungmann, eds. Volume I. Münster: Aschendorff, 1970.

Latko, Ernest F. *Origen's Concept of Penance*. Quebec: Université Laval, 1949.

Latourette, Kenneth S. *History of Christianity*. New York: Harper, 1953.

Lebeau, P. "L'interpretation origénienne de Rm. 8, 19–22." In *Kyriakon* (see Laporte above), I, 336–345.

Le Boulleuc, A. "De la croissance selon les Stoiciens à la Résurrection selon Origène." *Revue des études grecques*, 88 (1975–1976), 143–155.

Lécuyer, J. "Sacerdoce des fidèles et sacerdoce ministériel chez Origène." *Vetera Christianorum*, 7 (1970), 253–264.

Lenz, C. "Apokatastasis." *Reallexikon für Antike und Christentum*, 1 (1954), 510–516.

Letocha, Danièle. "L'affrontement entre le christianisme et le paganisme dans le Contre Celse d'Origène." *Dialogue*, 19 (1980), 373–395.

Levine, Lee. *Caesarea under Roman Rule*. Leiden: Brill, 1975.

Lienhard, J. T. "On 'Discernment of Spirits' in the Early Church." *Theological Studies*, 41 (1980), 5–529.

Lies, Lothar. *Wort und Eucharistie bei Origenes. Zur Spiritualisie-rungstendenz des Eucharistieverständnisses*. Innsbruck: Tyrolia, 1978.

_____. "Zum Stand heutige Origenesforschung." *Zeitschrift für katholische Theologie*, 102 (1980), 190–205.

Lieske, Aloysius. *Die Theologie der Logosmystik bei Origenes*. Münster: Aschendorff, 1938.

Lilla, Salvatore. *Clement of Alexandria*. Oxford: University Press, 1971.

Lomiento, Gennario. *L'esegesi origeniana del Vangelo di Luca*. Bari: Universita di Bari, 1966.

_____. *Il dialogo di Origene con Eraclide*. Bari: Quaderni di "Vetera Christianorum" 4, 1971.

_____. "Cristo didaskalos dei pochi e la communicazione ai molti secondo Origene." *Vet. Chr.* 9 (1972), 32–37.

Long, A. *Hellenistic Philosophy*. London: Duckworth, 1974.

Losada, J. "La Iglesia Kosmos en Origenes." *Miscellanea Commillas*, 51 (1959), 33–112.

Lubac, Henri de. *Histoire et esprit. L'intelligence de l'écriture d'après Origène*. Paris: Aubier, 1950.

Luneau, Auguste. *L'histoire du salut chez les pères de l'Église. La doctrine des ages du monde*. Paris: Beauchesne, 1964.

Lyons, J.A. *The Cosmic Christ in Origen and Teilhard de Chardin*. Oxford: University Press, 1982.

Macleod, C. W. "Allegory and Mysticism in Origen and Gregory of Nyssa." *JTS*, 22 (1971), 362–379.

Marias, J. *History of Philosophy*. 22nd ed. Trans. S. Appelbaum and C. Strowbridge. New York: Dover, 1967.

Mariño, P. "Los agapes cristianos como 'colegios' dentro del derecho romano? Acusacion del filosofo pagano Celso (siglo III) y respuesta de Origenes cristiano (siglo III." *Revista international de sociologia*, 33, nos. 13–14 (1975), 51–107.

_____. "La guerra en la pensamiento de Origenes y en su entorno cristiano." *Revista internacional de sociologia*, 34, no. 17 (1976), 7–37.

Martinez Pastor, Marcelo. *Teologia de la luz en Origenes*. Santander: Universidad Pontificia, 1963.

_____. "La simbologia y su desarrollo en el campo semantico de lux, in Origenes-Rufino." *Emerita*, 41, no. 1 (1973), 183–208.

Mattingly, Harold. *Christianity in the Roman Empire*. New York: Norton, 1967.

McLelland, J. C. "The Alexandrian Quest of the Non-Historical Christ." *Church History*, 37 (1968), 355–364.

_____. *God the Anonymous*. Philadelphia: Patristic Foundation, 1976.

Méhat, A. "Pour l'histoire du mot epistrophē: aux origines de l'idée de conversion." *Revue des études grecgues*, 68 (1975), ix.

_____. "Apocatastase." *Vigiliae Christianae*, 10 (1956), 196–214.

Ménard, J. E. "Transfiguration et polymorphic chez Origène." in *Epektasis* (see Hanson above), pp. 327–334.

Merino, M. "La conversion cristiana. El concepto de epistrephein y metanoia en San Justino." *Studium legionense*, 20 (1979), 89–126.

Merivale, Charles. *The Conversion of the Roman Empire*. New York: Appleton, 1865.

Merlan, P. "Greek Philosophy from Plato to Plotinus." *The Cambridge History of Later Greek and Early Medieval Philosophy*. Ed. A. H. Armstrong. Cambridge: University Press, 1967.

Messier, M. "Les rapports aves autrui dans le Contre Celse d'Origène." *Mélanges de science religieuse*, 28 (1971), 189–196.

Michiels, R. "La conception lucanienne de la conversion." *Eph. theo. lov.*, 41 (1965), 42–78.

Milburn, R. L. P. *Early Christian Interpretations of History.* London: Black, 1954.

Miura-Stange, Anne. *Celsus und Origenes.* Berlin: Töpelmann, 1926.

Mollat, D. "IIs regarderont celui qu'ils ont transpercé." *Lumière et vie*, No. 47 (1960), 95–114.

Monaci, A. "Apocalisse ed escatologia nell'opera de Origene." *Augustinianum*, 18 (1978), 139–151.

———. "Origene ed 'i molti': due religiosità a contrasto." *Augustinianum* 21 (1981), 99–117.

Mondésert, C. *Clément d'Alexandrie.* Paris: Aubier, 1944.

Mosetto, Francesco. *I miracoli evangelici nel dibattito fra Celso e Origene.* Rome: LAS, 1986.

Mott. Stephen C. "Greek Ethics and Christian Conversion: The Philonic Background of Titus 2: 10–14 and 3:3–7." *Novum Testamentum*, 20 (1978), 22–48.

Mühlenberg, E. "Das Verständnis des Bösen in neuplatonischen und früh-christlisher Sicht." *Kerygma und Dogma*, 15 (1969), 226–238.

Müller, G. "Origenes und die Apokatastasis." *Theologische Zeitschrift* 14 (1958), 174–190.

Musurillo, H. "The Recent Revival of Origen Studies." *Theological Studies*, 24 (1963), 250–263.

Nautin, Pierre. "Une citation meconnue des Stromates d'Origène." in *Epektasis* (see Hanson above), pp. 373–374.

———. "Note sur Origène, Hom. Luc. IV. 4 (substantia et natura = ousia)?" *Revue des études augustiniennes*, 22 (1976), 78–81.

———. *Origène, sa vie et son oeuvre.* Paris: Beauchesne, 1977.

Nemeshegyi, Peter. *La paternité de Dieu chez Origène.* Tournai: Desclée, 1960.

Neuschäfer, Bernhard. *Origenes als Philologe.* Basle: Fr. Reinhardt, 1987.

Nilsson, Martin P. *A History of Greek Religion.* Trans. F. Fielden. 2nd ed. (1952) New York: Norton, 1964.

———. *Greek Piety.* Trans. H. Rose. 1948 ed. New York: Norton, 1969.

Noce, C. "Il nome di Dio. Origene e l'interpretazione dell'Es. 3, 14." *Divinitas* 21 (1977), 23–50.

Nock, A. D. *Conversion: The Old and the New in Religion from Alexander the Great to Augustine of Hippo.* Oxford: University Press, 1933.

———. "Bekehrung." in Klauser's *Reallexikon für Antike und Christentum* (1951), II, 105–118.

———. *Early Gentile Christianity and its Hellenistic Background.* New York: Harper, 1964.

Oepke, A. *apokatastasis.* In G. Kittel, ed. *Theological Dictionary of the New Testament*, I (1964), 389–393.

Ogilvie, R. *The Romans and their Gods in the Age of Augustus.* London: Chatto and Windus, 1969.

Orbe, Antonio. *Hacia la primera teologia de la procession del Verbo.* Rome: Gregorian University Press, 1958.

_____. *La teologia del Espiritu Santo*. Rome: Gregorian University Press Library Edition, 1966.

_____. *Antropologia de San Ireneo*. Madrid: BAC, 1969.

_____. "Los valentinianos y el matrimonio espiritual. Hacia los origenes de la mistica nupcial." *Gregorianum*, 58 (1977), 5–53.

Origeniana, Origeniana Secunda and *Origeniana Tertia*. See Crouzel.

Osborn, Eric. *The Philosophy of Clement of Alexandria*. Cambridge: University Press, 1957.

_____. *Justin Martyr*. Tubingen: Mohr, 1973.

_____. "Origen and Justification." *Australian Biblical Review* 24 (1976), 18–19.

Otto, W. *The Homeric Gods. The Spiritual Significance of Greek Religion*. Trans. M. Hadas. 1954 ed. London: Thames and Hudson, 1979.

Outler, Albert C. "Faith and Reason in the Theology of Origen." Diss. Yale University, 1938.

_____. "Origen and the Regulae Fidei." *Church History* 8 (1939), 212–221.

Pagels, E. H. "Origen and the Prophets of Israel: A Critique of Christian Typology." *Journal of the Ancient Near Eastern Society of Columbia University* 5 (1973–1974), 335–344.

_____. *The Gnostic Gospels*. New York: Random House, 1979.

Papagno, J. L. "Flp. 2, 6–11 en la cristologia y soteriologia de Origenes." *Burgense collectanea scientifica* (Burgos) 17, no. 1 (1976), 395–429.

Papanikolaou, A. D. "The Allegorical Exegetical Method of Origen." *Theologia* (In Greek) 45, no. 2 (1974), 347–359.

Parker, H. M. D. *History of Roman World A. D. 138–337 A. D.* 2nd ed. London: Methuen, 1970.

Pazzini, Domenico. *In principio era il Logos. Origene e il prologo del vangelo di Giovanni*. Brescia: Paideia, 1983.

Pelikan, Jaroslav. *The Emergence of The Catholic Tradition (100–600)*. Chicago: University Press, 1971.

Pépin, J. *Théologie cosmigue et théologie chrétienne*. Paris, 1964.

Peri, Vittorio. "I passi sulla Trinità nelle omelie origeniane tradotte in latino da San Girolamo." *Studia Patristica* 6 (1962), 155–180.

_____. "Geremia secondo Origene. Esegesi e psicologia della testimonianza profetica." *Aevum* 48, nos. 1–2 (1974), 1–57.

_____. "Criteri di critica semantica dell'esegesi origeniana." *Augustinianum*, 15 (1975), 5–27.

_____. *Omelie origeniane sui Salmi. Contributo all'identificazione del testo latino*. Vatican: Biblioteca apostolica Vaticana, 1980.

Peri, C. "La Vita di Mose di Gregorio di Nissa: un viaggio verso l' aretè cristiana." *Vetera Christianorum* 11 (1974), 313–332.

Peters, F. E. *Greek Philosophical Terms*. New York: New York University press, 1967.

Petry, R. C. *Preaching in the Great Tradition. Neglected Chapters in the History of Preaching*. Philadelphia: Westminster Press, 1950.

Philippou, A. J. "Origen and the Early Jewish-Christian Debate." *Greek Orthodox Theological Review*, 15 (1970), 140–152.

354   BIBLIOGRAPHY

Plato, *The Laws*. Trans. T. J. Saunders. Corrected ed. London: Penguin, 1975.

———. *The Republic*. Trans. Paul Shorey. 2 Vols. Loeb ed. Cambridge, Mass.: Harvard University Press, 1937.

———. *Timaeus*. Trans. R. G. Bury. Loeb ed. Cambridge, Mass.: Harvard University Press, 1929.

———. *Phaedo*. Trans. H. N. Fowler. Loeb ed. Cambridge, Mass.: Harvard University Press, 1914.

Plotinus. *The Enneads*. Trans. A. H. Armstrong. Loeb ed. Cambridge, Mass.: Harvard University Press, 1966, ff.

Prestige, G. L. *God in Patristic Thought*. London: S.P.C.K., 1936.

———. *Fathers and Heretics*. London: S.P.C.K., 1975.

Prunet, O. *La morale de Clément d'Alexandrie et le Nouveau Testament*. Paris: Presses Universitaires, 1966.

Quasten, Johannes. *Patrology*. Volume 2: The Ante-Nicene Literature after Irenaeus. Paramus, N.J.: Newman, 1953.

Quispel, G. "Origen and the Valentinian Gnosis." *Vigiliae Christianae* 28 (1974), 29–42.

Rahner, Hugo. "Taufe und geistliches Leben bei Origenes." *Zeitschrift für Aszese und Mystik* 7 (1932), 205–223.

———. "Das Menschbild des Origenes." *Eranos Jahrbuch* 15 (1947), 197–248.

———. *Symbole der Kirche: Die Ekklesiologie der Väter*. Salzburg: Müller, 1965.

Rahner, Karl. "La doctrine d'Origène sur la pénitence." *Recherches de science religieuse* 37 (1950), 47–97, 252–286, 422–456.

Redepenning, E. R. *Origenes*. 2 Volumes. Bonn: E. Weber, 1841–1846.

Reijners, Gerardus. *Das Wort von Kreuz: Kreuzes — und Erlösungssymbolik ber Origenes*. Cologne: Böhlau, 1983.

Richard, M. "Les fragments d'Origène sur Prov. XXX, 15–31." In *Epektasis* (See Hanson above), pp. 385–394.

Rist, J. M. *Eros and Psyche: Studies in Plato, Plotinus and Origen*. Toronto: University Press, 1964.

———. *Stoic Philosophy*. Cambridge: University Press, 1969.

———. *Epicurus: An Introduction*. Cambridge: University Press, 1972.

———. "The Greek and Latin Texts of the Discussion on Free Will in De principiis, Book III." In *Origeniana* (see above under Crouzel), pp. 97–111.

Rius-Camps, J. *El dinamismo trinitario en la divinizacion de los seres racionales segun Origenes*. Rome: Pontifical Institute of Oriental Studies, 1970.

———. "Communicabilidad de la naturaleza de Dios segun el PeriArchon de Origenes." *Orientialia Christiana*, 36 (1968), 201–247; 38 (1970), 1430–1453; 40 (1974), 344–363.

———. "La suerte final de la naturaleza corporea segun el Peri Archon de Origenes." *Vetera Christianorum*, 10 (1973), 291–304.

Roberts, L. "Contra Celsum 1, 48." *Mnemosyne*, 26, no. 3 (1973), 286.

Robinson, James M., ed. *The Nag Hammadi Library in English*. New York: Harper, 1977.

Roncaglia, M. P. "Quelques questions ecclésiastique et d'ecclésiologie au IIIe siècle à Alexandre." *Proche-Orient chrétien*, 20, no. 1 (1970), 20–30.

Rondet, Henri. "Le péche originel dans le tradition Tertullien, Clément et Origène." *BLE*, 67 (1966), 133–148.

Rose, H. *Religion in Greece and Rome*. New York: Harper, 1959.

Rostovtzeff, M. *The Social and Economic History of the Hellenistic World*. Rev. by P. M. Fraser. Oxford: University Press, 1957.

_____. *A History of the Ancient World*. 2nd corr. ed. Oxford: University Press, 1928.

Rowe, J. Nigel. *Origen's Doctrine of Subordination: A Study in Origen's Christology*. Bern: Peter Lang, 1987.

Ruiz Jurado, M. "Le concept de 'Monde' chez Origène." *BLE*, 75 (1974), 3–24.

Saake, H. "Der Tractatus pneumatico-philosophicus des Origenes in Peri Archon 1, 3." *Hermes* 101, no. 1 (1973), 91–114.

Salmona, B. "Origene e Gregorio di Nissa salla resurrezione dei corpi e l'apocatastasi." *Augustinianum* 18 (1978), 383–388.

Sanchini, R. "Il simbolismo della traccia in Origene." *Studi storico religiosi anc. religioni e civiltà* 2, no. 2 (1978), 381–389.

Sandmel, S. *Philo of Alexandria: An Introduction*. Oxford: University Press, 1979.

Schafer, Theo. *Das Priester-Bild im Leben und Werk des Origenes*. Frankfort: Peter Lang, 1977.

Schär, Max. *Das Nachleben des Origenes in Zeitalter des Humanismus*. Basel: Helbing and Lichtenbahn, 1979.

Schäublin, Christoph. "Origenes und stoische Logik." *Museum Helveticum* [Fribourg] 36 (1979), 166–167.

Scheffczyk, L. "Exegese und Dogmatik zur virginitas post partum." *Münchener Theologische Zeitschrift* 28 (1977), 291–301.

Schendel, E. *Herrscchaft und Unterwerfung Christi*. Tübingen: Mohr, 1971.

Schultze, B. "Origenes über Bekenntnis und Fall des Petrus." *Orientalis Christiana* 41 (1974), 286–313.

Schwartz, J. "Origène, Contre Celse." *Revue d'histoire et de philosophie religieuses* 58, no. 3 (1978), 299–303.

Seeburg, Reinhold. *Text-Book of the History of Doctrines*. Trans. C. Hay. Volume I. 1900; rpt. Grand Rapids, Mich.: Baker Book House, 1977.

Sell, A. P. F. "Platonists (Ancient and Modern) and the Gospel." *Irish Theological Quarterly* 44 (1977), 153–174.

Sgherri, G. "A proposito di Origene e la lingua ebraica." *Augustinianum* 14 (1974), 223–257.

_____. "Sulla valutazione origeniana del LXX." *Biblica* 58 (1977), 1–28.

_____. *Chiesa e Sinagoga nelle opere di Origene*. Milan: Vita e Pensiero, 1982.

Simon, M. *La civilisation de l'antiquité et le christianisme*. Paris: Arthaud, 1972.

Simonetti, Manlio. "Alcune osservazione sull'interpretazione origeniana di Genesi, 2, 7 e 3, 21." *Aevum* 36 (1962), 370–81.

_____. "Due note sull'angelologia origeniana." *Rivista di cultura classica e medioevale* 4 (1962), 165–208.

_____. "Note sulla teologia trinitaria di Origene." *Vetera Christianorum*, 8 (1971), 273–307.

_____. "La morte di Gesù in Origene." *Revista di storia letteratura religiosa*, 8 (1972), 3–41.

————. "Teologia alessandrina e teologia asiatica al concilo di Nicea." *Augustinianum*, 13 (1973), 369–398.

————. "Origene." *Salesianum* 41 (1979), 299–308.

————. "Variazioni gnostiche e origeniana sul tema della storia della salvezza." *Augustinianum* 16 (1976), 7–21.

Skarsaune, Oskar. "Conversion of Justin Martyr." *Studia Theologica* 30 (1976), 53–73.

Spanneut, M. *Le stoîcisme de pères de l'Église: De Clément de Rome à Clément d'Alexandrie.* Paris: Seuil, 1957.

Stelzenberger, Johannes. *Syneidesis bei Origenes.* Paderborn: Schöningh, 1963.

Stritzky, M–B von. "Die Bedeutung der Phaidrosinterpretation für die Apokatastasis des Origenes." *Vigilias Christianae* 31 (1977), 283–297.

————. "Der Begriff der Eusebeia und seine Voraussetzungen in der Interpretation des Origenes." In *Festschrift für Bernhard Kotting* (1980), pp. 155–164.

Studer, B. "Zur Frage der dogmatischen Terminologie in der lateinische übersetzung von Origenes' de Principiis." In *Epektasis* (See Hanson above), 403–414.

————. "La résurrection de Jésus d'après le Peri Archon d'Origène." *Augustinianum*, 18 (1978), 279–309.

Suso, Frank K. "Vita apostolica als Lebensnorm in der Alten Kirche." *Internationale katholische Zeitschrift*, 8 (1979), 106–120.

Teichtweier, Georg. *Das Sein des Menschen.* Regensburg: F. Pustet, 1953.

————. *Die Sundenlehre des Origenes.* Regensburg: F. Pustet, 1958.

Torjesen, Karen J. "Origen's Interpretation of the Psalms." *Studia Patristica*, 17 (1983), 944–958.

Torjesen, Karen J. *Hermeneutical Procedure and Theological Method in Origen's Exegesis.* Berlin: De Gruyter, 1986.

Townsley, A. L. "Origen's 'ho Theos', Anaximander's 'to theion' and a Series of Worlds. Some Remarks." *Orientalia Christiana* 41 (1975), 140–149 and in *Revista di studi classici* 23, no. 1 (1975), 5–13.

Trevijano Etcheverria, R. *En luncha contra las Potestades. Execesis primitiva de Ef. 6, 11–17 hasta Origenes.* Victoriensia: Seminary of Victoria Press, 1968. Origen: pp. 151–373.

————. "Origenes y la regula fidei." In *Origeniana* (see Crouzel above), pp. 327–338.

Trigg, Joseph. "A Decade of Origen Studies." *Religious Studies Review* 7 (1981), 21–27.

————. "The Charismatic Intellectual. Origen's Understanding of Religious Leadership." *Church History* 50 (1981), 5–19.

————. *Origen: The Bible and Philosophy in the Third-Century Church.* Atlanta, Ga.: Knox, 1983.

————. "A Fresh Look at Origen's Understanding of Baptism." *Studia Patristica*, 17 (1982), 959–965.

Tsirpaulis, C. N. "The Concept of Universal Salvation in Saint Gregory of Nyssa." *Kleronomia* 12 (1980), 19–35.

Tripolitis, Antonia. *The Doctrine of the Soul in the Thought of Plotinus and Origen.* Roslyn Heights, N.Y.: Libra, 1978.

Turner, H. E. W. *The Pattern of Christian Truth: A Study in the Relations between Orthodoxy and Heresy in the Early Church.* London: Mobray, 1954.

Van De Paverd, F. "Disciplinarian Procedures in the Early Church." *Augustinianum* 21 (1981), 291–316.

Turney, A. "Apocatastasis." *New Catholic Encyclopedia*, I (1967), 665.

Van Andel, G. K. "Severus and Origenism." *Vigiliae Christianae*, 34 (1980), 278–287.

Van Eijk, A. H. C. "Only That Can Rise Which Has Previously Fallen: The History of a Formula." *JTS*, 22 (1971), 517–529.

Van Parys, M. "Unification de l'homme dans le Nom. exègése de Mt. 18:19–20." *Irenikon* 50 (1977), 345–358.

Van Winden, J. C. M. "Le christianisme et la philosophie. Le commencement du dialogue entre la foi et la raison." In *Kyriakon, Festschrift J. Quasten*. Münster: Aschendorff, 1970. I: 205–213.

_____. "Origen's Definition of Eucharistia in De oratione 14, 2." *Vigiliae Christianae* 28 (1974), 139–140.

Verdenius, W. J. "Plato and Christianity." *Ratio* 5 (1963), 15–32.

Vogt, H. *Das Kirchenverständnis des Origenes*. Vienna: Böhlau, 1974.

_____. "Eucharistielehre des Origenes?" *Freiburg Zeitschrift für Philosophie und Theologie* 25, no. 3 (1978), 428–442.

_____. "Falsche Ergänzungen oder Korrekturen in Mattäus-Kommentar des Origenes." *Theologische Quartalschrift*, 160 (1980), 207–212.

Völker, W. *Das Vollkommenheisideal des Origenes*. Tübingen: Mohr, 1935.

Warkotsch, Albert. *Antike Philosophie im Urteil der Kirchenväter. Christlicher Glaube im Widerstreit der Philosophien*. München: Schöningh, 1973.

Weiss, B. "Die Unsterblichkeit der Seele als eschatologisches Heitsgut nach Origenes." *Trierer Theologische Zeitschrift* 80, no. 3 (1971), 156–169.

Westcott, B. F. "Origenes." in *A Dictionary of Christian Biography* 4 (1887), 96–142.

_____. *Essays in the History of Religious Thought*. London: Macmillan & Co., 1891.

Wiles, Maurice F. *The Spiritual Gospel*. Cambridge: University Press, 1960.

_____. *The Divine Apostle*. Cambridge: University Press, 1967.

_____. "Origen as Biblical Scholar." *The Cambridge History of the Bible*, I (1970), 454–489.

Williams, Raymond B. "Origen's Interpretation of the Gospel of John." Diss. University of Chicago, 1966.

Wilson, R. "Slippery Words II: Gnosis, Gnostic, Gnosticism." *Expository Times*, 89 (1978), 296–301.

Winston, D. "Introduction." In *Philo of Alexandria — Selections*. New York: Paulist Press, 1981.

Wolfson, Harry A. *The Philosophy of the Church Fathers*, I. 2nd ed. Cambridge, Mass.: Harvard University Press, 1965.

_____. *Philo*. 2 Volumes. Cambridge, Mass.: Harvard University Press, 1947.

Würthwein, E. *metanoeō/metanoia*. *TDNT*, IV, 984–985.

Young, F. M. *The Use of Sacrificial Ideas in Greek Christian Writers from the New Testament to John Chrysostom*. Philadelphia: Patristic Foundation, 1979.

Zeller, E. *Outlines of the History of Greek Philosophy*. 13th ed. (1931) Trans. L. Palmer. Rev. W. Nestle. New York: Dover, 1980.

Index of Cited Texts of Origen

HOMILIES

Homilies on Genesis (Hom. in Gen.): 1.1, 290 n.139; *1.5*, 302 nn. 180-181; *1.13*, 295 n.59; *7.2*, 329 n.315; *13.4*, 294 n.42, 298 n.127

Homilies on Exodus (Hom. in Ex.): 2.1, 304 nn. 26-27; *2.3*, 307 n.90; *3.3*, 316 n.215; *5.5*, 319 n.275; *9.13*, 311 n.144; *11.3*, 306 n.59; *11.6*, 318 n.264; *11.7*, 331 n.360; *13.7*, 306 n.64

Homilies on Leviticus (Hom. in Lev.): 1.4, 318 nn. 254-255; *2.4*, 331 n.351; *5.1*, 300 n.148, n.152; *5.8*, 317 n.240; *6.3*, 315 n.207; *6.6*, 316 n.214; *7.4*, 318 n.261; *8.11*, 330 n.338; *9.4*, 331 n.343; *9.6*, 300 n.157, n.159; *9.8*, 312 n.144; *12.4*, 313 n.164; *12.5*, 317 n.251; *12.6*, 314 n.187; *12.7*, 318 n.252

Homilies on Numbers (Hom. in Num.): 2.1, 316 n.214; *3.1*, 331 n.350; *4.3*, 318 n.252, n.259; *6.3*, 330 n.338; *10.1*, 314 n.186, 319 n.287; *11.3*, 317 n.245; *11.8*, 311 n.144; *11.9*, 312 n.144; *12.4*, 297 n.99, n.103, nn. 119-120; *13.7*, 303 n.191; *17.4*, 332 n.371; *21.1*, 306 n.60; *22.4*, 315 n.207; *23.3*, 312 n.144; *23.6*, 317 n.250, 218 n.260; *23.8*, 317 n.246; *24.2*, 308 n.95; *27.1*, 318 nn. 256-258; *27.3*, 326 n.199; *27.12*, 333 n.401

Homilies on Joshua (Hom. in Jesu Nave): 1.6, 303 n.191; *3.2*, 321 n.66; 330 n.331; *3.5*, 302 nn. 184-185; *4.1*, 331 n.347; *5.6*, 314 n.190; *6.1*, 322 n.91, 333 n.396; *7.6*, 314 n.192; *9.9*, 318 n.260, 333 n.396; *10.1*, 306 n.61, n.62; *10.2*, 306 n.63; *10.3*, 306 n.65; *13.4*, 324 n.158; *15.5*, 296 n.96; *17.2*, 321 n.37; *20.1 (Phil.12)*, 301 n.160; *20.3 (Phil.12)*, 301 n.161; *21.2*, 313 n.181; *22.2*, 322 nn. 87-89; *23.4*, 332 n.281; *24.3*, 324 n.163

Homilies on Judges (Hom. in Jud.): 7.7, 331 n.360

Homilies on Psalms (Hom. in Ps.): 3.6, 327 n.242, 332 n.386; *38.1*, 314 n.199; *38.2*, 314 n.199

Homilies on the Song of Songs (Hom. in Cant.): 1.6, 307 n.93, 328 n.254; *2.12*, 307 n.90

Homilies on Jeremiah (Hom. in Jer.): 1.1-2, 328 n.262; *1.3*, 297 n.122, 313 n.172, 328 n.261; *1.4*, 297 n.123, 326 n.190, 328 n.286; *1.7*, 296 n.81, 300 n.153, 320 n.5, 321 nn. 45-46; *1.8*, 322 n.71; *1.10*, 281 n.9,

304 n.12, 322 n.71, 333 n.403; *1.12*, 321 n.47, 324 n.144; *1.14*, 293 n.33, 296 n.81; *1.15*, 296 n.81; *1.16*, 289 n.116, 296 n.81, 301 n.160, 331 n.341; *2.1*, 282 n.10, 291 n.3, 294 n.44, 297 n.114, n.115, 328 n.289; *2.2-3*, 292 n.16; *2.2*, 300 n.158, 326 n.202; *2.3*, 304 n.12, 326 n.202, 331 n.340; *3.2*, 286 nn. 67-68, 291 n.6, 293 n.30, 321 n.53, 328 n.253; *4.1-6*, 299 n.140; *4.1*, 320 n.7; *4.2-3*, 306 n.74; *4.2-4*, 321 n.52; *4.3*, 306 n.75, 326 n.211, 327 n.236; *4.4*, 316 n.220, 328 n.287; *4.5*, 298 n.124, 299 n.140, 316 n.232; *4.6*, 299 n.140, 301 n.166, 316 n.233, 317 n.235; *5.2*, 292 n.22, 297 n.112, 303 n.1, 320 nn. 9-14; *5.5*, 328 n.277, n.279; *5.6*, 295 n.53, n.54, 300 n.154, 324 n.151; *5.7*, 297 n.177, 303 n.5, 304 n.19, 314 n.188; *5.8*, 299 n.141, 304 n.6; *5.9*, 292 n.15, 299 n.142; *5.10*, 304 n.18, 317 n.243, 320 n.15; *5.11*, 317 n.243; *5.13*, 292 n.14, 317 n.250; *5.14*, 281 n.9, 294 n.42, 302 n.184; *5.15-16*, 299 n.134; *5.16-17*, 297 n.107; *5.16*, 302 n.176, 316 n.215, n.216, n.217; *5.17*, 316 n.218, 329 n.299; *6.1*, 326 n.198; *6.2*, 307 n.81; *6.3*, 319 nn. 277-279; *7.1*, 328 n.266; *7.2*, 287 n.90; *7.3*, 292 n.22, 295 n.68, 298 n.128, 302 n.184; 313 n.180, 314 n.187; *8.1*, 281 n.4, 288 n.104, 295 n.74, 304 n.7, 325 nn. 166-167, 330 n.323; *8.2*, 292 n.22, 304 n.8, 322 n.72, 324 n.125, 330 n.324; *8.3*, 322 n.95; *8.4*, 322 n.96; *8.6*, 322 n.73; *8.7*, 332 n.396; *8.8*, 332 n.384; *8.9*, 332 n.385; *9.1*, 298 n.129, 308 n.105, 324 nn. 146-149; *9.2*, 302 n.179, 313 nn. 165-166, 313 n.172; *9.3*, 308 n.106, 313 n.167, n.169, 328 n.268; *9.4*, 297 n.97, 303 n.4, 308 nn. 108, 109-111, 313 n.168, 325 n.184, 328 n.267; *10.1*, 299 n.134, 301 n.162, 307 n.79, 323 n.111, n.117; *10.5*, 316 n.227; *10.6*, 303 n.193, n.194; *10.8*, 303 n.194, 328 n.278; *11.2*, 292 n.13, 295 n.76, 304 n.7, 325 n.169; *11.3*, 314 n.199; *11.5*, 287 n.79, 291 n.13; *11.6*, 289 n.122, 294 n.42, 322 n.74, 326 n.201; *12.2*, 303 n.3, 304 n.12; *12.5*, 314 n.189, n.192; *12.6*, 314 n.193, 318 n.253, 322 n.75; *12.7-8*, 297 n.120, 300 n.153; *12.7*, 312 n.149, 332 n.365; *12.8*, 312 n.148; *12.11*, 304 n.12,

Index of Modern Writers Cited

Index of Subjects

Actions, moral: connection to contemplation, 96–98, 170–174, 304 n.21; and doctrine, 319 n.286, n.287; needed in higher life, 243; not prior to inner growth, 174; Origen's terminology of, 93–94. *See also Arete; Ergon; Logos; Praxis; Theoria*

Adam, 38, 53, 162; and Christ, 318 n.262

Aid, divine: comes when one has done everything in his power, 103; necessary for change to occur, 100–101

Aisthesis (sense-perception): definition of, 61, 292 n.16

Albinus: epistemology of, 292 n.16; view of conversion of, 20

Allegorical method: how Origen used, 38, 47

Angels: alone cannot save, 303 n.191; divorce with men, 89–90; guardian, 307 n.85; help with good conduct, 111; kinds of, 303 n.200; not all fell, 283 n.23; and restoration, 53–54; and stars, 88, 303 n.193; way they influence soul, 88–90

Anthropology: of Irenaeus, 31; of Origen, 159–160; terms of Origen, 293 n.33

Apokatastasis (restoration): definition of, 42–43, 288 n.105, 303 n.188, 319 n.287; and universality, 52, 53–54; use in Scripture of, 284 n.27, n.28; use of word by others before Origen, 42, 284 n.26; of whole world, not just church, 53

Apologists: views on change, 29–30

Apostles: as models, 306 n.69

Apostolic fathers: views on change of, 28–29

Arete (virtue), 93, 94

Articles of faith, 19

Augustine, 260, 315 n.210

Aurelius, Marcus, 305 n.52

Axios (worthy), 164–165

Baptism: and conversion in New Testament, 26; and conversion in Tertullian, 32; on earth one, 227, of fire, 227; higher knowledge not guaranteed by, 331 n.353; kinds of, 331 n.339; not automatically confirmed by, 207 n.93; only one true, 215; preparation necessary for, 228–229; responsibility connected with, 230; and the spiritual life, 227–231; two levels of purification of, 228–229; requires repentance, 213; three facets concerning, 230

Behavior, Christian: connection with Christ, 113–117; terms explaining, 93–94

Belief: a foundation for more advanced levels, 157; immature and maturing, aspect of, 191–197; and scripture, 196; and sight, 157; stage of growth, 238–239

Biblical images of movement in spiritual change: bride/church, body/members, 122–123; building, 113, 121–122; "chains" and "bonds" as sins and oppression of governments, 313 n.168; clouds, 169–170; conversion as a healing, 154; "day of man," 119; field as soul of student, 140; from being fish to living on a mountain, 117; general list of, 310 n.122; God as gardener in soul, 147; going up and ahead, 117–118; Jerusalem as church, 124; journey of Israel to promised land, 191, 243; life and death in soul's transformation, 114–115, 184–185; mountains, 298 n.125; partridge as devil, 191; renouncing world, 119–120; of restoration, 183; the sea, 310 n.124; "straining forward to what lies ahead," 118–119; teacher as physician, 145; three levels of "nourishment," 81, 142, 155

Body: after-death and in the end, 57–60, 289 n.130, n.131, 289 n.134, 290 n.139, 290 n.2, n.3; dealing with in spiritual journey, 63–65; fall from spiritual to physical, 62; and flesh, 291 n.13; the importance of, 61–62; nature of, 59–60; *soma*, 40; the yoke of when mature, 156

Celsus: how Origen refutes, 304 n.13; view of Christians of, 305 n.52

Change, concept of: to non-Christian sects, 16–23

Charity: bond between Trinity and between man and God, 181–182

Christ: absolute virtue, 116–117, 308 n.99, 309 n.112; and Adam, 162; aids those who "strain forward," 119; becoming a christ in oneself, 113–117, 180–181, 309 n.119, 312 n.159; bringer of knowledge, 163; the catalyst in moral change, 115–116; charity in the revelation of, 181–182; connection of his Sonship with man's, 116–117, 308 n.111, 309 n.117; conquers devil, 78; as converter, 175;

366

Rufinus: as translator of Origen's works, 265–266, 281 n.3, 321 n.55, 335 n.31
Rule of faith: Origen's fidelity to, 281 n.9; on subjects not mentioned in, 37, 38

Saints: can sin, 127; models, 109–110
Salvation: different from spiritual growth, 106–108; each man can attain, 209; and freedom, 107; from Christ alone, 110; is it universal, 51–57; two kinds of, 106–108
Scripture: as agent of Logos to help men rule the senses, 79–83; allegorical interpretation, 47; as a book used in teaching, 133-138; and conduct, 137; conversion by, 81; different spiritual levels correspond to different books of, 142; difficult to understand, 80; difficulty of, 300 n.146; dimensions of, 300 nn.146, 148, 153; each person understands according to capacity, 81; as an epistemological journey, 236; and faith, 189, 196; to follow the models in, is the true conversion, 137; and the higher life, 232-236; kind of intensity required to understand the, 235; knowledge beyond, 236–237; the literal versus spiritual sense of, 236; levels of interpretation, 48; magical powers, 83; for the mature, 156; the mature search the, 234–236; mysterious ideas of, 233; need to repent of interpretations of, 214–215; no one fully understands, 232; Origen's defense of, 36–37; Origen's method in interpreting, 300 n.148, n.153; power from God, 305 n.38; power in words alone of, 301 n.160, n.162; role of body of, 81; soul comes first to know through bodily sense of, 300 n.147, n.150; three dimensions for salvation, 81; understanding of dependent on willingness and logos, 300 n.156; as a vehicle to change conduct, 133–144; view of conversion in, 23–27
Seeing: in contrast to believing, 157, 200
Seminal principle: through all stages of change, the body has a, 59; resurrection and, 59
Sense, divine: gift of God to master and transcend senses, 65–66
Senses, corporeal/spiritual, 292 n.16; mastering the, 63–65; and Prov. 2:5, 292 n.25; to know God, use of, 292 n.26
Sexual imagery: used by Origen to explain relationship of man and divine, 240–242
Shame: an integral of repentance, 210–211
Shub, 24, 25, 277 n.50
Sin: effect of, 209, 213; every spiritual stage has, 127; in Greco-Roman religions, 17; in New Testament, 25, 76; and repentance, 207–209, 328 n.294; saints can, 127; ways to be forgiven for, 229
Slaves: necessary for true Christians to be, 309 n.115; servants and, 309 n.115; those on the path, 116
Soma (body): irrational part of soul is, 40

Sominal principle: maintaining personality in resurrection, 59
Sons of God: becoming, 115–116
Soul (psyche): death of, 286 n.73; definition of Greek word for, 293 n.33; fundamental powers of, 67–69; initially good, 77; prayers lift up, 158; upper and lower dimensions, 38, 40
Spirit: Celsus's material view of, 329 n.315; and conduct, 310 n.124; in contrast to the material/physical, 219; definition of, 329 n.305; distinguishing soul, flesh, and, 220; and flesh in restoration of soul, 184; and Holy Spirit, 222–223; inspiration and source of strength for the mature, 157–159; needed for faith, 166; role of, in the higher life, 163–164; soul is not the, 219–220; work and effect of the, 219–220. See also Pneuma
Spirit, Holy. See Holy Spirit
Spiritual movement or growth: arises from knowledge of faith, 198; choice not nature causes, 46–47; Christ overcoming death brings, 72; continues after death, 106, 306 n.60; each level of, an aspect of Christ, 178; the heart and Holy Spirit in making, 226–227; key terms, 93, 96–98; laying holding of wisdom brings, 177; like healing, 154; love and fear and, 309 n.116; mastering senses in, 63–65; needs good conduct and doctrine, 147–148; prayer a pattern for, 218; and repentance, 205–206; role of Holy Spirit in, 223– 227; role of spirit in, 218–220; stages for Origen, 37; strength and capacity of will and mind leads to, 245–246; in terms of faith, 187–188, 192, 196–197; three inner spiritual activities of Christ corresponding to three modes of, 179–180; three modes, 167–174, 298 n.131, 322 n.86; through Scripture, 81, 143; transcendence of body, worship, human knowledge, etc., is, 152–159; vacillates and relapses, 95, 102–105, 129; works written on, 262–263. See also Conversion
Stability: as factor in growth of faith, 193–194, 201; as factor in growth of knowledge, 244–245
Stars: and angels, 88, 303 n.193
Stoics: Origen's view of knowledge similar to, 239–240; view of conversion, 18–19, 273 n.20, n.23; 274 n.25; view of knowledge different from Origen, 292 n.16; view of soul, 293 n.33
Suffering: use by God to change man, 48

Teacher/teaching: behavior of influential, 133; and Christ, 307 n.92; effect of conduct of, 132-133; the false, 134–135; guide in Scripture, 138–144; importance in spiritual growth, 132-149, 307 n.88; importance of kind of, 146–148; method of, depends upon the needs of student, 139; methodology of,

DATE DUE